# TRADE DRESS AND DESIGN LAW

**EDITORIAL ADVISORS**

**Vicki Been**
Elihu Root Professor of Law
New York University School of Law

**Erwin Chemerinsky**
Dean and Distinguished Professor of Law
University of California, Irvine, School of Law

**Richard A. Epstein**
James Parker Hall Distinguished Service Professor of Law
University of Chicago Law School
Peter and Kirsten Bedford Senior Fellow
The Hoover Institution
Stanford University

**Ronald J. Gilson**
Charles J. Meyers Professor of Law and Business
Stanford University
Marc and Eva Stern Professor of Law and Business
Columbia Law School

**James E. Krier**
Earl Warren DeLano Professor of Law
The University of Michigan Law School

**Richard K. Neumann, Jr.**
Professor of Law
Hofstra University School of Law

**Robert H. Sitkoff**
John L. Gray Professor of Law
Harvard Law School

**David Alan Sklansky**
Professor of Law
University of California at Berkeley School of Law

**Kent D. Syverud**
Dean and Ethan A. H. Shepley University Professor
Washington University School of Law

**Elizabeth Warren**
Leo Gottlieb Professor of Law
Harvard Law School

ASPEN PUBLISHERS

# TRADE DRESS AND DESIGN LAW

**Graeme B. Dinwoodie**
*Professor of Intellectual Property and
Information Technology Law
University of Oxford*

**Mark D. Janis**
*Professor of Law and Ira C. Batman Faculty Fellow
Indiana University—Bloomington*

Law & Business

AUSTIN   BOSTON   CHICAGO   NEW YORK   THE NETHERLANDS

© 2010 Aspen Publishers
Published by Aspen Publishers. All Rights Reserved.

No part of this publication may be reproduced or transmitted in any form or by any means, electronic or mechanical, including photocopy, recording, or any information storage and retrieval system, without permission in writing from the publisher. Requests for permission to make copies of any part of this publication should be mailed to:

Aspen Publishers
Attn: Permissions Department
76 Ninth Avenue, 7th Floor
New York, NY  10011-5201

To contact Customer Care, e-mail customer.care@aspenpublishers.com, call 1-800-234-1660, fax 1-800-901-9075, or mail correspondence to:

Aspen Publishers
Attn: Order Department
PO Box 990
Frederick, MD 21705

Printed in the United States of America.

1 2 3 4 5 6 7 8 9 0

ISBN 978-0-7355-6832-7

**Library of Congress Cataloging-in-Publication Data**

Dinwoodie, Graeme B.
  Trade dress and design law / Graeme B. Dinwoodie, Mark D. Janis.
    p. cm.
    Includes bibliographical references and index.
    ISBN 978-0-7355-6832-7 (perfectbound : alk. paper) 1. Design protection—United States. 2. Trademarks—Law and legislation—United States. 3. Actions and defenses—United States. I. Janis, Mark D. II. Title.
  KF3086.D56 2010
  346.7304′84—dc22                                           2010010762

COVER ART: The Legless Glass Table and sketch on the cover of this book are both the creation of Peter Devins, designer and artist. Web site: www.devinsdesign.com

This book contains paper from well-managed forests to SFI standards.

# About Wolters Kluwer Law & Business

Wolters Kluwer Law & Business is a leading provider of research information and workflow solutions in key specialty areas. The strengths of the individual brands of Aspen Publishers, CCH, Kluwer Law International and Loislaw are aligned within Wolters Kluwer Law & Business to provide comprehensive, in-depth solutions and expert-authored content for the legal, professional and education markets.

**CCH** was founded in 1913 and has served more than four generations of business professionals and their clients. The CCH products in the Wolters Kluwer Law & Business group are highly regarded electronic and print resources for legal, securities, antitrust and trade regulation, government contracting, banking, pension, payroll, employment and labor, and healthcare reimbursement and compliance professionals.

**Aspen Publishers** is a leading information provider for attorneys, business professionals and law students. Written by preeminent authorities, Aspen products offer analytical and practical information in a range of specialty practice areas from securities law and intellectual property to mergers and acquisitions and pension/benefits. Aspen's trusted legal education resources provide professors and students with high-quality, up-to-date and effective resources for successful instruction and study in all areas of the law.

**Kluwer Law International** supplies the global business community with comprehensive English-language international legal information. Legal practitioners, corporate counsel and business executives around the world rely on the Kluwer Law International journals, loose-leafs, books and electronic products for authoritative information in many areas of international legal practice.

**Loislaw** is a premier provider of digitized legal content to small law firm practitioners of various specializations. Loislaw provides attorneys with the ability to quickly and efficiently find the necessary legal information they need, when and where they need it, by facilitating access to primary law as well as state-specific law, records, forms and treatises.

Wolters Kluwer Law & Business, a unit of Wolters Kluwer, is headquartered in New York and Riverwoods, Illinois. Wolters Kluwer is a leading multinational publisher and information services company.

# SUMMARY OF CONTENTS

| | |
|---|---|
| *Contents* | *ix* |
| *Preface* | *xvii* |

### PART I. INTRODUCTION — 1

1  **INTRODUCTION TO TRADE DRESS AND DESIGN LAW** — 3

### PART II. TRADE DRESS — 39

2  **DISTINCTIVENESS** — 41

3  **FUNCTIONALITY** — 107

4  **ENFORCEMENT AND DEFENSES** — 211

### PART III. DESIGN PATENTS — 295

5  **SECURING RIGHTS** — 297

6  **ENFORCING RIGHTS** — 381

### PART IV. COPYRIGHT — 431

7  **COPYRIGHT** — 433

## PART V. SUI GENERIS REGIMES — 525
## 8  SUI GENERIS DESIGN PROTECTION — 527

*Table of Cases* — 573
*Index* — 579

# CONTENTS

Preface — xvii

## PART I. INTRODUCTION — 1

## 1 INTRODUCTION TO TRADE DRESS AND DESIGN LAW — 3

### A. INTRODUCTION: WHAT IS DESIGN? — 4
- Alice Rawsthorn, What Defies Defining, but Exists Everywhere? — 5
- Graeme B. Dinwoodie, Federalized Functionalism: The Future of Design Protection in the European Union — 6
- Robert C. Denicola, Applied Art And Industrial Design: A Suggested Approach to Copyright in Useful Articles — 9
- Orit Fischman Afori, Reconceptualizing Property in Designs — 11

Notes and Questions — 13

### B. THE MODERN LEGISLATIVE LANDSCAPE FOR TRADE DRESS AND DESIGN PROTECTION — 15

1. The International Intellectual Property Law of Design — 16
   a. TRIPS — 16
   b. The Hague Agreement Concerning the International Registration of Industrial Designs — 16
2. U.S. Intellectual Property Laws Regarding Design — 17
   a. Trademark and Unfair Competition Protection — 17
   b. Patent Protection — 18
   c. Copyright Protection — 19

ix

3. European Union Design Law 20
　　　　　Notes and Questions 20
　C. THE "CUMULATION/PREEMPTION" PROBLEM IN
　　　DESIGN LAW 24
　　　• *Sears, Roebuck & Co. v. Stiffel Co.* 24
　　　　Notes and Questions 27
　　　• *Bonito Boats, Inc. v. Thunder Craft Boats, Inc.* 28
　　　　Notes and Questions 36

# PART II. TRADE DRESS 39

# 2 DISTINCTIVENESS 41

　A. TRADE DRESS AND DESIGNS AS PROTECTABLE
　　　SUBJECT MATTER UNDER TRADEMARK AND
　　　UNFAIR COMPETITION PRINCIPLES 41
　　　• *Flagg Mfg. Co. v. Holway* 42
　　　• *George G. Fox Co. v. Hathaway* 43
　　　• *Enterprise Mfg. Co. v. Landers, Frary & Clark* 45
　　　• *Crescent Tool Co. v. Kilborn & Bishop Co.* 46
　　　　Notes and Questions 47
　　　• Lanham Act, Section 45 48
　　　• *Kohler Co. v. Moen Inc.* 48
　　　　Notes and Questions 63
　B. THE SUPREME COURT'S FRAMEWORK
　　　FOR DISTINCTIVENESS IN TRADE DRESS
　　　AND DESIGN CASES 64
　　　1. Fundamentals of Distinctiveness: The *Abercrombie*
　　　　　Spectrum 64
　　　2. The *Seabrook* Analysis 67
　　　3. The Supreme Court's Framework for Trade Dress
　　　　　Distinctiveness 67
　　　　• *Two Pesos, Inc. v. Taco Cabana, Inc.* 68
　　　　　Notes and Questions 76
　　　　• *Qualitex Co. v. Jacobson Products Co., Inc.* 78
　　　　　Notes and Questions 84
　　　　• *Wal-Mart Stores, Inc. v. Samara Brothers, Inc.* 85
　　　　　Notes and Questions 90
　C. TRADE DRESS AND DESIGN DISTINCTIVENESS
　　　AFTER *WAL-MART* 92
　　　1. Product Design v. Product Packaging 92
　　　　• *In re Slokevage* 92
　　　　　Notes and Questions 95

|   |   |
|---|---|
| 2. Secondary Meaning | 96 |
| • Restatement (Third) of Unfair Competition (1995) Section 13, Comment (e) | 96 |
| • *Yankee Candle Co., Inc. v. Bridgewater Candle Co., LLC* | 98 |
| Notes and Questions | 103 |

# 3 FUNCTIONALITY 107

## A. INTRODUCTION TO THE CONCEPT OF FUNCTIONALITY 107
- *Kellogg Co. v. National Biscuit Co.* — 108
- Notes and Questions — 111

## B. THE SCOPE OF THE FUNCTIONALITY DOCTRINE 112

### 1. Utilitarian Features 112
- *In re Morton-Norwich Products, Inc.* — 112
- Notes and Questions — 122

### 2. Aesthetic Features 123
- *Wallace Int'l Silversmiths, Inc. v. Godinger Silver Art Co., Inc.* — 124
- *Brunswick Corp. v. British Seagull Ltd.* — 129
- Notes and Questions — 131

## C. THE MODERN APPROACH TO FUNCTIONALITY 132

### 1. The U.S. Supreme Court Framework 132
- *Qualitex Co. v. Jacobson Prods. Co., Inc.* — 133
- *TrafFix Devices, Inc. v. Marketing Displays, Inc.* — 135
- Notes and Questions — 141

### 2. Applying the Modern Supreme Court Framework after *TrafFix* 143

  a. Utilitarian Features — 143
  - *Valu Engineering, Inc. v. Rexnord Corp.* — 143
  - *Eppendorf-Netheler-Hinz Gmbh v. Ritter Gmbh* — 147
  - *Fuji Kogyo Co., Ltd. v. Pacific Bay Int'l, Inc.* — 149
  - Notes and Questions — 156

  b. Aesthetic Features — 160
  - *Abercrombie & Fitch Stores, Inc. v. American Eagle Outfitters* — 160
  - *Au-Tomotive Gold, Inc. v. Volkswagen of America, Inc.* — 165
  - Notes and Questions — 169

  c. The Relationship between the Tests — 171
  - Notes and Questions — 173

### 3. Functionality in the European Union 174
- *Koninklijke Philips Electronics NV v. Remington Consumer Products Ltd* — 174

- *Case C-48/09 P, Lego Juris A/S v. Office for Harmonisation in the Internal Market* — 177
- *Benetton Group Spa v. G-Star International BV 2007 E.C.R. I-07709 (ECJ 2007)* — 181
  Notes and Questions — 184

### D. BEYOND FUNCTIONALITY? — 185
- *Vornado Air Circulation Sys., Inc. v. Duracraft Corp.* — 186
  Notes and Questions — 197
- *Bretford Mfg., Inc. v. Smith System Mfg. Corp.* — 204
  Notes and Questions — 208

## 4 ENFORCEMENT AND DEFENSES — 211

### A. TRADE DRESS INFRINGEMENT — LIKELIHOOD OF CONFUSION — 211
- Figure 4-1: Likelihood of Confusion Factor Tests — 214

1. Applying the Multifactor Confusion Test in Trade Dress Cases — 219
   a. Product Packaging — 219
   - *Ambrit, Inc. v. Kraft, Inc.* — 219
     Notes and Questions — 228
     Problem 4-1: Likelihood of Confusion in Private-Label Goods Cases — 235
   b. Product Design — 239
   - *Versa Products Company, Inc. v. Bifold Company (Manufacturing) Ltd.* — 239
     Notes and Questions — 252

2. Confusion away from the Point of Sale — 255
   - *Ferrari S.P.A. Esercizio Fabriche Automobili e Corse v. Roberts* — 255
     Notes and Questions — 260
   - *Gibson Guitar Corp. v. Paul Reed Smith Guitars, LP* — 262
     Notes and Questions — 269

### B. TRADE DRESS DILUTION AND OTHER NON-CONFUSION-BASED THEORIES — 270

1. Protection against Dilution — 271
   - Lanham Act Section 43(c) — 271
     Notes and Questions — 273

2. Protection against Counterfeiting — 276

### C. PERMISSIBLE USE OF ANOTHER'S TRADE DRESS — 277
- *Herman Miller, Inc. v. A. Studio S.R.L.* — 277
  Notes and Questions — 281

- *Mattel Inc. v. Walking Mountain Productions*    284
  - Notes and Questions    291
- **D. REMEDIES**    292

# PART III. DESIGN PATENTS    295

# 5 SECURING RIGHTS    297

- Patent and Trademark Office Manual of Patent Examining Procedure    300

## A. WHAT IS A "DESIGN FOR AN ARTICLE OF MANUFACTURE"?    301
- *Hoop v. Hoop*    301
- Notes and Questions    304
- Problem 5-1: Computer-Generated Icons    312

## B. ORNAMENTALITY AND FUNCTIONALITY    312
- *In re Webb*    312
- Notes and Questions    315
- *Best Lock Corp. v. Ilco Unican Corp.*    320
- *PHG Technologies, LLC v. St. John Companies, Inc.*    325
- Notes and Questions    330

## C. NOVELTY AND NONOBVIOUSNESS    335
- *Door-Master Corp. v. Yorktowne, Inc.*    335
- Notes and Questions    339
- *International Seaway Trading Corp. v. Walgreens Corp.*    341
- Notes and Questions    351
- Problem 5-2: The Middle Finger Design    352
- Problem 5-3: Experimenting with Designs    352
- *Durling v. Spectrum Furniture Co., Inc.*    355
- Notes and Questions    359
- Problem 5-4: The Football Helmet Birdhouse    363
- Problem 5-5: Priority    364
- Appendix A: U.S. Design Patent No. 543,681    367
- Appendix B: U.S. Design Patent No. 367,440    373

# 6 ENFORCING RIGHTS    381

## A. THE INFRINGEMENT ANALYSIS    381
### 1. The *Gorham* "Substantial Similarity" Test    382
- *Gorham Co. v. White*    382
- Notes and Questions    386

### 2. Substantial Similarity Under *Egyptian Goddess*    391
- *Egyptian Goddess, Inc. v. Swisa, Inc.*    392

|  | Notes and Questions | 407 |
| --- | --- | --- |
|  | *Crocs, Inc. v. International Trade Commission* | 410 |
|  | *Richardson v. Stanley Works, Inc.* | 417 |
|  | Problem 6-1: Applying *Egyptian Goddess*: The Giant Stuff-A-Pumpkin | 422 |
|  | Problem 6-2: Design Patents and the Repair/Reconstruction Distinction | 424 |
| **B.** | **REMEDIES** | **425** |
|  | • *Nike, Inc. v. Wal-Mart Stores, Inc.* | 425 |
|  | Notes and Questions | 429 |

# PART IV. COPYRIGHT — 431

# 7 COPYRIGHT — 433

## A. COPYRIGHTABILITY IN GENERAL — 433

### 1. Originality — 434
- *Yurman Studio, Inc. v. Castaneda* — 434
- Notes and Questions — 436

### 2. The Section 102(b) Exclusions — 437
- *Herbert Rosenthal Jewelry Corp. v. Kalpakian* — 437
- Notes and Questions — 440

## B. "PICTORIAL, GRAPHIC AND SCULPTURAL WORKS": USEFUL ARTICLES AND THE SEPARABILITY DOCTRINE — 440

### 1. Copyright Protection for Useful Articles — 441
- *Mazer v. Stein* — 441
- Notes and Questions — 444

### 2. The Separability Doctrine Under the 1976 Act — 445
- *Pivot Point Int'l, Inc. v. Charlene Products, Inc.* — 446
- Notes and Questions — 462

## C. SCOPE OF COPYRIGHT PROTECTION — 464

### 1. Copyright Infringement — 465
- *Peter Pan Fabrics, Inc. v. Martin Weiner Corp.* — 465
- *Ty, Inc. v. GMA Accessories, Inc.* — 466
- *JCW Investments, Inc. v. Novelty, Inc.* — 470
- Notes and Questions — 474

### 2. Fair Use — 475
- *Mattel Inc. v. Walking Mountain Productions* — 475
- Notes and Questions — 482

### D. ARCHITECTURAL WORKS — 483
- *T-Peg, Inc. v. Vermont Timber Works, Inc.* — 483
  Notes and Questions — 490
- *Leicester v. Warner Brothers* — 491
  Notes and Questions — 506

### E. WORKS OF VISUAL ART — 507
- *Martin v. City of Indianapolis* — 507
- *Massachusetts Museum of Contemporary Art Foundation Inc. v. Büchel* — 513
  Notes and Questions — 523

## PART V. SUI GENERIS REGIMES — 525

## 8 SUI GENERIS DESIGN PROTECTION — 527

### A. EUROPEAN DESIGN RIGHTS — 528
- Community Design Regulation Article 7 — 533
- *Green Lane Products Ltd. v. PMS International Group Plc.* — 534
- Community Design Regulation Articles 10 and 19(1) — 543
- *Proctor & Gamble Co. v. Reckitt Benckiser (UK) Ltd* — 544
- *J Choo (Jersey) Ltd v. Towerstone Ltd.* — 556
  Notes and Questions — 560

### B. SUI GENERIS REGIMES UNDER U.S. LAW — 566
- Vessel Hull Design Protection Act — 567
  Notes and Questions — 571
- Epilogue — 572

*Table of Cases* — 573
*Index* — 579

# *PREFACE*

As Jerry Reichman suggests in the quote with which we begin this book, the protection of design is a fascinating and arguably still-unsolved challenge for intellectual property law. Jerry's observation resonated easily with both of us: design protection was the focus of Graeme's doctoral research, and Mark litigated design patents in practice. In part for that reason, we decided that it merited the in-depth treatment that we provide in this book. But there are other reasons too. Of course, design is crucially important in today's economy, across virtually all industries. The legal protection offered to such an economically significant enterprise is thus important in and of itself. However, a number of pedagogical considerations also prompted this book. Design raises many of the policy puzzles that arise in the better known intellectual property regimes (such as copyright, patent, and trademark). Design protection law offers an efficient vehicle for addressing the sorts of policy choices that are debated throughout intellectual property law. Moreover, because design protection implicates a number of intellectual property regimes, students who have studied those regimes can apply their knowledge in an intensive manner that allows consideration of a wide range of social and commercial contexts. Finally, because discussions of design protection frequently contemplate departures from the traditional regimes in favor of sui generis protection, the study of design protection offers a theoretical window into possible new paradigms of intellectual property protection (especially for new types of subject matter). Thus, materials on design protection are versatile, and capable of being used for a survey exploration of intellectual property, for an advanced course in applied intellectual property, or for a seminar that probes recurring theoretical dilemmas—not to mention, for simply learning about design protection law.

One way to view design protection is through a trademark lens, a perspective that generous judicial decisions (especially, but not exclusively, in the United States) have periodically encouraged. We explore that perspective in Chapters 2-4 of this book. In that part of the book, we borrow some core materials from our book *Trademarks and Unfair Competition: Law and Policy*,

xvii

and we augment those materials with new cases, notes, questions, and problems applying general trademark principles specifically to trade dress.

In the United States, the design patent regime has long been part of the design protection landscape. But it receives cursory treatment in most intellectual property casebooks. In Chapters 5 and 6, we hope to remedy this deficiency by addressing all aspects of design patent validity and enforcement. The lack of any sustained, prior treatment of design patents may have reflected design's position at the intersection of other major intellectual property rights as well as the lack of confidence in design patents as effective instruments of protection. But, as will be seen from the very recent date-stamp on many appellate decisions in Chapters 5 and 6, there has been a contemporary rejuvenation of interest in design patent protection. The materials in these chapters are the first to tackle that rejuvenation.

Copyright protection also remains an alternative for producers of innovative designs. The cases and materials in Chapter 7 allow the instructor to explore not only the core question of how copyright protects designs generally, but also the more specific treatment of architectural designs by the Copyright Act. Finally, in Chapter 8, we discuss sui generis design regimes, using the prominent example of the free-standing design protection regimes available in the European Union. American producers are heavy users of the EU regimes, and the treatment in this Chapter allows us to pursue the comparative dimension to the topic that we otherwise weave throughout the materials (especially in our treatment of trademark law). Moreover, the EU system is often offered as a model for potential adoption in the United States; a detailed analysis also enables the instructor to raise questions about whether the U.S. should consider its own stand-alone, comprehensive design protection scheme (taking into account the limited sui generis design protection regimes, such as those for boat hulls, which we also address in Chapter 8).

We are indebted to many people who were crucial to the completion of this book. Carol McGeehan first persuaded us that the innovations we tried in our *Trademarks and Unfair Competition* book could successfully transfer to the topic of designs. John Devins helped us immensely, and displayed great patience in allowing us to explore design protection in the way and to the extent that we thought it warranted. And he also introduced us to his brother Peter, whose design graces the front cover of this book, for which we are grateful. Erica Anderson, Julie Mowers, Liz Peters, and many other research assistants helped us with early drafts, and Mike Morris and Leslie Prill assisted with more recent incarnations of the manuscript. Kati Jumper provided outstanding secretarial support, as always.

Finally, to our considerable amazement, Brian, Julie, and our respective families all permitted us to work on yet another book. As they occasionally remind us, we owe them big time for their limitless support, patience and love.

Graeme B. Dinwoodie<br>
Mark D. Janis

April 2010

# PART I
# INTRODUCTION

# CHAPTER 1
# INTRODUCTION TO TRADE DRESS AND DESIGN LAW

[I]ndustrial design has posed the intellectual property world's single most complicated puzzle.
    J.H. Reichman, *Past and Current Trends in the Evolution of Design Protection Law—A Comment*, 4 Fordham Intell. Prop. Media & Ent. L.J. 387 (1993).

Fabulous amounts of time and effort have been poured into solving the design protection problem with, to date, no legislative solution.
    *In re Nalbandian*, 661 F.2d 1214, 1218 n. 1 (CCPA 1981) (Rich, J., concurring).

This book addresses one of the most difficult issues in intellectual property law: how to provide optimal protection for designs. It is also one of the oldest dilemmas in world intellectual property law, and one that played a prominent (albeit often overlooked) role in the development of modern intellectual property law. *See* Brad Sherman & Lionel Bently, The Making of Modern Intellectual Property Law (1999) (addressing the role of design legislation in early British intellectual property law). The enterprise of industrial design has been commercially important for many decades, and design endeavors more broadly speaking trace back for centuries. Although intellectual property laws were applied quite early on to protect designs, there remains no international consensus on the precise form that design protection should take. Nor have national approaches remained consistent over time. As we will see, the U.S. Supreme Court has vacillated in its jurisprudence on designs, and Congress has contemplated free-standing design protection legislation some seventy times without enacting it.

At the same time, visual imagery has become predominant in modern culture. Accordingly, the pressure is mounting to provide an adequately balanced scheme of design protection. This book examines domestic and foreign intellectual property law pertaining to designs, exploring both doctrine and policy in some detail.

In Part A of this chapter, we first provide background information on design and the design process, and we consider what is meant by "design" in the context of intellectual property protection. We then provide, in Part B, a brief overview of international, U.S., and European legal regimes that govern the intellectual property law of designs, to provide an introduction to the materials in the remainder of the book. Finally, in Part C we conclude by examining a key problem in U.S. design law: whether securing protection for a design under one intellectual property regime should preclude protection for the same design under another regime. We refer to this as the "cumulation/preemption" problem. We return to each of these themes in subsequent chapters of the book.

## A. INTRODUCTION: WHAT IS DESIGN?

Apple Inc. markets a family of digital electronic devices—iPods. Through mid-2008, Apple had sold over 150 million iPods. The iPod "is equal parts MP3 player and fashion accessory, and it owes its mainstream success probably more to the latter." Matt Buchanan, *The Siren Song of iPod Love*, Washington Square News, April 8, 2004, *available at* http://media.www.nyunews.com/media/storage/paper869/news/2004/04/08/Opinionshardwired/The-Siren.Song.Of.Ipod.Love-2389990.shtml. Commentators refer to the iPod's "sleek" and "minimalist" design. A sketch representing one version of the iPod is reproduced below.

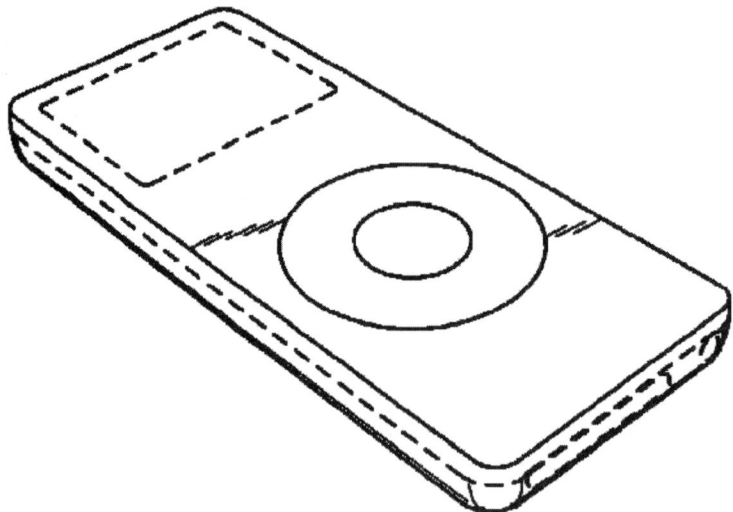

The overall visual appearance of the iPod product is commercially valuable to Apple. Accordingly, to the extent that the appearance is protectable by intellectual property laws, Apple might be well-advised to take steps to do so. The iPod player is surely an example of successful "design". But the concept of design is elusive and complex, as the following excerpts indicate.

## ALICE RAWSTHORN, WHAT DEFIES DEFINING, BUT EXISTS EVERYWHERE?

International Herald Tribune, Aug. 19, 2008
http://www.iht.com/articles/2008/08/18/arts/DESIGN18.php[*]

What is design? It's a seemingly simple question, that's very hard to answer. Think about it, and you'll realize why.

The word itself has several uses. It's a verb and a noun, which can mean design as in the practice of design, but also the process of doing it, as well as the end-result. Confused? No wonder. A sentence coined by the American design historian John Heskett may help to make things clearer: "Design is to produce a design to design a design." He might have added the fourth use of design as a noun, the 17th-century definition of "a design" as a dastardly plan.

Then there are all of the areas where design is deployed. Architecture. Engineering. Products. Transport. Fashion. Graphics. Multimedia. Information technology. Social services. Disaster relief, and so on. How can it be expected to have a coherent meaning across all of them? Or when it means different things in different countries? It can't, which is why design has become such an ambiguous term, complex and often contradictory with a range of meanings that change over time. So what does it mean now?

1. Design and things.

Ambiguous though it is, design has held on to one meaning for centuries: the process of conceiving and creating things in the hope of making life easier and more enjoyable. Originally this was the role of craftsmen, who also made their own work, but since the Industrial Revolution, it has become the province of designers, who conceive, but don't necessarily make, whatever they design.

Among the pioneers was the British sculptor John Flaxman, who designed vases, plates and other ceramic pieces for Wedgwood in the late 1700s. A century later, another Briton, Christopher Dresser, pioneered the role of the professional designer by developing products for different manufacturers. The mid-20th century gave us such exemplars as Dieter Rams, the German designer of gorgeous electronic products for Braun, and Ladislav Sutnar, the Czech graphic designer whose information design projects are the precursors of computer icons and Web navigation systems in use today.

This traditional meaning of design is now perpetuated by Vitra with its beautifully engineered furniture, but new interpretations are emerging. One is to use design to reduce the number of objects in our lives, rather than to create new ones. As the environmental crisis deepens, it makes sense to save materials and energy by combining the functions of several products into one, so we can dispense with the rest. Take Apple's iPhone or the BlackBerry Bold, which play

---

[*]©2008. *The New York Times*. All rights reserved. Used by permission and protected by the Copyright Laws of the United States. The printing, copying, redistribution or retransmission of the Material without express written permission is prohibited.

the multiple roles of a phone, watch, alarm clock, diary, barometer, Internet browser and atlas.

2. Design and formulas.

What do a BlackBerry, an 18th-century Wedgwood vase and Sutnar's instruction manuals have in common? They were all designed in the expectation that they'd always take exactly the same form. But designers are now also working more flexibly by developing formulas to produce things that can be interpreted differently by different people, rather than finished objects.

An early example is the geodesic dome, the emergency shelter designed in 1948 by the American inventor Richard Buckminster Fuller. Rather than envisioning it as a completed structure, he prescribed instructions to build it anywhere in the world, using whatever materials might be available. Hundreds of thousands of geodesic domes have since been constructed using everything from plastic sheeting and old clothes, to scraps of wood and metal.

. . .

3. Design and behavior.

One of the most powerful, and often unsung roles of design is regulating behavior. Think of how traffic signs influence our driving, or maps guide us to our destinations. This element of design is becoming increasingly important, not least in helping us to use digital devices, like cellphones. As their form gives few clues as to their function, the quality of the user interface design (the software that determines whether or not they can be operated easily and intuitively) is as important in determining if we'll enjoy using them as how they look.

. . .

4. Meaningless design.

The contemporary equivalent of design's 17th-century guise as a "dastardly plan" is the use of the word "design" as a marketing ploy. Think of all the shoddily designed cars with "design" emblazoned on their tailgates, and even shoddier furniture stores that include the word in their advertising slogans. Such promotional stunts confused design with styling, design purists used to complain, but these days the situation is worse. The word has been so drained of meaning, that whatever is billed as "design" will almost certainly be badly designed, just as self-styled "icons" and "classics" are anything but.

### GRAEME B. DINWOODIE, FEDERALIZED FUNCTIONALISM: THE FUTURE OF DESIGN PROTECTION IN THE EUROPEAN UNION
24 AIPLA Q.J. 611, 626-632 (1996)[*]

As first understood, "industrial design" described the form given to products, quite distinct from their function.[37] Design was an essentially supplementary

---

[*]Copyright 1996 Graeme B. Dinwoodie. Reprinted with permission.

37. *See* CHRISTOPHER LORENZ, THE DESIGN DIMENSION 10 (1986). The origin of modern industrial design can be traced to late nineteenth and early twentieth century England and, paradoxically, to

process, an afterthought that by its concealment of the ugliness of utilitarian parts contributed to post-production marketing efforts. The primary unfinished functional design of the product was conceived of without reference to aesthetic considerations. In the early twentieth century, however, following the Bauhaus[38] emphasis upon form following function,[39] industrial design evolved to include the consideration and application of aesthetic design features as an integral part of the overall product development process.

Industrial design in this modern sense — which might, with some overgeneralization, be called "functionalist" design — began to figure prominently in the priorities of management in Europe by the late 1950s. Although U.S. industry had deployed industrial design since the 1920s,[41] the conversion of U.S. industry to fully integrated functionalism occurred later than in Europe.[42] Until the latter half of the twentieth century, industrial design in the United States still consisted of efforts to "stylize" the appearance of a product in a supplementary (almost obsolete) fashion that resonated more in the fields of advertising or sales than in the development of the product's features.[43]

---

the Arts and Crafts movement, which sprung from a *dissatisfaction* with manufactured goods and a renewed respect for the individual craftsman. *See id.* at 10-24; JOHN HESKETT, INDUSTRIAL DESIGN 85 (1980). Led by William Morris and Philip Webb, the Arts and Crafts Movement rebelled against the values and aesthetics of the Industrial Revolution and the division of design and manufacture that had occurred during that period. *See* RALPH CAPLAN, BY DESIGN 40 (1982). *But see* HESKETT, *supra* at 19-20 (suggesting that the influence of Morris and followers, while great abroad, was limited in Britain, where industry perceived their views as based on a nostalgia for the craft and culture of the past). Its advocacy of pre-industrial values and its aversion to the ugliness of machine-made functional products had an incidental effect in the industrial arena, however, and led to the innovation of what literally might be called "applied art," i.e., art applied to a product in the final stages of its manufacture. This indiscriminate application of ornament was the earliest and most crude form of industrial design, allowing manufacturers to cater to the demands of novelty and fashion while retaining the constancy and standardization of product that contributed toward cheap production. *See id.* at 72 (discussing concept with respect to the commercial considerations of the U.S. automobile industry in the 1920s).

38. The Bauhaus School of architecture, design and craftsmanship, was founded in Germany in 1919 by Walter Gropius (1883-1969) and was later led by Ludwig Mies van der Rohe. The Bauhaus emphasized the importance of simplicity and economy, and attempted to reconcile art and design with industrial techniques. Its historical significance lies not in the range of designed products emanating from it, but in its philosophical and educational influence. *See* HESKETT, *supra* note 37, at 103-104 ("Bauhaus products appear no more than a minuscule contribution from an avant garde fringe group . . . [but] the fact of its enormous influence is undeniable. . . . What the Bauhaus was appears to have been less important than what its members and followers believed it to be. Its influence, far greater than the sum of its practical achievements, is above all a testimony to the power of ideas.").

39. The precept that form should follow function was, of course, not exclusive to the Bauhaus. The phrase itself is often credited to Louis Sullivan, the important late nineteenth and early twentieth century architect.

41. "Furniture and textiles, their usefulness taken for granted, had long sold on design. Now it was the turn of washing machines, furnaces, switchboards, and locomotives." LORENZ, *supra* note 37, at 14 (citation omitted).

42. The [1985 launch of the Ford Taurus and Mercury Sable] marked the conversion of the world's second largest motor company to a strategy of competing through adventurous, aerodynamic product design. Gone was the traditional policy, common to all American motor manufacturers, of cladding a lackluster and unimaginative vehicle in an unwieldy, boxy, battering-ram shape, garnished with all sorts of ritzy, angular radiator grilles, tail fins and chromium strips. In its place was a policy of integral design, in which the car's uncluttered shape was heavily influenced by the need to reduce wind drag in order to improve its fuel consumption.

LORENZ, *supra* note 37, at 15.

43. *See* HENRY DREYFUSS, DESIGNING FOR PEOPLE 69 (1955) (criticizing Detroit's habit of disguising form related to function with appendages of chrome teeth, disks, and wings), *cited in* LORENZ, *supra*

Indeed, early U.S. efforts at more integrated design were commercially unsuccessful.[44] Eventually, however, led by designers such as Henry Dreyfuss, the integrated functionalism of the Europeans came to the United States and replaced the supplementary "styling" of the earlier years.[45]

Design made the transition to mass-produced goods not just as the reflection of a dominant artistic philosophy but also as a commercially dictated marketing strategy. Properly effected, the process of making functional products appear more aesthetically pleasing resulted in greater commercial success.[46] Manufacturers now attribute a significant portion of a product's success, and thus allocate a substantial portion of investment in product development, to design.[47] "Design is no longer a luxury, . . . it is a necessity."[48] And the commercial significance (and necessity) of industrial design is likely only to grow. As the world consumer product market integrates, the consumer is faced with a larger array of relatively standardized products. Discrimination among these similar products will depend increasingly upon design innovation: in the era of product proliferation, superior design is one of the primary means by which consumers will differentiate [among] products.[49]

More idealistically, to the extent that society is experiencing the indiscriminate expansion of product availability, the consequent "variable banality" can be overcome only by meaningful product innovation rather than superficial variation imposed as a decorative afterthought.[50] Lack of protection for those

---

note 37, at 15. "From the very start, a yawning gulf developed between European and U.S. conceptions of industrial design: the one highly intellectual and dedicated to functional simplicity (what has often been described as 'working from the inside out'), the other a styling tool at the service of sales and advertising, where the exterior was all-important, and the inside mattered little." LORENZ, *supra* note 37, at 11.

44. *See* LORENZ, *supra* note 37, at 15 (noting the failure of the Chrysler "Airflow").

45. Arguably, European manufacturers also began paying greater heed to "styling," suggesting not so much a fundamental shift in world design but rather an assimilation that has tended to drift in favor of integrated functionalism. *See* HESKETT, *supra* note 37, at 123 & 126 (impact of "streamlining" felt outside the United States, the image conveyed by publications and films). Raymond Loewy, (1893-1984), a French-born designer who immigrated to America in 1919, claimed his design of the Sears, Roebuck Coldspot refrigerator to be the "first work commissioned as industrial design in America." RAYMOND LOEWY, INDUSTRIAL DESIGN 13 (1979).

46. *See* LOEWY, *supra* note 45, at 10 (1979) ("Between two products equal in price, function and quality, the better looking will outsell the other"); *cf.* PAUL INGRASSIA AND JOSEPH B. WHITE, COMEBACK: THE FALL & RISE OF THE AMERICAN AUTOMOBILE INDUSTRY 179 (Simon & Schuster 1994) ("Because of dated designs [of the Chevrolet Cavalier] and poor quality, GM was forced to shell out $700 in retail discounts for every vehicle it sold in North America—a 40 percent increase from the year before.").

47. A study conducted by the Gallup Organization in 1985 revealed that senior U.S. business executives attributed 60% of the success of a new product to industrial design. *See Hearings on S. 791 Before the Subcomm. on Patents, Copyrights and Trademarks of the Senate Comm. on the Judiciary,* 100th Cong. 32 (1987) (statement of Cooper C. Woodring, Chairman of the Board, Industrial Designers Society of America).

48. LORENZ, *supra* note 37, at 4.

49. *See id.* ("One of the few hopes companies have to stand out from the crowd is to produce superiorly designed products for their target markets.") (citation omitted).

50. Cristina Morozzi, *E' Possibile la bellezza?,* 154 MODO 16, 17 (1994) ("To counter standardization and the pointless multiplicity of styles, there is no point going back to the basics: radical innovation is necessary. . . . Avant-garde has to become a permanent, rather than a temporary condition.") (translated by publisher at 4). *See also* LORENZ, *supra* note 37, at 24 ("As the new corporate design converts have learned in recent years, it is in helping to achieve *real* differentiation

who assume risk and discard the shackles of orthodoxy contributes to design conservatism, and to the banality that such conservatism inevitably engenders.[51]

Yet, many national laws offer only limited protection to the functional (as opposed to ornamental) aspects of a product's design, although designs integrating form and function have become the most valuable facet of modern industrial design. Acting on this premise, the [European] Commission perceived a Community interest in protecting that increasingly-valuable form of design against misappropriation.

### Robert C. Denicola, Applied Art And Industrial Design: A Suggested Approach to Copyright in Useful Articles
67 Minn. L. Rev. 707, 738-741 (1983)[*]

### III. Applied Art and Industrial Design

#### A. The Design Process

. . .

In a sense, the origins of industrial design can be traced to the earliest attempts to fashion natural materials into more useful forms. Not until the Industrial Revolution brought the capacity to manufacture unlimited quantities of identical products, however, did a discreet conception of industrial design begin to emerge. Initially, industrial design was little more than a belated attempt to conceal the patent ugliness proliferated by developing technologies. This concept of industrial design as decoration, however, was gradually replaced by a vision premised on a more intimate relationship between the nature of a product and its appearance. In 1894, Frank Lloyd Wright declared that "the machine is here to stay," and challenged the designer to "use this normal tool of civilization to best advantage instead of prostituting it as he has hitherto done in reproducing with murderous ubiquity forms born of

---

that industrial design can play such a valuable part. To do that, . . . [r]ather than just tinkering around with the product's wrapping, he or she must start with the complete product as it would be used by someone. . . .").

51. *Cf.* Robin Laurence, *Appeal of Steel Enjoys A Retro-Revival,* Vancouver Sun, Aug. 12, 1995, at D5 (noting idealist beliefs concerning the effect of modernist industrial design on social and economic affairs). A legal regime that encourages minor ornamental variations on an uninspired theme also disserves the consuming public. A choice of similar variants may be no choice at all. Plentiful homogeneity may be particularly destructive of choice and diversity because the purchasing resistance to radical innovation induced by similar variants ultimately snowballs and affects the creative process itself. To deal with this problem, Raymond Loewy formulated the principle of "MAYA" (most advanced yet acceptable) by which to design consumer products. *See* Heskett, *supra* note 37, at 178; *see also* Gillo Dorfles, *Sociological and Semiological Aspects of Design,* in Design History: Past, Process, Product 11, 12-13 (1979) ("An incessant supply of graphic, cinematic, televisual and musical images, unanswered by an equivalent response on the part of the consumer, may lead to a sterilization of the imaginative quality of the individual. . . . There is a pressing need to restore to the consumer the possibility of exercising his own choice and of enhancing his own preferential capacity, in rebellion against the framework of pre-established conformism—even though that conformism is an avant-garde one."); John F. Pile, Design: Purpose, Form and Meaning 2 (1979) ("In spite of our belief that we live in the civilization with the highest level of technical achievement in history, we accept with enthusiasm some of the worst artifacts that humanity has ever endured.").

*Copyright 1983 Robert C. Denicola. Reprinted with permission.

other times and other conditions."[152] The twentieth century soon saw industrial design become an integral aspect of product development.

The dominant feature of modern industrial design is the merger of aesthetic and utilitarian concerns. It is the influence of nonaesthetic factors, the nexus between what the product must do and how it must look, that distinguishes true industrial design from other artistic endeavors. The industrial designer as engineer—a perspective no less valid than industrial designer as artist—is subject to the functional constraints inherent in each undertaking. The designer cannot follow wherever aesthetic interests might lead. Utilitarian concerns influence, and at times dictate, available choices. Indeed, aesthetic success is often measured in terms of the harmony achieved between competing interests. The merger of aesthetics and utility defines the designer's craft, so that "whatever else he is or isn't—artist, engineer, salesman, planner, management consultant, inventor—the industrial designer is a problem solver."[155]

The most obvious factor influencing and directing the designer's creativity is the necessity of accommodating the functional operation of the product. At its most fundamental level, this consideration simply excludes any form that significantly interferes with the utility of the article. Modern approaches to industrial design, however, generally seek a relationship between form and function far more intimate than simple compatibility. Raymond Loewy, perhaps the design profession's most celebrated practitioner, speaks of the "natural form" and "self-expression of the machine."[156] The notion of form reflecting function is a basic tenet of contemporary design: "The best designs are those in which the appearance springs truly from the structure, and is a logical expression of it."[157] Perusal of any of the multitude of books collecting illustrations of "modern" design confirms the general acceptance of this fundamental credo. The notion of expressing function through form differs in an important respect from the more primitive requirement that form be compatible with function, since the former is itself a purely aesthetic concern, expressing one conception of "good" design. In this sense, the principle suggests limitations not unlike those imposed on any artist by internal or external conceptions of artistic merit or worth. When practiced, however, the principle operates to intensify the nexus between form and function.

Other utilitarian considerations can, of course, be identified: "[T]he following things should be treated respectfully: function, ease of operation, maintenance, cost of upkeep, storage, cost of manufacturing, packing, shipping, display, safety, fail-safe operations, . . . all these and more are involved in doing the job properly. . . ."[160] Such concerns can be served poorly or well, but they cannot be ignored. Their cumulative influence can render the designer's task quite unlike that confronting the painter or sculptor.

---

152. [V. Papanek, Design for the Real World 22-23 (1971)].
155. Industrial Designers Society of America, Design in America 5 (1969).
156. [R. Loewy, Industrial Design 13 (1979).]
157. [W. Cain, Engineering Product Design 157 (1969).]
160. [R. Loewy, *supra* note 156, at 18.]

Orit Fischman Afori, Reconceptualizing Property in Designs
25 Cardozo Arts & Ent. L.J. 1105, 1110-1115 (2008)*

## What Is a Design, and What Functions Does It Serve?

. . .

Industrial designs first emerged in the nineteenth century, with the Industrial Revolution. As the costs of production of goods dropped, the foundations of the current "consumer society" were laid: supply grew, competition was created, and producers had to attract consumers by improving the quality and appeal of their merchandise. This historical process led to the development of a new profession, that of "art-workers," whose job it was to adapt the artistic skills of the old-world fine-arts realm into the service of modern consumer society, including the artistic shaping of industrialized merchandise. In the twentieth century there were further developments in conceptualizing designs, as art and industry merged, and the designer began to be seen as an artist in his own right. In response, social definitions strengthened the differentiation between implicitly lower-class artisans and implicitly upper-class artists, with the former in charge of utility and the latter in control of beauty, or art for art's sake. Oscar Wilde captured this insight by stating: "[a]ll art is quite useless."[21] Wilde's view dominated the nineteenth century, and ran counter to a tradition established much earlier by Horace that good art is "dulce et ultile," or instructive and pleasant. The utilitarian emphasis allied craftsmanship, and later mass production techniques, with diminished artistic worth, and these social practices were reflected and enshrined in legislation. The cross-fertilization of high art and design in the past hundred years led to the present questioning of this rationale. Yet the development of a body of law pertaining to design was a long and essentially random process. The problem of defining designed products has remained relevant because the question of whether designs are industrial or artistic property remains unresolved. Even without assigning an appropriate classification on design, there are many utilitarian justifications for commodification of designs and acknowledging their proprietary character, per se.

Investment in product design increases attractiveness and furthers market competition, which enhance the market's efficiency. Investment in product design furthers efficiency by serving customers' benefit in terms of both quality and the aesthetic appearance of the product. By furthering a product's aesthetic appearance, design makes a positive contribution to market efficiency because the product increases the consumer's aesthetic pleasure, aside from its utility. Furthering enjoyment by aesthetic products has a positive value, per se, which enhances public welfare, even if such investment might make the product more expensive. This benefit stemming from advancing design is also rooted in a socio-economic context which encourages personal preferences of taste, style, etc. As there is room for different flavors

---

*Copyright 2008 Orit Fischman Afori. Reprinted with permission.
21. Oscar Wilde, Preface to The Picture of Dorian Gray (1891).

of the same foodstuff to suit consumers' likes and dislikes, the same logic applies to other products, such as furniture and fashion. In today's consumer society, consumption of goods no longer depends only on necessity, but has multiple sociological and psychological functions. Consumption symbolizes a certain life-style and socio-economic status, but it also serves various goals, such as social equalization, self-identification, etc. Consumers are divided into varied subgroups which enables the formation of market segments (sometimes accompanied with price discrimination mechanisms) according to potential profits from the differences in their needs and preferences. Design in this context serves as a means to communicate information, such as cultural values (of taste and style), social values (of environmental impact and equal availability), and also more "objective" attributes (of ease of use and durability).

Opponents of making design rights proprietary contend that the only beneficiary of design protection is whoever commissions the design, not the end-customer. The end-user does not benefit because the principle [sic.] economic function of applied or industrial design is to increase product competitiveness to increase returns. Design rights, so goes the argument, are not justified from a utilitarian point of view. The industrial designer's role, it is claimed, is to introduce false distinctions among identical products in order to artificially increase sales. Therefore, even if a competitor copies a design, it would not significantly alter the first producer's incentive to further invest in product design since he must maintain the product's attractiveness to remain competitive. Furthermore, if copying the design will cause customers to confuse the products of two producers, a cause of action already exists under trademark's tort law. This ... confuses design as a category with designs that have indeed been made into trademarks. Thus, according to the opposing line of reasoning, there is no justification for the commodification of designs, and trademark torts satisfactorily deal with cases of improper use.

Notably, the opposition to design as a proprietary right fails to consider the role of aesthetics from promoting the product's competitiveness and economic efficiency. In fact, the contrary is true: aesthetics is part of an efficient consumption process, which is aimed to fulfill customers' needs, expectations, etc. In this respect, one of the most insightful redefinitions of design's aesthetic is that:

> [A]esthetics is not simply a visual exercise, but rather the appropriate and harmonious balancing of all user needs and wants within technical and social constraints. The designer must successfully integrate all the requirements that balance the rational, sensory, and emotional expectations of the individual user and of society as a whole.[42]

Furthermore, the information communicated through the product's design is much more than the origin of the goods, as it is with respect to trademarks. Communication of all the various elements of information-from cultural and social values to "objective" attributes—through the product's

---

42. [Gianfranco Zaccai, *Art and Technology, Aesthetic Redefined*, in Discovering Design: Explorations in Design Studies 3, 6 (Richard Buchanan & Victor Margolin eds., Univ. of Chicago Press 1995).]

appearance—increases market efficiency since it enhances market segmentation and makes the consuming process short and satisfactory. The social, cultural and political impact of design on consumer society is well known and hard to overstate. There is vast scholarly research on consumer behavior and the sociological effects of consumption on self-concept and cultural identity, which in turn further both market efficiency and other cultural goals.

As to product quality, the role of design in furthering the public's welfare is profound since the differentiation of products involves the physical and intrinsic change of their appearance, in matters such as size, weight, form, and material, which might have as goals comfort and suitability to meet personal needs and individual requirements. The differentiation accomplished by design to increase sales may also increase the product's functional quality, beyond just appealing to buyers' personal aesthetic preferences. Nevertheless, the aesthetic pleasure in a product is in and of itself a utilitarian value, and hovers between objective, functional benefit and non-objective, personal sensory benefit. Thus, the dichotomy between the two qualities, the functional and the aesthetic, soon breaks down and is further challengeable, since functional, utilitarian features are themselves subject to a dynamic socio-economic and cultural context. Design asks first for whom the product is intended, then determines the appropriate featurers [sic] for his or her socio-economic cohort. In other words, the utilitarian justification for design as an incentive to invest in a product's appearance is concerned with furthering both quality and aesthetics equally.

To conclude, design satisfies the needs and desires of heterogeneous consumers. Accordingly, design may be defined as both a result of human imaginative endeavor in contrast to the purely mechanistic, but guided also by certain [immanent] features, such as technology, function, and fashion.

## NOTES AND QUESTIONS

1. ***Art vs. engineering.*** Is design more about art or engineering? In fashioning appropriate intellectual property rules, is it important to know the answer to that question? Suppose, as Denicola suggests, that the design process entails a complicated merging of aesthetic and utilitarian considerations. Do you expect that traditional intellectual property regimes, such as the utility patent system or the copyright system, are well suited to accommodate such endeavors? If not, should designs be protected by a sui generis (stand-alone) design protection regime? Or is design about something else entirely, besides (or in addition to) art or engineering?

2. ***Distinguishing ornamental from functional.*** In the intellectual property law of design protection, a major theme is the distinction between ornamental and functional features. Does Denicola's description of the design process suggest that making this distinction will be exceptionally difficult? In the Apple iPod design, which features are ornamental and which are functional, in the colloquial sense of those terms? Can you think of other intellectual property doctrines that might be used as the principal criteria for distinguishing between protectable and unprotectable designs? Novelty? Distinctiveness? Originality?

3. ***Verbalizing design.*** Nonverbal designs are difficult to render verbally—as we all know from the saying "A picture is worth a thousand words." How would you characterize, in words, the Apple iPod design depicted above? Is it even possible to do so? The difficulty of translating pictures to words has been a major hurdle in the law of design protection, as the materials in this book illustrate.

4. ***Economic justifications for design protection.*** Are you surprised by the assertion in the Afori excerpt that there is an economic efficiency justification for investing in a product's aesthetic appeal? Do you expect that it would be difficult to quantify aesthetic matters in terms of costs and benefits? If so, what sorts of proxies might the law attempt to develop to alleviate any such difficulty?

5. ***Incentives and the designer.*** Does the law need to provide incentives for producers to invest in aesthetically appealing products such as the Apple iPod? Or will producers do so anyway, even without the promise of exclusivity? Should this matter? That is, should we only recognize intellectual property rights in subject matter that would not be produced but for the promise of intellectual property rights?

6. ***Design innovation in the absence of IP protection?*** An orthodox view of intellectual property's incentive effect is that intellectual property rights supply producers with an incentive to invest in innovation, an incentive that would be dampened if rivals could freely appropriate the producer's innovations and sell them in competition with the producer at low cost. Kal Raustiala & Christopher Sprigman, *The Piracy Paradox: Intellectual Property and Innovation in Fashion Design*, 92 VA. L. REV. 1687 (2006). Raustiala and Sprigman contrast the orthodox view with the reality of the fashion design industry:

> IP law fails to protect the core of fashion, the design. Despite this lack of protection, the fashion industry continues to create new designs on a regular basis. The lack of copyright protection for fashion designs has not deterred investment in the industry. Nor has it reduced innovation in designs, which are plentiful each season. Fashion plainly provides an interesting and important challenge to IP orthodoxy.
>
> . . . [T]he lack of IP rights for fashion design has not quashed innovation, as the orthodox account would predict, and this has in turn reduced the incentive for designers to seek legal protection for their creations. Not only has the lack of copyright protection for fashion designs not destroyed the incentive to innovate in apparel, it may have actually promoted it. This claim—that piracy is paradoxically beneficial for fashion designers—rests on attributes specific to fashion, in particular the status-conferring, or positional, nature of clothing. We do not claim that fashion designers chose this low-IP system in any conscious or deliberate way. But we do claim that the highly unusual political equilibrium in fashion is explicable once we recognize its dynamic effects: that fashion's cyclical nature is furthered and accelerated by a regime of open appropriation.

*Id.* at 1775-76. Would you predict that Raustiala and Sprigman's conclusions about the fashion industry apply equally to design in other fields? Does the incentives story concerning fashion designs remind you of the story one might tell about whether a poet requires an incentive to produce and disseminate poetry? About whether a molecular biologist requires an incentive to investigate the genetic basis for a disease? Or is design a unique endeavor? If the public's aesthetic preferences shift frequently, does this alone make the enterprise of design different? The answers to these questions would seem to be particularly important if we are to fit traditional intellectual property regimes (and their traditional incentive structures) to designs. Other scholars who have studied the dynamics of innovation in fashion design have concluded that a limited right against copying is warranted, particularly to encourage innovation among smaller, less well-established designers. *See* C. Scott Hemphill & Jeannie Suk, *The Law, Culture, and Economics of Fashion*, 61 STAN. L. REV. 1147 (2008-2009).

7. *Other utilitarian justifications for design protection.* Dinwoodie cites the proposition that "[d]esign is no longer a luxury, . . . it is a necessity" (referring to Christopher Lorenz, The Design Dimension (1986)). Do Dinwoodie's arguments support the related proposition that design *protection* is now a necessity? If, as Dinwoodie suggests, design facilitates consumer differentiation among products, how should a design protection law be crafted in order to vindicate this function? Dinwoodie also asserts that without design protection, the visual/cultural landscape would be impoverished. Accepting this premise, how might one structure intellectual property rules so as to promote more adventuresome designs? How would we measure whether such rules were successful in achieving that goal?

8. *Whose interests are served?* When we set about the task of creating intellectual property protection for designs, whose interests are we seeking to serve? Those of the designer? Those of the owner of the intellectual property (which may be the designer, or the designer's employer or assignee)? Of the competitors of the designer? Of the consumers of the products in which the designs are embodied? Of the public? A standard response is that the law should strive to achieve a balance of all of these interests. As you study the materials in this book, consider whether that balance is evident in the law of design protection—or even in the way that judges and legislators talk about the law of design protection.

# B. THE MODERN LEGISLATIVE LANDSCAPE FOR TRADE DRESS AND DESIGN PROTECTION

This book features the U.S. intellectual property law of designs, but also includes significant coverage of international standards and design law in other regions and countries, notably Europe. Many American commentators find the European model to be attractive as a model for reform in the United States.

## 1. THE INTERNATIONAL INTELLECTUAL PROPERTY LAW OF DESIGN

### (a) TRIPS

The TRIPS Agreement, the WTO agreement dealing in detail with intellectual property, sets out minimum substantive standards for intellectual property protection to which WTO members must adhere in fashioning their national laws. TRIPS Part II, Section 4, deals with industrial designs, establishing standards for securing protection (Article 25) and for the nature and scope of protection (Article 26). *See also* art. 2(1) (incorporating Paris convention). Article 25(1) requires members to protect "independently created industrial designs that are new or original," and permits members to decline to extend protection "to designs dictated essentially by technical or functional considerations." Article 25(2) requires members to provide for effective protection specifically for textile designs, and allows members to satisfy this mandate either through "industrial design law or copyright law."

Article 26(1) requires that protected industrial designs enjoy a set of exclusive rights reminiscent of patent rights—that is, rights to prevent the unauthorized making, selling, or importing of articles "bearing or embodying a design which is a copy, or substantially a copy, of the protected design. . . ." Article 26(1) also adds an important caveat, specifying that the unauthorized activities violate the exclusive rights "when such acts are undertaken for commercial purposes." Article 26(2) allows members to provide limited exceptions to the exclusive rights, and Article 26(3) specifies that the protection available to designs must endure for at least ten years. *See generally* Ana Gerdau de Borja, *Exceptions to Design Rights: The Potential Impact of Article 26(2) TRIPS*, 30 EUR. INTELL. PROP. REV. 500 (2008) (offering predictions about the scope of the Article 26(2) exception and analyzing whether a proposed repair exception under the EU Design Directive would conform with Article 26(2)). As you proceed through the book, you should consider how well the various forms of intellectual property protection for design fit with the TRIPS standards.

### (b) The Hague Agreement Concerning the International Registration of Industrial Designs

The Hague Agreement offers the possibility that a designer may obtain protection for a design in a number of designated countries by filing a single application with the World Intellectual Property Organization (WIPO). Older texts of the Hague Agreement, such as the 1934 London Act and the 1960 Hague Act, were crafted to cater to countries that did not carry out substantial examination of design registration applications and thus relied essentially on a deposit system. In the late 1990s, however, efforts were made to conclude a revised version of the agreement, with a view to persuading other countries (such as the United States, Japan, and the United Kingdom) to join the system. These efforts reached fruition at a diplomatic conference in July 1999 in Geneva; it is the Geneva Act that the United States will implement. Although the United States is not currently a member of the Hague Union, on

December 7, 2007, the United States Senate approved ratification of the Geneva Act of the Agreement, and thus U.S. participation in the Hague system is on the horizon.

A Hague application must comply with a series of mandatory content requirements as well as with the specific requirements of those contracting states (so-called additional mandatory content requirements) designated as countries in which protection is sought. These additional requirements come from states with an administrative examination of novelty (termed "Examination Offices"). The United States had indicated in negotiations that the only additional requirements from Article 5(2)(b) of the Geneva Act that it will impose are the inclusion of a claim and the name of the creator of the design. Determinations that the application satisfies the requirements of the Hague Agreement as to form and content are to be made by WIPO. Once the international design registration (IDR) is received by the designated countries, it will be examined as would any domestic application. Thus, the United States PTO would subject the IDR to the same examination process as it would a domestic design patent application. The grounds for refusal will be determined by U.S. law, with the exception that refusal cannot be based on noncompliance with a requirement relating to the form or content of the international application. *See* Geneva Act, art. 12(1). For example, a designated state cannot require applicants to provide a translation of the application into a language that is not required by the agreement. Any notification of refusal to register must be communicated to WIPO within six months, or twelve months in the case of countries (such as the United States) with Examining Offices. *See* Geneva Act Regulations, Rule 18.

## 2. U.S. INTELLECTUAL PROPERTY LAWS REGARDING DESIGN

In the United States, there is no single, free-standing design law. Rather, U.S. intellectual property law on design is composed of a complex of legal regimes: the general trademark and copyright regimes (which encompass design as well as other subject matter) along with the design patent regime (which is devoted specifically to protecting design). The vessel hull protection scheme, housed in Chapter 13 of the U.S. Copyright Act, resembles sui generis design protection in certain respects, as does the Semiconductor Chip Protection Act of 1984, 17 U.S.C. §§901-914. Thus, design law is an especially complex and interesting subject in the United States, one that requires both familiarity with multiple intellectual property regimes and a sense for balancing them optimally. We provide a brief overview of the pertinent regimes in the following discussion to set the stage for the more detailed discussions appearing in the remainder of the book.

### (a) Trademark and Unfair Competition Protection

Trademark law provides one form of protection available to designers. Trademark protection is potentially available for a broad range of subject matter that may include elements of its packaging, its shape, or other nonverbal attributes. These elements, which may extend to the "total image" of a product or service, are often referred to as "trade dress."

The Lanham Act, 15 U.S.C. §§1051-1141n, governs the federal trademark regime. The modern Lanham Act defines the concept of a mark liberally, to include "any word, name, symbol, or device" that identifies or distinguishes one producer's goods or services from another's. 15 U.S.C. §1127 (Lanham Act §45). Mark owners can obtain registered rights through the Lanham Act's "Principal Register" registration scheme by applying to the U.S. Patent and Trademark Office under the procedures specified in Lanham Act §1. Marks must be distinctive and nonfunctional in order to be protectable on the Principal Register, and must not run afoul of any of the various substantive bars to registration set forth in Lanham Act §2. An application for a Lanham Act registration must allege that the applicant has put the mark into use or that the applicant intends to use the mark within a prescribed time subject to certain exceptions pertaining to foreign applicants, a registration only issues upon use. A successful registrant may maintain the registration in force indefinitely if the registrant complies with specified requirements, including the requirement to keep the mark in use. A registrant can enforce rights in a mark through a civil suit for trademark infringement under Lanham Act §32(1)(a) against third party uses that are likely to cause confusion and/or for dilution under §43(c), although the latter is available only to marks qualifying as famous under §43(c)(2)(A).

Federal trademark law also recognizes common law trademark rights, which come into existence when a mark owner puts a mark into use, if the mark is distinctive and nonfunctional. Although a mark owner who has secured only common law rights does not enjoy various procedural advantages available to registrants, the Lanham Act does permit owners of common law marks to enforce them in a federal action for unfair competition under Lanham Act §43(a) that closely approximates those available to registrants under section 32. The Lanham Act remedy against dilution in §43(c) is also available to owners of common law rights in famous marks.

Chapters 2-4 of this book cover trade dress protection. Chapter 2 covers the distinctiveness prerequisite, long a source of conflict in the law of trade dress. Chapter 3 covers functionality, a conceptually difficult protectability doctrine. Finally, Chapter 4 covers trade dress enforcement, focusing on confusion and dilution actions.

### (b) Patent Protection

The U.S. Patent Act, codified at 35 U.S.C. §§1-376, is composed predominantly of provisions that make up the more familiar utility patent system. Embedded within Title 35 are a small number of provisions (most of them in Chapter 16 of that title) that together establish a design patent system, a system that is formally independent of the utility patent system but incorporates many of its features by reference. Design patents are available to inventors of "any new, original and ornamental design for an article of manufacture."

35 U.S.C. §171. Courts have also required that the design not be dictated by function, typically tying this requirement to the ornamentality criterion. Section 171 also specifies that the other provisions of Title 35 relating to utility patents apply to design patents unless otherwise specified. Accordingly, to qualify for a design patent, the design must not only be new, original, and ornamental (not functional), it must also be nonobvious (a requirement for utility patents codified in Section 103). As we will see in Chapter 5, which covers patentability rules for design patents, these requirements can be quite different from trademark law's distinctiveness requirement.

Design patents last for a term of fourteen years, measured from the date of issuance. 35 U.S.C. §173. There are no design patent provisions specifying the nature of the exclusive rights, so the provisions from utility patent law apply. Section 271 specifies that a patent owner has the right to exclude others from making, using, selling, offering to sell, or importing the patented invention. To determine whether these rights have been violated in the design patent context, one must compare the visual appearance of the accused design with that of the patented design, guided by a framework of rules that judges have developed over time. Some commentators view those rules as having the practical effect of restricting the scope of design patent protection to something approaching the exact visual appearance of the design as depicted in the patent drawings.

The Patent Act also contains a special remedy provision for design patents, 35 U.S.C. §289. Section 289 provides that a design patent owner who proves infringement may choose to collect the infringer's total profit from the sale of articles to which the infringing design has been applied. We cover design patent infringement and remedies in Chapter 6.

### (c) Copyright Protection

Copyright law is yet another design protection mechanism, as explored in Chapter 7 of this book. In the United States, copyright law is governed by the Copyright Act of 1976, codified at 17 U.S.C. §§101 et seq. Included among the subject matter eligible for copyright protection under the Act are "pictorial, graphic and sculptural" works (PGS works). 17 U.S.C. §102(a)(5). Section 101 of the Act defines PGS works generously, except that for the design of a "useful article," such a design is copyrightable only to the extent that the pictorial, graphic, or sculptural features "can be identified separately from, and are capable of existing independently of, the utilitarian aspects of the article." Courts have struggled with the task of separating PGS features from utilitarian features. PGS works, like other potentially copyrightable works, must also satisfy the other core copyrightability requirements—i.e., the works must be original and fixed in a tangible medium of expression. 17 U.S.C. §102(a).

The owner of a U.S. copyright in a PGS work enjoys a set of exclusive rights to reproduce the copyrighted work, prepare derivative works based on the copyrighted work, distribute copies of the work to the public and display the PGS work publically. 17 U.S.C. §§106(1), (2), (3), (5). Section 113 of the

Act particularizes the scope of exclusive rights in PGS works in various ways—such as by specifying that the §106(1) right to reproduce a PGS works includes the right to reproduce the work "in or on any kind of article, whether useful or otherwise." 17 U.S.C. §113(a).

In 1990, Congress designated architectural works as a category of copyrightable works of authorship, 17 U.S.C. §102(a)(8), and defined "architectural work" in 17 U.S.C. §101 as "the design of a building as embodied in any tangible means of expression." One purpose for this legislative change was to disentangle architectural works from the debates that had surrounded PGS features embodied in useful articles. Congress also enacted certain limitations on the scope of exclusive rights in architectural works, as specified in 17 U.S.C. §120.

The Copyright Act also includes a chapter entitled "Protection of Original Designs," comprised of provisions codified at 17 U.S.C. §§1301-1332. Notwithstanding its general title, the provisions offer special protection only to the designs of vessel hulls. *See* 17 U.S.C. §1301(a)(1) (extending protection to the "design of a useful article which makes the article attractive or distinctive in appearance to the purchasing or using public"); 17 U.S.C. §1301(b)(2) (defining "useful article" as "a vessel hull, including a plug or mold . . ."). The legislation responds to the *Bonito Boats* decision excerpted below, but also may set the stage for comprehensive design protection legislation, a topic of periodic debate in the United States. We cover design protection legislation—as it exists abroad and as it has been proposed in the United States—in Chapter 8.

## 3. EUROPEAN UNION DESIGN LAW

The EU Regulation on Community Designs establishes a design registration system (and recognizes unregistered rights in designs) having effect across the entire European Union. Registrations are granted by the Office for Harmonisation in the Internal Market (OHIM), which also administers the Community Trademark system. No comparable system of sui generis design protection exists in the United States. In Chapter 8, we discuss the Community Design regime and the debate in the United States over whether to adopt sui generis design protection.

### NOTES AND QUESTIONS

1. *Protecting the iPod design in the United States.* Based on the overview of U.S. intellectual property regimes discussed above, consider how Apple might secure and enforce rights in the designs for the family of iPod products. How heavily would your strategy rely on trademark protection? Apple owns at least two trademark registrations on the design of iPod products. Registration No. 3,341,214, issued on November 20, 2007, depicts the following design, used in connection with "[p]ortable and handheld digital electronic devices for recording, organizing, transmitting, manipulating, and reviewing text, data, audio and video files," and many other enumerated products:

## B. The Modern Legislative Landscape for Trade Dress and Design Protection 21

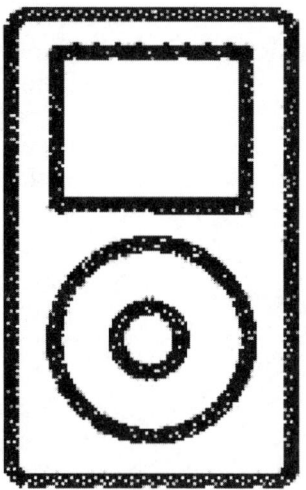

Registration No. 3,365,816, issued on January 8, 2008, depicts the following design used in connection with the same products.

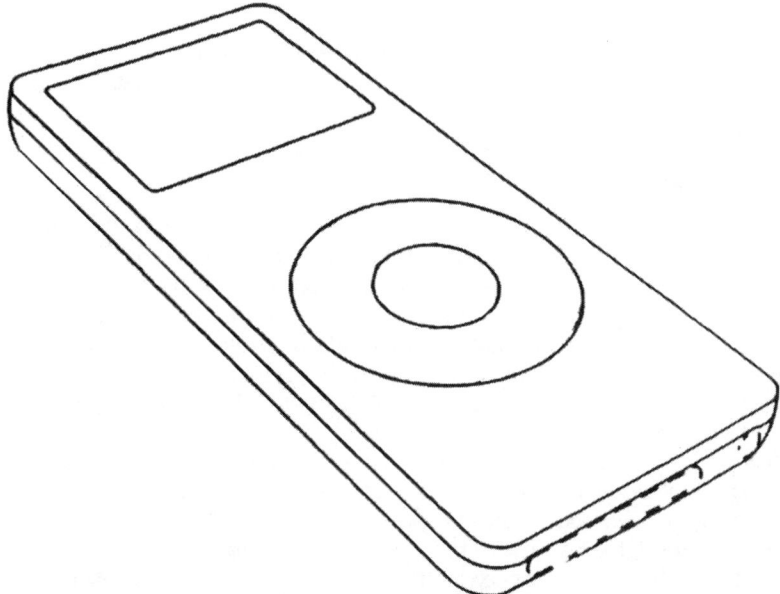

In addition, Apple owns numerous design patents claiming various iPod designs, including U.S. Design Pat. Nos. D572267, D570372, D568338, D562847, D562348, D558756, D558757, and D558758. The design depicted at the beginning of this chapter is from U.S. Design Patent No. D570372; the design depicted below appears in D562348:

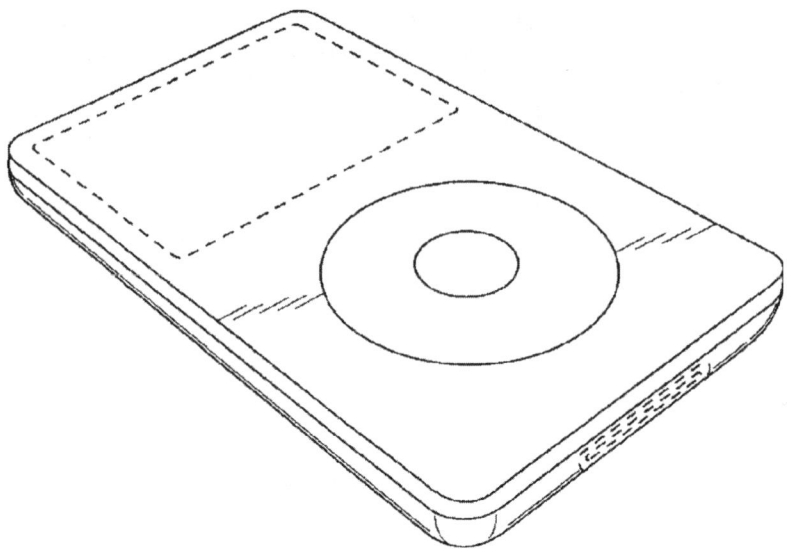

Does the large number of iPod design patents listed surprise you? Does that number raise inferences as to the likely scope of protection of each of the individual design patents?

**2. *A cyclical pattern in design protection?*** In this book, you will regularly be confronted with questions about whether a given mixture of forms of intellectual property protection adequately protects designs. In remarks delivered in 1993, Jerry Reichman spoke of a recurring cyclical pattern of overprotection and underprotection of designs.

> The initial condition of underprotection typically stems from the full patent approach, which the United States still adheres to; Switzerland is also one of the last few countries, plus maybe Ireland, to follow the full patent model. Very few designs ever qualify for protection under a full patent approach because patent law imposes a nonobviousness standard, whereas commercial designs normally partake of small variations upon themes already known to the prior art. Such variations, though commercially valuable, seldom constitute an "inventive step" away from the prior art.
>
> Historically, many countries tried to rectify the underprotection characteristic of a full patent model by opening their copyright laws to industrial designs, and France remains the most prominent adherent to this "unity of art" approach. However, copyright law inevitably overprotects product designs to such a degree that, outside of France, legislators soon tended to fall back on some form of industrial property protection once again—especially a modified patent approach—which, however, also breeds new states of underprotection. . . .
>
> And so it goes, round and round across the world's intellectual property system, from one generation to the next without breaking the cyclical pattern. Chronic underprotection in industrial property law leads to chronic overprotection in artistic property law, which in turn inspires further reactive reforms of industrial property law tending to reinstate levels of underprotection that will foster renewed appeals to copyright law.
>
> J.H. Reichman, *Past and Current Trends in the Evolution of Design Protection Law—A Comment,* 4 FORDHAM INTELL. PROP. MEDIA & ENT. L.J. 387, 388-89 (1993).

Unfair competition laws (built in part around the misappropriation concept) may also become part of the cycle, as a response to underprotection but as a potential source of overprotection. *Id.* As you study the cases and legislation in this book, consider whether they reflect an awareness of Reichman's cyclical pattern. Do judges deciding cases that involve, say, protection of a design via a design patent, consider how their decision meshes with design protection under copyright, or other intellectual property regimes? Should they consider such matters? Should legislators consider such matters?

**3. *Designs as incremental (subpatentable) improvements?*** Are most designs mere incremental improvements? If so, what does this suggest about the intellectual property regime (or mix of regimes) that would best balance private and public interests in the protection of designs? Patent regimes seek to facilitate innovation, but are patent regimes generally suited to protect incremental advances? *See* Gerard N. Magliocca, *Ornamental Design and Incremental Innovation*, 86 MARQ. L. REV. 845 (2003) (exploring the role of the patent system in protecting designs). Is copyright a better fit, or does copyright's focus on promoting advances in the arts square well with incremental improvements in industrial design? To what extent do the goals of trademark regimes reflect a concern with promoting (incremental) innovation? *See* Jay Dratler, Jr., *Trademark Protection for Industrial Designs*, 1988 U. ILL. L. REV. 887 (1988). Dratler argues that trademark law's flexibility makes it a better vehicle than patent or copyright for protecting designs. Trademark law, he asserts, relies on fluid notions of consumer confusion and distinctiveness, and on equitable remedies that can be tailored to minimize confusion in particular cases, while preserving competition. Patent and copyright rely on more rigid notions of property rights. As you study the materials in this book, consider whether you agree with this assessment.

**4. *Sui generis protection*.** Based on what you have learned so far about the state of design law in the United States, should the United States adopt a freestanding design regime?

Consider one commentator's arguments in favor of such a regime:

> 1. The current laws on the books for protecting designs [in the United States] . . . have been rendered almost impotent;
> 2. Increased globalization has made many more consumer products available whose only distinguishing characteristic, in many cases, is their outward appearance, i.e., their design;
> 3. Corporate America[] digs good design and appreciates the value that good design brings to the bottom line;
> 4. The U.S. is arguably in violation of the 1995 TRIPS agreement for not providing for a system to protect "new or original" industrial designs.
> 5. The Vessel Hull Protection Act and Fashion Bill [both discussed in Chapter 8] have demonstrated Congress' willingness to consider and pass *sui generis* design protection laws, albeit special purpose ones.
> 6. The Internet has emerged as an incredibly effective and inexpensive organizing and communicating tool.

> The time has come to solve the current crisis in U.S. design law by reconstituting a coalition of designers, manufacturers, and allied trade associations to protect industrial designs quickly, easily, and inexpensively, before this last bastion of American creativity is knocked off out of existence.

Perry J. Saidman, *The Crisis in the Law of Designs*, 89 J. Pat. & Trademark Off. Soc'y 301, 337-338 (2007). We take up the question of sui generis design protection in detail in Chapter 8. As you study the materials in the intervening chapters, you should keep in mind the arguments pro and con relating to sui generis legislation.

## C. THE "CUMULATION/PREEMPTION" PROBLEM IN DESIGN LAW

Design protection law in the United States is composed of a combination of several intellectual property regimes. United States design protection law thus presents a particularly difficult "cumulation/preemption" problem: should a designer be entitled to claim rights in the same design under multiple regimes ("cumulation"), or should protection under one regime preclude protection under another ("preemption")? The cumulation/preemption problem also arises in foreign jurisdictions where designs are protected by a sui generis design protection law. There, the question is whether an applicant for protection under the sui generis law should be required to forgo other forms of intellectual property protection. *See, e.g.,* Ralph S. Brown, *Design Protection: An Overview*, 34 UCLA L. Rev. 1341, 1401-02 (1987) (asserting that proposals for a U.S. sui generis design protection law should include a requirement that intellectual property owners elect one form of protection or another). The cumulation/preemption problem is not unique to designs, but design law illustrates the problem starkly.

In the United States, the cumulation/preemption problem for designs is further complicated by the fact that under certain circumstances, designs may qualify for protection under state law, in addition to federal law. In a series of famous cases, some of which are excerpted below, the Supreme Court considered the extent to which the Supremacy Clause forced state protections for designs to give way in the face of conflicting federal protections. As you read the cases, consider whether the policy analysis that undergirds the Court's conclusion, that there is a conflict between federal and state laws, might also apply in a case in which a designer invokes protection under multiple, arguably conflicting, *federal* intellectual property regimes.

### Sears, Roebuck & Co. v. Stiffel Co.
376 U.S. 225 (1964)

Mr. Justice Black delivered the opinion of the Court:
The question in this case is whether a State's unfair competition law can, consistently with the federal patent laws, impose liability for or prohibit the copying of an article which is protected by neither a federal patent nor a copyright. The respondent, Stiffel Company, secured design and mechanical

patents on a "pole lamp"—a vertical tube having lamp fixtures along the outside, the tube being made so that it will stand upright between the floor and ceiling of a room. Pole lamps proved a decided commercial success, and soon after Stiffel brought them on the market Sears, Roebuck & Company put on the market a substantially identical lamp, which it sold more cheaply, Sears' retail price being about the same as Stiffel's wholesale price. Stiffel then brought this action against Sears in the United States District Court for the Northern District of Illinois, claiming in its first count that by copying its design Sears had infringed Stiffel's patents and in its second count that by selling copies of Stiffel's lamp Sears had caused confusion in the trade as to the source of the lamps and had thereby engaged in unfair competition under Illinois law. There was evidence that identifying tags were not attached to the Sears lamps although labels appeared on the cartons in which they were delivered to customers, that customers had asked Stiffel whether its lamps differed from Sears', and that in two cases customers who had bought Stiffel lamps had complained to Stiffel on learning that Sears was selling substantially identical lamps at a much lower price.

The District Court, after holding the patents invalid for want of invention, went on to find as a fact that Sears' lamp was "a substantially exact copy" of Stiffel's and that the two lamps were so much alike, both in appearance and in functional details, "that confusion between them is likely, and some confusion has already occurred." On these findings the court held Sears guilty of unfair competition, enjoined Sears "from unfairly competing with (Stiffel) by selling or attempting to sell pole lamps identical to or confusingly similar to" Stiffel's lamp, and ordered an accounting to fix profits and damages resulting from Sears' "unfair competition."

The Court of Appeals affirmed. That court held that, to make out a case of unfair competition under Illinois law, there was no need to show that Sears had been "palming off" its lamps as Stiffel lamps; Stiffel had only to prove that there was a "likelihood of confusion as to the source of the products"—that the two articles were sufficiently identical that customers could not tell who had made a particular one. Impressed by the "remarkable sameness of appearance" of the lamps, the Court of Appeals upheld the trial court's findings of likelihood of confusion and some actual confusion, findings which the appellate court construed to mean confusion "as to the source of the lamps." The Court of Appeals thought this enough under Illinois law to sustain the trial court's holding of unfair competition, and thus held Sears liable under Illinois law for doing no more than copying and marketing an unpatented article. We granted certiorari to consider whether this use of a State's law of unfair competition is compatible with the federal patent law.

Before the Constitution was adopted, some States had granted patents either by special act or by general statute, but when the Constitution was adopted provision for a federal patent law was made one of the enumerated powers of Congress because, as Madison put it in The Federalist No. 43, the States "cannot separately make effectual provision" for either patents or copyrights.[4] That constitutional provision is Art. I, §8, cl. 8, which empowers

---

4. The Federalist (Cooke ed. 1961) 288.

Congress "To promote the Progress of Science and useful Arts, by securing for limited Times to Authors and Inventors the exclusive Right to their respective Writings and Discoveries." Pursuant to this constitutional authority, Congress in 1790 enacted the first federal patent and copyright law, 1 Stat. 109, and ever since that time has fixed the condition upon which patents and copyrights shall be granted, see 17 U.S.C. §§1-216; 35 U.S.C. §§1-293. These laws, like other laws of the United States enacted pursuant to constitutional authority, are the supreme law of the land. [cit.] When state law touches upon the area of these federal statutes, it is "familiar doctrine" that the federal policy "may not be set at naught, or its benefits denied" by the state law. [cit.] This is true, of course, even if the state law is enacted in the exercise of otherwise undoubted state power.

The grant of a patent is the grant of a statutory monopoly; indeed, the grant of patents in England was an explicit exception to the statute of James I prohibiting monopolies. Patents are not given as favors, as was the case of monopolies given by the Tudor monarchs, [cit.], but are meant to encourage invention by rewarding the inventor with the right, limited to a term of years fixed by the patent, to exclude others from the use of his invention. During that period of time no one may make use, or sell the patented product without the patentee's authority. 35 U.S.C. §271. But in rewarding useful invention, the "rights and welfare of the community must be fairly dealt with and effectually guarded." *Kendall v. Winsor*, 21 How. 322, 328 (1859). To that end the prerequisites to obtaining a patent are strictly observed, and when the patent has issued the limitations on its exercise are equally strictly enforced. To begin with, a genuine "invention" or "discovery" must be demonstrated "lest in the constant demand for new appliances the heavy hand of tribute be laid on each slight technological advance in an art." *Cuno Engineering Corp. v. Automatic Devices Corp.*, 314 U.S. 84, 92 (1941). . . . Finally, and especially relevant here, when the patent expires the monopoly created by it expires, too, and the right to make the article—including the right to make it in precisely the shape it carried when patented—passes to the public. *Kellogg Co. v. National Biscuit Co.*, 305 U.S. 111, 120-122 (1938); *Singer Mfg. Co. v. June Mfg. Co.*, 163 U.S. 169, 185 (1896).

Thus the patent system is one in which uniform federal standards are carefully used to promote invention while at the same time preserving free competition. Obviously a State could not, consistently with the Supremacy Clause of the Constitution, extend the life of a patent beyond its expiration date or give a patent on an article which lacked the level of invention required for federal patents. To do either would run counter to the policy of Congress of granting patents only to true inventions, and then only for a limited time. Just as a State cannot encroach upon the federal patent laws directly, it cannot, under some other law, such as that forbidding unfair competition, give protection of a kind that clashes with the objectives of the federal patent laws.

In the present case the "pole lamp" sold by Stiffel has been held not to be entitled to the protection of either a mechanical or a design patent. An unpatentable article, like an article on which the patent has expired, is in the public domain and may be made and sold by whoever chooses to do so. What Sears did was to copy Stiffel's design and to sell lamps almost identical to those sold by Stiffel. This it had every right to do under the federal patent laws. That Stiffel originated the pole lamp and made it popular is immaterial. "Sharing in the goodwill of an article unprotected by patent or trade-mark is the exercise of a right possessed by all — and in the free exercise of which the consuming public is deeply interested." *Kellogg Co. v. National Biscuit Co., supra*, 305 U.S. at 122. To allow a State by use of its law of unfair competition to prevent the copying of an article which represents too slight an advance to be patented would be to permit the State to block off from the public something which federal law has said belongs to the public. The result would be that while federal law grants only 14 or 17 years' protection to genuine inventions, see 35 U.S.C. §§154, 173, States could allow perpetual protection to articles too lacking in novelty to merit any patent at all under federal constitutional standards. This would be too great an encroachment on the federal patent system to be tolerated.

Sears has been held liable here for unfair competition because of a finding of likelihood of confusion based only on the fact that Sears' lamp was copied from Stiffel's unpatented lamp and that consequently the two looked exactly alike. Of course there could be "confusion" as to who had manufactured these nearly identical articles. But mere inability of the public to tell two identical articles apart is not enough to support an injunction against copying or an award of damages for copying that which the federal patent laws permit to be copied. Doubtless a State may, in appropriate circumstances, require that goods, whether patented or unpatented, be labeled or that other precautionary steps be taken to prevent customers from being misled as to the source, just as it may protect businesses in the use of their trademarks, labels, or distinctive dress in the packaging of goods so as to prevent others, by imitating such markings, from misleading purchasers as to the source of the goods. But because of the federal patent laws a State may not, when the article is unpatented and uncopyrighted, prohibit the copying of the article itself or award damages for such copying. [cit.] The judgment below did both and in so doing gave Stiffel the equivalent of a patent monopoly on its unpatented lamp. That was error, and Sears is entitled to a judgment in its favor.

*Reversed.*

## NOTES AND QUESTIONS

1. *The companion case* — Compco. In a companion case decided on the same day, *Compco*, Day-Brite sued its competitor Compco for alleged infringement of Day-Brite's design patent on a lighting fixture, and also asserted a state law unfair competition claim. *Compco Corp. v. Day-Brite Lighting, Inc.*, 376 U.S. 234 (1964). The lower courts had invalidated the design patent but had sustained Day-Brite's state law claim. The Supreme Court reversed on the state law claim, reiterating its holding in *Sears*:

> Here Day-Brite's fixture has been held not to be entitled to a design or mechanical patent. Under the federal patent laws it is, therefore, in the public domain and can be copied in every detail by whoever pleases. . . . [I]f the design is not entitled to a design patent or other federal statutory protection, then it can be copied at will.

*Id.* at 237-238. Though a state had a legitimate interest in preventing the public from being deceived in the marketplace, the state could not vindicate that interest by prohibiting the copying of unpatented articles:

> That an article copied from an unpatented article could be made in some other way, that the design is "nonfunctional" and not essential to the use of either article, that the configuration of the article copied may have a "secondary meaning" which identifies the maker to the trade, or that there may be "confusion" among purchasers as to which article is which or as to who is the maker, may be relevant evidence in applying a State's law requiring such precautions as labeling; however, and regardless of the copier's motives, neither these facts nor any others can furnish a basis for imposing liability for or prohibiting the actual acts of copying and selling. *Cf. Kellogg Co. v. National Biscuit Co.*, 305 U.S. 111, 120 (1938).

*Id.* at 238. Does this clarify the scope of *Sears*?

**2. *Justice Harlan's concurring opinion*.** Justice Harlan concurred in the result in *Compco*, and noted that his concurrence also applied to *Sears*. Justice Harlan would have given the states "more leeway" in regulating unfair competition where the defendant was confusing customers as to the source of the goods. Justice Harlan opined that "[v]indication of the paramount federal interest at stake does not require a State to tolerate such specifically oriented predatory business practices." 376 U.S. at 239 (Harlan, J., concurring). Do you agree?

### Bonito Boats, Inc. v. Thunder Craft Boats, Inc.
### 489 U.S. 141 (1989)

Justice O'Connor delivered the opinion of the Court:

I

In September 1976, petitioner Bonito Boats, Inc. (Bonito), a Florida corporation, developed a hull design for a fiberglass recreational boat which it marketed under the trade name Bonito Boat Model 5VBR. Designing the boat hull required substantial effort on the part of Bonito. A set of engineering drawings was prepared, from which a hardwood model was created. The hardwood model was then sprayed with fiberglass to create a mold, which then served to produce the finished fiberglass boats for sale. The 5VBR was placed on the market sometime in September 1976. There is no indication in the record that a patent application was ever filed for protection of the utilitarian or design aspects of the hull, or for the process by which the hull was manufactured. The 5VBR was favorably received by the boating public, and "a broad interstate market" developed for its sale.

In May 1983, after the Bonito 5VBR had been available to the public for over six years, the Florida Legislature enacted Fla. Stat. §559.94 (1987). The statute makes "[i]t . . . unlawful for any person to use the direct molding process to duplicate for the purpose of sale any manufactured vessel hull or component part of a vessel made by another without the written permission of that other person." §559.94(2). The statute also makes it unlawful for a person to "knowingly sell a vessel hull or component part of a vessel duplicated in violation of subsection (2)." §559.94(3). Damages, injunctive relief, and attorney's fees are made available to "[a]ny person who suffers injury or damage as the result of a violation" of the statute. §559.94(4). The statute was made applicable to vessel hulls or component parts duplicated through the use of direct molding after July 1, 1983. §559.94(5).

[Bonito sued in Florida state court, asserting that Thunder Craft was duplicating the 5VBR hull in violation of the Florida statute and seeking injunctive and other relief. The trial court concluded that the Florida statute conflicted with federal patent law and must be struck down in accordance with the *Sears* and *Compco* decisions. The Court of Appeals affirmed, as did the Florida Supreme Court, over a dissent. The U.S. Supreme Court then took up the case.]

II

Article I, §8, cl. 8, of the Constitution gives Congress the power "[t]o promote the Progress of Science and useful Arts, by securing for limited Times to Authors and Inventors the exclusive Right to their respective Writings and Discoveries." The Patent Clause itself reflects a balance between the need to encourage innovation and the avoidance of monopolies which stifle competition without any concomitant advance in the "Progress of Science and useful Arts." As we have noted in the past, the Clause contains both a grant of power and certain limitations upon the exercise of that power. Congress may not create patent monopolies of unlimited duration, nor may it "authorize the issuance of patents whose effects are to remove existent knowledge from the public domain, or to restrict free access to materials already available." *Graham v. John Deere Co. of Kansas City*, 383 U.S. 1, 6 (1966).

From their inception, the federal patent laws have embodied a careful balance between the need to promote innovation and the recognition that imitation and refinement through imitation are both necessary to invention itself and the very lifeblood of a competitive economy....

[Under today's patent statute] [p]rotection is offered to "[w]hoever invents or discovers any new and useful process, machine, manufacture, or composition of matter, or any new and useful improvement thereof." 35 U.S.C. §101. Since 1842, Congress has also made protection available for "any new, original and ornamental design for an article of manufacture." 35 U.S.C. §171. To qualify for protection, a design must present an aesthetically pleasing appearance that is not dictated by function alone, and must satisfy the other criteria of patentability.

[The Court discussed the utility patent law's requirements for utility, novelty, and nonobviousness.]

The applicant whose invention satisfies the requirements of novelty, nonobviousness, and utility, and who is willing to reveal to the public the substance of his discovery and "the best mode ... of carrying out his invention," 35 U.S.C. §112, is granted "the right to exclude others from making, using, or selling the invention throughout the United States," for a period of 17 years. 35 U.S.C. §154. The federal patent system thus embodies a carefully crafted bargain for encouraging the creation and disclosure of new, useful, and nonobvious advances in technology and design in return for the exclusive right to practice the invention for a period of years. "[The inventor] may keep his invention secret and reap its fruits indefinitely. In consideration of its disclosure and the consequent benefit to the community, the patent is granted. An exclusive enjoyment is guaranteed him for seventeen years, but upon expiration of that period, the knowledge of the invention inures to the people, who are thus enabled without restriction to practice it and profit by its use." *United States v. Dubilier Condenser Corp.*, 289 U.S. 178 (1933).

The attractiveness of such a bargain, and its effectiveness in inducing creative effort and disclosure of the results of that effort, depend almost entirely on a backdrop of free competition in the exploitation of unpatented designs and innovations. The novelty and nonobviousness requirements of patentability embody a congressional understanding, implicit in the Patent Clause itself, that free exploitation of ideas will be the rule, to which the protection of a federal patent is the exception. Moreover, the ultimate goal of the patent system is to bring new designs and technologies into the public domain through disclosure. State law protection for techniques and designs whose disclosure has already been induced by market rewards may conflict with the very purpose of the patent laws by decreasing the range of ideas available as the building blocks of further innovation. The offer of federal protection from competitive exploitation of intellectual property would be rendered meaningless in a world where substantially similar state law protections were readily available. To a limited extent, the federal patent laws must determine not only what is protected, but also what is free for all to use. [cit.].

Thus our past decisions have made clear that state regulation of intellectual property must yield to the extent that it clashes with the balance struck by Congress in our patent laws. The tension between the desire to freely exploit the full potential of our inventive resources and the need to create an incentive to deploy those resources is constant. Where it is clear how the patent laws strike that balance in a particular circumstance, that is not a judgment the States may second-guess. We have long held that after the expiration of a federal patent, the subject matter of the patent passes to the free use of the public as a matter of federal law. [cit.]; *Kellogg Co. v. National Biscuit Co.*, 305 U.S. 111 (1938); *Singer Mfg. Co. v. June Mfg. Co.*, 163 U.S. 169 (1896). Where the public has paid the congressionally mandated price for disclosure, the States may not render the exchange fruitless by offering patent-like protection to the subject matter of the expired patent. "It is self-evident that on the expiration of a patent the monopoly created by it ceases to exist, and the right to make the thing formerly covered by the patent becomes public property." *Singer, supra*, at 185.

In our decisions in [*Sears* and *Compco*], we found that publicly known design and utilitarian ideas which were unprotected by patent occupied much the same position as the subject matter of an expired patent. . . .

The pre-emptive sweep of our decisions in *Sears* and *Compco* has been the subject of heated scholarly and judicial debate. *See, e.g.*, Symposium, *Product Simulation: A Right or a Wrong?*, 64 COLUM. L. REV. 1178 (1964); *Lear, Inc. v. Adkins*, 395 U.S. 653, 676 (1969) (Black, J., concurring in part and dissenting in part). Read at their highest level of generality, the two decisions could be taken to stand for the proposition that the States are completely disabled from offering any form of protection to articles or processes which fall within the broad scope of patentable subject matter. *See id., at 677.* Since the potentially patentable includes "anything under the sun that is made by man," *Diamond v. Chakrabarty*, 447 U.S. 303, 309 (1980) (citation omitted), the broadest reading of *Sears* would prohibit the States from regulating the deceptive simulation of trade dress or the tortious appropriation of private information.

That the extrapolation of such a broad pre-emptive principle from *Sears* is inappropriate is clear from the balance struck in *Sears* itself. The *Sears* Court made it plain that the States "may protect businesses in the use of their trademarks, labels, or distinctive dress in the packaging of goods so as to prevent others, by imitating such markings, from misleading purchasers as to the source of the goods." *Sears, supra*, 376 U.S., at 232 (footnote omitted). Trade dress is, of course, potentially the subject matter of design patents. *See W.T. Rogers Co. v. Keene*, 778 F.2d 334, 337 (7th Cir. 1985). Yet our decision in *Sears* clearly indicates that the States may place limited regulations on the circumstances in which such designs are used in order to prevent consumer confusion as to source. Thus, while *Sears* speaks in absolutist terms, its conclusion that the States may place some conditions on the use of trade dress indicates an implicit recognition that all state regulation of potentially patentable but unpatented subject matter is not ipso facto pre-empted by the federal patent laws.

What was implicit in our decision in *Sears*, we have made explicit in our subsequent decisions concerning the scope of federal pre-emption of state regulation of the subject matter of patent. Thus, in *Kewanee Oil Co. v. Bicron Corp.*, 416 U.S. 470 (1974), we held that state protection of trade secrets did not operate to frustrate the achievement of the congressional objectives served by the patent laws. Despite the fact that state law protection was available for ideas which clearly fell within the subject matter of patent, the Court concluded that the nature and degree of state protection did not conflict with the federal policies of encouragement of patentable invention and the prompt disclosure of such innovations.

[The Court cited several reasons for its conclusion in *Kewanee Oil*, including the fact that trade secret protection did not extend to acts of reverse engineering or independent development, and so was relatively weak compared to patent protection.]

We have since reaffirmed the pragmatic approach which *Kewanee* takes to the pre-emption of state laws dealing with the protection of intellectual property. *See Aronson* [*v. Quick Point Pencil Co.*, 440 U.S. 257, 262 (1979)] ("State law is not displaced merely because the contract relates to intellectual property which may or may not be patentable; the states are free to regulate the use of such intellectual property in any manner not inconsistent with federal law."). At the same time, we have consistently reiterated the teaching of *Sears* and *Compco* that ideas once placed before the public without the protection of a valid patent are subject to appropriation without significant restraint. *Aronson, supra*, at 263.

At the heart of *Sears* and *Compco* is the conclusion that the efficient operation of the federal patent system depends upon substantially free trade in publicly known, unpatented design and utilitarian conceptions. In *Sears*, the state law offered "the equivalent of a patent monopoly," 376

U.S., at 233, in the functional aspects of a product which had been placed in public commerce absent the protection of a valid patent. While, as noted above, our decisions since *Sears* have taken a decidedly less rigid view of the scope of federal pre-emption under the patent laws, *e.g.*, *Kewanee, supra*, 416 U.S., at 479-480, we believe that the *Sears* Court correctly concluded that the States may not offer patent-like protection to intellectual creations which would otherwise remain unprotected as a matter of federal law. Both the novelty and the nonobviousness requirements of federal patent law are grounded in the notion that concepts within the public grasp, or those so obvious that they readily could be, are the tools of creation available to all. They provide the baseline of free competition upon which the patent system's incentive to creative effort depends. A state law that substantially interferes with the enjoyment of an unpatented utilitarian or design conception which has been freely disclosed by its author to the public at large impermissibly contravenes the ultimate goal of public disclosure and use which is the centerpiece of federal patent policy. Moreover, through the creation of patent-like rights, the States could essentially redirect inventive efforts away from the careful criteria of patentability developed by Congress over the last 200 years. We understand this to be the reasoning at the core of our decisions in *Sears* and *Compco*, and we reaffirm that reasoning today.

### III

We believe that the Florida statute at issue in this case so substantially impedes the public use of the otherwise unprotected design and utilitarian ideas embodied in unpatented boat hulls as to run afoul of the teaching of our decisions in *Sears* and *Compco*. It is readily apparent that the Florida statute does not operate to prohibit "unfair competition" in the usual sense that the term is understood. The law of unfair competition has its roots in the common law tort of deceit: its general concern is with protecting consumers from confusion as to source. While that concern may result in the creation of "quasi-property rights" in communicative symbols, the focus is on the protection of consumers, not the protection of producers as an incentive to product innovation.

With some notable exceptions, including the interpretation of the Illinois law of unfair competition at issue in *Sears* and *Compco*, [cit.], the common law tort of unfair competition has been limited to protection against copying of nonfunctional aspects of consumer products which have acquired secondary meaning such that they operate as a designation of source. [cit.] The "protection" granted a particular design under the law of unfair competition is thus limited to one context where consumer confusion is likely to result; the design "idea" itself may be freely exploited in all other contexts.

In contrast to the operation of unfair competition law, the Florida statute is aimed directly at preventing the exploitation of the design and utilitarian conceptions embodied in the product itself. The sparse legislative history surrounding its enactment indicates that it was intended to create an inducement for the improvement of boat hull designs. *See* Tr. of Meeting of Transportation Committee, Florida House of Representatives, May 3, 1983 ("[T]here is no inducement for [a] quality boat manufacturer to improve these designs and secondly, if he does, it is immediately copied. This would prevent that and allow him recourse in circuit court."). To accomplish this goal, the Florida statute endows the original boat hull manufacturer with rights against the world, similar in scope and operation to the rights accorded a federal patentee. Like the patentee, the beneficiary of the Florida statute may prevent a competitor from "making" the product in what is evidently the most efficient manner available and from "selling" the product when it is produced in that fashion. Compare 35 U.S.C. §154. The Florida scheme offers this protection for an unlimited number of years to all boat hulls and their component parts, without regard to their ornamental or technological merit. Protection is available for subject matter for which patent protection has been denied or has expired, as well as for designs which have been freely revealed to the consuming public by their creators.

In this case, the Bonito 5VBR fiberglass hull has been freely exposed to the public for a period in excess of six years. For purposes of federal law, it stands in the same stead as an item for which a patent has expired or been denied: it is unpatented and unpatentable. See 35 U.S.C. §102(b). Whether because of a determination of unpatentability or other commercial concerns, petitioner chose to expose its hull design to the public in the marketplace, eschewing the bargain held out by the federal patent system of disclosure in exchange for exclusive use. Yet, the Florida statute allows petitioner to reassert a substantial property right in the idea, thereby constricting the spectrum of useful public knowledge. Moreover, it does so without the careful protections of high standards of innovation and limited monopoly contained in the federal scheme. We think it clear that such protection conflicts with the federal policy "that all ideas in general circulation be dedicated to the common good unless they are protected by a valid patent." *Lear, Inc. v. Adkins*, 395 U.S., at 668.

That the Florida statute does not remove all means of reproduction and sale does not eliminate the conflict with the federal scheme. *See Kellogg*, 305 U.S., at 122. In essence, the Florida law prohibits the entire public from engaging in a form of reverse engineering of a product in the public domain. This is clearly one of the rights vested in the federal patent holder, but has never been a part of state protection under the law of unfair competition or trade secrets. *See Kewanee*, 416 U.S., at 476 ("A trade secret law, however, does not offer protection against discovery by . . . so-called reverse engineering, that is by starting with the known product and working backward to divine the process which aided in its development or manufacture."); [cit.]. The duplication of boat hulls and their component parts may be an essential part of innovation in the field of hydrodynamic design. Variations as to size and combination of various elements may lead to significant advances in the field. Reverse engineering of chemical and mechanical articles in the public domain often leads to significant advances in technology. If Florida may prohibit this particular method of study and recomposition of an unpatented article, we fail to see the principle that would prohibit a State from banning the use of chromatography in the reconstitution of unpatented chemical compounds, or the use of robotics in the duplication of machinery in the public domain.

[The Court also asserted that by eliminating the threat of reverse engineering, the Florida statute might reduce the incentives for inventors to develop inventions that actually meet the "rigorous requirements of patentability." In addition, allowing states to create patent-like rights would impose administrative costs on competitors, in that they could not merely rely on the absence of a patent notice to conclude that a particular design was in the public domain.]

The Florida scheme blurs this clear federal demarcation between public and private property. One of the fundamental purposes behind the Patent and Copyright Clauses of the Constitution was to promote national uniformity in the realm of intellectual property. *See* The Federalist No. 43, p. 309 (B. Wright ed. 1961). Since the Patent Act of 1800, Congress has lodged exclusive jurisdiction of actions "arising under" the patent laws in the federal courts, thus allowing for the development of a uniform body of law in resolving the constant tension between private right and public access. *See* 28 U.S.C. §1338; [cit.]. Recently, Congress conferred exclusive jurisdiction of all patent appeals on the Court of Appeals for the Federal Circuit, in order to "provide nationwide uniformity in patent law." H.R. Rep. No. 97-312, p. 20 (1981). This purpose is frustrated by the Florida scheme, which renders the status of the design and utilitarian "ideas" embodied in the boat hulls it protects uncertain. Given the inherently ephemeral nature of property in ideas, and the great power such property has to cause harm to the competitive policies which underlay the federal patent laws, the demarcation of broad zones of public and private right is "the type of regulation that demands a uniform national rule." [cit.]. Absent such a federal rule, each State could afford patent-like protection to particularly favored home industries, effectively insulating them from competition from outside the State.

. . .

It is difficult to conceive of a more effective method of creating substantial property rights in an intellectual creation than to eliminate the most efficient method for its exploitation. *Sears* and *Compco* protect more than the right of the public to contemplate the abstract beauty of an otherwise unprotected intellectual creation—they assure its efficient reduction to practice and sale in the marketplace.

Appending the conclusionary label "unscrupulous" to such competitive behavior merely endorses a policy judgment which the patent laws do not leave the States free to make. Where an item in general circulation is unprotected by patent, "[r]eproduction of a functional attribute is legitimate competitive activity." *Inwood Laboratories, Inc. v. Ives Laboratories, Inc.*, 456 U.S. 844, 863 (1982) (White, J., concurring in result).

. . . [T]he federal standards for patentability, at a minimum, express the congressional determination that patent-like protection is unwarranted as to certain classes of intellectual property. The States are simply not free in this regard to offer equivalent protections to ideas which Congress has determined should belong to all. For almost 100 years it has been well established that in the case of an expired patent, the federal patent laws do create a federal right to "copy and to use." *Sears* and *Compco* extended that rule to potentially patentable ideas which are fully exposed to the public.

Our decisions since *Sears* and *Compco* have made it clear that the Patent and Copyright Clauses do not, by their own force or by negative implication, deprive the States of the power to adopt rules for the promotion of intellectual creation within their own jurisdictions. *See* Aronson, 440 U.S. at 262; *Goldstein v. California*, 412 U.S. 546, 552-561 (1973); *Kewanee*, 416 U.S. at 478-479. Thus, where "Congress determines that neither federal protection nor freedom from restraint is required by the national interest," *Goldstein, supra*, 412 U.S. at 559, the States remain free to promote originality and creativity in their own domains.

Nor does the fact that a particular item lies within the subject matter of the federal patent laws necessarily preclude the States from offering limited protection which does not impermissibly interfere with the federal patent scheme. As *Sears* itself makes clear, States may place limited regulations on the use of unpatented designs in order to prevent consumer confusion as to source. In *Kewanee*, we found that state protection of trade secrets, as applied to both patentable and unpatentable subject matter, did not conflict with the federal patent laws. In both situations, state protection was not aimed exclusively at the promotion of invention itself, and the state restrictions on the use of unpatented ideas were limited to those necessary to promote goals outside the contemplation of the federal patent scheme. Both the law of unfair competition and state trade secret law have coexisted harmoniously with federal patent protection for almost 200 years, and Congress has given no indication that their operation is inconsistent with the operation of the federal patent laws. [cit.].

Indeed, there are affirmative indications from Congress that both the law of unfair competition and trade secret protection are consistent with the balance struck by the patent laws. Section 43(a) of the Lanham Act, 60 Stat. 441, 15 U.S.C. §1125(a), creates a federal remedy for making "a false designation of origin, or any false description or representation, including words or other symbols tending falsely to describe or represent the same. . . ." Congress has thus given federal recognition to many of the concerns that underlie the state tort of unfair competition, and the application of *Sears* and *Compco* to nonfunctional aspects of a product which have been shown to identify source must take account of competing federal policies in this regard. Similarly, as Justice MARSHALL noted in his concurring opinion in *Kewanee*: "State trade secret laws and the federal patent laws have co-existed for many, many, years. During this time, Congress has repeatedly demonstrated its full awareness of the existence of the trade secret system, without any indication of disapproval. Indeed, Congress has in a number of instances given explicit federal protection to trade secret information provided to federal agencies." *Kewanee, supra*, 416 U.S. at 494 (concurring in result) (citation omitted). The case for federal preemption is particularly weak where Congress has indicated its awareness of the operation of state law in a field of federal interest, and has nonetheless decided to "stand by both concepts and to tolerate whatever tension there [is] between them." [cit.] The same cannot be said of the Florida statute at issue here, which offers protection beyond that available under the law of unfair competition or trade secret, without any showing of consumer confusion, or breach of trust or secrecy.

The Florida statute is aimed directly at the promotion of intellectual creation by substantially restricting the public's ability to exploit ideas that the patent system mandates shall be free for all to use. Like the interpretation of Illinois unfair competition law in *Sears* and *Compco*, the Florida statute represents a break with the tradition of peaceful co-existence between state market regulation and federal patent policy. The Florida law substantially restricts the public's ability to exploit an unpatented design in general circulation, raising the specter of state-created monopolies in a host of useful shapes and processes for which patent protection has been denied or is otherwise unobtainable. It thus enters a field of regulation which the patent laws have reserved to Congress. The patent statute's careful balance between public right and private monopoly to promote certain creative activity is a "scheme of federal regulation . . . so pervasive as to make reasonable the inference that Congress left no room for the States to supplement it." [cit.].

Congress has considered extending various forms of limited protection to industrial design either through the copyright laws or by relaxing the restrictions on the availability of design patents. *See generally* Brown, *Design Protection: An Overview*, 34 UCLA L. Rev. 1341 (1987). Congress explicitly refused to take this step in the copyright laws, *see* 17 U.S.C. §101; H.R. Rep. No. 94-1476, p. 55 (1976), U.S. Code Cong. & Admin. News 1976, pp. 5659, 5668, and despite sustained criticism for a number of years, it has declined to alter the patent protections presently available for industrial design. *See* Report of the President's Commission on the Patent System, S. Doc. No. 5, 90th Cong., 1st Sess., 20-21 (1967); Lindgren, *The Sanctity of the Design Patent: Illusion or Reality?*, 10 OKLA. CITY L. REV. 195 (1985). It is for Congress to determine if the present system of design and utility patents is ineffectual in promoting the useful arts in the context of industrial design. By offering patent-like protection for ideas deemed unprotected under the present federal scheme, the Florida statute conflicts with the "strong federal policy favoring free competition in ideas which do not merit patent protection." *Lear, Inc.*, 395 U.S. at 656. We therefore agree with the majority of the Florida Supreme Court that the Florida statute is preempted by the Supremacy Clause, and the judgment of that court is hereby *affirmed*.

## NOTES AND QUESTIONS

1. *Cumulation as a policy matter.* Under what circumstances, if any, is more intellectual property protection better? Does the cumulation of intellectual property protections distort the private-public balance that the respective individual intellectual property regimes strive to effectuate? Or is "cumulation" a mildly argumentative label for the grant of slightly different intellectual property rights designed to provide distinct sorts of incentives or serve different social purposes?

2. *The "absolutist" reading of* **Sears** *and* **Compco**. The *Bonito Boats* Court rejected the "absolutist" reading of *Sears*—the reading that after *Sears*, the states "are completely disabled from offering any form of protection to articles or processes which fall within the broad scope of patentable subject matter." By rejecting that view, the Court left room for states to regulate trade dress and trade secrets (in harmony with the Court's prior ruling in *Kewanee Oil*). Are you persuaded that state regulation of trade dress and trade secrets poses a lesser

conflict with federal patent law than does the Florida statute at issue in *Bonito Boats*, or the application of state unfair competition law to designs as in *Sears* or *Compco*? Is there a clear answer? Or do you find the *Kewanee* "pragmatic approach" more helpful in determining whether a federal intellectual property statute should preempt state regulation?

3. ***Vessel hull legislation.*** Congress responded to *Bonito Boats* by passing design protection legislation for the designs of vessel hulls — and tacking the legislation onto the copyright statute. Although the federal vessel hull legislation presents no federal/state preemption issue, doesn't the federal legislation raise the same concerns as the Florida statute about compromising the so-called right to copy? Should the Court strike down the legislation if the issue were presented to it? On what grounds?

4. ***The "limited times" clause of Article 1, Section 8, Clause 8.*** Trademark/unfair competition protection (such as that at issue in *Sears* and *Compco*) potentially has no expiration date. Are there circumstances under which the application of trademark or unfair competition protection to designs (even under federal law) violates the limited times clause of Article 1, Section 8, Clause 8? In determining whether one federal intellectual property law conflicts with another, is Article 1, Section 8, Clause 8 the likely starting point for constitutional analysis?

# PART II
# TRADE DRESS

# CHAPTER 2
# *DISTINCTIVENESS*

The next three chapters discuss the protection of designs as "trade dress" under U.S. trademark law. Trade dress refers to the total image of a product or service, which may include the colors and graphics on product labels, the appearance of product packaging, the shape of the product itself (sometimes referred to as the product's "configuration," or, perhaps too loosely, as the product's "design"), or even the product's color. We devote the bulk of our attention to product shapes as trade dress, alongside some materials on color and product packaging.

As we discussed in Chapter 1, the Lanham Act governs U.S. trademark law, but the Act evolved from the common law of unfair competition, and U.S. law remains a blend of statutory and common law concepts. That blend will be evident from the materials in this chapter. This chapter introduces the protection of trade dress and product design under trademark and unfair competition law, and addresses one of the core requirements for securing either form of protection: distinctiveness. Many of the distinctiveness rules spring from the common law. Chapter 3 covers non-functionality, another requirement for obtaining trademark rights and a crucial concept in design protection. In Chapter 4, the focus shifts to enforcement: the theories of trade dress infringement and related causes of action, and defenses to those causes of action.

## A. TRADE DRESS AND DESIGNS AS PROTECTABLE SUBJECT MATTER UNDER TRADEMARK AND UNFAIR COMPETITION PRINCIPLES

Many familiar trademarks are word marks: COCA-COLA for a soft drink, for example. Under the traditional view, COCA-COLA functions as a trademark for soft drink because the term identifies the origin of the soft drink and symbolizes the reputation and goodwill of the soft drink producer. *See, e.g., Hanover Star Milling Co. v. Metcalf*, 240 U.S. 403, 412 (1916) ("The primary and proper function of a trademark is to identify the origin or ownership of the article to which it is affixed."); *see also Prestonettes, Inc. v. Coty*, 264 U.S. 359, 368 (1924) ("A trade-mark only gives the right to prohibit the use of it so far as to protect the owner's good will against the sale of another's product as his."); *Mishawaka Rubber & Woolen Mfg. Co. v. S.S. Kresge Co.*, 316 U.S. 203, 205 (1942) ("The protection of trade-marks is the law's recognition of the psychological function of symbols. . . . A trade-mark is a merchandising short-cut which induces a purchaser to select what he wants."). Trademark protection is thought to encourage producers to invest in maintaining consistent product quality, and to protect consumers from being deceived as to the source or sponsorship of products or services.

On the other hand, some of the most potent elements of many brands are nonverbal. Consider the Coca-Cola product: the red-and-white color combination, the "ribbon" graphic, and the shape of the Coca-Cola bottle all contribute significantly to Coca-Cola's brand recognition. Might these elements—alone or in combination—function to identify source and symbolize goodwill just as effectively as words do? More effectively? If so, it would seem that nonverbal source indicators such as the graphics on packaging or the shapes of products would be recognized as potentially protectable subject matter under the rules of trademark and unfair competition law.

In this section, we consider cases that discuss the fundamental idea of using trademark and unfair competition law to protect trade dress. We look first to older cases that rely on unfair competition principles. We then turn to the modern statutory definition of the term "trademark" from Lanham Act §45.

### FLAGG MFG. CO. v. HOLWAY
178 Mass. 83 (Mass. 1901)

HOLMES, Chief Justice:

This is a bill brought to restrain the defendant from selling zithers which imitate the plaintiff's, or with strings arranged and spaced as the plaintiff's strings are arranged and spaced, and specifically to restrain it from selling a particular form of zither heretofore sold by it and exhibited by the bill. The case was sent to a master, who reported what is manifest on inspection, when the time of the respective manufactures is known, that the defendant deliberately copied the plaintiff's instrument in all essential and many non essential details, adding that this was done for a wrongful purpose. The Superior Court made a decree for the plaintiff, in terms almost as broad as the prayers of the bill, and the defendant appealed.

We are of opinion that the decree was wrong in principle. Both zithers are adapted for the use of patented sheets of music, but the zithers are not patented. Under such circumstances the defendant has the same right that the plaintiff has to manufacture instruments in the present form, to imitate the arrangement of the plaintiff's strings or the shape of the body. In the absence of a patent the freedom of manufacture cannot be cut down under the name of preventing unfair competition. [cit.]. *See Singer Mfg. Co. v. June Mfg. Co.*, 163 U.S. 169 [1896]. All that can be asked is that precautions shall be taken, so far as are consistent with the defendant's fundamental right to make and sell what it chooses, to prevent the deception which no doubt it desires to practice.

It is true that a defendant's freedom of action with regard to some subsidiary matter of ornament or label may be restrained, although a right of the same nature with its freedom to determine the shape of the articles which it sells. But the label or ornament is a relatively small and incidental affair, which would not exist at all, or at least would not exist in that shape but for the intent to deceive; whereas the instrument sold is made as it is, partly at least, because of a supposed or established desire of the public for instruments in that form. The defendant has the right to get the benefit of that desire even if created by the plaintiff. The only thing it has not the right to steal is the good will attaching to the plaintiff's personality, the benefit of the public's desire to have goods made by the plaintiff. Probably if there were an absolute conflict between the defendant's right as we have stated it and that of the plaintiff's, the defendant's would prevail. *American Waltham Watch Co. v. United States Watch Co.*, 173 Mass. 85, 86, 87 [1899]. But the plaintiff's right can be protected sufficiently by requiring the defendant's zithers to be clearly marked so as to indicate unmistakably that they are the defendant's and not the plaintiff's goods. This is the relief which the master found to be proper, and we are of opinion that he was right. To go further is to save the plaintiff from a competition from which it has no right to be exempt.

Reversed.

## GEORGE G. FOX CO. v. HATHAWAY
### 199 Mass. 99 (Mass. 1908)

KNOWLTON, Chief Justice:

This is a suit founded on the alleged unfair competition of the defendants, through the sale of a certain kind of bread made in imitation of bread previously manufactured and sold by the plaintiff. The plaintiff's bread is called "Creamalt," and the loaves are of a size, shape, color and condition of surface that gives them a peculiar visual appearance which has come to be recognized by customers in connection with the name, as indicating the place of manufacture and the quality of the bread. There was evidence at the hearing that, by extensive advertising and by its method of conducting its business, a very valuable good will had been acquired by the plaintiff in connection with the manufacture and sale of this bread. . . .

It appeared at the hearing that the defendants began to manufacture and sell bread in loaves of the same size, shape, color and general visual appearance as the plaintiff's, such that an ordinary purchaser, not making a careful examination, would be likely to be deceived, and to buy the defendants' bread in the belief that it was of the same kind that he had previously bought of the plaintiff's manufacture. Not only was the general appearance of the defendants' loaf such as to indicate that it might easily be used to deceive purchasers who called for the plaintiff's bread, but there was considerable testimony to show that it was in fact so used by retail dealers. The evidence introduced by the plaintiff tended strongly to establish its contention that the defendants were taking advantage of the good will of its business and of the demand for its bread by putting upon the market loaves similar in appearance, of their own manufacture.

. . .

The principal contention of the defendants is that the use by the plaintiff of this combination of size, shape, color and condition of the surface, to produce a general visual appearance for its loaf of bread, made in part of malt and milk, gives it no rights, or at least, gives it no rights against one who uses only this combination, without using the same or a similar name. It also contends that, if such a combination calls for any precautions against deception, the defendants did all that they were called upon to do for that purpose.

In the first place it appears that the oval shape adopted by the plaintiff was uncommon, although not entirely novel, and that it was uneconomical, and less convenient and satisfactory generally for the cutting of slices for all kinds of uses than the shapes generally adopted. There was nothing to show that the defendants' business interests required the combination of this shape with the same size, color and general visual appearance that had become associated with the plaintiff's trade in this Creamalt bread.

. . . There are numberless shapes and sizes in which loaves of bread may be produced, and various peculiarities of appearance in color and condition of surface. These that the defendants adopted had been combined to distinguish the plaintiff's Creamalt bread, and it was the duty of other manufacturers to recognize this fact. Not, indeed, to the abandonment of their right to do what was reasonably necessary to success in the management of their own business; but to the extent of so conducting their business as not unreasonably and unnecessarily to interfere with the plaintiff's business through deception of the public.

[Defendants had placed a paper band on their loaves containing the words "Hathaway's Log Cabin Bread," and stamped the letters "C.F.H." on the bottoms of its baking tins. According to the defendant, these features distinguished its bread from the plaintiff's bread, which was sold under the label "Fox's Creamalt." But the court doubted whether retailers would retain the labels when selling bread to customers, and questioned whether retail consumers would notice any letters on the undersides of the loaves.]

We are of opinion that the defendants unnecessarily, with no apparent reason except to take advantage of the reputation built up by the plaintiff, produced and put upon the market an imitation of its loaves, adapted to use in deceiving that part of the public who had only a general knowledge and recollection of that which had been recommended to them, or which they had been accustomed to buy. . . .

The case of *Flagg Mfg. Co. v. Holway* . . . , relied on by the defendants, is materially different from the one at bar. In that case it was assumed in the opinion, upon findings of the master, that the form of zither that the plaintiff made, which the defendant imitated, and which was not patented, had in it certain elements of value for use and for sale which were peculiar to that form. If, quite apart from the plaintiff's good will, belonging to him as a particular manufacturer, this form of instrument was peculiarly valuable, the defendant had a right to make others like it. The only right of the plaintiff was to have the defendants' goods so marked as to indicate unmistakably that they were the defendants' and not the plaintiff's goods. Such marking, so made that persons observing as particularly as they would be likely to observe in buying a musical instrument, could easily be put upon the instruments.

In the present case there are no intrinsic advantages in the combination which produces this general visual appearance, and there are some disadvantages in it. A very different general appearance will be just as advantageous to the defendants, unless they wish by deceit to get away the plaintiff's customers.

Moreover, it is not so easy to mark loaves of bread of the same size, shape and color, in such a way that they will readily be distinguished from one another by purchasers generally, as it is so to mark musical instruments. The fundamental question in every such case is: How can the rights and interests of both parties be protected most completely and equitably?

Reversed.

## Enterprise Mfg. Co. v. Landers, Frary & Clark
131 F. 240 (2d Cir. 1904)

Lacombe, Circuit Judge:

This is a most aggravated case of unfair trading. Usually in these case[s] the defendants so dress their goods as to present a number of points of difference, on which they rely when charged with intent to deceive; insisting that, although there may be resemblances, the differences are so great as to preclude any idea that they had sought to produce confusion. Here, on the contrary, they have not only conformed their goods to complainant's in size and general shape, which was to be expected, but also in all minor details of structure — every line and curve being reproduced, and superfluous metal put into the driving wheels to produce a strikingly characteristic effect — while the goods are so dressed with combinations of color, with decorations reproduced or closely simulated, with style of lettering and details of ornamentation, that, except for the fact that on the one mill is found the complainant's name, and on the other the defendants', it would be very difficult to tell them apart. It is elementary law that, when the simulation of well-known and distinctive features is so close, the court will assume that defendants intended the result they have accomplished, and will find an intent to appropriate the trade of their competitor, even though in their instructions to their own selling agents they may caution against oral misrepresentations as to the manufacture of the goods. There is evidence to show that purchasers have been deceived as to the identity of these mills, but, in the case of [an exact] copy, such as defendants offer to the public, such proof is hardly needed.

It is to defendants' credit that, when confronted with the charge of copying, they have not denied it, nor asserted that they were trying to differentiate their own products. On the contrary, they admit that they "concluded they could profitably manufacture this same line of hardware and sell it in competition with the Enterprise Company," and accordingly commenced the manufacture thereof, "using parts of mills sold by the Enterprise Company as patterns wherever it was convenient or profitable to do so," with the result that they are "now making and selling coffee mills which in all substantial respects, and especially in their effectiveness in use and attractiveness, are the same goods as those made and sold by the Enterprise Company."

No doubt, with such identity in attractiveness, competition with complainant's mills would be much more effective; but defendants overlooked the fact that a court of equity will not allow a man to palm off his goods as those of another, whether his misrepresentations are made by mouth, or, more subtly, by simulating the collocation of details of appearance by which the consuming public has come to recognize the product of his competitor.

. . .

*Affirmed.*

## CRESCENT TOOL CO. v. KILBORN & BISHOP CO.
247 F. 299 (2d Cir. 1917)

LEARNED HAND, District Judge:

[Plaintiff made an adjustable wrench under the mark CRESCENT. As the court described it (paraphrasing the parties' affidavits), "[t]he wrench, on account of its appearance and new and original shape, pleased the public, and its sales grew rapidly from year to year, so that it became known to the jobbing trade and retailers and consumers as the 'Crescent' type of wrench. Its main structural features were all old in detail. It was adjustable to bolts and nuts of different sizes somewhat after the manner of a monkey wrench, but it was nevertheless quite different mechanically from a monkey wrench. It had a straight handle of web and rib construction, spreading slightly from the neck to the end, with a hole in the end of the web by which it could be hung up. No adjustable wrench of precisely the same character had ever appeared upon the market. There had, however, been adjustable wrenches, some with straight handles, some with web and rib curved handles, and there had been other tools with straight web and rib handles, somewhat broader at the end than at the neck. Plaintiff's name is plainly printed upon the web of the handle in raised letters."

Defendant sold a competing wrench under a different name. The defendant's wrench was "substantially a direct facsimile" of the plaintiff's. There was some evidence of confusion among wrench buyers.]

The cases of so-called "nonfunctional" unfair competition, starting with the "coffee mill case," *Enterprise Mfg. Co. v. Landers, Frary & Clark*, [131 F. 240 (2d Cir. 1904)] are only instances of the doctrine of "secondary" meaning. All of them presuppose that the appearance of the article, like its descriptive title in true cases of "secondary" meaning, has become associated in the public mind with the first comer as manufacturer or source, and, if a second comer imitates the article exactly, that the public will believe his goods have come from the first, and will buy, in part, at least, because of that deception. Therefore it is apparent that it is an absolute condition to any relief whatever that the plaintiff in such cases show that the appearance of his wares has in fact come to mean that some particular person—the plaintiff may not be individually known—makes them, and that the public cares who does make them, and not merely for their appearance and structure. It will not be enough only to show how pleasing they are, because all the features of beauty or utility which commend them to the public are by hypothesis already in the public domain. The defendant has as much right to copy the "nonfunctional" features of the article as any others, so long as they have not become associated with the plaintiff as manufacturer or source.

The critical question of fact at the outset always is whether the public is moved in any degree to buy the article because of its source and what are the features by which it distinguishes that source. Unless the plaintiff can answer this question he can take no step forward; no degree of imitation of details is actionable in its absence.

In the case at bar it nowhere appears that before 1910, when the defendant began to make its wrenches, the general appearance of the plaintiff's wrench had come to indicate to the public any one maker as its source, or that the wrench had been sold in any part because of its source, as distinct from its utility or neat appearance. It is not enough to show that the wrench became popular under the name "Crescent"; the plaintiff must prove that before 1910 the public had already established the habit of buying it, not solely because they wanted that kind of wrench, but because they also wanted a Crescent, and thought all such wrenches were Crescents.

Upon the trial the plaintiff may, however, be able to establish this, and it is only fair to indicate broadly the considerations which will then determine the scope of his relief. In such cases neither side has an absolute right, because their mutual rights conflict. Thus the plaintiff has the right not to lose his customers through false representations that those are his wares which in fact are not, but he may not monopolize any design or pattern, however trifling. The defendant, on the other hand, may copy the plaintiff's goods slavishly down to the minutest detail; but he may not represent himself as the plaintiff in their sale. When the appearance of the goods has in fact come to represent a given person as their source, and that person is in fact the plaintiff, it is impossible to make these rights absolute; compromise is essential, exactly as it is with the right to use the common language in cases of "secondary" meaning....

[Reversed.]

## NOTES AND QUESTIONS

1. *Defining "trade dress."* Review the descriptions of the subject matter at issue in the above cases. In contemporary terms, the subject matter might be thought of as trade dress. From those descriptions, can you derive a general definition of trade dress? Are you surprised that the opinions do not delineate in much detail the precise boundaries of the subject matter? Why or why not?

2. *Holmes' view.* In the zither case (*Flagg*), does Holmes exclude product shapes altogether from protection under unfair competition laws? Or does *Flagg* stand for the proposition that such protection will be available, but only under limited circumstances, as Judge Knowlton suggests in the bread case (*Fox*)? If the latter, what are the limited circumstances?

3. *Hand's view.* In the *Crescent Tool* case, is Learned Hand excluding product shapes altogether from protection under the unfair competition laws, or is he limiting protection to cases in which the subject matter has "secondary meaning" and is "nonfunctional"? Does Learned Hand explain those concepts adequately? Hand also says that there must be evidence that the public cares who makes the products at issue. Was this an additional requirement of

"materiality"? Learned Hand characterizes the coffee mill case, *Enterprise*, as a case of "nonfunctional unfair competition." Is that a fair characterization of the court's rationale for granting relief in that case?

**4. *A modern translation.*** The concerns voiced in these older cases remain relevant today. Sometimes, modern courts debate those concerns by reference to foundational principles—such as the definition of trademark, interpreted below in the *Kohler* case. More commonly, courts invoke doctrines of distinctiveness and functionality. For example, a modern decision in *Flagg* might turn on the functionality doctrine. The cases in the next section of Chapter 2 illustrate the emergence and application of distinctiveness as one dominant prerequisite for modern trade dress and design protection, and the cases in Chapter 3 illustrate the same for the functionality doctrine.

## Lanham Act
### Section 45

The term "trademark" includes any word, name, symbol, or device, or any combination thereof . . . used by a person . . . to identify and distinguish his or her goods, including a unique product, from those manufactured or sold by others and to indicate the source of the goods, even if that source is unknown. . . .

## Kohler Co. v. Moen Inc.
### 12 F.3d 632 (7th Cir. 1993)

Coffey, Circuit Judge:

### I. Background

Kohler and Moen are competitors in the business of manufacturing and selling plumbing products, including faucets and faucet handles. Moen sought and obtained trademark registration of its "LEGEND" kitchen faucet and the appearance of the handle used on the "LEGEND" and other Moen faucets. In support of registration of its product configurations as trademarks, Moen introduced voluminous evidence of sales and promotional expenses with respect to each design, and also submitted substantial evidence that purchasers of its products recognized the source of the faucets by their distinctive shapes. The record included hundreds of declarations from persons in the plumbing business and from individual purchasers attesting to the distinctiveness of the shape of Moen's faucet and handle without reference to any markings. One of Moen's vice-presidents submitted a declaration stating that Moen's faucet design is not based upon utility or function, is not inexpensive to manufacture, and is only one of many competitive designs in the industry performing the same function. Moen also submitted a declaration from the chairman of one of its chief competitors, Price Pfister, that stated that Moen's faucet is distinctive, its design indicates a single point of origin, the design is neither functional nor utilitarian, and that trademark protection for the configuration would not hinder competition in the plumbing trade. Finally, a market research survey of 273 licensed plumbers in six cities revealed that eighty-two percent of those surveyed identified the faucet as a Moen product, and eighty-three percent identified the handle as a Moen product.

[Kohler opposed Moen's applications on the ground that product shapes were not registrable as trademarks. The TTAB dismissed the oppositions and Kohler sought review in the district court under 15 U.S.C. §1071(b). The district court granted summary judgment in favor of Moen; Kohler appealed.] In proceedings before the TTAB, in the district court, and in this court, Kohler has forthrightly conceded that if product shapes can receive protection under federal trademark law, Moen is entitled to registration of its LEGEND faucet and faucet handle. Thus, the issue before the district court and this court is legal in nature: does the §45 definition of "Trademark" in the Lanham Act, 15 U.S.C. §1127 (1988), ("the Act") exclude trademark protection of product configurations?

. . .

### III. Analysis

In dismissing Kohler's oppositions, the TTAB necessarily concluded that §45 of the Act provides trademark protection for product configurations. Section 45 of the Act defines trademark to "*include*[] any word, name, symbol, or device or any combination thereof adopted and used by a manufacturer or merchant to identify his goods and distinguish them from those manufactured or sold by others." 15 U.S.C. §1127 (1988). As Kohler notes, §45 does not list "product configuration" among its examples of trademarks. Early decisions under the Act strictly construed the language of §45 and held that a product or container shape was not entitled to trademark protection. *See* 1 McCarthy, *McCarthy on Trademarks and Unfair Competition*, §7.31 (3d ed. 1992) [hereinafter *McCarthy on Trademarks*]; *Ex Parte Minnesota Mining & Mfg. Co.*, 92 U.S.P.Q. 74 (1952). Subsequent TTAB decisions and the courts reviewing TTAB rulings, however, have interpreted §45 to allow trademark protection for product configurations.

In *Application of Kotzin*, 276 F.2d 411, 414-15 (C.C.P.A. 1960), the Court of Customs and Patent Appeals ("C.C.P.A.") held that the §45 list ("word, name, symbol or device") did not restrict other items from receiving trademark protection if they satisfied the requirements for registration on the Principal Register. The court in *Kotzin* supported its interpretation of the statute by noting that the provision stated that trademarks "*include*" words, names, symbols or devices, not that "trademark" "*means*" words, names, symbols or devices. Furthermore, the court noted that the language of §2 of the Act, 15 U.S.C. §1052, which lists exceptions to registrability under the Act, supported its ruling that Congress did not intend §45 to be an all-inclusive list. *Id.* at 414. Section 2 states that "[n]o trademark . . . shall be refused registration on the principal register *on account of its nature*," unless one or more of the specified exceptions to registrability set forth in the statute apply. 15 U.S.C. §1052 (emphasis added). Neither trouser tags (the item the applicant sought to register in *Kotzin*) nor product configurations fall within any of the exceptions to registrability set forth in §2.

In *Application of Mogen David*, 328 F.2d 925 (C.C.P.A.1964), the C.C.P.A. held that the configuration of a container could be registered as a trademark for the product it contains. *Id.* at 929-30. The C.C.P.A. thereafter held that a product configuration itself could be registered as a trademark in *Application of Honeywell, Inc.*, 497 F.2d 1344 (C.C.P.A.), *cert. denied*, 419 U.S. 1080, (1974). The C.C.P.A., the Federal Circuit, and the TTAB have since interpreted §45 to allow trademark protection for qualifying product configurations. [cit.] Because Congress did not specify in §45 that product configurations are entitled to trademark protection, however, we must determine whether Congress authorized the Commissioner of Patents and Trademarks and the TTAB to interpret §45 of the Act.

[In accordance with applicable administrative law principles, the court considered whether the TTAB's conclusion that product configurations are eligible for trademark status was based on a permissible construction of Lanham Act §45.] The persuasiveness of the TTAB and the Federal Circuit's interpretation of §45 is reinforced by the legislative history accompanying the 1988 Lanham Act amendments. *See* Trademark Law Revision Act of 1988, Pub. L. 100-667, §38, S. Rep. 515, 100th Cong., 2d Sess. 44 (1988), *reprinted in*, 1988 U.S.C.C.A.N. 5577, 5607. Although these amendments did not take effect until November 1989, approximately two years after the TTAB's decision in this case, as a codification of prior case law they validate the uniform preamendment interpretation of §45 on the Act. The Senate Report accompanying the 1988 amendments specifically states "the words 'symbol or device,'" were retained in the Trademark Revision Act's revised definition of trademark "so as not to preclude the registration of colors, shapes, sounds *or configurations* where they function as trademarks." S. Rep. 100-515, 100th Cong., 2d Sess. at 44, *reprinted in*, 1988 U.S.C.C.A.N. at 5607 (emphasis added). Congress thus specifically approved the broad judicial interpretation of §45's definition of "trademark" to include product configurations. In light of uniform and persuasive judicial authority and the subsequent congressional approval of those judicial interpretations of §45, we conclude Congress intended that product configurations were eligible for trademark status under §45 of the Lanham Act. Therefore, we hold now, as we have in the past, that §45 of the Act allows product configurations to be eligible for trademark status. [cit.] Having determined that the TTAB's construction of §45 is permissible and is consistent with our construction thereof, we turn to the specific challenges to the TTAB's interpretation.

In its brief, Kohler restates essentially two arguments in various forms. Initially, Kohler argues that granting trademark protection to product configurations impermissibly conflicts with the Patent Clause of the United States Constitution and the implementing patent law because it is the equivalent of a perpetual patent. Second, Kohler alleges trademark protection for product configurations is anticompetitive and inhibits product development because it precludes manufacturers from using product configurations resembling trademarked configurations.

### A. Trademark Protection Is Not Equivalent to a Perpetual Patent

Kohler asserts that granting trademark protection and allowing trademark registration for a product configuration directly conflicts with the rationale of the Constitution's Patent Clause and the Patent Act, 35 U.S.C. §§1-376 (1988). Kohler alleges that the Supreme Court's interpretation of the Patent Clause in *Bonito Boats, Inc. v. Thunder Craft Boats, Inc.*, 489 U.S. 141, 146 (1989); *Sears Roebuck & Co. v. Stiffel Co.*, 376 U.S. 225 (1964), and *Compco Corp. v. Day-Brite Lighting, Inc.*, 376 U.S. 234 (1964), indicates that the TTAB and lower courts' interpretation of the Act to allow trademark protection for product configurations contravenes the Patent Clause's requirement that the exclusive right to "Writings and Discoveries" be for a "limited Time[]." To analyze the soundness of Kohler's claim that courts' interpretation of the Act runs afoul of the Patent Clause and implementing patent law, a brief discussion of the purpose of each is necessary.

To obtain patent protection, an applicant has to show that an invention or design is both novel and "not obvious at the time the invention was made to a person having ordinary skill in the art to which said art pertains." 35 U.S.C. §103 (1988). Patent protection is limited in duration: utility patents last for seventeen years, 35 U.S.C. §154* (1988), and design patents extend for fourteen years, 35 U.S.C. §173 (1988). The innovation passes into the public domain after the patent expires.

Compared to patent protection, trademark protection is relatively weak because it precludes competitors only from using marks that are likely to confuse or deceive the public. Trademark protection is dependent only on public reaction to the trademark in the marketplace rather than solely on the similarity of the configurations. *See* Jay Dratler, *Trademark Protection for Industrial Designs*, 1988 U. Ill. L. Rev. 887, 896 (1988) [hereinafter Dratler, *Industrial Designs*]. An applicant for trademark protection need prove only that the proposed trademark is distinctive; that is, that it is either arbitrary, suggestive, or descriptive and has secondary meaning. Although patent rights are limited in duration by statute, trademark rights may continue as long as the mark is used to distinguish and identify. Significantly, while a patent creates a type of monopoly pricing power by giving the patentee the exclusive right to make and sell the innovation, a trademark gives the owner only the right to preclude others from using the mark when such use is likely to cause confusion or to deceive. *See* 1 McCarthy on Trademarks §2.05[1].

. . .

Kohler forthrightly concedes that in *W.T. Rogers Co. v. Keene*, 778 F.2d 334 (7th Cir. 1985), this court considered and rejected the claim that granting trademark protection for product configurations conflicts with the Patent Clause and patent law. As Judge Posner noted in *W.T. Rogers:*

> [P]rovided that a defense of functionality is recognized, there is no conflict with federal patent law, save possibly with 35 U.S.C. §171, which allows a 14-year patent to be granted for a nonfunctional ornamental design—a design patent. But the courts that have considered the issue have concluded,

---

*[Ed. note: Congress has since amended the Patent Act. U.S. utility patents now last for twenty years from the application filing date.]

rightly in our view, that this section does not prevent the enforcement of a common law trademark in a design feature. See discussion in 1 Chisum, Patents §1.04[6] (1985). The trademark owner has an indefinite term of protection, it is true, but in an infringement suit must also prove secondary meaning and likelihood of confusion, which the owner of a design patent need not do; there is therefore no necessary inconsistency between the two modes of protection.

*Id.* at 337.[8]

In sum, courts have consistently held that a product's different qualities can be protected simultaneously, or successively, by more than one of the statutory means for protection of intellectual property. [cit.]

Kohler disagrees with our view that patent and trademark law are distinct areas of law. Instead, Kohler maintains that in light of the Supreme Court's holdings in *Bonito Boats, Inc. v. Thunder Craft Boats, Inc.*, 489 U.S. 141 (1989); *Compco Corp. v. Day-Brite Lighting, Inc.*, 376 U.S. 234 (1964), and *Sears Roebuck & Co. v. Stiffel Co.*, 376 U.S. 225 (1964), Moen's faucet and faucet handle are not protected under the Act because unpatented goods may be freely copied. In all three cases that Kohler relies upon, the Supreme Court examined state unfair competition laws to evaluate whether federal patent law preempted their application. The Court in each case held that a state's unfair competition laws could not extend patent-like protection to otherwise unprotected designs because such protection conflicted with the federal policy expressed in the patent clause and patent laws of generally free trade in unpatented design and utilitarian concepts. *See Bonito Boats*, 489 U.S. at 152-54 (discussing *Sears* and *Compco* decisions). We disagree with Kohler's sweeping conclusion that the Supreme Court's holdings in *Sears, Compco*, and *Bonito Boats* preclude trademark protection for product configurations.[9]

---

8. Kohler questions the reasoning in *W.T. Rogers* by noting that likelihood of confusion relates only to whether there has been an infringement, not whether product configuration is entitled to trademark protection in the first place. Of course, the "likelihood of confusion" requirement referred to in *W.T. Rogers* for infringement actions emphasizes that a trademark right is not equivalent to a patent right. A design patent gives the patentee a virtually absolute monopoly in the design, while a trademark allows competitive uses of a protected design so long as such uses do not create consumer confusion. We disagree with Kohler's claim that the test for infringement in a design patent case is "essentially the same" as the infringement test for a trademark infringement case. Kohler maintains that this purported equivalency in the two tests indicates that design patent plaintiffs must establish "some degree of product recognition among purchasers." Kohler oversimplifies. The test for trademark infringement requires proof that the trademark has acquired secondary meaning or is a distinctive, identifying mark, and that consumers are likely to be confused by the similarity of appearance. *Schwinn Bicycle Co. v. Ross Bicycles, Inc.*, 870 F.2d 1176, 1182 (7th Cir. 1989). Likelihood of confusion is measured by considering numerous factors; similarity of appearance is only one of those factors. *See id.* at 1185; *Wesley-Jessen, Div. v. Bausch & Lomb, Inc.*, 698 F.2d 862, 866 (7th Cir. 1983).

By contrast, infringement of a design patent is established by proof that the designs look alike to the eye of the ordinary observer. *See Gorham Co. v. White*, 81 U.S. 511, 528 (1872). . . .

9. In agreeing with Kohler's contentions, the dissent fundamentally departs from our interpretation of the Lanham Act as applied to product configurations by viewing this judicially accepted application of the Act as conferring patent-like protection. Only if one accepts the dissent's characterization of federal trademark protection as "patent-like" can the snippets of dicta drawn from Supreme Court cases involving state laws conferring perpetual patent-like protection be viewed as indirect support for the dissent's position. We believe that our discussion of the relevant Supreme Court cases supports our holding and refutes Kohler's claim that the Court has hinted in dicta that product configurations are not entitled to the limited protection available under the Lanham Act.

In the *Sears/Compco* decisions, the Supreme Court reviewed two decisions from this court which held that Illinois unfair competition law prohibited unauthorized copying of unpatentable lighting fixture designs. The Supreme Court held in both cases that federal copyright and patent law preempted the state unfair competition law which prohibited the copying of a nonpatented product. *Sears*, 376 U.S. at 231-32; *Compco*, 376 U.S. at 237-38. Kohler argues that because state unfair competition and federal trademark law serve the same purpose, federal patent law also conflicts with federal trademark law.[10] Kohler is mistaken. First, no Lanham Act issue was raised in either *Sears* or *Compco;* the decision in each case was based on the Supremacy Clause. Second, the Court in *Compco* noted that a defendant may copy at will if the design is "not entitled to a design patent *or other federal statutory protection.* . . ." *Compco*, 376 U.S. at 238. Of course, the Lanham Act falls under the rubric of "other federal statutory protection," and courts have expressly held that *Sears* and *Compco* do not preclude federal trademark protection of designs. [cit.]

In *Bonito Boats*, the Supreme Court unanimously held that a Florida statute granting perpetual patent-like protection to a boat hull design already on the market conflicted with federal patent law and was therefore invalid under the Supremacy Clause. In arriving at this holding, the Court reaffirmed the proposition stated in *Sears* and *Compco* that "publicly known design and utilitarian ideas which were unprotected by patent occupied much the same position as the subject matter of an expired patent" — they were unprotected. *Bonito Boats*, 489 U.S. at 152. Kohler seizes upon this language as a broad proclamation that the preemption principles set forth in *Sears* and *Compco* stand unaltered. Kohler argues that *Bonito Boats* reaffirmed the *Sears* and

---

10. An exaggeration of the relationship between the Lanham Act and state law of unfair competition leads the dissent, in our view, to erroneously conclude that the Lanham Act merely federalizes the common law of trademarks and unfair competition. The Lanham Act was drafted in *reaction* to draconian state trademark legislation that threatened to interfere with interstate commerce. [cit.] The Lanham Act and state common law are independent of each other, although the standards of federal registrability use terminology similar to state common law trademark standards. [cit.] That the Supreme Court has held that extraordinarily protective state trademark law runs afoul of the Patent Clause and Patent Act does not threaten the constitutionality of the Lanham Act as courts have applied it. The Lanham Act differs in many respects from the common law standards. As one commentator has noted:

> Things such as service marks, collective and certification marks, are federally registrable, even though their common law status is doubtful. Conversely, although corporate and commercial trade names are protected by the common law, they are *not* federally registrable.

*McCarthy on Trademarks*, §7.33[2] (footnotes omitted).

The Lanham Act as written and applied is not "exactly the same" as the state laws at issue in *Sears, Compco*, and *Bonito Boats*. Thus, this court's holding, and that of every circuit to consider the issue, does not create any conflict with the Constitution, the patent laws, or Supreme Court decisions. The dissent's conjuring up of the specter of design patents "made perpetual by trademarking the design" is inapposite to our holding and the facts of this case. First, there is no indication that Moen ever had or could qualify for a design patent on its products. Second, federal trademark protection does not transform the durationally limited monopoly of a design patent into a perpetual right. As we have noted, federal trademark protection for a product's configuration does not create a *monopoly* in the use of the product's shape. Moen is not "free from effective competition in the market for a popular brand of faucet." Moen simply has the right to preclude others from copying its trademarked product for the purpose of confusing the public as to its source. Kohler is free to copy Moen's design so long as it insures that the public is not thereby deceived or confused into believing that its copy is a Moen faucet.

*Compco* and that the preemption principles set forth in those cases should be read to preclude federal trademark protection for product configurations.

As in *Sears*, however, the *Bonito Boats* Court recognized that states have the power to give unfair competition and trademark protection to trade dress.... The Court's holding in *Bonito Boats* is also inapplicable to federal trademark law because the Florida statute granted boat manufacturers patent-like rights far exceeding any right available under the Lanham Act.... [T]he underlying policies of federal trademark law, and the nature of the protection afforded, do not approximate the sweeping, perpetual patent-like state statutes that the Supreme Court found impermissible in *Sears, Compco,* and *Bonito Boats*.

[The court reviewed the *Two Pesos* decision.]** The Court was not directly confronted in *Two Pesos* with the issue of whether product configurations were protected trade dress under §43 of the Act. Nonetheless, the Court's discussion of the Fifth Circuit's approach to trade dress protection suggested that any conflicts between the patent laws and the Lanham Act should be resolved by a careful application of traditional bases for determining the propriety of trademark protection such as likelihood of confusion, functionality, and distinctiveness....

Kohler's contention that even a remote potential for conflict between trademark law and design patent law requires the reversal of this circuit's settled precedent and rejection of the uniform holdings of every court to consider the issue, ignores the Supreme Court's observation in *Two Pesos* that sensitive application of the principles governing trademark recognition can avert the threat of a perpetual trademark "monopoly." *See also* Dratler, *Industrial Design*, 1988 U. ILL. L. REV. 887, 936 ("Because trademark principles reveal their potential for conflict with patent goals only when applied to specific facts, courts should attempt to achieve that harmony by analyzing the conflict in the context of specific facts. In short, any perceived conflict should be resolved not on the face of the law, but only on the law as applied."). Furthermore, a fundamental rule of statutory construction requires that statutes are to be construed, if possible, in harmony with the Constitution and other applicable statutes. [cit.] Indisputably, some of the concerns expressed in *Sears, Compco,* and *Bonito Boats* regarding state law conflicts with the patent laws are also valid with respect to federal legislation. It could be argued that Congress could conceivably enact legislation conferring perpetual patent-like monopolies that would conflict with the patent clause's requirement that exclusive rights to authors and inventors be only "for limited Times." U.S. Const. art. I, §8, cl. 8. It is apparent, however, that perpetual trademark protection under the Lanham Act for a product configuration or design is not the equivalent of impermissible perpetual patent protection.

Kohler has conceded that under the facts of this case, Moen satisfied all of the requirements for trademark protection for product configurations. The Supreme Court's holdings and dicta in *Sears, Compco, Bonito Boats,* and *Two Pesos* offer no reason for this court to hold that every court that has allowed federal trademark protection for product configurations was mistaken.

---

**[Ed. Note: The Supreme Court may have since limited *Two Pesos*, as discussed in the *Samara* case in this chapter.]

## B. Trademark Protection

Kohler also alleges that allowing tra[demark protection for product config]urations is anticompetitive and inhibi[ts product development. Kohler argues] extending trademark protection to p[roduct configurations is unnecessary and] courts should refuse such protection [because producers can simply label] their products to prevent consumer [confusion. Finally, Kohler contends] that any change in the extent of trad[emark protection available for product] configurations should come only from [Congress.]

Kohler contends that granting trad[emark protection to product configura]tions conflicts with public policy favori[ng competition and disfavoring monop]olies. As we noted earlier, trademarks a[re narrow monopolies that allow other] designs similar to the trademark so lo[ng as they do not create a likelihood of] confusion. Furthermore, Kohler conc[edes that Moen's alleged] trademark protection to Moen will n[ot prevent Kohler from producing faucets] or faucet handles. We recognized in *W.T. Rogers Co. v. Keene,* [778 F.2d 334,] that granting trademark protection to a nongeneric and nonfunctional product design does not stifle competition. We noted that, "[s]ince the supply of distinctive names and symbols usable for brand identification is very large, indeed for all practical purposes infinite, competition is not impaired by giving each manufacturer a perpetual 'monopoly' of his identifying mark; such marks are not a scarce input into the production of goods." *W.T. Rogers,* 778 F.2d at 339.

Kohler admits the configuration of Moen's faucet and faucet handle is not functional; i.e. the trademarked feature would not be "found in all or most brands of the product even if no producer had any desire to have his brand mistaken for that of another producer. . . . [A] functional feature is one which competitors would have to spend money not to copy but to design around." *W.T. Rogers,* 778 F.2d at 339; [cit.]. Kohler has not challenged Moen's claim that the configuration of its faucet and faucet handle is designed solely to differentiate the source of these particular products from those of other manufacturers. We decline to accept Kohler's invitation to overrule our decisions holding that functionality is a valid criterion for evaluating the propriety of trademark protection.

Kohler's claim that trademark protection for product configurations undermines product development is both unpersuasive and unsupported. As discussed earlier, such a conclusion is possible only if the underlying policies and protections of federal trademark and patent law are ignored. Patents encourage the type of innovation that advances the progress of "Science and the useful Arts," and patent law imposes a high standard for patentable protection and limits patent grants to a fixed term. Trademark law protects a producer's right to select an identifying name or symbol for his brand and exclude others from using it. Moreover, "[j]ust as the economic rewards of trademark protection encourage discovery and invention, so do the economic rewards of trademark protection encourage creative effort in marketing." Dratler, *Industrial Designs,* 1988 U. Ill. L. Rev. 887, 927-28. Innovation in product design and marketing for the purpose of enhancing producer identity reduces the costs to consumers of informing themselves about the product source so that they can either continue purchasing the products from particular

...e products from those producers altogether. *See W.T.* ...38; [cit.].

...ention that Congress must amend federal trademark law to ...r courts' "novel and expansive interpretation of the trademark ...termined by the Supreme Court in *Bonito Boats*. There the Court ... Congress's adoption of §43(a) of the Lanham Act and the long-... coexistence of the patent statute with unfair competition law are ...native indications" that unfair competition law is "consistent with the ...licy] balance struck by the patent laws." *Bonito Boats*, 489 U.S. at 166. As noted earlier, we perceive no unavoidable conflict between the patent law and federal trademark law as applied to product configurations.

[*Affirmed.*]

CUDAHY, Circuit Judge, dissenting:

The majority opinion is an admirably lucid presentation of the point of view adopted by the Court of Appeals for the Federal Circuit and its predecessor, the Court of Customs and Patent Appeals, during about the last twenty years. Unfortunately, this view notoriously lacks the support and endorsement of the Supreme Court. *See Application of Honeywell, Inc.*, 497 F.2d 1344 (C.C.P.A.), *cert. denied*, 419 U.S. 1080 (1974); *In re Teledyne*, 696 F.2d 968 (Fed. Cir. 1982).[1] [cit.] In adopting the position that the configuration or design of products themselves may be the subject of federal trademark protection, the Federal Circuit and the courts that have followed it seem to have taken lightly the emphasis placed on the *right to copy* by decisions of the Supreme Court not only recently but stretching back for a century. *See Bonito Boats, Inc. v. Thunder Craft Boats, Inc.*, 489 U.S. 141 (1989); *Sears, Roebuck & Co. v. Stiffel*, 376 U.S. 225 (1964); *Compco Corp. v. Day-Brite Lighting, Inc.*, 376 U.S. 234 (1964); *Kellogg Co. v. National Biscuit Co.*, 305 U.S. 111 (1938); *Singer Mfg. Co. v. June Mfg. Co.*, 163 U.S. 169 (1896). While I have the greatest respect for the Federal Circuit, its decisions do not bind us. I think those decisions should not be followed when they seem to be so much in conflict with relevant Supreme Court authority. The essential issue before us is whether to follow lower court cases that lack the endorsement of the Supreme Court and that defeat the important right to copy unpatented articles recently proclaimed yet again by the Supreme Court in *Bonito Boats*, 489 U.S. at 151-153. [cit.] This is a crucially important issue for the maintenance of a free and competitive economy. We should not hesitate to go back to fundamentals in the analysis of the problem.

The majority correctly states the two basic arguments presented by Kohler for denying federal trademark registration to product configurations. Kohler contends that the practice is an unconstitutional violation of the Patent Clause of the Constitution *and* is anticompetitive. These are both fundamental questions and the majority has been unable to answer them at a fundamental level.

---

1. While Moen and the majority on the subject of product configuration trademarks trace the relatively recent departure of the Federal Circuit from *Application of Mogen David Wine Corp.*, 328 F.2d 925 (C.C.P.A. 1964), that case involved not the configuration of the product itself (wine) but the shape of a wine *bottle*-a container. *See Application of Mogen David Wine Corp.*, 372 F.2d 539, 544 (C.C.P.A. 1967) (Smith J., concurring) (later proceeding). *Mogen David* did not therefore directly confront the issue raised here, although it lays some of the groundwork.

The Supreme Court has made clear that the patent monopoly which may be secured by obtaining a design patent on a product may not be indefinitely extended through the use of a federal trademark on the product configuration. Thus, in *Scott Paper Co. v. Marcalus Mfg. Co.*, 326 U.S. 249 (1945), the Court summarized the rationale for this rule:

> The public has invested in such free use by the grant of a monopoly to the patentee for a limited time. Hence any attempted reservation or continuation in the patentee or those claiming under him of the patent monopoly, after the patent expires, *whatever the legal device employed*, runs counter to the policy and purpose of the patent laws. . . .
>
> By the force of the patent laws not only is the invention of a patent dedicated to the public upon its expiration, but the public thereby becomes entitled to share in the good will which the patentee has built up in the patented article or product through the enjoyment of his patent monopoly. *Hence we have held that the patentee may not exclude the public from participating in that good will or secure, to any extent, a continuation of his monopoly by resorting to the trademark law and registering as a trademark any particular descriptive matter appearing in the specifications, drawings or claims of the expired patent, whether or not such matter describes essential elements of the invention or claims.*

*Id.* at 256 (emphasis supplied) (citations omitted).

In *Singer Mfg. Co. v. June Mfg. Co.*, 163 U.S. 169 (1896), Singer made patented sewing machines for several years having a distinctive form and appearance. 163 U.S. at 175. After the expiration of the principal patents, June Manufacturing Company began making sewing machines with the same appearance. *Id.* Singer complained that June, "for the purpose of inducing the belief that sewing machines manufactured and sold by it [June] were made by [Singer], was making and selling machines of the exact size, shape, ornamentation, and general appearance as" Singer's machines. *Id.* at 170. The Court refused to enjoin the copying of Singer's product configuration and held:

> It is self-evident that on the expiration of a patent the monopoly created by it ceases to exist, and the right to make the thing formerly covered by the patent becomes public property. It is upon this condition that the patent is granted. *It follows, as a matter of course, that on the termination of the patent there passes to the public the right to make the machine in the form in which it was constructed during the patent.* We may, therefore, dismiss without further comment the complaint as to the form in which the defendant made his machines.

*Id.* at 185 (emphasis supplied).

In *Kellogg Co. v. National Biscuit Co.*, 305 U.S. 111 (1938) the shredded wheat biscuit was the subject of a design patent held by National Biscuit covering the pillow-shaped form. Upon the expiration of the patent, the Court allowed Kellogg to manufacture the same biscuit under the name "shredded wheat." The Court held that "upon expiration of the patents the form . . . was dedicated to the public." 305 U.S. at 119-20.

Certainly, if the Patent Clause gives the right to copy an article which was once covered by a patent, the public must also retain the right to copy an article which has never been even temporarily removed from the public domain by reason of being patented. [Judge Cudahy reviewed *Sears, Compco,* and *Bonito Boats.*]

Moen — and the majority here — argue that *Sears, Compco* and *Bonito Boats* are concerned with the interface between federal patent law and the *state* law of unfair competition. The cases therefore merely involve application of the Supremacy Clause and federal preemption of state law. Superficially, this argument may have some appeal but it ignores the fact that the Lanham Act (comprising the federal law of trademarks and unfair competition) essentially federalizes the common law of trademarks and unfair competition. And the Lanham Act provides a federal trademark register to which generally recognized principles of notice may be applied. Therefore, the conflict that the Court found between state law and federal patent law as a prerequisite to preemption in *Sears, Compco* and *Bonito Boats* is exactly the same conflict as would develop between federal patent law and federal trademark law if a design patent could be made perpetual by trademarking the design. As a matter of commercial reality, therefore, the relation of patent law to state unfair competition law is exactly the same as its relation to federal trademark law.[3]

The conflict, then, is directly between a federal statutory scheme rooted in the Constitution and a federal codification of the common law.[4] As the Court noted in *Bonito Boats*, the Lanham Act's federalization of the common law of unfair competition reflects a congressional affirmation of policies that must be made conformable with the constitutionally rooted patent laws:

> Congress has thus given federal recognition to many of the concerns that underlie the state tort of unfair competition, and the application of *Sears* and *Compco* to nonfunctional aspects of a product which has been shown to identify sources must take account of competing federal policies in this regard.

489 U.S. at 166. Mindful of the policies underlying federal trademark law as succinctly described by the majority here, we must determine whether any

---

3. The majority argues that differences between stringent state unfair competition laws and the Lanham Act require us to distinguish the entire line of Supreme Court authority articulating a constitutional policy favoring a right to copy. I do not agree that one hundred years of policy can be ignored merely because the Lanham Act may differ somewhat from the state laws considered by the Court. The *conflict* posed by these state laws and the Lanham Act remains the same: whether trademark can be used as a back door to protection properly acquired by a design patent.

4. The majority opinion cites part of one paragraph of this court's opinion in *W.T. Rogers Co. v. Keene*, 778 F.2d 334 (7th Cir. 1985), for the proposition that we have already decided that there is no conflict between patent law and trademark protection of product configurations. *See id.* at 337. I do not agree that *W.T. Rogers* disposed of this issue. In *W.T. Rogers*, Judge Posner traversed the rocky terrain of "functionality." He indicated that although a functionality defense could avert a conflict between trademark and utility patent law, there might still be a clash with design patent law. *Id.* He pointed to the different standards for proving trademark and design patent infringement to harmonize the two modes of protection. But, respectfully, this is not an adequate answer to the anticompetitive features of trademark protection for product configurations. Judge Posner's conclusion that there is no "necessary inconsistency" between trademark and patent law does not, as the majority states, tell us there is no *possible* inconsistency. And indeed, this inconsistency arises when, as here, a company resorts to trademark law to protect the very product itself.

Moreover, I am not persuaded that passing references to trademarks for designs in *Two Pesos, Inc. v. Taco Cabana, Inc.*, 505 U.S. 763 (1992), which does not even indirectly address the issues here, sheds any light on the conflict between patent law and trademarks for product configurations.

A. Trade Dress and Designs as Protecta[ble]

trademark interests served by recognizing entire prod[uct ...]
sufficiently weighty to defeat the crucial policies served b[y ...]

What is at stake here is the right to copy the thing itself—[the]
configuration or design. The configuration or design of a produ[ct ...]
as the name of the product. As the Supreme Court cases demo[nstrate,]
constitutional right to copy after a patent expires or in the absence o[f ...]
is the reciprocal of the constitutional right to prohibit copying for a l[imited]
term under the Patent Clause. To ignore this principle is to permit perpe[tual]
monopolies on product ideas or particular product designs and to inhibit product development. Kohler has provided some horrible examples of allowing federal trademark registration to substitute for the grant of a design patent. One example consists of what appears to be a simple white disc. This product is a round beach towel, which has been granted registration as a trademark on the Principal Register. The registrant presumably has a monopoly on the production of beach towels that are round. Other registrations (and monopolies) may follow for triangular beach towels, trapezoidal beach towels or whatever. As a result of the case now before us, only Moen will be legally entitled to supply replacement handles for Moen faucets. Moen will have the equivalent of a perpetual design patent on its faucets and faucet handles—in violation of the Constitution.

Courts have attempted to reconcile any conflict between trademark and patent law by invoking the rubric of functionality. The functionality defense seeks to protect the integrity of the utility patent system by excepting from configuration trademarks those products for which trademark protection would result in a perpetual monopoly inconsistent with the utility patent laws. *Vaughn Mfg. Co. v. Brikam Int'l Inc.*, 814 F.2d 346, 349 (7th Cir. 1987) ("The defense exists because granting exclusive rights to functional features of products is the domain of patent, not trademark, law."); *W.T. Rogers*, 778 F.2d at 338. No one questions that functional features not protected by a valid utility patent, or for which the patent has expired, are open to everyone to copy. Trademarks may not be acquired to defeat the right to copy. Yet Moen and the courts on which it relies (and the majority here) claim that this should not also be the case with respect to nonfunctional features when design patents are not available to protect them. *See Honeywell*, 497 F.2d at 1347-49.[5]

Yet there is no basis for treating the subject matter of design and utility patents differently: if functional matter not protected by a utility patent is available for all to copy, then it follows that ornamental or aesthetic designs

---

5. This perhaps unfortunate distinction between the functional and the nonfunctional seems to have taken root in *Honeywell*. The Court of Customs and Patent Appeals recognized that trademark rights are not available for functional—defined as "in essence utilitarian or dictated by reasons of engineering efficiency"—subject matter disclosed in a utility patent because such protection would conflict with public policy favoring competition and the "right to copy." 497 F.2d at 1348. When trademark rights were sought for nonfunctional elements of a design patent, however, the court did not pursue the same policy. Rather, the court said it had "decided that the public interest—protection from confusion, mistake, and deception in the purchase of goods and services—must prevail over any alleged extension of design patent rights when a trademark is nonfunctional." *Id.*

so free for everyone to copy. Design and ⟨...⟩ law, 35 U.S.C. §§1-376 (1984). There is ⟨...⟩ would allow a distinction to be made ⟨...⟩ purposes of extending trademark pro- ⟨...⟩ the contrary, the law applicable to utility ⟨...⟩ll: "The provisions of this title relating to ⟨...⟩ patents for designs, except as otherwise

⟨...⟩g between the subjects of design and ⟨...⟩ freedom to copy functional features ⟨...⟩edom to copy aesthetic features is not ⟨...⟩9 (trademark for "ornamental, fanciful ⟨...⟩er competition). In this circuit, "func- ⟨...⟩ feature serves a function, but that ⟨...⟩ a competitor the means to compete effectively. . . . A feature is functional if it is one that is costly to design around or do without, rather than one that is costly to have." *Schwinn Bicycle Co. v. Ross Bicycles, Inc.*, 870 F.2d 1176, 1188-89 (7th Cir. 1989). The Court of Customs and Patent Appeals described in even stronger terms "the public policy . . . as not the *right* to slavishly copy articles which are not protected by patent or copyright, but the *need* to copy those articles, which is more properly termed the right to compete *effectively*." *In re Morton-Norwich Products, Inc.*, 671 F.2d 1332, 1339 (C.C.P.A. 1982). [cit.]

Courts have struggled with the obvious fact that design features can be as essential to competition—"functional"—as utilitarian features. Some have developed the doctrine of "aesthetic functionality" to reconcile this conflict. [cit.] Although this circuit has apparently rejected that view, *W.T. Rogers*, 778 F.2d at 340, we have recognized that "there may come a point where the design feature is so important to the value of the product to consumers that continued trademark protection would deprive them of competitive alternatives." *W.T. Rogers*, 778 F.2d at 347; *Schwinn*, 870 F.2d at 1191. More succinctly, we have found "beauty is function." *W.T. Rogers*, 778 F.2d at 343. At the same time, not all designs that enhance a product's appeal have been found to be "functional." *Schwinn*, 870 F.2d at 1191. We are therefore left with a significant "undistributed middle" in applying this doctrine to aesthetic features. Ralph Brown, *Design Protection*, at 1366-67.

This functional/nonfunctional dichotomy is purely judge-made and is not based on the patent law. Nor, for that matter, is it based on the trademark law. Patent law does not require that an invention—whether protected by a utility patent or by a design patent—be something that is essential for competition. For utility patents, the invention need only be useful, 35 U.S.C. §101 (1984). Competitors often design around a utility patent. Design patents, on the other hand, protect ornamental designs of an article of manufacture, 35 U.S.C. §171 (1984), whether or not they are essential for competition. If we are to rely on the patent law, we know that that which is not protected by a utility patent or that on which a utility patent has expired is free for everyone to copy, regardless whether the matter in question is needed to compete or not. The same should be true of design features which are unprotected by a design patent. It does not matter that the design may not be necessary for competition. And, in any event, the attempt to categorize product features as "essential" or "non-essential" for competition is perplexing and ultimately vain.

The "functionality" doctrine has proved to be at best an extremely fuzzy border between design patent and trademark law. While utility patents and trademarks usually encompass unrelated subject matter, Judge Rich accurately noted that "functionality, ornamental appearance, and good industrial design are matters which are closely intermingled. The very best product design has long been called functional design." *Honeywell*, 497 F.2d at 1351 (Rich, J., concurring). The line between nonfunctional and functional is difficult to draw and an obvious source of litigation.

It is also incorrect or irrelevant to say that there is no conflict between configuration trademarks and the design patent law, because in a trademark case a plaintiff must also prove secondary meaning and likelihood of confusion. Likelihood of confusion only relates to whether there has been an infringement, not whether a product configuration is entitled to protection in the first place. In fact, *Compco* explicitly rejected likelihood of confusion and secondary meaning as sufficient reasons to grant a monopoly.... Even where a product configuration has achieved significance as an identifier of the source of the goods, the remedy is not to create a monopoly in the configuration. In *Kellogg v. National Biscuit*, the Court observed,

> [D]ue to the long period in which the plaintiff or its predecessor was the only manufacturer of the product, many people have come to associate the product, and as a consequence the name by which the product is generally known, with the plaintiff's factory at Niagara Falls.

305 U.S. at 118.

And the Court concluded:

> Where an article may be manufactured by all, a particular manufacturer can no more assert exclusive rights in a form in which the public has become accustomed to see the article and which, in the minds of the public, is primarily associated with the article rather than a particular producer, than it can in the case of a name with similar connections in the public mind. Kellogg Company was free to use the pillow-shaped form, subject only to the obligation to identify its product lest it be mistaken for that of the plaintiff.

305 U.S. at 120.

Thus, in *Kellogg* the shape of National Biscuit's "shredded wheat" was held to be generic and unprotectable as a trademark even though it was associated in the public mind with a particular producer. The shape of the product was like its name. The appropriate method of identifying it with its producer was to mark it with the distinctive mark or name of its manufacturer—not to grant a monopoly on its shape. Adequate labeling is sufficient and is the appropriate way to avoid source confusion.

Granting trademark protection to product configurations conflicts directly and importantly with the public policy favoring competition and disfavoring monopolies and monopolistic practices. In *American Safety Table Co., Inc. v. Schreiber*, 269 F.2d 255 (2d Cir.), *cert. denied*, 361 U.S. 915 (1959), the Second Circuit declared:

> In approaching the question of whether Schreiber & Goldberg's copying of the Amco machine is actionable, it must be remembered that the interests and equities of the litigants at bar are not the only ones which must be considered. Indeed, the underlying principles of our competitive economy and the desirability of passing on to the American public the advances of technical progress not only are entitled to consideration, in fact they dominate the picture although the interests of the public are not represented by either of the parties to the action. . . .
>
> [I]mitation is the life blood of competition. It is the unimpeded availability of substantially equivalent units that permits the normal operation of supply and demand to yield the fair price society must pay for a given commodity. [Citations omitted.] Unless such duplication is permitted, competition may be unduly curtailed with the possible resultant development of undesirable monopolistic conditions.

*Id.* at 271-72.

Chief Judge Charles E. Clark in dissent in *American Safety Table* put it even more strongly:

> We have only recently unequivocally reaffirmed these principles in *Modern Aids Inc. v. R.H. Macy & Co.*, 2d Cir., 264 F.2d 93, 94, where the court stated *Per Curiam:* "The plaintiff had no patent, and except for one proviso the defendant was free to imitate its machine as closely as it chose, no matter how much the competition might lessen the plaintiff's sales. That proviso was that, if the buying public had come to believe that every machine made after the plaintiff's model was the plaintiff's product, and had in any degree relied upon the source of the machine, rather than its performance, the plaintiff might have some relief. *Even then, however, the relief would go no further than to require the defendant to make plain to buyers that the plaintiff was not the source of the machines sold by it.*"

*Id.* at 281-82 (emphasis supplied).

It is also no answer to Kohler's argument that trademark registration for product configurations is anticompetitive to say that such a trademark creates only a relatively weak monopoly, or, as the majority contends, that it creates no "monopoly" at all. A restraint on competition need not be absolute to be effective. Kohler cannot copy Moen's unpatented faucet and handle unless it knows that Moen will be unable to prove a likelihood of confusion. At the end of the day, Moen has no patent, yet remains free from effective competition in the market for a popular brand of faucet.

[Judge Cudahy also expressed doubt that administrative law principles called for deference to the PTO's practice of registering product shapes.] In any event, the Patent and Trademark Office historically refused registration of overall product configurations as trademarks. *See Ex Parte Mars Signal-Light Co.*, 85 U.S.P.Q. (BNA) 173 (Comm. Patents 1950); *In re Duro-Test Corp.*, 134 U.S.P.Q. (BNA) 137 (TTAB 1962). Only when the Court of Customs and Patent Appeals took its misguided step in *Honeywell* in 1974 did the Patent and

Trademark Office practice change. Further, it is common kn persistence of skilled intellectual property practitioners may registration for purported marks whose registrability is, to say ι ginal. The courts must be vigilant to sustain constitutional limita give appropriate weight to basic economic considerations like th competition.

With respect to the 1988 amendments of the Lanham Act, the lisι demarkable categories was not changed. Both sides claim that this indicaι intent of Congress to either favor or disfavor trademarks on product con urations. It seems to me that the congressional action or inaction shows ve little one way or the other.

. . .

If the issue before us is a conflict between a well-defined statutory scheme (the design patent laws) enacted under a specific and limited constitutional directive (the Patent Clause) and a judicial doctrine (protection of product configurations as trademarks) only remotely incident to a general statutory scheme (the Lanham Act), the specific, constitutionally-mandated provisions should control. *See Morton v. Mancari*, 417 U.S. 535, 550-51 (1974).

In my view, whatever new law has been developed in the lower courts to authorize the use of product configuration trademarks as a substitute for design patents is without sanction from the Supreme Court. The Court has spoken repeatedly to disfavor the use of unfair competition law to avoid the "limited times" provision of the Patent Clause. The Court has emphasized the importance of the right to copy as an aspect of the Patent Clause. The right to copy is constitutionally protected and is absolutely essential to the successful long-term operation of a free and competitive economy. I therefore respectfully dissent.

## NOTES AND QUESTIONS

1. ***Lanham Act protection for designs under Section 43(a) after* Sears *and* Compco.** In *Kohler*, the court discusses Lanham Act protection for designs under Lanham Act Section 43(a). That provision recognizes protection for subject-matter that has not been registered with the U.S. Patent and Trademark Office. Kohler was not the first defendant to assert that the *Sears* and *Compco* decisions precluded a Lanham Act Section 43(a) action for product design under the Lanham Act. The Eighth Circuit had rejected the same argument in *Truck Equip. Service Co. v. Fruehauf Corp.*, 536 F.2d 1210 (8th Cir. 1976). Over time, other circuits followed suit. Do you find it surprising that the views expressed in Judge Cudahy's dissent have been largely rejected?

2. ***Lanham Act registration for designs.*** In *Kohler*, the design at issue was not registered. It is now well established that designs are potentially registrable on the Principal Register, and are therefore entitled to the benefits of Principal Register registration: a presumption of validity, ownership, and the exclusive right to use under Lanham Act Sections 7(b) and 33(a); incontestability (if additional requirements are met) in accordance with Lanham Act Sections 15

ity of use under Lanham Act Section 7(c). [...] the TTAB had concluded in a series of [...] registrable, based on the Lanham Act [...] noted above, the Lanham Act definition [...] encompasses "symbols" and "devices," [...] guage ("the term 'trademark' *includes* [...] any combination thereof") (emphasis [...]-ended list. In addition, as the *Kohler* [...] from the 1988 amendments to the [...] phrase "symbol or device" was [...] design protection. One scholar asserts [...] Section 45 definition to extend to product [...]. Lunney, Jr., *The Trade Dress Emperor's New Clothes: [...]oes Not Belong on the Principal Register*, 51 HASTINGS L.J. 1131 [...]nney reads the legislative history of the Lanham Act to say that [...]ngress intended product designs to be registrable only on the Supplemental Register, and that Assistant Commissioner Daphne Leeds ignored that history when she held in *Ex Parte Haig & Haig Ltd.*, 118 U.S.P.Q. (BNA) 229 (Comm'r Pat. 1958), that a product design could be registered on the Principal Register because it qualified as a "symbol or device." Not everyone concurs with this reading. But suppose that you do concur. Should Congress revise the Lanham Act? How so?

**3. *The role of aesthetic functionality.*** In Chapter 3, we take up doctrines of functionality, including the doctrine of aesthetic functionality. As we will discuss, "utilitarian" functionality is a doctrine that seeks to police the boundary between the utility patent and trademark regimes. Some have suggested that "aesthetic" functionality regulates the boundary between the *design* patent and trademark regimes. *See* Jay Dratler, Jr., *Trade Dress Protection for Product Configurations: Is There a Conflict with Patent Policy?*, 24 AIPLA Q.J. 427, 510 (1996). As you learn more about the doctrines—and the regimes—consider whether these propositions about functionality are descriptively accurate, and, if so, whether functionality doctrines are operating effectively in these roles.

## B. THE SUPREME COURT'S FRAMEWORK FOR DISTINCTIVENESS IN TRADE DRESS AND DESIGN CASES

### 1. FUNDAMENTALS OF DISTINCTIVENESS: THE *ABERCROMBIE* SPECTRUM

Distinctiveness concerns the relationship between a term (or symbol or other indicia) and the underlying products or services with which the term is used. A term is distinctive when it serves to identify the source or sponsorship of goods or services with which the term is used. A term may be distinctive because of its inherent nature and the context in which it is used, or it may become distinctive over time as a result of its use. Restatement (Third) of Unfair Competition §13 (1995). In *Abercrombie & Fitch Co. v. Hunting World, Inc.*, 531 F.2d 4 (2d Cir. 1976), Judge Friendly laid out a distinctiveness framework (the "*Abercrombie* spectrum") that is now universally followed in cases involving word marks. Friendly suggested that marks could be categorized as either (1) generic, (2) descriptive, (3) suggestive, or (4) arbitrary or fanciful. A generic term—a term that restates the genus to which the product or service at issue belongs—can never qualify as distinctive. *See also* Lanham Act §14(3) (providing that a registration may be cancelled at any time if the registered mark becomes the generic name of the underlying products or services). A term that merely describes the qualities of the underlying products or services cannot receive trademark protection unless the mark acquires distinctiveness through use—i.e., possesses secondary meaning. *See also* Lanham Act §2(e)(1) (barring registration for merely descriptive marks); Lanham Act §2(f) (carving out an exception for marks having secondary meaning, and providing that marks in continuous use for five years are presumed to have secondary meaning).

A term that suggests (i.e., does not merely describe) the qualities or features of the underlying products or services receives trademark protection under the *Abercrombie* spectrum without any showing of secondary meaning. The distinction between suggestive marks and merely descriptive marks is often a subtle one, and courts have developed a variety of approaches to analyze the issue. In *Zatarains, Inc. v. Oak Grove Smokehouse, Inc.*, 698 F.2d 786 (5th Cir. 1983), the court offered four tests for distinguishing between suggestive and merely descriptive marks: a test based on the dictionary definition of the term at issue (asking whether the definition refers to the qualities of the product); the "imagination" test (asking whether it requires a certain effort of imagination to jump from the term at issue to the underlying products); the competitors' need test (asking whether competitors would need to have access to the term at issue in order to sell their products); and the third-party use test (asking about the extent to which others have used the term in marketing similar products).

Finally, a term may be categorized as arbitrary or fanciful, in which case it will qualify for trademark protection without any showing of secondary meaning. An arbitrary term is a conventional English word that bears no apparent relationship to the underlying products or services (e.g., APPLE for computers). A fanciful term is a coined term having no meaning other than as a source indicator for the underlying products and services. Marks that are suggestive or arbitrary or fanciful are referred to as inherently distinctive marks because they are thought likely to possess distinctiveness intrinsically, with no need to resort to evidence of actual reception in the marketplace. *See* Graeme B. Dinwoodie, *Reconceptualizing the Inherent Distinctiveness of Product Design Trade Dress*, 75 N.C. L. Rev. 471 (1997). Merely descriptive marks for which secondary meaning has developed may be referred to as noninherently distinctive marks, or as marks having acquired distinctiveness. *See* Restatement (Third) of Unfair Competition §13 (1995) (defining the terms).

Like most rules in trademark law, the distinctiveness rules summarized in *Abercrombie* emerged from cases involving word marks. How should courts and the PTO analyze distinctiveness in cases involving trade dress or other nonverbal marks? Start by considering a simple example of a nonverbal mark: a logo, such as the Nike Co. "swoosh" logo used on shoes and other merchandise. If you assess the distinctiveness of the swoosh logo (used on shoes) under the *Abercrombie* spectrum, what result?

What if the swoosh mark is, at least in part, a decorative touch? Does this affect the distinctiveness analysis under *Abercrombie*? Should it? *See J.M. Hollister, LLC v. American Eagle Outfitters*, 2005 WL 1076246 (S.D. Ohio May 5, 2005) (number 22 emblazoned on a sweatshirt); *cf.* TMEP §1202.03 ("Subject matter that is merely a decorative feature does not identify and distinguish the applicant's goods and, thus, does not function as a trademark. A decorative feature may include words, designs, slogans or other trade dress. . . . Matter that serves primarily as a source-indicator, either inherently or as a result of acquired distinctiveness, and that is only incidentally ornamental or decorative, can be registered as a trademark."). Suppose that Nike asserted that the swoosh mark is *inherently* distinctive. How would you analyze that claim?

In *Kendall-Jackson Winery, Ltd. v. E. & J. Gallo Winery*, 150 F.3d 1042 (9th Cir. 1998), the court attempted to apply the *Abercrombie* spectrum to determine whether Kendall-Jackson's grape leaf logo on its wine bottle labels was distinctive. The court first suggested that such a logo might be inherently distinctive under a "standard" application of *Abercrombie*:

> The use of a grape leaf as a mark for wine would normally be inherently distinctive because it suggests, rather than describes, the product. One has to go through two or three steps to associate the leaf with the product—i.e., a grape leaf comes from a grapevine, which has grapes from which wine is produced. Under the standard test, a grape leaf could be suggestive and thus inherently distinctive. [cit].

*Id.* at 1048-49. However, because many wine producers had used grape leaf logos on their bottles, grape leaf logos had become generic:

> By itself, a grape leaf cannot differentiate one brand from another because precisely the same reasoning links the same emblem to the product in each case: A grape leaf suggests a grapevine, which suggests a grape, which suggests wine. Because the grape leaf is used widely in the industry, it has lost the power to differentiate brands. . . .

*Id.* Still, the court conceded, *particular depictions* of grape leaves used on wine bottles might incorporate distinctive features. *Id.* Nevertheless, the court concluded that to the extent that Kendall-Jackson's particular grape leaf logo included any distinctive features, Gallo had not appropriated them.

## 2. THE *SEABROOK* ANALYSIS

In *Seabrook Foods, Inc. v. Bar-Well Foods, Ltd.*, 568 F.2d 1342 (C.C.P.A. 1977), the Court of Customs and Patent Appeals was faced with the question whether the packaging for frozen foods was distinctive. The packaging is reproduced here.

The court fashioned a test for inherent distinctiveness that has since been adopted by many courts and the PTO to help assess whether logos are inherently distinctive:

> In determining whether a design is arbitrary or distinctive this court has looked to whether it was a "common" basic shape or design, whether it was unique or unusual in a particular field, whether it was a mere refinement of a commonly adopted and well-known form of ornamentation for the goods, or whether it was capable of creating a commercial impression distinct from the accompanying words.

Do you think that this test is superior to the *Abercrombie* test, at least as applied to claims of inherent distinctiveness? Do you think that the test could readily be adapted for determining the inherent distinctiveness of other categories of nonverbal source indicators?

## 3. THE SUPREME COURT'S FRAMEWORK FOR TRADE DRESS DISTINCTIVENESS

The framework for analysis of distinctiveness for trade dress now rests primarily on two Supreme Court decisions, *Two Pesos* and *Wal-Mart*, excerpted below. An intervening decision, *Qualitex*, is also relevant to understanding the modern framework. As you read the cases, consider both the substantive rules that the Court articulates, and the apparent shift in the Court's attitudes about the social utility of trade dress (especially design trade dress) protection.

### Two Pesos, Inc. v. Taco Cabana, Inc.
505 U.S. 763 (1992), reh'g denied, 505 U.S. 1244 (1992)

Justice WHITE delivered the opinion of the Court:

The issue in this case is whether the trade dress[1] of a restaurant may be protected under §43(a) of the Trademark Act of 1946 (Lanham Act), based on a finding of inherent distinctiveness, without proof that the trade dress has secondary meaning.

I

Respondent Taco Cabana, Inc., operates a chain of fast-food restaurants in Texas. The restaurants serve Mexican food. The first Taco Cabana restaurant was opened in San Antonio in September 1978, and five more restaurants had been opened in San Antonio by 1985. Taco Cabana describes its Mexican trade dress as "a festive eating atmosphere having interior dining and patio areas decorated with artifacts, bright colors, paintings and murals. The patio includes interior and exterior areas with the interior patio capable of being sealed off from the outside patio by overhead garage doors. The stepped exterior of the building is a festive and vivid color scheme using top border paint and neon stripes. Bright awnings and umbrellas continue the theme."

In December 1985, a Two Pesos, Inc., restaurant was opened in Houston. Two Pesos adopted a motif very similar to the foregoing description of Taco Cabana's trade dress. Two Pesos restaurants expanded rapidly in Houston and other markets, but did not enter San Antonio. In 1986, Taco Cabana entered the Houston and Austin markets and expanded into other Texas cities, including Dallas and El Paso, where Two Pesos was also doing business.

In 1987, Taco Cabana sued Two Pesos in the United States District Court for the Southern District of Texas for trade dress infringement under §43(a) of the Lanham Act, 15 U.S.C. §1125(a) (1982 ed.), and for theft of trade secrets under Texas common law. The case was tried to a jury, which was instructed to return its verdict in the form of answers to five questions propounded by the trial judge. The jury's answers were: Taco Cabana has a trade dress; taken as a whole, the trade dress is nonfunctional; the trade dress is inherently distinctive; the trade dress has not acquired a secondary meaning in the Texas market; and the alleged infringement creates a likelihood of confusion on the part of ordinary customers as to the source or association of the restaurant's goods or services.

---

1. The District Court instructed the jury: "'[T]rade dress' is the total image of the business. Taco Cabana's trade dress may include the shape and general appearance of the exterior of the restaurant, the identifying sign, the interior kitchen floor plan, the decor, the menu, the equipment used to serve food, the servers' uniforms and other features reflecting on the total image of the restaurant." The Court of Appeals accepted this definition and quoted from *Blue Bell Bio-Medical v. Cin-Bad, Inc.*, 864 F.2d 1253, 1256 (CA5 1989): "The 'trade dress' of a product is essentially its total image and overall appearance." It "involves the total image of a product and may include features such as size, shape, color or color combinations, texture, graphics, or even particular sales techniques." *John H. Harland Co. v. Clarke Checks, Inc.*, 711 F.2d 966, 980 (CA11 1983). . . .

Because, as the jury was told, Taco Cabana's trade dress was protected if it either was inherently distinctive or had acquired a secondary meaning, judgment was entered awarding damages to Taco Cabana. In the course of calculating damages, the trial court held that Two Pesos had intentionally and deliberately infringed Taco Cabana's trade dress.

The Court of Appeals ruled that the instructions adequately stated the applicable law and that the evidence supported the jury's findings. In particular, the Court of Appeals rejected petitioner's argument that a finding of no secondary meaning contradicted a finding of inherent distinctiveness.

In so holding, the court below followed precedent in the Fifth Circuit. In *Chevron Chemical Co. v. Voluntary Purchasing Groups, Inc.*, 659 F.2d 695, 702 (CA5 1981), the court noted that trademark law requires a demonstration of secondary meaning only when the claimed trademark is not sufficiently distinctive of itself to identify the producer; the court held that the same principles should apply to protection of trade dresses. The Court of Appeals noted that this approach conflicts with decisions of other courts, particularly the holding of the Court of Appeals for the Second Circuit in *Vibrant Sales, Inc. v. New Body Boutique, Inc.*, 652 F.2d 299 (1981), *cert. denied*, 455 U.S. 909 (1982), that §43(a) protects unregistered trademarks or designs only where secondary meaning is shown. We granted certiorari to resolve the conflict among the Courts of Appeals on the question whether trade dress that is inherently distinctive is protectable under §43(a) without a showing that it has acquired secondary meaning. We find that it is, and we therefore affirm.

II

The Lanham Act was intended to make "actionable the deceptive and misleading use of marks" and "to protect persons engaged in . . . commerce against unfair competition." §45. Section 43(a) "prohibits a broader range of practices than does §32," which applies to registered marks, *Inwood Laboratories, Inc. v. Ives Laboratories, Inc.*, 456 U.S. 844, 858 (1982), but it is common ground that §43(a) protects qualifying unregistered trademarks and that the general principles qualifying a mark for registration under §2 of the Lanham Act are for the most part applicable in determining whether an unregistered mark is entitled to protection under §43(a). *See Thompson Medical Co. v. Pfizer Inc.*, 753 F.2d 208, 215-216 (CA2 1985); [cit.]. . . .

The general rule regarding distinctiveness is clear: An identifying mark is distinctive and capable of being protected if it either (1) is inherently distinctive or (2) has acquired distinctiveness through secondary meaning. [cit.] It is also clear that eligibility for protection under §43(a) depends on nonfunctionality. [cit.] It is, of course, also undisputed that liability under §43(a) requires proof of the likelihood of confusion. [cit.]

The Court of Appeals determined that the District Court's instructions were consistent with the foregoing principles and that the evidence supported the jury's verdict. Both courts thus ruled that Taco Cabana's trade dress was not descriptive but rather inherently distinctive, and that it was not functional. None of these rulings is before us in this case, and for present purposes we assume, without deciding, that each of them is correct. In going on to affirm the judgment for respondent, the Court of Appeals, following its prior decision in *Chevron*, held that Taco Cabana's inherently distinctive trade dress was entitled to protection despite the lack of proof of secondary meaning. It is this issue that is before us for decision, and we agree with its resolution by the Court of Appeals. There is no persuasive reason to apply to trade dress a general requirement of secondary meaning which is at odds with the principles generally applicable to infringement suits under §43(a). . . .

Petitioner argues that the jury's finding that the trade dress has not acquired a secondary meaning shows conclusively that the trade dress is not inherently distinctive. The Court of Appeals' disposition of this issue was sound:

> Two Pesos' argument—that the jury finding of inherent distinctiveness contradicts its finding of no secondary meaning in the Texas market—ignores the law in this circuit. While the necessarily imperfect (and often prohibitively difficult) methods for assessing secondary meaning address the empirical question of current consumer association, the legal recognition of an inherently distinctive trademark or trade dress acknowledges the owner's legitimate proprietary interest in its unique and valuable informational device, regardless of whether substantial consumer association yet bestows the additional empirical protection of secondary meaning.

932 F.2d, at 1120, n.7.

Although petitioner makes the above argument, it appears to concede elsewhere in its brief that it is possible for a trade dress, even a restaurant trade dress, to be inherently distinctive and thus eligible for protection under §43(a). . . .

This brings us to the line of decisions by the Court of Appeals for the Second Circuit that would find protection for trade dress unavailable absent proof of secondary meaning. . . . In *Vibrant Sales, Inc. v. New Body Boutique, Inc.*, 652 F.2d 299 (1981), the plaintiff claimed protection under §43(a) for a product whose features the defendant had allegedly copied. The Court of Appeals held that unregistered marks did not enjoy the "presumptive source association" enjoyed by registered marks and hence could not qualify for protection under §43(a) without proof of secondary meaning. *Id.*, at 303, 304. The court's rationale seemingly denied protection for unregistered, but inherently distinctive, marks of all kinds, whether the claimed mark used distinctive words or symbols or distinctive product design. The court thus did not accept the arguments that an unregistered mark was capable of identifying a source and that copying such a mark could be making any kind of a false statement or representation under §43(a).

This holding is in considerable tension with the provisions of the Lanham Act. If a verbal or symbolic mark or the features of a product design may be registered under §2, it necessarily is a mark "by which the goods of the applicant may be distinguished from the goods of others," 60 Stat. 428, and must be registered unless otherwise disqualified. Since §2 requires secondary meaning only as a condition to registering descriptive marks, there are plainly marks that are registrable without showing secondary meaning. These same marks, even if not registered, remain inherently capable of distinguishing the goods of the users of these marks. Furthermore, the copier of such a mark may be seen as falsely claiming that his products may for some reason be thought of as originating from the plaintiff.

Some years after *Vibrant*, the Second Circuit announced in *Thompson Medical Co. v. Pfizer Inc.*, 753 F.2d 208 (1985), that in deciding whether an unregistered mark is eligible for protection under §43(a), it would follow the classification of marks set out by Judge Friendly in *Abercrombie & Fitch*. Hence, if an unregistered mark is deemed merely descriptive, which the verbal mark before the court proved to be, proof of secondary meaning is required; however, "[s]uggestive marks are eligible for protection without any proof of secondary meaning, since the connection between the mark and the source is presumed." [cit.] The Second Circuit has nevertheless continued to deny protection for trade dress under §43(a) absent proof of secondary meaning, despite the fact that §43(a) provides no basis for distinguishing between trademark and trade dress. *See, e.g., Stormy Clime Ltd. v. ProGroup, Inc.*, 809 F.2d, at 974; *Union Mfg. Co. v. Han Baek Trading Co.*, 763 F.2d 42, 48 (1985); *LeSportsac, Inc. v. K Mart Corp.*, 754 F.2d 71, 75 (1985).

The Fifth Circuit was quite right in *Chevron*, and in this case, to follow the *Abercrombie* classifications consistently and to inquire whether trade dress for which protection is claimed under §43(a) is inherently distinctive. If it is, it is capable of identifying products or services as coming from a specific source and secondary meaning is not required. This is the rule generally applicable to trademarks, and the protection of trademarks and trade dress under §43(a) serves the same statutory purpose of preventing deception and unfair competition. There is no persuasive reason to apply different analysis to the two. The "proposition that secondary meaning must be shown even if the trade dress is a distinctive, identifying mark, [is] wrong, for the reasons explained by Judge Rubin for the Fifth Circuit in *Chevron*." *Blau Plumbing, Inc. v. S.O.S. Fix-It, Inc.*, 781 F.2d 604, 608 (CA7 1986). The Court of Appeals for the Eleventh Circuit also follows *Chevron, AmBrit, Inc. v. Kraft, Inc.*, 805 F.2d 974, 979 (1986), and the Court of Appeals for the Ninth Circuit appears to think that proof of secondary meaning is superfluous if a trade dress is inherently distinctive, *Fuddruckers, Inc. v. Doc's B.R. Others, Inc.*, 826 F.2d 837, 843 (1987).

It would be a different matter if there were textual basis in §43(a) for treating inherently distinctive verbal or symbolic trademarks differently from inherently distinctive trade dress. But there is none. The section does not mention trademarks or trade dress, whether they be called generic, descriptive, suggestive, arbitrary, fanciful, or functional. Nor does the concept of secondary meaning appear in the text of §43(a). Where secondary meaning does appear in the statute, 15 U.S.C. §1052 (1982 ed.), it is a requirement that applies only to merely descriptive marks and not to inherently distinctive ones. We see no basis for requiring secondary meaning for inherently distinctive trade dress protection under §43(a) but not for other distinctive words, symbols, or devices capable of identifying a producer's product.

Engrafting onto §43(a) a requirement of secondary meaning for inherently distinctive trade dress also would undermine the purposes of the

Lanham Act. Protection of trade dress, no less than of trademarks, serves the Act's purpose to "secure to the owner of the mark the goodwill of his business and to protect the ability of consumers to distinguish among competing producers. National protection of trademarks is desirable, Congress concluded, because trademarks foster competition and the maintenance of quality by securing to the producer the benefits of good reputation." *Park 'N Fly*, 469 U.S., at 198, citing S. Rep. No. 1333, 79th Cong., 2d Sess., 3-5 (1946) (citations omitted). By making more difficult the identification of a producer with its product, a secondary meaning requirement for a nondescriptive trade dress would hinder improving or maintaining the producer's competitive position.

Suggestions that under the Fifth Circuit's law, the initial user of any shape or design would cut off competition from products of like design and shape are not persuasive. Only nonfunctional, distinctive trade dress is protected under §43(a). The Fifth Circuit holds that a design is legally functional, and thus unprotectible, if it is one of a limited number of equally efficient options available to competitors and free competition would be unduly hindered by according the design trademark protection. *See Sicilia Di R. Biebow & Co. v. Cox*, 732 F.2d 417, 426 (1984). This serves to assure that competition will not be stifled by the exhaustion of a limited number of trade dresses.

On the other hand, adding a secondary meaning requirement could have anticompetitive effects, creating particular burdens on the startup of small companies. It would present special difficulties for a business, such as respondent, that seeks to start a new product in a limited area and then expand into new markets. Denying protection for inherently distinctive nonfunctional trade dress until after secondary meaning has been established would allow a competitor, which has not adopted a distinctive trade dress of its own, to appropriate the originator's dress in other markets and to deter the originator from expanding into and competing in these areas.

[P]etitioner concedes that protecting an inherently distinctive trade dress from its inception may be critical to new entrants to the market and that withholding protection until secondary meaning has been established would be contrary to the goals of the Lanham Act. Petitioner specifically suggests, however, that the solution is to dispense with the requirement of secondary meaning for a reasonable, but brief, period at the outset of the use of a trade dress. If §43(a) does not require secondary meaning at the outset of a business' adoption of trade dress, there is no basis in the statute to support the suggestion that such a requirement comes into being after some unspecified time.

### III

We agree with the Court of Appeals that proof of secondary meaning is not required to prevail on a claim under §43(a) of the Lanham Act where the trade dress at issue is inherently distinctive, and accordingly the judgment of that court is affirmed.

It is so ordered.

Justice STEVENS, concurring in the judgment:

As the Court notes in its opinion, the text of §43(a) of the Lanham Act, 15 U.S.C. §1125(a) (1982 ed.), "does not mention trademarks or trade dress." Nevertheless, the Court interprets this section as having created a federal cause of action for infringement of an unregistered trademark or trade dress and concludes that such a mark or dress should receive essentially the same protection as those that are registered. Although I agree with the Court's conclusion, I think it is important to recognize that the meaning of the text has been transformed by the federal courts over the past few decades. I agree with this transformation, even though it marks a departure from the original text, because it is consistent with the purposes of the statute and has recently been endorsed by Congress.

## I

It is appropriate to begin with the relevant text of §43(a). [cit.] Section 43(a) provides a federal remedy for using either "a false designation of origin" or a "false description or representation" in connection with any goods or services. The full text of the section makes it clear that the word "origin" refers to the geographic location in which the goods originated. . . . For example, the "false designation of origin" language contained in the statute makes it unlawful to represent that California oranges came from Florida, or vice versa.

For a number of years after the 1946 enactment of the Lanham Act, a "false description or representation," like "a false designation of origin," was construed narrowly. The phrase encompassed two kinds of wrongs: false advertising and the common law tort of "passing off." False advertising meant representing that goods or services possessed characteristics that they did not actually have and passing off meant representing one's goods as those of another. Neither "secondary meaning" nor "inherent distinctiveness" had anything to do with false advertising, but proof of secondary meaning was an element of the common law passing-off cause of action. *See, e.g., G. & C. Merriam Co. v. Saalfield*, 198 F. 369, 372 (CA6 1912) ("The ultimate offense always is that defendant has passed off his goods as and for those of the complainant.").

## II

Over time, the Circuits have expanded the categories of "false designation of origin" and "false description or representation." . . . Although some have criticized the expansion as unwise, it is now "a firmly embedded reality." The United States Trade Association Trademark Review Commission noted this transformation with approval: "Section 43(a) is an enigma, but a very popular one. Narrowly drawn and intended to reach false designations or representations as to the geographical origin of products, the section has been widely interpreted to create, in essence, a federal law of unfair competition. . . . It has definitely eliminated a gap in unfair competition law, and its vitality is showing no signs of age."

[Justice Stevens noted that "whether we call the violation infringement, unfair competition, or false designation of origin, the test is identical — is there a 'likelihood of confusion?'" And he noted further that although "consistent with the common law background of §43(a), the Second Circuit has said that proof of secondary meaning is required to establish a claim that the defendant has traded on the plaintiff's good will by falsely representing that his goods are those of the plaintiff, . . . the Second Circuit has not explained why 'inherent distinctiveness' is not an appropriate substitute for proof of secondary meaning in a trade dress case. Most of the cases in which the Second Circuit has said that secondary meaning is required did not involve findings of inherent distinctiveness."]

### III

[Justice Stevens concluded that "even though the lower courts' expansion of the categories contained in §43(a) is unsupported by the text of the Act, . . . it is consistent with the general purposes of the Act." In particular, he invoked the stated concerns of Congressman Lanham, who suggested that one way the dual goals of the statute (protecting legitimate business and consumers) could be accomplished was by creating uniform legal rights and remedies that were appropriate for a national economy. Although the protection of trademarks had once been entirely a State matter, trade was no longer local, and national legislation was necessary to secure to the owners of trademarks in interstate commerce definite rights.]

Congress has revisited this statute from time to time, and has accepted the "judicial legislation" that has created this federal cause of action. Recently, for example, in the Trademark Law Revision Act of 1988, 102 Stat. 3935, Congress codified the judicial interpretation of §43(a), giving its *imprimatur* to a growing body of case law from the Circuits that had expanded the section beyond its original language.

Although Congress has not specifically addressed the question whether secondary meaning is required under §43(a), the steps it has taken in this subsequent legislation suggest that secondary meaning is not required if inherent distinctiveness has been established.[17] First, Congress broadened the language of §43(a) to make explicit that the provision prohibits "any word, term, name, symbol, or device, or any combination thereof" that is "likely to cause confusion, or to cause mistake, or to deceive as to the affiliation, connection, or association of such person with another person, or as to the origin, sponsorship, or approval of his or her goods, services, or commercial activities by another person." 15 U.S.C. §1125(a). That language makes clear that a confusingly similar trade dress is actionable under §43(a), without necessary reference to "falsity." Second, Congress approved and confirmed the extensive judicial development under the provision, including its application to trade dress that the federal courts had come to apply.[18] Third, the legislative history

---

17. "When several acts of Congress are passed touching the same subject-matter, subsequent legislation may be considered to assist in the interpretation of prior legislation upon the same subject." [cit.]

18. As the Senate Report explained, revision of §43(a) is designed "to codify the interpretation it has been given by the courts. Because Section 43(a) of the Act fills an important gap in federal unfair competition law, the committee expects the courts to continue to interpret the section.

"As written, Section 43(a) appears to deal only with false descriptions or representations and false designations of geographic origin. Since its enactment in 1946, however, it has been widely interpreted as creating, in essence, a federal law of unfair competition. For example, it has been applied to cases involving the infringement of unregistered marks, violations of trade dress and certain nonfunctional configurations of goods and actionable false advertising claims." S. Rep. No. 100-515, p. 40 (1988), U.S. Code Cong. & Admin. News 1988, pp. 5577, 5605.

of the 1988 amendments reaffirms Congress' goals of protecting both businesses and consumers with the Lanham Act. And fourth, Congress explicitly extended to any violation of §43(a) the basic Lanham Act remedial provisions whose text previously covered only registered trademarks. . . . These steps buttress the conclusion that §43(a) is properly understood to provide protection in accordance with the standards for registration in §2. These aspects of the 1988 legislation bolster the claim that an inherently distinctive trade dress may be protected under §43(a) without proof of secondary meaning.

### IV

In light of the consensus among the Courts of Appeals that have actually addressed the question, and the steps on the part of Congress to codify that consensus, *stare decisis* concerns persuade me to join the Court's conclusion that secondary meaning is not required to establish a trade dress violation under §43(a) once inherent distinctiveness has been established. Accordingly, I concur in the judgment, but not in the opinion, of the Court.

Justice THOMAS, concurring in the judgment.

Both the Court and Justice STEVENS decide today that the principles that qualify a mark for registration under §2 of the Lanham Act apply as well to determining whether an unregistered mark is entitled to protection under §43(a). The Court terms that view "common ground," though it fails to explain why that might be so, and Justice STEVENS decides that the view among the Courts of Appeals is textually insupportable, but worthy nonetheless of adherence. I see no need in answering the question presented either to move back and forth among the different sections of the Lanham Act or to adopt what may or may not be a misconstruction of the statute for reasons akin to *stare decisis*. I would rely, instead, on the language of §43(a).

Section 43(a) . . . codified, among other things, the related common law torts of technical trademark infringement and passing off, which were causes of action for false descriptions or representations concerning a good's or service's source of production. [cit.]

At common law, words or symbols that were arbitrary, fanciful, or suggestive (called "inherently distinctive" words or symbols, or "trademarks") were presumed to represent the source of a product, and the first user of a trademark could sue to protect it without having to show that the word or symbol represented the product's source in fact. See, *e.g.*, *Heublein v. Adams*, 125 F. 782, 784 (CC Mass. 1903). . . . Trade dress, which consists not of words or symbols, but of a product's packaging (or "image," more broadly), seems at common law to have been thought incapable ever of being inherently distinctive, perhaps on the theory that the number of ways to package a product is finite. Thus, a user of trade dress would always have had to show secondary meaning in order to obtain protection. [cit.]

Over time, judges have come to conclude that packages or images may be as arbitrary, fanciful, or suggestive as words or symbols, their numbers limited only by the human imagination. . . . A particular trade dress, then, is now considered as fully capable as a particular trademark of serving as a "representation or designation" of source under §43(a). As a result, the first user of an arbitrary package, like the first user of an arbitrary word, should be entitled to the presumption that his package represents him without having to show that it does so in fact. This rule follows, in my view, from the language of §43(a), and this rule applies under that section without regard to the rules that apply under the sections of the Lanham Act that deal with registration.

Because the Court reaches the same conclusion for different reasons, I join its judgment.

## NOTES AND QUESTIONS

1. *The holding in* Two Pesos. What precisely did the Court hold in *Two Pesos?* Are there any limits to its apparent holding that trade dress can be inherently distinctive? According to what test are courts instructed to determine whether trade dress is inherently distinctive? Which issues, if any, are left open by the Court?

2. *The test for inherent distinctiveness of product design trade dress in the wake of* Two Pesos. Immediately after *Two Pesos,* almost all courts read the decision as applying to product design trade dress, thus permitting the possibility of inherently distinctive product design trade dress. But courts differed widely on the appropriate *tests* to be applied to determine the distinctiveness of product design trade dress. Some courts continued to apply to product design claims the classical (*Abercrombie*) test used with respect to word marks. See, e.g., *Stuart Hall Co. v. Ampad Corp.*, 51 F.3d 780, 788 (8th Cir. 1995) (applying same doctrinal tests to trade dress and trademarks). Others applied the *Seabrook* test. Still others differentiated between product packaging and product design, and developed complex tests that seemed to afford lesser protection to product design. The two leading tests of this final kind were formulated by the Court of Appeals for the Third and Second Circuits. In *Duraco Prods. v. Joy Plastic Enters.*, 41 F.3d 1431, 1434 (3d Cir. 1994), involving rights claimed in the design of Grecian urn–style planters, the Third Circuit held that "to be inherently distinctive, a product feature or a combination or arrangement of features, *i.e.*, a product configuration, for which Lanham Act protection is sought must be (i) unusual and memorable, (ii) conceptually separable from the product, and (iii) likely to serve primarily as a designator of origin of the product." In *Knitwaves, Inc. v. Lollytogs Ltd.*, 71 F.3d 996 (2d Cir. 1995), which involved the design of sweaters, the Court of Appeals for the Second Circuit held that in determining whether a product design is inherently distinctive, "we ask whether it is likely to serve primarily as a designator of origin of the product." What characteristics of product design (as opposed to packaging or words) might have caused these courts to develop different tests for product design? Are the *Abercrombie* or *Seabrook* tests appropriate mechanisms for determining the protectability of product designs? Are the *Duraco* and *Knitwaves* tests superior? Revisit these questions after you read *Wal-Mart.*

3. *The test for inherent distinctiveness of product packaging trade dress in the wake of* Two Pesos. After *Two Pesos,* it was also unclear what test should

## B. The Supreme Court's Framework for Distinctiveness in Trade Dress and Design Cases

be applied to determine the inherent distinctiveness of *packaging* trade dress. The Second Circuit took up the question in *Fun-damental Too, Ltd. v. Gemmy Indus., Inc.*, 111 F.3d 993 (2d Cir. 1997). Fun-damental asserted trade dress in the packaging (shown here) for its "Toilet Bank" product, a coin bank that resembled a flush toilet.

Defendant Gemmy argued that to determine inherent distinctiveness, the court should rely on the *Seabrook* test. Instead, the court applied *Abercrombie*, for three reasons: (1) the court had previously applied *Abercrombie* in packaging cases; (2) product packaging was more suitable for treatment under *Abercrombie* than product design (and thus *Knitwaves* was distinguishable), because product packaging was more readily separated from the product itself and there were many alternatives for packaging (but possibly not for design); and (3) the *Abercrombie* test tracked the purpose of the Lanham Act to protect source identifiers. Regarding the third reason, the court explained that

> [w]hile a more stringent test is necessary in the product configuration context, applying *Abercrombie* to product packaging serves the aims of the Lanham Act because consumers are more likely to rely on the packaging of a product than on the product's design as an indication of source. Restatement (Third) of Unfair Competition §16 cmt. b (1995). In contrast, over-inclusive protection of the product design risks conferring benefits beyond the intended scope of the Lanham Act and entering what is properly the realm of patent law. [cit.]. Thus, though the *Abercrombie* classifications were originally developed for analysis of word marks, we conclude that because of the endless number of product packaging options the *Abercrombie* test is appropriately applied in this trade dress case.

*Fun-damental Too*, 111 F.3d at 1000. Do you agree with this reasoning? We will revisit this issue in *Yankee Candle*, which appears later in this chapter.

**4. Rationale of *Two Pesos*.** Why did the Court reach its conclusion in *Two Pesos*? Statutory language? Statutory purpose? Trademark policy? Other considerations? Where did Justice Stevens and Justice Thomas differ from Justice White?

## Qualitex Co. v. Jacobson Products Co., Inc.
514 U.S. 159 (1995)

Justice Breyer delivered the opinion of the Court:

The question in this case is whether the Trademark Act of 1946 (Lanham Act), 15 U.S.C. §§1051-1127 (1988 ed. and Supp. V), permits the registration of a trademark that consists, purely and simply, of a color. We conclude that, sometimes, a color will meet ordinary legal trademark requirements. And, when it does so, no special legal rule prevents color alone from serving as a trademark.

### I

The case before us grows out of petitioner Qualitex Company's use (since the 1950's) of a special shade of green-gold color on the pads that it makes and sells to dry cleaning firms for use on dry cleaning presses. In 1989, respondent Jacobson Products (a Qualitex rival) began to sell its own press pads to dry cleaning firms; and it colored those pads a similar green gold. In 1991, Qualitex registered the special green-gold color on press pads with the Patent and Trademark Office as a trademark. Registration No. 1,633,711 (Feb. 5, 1991). Qualitex subsequently added a trademark infringement count, 15 U.S.C. §1114(1), to an unfair competition claim, §1125(a), in a lawsuit it had already filed challenging Jacobson's use of the green-gold color.

Qualitex won the lawsuit in the District Court. But, the Court of Appeals for the Ninth Circuit set aside the judgment in Qualitex's favor on the trademark infringement claim because, in that Circuit's view, the Lanham Act does not permit Qualitex, or anyone else, to register "color alone" as a trademark. [However, the Court of Appeals upheld the judgment in Qualitex's favor under Section 43(a) of the Lanham Act. *See* 13 F.3d 1297 (9th Cir. 1994).]

The Courts of Appeals have differed as to whether or not the law recognizes the use of color alone as a trademark. *Compare NutraSweet Co. v. Stadt Corp.*, 917 F.2d 1024, 1028 (CA7 1990) (absolute prohibition against protection of color alone), *with In re Owens-Corning Fiberglas Corp.*, 774 F.2d 1116, 1128 (CA Fed. 1985) (allowing registration of color pink for fiberglass insulation), and *Master Distributors, Inc. v. Pako Corp.*, 986 F.2d 219, 224 (CA8 1993) (declining to establish per se prohibition against protecting color alone as a trademark). Therefore, this Court granted certiorari. We now hold that there is no rule absolutely barring the use of color alone, and we reverse the judgment of the Ninth Circuit.

### II

The Lanham Act gives a seller or producer the exclusive right to "register" a trademark, 15 U.S.C. §1052 (1988 ed. and Supp. V), and to prevent his or her competitors from using that trademark, §1114(1). Both the language of the Act and the basic underlying principles of trademark law would seem to include color within the universe of things that can qualify as a trademark. The language of the Lanham Act describes that universe in the broadest of terms. It says that trademarks "includ[e] any word, name, symbol, or device, or any combination thereof." §1127. Since human beings might use as a "symbol" or "device" almost anything at all that is capable of carrying meaning, this language, read literally, is not restrictive. The courts and the Patent and Trademark Office have authorized for use as a mark a particular shape (of a Coca-Cola bottle), a particular sound (of NBC's three chimes), and even a particular scent (of plumeria blossoms on sewing thread). *See, e.g.*, Registration No. 696,147 (Apr. 12, 1960); Registration Nos. 523,616 (Apr. 4, 1950) and 916,522 (July 13, 1971); *In re Clarke*, 17 U.S.P.Q.2d (BNA) 1238, 1240 (T.T.A.B. 1990). If a shape, a sound, and a fragrance can act as symbols why, one might ask, can a color not do the same?

A color is also capable of satisfying the more important part of the statutory definition of a trademark, which requires that a person "us[e]" or "inten[d] to use" the mark "to identify and distinguish his or her goods, including a unique product, from those manufactured or sold by others and to indicate the source of the goods, even if that source is unknown." 15 U.S.C. §1127.

True, a product's color is unlike "fanciful," "arbitrary," or "suggestive" words or designs, which almost automatically tell a customer that they refer to a brand. *Abercrombie & Fitch Co. v. Hunting World, Inc.*, 537 F.2d 4, 9-10 (CA2 1976) (Friendly, J.); *see Two Pesos, Inc. v. Taco Cabana, Inc.*, 505 U.S. 763, 768 (1992). The imaginary word "Suntost," or the words "Suntost Marmalade," on a jar of orange jam immediately would signal a brand or a product "source"; the jam's orange color does not do so. But, over time, customers may come to treat a particular color on a product or its packaging (say, a color that in context seems unusual, such as pink on a firm's insulating material or red on the head of a large industrial bolt) as signifying a brand. And, if so, that color would have come to identify and distinguish the goods—i.e., "to indicate" their "source"—much in the way that descriptive words on a product (say, "Trim" on nail clippers or "Car-Freshner" on deodorizer) can come to indicate a product's origin. *See, e.g., J. Wiss & Sons Co. v. W.E. Bassett Co.*, 462 F.2d 567, 569 (1972); *Car-Freshner Corp. v. Turtle Wax, Inc.*, 268 F. Supp. 162, 164 (S.D.N.Y. 1967). In this circumstance, trademark law says that the word (e.g., "Trim"), although not inherently distinctive, has developed "secondary meaning." *See Inwood Laboratories, Inc. v. Ives laboratories, Inc.*, 456 U.S. 844, 851, n.11 (1982) ("[S]econdary meaning" is acquired when "in the minds of the public, the primary significance of a product feature . . . is to identify the source of the product rather than the product itself"). Again, one might ask, if trademark law permits a descriptive word with secondary meaning to act as a mark, why would it not permit a color, under similar circumstances, to do the same?

We cannot find in the basic objectives of trademark law any obvious theoretical objection to the use of color alone as a trademark, where that color has attained "secondary meaning" and therefore identifies and distinguishes a particular brand (and thus indicates its "source"). In principle, trademark law, by preventing others from copying a source-identifying mark, "reduce[s] the customer's costs of shopping and making purchasing decisions," 1 J. McCarthy, *McCarthy on Trademarks and Unfair Competition* §2.01[2], p. 2-3 (3d ed. 1994) (hereinafter McCarthy), for it quickly and easily assures a potential customer that this item—the item with this mark—is made by the same producer as other, similarly marked items that he or she liked (or disliked) in the past. At the same time, the law helps assure a producer that it (and not an imitating competitor) will reap the financial, reputation-related rewards associated with a desirable product. The law thereby "encourage[s] the production of quality products," *ibid.*, and simultaneously discourages those who hope to sell inferior products by capitalizing on a consumer's inability quickly to evaluate the quality of an item offered for sale. [cit.] It is the source-distinguishing ability of a mark—not its ontological status as color, shape, fragrance, word, or sign—that permits it to serve these basic purposes. *See* Landes & Posner, *Trademark Law: An Economic Perspective*, 30 J.L. & Econ. 265, 290 (1987). And, for that reason, it is difficult to find, in basic trademark objectives, a reason to disqualify absolutely the use of a color as a mark. . . .

It would seem, then, that color alone, at least sometimes, can meet the basic legal requirements for use as a trademark. It can act as a symbol that distinguishes a firm's goods and identifies their source, without serving any other significant function. *See* U.S. Dept. of Commerce, Patent and Trademark Office, *Trademark Manual of Examining Procedure* §1202.04(e), p. 1202-13 (2d ed. May, 1993) (hereinafter PTO Manual) (approving trademark registration of color alone where it "has become distinctive of the applicant's goods in commerce," provided that "there is [no] competitive need for colors to remain available in the industry" and the color is not "functional"); *see also* 1 McCarthy §§3.01[1], 7.26, pp. 3-2, 7-113 ("requirements for qualification of a word or symbol as a trademark" are that it be (1) a "symbol," (2) "use[d] . . . as a mark," (3) "to identify and distinguish the seller's goods from goods made or sold by others," but that it not be "functional"). Indeed, the District Court, in this case, entered findings (accepted by the Ninth Circuit) that show Qualitex's green-gold press pad color has met these requirements. The green-gold color acts as a symbol. Having developed secondary meaning (for customers identified the green-gold color as Qualitex's), it identifies the press pads' source. And, the green-gold color serves no other function. (Although it is important to use some color on press pads to avoid noticeable stains, the court found "no competitive need in the press pad industry for the green-gold color, since other colors are equally usable.") Accordingly, unless there is some special reason that convincingly militates against the use of color alone as a trademark, trademark law would protect Qualitex's use of the green-gold color on its press pads.

### III

Respondent Jacobson Products says that there are four special reasons why the law should forbid the use of color alone as a trademark. We shall explain, in turn, why we, ultimately, find them unpersuasive.

*First*, Jacobson says that, if the law permits the use of color as a trademark, it will produce uncertainty and unresolvable court disputes about what shades of a color a competitor may lawfully use. Because lighting (morning sun, twilight mist) will affect perceptions of protected color, competitors and courts will suffer from "shade confusion" as they try to decide whether use of a similar color on a similar product does, or does not, confuse customers and thereby infringe a trademark. Jacobson adds that the "shade confusion" problem is "more difficult" and "far different from" the "determination of the similarity of words or symbols."

## B. The Supreme Court's Framework for Distinctiveness in Trade Dress and Design Cases

We do not believe, however, that color, in this respect, is special. Courts traditionally decide quite difficult questions about whether two words or phrases or symbols are sufficiently similar, in context, to confuse buyers. They have had to compare, for example, such words as "Bonamine" and "Dramamine" (motion-sickness remedies); "Huggies" and "Dougies" (diapers); "Cheracol" and "Syrocol" (cough syrup); "Cyclone" and "Tornado" (wire fences); and "Mattres" and "1-800-Mattres" (mattress franchisor telephone numbers); [cit.]. Legal standards exist to guide courts in making such comparisons. *See, e.g.*, 2 McCarthy §15.08; 1 McCarthy §§11.24-11.25 ("strong" marks, with greater secondary meaning, receive broader protection than "weak" marks). We do not see why courts could not apply those standards to a color, replicating, if necessary, lighting conditions under which a colored product is normally sold. *See* Ebert, *Trademark Protection in Color: Do It by the Numbers!*, 84 T.M. Rep. 379, 405 (1994). Indeed, courts already have done so in cases where a trademark consists of a color plus a design, i.e., a colored symbol such as a gold stripe (around a sewer pipe), a yellow strand of wire rope, or a "brilliant yellow" band (on ampules). [cit.]

*Second*, Jacobson argues, as have others, that colors are in limited supply. Jacobsen claims that, if one of many competitors can appropriate a particular color for use as a trademark, and each competitor then tries to do the same, the supply of colors will soon be depleted. Put in its strongest form, this argument would concede that "hundreds of color pigments are manufactured and thousands of colors can be obtained by mixing." L. Cheskin, *Colors: What They Can Do for You* 47 (1947). But, it would add that, in the context of a particular product, only some colors are usable. By the time one discards colors that, say, for reasons of customer appeal, are not usable, and adds the shades that competitors cannot use lest they risk infringing a similar, registered shade, then one is left with only a handful of possible colors. And, under these circumstances, to permit one, or a few, producers to use colors as trademarks will "deplete" the supply of usable colors to the point where a competitor's inability to find a suitable color will put that competitor at a significant disadvantage.

This argument is unpersuasive, however, largely because it relies on an occasional problem to justify a blanket prohibition. When a color serves as a mark, normally alternative colors will likely be available for similar use by others. Moreover, if that is not so—if a "color depletion" or "color scarcity" problem does arise—the trademark doctrine of "functionality" normally would seem available to prevent the anticompetitive consequences that Jacobsen's argument posits, thereby minimizing that argument's practical force.

The functionality doctrine, as we have said, forbids the use of a product's feature as a trademark where doing so will put a competitor at a significant disadvantage because the feature is "essential to the use or purpose of the article" or "affects [its] cost or quality." *Inwood Labs.*, 456 U.S. at 850, n.10. The functionality doctrine thus protects competitors against a disadvantage (unrelated to recognition or reputation) that trademark protection might otherwise impose, namely their inability reasonably to replicate important non-reputation–related product features. . . .

The upshot is that, where a color serves a significant non-trademark function—whether to distinguish a heart pill from a digestive medicine or to satisfy the "noble instinct for giving the right touch of beauty to common and necessary things," G. Chesterton, *Simplicity and Tolstoy* 61 (1912)—courts will examine whether its use as a mark would permit one competitor (or a group) to interfere with legitimate (non-trademark–related) competition through actual or potential exclusive use of an important product ingredient. That examination should not discourage firms from creating esthetically pleasing mark designs, for it is open to their competitors to do the same. *See, e.g., W. T. Rogers Co. v. Keene*, 778 F.2d 334, 343 (7th Cir. 1985) (Posner, J.). But, ordinarily, it should prevent the anticompetitive consequences of Jacobsen's hypothetical "color depletion" argument, when, and if, the circumstances of a particular case threaten "color depletion."

*Third*, Jacobson points to many older cases—including Supreme Court cases—in support of its position. In 1878, this Court described the common law definition of trademark rather broadly to "consist of a name, symbol, figure, letter, form, or device, if adopted and used by a manufacturer or merchant in order to designate the goods he manufactures or sells to distinguish the same from those manufactured or sold by another." *McLean v. Fleming*, 96 U.S. 245, 254. Yet, in interpreting the Trademark Acts of 1881 and 1905, which retained that common law definition, the Court questioned "[w]hether mere color can constitute a valid trade-mark," *A. Leschen & Sons Rope Co. v. Broderick & Bascom Rope Co.*, 201 U.S. 166, 171 (1906), and suggested that the "product including the coloring matter is free to all who make it," *Coca-Cola Co. v. Koke Co. of America*, 254 U.S. 143, 147 (1920). Even though these statements amounted to dicta, lower courts interpreted them as forbidding protection for color alone. . . .

These Supreme Court cases, however, interpreted trademark law as it existed before 1946, when Congress enacted the Lanham Act. The Lanham Act significantly changed and liberalized the common law to "dispense with mere technical prohibitions," S. Rep. No. 1333, 79th Cong., 2d Sess., 3 (1946), most notably, by permitting trademark registration of descriptive words (say, "U-Build-It" model airplanes) where they had acquired "secondary meaning." *See Abercrombie & Fitch Co.*, 537 F.2d, at 9 (Friendly, J.). The Lanham Act extended protection to descriptive marks by making clear that (with certain explicit exceptions not relevant here), "nothing . . . shall prevent the registration of a mark used by the applicant which has become distinctive of the applicant's goods in commerce." 15 U.S.C. §1052(f) (1988 ed., Supp. V).

This language permits an ordinary word, normally used for a non-trademark purpose (e.g., description), to act as a trademark where it has gained "secondary meaning." Its logic would appear to apply to color as well. Indeed, in 1985, the Federal Circuit considered the significance of the Lanham Act's changes as they related to color and held that trademark protection for color was consistent with the "jurisprudence under the Lanham Act developed in accordance with the statutory principle that if a mark is

## B. The Supreme Court's Framework for Distinctiveness in Trade Dress and Design Cases

capable of being or becoming distinctive of [the] applicant's goods in commerce, then it is capable of serving as a trademark." *Owens-Corning,* 774 F.2d, at 1120.

In 1988, Congress amended the Lanham Act, revising portions of the definitional language, but left unchanged the language here relevant. §134, 102 Stat. 3946, 15 U.S.C. §1127. It enacted these amendments against the following background: (1) the Federal Circuit had decided *Owens-Corning;* (2) the Patent and Trademark Office had adopted a clear policy (which it still maintains) permitting registration of color as a trademark, *see* PTO Manual §1202.04(e) (at p. 1200-12 of the January 1986 edition and p. 1202-13 of the May 1993 edition); and (3) the Trademark Commission had written a report, which recommended that "the terms 'symbol, or device' . . . not be deleted or narrowed to preclude registration of such things as a color, shape, smell, sound, or configuration which functions as a mark," The United States Trademark Association Trademark Review Commission Report and Recommendations to USTA President and Board of Directors, 77 T.M. Rep. 375, 421 (1987); *see also* 133 Cong. Rec. 32812 (1987) (statement of Sen. DeConcini) ("The bill I am introducing today is based on the Commission's report and recommendations."). This background strongly suggests that the language "any word, name, symbol, or device," 15 U.S.C. §1127, had come to include color. And, when it amended the statute, Congress retained these terms. Indeed, the Senate Report accompanying the Lanham Act revision explicitly referred to this background understanding, in saying that the "revised definition intentionally retains . . . the words 'symbol or device' so as not to preclude the registration of colors, shapes, sounds or configurations where they function as trademarks." S. Rep. No. 100-515, at 44 U.S. Code Cong. & Admin. News, 1988, p. 5607. (In addition, the statute retained language providing that "[n]o trademark by which the goods of the applicant may be distinguished from the goods of others shall be refused registration . . . on account of its nature" (except for certain specified reasons not relevant here). 15 U.S.C. §1052 (1988 ed., Supp. V).)

This history undercuts the authority of the precedent on which Jacobson relies. Much of the pre-1985 case law rested on statements in Supreme Court opinions that interpreted pre–Lanham Act trademark law and were not directly related to the holdings in those cases. Moreover, we believe the Federal Circuit was right in 1985 when it found that the 1946 Lanham Act embodied crucial legal changes that liberalized the law to permit the use of color alone as a trademark (under appropriate circumstances). At a minimum, the Lanham Act's changes left the courts free to reevaluate the preexisting legal precedent which had absolutely forbidden the use of color alone as a trademark. Finally, when Congress reenacted the terms "word, name, symbol, or device" in 1988, it did so against a legal background in which those terms had come to include color, and its statutory revision embraced that understanding.

*Fourth,* Jacobson argues that there is no need to permit color alone to function as a trademark because a firm already may use color as part of a trademark, say, as a colored circle or colored letter or colored word, and may rely upon "trade dress" protection, under §43(a) of the Lanham Act, if a competitor copies its color and thereby causes consumer confusion regarding the overall appearance of the competing products or their packaging, *see* 15 U.S.C. §1125(a) (1988 ed., Supp. V). The first part of this argument begs the question. One can understand why a firm might find it difficult to place a usable symbol or word on a product (say, a large industrial bolt that customers normally see from a distance); and, in such instances, a firm might want to use color, pure and simple, instead of color as part of a design. Neither is the second portion of the argument convincing. Trademark law helps the holder of a mark in many ways that "trade dress" protection does not. *See* 15 U.S.C. §1124 (ability to prevent importation of confusingly similar goods); §1072 (constructive notice of ownership); §1065 (incontestable status); §1057(b) (prima facie evidence of validity and ownership). Thus, one can easily find reasons why the law might provide trademark protection in addition to trade dress protection.

IV

Having determined that a color may sometimes meet the basic legal requirements for use as a trademark and that respondent Jacobson's arguments do not justify a special legal rule preventing color alone from serving as a trademark (and, in light of the District Court's here undisputed findings that Qualitex's use of the green-gold color on its press pads meets the basic trademark requirements), we conclude that the Ninth Circuit erred in barring Qualitex's use of color as a trademark. For these reasons, the judgment of the Ninth Circuit is

*Reversed.*

## NOTES AND QUESTIONS

1. **"Trademarks" v. "Trade Dress."** Near the end of the opinion, the Court remarks that trademark protection may help the owner in ways that trade dress protection does not. From the context, it is evident that the Court means that *registered* rights in trade dress help the owner in ways that *unregistered* rights in trade dress (which are vindicated under Lanham Act §43(a)) do not. Should the prerequisites for trade dress protection differ depending on whether the owner is asserting registered or unregistered rights?

2. **The** Qualitex *treatment of* **Two Pesos.** In *Qualitex*, the Court cited *Two Pesos*, but was the Court applying *Two Pesos*? Was it modifying *Two Pesos*? Even if the Court did not mean to modify *Two Pesos*, did its opinion have that effect anyway? These questions were (and are) important, because they suggest that the impact of the *Qualitex* case was not to be confined to the relatively obscure area of color marks, but was instead to be felt in the broader field of trade dress, as the Supreme Court's next foray into trade dress made plain.

## B. The Supreme Court's Framework for Distinctiveness in Trade Dress and Design Cases

 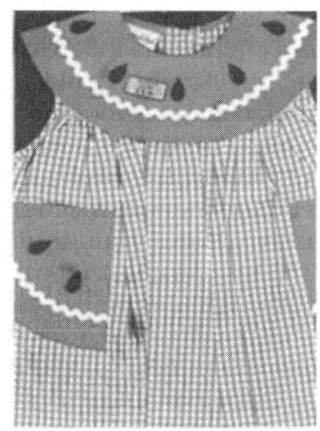 

### WAL-MART STORES, INC. v. SAMARA BROTHERS, INC.
529 U.S. 205 (2000)

Justice SCALIA delivered the opinion of the Court:

In this case, we decide under what circumstances a product's design is distinctive, and therefore protectible, in an action for infringement of unregistered trade dress under §43(a) of the Trademark Act of 1946 (Lanham Act), 60 Stat. 441, as amended, 15 U.S.C. §1125(a).

I

Respondent Samara Brothers, Inc., designs and manufactures children's clothing. Its primary product is a line of spring/summer one-piece seersucker outfits decorated with appliques of hearts, flowers, fruits, and the like. A number of chain stores, including JCPenney, sell this line of clothing under contract with Samara.

Petitioner Wal-Mart Stores, Inc., is one of the nation's best known retailers, selling among other things children's clothing. In 1995, Wal-Mart contracted with one of its suppliers, Judy-Philippine, Inc., to manufacture a line of children's outfits for sale in the 1996 spring/summer season. Wal-Mart sent Judy-Philippine photographs of a number of garments from Samara's line, on which Judy-Philippine's garments were to be based; Judy-Philippine duly copied, with only minor modifications, 16 of Samara's garments, many of which contained copyrighted elements. In 1996, Wal-Mart briskly sold the so-called knockoffs, generating more than $1.15 million in gross profits.

In June 1996, a buyer for JCPenney called a representative at Samara to complain that she had seen Samara garments on sale at Wal-Mart for a lower price than JCPenney was allowed to charge under its contract with Samara. The Samara representative told the buyer that Samara did not supply its clothing to Wal-Mart. Their suspicions aroused, however, Samara officials launched an investigation, which disclosed that Wal-Mart and several other major retailers—Kmart, Caldor, Hills, and Goody's—were selling the knockoffs of Samara's outfits produced by Judy-Philippine.

After sending cease-and-desist letters, Samara brought this action in the United States District Court for the Southern District of New York against Wal-Mart, Judy-Philippine, Kmart, Caldor, Hills, and Goody's for copyright infringement under federal law, consumer fraud and unfair competition under New York law, and—most relevant for our purposes—infringement of unregistered trade dress under §43(a) of the Lanham Act, 15 U.S.C. §1125(a). All of the defendants except Wal-Mart settled before trial.

After a weeklong trial, the jury found in favor of Samara on all of its claims. Wal-Mart then renewed a motion for judgment as a matter of law, claiming, inter alia, that there was insufficient evidence to support a conclusion that Samara's clothing designs could be legally protected as distinctive trade dress for purposes of §43(a). The District Court denied the motion, and awarded Samara damages, interest, costs, and fees totaling almost $1.6 million, together with injunctive relief. The Second Circuit [found that the design trade dress was inherently distinctive and] affirmed the denial of the motion for judgment as a matter of law, and we granted certiorari.

II

The Lanham Act [in section 2] provides for the registration of trademarks, which it defines in §45 to include "any word, name, symbol, or device, or any combination thereof [used or intended to be used] to identify and distinguish [a producer's] goods . . . from those manufactured or sold by others and to indicate the source of the goods. . . ." 15 U.S.C. §1127. . . . In addition to protecting registered marks, the Lanham Act, in §43(a), gives a producer a cause of action for the use by any person of "any word, term, name, symbol, or device, or any combination thereof . . . which . . . is likely to cause confusion . . . as to the origin, sponsorship, or approval of his or her goods. . . ." 15 U.S.C. §1125(a). It is the latter provision that is at issue in this case.

The breadth of the definition of marks registrable under §2, and of the confusion-producing elements recited as actionable by §43(a), has been held to embrace not just word marks, such as "Nike," and symbol marks, such as Nike's "swoosh" symbol, but also "trade dress"—a category that originally included only the packaging, or "dressing," of a product, but in recent years has been expanded by many courts of appeals to encompass the design of a product. *See, e.g., Ashley Furniture Industries, Inc. v. Sangiacomo N. A., Ltd.*, 187 F.3d 363 (C.A.4 1999) (bedroom furniture); *Knitwaves, Inc. v. Lollytogs, Ltd.*, 71 F.3d 996 (C.A.2 1995) (sweaters); *Stuart Hall Co., Inc. v. Ampad Corp.*, 51 F.3d 780 (C.A.8 1995) (notebooks). These courts have assumed, often without discussion, that trade dress constitutes a "symbol" or "device" for purposes of the relevant sections, and we conclude likewise. "Since human beings might use as a 'symbol' or 'device' almost anything at all that is capable of carrying meaning, this language, read literally, is not restrictive." *Qualitex Co. v. Jacobson Products Co.*, 514 U.S. 159, 162 (1995). This reading of §2 and §43(a) is buttressed by a recently added subsection of §43(a), §43(a)(3), which refers specifically to "civil action[s] for trade dress infringement under this chapter for trade dress not registered on the principal register." 15 U.S.C.A. §1125(a)(3) (Oct. 1999 Supp.).

The text of §43(a) provides little guidance as to the circumstances under which unregistered trade dress may be protected. It does require that a producer show that the allegedly infringing feature is not "functional," *see*

§43(a)(3), and is likely to cause confusion with the product for which protection is sought, *see* §43(a)(1)(A), 15 U.S.C. §1125(a)(1)(A). Nothing in §43(a) explicitly requires a producer to show that its trade dress is distinctive, but courts have universally imposed that requirement, since without distinctiveness the trade dress would not "cause confusion . . . as to the origin, sponsorship, or approval of [the] goods," as the section requires. Distinctiveness is, moreover, an explicit prerequisite for registration of trade dress under §2, and "the general principles qualifying a mark for registration under §2 of the Lanham Act are for the most part applicable in determining whether an unregistered mark is entitled to protection under §43(a)." *Two Pesos, Inc. v. Taco Cabana, Inc.*, 505 U.S. 763, 768 (1992) (citations omitted).

In evaluating the distinctiveness of a mark under §2 (and therefore, by analogy, under §43(a)), courts have held that a mark can be distinctive in one of two ways. First, a mark is inherently distinctive if "[its] intrinsic nature serves to identify a particular source." *Ibid.* In the context of word marks, courts have applied the now-classic test originally formulated by Judge Friendly, in which word marks that are "arbitrary" ("Camel" cigarettes), "fanciful" ("Kodak" film), or "suggestive" ("Tide" laundry detergent) are held to be inherently distinctive. *See Abercrombie & Fitch Co. v. Hunting World, Inc.*, 537 F.2d 4, 10-11 (C.A.2 1976). Second, a mark has acquired distinctiveness, even if it is not inherently distinctive, if it has developed secondary meaning, which occurs when, "in the minds of the public, the primary significance of a [mark] is to identify the source of the product rather than the product itself." *Inwood Laboratories, Inc. v. Ives Laboratories, Inc.*, 456 U.S. 844, 851, n.11 (1982).[4]

The judicial differentiation between marks that are inherently distinctive and those that have developed secondary meaning has solid foundation in the statute itself. Section 2 requires that registration be granted to any trademark "by which the goods of the applicant may be distinguished from the goods of others"—subject to various limited exceptions. 15 U.S.C. §1052. It also provides, again with limited exceptions, that "nothing in this chapter shall prevent the registration of a mark used by the applicant which has become distinctive of the applicant's goods in commerce"—that is, which is not inherently distinctive but has become so only through secondary meaning. §2(f), 15 U.S.C. §1052(f). Nothing in §2, however, demands the conclusion that every category of mark necessarily includes some marks "by which the goods of the applicant may be distinguished from the goods of others" without secondary meaning—that in every category some marks are inherently distinctive.

Indeed, with respect to at least one category of mark—colors—we have held that no mark can ever be inherently distinctive. *See Qualitex*, 514 U.S., at 162-163. . . .

It seems to us that design, like color, is not inherently distinctive. The attribution of inherent distinctiveness to certain categories of word marks

---

4. The phrase "secondary meaning" originally arose in the context of word marks, where it served to distinguish the source-identifying meaning from the ordinary, or "primary," meaning of the word. "Secondary meaning" has since come to refer to the acquired, source-identifying meaning of a non-word mark as well. It is often a misnomer in that context, since non-word marks ordinarily have no "primary" meaning. Clarity might well be served by using the term "acquired meaning" in both the word-mark and the non-word-mark contexts—but in this opinion we follow what has become the conventional terminology.

and product packaging derives from the fact that the very purpose of attaching a particular word to a product, or encasing it in a distinctive packaging, is most often to identify the source of the product. Although the words and packaging can serve subsidiary function—a suggestive word mark (such as "Tide" for laundry detergent), for instance, may invoke positive connotations in the consumer's mind, and a garish form of packaging (such as Tide's squat, brightly decorated plastic bottles for its liquid laundry detergent) may attract an otherwise indifferent consumer's attention on a crowded store shelf—their predominant function remains source identification. Consumers are therefore predisposed to regard those symbols as indication of the producer, which is why such symbols "almost automatically tell a customer that they refer to a brand," *id.*, at 162-163, and "immediately . . . signal a brand or a product 'source,'" *id.*, at 163. And where it is not reasonable to assume consumer predisposition to take an affixed word or packaging as indication of source—where, for example, the affixed word is descriptive of the product ("Tasty" bread) or of a geographic origin ("Georgia" peaches)—inherent distinctiveness will not be found. That is why the statute generally excludes, from those word marks that can be registered as inherently distinctive, words that are "merely descriptive" of the goods, §2(e)(1), 15 U.S.C. §1052(e)(1), or "primarily geographically descriptive of them," *see* §2(e)(2), 15 U.S.C. §1052(e)(2). In the case of product design, as in the case of color, we think consumer predisposition to equate the feature with the source does not exist. Consumers are aware of the reality that, almost invariably, even the most unusual of product designs—such as a cocktail shaker shaped like a penguin—is intended not to identify the source, but to render the product itself more useful or more appealing.

The fact that product design almost invariably serves purposes other than source identification not only renders inherent distinctiveness problematic; it also renders application of an inherent-distinctiveness principle more harmful to other consumer interests. Consumers should not be deprived of the benefits of competition with regard to the utilitarian and esthetic purposes that product design ordinarily serves by a rule of law that facilitates plausible threats of suit against new entrants based upon alleged inherent distinctiveness. How easy it is to mount a plausible suit depends, of course, upon the clarity of the test for inherent distinctiveness, and where product design is concerned we have little confidence that a reasonably clear test can be devised. Respondent and the United States as amicus curiae urge us to adopt for product design relevant portions of the test formulated by the Court of Customs and Patent Appeals for product packaging in *Seabrook Foods, Inc. v. Bar-Well Foods, Ltd.*, 568 F.2d 1342 (1977). That opinion, in determining the inherent distinctiveness of a product's packaging, considered, among other things, "whether it was a 'common' basic shape or design, whether it was unique or unusual in a particular field, [and] whether it was a mere refinement of a commonly-adopted and well-known form of ornamentation for a particular class of goods viewed by the public as a dress or ornamentation for the goods." *Id.*, at 1344 (footnotes omitted). Such a test would rarely provide the basis for summary disposition of an anticompetitive strike suit. Indeed, at oral argument, counsel for the United States quite understandably would not give a definitive answer as to whether the test was met in this very case, saying only that "[t]his is a very difficult case for that purpose." Tr. of Oral Arg. 19.

It is true, of course, that the person seeking to exclude new entrants would have to establish the nonfunctionality of the design feature, *see* §43(a)(3), 15 U.S.C.A. §1125(a)(3) (Oct. 1999 Supp.) — a showing that may involve consideration of its esthetic appeal, *see Qualitex*, 514 U.S., at 170. Competition is deterred, however, not merely by successful suit but by the plausible threat of successful suit, and given the unlikelihood of inherently source-identifying design, the game of allowing suit based upon alleged inherent distinctiveness seems to us not worth the candle. That is especially so since the producer can ordinarily obtain protection for a design that is inherently source identifying (if any such exists), but that does not yet have secondary meaning, by securing a design patent or a copyright for the design — as, indeed, respondent did for certain elements of the designs in this case. The availability of these other protections greatly reduces any harm to the producer that might ensue from our conclusion that a product design cannot be protected under §43(a) without a showing of secondary meaning.

Respondent contends that our decision in *Two Pesos* forecloses a conclusion that product-design trade dress can never be inherently distinctive. . . . *Two Pesos* unquestionably establishes the legal principle that trade dress can be inherently distinctive, but it does not establish that product-design trade dress can be. *Two Pesos* is inapposite to our holding here because the trade dress at issue, the decor of a restaurant, seems to us not to constitute product design. It was either product packaging — which, as we have discussed, normally is taken by the consumer to indicate origin — or else some tertium quid that is akin to product packaging and has no bearing on the present case.

Respondent replies that this manner of distinguishing *Two Pesos* will force courts to draw difficult lines between product-design and product-packaging trade dress. There will indeed be some hard cases at the margin: a classic glass Coca-Cola bottle, for instance, may constitute packaging for those consumers who drink the Coke and then discard the bottle, but may constitute the product itself for those consumers who are bottle collectors, or part of the product itself for those consumers who buy Coke in the classic glass bottle, rather than a can, because they think it more stylish to drink from the former. We believe, however, that the frequency and the difficulty of having to distinguish between product design and product packaging will be much less than the frequency and the difficulty of having to decide when a product design is inherently distinctive. To the extent there are close cases, we believe that courts should err on the side of caution and classify ambiguous trade dress as product design, thereby requiring secondary meaning. The very closeness will suggest the existence of relatively small utility in adopting an inherent-distinctiveness principle, and relatively great consumer benefit in requiring a demonstration of secondary meaning.

We hold that, in an action for infringement of unregistered trade dress under §43(a) of the Lanham Act, a product's design is distinctive, and therefore protectible, only upon a showing of secondary meaning. The judgment of the Second Circuit is reversed and the case is remanded for further proceedings consistent with this opinion. It is so ordered.

## NOTES AND QUESTIONS

1. *The question before the Court.* In *Wal-Mart*, the Court granted certiorari on the question "what must be shown to establish that a product's design is inherently distinctive for purposes of Lanham Act trade-dress protection?" *See* 120 S. Ct. 308 (1999). Why is there no discussion in the Court's opinion of the post–*Two Pesos* case law discussing inherent distinctiveness of product design trade dress or of the issue presented in the petition for certiorari?

2. *Consistency with prior Supreme Court case law.* Do you agree with the reading of *Two Pesos* and *Qualitex* offered by the *Wal-Mart* Court? To what extent has the Court offered an elaboration upon the meaning of its earlier opinions? To what extent is the Court backtracking on its earlier opinions? Does the *Wal-Mart* Court look to the same sources as the *Two Pesos* and *Qualitex* Courts? What is the respective significance of statutory language, legislative history, trademark policy, or other concerns in each of the Court's decisions? How does the Court's concern for competition manifest itself in each of the three cases? *See* Graeme B. Dinwoodie, *The Rational Limits of Trademark Law, in* UNITED STATES INTELLECTUAL PROPERTY: LAW AND POLICY (Hansen ed. 2006); *see also* Graeme B. Dinwoodie, *The Seventh Annual Honorable Helen Wilson Nies Memorial Lecture on Intellectual Property Law: The Trademark Jurisprudence of the Rehnquist Court*, 8 MARQ. INTELL. PROP. L. REV. 187 (2004) (suggesting various influences); Robert G. Bone, *Enforcement Costs and Trademark Puzzles*, 90 VA. L. REV. 2099 (2004) (suggesting that trade dress law reflects attention to enforcement costs); David S. Welkowitz, *The Supreme Court and Trademark Law in the New Millennium*, 30 WM. MITCHELL L. REV. 1659 (2004) (linking current influences to historical developments).

3. *Consistency with lower court approaches.* How is the test announced by the Court in *Wal-Mart* different from the approach of the Third Circuit in *Duraco* and the Second Circuit in *Knitwaves*?

4. *Rationales for a secondary meaning requirement.* What are the reasons the Court imposed a secondary meaning requirement on product design trade dress claims? (You may find several variables or reasons in the opinion.) Are these reasons persuasive? To what extent do these reasons apply to other types of trademark? Did Judge Learned Hand contemplate a blanket secondary meaning requirement for product design trade dress in the *Crescent Tool* case, in Section A of this chapter?

5. *Assigning significance to categories.* Classical trademark distinctiveness analysis assigns marks to different categories (e.g., descriptive terms), which in turn affects the ability of those marks to receive protection absent secondary meaning. Is the Court simply saying that product design marks are, as a legal matter, to be treated as descriptive marks? Is the classification of a mark as descriptive (thus requiring secondary meaning for protection) different from classifying a mark as a product design (thus requiring the same proof for protection)?

6. *The line between packaging and design.* The Court has now created a different rule for product design than for product packaging. How did the *Wal-Mart* Court draw the line between packaging and design? Consider whether your answer to the last question would vary depending on whether the line were drawn by reference to (a) the examples cited by the *Wal-Mart* Court of different types of mark, (b) the different variables that made the *Wal-Mart* Court treat design differently, or (c) a conceptual definition of what is a design and what is packaging. *Cf.* Graeme B. Dinwoodie, *Reconceptualizing the Inherent*

*Distinctiveness of Product Design Trade Dress*, 75 N.C. L. Rev. 471, 573-585 (1997). We explore this issue further in Section C.1 of this chapter.

**7. "*Some tertium quid.*"** The Court distinguished *Two Pesos* by describing that case as involving "product packaging" (which the Court implies can be inherently distinctive) "or else some *tertium quid* that is akin to product packaging and has no bearing on the present case." Might there be other types of mark that one could categorize as "some *tertium quid*," such that the less demanding *Two Pesos* rule would apply? What is there about restaurant decor that warrants abrogation from the *Wal-Mart* rule?

**8. *Alternative approaches.*** The government refused at oral argument in *Wal-Mart* to answer questions regarding how *Seabrook* would be applied in the case before the Court. Would the *Seabrook* test have supported a finding of inherent distinctiveness in *Wal-Mart*?

**9. *Legislative reform.*** In the wake of *Wal-Mart*, the Board of the American Intellectual Property Law Association adopted the following resolutions:

> RESOLVED, that the American Intellectual Property Law Association ("AIPLA") favors, in principle, revision of the Lanham Act, 15 U.S.C. §1051, *et seq.*, to provide that a non-functional product configuration or design can be deemed inherently distinctive when the requirements for inherent distinctiveness applied to trade dress are met.
>
> RESOLVED, that the American Intellectual Property Law Association ("AIPLA") favors amending the Lanham Act by adding the following to Section 45, 15 U.S.C. §1127:
>
>> Non-functional trade dress (including a product configuration or design) which is "inherently distinctive" is registrable under section 2 and protectable under section 43 of this Act. In determining whether a product configuration or design is "inherently distinctive" under this Act, the following factors shall be considered—
>>
>>> (1) whether the configuration or design is a common basic shape or design;
>>>
>>> (2) whether the configuration or design is unique or unusual in the particular field involved;
>>>
>>> (3) whether the configuration or design is a mere refinement of a commonly-adopted and well-known form of ornamentation for the particular class of goods involved;
>>>
>>> (4) whether the configuration or design is capable of creating a commercial impression distinct from any accompanying words; and
>>>
>>> (5) any other factor which may tend to show that the configuration or design would be inherently recognized by members of the relevant public as an indication of the source of the goods.

Would you support these amendments to the Lanham Act? In what ways (if any) is this proposal different from the *Seabrook* test? Does this suggest any weaknesses in the *Seabrook* test? Could you rewrite this proposal in any way that makes the test clearer, or that avoids the problems with which the *Wal-Mart* Court was concerned? *See* Trade Dress Protection Act, H.R. 3163, 105th Cong. (1998). *See also* Lars Smith, *Trade Distinctiveness: Solving Scalia's Tertium Quid Conundrum*, 2005 Mich. St. L. Rev. 243 (2005) (suggesting a "trade distinctiveness" test for trade dress distinctiveness that does not distinguish between design and packaging: "First, the party claiming that its trade dress has trade distinctiveness would have to prove that there is a custom in the trade to use the claimed design features as source-identifying. Second, the party would have to show that their trade dress is unusual in light of the nature of the design features common for the product or service."); *cf.* Graeme B. Dinwoodie, *Reconceptualizing the Inherent Distinctiveness of Product Design Trade Dress*, 75 N.C. L. REV. 471, 585-597 (1997) (incorporating industry custom within the *Seabrook* test).

## C. TRADE DRESS AND DESIGN DISTINCTIVENESS AFTER *WAL-MART*

Courts have applied *Wal-Mart* in a variety of cases. In a few cases, such as *Slokevage*, excerpted below, courts have discussed the threshold distinction between product design (or configuration) and product packaging. Taking their cue from *Wal-Mart*, courts almost invariably characterize trade dress as design in close cases. As a result, trade dress owners routinely must produce evidence of secondary meaning. The *Yankee Candle* case, also excerpted below, illustrates one court's approach to reviewing that evidence.

As you study these cases, review the older cases found at the beginning of this chapter. Courts in the older cases grappled with the fundamental notion that product shapes could signify origin. Are courts in these newer cases still struggling with the fundamentals, even if they are speaking in terms of modern doctrine?

### 1. PRODUCT DESIGN VS. PRODUCT PACKAGING

IN RE SLOKEVAGE

441 F.3d 957 (Fed. Cir. 2006)

LOURIE, Circuit Judge:

Background

[Joanne] Slokevage filed an application to register a mark on the Principal Register for "pants, overalls, shorts, culottes, dresses, skirts." Slokevage described the mark in her application as a "configuration" that consists of a label with the words "FLASH DARE!" in a V-shaped background, and cut-out areas located on each side of the label. The cut-out areas consist of a hole in a garment and a flap attached to the garment with a closure device. This trade dress configuration, which is located on the rear of various garments, is depicted [below].

Although Slokevage currently seeks to register a mark for the overall configuration of her design, she has already received protection for various aspects of the trade dress configuration. For example, she received a design patent for the cut-out area design. She also registered on the Supplemental Register a design mark for the cut-out area.[1] In addition, she registered the word mark "FLASH DARE!" on the Principal Register.

[The trademark examiner initially refused registration of the proposed mark inter alia on the ground that it constituted a clothing configuration that is not inherently distinctive. Slokevage chose not to submit evidence of acquired distinctiveness. The examiner made final his refusal to register the mark on the ground that the clothing configuration constitutes "product design/configuration," which cannot be inherently distinctive. The examiner noted that Slokevage's reference in her application to the trade dress as a "cut-away flap design" supported a determination that the configuration constitutes product design. Slokevage appealed the refusal of the examiner to register the trade dress configuration, and the Board affirmed the examiner's decision.]

Discussion

. . . .

As a preliminary matter, Slokevage argues that whether trade dress is product design or not is a legal determination, whereas the government asserts that it is a factual issue. The resolution of that question is an issue of first impression for this court. We conclude that the determination whether trade dress is product design is a factual finding because it is akin to determining whether a trademark is inherently distinctive or whether a mark is descriptive, which are questions of fact. *See, e.g., Hoover Co. v. Royal Appliance Mfg. Co.*, 238 F.3d 1357, 1359 (Fed. Cir. 2001) ("The issue of inherent distinctiveness is a factual determination made by the board."); [cit.]. Inherent distinctiveness or descriptiveness involves consumer perception and whether consumers are predisposed towards equating a symbol with a source. *See In re MBNA Am. Bank, N.A.*, 340 F.3d 1328, 1332 (Fed. Cir. 2003); *In re Nett Designs, Inc.*, 236 F.3d at 1341-42. Such issues are determined based on testimony, surveys, and other evidence as questions of fact. Determining whether trade dress is product design or product packaging involves a similar inquiry. *Wal-Mart*, 529 U.S. at 213 (discussing product packaging and design in the context of consumers' ability to equate the product with the source). We therefore will defer to the Board's finding on product design, affirming the Board if its decision is supported by substantial evidence. . . .

I. Trade Dress and Product Design

On appeal, Slokevage argues that the Board erred in determining that the trade dress for which she seeks protection is product design and thus that it cannot be inherently distinctive. She asserts that the Board's reliance on the Supreme Court's decision in *Wal-Mart* to support its position that Slokevage's

---

1. Pursuant to section 23 of the Lanham Act, the United States Patent and Trademark Office ("PTO") maintains a Supplemental Register for marks "capable of distinguishing applicant's goods or services and not registrable on the principal register." 15 U.S.C. §1091(a).

trade dress is product design is misplaced. In particular, she contends that *Wal-Mart* does not provide guidance on how to determine whether trade dress is product design. Moreover, she maintains that the trade dress at issue in *Wal-Mart*, which was classified as product design without explanation, is different from Slokevage's trade dress because the *Wal-Mart* trade dress implicated the overall appearance of the product and was a theme made up of many unique elements. Slokevage argues that her trade dress, in contrast, involves one component of a product design, which can be used with a variety of types of clothing. Slokevage further asserts that her trade dress is located on the rear hips of garments, which is a location that consumers frequently recognize as identifying the source of the garment.

The PTO responds that the Board correctly concluded that Slokevage's trade dress is product design and that it properly relied on *Wal-Mart* for support of its determination. According to the PTO, in the *Wal-Mart* decision the Supreme Court determined that a design of clothing is product design. The PTO further asserts that the trade dress at issue in *Wal-Mart*, which was classified as product design, is similar to Slokevage's trade dress. The trade dress in *Wal-Mart* consists of design elements on a line of garments, and Slokevage's trade dress similarly consists of a design component common to the overall design of a variety of garments. The PTO notes that Slokevage's trade dress application refers to her trade dress as a "configuration" including a "clothing feature," and that "product configuration" is synonymous with "product design." The PTO also argues that under *Wal-Mart* product design cannot be inherently distinctive, the rationale being that consumers perceive product design as making the product more useful or desirable, rather than indicating source. According to the PTO, the trade dress at issue here makes the product more desirable to consumers, rather than indicates source. Finally, the PTO notes that even if it were a close case as to whether Slokevage's trade dress constitutes product design, the Court's opinion in *Wal-Mart* states that in "close cases," trade dress should be categorized as product design, thereby requiring proof of acquired distinctiveness for protection. 529 U.S. at 215.

We agree with the Board that Slokevage's trade dress constitutes product design and therefore cannot be inherently distinctive. . . .

. . . [A]lthough the decision in *Wal-Mart* does not expressly address the issue of what constitutes product design, it is informative to this case because it provides examples of trade dress that are product design. The Court observed that a "cocktail shaker shaped like a penguin" is product design and that the trade dress at issue in that case, "a line of spring/summer one-piece seersucker outfits decorated with appliques of hearts, flowers, fruits, and the like" is product design. *Wal-Mart*, 529 U.S. at 207, 213. These examples demonstrate that product design can consist of design features incorporated into a product. Slokevage urges that her trade dress is not product design because it does not alter the entire product but is more akin to a label being placed on a garment. We do not agree. The holes and flaps portion are part of the design of the clothing—the cut-out area is not merely a design placed on top of a garment, but is a design incorporated into the garment itself. Moreover, while Slokevage urges that product design trade dress must implicate the entire product, we do not find support for that proposition. Just as the product design in *Wal-Mart* consisted of certain design features featured on clothing, Slokevage's trade dress similarly consists of design features, holes and flaps, featured in clothing, revealing the similarity between the two types of design.

In addition, the reasoning behind the Supreme Court's determination that product design cannot be inherently distinctive is also instructive to our case. The Court reasoned that, unlike a trademark whose "predominant function" remains source identification, product design often serves other functions, such as rendering the "product itself more useful or more appealing." *Wal-Mart*, 529 U.S. at 212, 213. The design at issue here can serve such utilitarian and aesthetic functions. For example, consumers may purchase Slokevage's clothing for the utilitarian purpose of wearing a garment or because they find the appearance of the garment particularly desirable. Consistent with the Supreme Court's analysis in *Wal-Mart*, in such cases when the purchase implicates a utilitarian or aesthetic purpose, rather than a source-identifying function, it is appropriate to require proof of acquired distinctiveness.

Finally, the Court in *Wal-Mart* provided guidance on how to address trade dress cases that may be difficult to classify: "To the extent that there are close cases, we believe that courts should err on the side of caution and classify ambiguous trade dress as product design, thereby requiring secondary meaning." 529 U.S. at 215. Even if this were a close case, therefore, we must follow that precedent and classify the trade dress as product design. We thus agree with the Board that Slokevage's trade dress is product design and therefore that she must prove acquired distinctiveness in order for her trade dress mark to be registered.

[*Affirmed*].

## NOTES AND QUESTIONS

1. ***The "product being purchased and consumed."*** In *McKernan v. Burek*, 118 F. Supp. 2d 119 (D. Mass. 2000), the plaintiff sold, and sought trade dress protection for, popular novelty stickers that purported to be permits for an imaginary Cape Cod Canal Tunnel. The district court concluded that

> the example given in *Wal-Mart*, of the classic Coca-Cola bottle is instructive: an item is the product if it is the essential commodity being purchased and consumed rather than the dress which presents the product. Here, the essential commodity being purchased is a joke on a bumper sticker. All of the visual elements contained in the Tunnel Permit are a part of this joke and indispensable to it. What is being purchased and consumed is the novelty sticker, not dress identifying the prestige or standing of its source. Because McKernan is seeking protection for the product being consumed, the proper classification of what McKernan seeks to protect is product design. This view of the matter is strengthened by the *Wal-Mart* Court's remarkably clear advice that in close cases trial courts should "err on the side of caution and classify ambiguous trade dress as product design."

Are you persuaded by the court's explanation of the design-packaging definitional divide or by the court's application of its test in the case before it? If the novelty sticker were sold as a free gift accompanying the sale of breakfast cereal, would your analysis change? Is the approach of the *McKernan* court consistent with the approach of the *Wal-Mart* Court? Would the plaintiff's claimed trade dress in *Slokevage* have been treated as design or packaging under the approach articulated by the district court in *McKernan*?

2. *"Features inherent to the actual physical product."* In the next case, *Yankee Candle*, the court defines product design cases as involving "features inherent to the actual physical product." Is this a workable definition? Does this definition align with the notions of design that we discussed in Chapter 1? How would it apply to the subject matter of *Slokevage*? Among other things, the *Yankee Candle* case involves a claim of trade dress in the appearance of labels on jars that hold individual candles. The court states that "detachable labels are a classic case of product packaging, and therefore may be inherently distinctive." Might there be a distinction between detachable and nondetachable labels? Between nondetachable labels and designs etched into the candles? Should the protectability of a mark consisting of the letter "W" stitched into the back pocket of a pair of jeans be treated differently than a leather label attached to the back pocket with the same "W" stitched into the leather label? Should your analysis of distinctiveness be affected by the existence of other registered marks consisting of pocket stitching designs for jeans? *See* Graeme B. Dinwoodie, *Reconceptualizing the Inherent Distinctiveness of Product Design Trade Dress*, 75 N.C. L. Rev. 471 (1997). How would the fact that jeans manufacturers commonly stitch decorative designs on back pockets affect your answer? *See In re Right-On Co., Ltd.*, 87 U.S.P.Q.2d (BNA) 1152 (TTAB 2008) (applying *Seabrook*). Would it matter whether consumers typically left the leather label on their jeans when worn?

3. *Revisiting* **Wal-Mart**? If the role of packaging in consumer purchasing decisions were to evolve over time, would you support reconsideration of the *Wal-Mart* rule? *See* Louise Story, *Product Packages Now Shout to Get Your Attention*, N.Y. Times, Aug. 10, 2007 (noting that "some brands are bragging that their bottles of cleansers and other household products are attractive enough to be left out in plain view, rather than hidden in a closet or drawer").

## 2. SECONDARY MEANING

Mark owners may attempt to establish secondary meaning in a variety of ways. The following excerpt summarizes the types of direct and circumstantial evidence that has routinely been found acceptable in cases involving word marks. Should courts (and trademark examiners) scrutinize secondary meaning evidence more strictly in cases involving trade dress? Should they develop different rules for proving secondary meaning in trade dress cases?

### Restatement (Third) of Unfair Competition (1995)
Section 13, Comment (e)

[S]econdary meaning does not connote a subordinate or rare meaning. It refers instead to a subsequent significance added to the original meaning of the term. . . .

Secondary meaning may be established by either direct or circumstantial evidence. Testimony from individual consumers is clearly relevant to the existence of secondary meaning, but the lack of a representative sample of consumers often undermines its probative value. Surveys of prospective purchasers, if properly formulated and conducted, can be particularly persuasive.

Proof of actual consumer confusion caused by another's use of the designation is also evidence of secondary meaning, since if the designation is not distinctive, use by another will not result in confusion. . . .

The length of time the designation has been in use is also relevant. Although secondary meaning may sometimes be inferred from evidence of long and continuous use, no particular length of use is required. In some cases distinctiveness is not acquired even after an extended period of time; in others it may be acquired soon after adoption. Section 2(f) of the Lanham Act, 15 U.S.C.A. §§1052(f), permits but does not require the Patent and Trademark Office to accept as prima facie evidence of distinctiveness proof of "substantially exclusive and continuous use" for five years. Advertising and other promotional efforts resulting in increased public exposure for the designation may also support an inference of secondary meaning. It is the likely effect rather than the effort invested in such activities, however, that is determinative, and the expenditure of substantial sums in advertising does not in itself create protectable rights. Advertisements that emphasize the source significance of the designation through prominent use of the term or symbol or that invite consumers to "look for" the designation when selecting goods, for example, are more likely to generate secondary meaning than are more descriptive advertising uses.

The physical manner in which the designation is used with the goods, services, or business can also affect the likelihood that the designation will acquire secondary meaning. A designation that is relatively inconspicuous or that is used only in conjunction with other trademarks may be less likely to acquire secondary meaning than a more prominently displayed designation. Similarly, prominent use of a designation in the manner typical of a trade name, such as its appearance on signs or correspondence, can emphasize its association with the particular business more clearly than less conspicuous uses.

Concurrent use of a term by competitors is relevant as tending to negate the existence of secondary meaning. If the term has been used in a descriptive sense or as part of a trademark or trade name by numerous sellers in the market, it is unlikely to become associated exclusively with a single producer.

The significance of the designation to prospective purchasers may also be demonstrated by the nature of its use in newspapers, popular magazines, or dictionaries, at least when the product is marketed to the general public. The significance of the term to professionals in the trade such as dealers or retailers is also relevant, although it may not be accorded substantial weight if the goods or services are marketed primarily to nonprofessionals.

Proof that a competing seller has intentionally copied a designation previously used by another is often accepted as evidence of secondary meaning on the theory that the copying was motivated by a desire to benefit from confusion with the prior user. The strength of the inference may be diminished, however, by other credible motives for the copying. Thus, if the designation is plainly descriptive and equally applicable to the products of both sellers, or consists of a feature that is functional or that otherwise enhances the value of the product for reasons unrelated to any alleged source significance, evidence of intentional copying may carry little weight on the issue of secondary meaning.

## YANKEE CANDLE CO., INC. v. BRIDGEWATER CANDLE CO., LLC
259 F.3d 25 (1st Cir. 2001)

TORRUELIA, Circuit Judge:

[Yankee Candle Company ("Yankee"), a leading manufacturer of scented candles, sued competitor Bridgewater Candle Company ("Bridgewater") on counts of inter alia copyright infringement and trade dress infringement under section 43(a) of the Lanham Act. The district court granted summary judgment to Bridgewater on both claims. The court of appeals affirmed the district court's judgment with respect to the copyright claim and proceeded to consider the trade dress claim.

The district court had identified three ways in which Yankee claimed that Bridgewater had infringed its trade dress: (i) by copying Yankee's method of shelving and displaying candles in its stores, called the "Vertical Display System"; (ii) by copying the overall "look and feel" of Yankee's Housewarmer line of candles; and (iii) by copying the design of Yankee's merchandise catalog, specifically its one fragrance per page layout.]

### C. Yankee's Claims

On appeal, Yankee argues that the district court erred in several ways. First, Yankee contends that the district court ignored its "combination" claim defining its trade dress as the *combination* of its Housewarmer series of labels, its choice of candle sizes and styles, its Vertical Design System, and its catalog layout. By disaggregating the features of its trade dress, says Yankee, the district court failed to analyze the "look and feel" of the entire Yankee product. Second, Yankee argues that the district court erroneously defined its trade dress as product design/configuration, and in so doing, proceeded directly to the question of secondary meaning without considering that the dress might be inherently distinctive. Third, Yankee argues that it introduced sufficient evidence of secondary meaning to survive summary judgment.... Although we agree with Yankee that the district court failed to address its combination claim as such and we entertain the possibility that the court incorrectly analyzed Yankee's claims under a product design/configuration rubric, we ultimately reach the same conclusion as the district court and affirm the grant of summary judgment, albeit using a different analysis. [cit.]

#### 1. Yankee's Trade Dress

We begin by sketching Yankee's claimed trade dress, which we read on appeal as defined in two possible ways. First, Yankee suggests that its trade dress is a combination of: (i) the Vertical Display System; (ii) the catalog, with an emphasis on its "one fragrance per page" layout; (iii) its candle shapes and sizes; (iv) the quantities of candles it sells as a unit; and (v) the Housewarmer labels, specifically their inclusion of (a) a full-bleed photograph, (b) a superimposed title plate with gold edging and lettering on a white background, (c) a rectangular shape, and (d) a reflective border.[8] Alternatively, Yankee describes its trade dress as the elements common to its Housewarmer labels. . . .

---

8. We note that Yankee has not been entirely consistent in its definition of its trade dress in its appellate brief. At times, it appears that Yankee is arguing that individual *features* of its product line, namely its labels, its catalogues and its Vertical Display System, deserve trade dress protection. This was

## 2. Inherent Distinctiveness

### a. The Combination Claim

Yankee argues that the distinct combination of elements comprising its candle sizes and shapes, quantities sold, labels, Vertical Design System, and catalog stem from "arbitrary" choices and are thus "inherently distinctive" and entitled to trademark protection. *See Two Pesos*, 505 U.S. at 768 (inherently distinctive marks are entitled to protection). Certain types of trade dress, however, can never be inherently distinctive. *Wal-Mart*, 529 U.S. at 212-14 (product design/configuration cannot be inherently distinctive); *Qualitex Co. v. Jacobson Prods. Co.*, 514 U.S. 159, 162 (1995) (color cannot be inherently distinctive). We find that Yankee's combination claim falls under the category of product design/configuration, and thus Yankee must prove that the dress has attained secondary meaning in order for it to be protected under the Lanham Act. *Wal-Mart*, 529 U.S. at 215.

Yankee argues that because its products are candles, all the trappings associated with the sale of the candle—i.e., the candle-holders, the Vertical Display System, the labels, and the catalog—constitute product packaging, or at the very least a *"tertium quid . . .* akin to product packaging," categories of trade dress that may be inherently distinctive. *See Wal-Mart*, 529 U.S. at 215 (citing *Two Pesos*, 505 U.S. at 773).

Although, as we explain below, Yankee's Housewarmer *labels* are product packaging and thus may be inherently distinctive, when combined with actual candle features, candle containers, the catalog,[9] and the in-store display system, the claim is no longer clearly a product-packaging one. Nor can the claim be categorized as product design/configuration, as that term has generally been defined to be limited to features inherent to the actual physical product: here, the candles. *See Wal-Mart*, 529 U.S. at 212 (describing cocktail shaker shaped as penguin as a product design); *Lund*, 163 F.3d at 34-36 (kitchen faucets). We also do not see this claim as akin to the restaurant decor upheld as potentially inherently distinctive in *Two Pesos*, which the Supreme Court later described as a *"tertium quid* that is akin to product packaging." *Wal-Mart*, 529 U.S. at 215. [cit.] Yankee has not made a claim as to the overall appearance of an entire store, but has instead isolated certain characteristics of its candle display in stores. This strikes us as far closer to the design/configuration category. The fact that Yankee points to particular aspects of the candles themselves, namely their shapes and sizes, only confirms our categorization.

---

the analysis undertaken by the district court. At other points, however, Yankee disclaims such an approach. We note that the burden to clearly identify the trade dress at issue is on the plaintiff. *See, e.g., Landscape Forms v. Columbia Cascade Co.*, 113 F.3d 373, 381 (2d Cir. 1997). Moreover, at least one federal court has previously criticized Yankee for failing in this regard. *Yankee Candle Co. v. New England Candle Co.*, 14 F. Supp. 2d 154, 162 (D. Mass. 1998), *vacated pursuant to settlement*, 29 F. Supp. 2d 44 (D. Mass. 1998). After a careful review of the record, we conclude that Yankee has been sufficiently consistent as to these two descriptions of its trade dress for us to evaluate them on appeal.

9. We note that we are troubled by the inclusion of Yankee's catalog in its combination trade dress claim. A combination trade dress claim is one that includes a number of different features of a product or its packaging which, *taken together*, are potentially indicative of source. In this case, although the candles, their labels, and the Vertical Display System are all seen at the same time, the catalog is a separate item mailed to consumers at their homes. . . . At any rate, because we conclude that Yankee must establish that its combination has acquired secondary meaning, and has not in fact done so, whether the catalog is included or not in the combination claim is ultimately irrelevant.

In *Wal-Mart*, the Supreme Court instructed us how to deal with claims that were at the margin of product design/configuration: "To the extent that there are close cases, we believe that courts should err on the side of caution and classify ambiguous trade dress as product design, thereby requiring secondary meaning." 529 U.S. at 215. We follow that advice here. To prevail on its combination claim, Yankee must show that its trade dress has acquired secondary meaning.

b. Labels

Yankee also claims that unique features of its Housewarmer labels constitute an inherently distinctive trade dress. The district court found that the labels were also product configuration/design, and thus could not be inherently distinctive as a matter of law. We disagree. Detachable labels are a classic case of product packaging, and therefore may be inherently distinctive. *See, e.g., Fun-Damental Too*, 111 F.3d at 1000-01. Although the district court did not determine whether the Housewarmer labels were inherently distinctive, we are convinced that the label elements highlighted by Yankee do not meet the inherent distinctiveness test of *Abercrombie & Fitch Co. v. Hunting World, Inc.*, 537 F.2d 4 (2d Cir. 1976). We therefore uphold the district court's grant of summary judgment on this basis.

. . . [B]ecause the *Abercrombie* test was first applied to word marks, it may be difficult to apply to visual marks or trade dress, *Lund*, 163 F.3d at 39. The Supreme Court, however, has endorsed the use of the *Abercrombie* test in the evaluation of visual marks, as well as in the assessment of product packaging trade dress claims. *Id.* (citing *Two Pesos*, 505 U.S. at 768-69).

This Court, however, has noted that "[w]e do not believe that the Supreme Court's endorsement of the *Abercrombie* test in *Two Pesos* requires a strict application of the *Abercrombie* test in all contexts. . . ." *Id.* at 40. Instead, we have found it appropriate to supplement the somewhat bare-boned *Abercrombie* categories with the questions asked in *Seabrook Foods, Inc. v. Bar-Well Foods Ltd.*, 568 F.2d 1342 (C.C.P.A. 1977). In *Seabrook*, inherent distinctiveness was determined by reference to: (i) whether the design was a common or basic one; (ii) whether it was "unique or unusual" in the field; (iii) whether it was a refinement of a common form of ornamentation; and (iv) "whether it was capable of creating a commercial impression distinct from the accompanying words."[10] *Wiley v. Am. Greetings Corp.*, 762 F.2d 139, 141 (1st Cir. 1985) (quoting *Seabrook*, 568 F.2d at 1344). "In reality [the question is] whether the [dress] is so unique, unusual or unexpected in this market that it will automatically be perceived by customers as an indicator of origin." *Lund*, 163 F.3d at 40 (citing 1 J. McCarthy, *McCarthy on Trademarks and Unfair Competition* §8.13 (4th ed. 1996)); *see also McKernan v. Burek*, 118 F. Supp. 2d 119, 124 (D. Mass. 2000) (describing this question as the "*Lund* test" for inherent distinctiveness).

Furthermore, in evaluating the inherent distinctiveness of Yankee's packaging, we must consider the fact that although Yankee's Housewarmer labels

---

10. We note that other circuits may be less willing to apply this "gloss" on the *Abercrombie* test when product packaging is at issue. For example, despite noting that "[w]e are not so confident that the *Abercrombie* analysis is more naturally fit for product packaging cases" than is a *Seabrook*-like test, the Second Circuit has resisted the temptation to refine the *Abercrombie* test for visual marks or trade dress. *Landscape Forms*, 113 F.3d at 379.

have obvious similarities, they also differ significantly from one another, in that they necessarily display different pictures corresponding to their particular candle fragrance. In other words, Yankee seeks to protect features common to a set of labels, as opposed to a specific label common to a host of Yankee goods. A trade dress plaintiff seeking to protect a series or line of products faces a particularly difficult challenge, as it must show that the appearance of the several products is "sufficiently distinct and unique to merit protection." *Landscape Forms*, 113 F.3d at 380; *Jeffrey Milstein, Inc. v. Greger, Lawlor, Roth, Inc.*, 58 F.3d 27, 32-33 (2d Cir. 1995). Moreover, trade dress claims across a line of products present special concerns in their ability to artificially limit competition, as such claims are generally broader in scope than claims relating to an individual item. *Landscape Forms*, 113 F.3d at 381.

Yankee has focused on the "arbitrary" choices it made in designing its label, and has for this reason introduced into evidence numerous possibilities of alternative label designs. While we appreciate that there are many different potential ways of creating a candle label, we think Yankee's approach ignores the focus of the inherent distinctiveness inquiry. . . . [Y]ankee's label is essentially a combination of functional and common features. *See Pubs. Int'l*, 164 F.3d at 341 (gold coloring is a prime example of aesthetic functionality, because it connotes opulence). Although such a combination may be entitled to protection where secondary meaning is shown, *Lund*, 163 F.3d at 37, it is less likely to qualify as inherently distinctive, *Jeffrey Milstein*, 58 F.3d at 32. While the particular combination of common features may indeed be "arbitrary," we do not think that any reasonable juror could conclude that these elements are so "unique and unusual" that they are source-indicative in the absence of secondary meaning. *Lund*, 163 F.3d at 40.

### 3. Secondary Meaning

Having concluded that neither trade dress claim made by Yankee qualifies for protection based on its inherent distinctiveness, we next address whether Yankee has introduced sufficient evidence to survive summary judgment on the question of secondary meaning. As evidence of secondary meaning,[11] Yankee points to: (i) its advertising campaign featuring pictures of its products with the claimed trade dress; (ii) its continuous and virtually exclusive use of its trade dress since 1995; (iii) its high sales figures for Housewarmer candles; (iv) evidence from Bridgewater's files indicating that retailers identify a resemblance between Bridgewater's styles and Yankee's; (v) testimony by a Bridgewater's sales agent as to the distinctiveness of the Yankee trade dress; (vi) testimony by Bridgewater and Yankee employees as to the distinctiveness of Yankee's claimed trade dress; (vii) evidence of actual consumer confusion between Bridgewater and Yankee products; and (viii) evidence of intentional copying by Bridgewater.

This Court has said that "[p]roof of secondary meaning entails vigorous evidentiary requirements." [cit.] The only direct evidence probative of

---

11. With respect to the question of secondary meaning, Yankee does not clearly distinguish the evidentiary support for its label claim from that supporting its combination claim. For purposes of this analysis, we assume that the adduced evidence may be relevant to both aspects of its claimed trade dress. We note, however, that secondary meaning faces a higher threshold in a product design/configuration case. *See Lund*, 163 F.3d at 42; *Duraco*, 40 F.3d at 1435.

secondary meaning is consumer surveys and testimony by individual consumers. *Id.* Although survey evidence is not required, "it is a valuable method of showing secondary meaning." *Lund*, 163 F.3d at 42. Yankee has introduced no survey evidence here.[12] Yankee also cites no evidence that individual consumers associate the particular features at issue with Yankee.[13]

Secondary meaning may also be proven through circumstantial evidence, specifically the length and manner of the use of the trade dress, the nature and extent of advertising and promotion of the trade dress, and the efforts made to promote a conscious connection by the public between the trade dress and the product's source. *See Boston Beer*, 9 F.3d at 182. Other factors may include the product's "established place in the market" and proof of intentional copying. *Lund*, 163 F.3d at 42. Yankee has introduced substantial evidence that the Housewarmer line of candles and corresponding display have been in circulation since 1995, that Yankee spends significant resources advertising its Housewarmer line, and that sales of Housewarmer candles have been extremely successful. However, in concluding that Yankee had not made a sufficient evidentiary showing of secondary meaning, the district court focused on the lack of evidence as to advertising of the *specific* trade dress claimed, as well as the lack of evidence demonstrating a conscious connection by the public between the claimed trade dress and the product's source.

We believe the district court emphasized the relevant issues in conducting its analysis of secondary meaning. Proof of secondary meaning requires at least *some* evidence that consumers associate the trade dress with the source. Although evidence of the pervasiveness of the trade dress may support the conclusion that a mark has acquired secondary meaning, it cannot stand alone. To find otherwise would provide trade dress protection for any successful product, or for the packaging of any successful product. *See Seabrook*, 568 F.2d at 1344 (evidence of sales volume may be relevant to secondary meaning, but "is not necessarily indicative"). Such an open standard hardly comports with the "vigorous" evidentiary showing required by this Court, nor does it comport with the purposes of trade dress protection, namely "to protect that which identifies a product's source." *Lund*, 163 F.3d at 35. In the absence of *any* evidence that the claimed trade dress actually *does* identify a product's source, the trade dress should not be entitled to protection.

That being said, Yankee argues that, because its advertising contained pictures of its products incorporating the claimed trade dress, it was the type of "look-for" advertising that can, on its own, support a finding of secondary meaning *See First Brands Corp. v. Fred Meyer, Inc.*, 809 F.2d 1378, 1383 (9th Cir. 1987). "Look-for" advertising is such that "encourages consumers to identify the claimed trade dress with the particular producer."

---

12. Yankee has cited surveys, taken by Bridgewater, indicating that Bridgewater's trade dress is substantially similar to Yankee's. Although this evidence, if admissible, would be probative of a likelihood of confusion, it does not indicate that Yankee's trade dress has acquired secondary meaning.

13. The evidence that Yankee's retailers and distributors viewed the trade dress as distinctive is not probative of secondary meaning. "[S]econdary meaning occurs when 'the primary significance [of the trade dress] *in the minds of the consuming public* is not the product but the producer.'" *Lund*, 163 F.3d at 42 (quoting *Kellogg v. Nat'l Biscuit Co.*, 305 U.S. 111 (1938)) (emphasis added). The opinions of retailers and distributors active in the scented candle field and extremely familiar with Yankee products is hardly evidence of whether the "consuming public" forms the same association.

*Thomas & Betts Corp. v. Panduit Corp.*, 65 F.3d 654, 662 (7th Cir. 1995). In other words, it is advertising that specifically directs a consumer's attention to a particular aspect of the product. To be probative of secondary meaning, the advertising must direct the consumer to those features claimed as trade dress. *Id.* Merely "featuring" the relevant aspect of the product in advertising is no more probative of secondary meaning than are strong sales; again, to provide protection based on extensive advertising would extend trade dress protection to the label (or to the combination claim) without any showing that the consumer associated the dress with the product's source. [cit.] The district court found that Yankee's advertising did not emphasize any particular element of its trade dress, and thus could not be probative of secondary meaning. We agree.

We also do not find Yankee's evidence of intentional copying probative of secondary meaning. First, to the extent Yankee seeks to use such evidence as secondary meaning of its *combination* trade dress, intent plays a particularly minor role in product design/configuration cases. *See, e.g., Duraco*, 40 F.3d at 1453 ("[A]ttempts to copy a product configuration [may] not be probative [because] the copier may very well be exploiting a particularly desirable feature, rather than seeking to confuse consumers as to the source of the product."). Given the highly functional nature of certain elements of Yankee's claimed combination trade dress, *see Yankee I*, 99 F. Supp. 2d at 151-52, the concern that protection could prevent healthy competition in the scented candle field weighs heavily in this case.

The testimony that Bridgewater designers were, at times, told to make the labels look more like Yankee's is more troubling. *See Blau Plumbing, Inc. v. S.O.S. Fix-it, Inc.*, 781 F.2d 604, 611 (7th Cir. 1986) (defendant's belief that trade dress has acquired secondary meaning provides some evidence that it actually has acquired secondary meaning). However, the relevant intent is not just the intent to copy, but to "pass off" one's goods as those of another. *Id.* Given that Bridgewater prominently displayed its trade name on its candles, we do not think that the evidence of copying was sufficiently probative of secondary meaning.

In sum, Yankee has not introduced any of the direct evidence — surveys or consumer testimony — traditionally used to establish secondary meaning. Although it has introduced some of the circumstantial evidence often used to support such a finding, the lack of any evidence that actual consumers associated the claimed trade dress with Yankee, as well as the lack of evidence as to confusion on the part of actual consumers, renders this circumstantial evidence insufficient for a reasonable juror to find that the trade dress had acquired a secondary meaning. Yankee has not made the vigorous evidentiary showing required by this Court. The grant of summary judgment on Yankee's Lanham Act claim is affirmed.

## NOTES AND QUESTIONS

1. *"Claiming" trade dress.* As the *Yankee Candle* court notes, courts have in recent years become more stringent in requiring careful (and consistent) definition of what plaintiffs claim as trade dress. *See New Colt Holding v. RJG Holdings of Florida*, 312 F. Supp. 2d 195, 206 n.6 (D. Conn. 2004) (noting consequences of loose drafting of the trade dress description); *General Motors Corp. v. Lanard Toys*,

*Inc.*, 80 U.S.P.Q.2d 1608, 1614 (6th Cir. 2006) (finding General Motors' identification of the trade dress of its HUMMER vehicles as "the exterior appearance and styling of the vehicle design which includes the grille, slanted and raised hood, split windshield, rectangular doors, squared edges etc." as sufficient); *Maharishi Hardy Blechman Ltd. v. Abercrombie & Fitch Co.*, 292 F. Supp. 2d 535, 542 (S.D.N.Y. 2003) (describing requirements as "specificity and consistency"). Most trade dress cases are litigated under Section 43(a), so there is rarely a registration record to assist; most definitions are crafted in litigation. Although the court concludes, *see* n.9, that the definition is sufficiently consistent to be evaluated, the closeness of that question does still affect the court's analysis. In what way? For a discussion of the interests served by requiring specificity in trade dress definition, *see New Colt*, 312 F. Supp. 2d at 203-204 (citing *Yurman Design, Inc. v. PAJ, Inc.*, 262 F.3d 101, 117 (2d Cir. 2001)). Are there any dangers in requiring that a complaint provide a written description of the claimed trade dress, rather than relying on visual representation? *See id.*

    **2. Written descriptions of trade dress: an example.** If you were counsel for Procter & Gamble, the manufacturer of BOUNTY kitchen towels, how would you define the trade dress of your client's product as shown below? (For one attempt, see *Procter & Gamble v. McLane Company*, Case No. 3:05CV 0427 (WHR) S.D. Ohio Feb. 23, 2006, available at www.shapeblog.com/2006/03/definition_of_confusingly_simi.html).

    **3. Timing of definition of trade dress.** If the trade dress is defined during the course of the litigation, when precisely must the plaintiff offer a definition? *Cf. Maharishi Hardy Blechman Ltd. v. Abercrombie & Fitch Co.*, 292 F. Supp. 2d 535, 545-546 (S.D.N.Y. 2003). What advantages does this "claiming practice" offer over regimes such as design patent, where the patentee must include in its application drawings that effectively define the property right? Are there ways of controlling any potential for abuse that "late claiming" opens up? (You might consider by way of comparison how a design patentee might seek to expand the scope of the property right it defined during the application process.) The claiming problem arises in many aspects of intellectual property law. *See* Jeanne Fromer, *Claiming Intellectual Property*, 76 U. CHI. L. REV. 719 (2009). It has been a particular focus of attention in modern utility patent law.

  4. ***Family trade dress.*** Courts are becoming particularly strict in their recognition of what is called "family trade dress," meaning a line of products with identical source-identifying design features. *See Landscape Forms, Inc. v. Columbia Cascade Co.*, 113 F.3d 373, 380 (2d Cir. 1997) (noting enhanced concern for competition where protection is sought for line of products); *Regal Jewelry Co. v. Kingsbridge Int'l Inc.*, 47 U.S.P.Q.2d 1074, 1081 (S.D.N.Y. 1998) (discussing difficulties of establishing family trade dress). Indeed, in *Rose Art Indus. v. Swanson*, 235 F.3d 165 (3d Cir. 2000), the Court of Appeals for the Third Circuit held that when the plaintiff in a trade dress action seeks protection under the Lanham Act for a series or line of products or packaging:

> [W]e will require [a] more stringent test before the nonfunctionality/distinctiveness/likelihood of confusion test is applied. A plaintiff, seeking protection for a series or line of products, must first demonstrate that the series or line has a recognizable and consistent overall look. Only after the plaintiff has established the existence of recognizable trade dress for the line or series of products should the trial court determine whether the trade dress is distinctive, whether the trade dress is nonfunctional, and whether the defendant's use of plaintiff's trade dress is likely to cause consumer confusion.

What is the purpose of this additional threshold requirement? What is a "consistent overall look"? How many products should be considered in determining whether such a look exists?

  5. ***Strategic definition of trade dress.*** Why might a plaintiff seek to define its trade dress broadly? What would be the advantages of a plaintiff defining its trade dress more narrowly? What policy concerns should guide a court assessing a claimed mark defined at a high stage of abstraction? In *Dyson Ltd. v. Registrar of Trade Marks*, Case C-321/03, [2007] E.T.M.R. 34 (ECJ 2007), the claimant was the manufacturer of a bagless vacuum cleaner in which dust is collected in a transparent container. It sought to register as a trademark in the United Kingdom "a transparent bin or collection chamber forming part of the external surface of a vacuum cleaner as shown in the representation [attached to the application]" for vacuum cleaners. The European Court of Justice upheld the refusal of the U.K. authorities to register the mark. The crux of the Court's concern was that Dyson did not seek to "obtain registration of a trade mark in one or more particular shapes of transparent collecting bin — the shapes represented graphically on the application form being only examples of such a bin — but rather to obtain registration of a trade mark in the bin itself." *See id.* at ¶20. The representations accompanying the application were merely examples of the form that the design could take. Stated differently, the Court was concerned that the registration sought to protect all "conceivable shapes of a transparent collecting bin forming part of the external surface of a vacuum cleaner" and that this was "an abuse of trade mark law in order to obtain an unfair competitive advantage". Doctrinally, under EU law, the Court held that the mark for which registration was sought was a "concept" that could be conceived only in the mind rather than a "sign . . . that is capable of being perceived visually," as required by Article 2 of the EU Trade Mark Directive. Do

you agree with the decision to refuse registration of such a mark, as a policy matter? If you do agree, does the case law just discussed provide the means for reaching that result? What does the reasoning of the Court of Justice mean for the protection of color per se as a mark? If you were counsel for Dyson, how might you reframe your application to ensure it passes muster, and what scope of protection do you think you would receive? (Assume that the public clearly associate the transparent bin with Dyson, as in fact they did.). *Cf. Maker's Mark Distillery, Inc. v. Diageo North. Am.*, 89 U.S.P.Q.2d (BNA) 1228 (W.D. Ky. 2008) (claimant relying on a registered trademark in the "wax-like coating covering the cap of the bottle and trickling down the neck of the bottle in a free-form irregular pattern" for alcoholic drinks, but stressing that it was not claiming a trademark in the general use of wax seals). How does the approach of the Court of Justice to subject matter fit with the approach taken by the Supreme Court in *Qualitex*? Is the distinction between "sign" and "concept" an appropriate line for trademark law to draw? *See Philips Elec. BV v. Remington Consumer Prods.* [1998] R.P.C. 283 (Ch. D. 1997) (Eng.).

6. ***Determining distinctiveness.*** In making its case for inherent distinctiveness, Yankee Candle emphasized the "arbitrary choices" that it made in designing its label and the fact that numerous alternative design possibilities existed. The court seemed unimpressed. Should these considerations be relevant? As regards its secondary meaning arguments, the court noted that "secondary meaning faces a higher threshold in a product design/configuration case." This proposition has support in modern case law. Why might this be so? *See* Ingrida Karins Berzins, *Comment: The Emerging Circuit Split over Secondary Meaning in Trade Dress Law*, 152 U. PA. L. REV. 1661 (2004) (suggesting that there is variation among the circuits regarding how strictly to apply the secondary meaning requirement, and identifying *Yankee Candle* as a case in which the court applied the requirement strictly). Some courts still place great weight on intentional copying, even in product design cases where alternative explanations of copying are even more likely. *See, e.g., Leviton Mfg. Co. v. Universal Sec. Instruments, Inc.*, 304 F. Supp. 2d 726 (D. Md. 2004) (allowing claim of secondary meaning of design of electrical ground fault interrupting system to go to trial based on evidence of intentional direct copying). Despite this, one commentator has recently noted that post–*Wal-Mart*, "[i]n all the cases where secondary meaning [of a design] was found, the product designs in question had been in use for years, if not decades." Berzins, *supra*, at 1673; *see also In re Howard Leight Indus.*, 80 U.S.P.Q.2d 1507 (T.T.A.B. 2006) (apparently unreceptive to claims of secondary meaning of product designs based largely on alleged long-term use). If this assessment is correct, has the *Wal-Mart* opinion had the effect that the Supreme Court sought?

7. ***Private labeling and secondary meaning.*** Should it matter to an analysis of the claimed secondary meaning in a product design that the producer has permitted private labeling of its product? *See Leviton Mfg. Co. v. Universal Sec. Instruments, Inc.*, 304 F. Supp. 2d 725, 736 n.7 (D. Md. 2004). *Cf. Malaco Leaf AB v. Promotion in Motion, Inc.*, 287 F. Supp. 2d 355, 370 (S.D.N.Y. 2003) (40 percent of product sold in packaging other than that for which the plaintiff claimed trade dress).

# CHAPTER 3
# *FUNCTIONALITY*

In this chapter, we cover the basic purposes of the functionality doctrine, its scope of application, and the different tests by which courts and the PTO determine whether a claimed trademark is functional. Along with distinctiveness, (non)functionality is one of the prerequisites to the establishment of trademark rights under current U.S. law. However, whereas distinctiveness is a requirement applicable to all trademarks, functionality in practice is of significance primarily in trade dress cases; as a result, it is (arguably) a trade dress–specific doctrine that is less influenced by general principles of trademark law. As you read the materials, you should consider whether this statement is fully accurate.

## A. AN INTRODUCTION TO THE CONCEPT OF FUNCTIONALITY

As trademark rights expanded to encompass new subject matter in general, and product designs or configurations in particular, courts (and the PTO) became concerned that trademark protection for this new subject matter might have substantial adverse consequences. As we have seen throughout this book, a particular concern is derived from overlapping intellectual property protection for designs—in particular, a concern that if designers can secure trademark protection for designs, they will be able to circumvent the limitations of utility patent law and copyright law in some instances. The functionality doctrine has been a central device (albeit not the exclusive device) for preventing or mitigating the adverse consequences that may arise from extending trademark protection to product designs. Many discussions of functionality start with the famous "Shredded Wheat" case, which at first glance has relatively little to say about functionality *doctrine*, but a good deal to say about the *concerns* underlying that doctrine.

## Kellogg Co. v. National Biscuit Co.
### 305 U.S. 111 (1938)

Mr. Justice Brandeis delivered the opinion of the Court:

This suit was brought in the federal court for Delaware by National Biscuit Company against Kellogg Company to enjoin alleged unfair competition by the manufacture and sale of the breakfast food commonly known as shredded wheat. The competition was alleged to be unfair mainly because Kellogg Company uses, like the plaintiff, the name shredded wheat and, like the plaintiff, produces its biscuit in pillow-shaped form.

Shredded wheat is a product composed of whole wheat which has been boiled, partially dried, then drawn or pressed out into thin shreds and baked. The shredded wheat biscuit generally known is pillow-shaped in form. It was introduced in 1893 by Henry D. Perky, of Colorado; and he was connected until his death in 1908 with companies formed to make and market the article. Commercial success was not attained until the Natural Food Company built, in 1901, a large factory at Niagara Falls, New York. In 1908, its corporate name was changed to "The Shredded Wheat Company"; and in 1930 its business and goodwill were acquired by National Biscuit Company.

Kellogg Company has been in the business of manufacturing breakfast food cereals since its organization in 1905. [Kellogg began manufacturing a product "whose form was somewhat like the product in question, but whose manufacture was different, the wheat being reduced to a dough before being pressed into shreds." Eventually, National Biscuit sued.]

In 1935, the District Court dismissed the bill. It found that the name "Shredded Wheat" is a term describing alike the product of the plaintiff and of the defendant; and that no passing off or deception had been shown. It held that upon the expiration of the Perky patent No. 548,086 issued October 15, 1895, the name of the patented article passed into the public domain. [The Court of Appeals affirmed, then vacated and reversed upon rehearing. The Court of Appeals directed the District Court to enjoin Kellogg from "the use of the name 'Shredded Wheat' as its trade-name" and from "advertising or offering for sale its product in the form and shape of plaintiff's biscuit." Kellogg nevertheless persisted in selling its product, claiming that the injunction only prevented it from selling a product called "Shredded Wheat," in the form of plaintiff's product, accompanied by a graphic of a dish with biscuits in it. National Biscuit petitioned to "clarify" the injunction, and prevailed in the lower courts. The Supreme Court ultimately granted certiorari.]

The plaintiff concedes that it does not possess the exclusive right to make shredded wheat. But it claims the exclusive right to the trade name "Shredded Wheat" and the exclusive right to make shredded wheat biscuits pillow-shaped. It charges that the defendant, by using the name and shape, and otherwise, is passing off, or enabling others to pass off, Kellogg goods for those of the plaintiff. Kellogg Company denies that the plaintiff is entitled to the exclusive use of the name or of the pillow-shape; denies any passing off; asserts that it has used every reasonable effort to distinguish its produce from that of the plaintiff; and contends that in honestly competing for a part of the market for shredded wheat it is exercising the common right freely to manufacture and sell an article of commerce unprotected by patent.

First. The plaintiff has no exclusive right to the use of the term "Shredded Wheat" as a trade name. For that is the generic term of the article, which describes it with a fair degree of accuracy; and is the term by which the biscuit in pillow-shaped form is generally known by the public. Since the term is generic, the original maker of the product acquired no exclusive right to use it. As Kellogg Company had the right to make the article, it had, also, the right to use the term by which the public knows it. [cit.] Ever since 1894 the article has been known to the public as shredded wheat. For many years, there was no attempt to use the term "Shredded Wheat" as a trade-mark. . . .

. . .

Moreover, the name "Shredded Wheat," as well as the product, the process and the machinery employed in making it, has been dedicated to the public. The basic patent for the product and for the process of making it, and many other patents for special machinery to be used in making the article, issued to Perky. In those patents the term "shredded" is repeatedly used as descriptive of the product. The basic patent expired October 15, 1912; the others soon after. Since during the life of the patents "Shredded Wheat" was the general designation of the patented product, there passed to the public upon the expiration of the patent, not only the right to make the article as it was made during the patent period, but also the right to apply thereto the name by which it had become known. As was said in *Singer Mfg. Co. v. June Mfg. Co.*, 163 U.S. 169, 185:

> It equally follows from the cessation of the monopoly and the falling of the patented device into the domain of things public that along with the public ownership of the device there must also necessarily pass to the public the generic designation of the thing which has arisen during the monopoly. . . .
>
> To say otherwise would be to hold that, although the public had acquired the device covered by the patent, yet the owner of the patent or the manufacturer of the patented thing had retained the designated name which was essentially necessary to vest the public with the full enjoyment of that which had become theirs by the disappearance of the monopoly.

It is contended that the plaintiff has the exclusive right to the name "Shredded Wheat," because those words acquired the "secondary meaning" of shredded wheat made at Niagara Falls by the plaintiff's predecessor. There is no basis here for applying the doctrine of secondary meaning. The evidence shows only that due to the long period in which the plaintiff or its predecessor was the only manufacturer of the product, many people have come to associate the product, and as a consequence the name by which the product is generally known, with the plaintiff's factory at Niagara Falls. But to establish a trade name in the term "shredded wheat" the plaintiff must show more than a subordinate meaning which applies to it. It must show that the primary significance of the term in the minds of the consuming public is not the product but the producer. This it has not done. The showing which it has made does not entitle it to the exclusive use of the term shredded wheat but merely entitles it to require that the defendant use reasonable care to inform the public of the source of its product.

. . .

Second. The plaintiff has not the exclusive right to sell shredded wheat in the form of a pillow-shaped biscuit—the form in which the article became known to the public. That is the form in which shredded wheat was made under the basic patent. The patented machines used were designed to produce only the pillow-shaped biscuits. And a design patent was taken out to cover the pillow-shaped form.[4] Hence, upon expiration of the patents the form, as well as the name, was dedicated to the public. As was said [in *Singer*, 163 U.S. at 185]: "It is self-evident that on the expiration of a patent the monopoly granted by it ceases to exist, and the right to make the thing formerly covered by the patent becomes public property. It is upon this condition that the patent is granted. It follows, as a matter of course, that on the termination of the patent there passes to the public the right to make the machine in the form in which it was constructed during the patent. We may therefore dismiss without further comment the complaint as to the form in which the defendant made his machines."

Where an article may be manufactured by all, a particular manufacturer can no more assert exclusive rights in a form in which the public has become accustomed to see the article and which, in the minds of the public, is primarily associated with the article rather than a particular producer, than it can in the case of a name with similar connections in the public mind. Kellogg Company was free to use the pillow-shaped form, subject only to the obligation to identify its product lest it be mistaken for that of the plaintiff.

Third. The question remains whether Kellogg Company in exercising its right to use the name "Shredded Wheat" and the pillow-shaped biscuit, is doing so fairly. Fairness requires that it be done in a manner which reasonably distinguishes its product from that of plaintiff.

Each company sells its biscuits only in cartons. The standard Kellogg carton contains fifteen biscuits; the plaintiff's twelve. The Kellogg cartons are distinctive. They do not resemble those used by the plaintiff either in size, form, or color. And the difference in the labels is striking. The Kellogg cartons bear in bold script the names "Kellogg's Whole Wheat Biscuit" or "Kellogg's Shredded Whole Wheat Biscuit" so sized and spaced as to strike the eye as being a Kellogg product. It is true that on some of its cartons it had a picture of two shredded wheat biscuits in a bowl of milk which was quite similar to one of the plaintiff's registered trade-marks. But the name Kellogg was so prominent on all of the defendant's cartons as to minimize the possibility of confusion.

Some hotels, restaurants, and lunchrooms serve biscuits not in cartons, and guests so served may conceivably suppose that a Kellogg biscuit served is one of the plaintiff's make. But no person familar [sic] with plaintiff's product would be misled. The Kellogg biscuit is about two-thirds the size of plaintiff's; and differs from it in appearance. Moreover, the field in which deception could be practiced is negligibly small. Only 2½ per cent of the Kellogg biscuits are sold to hotels, restaurants and lunchrooms. Of those so sold 98 per cent are sold in individual cartons containing two biscuits. These cartons are distinctive and bear prominently the Kellogg name. To put upon the individual

---

4. The design patent would have expired by limitations in 1909. In 1908 it was declared invalid by a district judge on the ground that the design had been in public use for more than two years prior to the application for the patent and theretofore had already been dedicated to the public. [cit.]

biscuit some mark which would identify it as the Kellogg product is not commercially possible. Relatively few biscuits will be removed from the individual cartons before they reach the consumer. The obligation resting upon Kellogg Company is not to insure that every purchaser will know it to be the maker but to use every reasonable means to prevent confusion.

It is urged that all possibility of deception or confusion would be removed if Kellogg Company should refrain from using the name "Shredded Wheat" and adopt some form other than the pillow-shape. But the name and form are integral parts of the goodwill of the article. To share fully in the goodwill, it must use the name and the pillow-shape. And in the goodwill Kellogg Company is as free to share as the plaintiff. [cit.] Moreover, the pillow-shape must be used for another reason. The evidence is persuasive that this form is functional — that the cost of the biscuit would be increased and its high quality lessened if some other form were substituted for the pillow-shape.

Kellogg Company is undoubtedly sharing in the goodwill of the article known as "Shredded Wheat"; and thus is sharing in a market which was created by the skill and judgment of plaintiff's predecessor and has been widely extended by vast expenditures in advertising persistently made. But that is not unfair. Sharing in the goodwill of an article unprotected by patent or trademark is the exercise of a right possessed by all — and in the free exercise of which the consuming public is deeply interested. There is no evidence of passing off or deception on the part of the Kellogg Company; and it has taken every reasonable precaution to prevent confusion or the practice of deception in the sale of its product.

Decrees reversed with direction to dismiss the bill.

Mr. Justice MCREYNOLDS and Mr. Justice BUTLER are of opinion that the decree of the Circuit Court of Appeals is correct and should be affirmed. To them it seems sufficiently clear that the Kellogg Company is fraudulently seeking to appropriate to itself the benefits of a goodwill built up at great cost by the respondent and its predecessors.

## NOTES AND QUESTIONS

1. **Kellogg *and the modern principles of functionality*.** In *Qualitex Co. v. Jacobson Products Co., Inc.*, 514 U.S. 159 (1995), the U.S. Supreme Court held that color per se could be registered as a trademark under the Lanham Act. In the course of addressing the respondent's argument that color per se could not be registered under the Lanham Act, the Supreme Court considered whether the functionality doctrine was in any way relevant to that issue. In so doing, the Court explained the purpose of the functionality doctrine:

> [T]he functionality doctrine prevents trademark law, which seeks to promote competition by protecting a firm's reputation, from instead inhibiting legitimate competition by allowing a producer to control a useful product feature. It is the province of patent law, not trademark law, to encourage invention by granting inventors a monopoly over new product designs or functions for a limited time, 35 U.S.C. §§154, 173, after which competitors are free to use the innovation. If a product's functional features could be used as trademarks,

however, a monopoly over such features could be obtained without regard to whether they qualify as patents and could be extended forever (because trademarks may be renewed in perpetuity). *See Kellogg Co. v. National Biscuit Co.*, 305 U.S. 111, 119-120 (1938) (Brandeis, J.). . . . Functionality doctrine therefore would require, to take an imaginary example, that even if customers have come to identify the special illumination-enhancing shape of a new patented light bulb with a particular manufacturer, the manufacturer may not use that shape as a trademark, for doing so, after the patent had expired, would impede competition — not by protecting the reputation of the original bulb maker, but by frustrating competitors' legitimate efforts to produce an equivalent illumination-enhancing bulb. *See, e.g., Kellogg Co., supra*, 305 U.S. at 119-120 (trademark law cannot be used to extend monopoly over "pillow" shape of shredded wheat biscuit after the patent for that shape had expired).

Identify precisely the concern(s) articulated by the Court in *Kellogg*, and reiterated in *Qualitex*. Is there more than one such concern? On what grounds would it be improper for trademark law to be used to extend a monopoly over the shape of the light bulb after its patent had expired? What if the manufacturer had not obtained a patent on that shape? What dangers does the Court see resulting from extensive trade dress protection?

2. ***Points of controversy in modern functionality jurisprudence.*** Through the years, a significant group of trademark law scholars have addressed the question of functionality. The single point upon which these scholars agree is that neither courts nor jurists have successfully formulated a consistent or workable approach to functionality. Disagreement centers on a variety of issues:

- The *rationales* underlying the functionality doctrine;
- The *test* for determining when a claimed mark is functional;
- The *scope* of the doctrine (in particular, whether it extends to aesthetic features);
- The *evidence* relevant to proof of functionality; and
- Whether existing functionality doctrine is *sufficient to effectuate* the rationales that undergird it.

Bear these points of controversy in mind as we review the cases in this chapter.

## B. THE SCOPE OF THE FUNCTIONALITY DOCTRINE

### 1. UTILITARIAN FEATURES

#### In Re Morton-Norwich Products, Inc.
671 F.2d 1332 (C.C.P.A. 1982)

Rich, Judge:

This appeal is from the ex parte decision of the United States Patent and Trademark Office (PTO) Trademark Trial and Appeal Board (Board), 209 USPQ 437 (TTAB 1980), in application serial No. 123,548, filed April 21, 1977, sustaining the examiner's refusal to register appellant's container configuration on the principal register. We reverse the holding on "functionality" and remand for a determination of distinctiveness.

## Background

Appellant's application seeks to register the following container configuration as a trademark for spray starch, soil and stain removers, spray cleaners for household use, liquid household cleaners and general grease removers, and insecticides:

Appellant owns U.S. Design Patent 238,655, issued Feb. 3, 1976, on the above configuration, and U.S. Patent 3,749,290, issued July 31, 1973, directed to the mechanism in the spray top.

The above-named goods constitute a family of products which appellant sells under the word-marks FANTASTIK, GLASS PLUS, SPRAY 'N WASH, GREASE RELIEF, WOOD PLUS, and MIRAKILL. Each of these items is marketed in a container of the same configuration but appellant varies the color of the body of the container according to the product. Appellant manufactures its own containers and stated in its application (amendment of April 25, 1979) that:

> Since such first use (March 31, 1974) the applicant has enjoyed substantially exclusive and continuous use of the trademark (i.e., the container) which has become distinctive of the applicant's goods in commerce.

The PTO Trademark Attorney (examiner), through a series of four office actions, maintained an unshakable position that the design sought to be registered as a trademark is not distinctive, that there is no evidence that it has become distinctive or has acquired a secondary meaning, that it is "merely functional," "essentially utilitarian," and non-arbitrary, wherefore it cannot function as a trademark. In the second action she requested applicant to "amplify the description of the mark with such particularity that *any portion* of the alleged mark considered to be non functional (sic) is incorporated in the description." (Emphasis ours.) She said, "The Examiner sees none." Having already furnished two affidavits to the effect that consumers spontaneously associate the package design with appellant's products, which had been sold in the container to the number of 132,502,000 by 1978, appellant responded to the examiner's request by pointing out, in effect, that it is the overall configuration of the container rather than any particular feature of it which is distinctive and that it was intentionally designed to be so, supplying several pieces of evidence showing several other containers of different appearance which perform the same functions. Appellant also produced the results of a survey conducted by an independent market research firm which had been made in response to the examiner's demand for evidence of distinctiveness. The examiner dismissed all of the evidence as "not persuasive" and commented that there had "still not been one iota of evidence offered that the subject matter of this application has been promoted as a trademark," which she seemed to consider a necessary element of proof. She adhered to her view that the design "is no more than a non-distinctive purely functional container for the goods plus a purely functional spray trigger controlled closure ... essentially utilitarian and non-arbitrary. . . ."

Appellant responded to the final rejection with a simultaneously filed notice of appeal to the board and a request for reconsideration, submitting more exhibits in support of its position that its container design was not "purely functional." The examiner held fast to all of her views and forwarded the appeal, repeating the substance of her rejections in her Answer to appellant's appeal brief. An oral hearing was held before the board.

## Board Opinion

The board, citing three cases, stated it to be "well-settled" that the configuration of a container "may be registrable for the particular contents thereof if the shape is non-functional in character, and is, in fact, inherently distinctive, or has acquired secondary meaning as an indication of origin for such goods." In discussing the "utilitarian nature" of the alleged trademark, the board took note of photographs of appellant's containers for FANTASTIK spray cleaner and GREASE RELIEF degreaser, the labels of which bore the words, respectively, "adjustable easy sprayer" and "NEW! Trigger Control Top," commenting that "the advertising pertaining to applicant's goods promotes the word marks of the various products and the desirable functional features of the containers."

[In light of the above, and after detailed review of appellant's survey evidence without any specific comment on it, the board concluded that "the container for applicant's products, the configuration of which it seeks to register, . . . is [functional], and therefore unregistrable, despite any de facto secondary meaning which applicant's survey and other evidence of record might indicate." The board noted that "not every word or configuration that has a de facto secondary meaning is protected as a trademark."]

## Issues

The parties do not see the issues in the same light. Appellant and the solicitor agree that the primary issue before us is whether the subject matter sought to be registered—the configuration of the container—is "functional."

Appellant states a second issue to be whether the configuration has the capacity to and does distinguish its goods in the marketplace from the goods of others.

The solicitor contends that it would be "premature" for us to decide the second issue if we disagree with the PTO on the first issue and have to reach it, and that we should, in that event, remand the case so the board can "consider" it. Whether to remand is, therefore, an issue.

## Opinion

As would be expected, the arguments made in this court are, except for the remand question, essentially the same as they were below. The question is not new and in various forms we have been over the ground before: is the design sought to be registered "functional"? There is a plethora of case law on this subject and it becomes a question of which precedents to follow here—and why. In our view, it would be useful to review the development of the principles which we must apply in order to better understand them. In doing so, it should be borne in mind that this is not a "configuration of *goods*" case but a "configuration of the *container* for the goods" case. . . .

A trademark is defined as "any word, name, symbol, or device or any combination thereof adopted and used by a manufacturer or merchant to *identify his goods* and distinguish them from those manufactured or sold by others" (emphasis ours). 15 U.S.C. §1127 (1976). Thus, it was long the rule that a trademark must be something other than, and separate from, the merchandise to which it is applied. *Davis v. Davis,* 27 F. 490, 492 (D. Mass. 1886). [cit.]

Aside from the trademark/product "separateness" rationale for not recognizing the bare design of an article or its container as a trademark, it was theorized that all such designs would soon be appropriated, leaving nothing for use by would-be competitors. One court, for example, feared that "[t]he forms and materials of packages to contain articles of merchandise . . . would be rapidly taken up and appropriated by dealers, until some one, bolder than the others, might go to the very root of things, and claim for his goods the primitive brown paper and tow string, as a peculiar property." *Harrington v. Libby,* 11 F. Cas. 605, 606 (C.C.S.D.N.Y 1877) (No. 6,107). Accord, *Diamond Match Co. v. Saginaw Match Co.,* 142 F. 727, 729-30 (6th Cir. 1906).

This limitation of permissible trademark subject matter later gave way to assertions that one or more features of a product or package design could legally function as a trademark. [cit.] It was eventually held that the entire design of an article (or its container) could, without other means of identification, function to identify the source of the article and be protected as a trademark. *E.g., In re Minnesota Mining and Manufacturing Co.,* 51 CCPA 1546, 1547-48, 335 F.2d 836, 837 (1964).

That protection was limited, however, to those designs of articles and containers, or features thereof, which were "nonfunctional." [cit.] This requirement of "nonfunctionality" is not mandated by statute, but "is deduced entirely from court decisions." *In re Mogen David Wine Corp.,* 51 CCPA 1260, 1269, 328 F.2d 925, 932 (1964) (Rich, J., concurring). It has as its genesis the judicial theory that there exists a fundamental right to compete through imitation of a competitor's product, which right can only be temporarily denied by the patent or copyright laws:

> If one manufacturer should make an advance in effectiveness of operation, or in simplicity of form, or in utility of color; and if that advance did not entitle him to a monopoly by means of a machine or process or a product or a design patent; and if by means of unfair trade suits he could shut out other manufacturers who plainly intended to share in the benefits of unpatented utilities . . . he would be given gratuitously a monopoly more effective than that of the unobtainable patent in the ratio of eternity to seventeen years.

[*Pope Automatic Merchandising Co. v. McCrum-Howell Co.*, 191 F. 979, 981-82 (7th Cir. 1911).]

An exception to the right to copy exists, however, where the product or package design under consideration is "nonfunctional" and serves to identify its manufacturer or seller, and the exception exists even though the design is not temporarily protectable through acquisition of patent or copyright. Thus, when a design is "nonfunctional," the right to compete through imitation gives way, presumably upon balance of that right with the originator's right to prevent others from infringing upon an established symbol of trade identification.

This preliminary discussion leads to the heart of the matter—how do we define the concept of "functionality," and what role does the above balancing of interests play in that definitional process?

## I. Functionality Defined

Many courts speak of the protectability as trademarks of product and package configurations in terms of whether a particular design is "functional" or "nonfunctional." Without proper definition, however, such a distinction is useless for determining whether such design is registrable or protectable as a trademark, for the label "functional" has dual significance. It has been used, on the one hand, in lay fashion to indicate "the normal or characteristic action of anything," and, on the other hand, it has been used to denote a legal conclusion. *Compare In re Penthouse International Ltd.*, 565 F.2d 679, 681 (CCPA 1977) (If the product configuration "has a non-trademark function, the inquiry is not at an end; possession of a function and of a capability of indicating origin are not in every case mutually exclusive."), *with In re Mogen David Wine Corp.*, 51 CCPA *supra* at 1270, 328 F.2d at 933 (Rich, J., concurring) ("The Restatement appears to use the terms 'functional' and 'nonfunctional' as labels to denote the legal consequence: if the former, the public may copy; and if the latter, it may not. This is the way the 'law' has been but it is not of much help in deciding cases.").

Accordingly, it has been noted that one of the "distinct questions" involved in "functionality" reasoning is, "In what way is (the) subject matter functional or utilitarian, factually or legally?" *In re Honeywell, Inc.*, 497 F.2d 1344, 1350 (CCPA 1974) (Rich, J., concurring). This definitional division . . . leads to the resolution that if the designation "functional" is to be utilized to denote the *legal* consequence, we must speak in terms of de facto functionality and de jure functionality, the former being the use of "functional" in the lay sense, indicating that although the design of a product, a container, or a feature of either is directed to performance of a function, it *may* be legally recognized as an indication of source. De jure functionality, of course, would be used to indicate the opposite—such a design may not be protected as a trademark.

This is only the beginning, however, for further definition is required to explain *how* a determination of whether a design is de jure functional is to be approached. We start with an inquiry into "utility."

### A. "Functional" Means "Utilitarian"[1]

From the earliest cases, "functionality" has been expressed in terms of "utility." In 1930, this court stated it to be "well settled that the configuration of *an article having utility* is not the subject of trade-mark protection." (Emphasis ours.) *In re Dennison Mfg. Co.*, 39 F.2d 720, 721 (1930) (Arbitrary urn or vase-like shape of reinforcing patch on a tag.). [cit.] This broad statement of the "law," that the design of an article "having utility" cannot be a trademark, is incorrect and inconsistent with later pronouncements.

We wish to make it clear . . . that a discussion of "functionality" is *always* in reference to the design of the thing under consideration (in the sense of its *appearance*) and *not* the thing itself. One court, for example, paraphrasing Gertrude Stein, commented that "a dish is a dish is a dish." *Hygienic Specialties Co. v. H. G. Salzman, Inc.*, 302 F.2d 614, 621 (2d Cir. 1962). No doubt, by definition, a dish always functions as a dish and has its utility, but it is the appearance of the dish which is important in a case such as this, as will become clear.

Assuming the *Dennison* court intended that its statement reference an article whose *configuration* "has utility," its statement is still too broad. Under that reasoning, the design of a particular article would be protectable as a trademark only where the design was useless, that is, wholly unrelated to the function of the article. . . .

Most designs, however, result in the production of articles, containers, or features thereof which are indeed utilitarian, and examination into the possibility of trademark protection is not to the mere *existence* of utility, but to the *degree* of design utility. . . .

Thus, it is the "utilitarian" *design* of a "utilitarian" *object* with which we are concerned, and the manner of use of the term "utilitarian" must be examined at each occurrence. The latter occurrence is, of course, consistent with the lay meaning of the term. But the former is being used to denote a *legal consequence* (it being synonymous with "functional"), and it therefore requires further explication.

---

1. It is well known that the law of "functionality" has been applied in both a "utilitarian" sense and in terms of "aesthetics." *See e.g., Vuitton et Fils S.A. v. J. Young Enterprises, Inc.*, 644 F.2d 769 (9th Cir. 1981); *International Order of Job's Daughters v. Lindeburg and Co.*, 633 F.2d 912 (9th Cir. 1980). Recognition of this provides an explanation for the statement that "the term 'functional' is not to be treated as synonymous with the literal significance of the term 'utilitarian.'" *J.C. Penney Co. v. H.D. Lee Mercantile Co.*, 120 F.2d 949, 954 (8th Cir. 1941). It will be so treated, however, where the issue is one of "utilitarian functionality" and not "aesthetic functionality." The PTO does not argue in this case that appellant's container configuration is aesthetically functional, notwithstanding appellant's argument that its design was adopted, in part, for aesthetic reasons.

B. "Utilitarian" Means "Superior in Function (De Facto) or Economy of Manufacture," Which "Superiority" Is Determined in Light of Competitive Necessity to Copy

Some courts have stated this proposition in the negative. In *American-Marietta Co. v. Krigsman*, 275 F.2d 287, 289 (2d Cir. 1960), the court stated that "those features of the original goods that are not in any way essential to their use" may be termed "nonfunctional." But what does this statement mean? In the case at bar, for example, we cannot say that it means that the subject *design* is "functional" merely because a hollow body, a handhold, and a pump sprayer are "essential to its use." What this phrase must mean is not that the generic *parts* of the article or package are essential, but, as noted above, that the particular *design* of the whole assembly of those parts must be essential. This, of course, leaves us to define "essential to its use," which is also the starting place for those courts which have set forth in positive fashion the reasons they believe that some product or package designs are not protectable as trademarks and thus not registrable.

In *Luminous Unit Co. v. Williamson*, 241 F. 265 (N.D. Ill. 1917), the court noted that "the owner of a fixture, machine, or device, patented or unpatented, who has obtained a trade in it, may simply exclude others from taking away that trade when they deceive the purchasing public as to the origin of the goods sold by them." *Id.* at 268. The court went on to state an exception to this rule, which is the public right to copy those "[n]ecessary elements of mechanical construction, essential to the practical operation of a device, and which cannot be changed without either lessening the efficiency or materially increasing expense." *Id.* at 269. . . . Another court framed the issue this way: Is the subject matter "made in the form it must be made if it is to accomplish its purpose"? *Marvel Co. v. Tullar Co.*, 125 F. 829, 830 (S.D.N.Y 1903).

Thus, it is clear that courts in the past have considered the public policy involved in this area of the law as, not the *right* to slavishly copy articles which are not protected by patent or copyright, but the *need* to copy those articles, which is more properly termed the right to compete *effectively*. Even the earliest cases, which discussed protectability in terms of exhaustion of possible packaging forms, recognized that the real issue was whether "the effect would be to gradually throttle trade." *Harrington v. Libby, supra* at 606.

More recent cases also discuss "functionality" in light of competition. One court noted that the "question in each case is whether protection against imitation will hinder the competitor in competition." *Truck Equipment Service Co. v. Fruehauf Corp.*, 536 F.2d 1210, 1218 (8th Cir. 1976). Another court, upon suit for trademark infringement (the alleged trademark being plaintiff's building design), stated that "enjoining others from using the building design (would not) inhibit competition in any way." *Fotomat Corp. v. Cochran*, 437 F. Supp. 1231, 1235 (D. Kan. 1977). This court has also referenced "hindrance of competition" in a number of the "functionality" cases which have been argued before it. [cit.] . . .

Given, then, that we must strike a balance between the "right to copy" and the right to protect one's method of trade identification, [cit.], what weights do we set upon each side of the scale? That is, given that "functionality" is a question of fact, *Vuitton et Fils S.A. v. J. Young Enterprises, Inc.*, 644 F.2d 769,

775 (9th Cir. 1981); *In re Deister Concentrator Co.*, 48 CCPA *supra* at 966, 289 F.2d at 504; [cit.], what facts do we look to in determining whether the "consuming public has an interest in making use of (one's design), superior to (one's) interest in being (its) sole vendor"? *Vaughan Novelty Mfg. Co. v. G. G. Greene Mfg. Corp.*, 202 F.2d 172, 176 (3d Cir.), *cert. denied,* 346 U.S. 820 (1953).

II. Determining "Functionality"

A. In General

Keeping in mind, as shown by the foregoing review, that "functionality" is determined in light of "utility," which is determined in light of "superiority of design," and rests upon the foundation "essential to effective competition," *Ives Laboratories, Inc. v. Darby Drug Co.*, 601 F.2d 631, 643 (2d Cir. 1979), and cases cited *supra,* there exist a number of factors, both positive and negative, which aid in that determination.

Previous opinions of this court have discussed what evidence is useful to demonstrate that a particular design is "superior." In *In re Shenango Ceramics, Inc.*, 53 CCPA 1268, 1273 (1966), the court noted that the existence of an expired utility patent which disclosed the utilitarian advantage of the design sought to be registered as a trademark was evidence that it was "functional." *Accord Mine Safety Appliances Co. v. Storage Battery Co.*, 56 CCPA 863, 864 (1969); *In re Deister Concentrator Co.*, 48 CCPA *supra* at 962; *Daniel v. Electric Hose & Rubber Co.*, 231 F. 827, 833 (3d Cir. 1916); [cit.]. It may also be significant that the originator of the design touts its utilitarian advantages through advertising. *Shenango, supra; Deister, supra; Mine Safety Appliances, supra; In re Pollak Steel Co.*, 50 CCPA 1045, 1046-47 (1963).

Since the effect upon competition "is really the crux of the matter," it is, of course, significant that there are other alternatives available. Nims, *Unfair Competition and Trade-Marks* at 377; compare *Time Mechanisms, Inc. v. Qonaar Corp.*, 422 F. Supp. 905, 913 (D.N.J. 1976) ("the parking meter mechanism can be contained by housings of many different configurations"), *and In re World's Finest Chocolate, Inc.*, 474 F.2d 1012, 1014 (CCPA 1973) ("We think competitors can readily meet the demand for packaged candy bars by use of other packaging styles, and we find no utilitarian advantages flowing from this package design as opposed to others as was found in the rhomboidally-shaped deck involved in *Deister.*"), *and In re Mogen David Wine Corp.*, 51 CCPA *supra* at 1270, 328 F.2d at 933 (Rich, J., concurring) ("Others can meet any real or imagined demand for wine in decanter-type bottles—assuming there is any such thing—without being in the least hampered in competition by inability to copy the Mogen David bottle design."), *and In re Minnesota Mining and Mfg. Co.*, 51 CCPA *supra* at 1551, 335 F.2d at 840 (It was noted to be an undisputed fact of record that the article whose design was sought to be registered "could be formed into almost any shape."), *and Fotomat Corp. v. Cochran,* 437 F. Supp. *supra* at 1235 (The court noted that the design of plaintiff's building functioned "no better than a myriad of other building designs.") with *In re Honeywell, Inc.*, 532 F.2d at 182 (A portion of the board opinion which the court adopted noted that there "are only so many basic shapes in which a thermostat or its cover can be made," but then concluded that "[t]he fact that thermostat covers may be produced in other forms or shapes does not and cannot detract from the functional character of the configuration here involved.").

It is also significant that a particular design results from a comparatively simple or cheap method of manufacturing the article. In *Schwinn Bicycle Co. v. Murray Ohio Mfg. Co.*, 339 F. Supp. 973, 980 (M.D. Tenn. 1971), *aff'd*, 470 F.2d 975 (6th Cir. 1972), the court stated its reason for refusing to recognize the plaintiff's bicycle rim surface design as a trademark:

> The evidence is uncontradicted that the various manufacturers of bicycle rims in the United States consider it commercially necessary to mask, hide or camouflage the roughened and charred appearance resulting from welding the tubular rim sections together. The evidence represented indicates that the only other process used by bicycle rim manufacturers in the United States is the more complex and more expensive process of grinding and polishing.

Accord, *In re Pollak Steel Co.*, 50 CCPA *supra* at 1050, 314 F.2d at 570; *Luminous Unit Co. v. R. Williamson & Co.*, *supra* at 269.

B. The Case at Bar

1. The Evidence of Functionality

We come now to the task of applying to the facts of this case the distilled essence of the body of law on "functionality" above discussed. The question is whether appellant's plastic spray bottle is de jure functional; is it the best or one of a few superior designs available? We hold, on the basis of the evidence before the board, that it is not.

The board thought otherwise but did not state a single supporting reason. In spite of her strong convictions about it, neither did the examiner. Each expressed mere opinions and it is not clear to us what either had in mind in using the terms "functional" and "utilitarian." Of course, the spray bottle is highly useful and performs its intended functions in an admirable way, but that is not enough to render the *design* of the spray bottle—which is all that matters here—functional.

As the examiner appreciated, the spray bottle consists of two major parts, a bottle and a trigger-operated, spray-producing pump mechanism which also serves as a closure. We shall call the latter the spray top. In the first place, a molded plastic bottle can have an infinite variety of forms or designs and still *function* to hold liquid. No one form is *necessary* or appears to be "superior." Many bottles have necks, to be grasped for pouring or holding, and the necks likewise can be in a variety of forms. The PTO has not produced one iota of evidence to show that the shape of appellant's bottle was *required* to be as it is for any de facto functional reason, which might lead to an affirmative determination of de jure functionality. The evidence, consisting of competitor's molded plastic bottles for similar products, demonstrates that the same functions can be performed by a variety of other shapes with no sacrifice of any functional advantage. There is no necessity to copy appellant's trade dress to enjoy any of the functions of a spray-top container.

As to the appearance of the spray top, the evidence of record shows that it too can take a number of diverse forms, all of which are equally suitable as housings for the pump and spray mechanisms. Appellant acquired a patent on the pump mechanism (No. 3,749,290), the drawings of which show it embodied in a structure which bears not the slightest resemblance to the appearance of appellant's spray top. The pictures of the competition's spray bottles further illustrate that no particular housing *design* is necessary to have a pump-type sprayer. Appellant's spray top, seen from the side, is rhomboidal, roughly speaking, a design which bears no relation to the shape of the pump mechanism housed within it and is an arbitrary decoration—no more de jure functional than is the grille of an automobile with respect to its under-the-hood power plant. The evidence shows that even the shapes of pump triggers can and do vary while performing the same function.

What is sought to be registered, however, is no single design feature or component but the overall composite design comprising both bottle and spray top. While that design must be *accommodated* to the functions performed, we see no evidence that it was *dictated* by them and resulted in a functionally or economically superior design of such a container.

Applying the legal principles discussed above, we do not see that allowing appellant to exclude others (upon proof of distinctiveness) from using this trade dress will hinder competition or impinge upon the rights of others to compete effectively in the sale of the goods named in the application, even to the extent of marketing them in *functionally* identical spray containers. The fact is that many others are doing so. Competitors have apparently had no need to simulate appellant's trade dress, in whole or in part, in order to enjoy all of the functional aspects of a spray top container. Upon expiration of any patent protection appellant may now be enjoying on its spray and pump mechanism, competitors may even copy and enjoy all of its functions without copying the external appearance of appellant's spray top.

If the functions of appellant's bottle can be performed equally well by containers of innumerable designs and, thus, no one is injured in competition, why did the board state that appellant's *design* is functional and for that reason not registrable?

2. The Relationship Between "Functionality" and Distinctiveness

One who seeks to register (or protect) a product or container configuration as a trademark must demonstrate that its design is "nonfunctional," as discussed above, and that the design functions as an indication of source, whether inherently so, because of its distinctive nature, [cit.], or through acquisition of secondary meaning. These two requirements must, however, be kept separate from one another.

The issues of distinctiveness and functionality may have been somewhat intermixed by the board. The design in issue appears to us to be relatively simple and plain, and the board, although not ruling upon appellant's contention that its design has acquired secondary meaning, discussed only distinctiveness before reaching its conclusion that the design was "functional." The unexpressed (and perhaps unconscious) thought may have been that if something is not inherently distinctive (appellant admits that its design is not), perhaps even austere, then, since it does not at a particular time function as a legally recognized indication of source, it probably never will. And since it is so plain that one may believe it is not and never will be a trademark, it will be perceived—not that the design is not inherently distinctive—but that it is "functional," without analysis of why it is believed to be "functional." The sole criterion seems to have been that the design is ordinary.[4]

. . . Whether in fact the design is "functional" requires closer and more careful scrutiny. We cannot say that there exists an inverse proportional relationship in all cases between distinctiveness of design and functionality (de facto or de jure). . . .

This court's past opinions which indicate that a particular design is "nonfunctional" because it is "arbitrary" are not to be construed as contrary to [our comments on this relationship]. In this situation, "arbitrary" is not used in the typical trademark (distinctiveness) sense of the word. It is used to indicate a design which may have been selected without complete deference to utility and, thus, is most likely "nonfunctional." That is, it is used to indicate the opposite side of the "functional" coin, since a design can be inherently distinctive (the usual trademark law meaning of the word "arbitrary") and still be "functional." . . .

*Reversed and Remanded.*

## NOTES AND QUESTIONS

1. ***The* Morton-Norwich *approach.*** What is the rationale for the functionality doctrine, according to the *Morton-Norwich* court? What is the test that the court applies? To what evidence does it look to determine the answer to the relevant question? Which of the evidentiary factors identified in *Morton-Norwich* appear to offer potential for expansive interpretation by courts?

2. *Limiting protection for designs: doctrinal vehicles.* What are the different doctrinal devices through which courts or the PTO might limit the protection of product designs under the trademark statute? Why might the classification of a design as "arbitrary" be relevant to its protection as a trademark? Why might the availability of alternative designs that perform the same function be relevant to the protection of a design as a trademark? Would it matter whether these alternative designs already existed in the marketplace or were simply possibilities? *See* Graeme B. Dinwoodie, *Reconceptualizing the Inherent Distinctiveness of Product Design Trade Dress*, 75 N.C. L. Rev. 471, 600-602 (1997).

3. *Product design and product packaging.* Judge Rich stresses that "it should be borne in mind that this is not a 'configuration *of goods*' case but a 'configuration of the *container* for the goods' case." Should that affect the functionality doctrine? In *Wal-Mart, supra* Chapter 2, Section B, the Supreme Court endorsed a different test by which to determine the distinctiveness of product

---

4. Perhaps the solicitor was of the same opinion. Continually referencing "the container," he concluded that " '[e]ssentially functional' subject matter is just that—it doesn't matter whether it results in a competitive edge or not. Either way, essentially functional subject matter is not registrable."

We have refrained from using phrases such as "essentially functional," "primarily functional," and "dictated primarily by functional considerations" to denote the legal consequence, all of which use the word "functional" in the lay sense of the term. If, in the legal sense, a particular design is functional, such adverbs as "essentially" and "primarily" are without meaning. Either a design is functional (de jure) or it is not.

design (as opposed to product packaging). Should we have different functionality doctrines for product configuration cases, on the one hand, and product container configuration cases, on the other?

**4. *The separateness argument.*** The court notes that the "separateness" rationale for not recognizing trademark rights in the design of an article had eventually given way to a more liberal approach to design trademark protection. Has the separateness rationale implicitly resurfaced in modern distinctiveness decisions? Another separateness rationale underlies decisions to recognize copyright protection for designs embodied in useful articles, as we discuss in Chapter 7.

**5. *Balancing interests.*** What interests or values cause the right to compete through imitation of a product unprotected by patent or copyright law to give way to the assertion of trademark rights? How should the interests served by trademark protection be balanced with the right to compete? The court concludes (pre-*Wal-Mart*, of course) that "a design can be inherently distinctive and still be functional." What protection *is* available to a distinctive but functional design? What protection *should be* available?

**6. *Design patent protection.*** The *Morton-Norwich* court mentions that the applicant owned a design patent on the configuration in question. Design patent protection is granted to new and nonobvious ornamental designs, as we discuss in Chapter 5. As you study the materials in this casebook, consider the ways in which U.S. design patent protection differs from U.S. trade dress protection. Likewise, consider how protections under both of these regimes differ from protection for designs under copyright law (discussed in Chapter 7). What explains those differences?

### 2. AESTHETIC FEATURES

Consider the following hypothetical. Dinwoodie and Janis open a chocolate store in Chicago just in time for St. Valentine's Day. To attract the crowd of overly sentimental romantics who rush mindlessly to the stores on February 13, they decide to market chocolates in red heart-shaped boxes. (Suppose, for the purpose of this hypothetical, that Dinwoodie and Janis were the first producers to package chocolates in heart-shaped boxes; indeed, they only hit upon the idea after months of thought.) Quickly, the chocolate lovers (and just plain lovers) of Chicago come to associate the heart-shaped box with the chocolates produced by Dinwoodie and Janis. Would you be willing to grant Dinwoodie and Janis trademark protection in the heart-shaped box for chocolates? What concerns might this raise? Are these concerns addressed by the rules articulated by the *Morton-Norwich* court? What is the "function" of the box shape? If the *Morton-Norwich* rules (and factors) were applied to the shape of the box, what would be the result? What interests might support giving Dinwoodie and Janis trademark rights in the shape of the box for chocolates?

Most early applications of the functionality rule involved denial of protection to mechanical or utilitarian features of a product's trade dress. But, as the *Morton-Norwich* court hints in footnote 1, the doctrine of functionality soon expanded to deny protection to certain design features that were not utilitarian in the mechanical sense (i.e., were aesthetic). This doctrine of "aesthetic functionality" is derived from commentary to the first Restatement of Torts. *See* Restatement of Torts §742, cmt. a (1938) ("When goods are bought largely for their aesthetic value, their features may be functional because they definitely contribute to that value and thus aid the performance of an object for which the goods are intended."). But the judicial opinion regarded as the effective starting point for aesthetic functionality is *Pagliero v. Wallace China Co.*, 198 F.2d 339, 343 (9th Cir. 1952) (articulating rule that a design that was "an important ingredient in the commercial success" of a product was *de jure* functional and thus unprotected even if that feature was aesthetic). In that case, the decorative design of hotel china was held to be aesthetically functional because it was "an essential selling feature" of the product. Although the *Pagliero* standard was heavily criticized and is now rarely used by courts—the Ninth Circuit has itself retreated from its standard in *Pagliero*—the doctrine of aesthetic functionality has survived.

Consider whether the rationales for the functionality doctrine articulated in *Morton-Norwich* apply with as much force to the design features for which trademark rights are claimed in the following cases. Are there alternative rationales that support the doctrine in these cases? Is the doctrine of "aesthetic functionality" a separate doctrine from a doctrine of "utilitarian functionality"? Do we need different tests to determine the limits of trademark protection for "aesthetic" as opposed to "utilitarian" features? Is this a viable distinction?

### Wallace Int'l Silversmiths, Inc. v. Godinger Silver Art Co., Inc.

916 F.2d 16 (2d Cir. 1990), cert. denied, 499 U.S. 976 (1991)

Winter, Circuit Judge:

Wallace International Silversmiths ("Wallace") appeals from Judge Haight's denial of its motion for a preliminary injunction under Section 43(a) of the Lanham Act prohibiting Godinger Silver Art Co., Inc. ("Godinger") from marketing a line of silverware with ornamentation that is substantially similar to Wallace's GRANDE BAROQUE line. Judge Haight held that the GRANDE BAROQUE design is "a functional feature of 'Baroque' style silverware" and thus not subject to protection as a trademark. We affirm.

#### Background

Wallace, a Delaware corporation, has sold sterling silver products for over one hundred years. Its GRANDE BAROQUE pattern was introduced in 1941 and is still one of the best-selling silverware lines in America. Made of fine sterling silver, a complete place setting costs several thousand dollars. Total sales of GRANDE BAROQUE silverware have exceeded fifty million dollars. The GRANDE BAROQUE pattern is fairly described as "ornate, massive and flowery [with] indented, flowery roots and scrolls and curls along the side of the shaft, and flower arrangements along the front of the shaft." Wallace owns a trademark registration for the GRANDE BAROQUE name as applied to sterling silver flatware and hollowware. The GRANDE BAROQUE design is not patented, but on December 11, 1989, Wallace filed an application for trademark registration for the GRANDE BAROQUE pattern. This application is still pending.

Godinger, a New York corporation, is a manufacturer of silver-plated products. The company has recently begun to market a line of baroque-style silver-plated serving pieces. The suggested retail price of the set of four serving pieces is approximately twenty dollars. Godinger advertised its new line under the name 20TH CENTURY BAROQUE and planned to introduce it at the Annual New York Tabletop and Accessories Show, the principal industry trade show at which orders for the coming year are taken. Like Wallace's silverware, Godinger's pattern contains typical baroque elements including an indented root, scrolls, curls, and flowers. The arrangement of these elements approximates Wallace's design in many ways, although their dimensions are noticeably different. The most obvious difference between the two designs is that the Godinger pattern extends further down the handle than the Wallace pattern does. The Wallace pattern also tapers from the top of the handle to the stem while the Godinger pattern appears bulkier overall and maintains its bulk throughout the decorated portion of the handle. Although the record does not disclose the exact circumstances under which Godinger's serving pieces were created, Godinger admits that its designers were "certainly inspired by and aware of [the Wallace] design when [they] created [the 20TH CENTURY BAROQUE] design."

On the afternoon of April 23, 1990, Leonard Florence of Wallace learned from a wholesale customer, Michael C. Fina Company, that Godinger had placed an advertisement for its 20TH CENTURY BAROQUE serving pieces in an industry trade magazine. George Fina, the company's president, said that he was "confused" when he saw what he believed to be a pattern identical to GRANDE BAROQUE being advertised by another company. He asked Mr. Florence whether Wallace had licensed the design to Godinger or whether "the Godinger product was simply a 'knock-off.'" Two days after this conversation, Wallace filed the complaint in the instant matter stating various federal trademark and state unfair competition claims. Wallace also filed a motion for a temporary restraining order and sought a preliminary injunction prohibiting Godinger from using the mark 20TH CENTURY BAROQUE or infringing the trade dress of Wallace's GRANDE BAROQUE product.

[T]he district court held a hearing on Wallace's application for preliminary relief . . . [and] concluded that the GRANDE BAROQUE design was a "functional" feature of baroque-style silverware and thus ineligible for trade dress protection under Section 43(a) of the Lanham Act. In so holding, [Judge Haight] stated:

> In the case at bar, the "Baroque" curls and flowers are not "arbitrary embellishments" adopted to identify plaintiff's product. Instead, all the "Baroque" style silverware use essentially the same scrolls and flowers as a way to compete in the free market. The "Baroque" style is a line of silverware which many manufacturers produce. Just like the patterns on the chinaware in *Pagliero* [*v. Wallace China Co.*, 198 F.2d 339 (9th Cir. 1952)], the "Grande Baroque" design is a functional feature of "Baroque" style silverware.
>
> Wallace may well have developed secondary meaning in the market of "Baroque"-styled silverware. In fact, I assume for purposes of this motion

that anyone that sees, for instance, five lines of Baroque silverware will single out the Wallace line as being the "classiest" or the most handsome looking and will immediately exclaim "Oh! That's the Wallace line. They make the finest looking 'Baroque' forks!" That is secondary meaning. However, that does not mean that plaintiff's design is subject to protection. The "Baroque" curls, roots and flowers are not "mere indicia of source." Instead, they are requirements to compete in the silverware market. This is a classic example of the proposition that "to imitate is to compete." *Pagliero, supra,* at 344. The designs are aesthetically functional.

Accordingly, I conclude that plaintiff does not have a trade dress subject to the protection of the Lanham Act. . . .

He therefore . . . denied Wallace's motion for a preliminary injunction.

## Discussion

. . .

In order to maintain an action for trade dress infringement under Section 43(a) of the Lanham Act, the plaintiff must show that its trade dress has acquired secondary meaning—that is, the trade dress identifies the source of the product—and that there is a likelihood of confusion between the original trade dress and the trade dress of the allegedly infringing product. *LeSportsac, Inc. v. K Mart Corp.*, 754 F.2d 71, 75 (2d Cir. 1985). Even if the plaintiff establishes these elements, the defendant may still avoid liability on a variety of grounds, including the so-called functionality doctrine. Our present view of that doctrine is derived from the Supreme Court's dictum in *Inwood Laboratories*, stating that "[i]n general terms, a product feature is functional if it is essential to the use or purpose of the article or if it affects the cost or quality of the article." [*Inwood Laboratories, Inc. v. Ives Laboratories, Inc.*, 456 U.S. 844, 850 n.10 (1982)]. Our most recent elaboration of the doctrine was in [*Stormy Clime, Ltd. v. ProGroup, Inc.*, 809 F.2d 971 (2d Cir. 1987)], where Judge Newman stated:

> [T]he functionality inquiry . . . should [focus] on whether bestowing trade dress protection upon [a particular] arrangement of features "'will hinder competition or impinge upon the rights of others to compete effectively in the sale of goods.'" *Sicilia di R. Biebow & Co. v. Cox*, 732 F.2d 417, 429 (5th Cir. 1984) (quoting *In re Morton-Norwich Products, Inc.*, 671 F.2d 1332, 1342 (Cust. & Pat. App. 1982)).

*Id.* at 976-77. . . .

. . . Judge Haight found that the similarities between the Godinger and Wallace designs involved elements common to all baroque-style designs used in the silverware market. He noted that many manufacturers compete in that market with such designs and found that "[t]he 'Baroque' curls, roots and flowers are not 'mere indicia of source.' Instead, they are requirements to compete in the silverware market." Judge Haight concluded that "the 'Grande Baroque' design is a functional feature of 'Baroque' style silverware," relying on *Pagliero v. Wallace China Co.*, 198 F.2d 339 (9th Cir. 1952).

Although we agree with Judge Haight's decision, we do not endorse his reliance upon *Pagliero*. That decision allowed a competitor to sell exact copies of china bearing a particular pattern without finding that comparably attractive patterns were not available to the competitor. It based its holding solely on the ground that the particular pattern was an important ingredient in the commercial success of the china. *Id.* at 343-44. We [have] rejected *Pagliero* [before] and reiterate that rejection here. Under *Pagliero,* the commercial success of an aesthetic feature automatically destroys all of the originator's trademark interest in it, notwithstanding the feature's secondary meaning and the lack of any evidence that competitors cannot develop non-infringing, attractive patterns. By allowing the copying of an exact design without any evidence of market foreclosure, the *Pagliero* test discourages both originators and later competitors from developing pleasing designs. *See Keene Corp. v. Paraflex Industries, Inc.*, 653 F.2d 822, 824-25 (3d Cir. 1981).

Our rejection of *Pagliero,* however, does not call for reversal. Quite unlike *Pagliero,* Judge Haight found in the instant matter that there is a substantial market for baroque silverware and that effective competition in that market requires "use [of] essentially the same scrolls and flowers" as are found on Wallace's silverware. Based on the record at the hearing, that finding is not clearly erroneous and satisfies the requirement of *Stormy Clime* that a design feature not be given trade dress protection where use of that feature is necessary for effective competition. 809 F.2d at 976-77.

*Stormy Clime* [which involved protection for the design of jackets that included side-vents in the jackets] is arguably distinguishable, however, because it involved a design that had both aesthetic and utilitarian features. If read narrowly, *Stormy Clime* might be limited to cases in which trademark protection of a design would foreclose competitors from incorporating utilitarian features necessary to compete in the market for the particular product. In the instant case, the features at issue are strictly ornamental because they neither affect the use of the silverware nor contribute to its efficient manufacture. The question, therefore, is whether the doctrine of functionality applies to features of a product that are purely ornamental but that are essential to effective competition.

Our only hesitation in holding that the functionality doctrine applies is based on nomenclature. "Functionality" seems to us to imply only utilitarian considerations and, as a legal doctrine, to be intended only to prevent competitors from obtaining trademark protection for design features that are necessary to the use or efficient production of the product. *See Keene, supra* at 825 ("inquiry should focus on the extent to which the design feature is related to the utilitarian function of the product or feature"). Even when the doctrine is referred to as "aesthetic" functionality, it still seems an apt description only of pleasing designs of utilitarian features. Nevertheless, there is no lack of language in caselaw endorsing use of the defense of aesthetic functionality where trademark protection for purely ornamental features would exclude competitors from a market. *See, e.g.,* [*W.T. Rogers Co. v. Keene*, 778 F.2d 334, 347 (7th Cir. 1985)] ("Though a producer does not lose a design trademark just because the public finds it pleasing, there may come a point where the design feature is so important to the value of the product to consumers that continued trademark protection would deprive them of competitive alternatives[.]") (Posner, J.). . . .

We put aside our quibble over doctrinal nomenclature, however, because we are confident that whatever secondary meaning Wallace's baroque silverware pattern may have acquired, Wallace may not exclude competitors from using those baroque design elements necessary to compete in the market for baroque silverware. It is a first principle of trademark law that an owner may not use the mark as a means of excluding competitors from a substantial market. Where a mark becomes the generic term to describe an article, for example, trademark protection ceases. [cit.] Where granting trademark protection to the use of certain colors would tend to exclude competitors, such protection is also limited. *See First Brands Corp. v. Fred Meyer, Inc.*, 809 F.2d 1378 (9th Cir. 1987); J. THOMAS MCCARTHY, TRADEMARKS AND UNFAIR COMPETITION, §7:16 et seq. Finally, as discussed *supra,* design features of products that are necessary to the product's utility may be copied by competitors under the functionality doctrine.

In the instant matter, Wallace seeks trademark protection, not for a precise expression of a decorative style, but for basic elements of a style that is part of the public domain. As found by the district court, these elements are important to competition in the silverware market. We perceive no distinction between a claim to exclude all others from use on silverware of basic elements of a decorative style and claims to generic names, basic colors or designs important to a product's utility. In each case, trademark protection is sought, not just to protect an owner of a mark in informing the public of the source of its products, but also to exclude competitors from producing similar products. We therefore abandon our quibble with the aesthetic functionality doctrine's nomenclature and adopt the Draft Restatement's view that, where an ornamental feature is claimed as a trademark and trademark protection would significantly hinder competition by limiting the range of adequate alternative designs, the aesthetic functionality doctrine denies such protection. *See* Third Restatement of the Law, Unfair Competition (Preliminary Draft No. 3), Ch. 3, §17(c) at 213-14. This rule avoids the overbreadth of *Pagliero* by requiring a finding of foreclosure of alternatives while still ensuring that trademark protection does not exclude competitors from substantial markets.

Of course, if Wallace were able to show secondary meaning in a precise expression of baroque style, competitors might be excluded from using an identical or virtually identical design. In such a case, numerous alternative baroque designs would still be available to competitors. Although the Godinger design at issue here was found by Judge Haight to be "substantially similar," it is not identical or virtually identical, and the similarity involves design elements necessary to compete in the market for baroque silverware. Because according trademark protection to those elements would significantly hinder competitors by limiting the range of adequate alternative designs, we agree with Judge Haight's denial of a preliminary injunction.

*Affirmed.*

Wallace's Grand Baroque Silverware

### BRUNSWICK CORP. v. BRITISH SEAGULL LTD.
35 F.3d 1527 (Fed. Cir. 1994)

RADER, Circuit Judge:
[Mercury manufactured and sold marine outboard engines for over 30 years, and for most of that time, all Mercury outboard engines were black. Some of Mercury's advertisements focused on Mercury's "all black" color. Mercury engines were not, however, the only black outboard engines on the market during that time. In 1998, Mercury filed an application to register the color black for outboard engines on the Principal Register. British Seagull Ltd. and Outboard Marine Corp. (the opposers) filed Opposition Nos. 80,900 and 80,901. The Board considered the proposed mark's functionality.]

> [A]lthough the color black is not functional in the sense that it makes these engines work better, or that it makes them easier or less expensive to manufacture, black is more desirable from the perspective of prospective purchasers because it is color compatible with a wider variety of boat colors and because objects colored black appear smaller than they do when they are painted other lighter or brighter colors. The evidence shows that people who buy outboard motors for boats like the colors of the motors to be harmonious with the colors of their vessels, and that they also find it desirable under some circumstances to reduce the perception of the size of the motors in proportion to the boats.

*British Seagull, Ltd. v. Brunswick Corp.*, 28 U.S.P.Q.2d 1197, 1199 (T.T.A.B. 1993).

[Accordingly, the Board concluded that the color black, applied to the engines, was de jure functional because of competitive need. Mercury appealed the Board's decision. The Court of Appeals for the Federal Circuit stressed that "contrary to Mercury's assertion, the test for de jure functionality does not involve inquiry into whether a particular feature is 'essential' to compete at all." Rather, "if the feature asserted to give a product distinctiveness is the best, or at least one, of a few superior designs for its de facto purpose, it follows that competition is hindered. *Morton-Norwich* does not rest on total elimination of competition in the goods." Thus, the Board did not err by basing its finding of de jure functionality on competitive need. The Court then turned to the facts of Mercury's application.]

Turning to the present case, the Board determined that "black, when applied to [Mercury's] outboard marine engines, is de jure functional because of competitive need." *British Seagull,* 28 U.S.P.Q.2d at 1199. The color black, as the Board noted, does not make the engines function better as engines. The paint on the external surface of an engine does not affect its mechanical purpose. Rather, the color black exhibits both color compatibility with a wide variety of boat colors and ability to make objects appear smaller. With these advantages for potential customers, the Board found a competitive need for engine manufacturers to use black on outboard engines. Based on this competitive need, the Board determined that the color was de jure functional. This court discerns no error in the Board's legal reasoning and no clear error in its factual findings.

This court's decision in [*In re Owens-Corning Fiberglass Corp.,* 774. F.2d 1116 (Fed. Cir. 1985)] does not compel a different result. In *Owens-Corning,* Owens-Corning sought to register the color pink as applied to its fibrous glass insulation. This court reversed the Board's refusal to register the color pink as Owens-Corning's trademark. The Board found that no other insulation manufacturer colored any of its products. The record revealed no reason to dye the insulation pink or any other color. Indeed, insulation in use is not open to general view at all. Owens-Corning alone undertook the additional, unnecessary step of coloring the insulation.

This court determined that no anti-competitive effects would follow from awarding Owens-Corning a mark for the color pink. . . .

This case, as the Board found, compels a different result. All outboard engine manufacturers color their products. These manufacturers seek colors that easily coordinate with the wide variety of boat colors. The Board found that the color black served this non-trademark purpose. In addition, the Board found that the color black serves the non-trademark purpose of decreasing apparent object size. The record showed that these features were important to consumers. Unlike the pink color in *Owens-Corning,* the Board found a competitive need for the color black. Thus, the Board concluded that registration of Mercury's proposed mark would hinder competition. This court discerns no clear error in the Board's findings.

[The court concluded that the Board properly considered whether alternative colors were available in order to avoid the fettering of competition. The court noted that "the functionality limitation on trademark protection properly subsumes any lingering policy concerns embodied in the 'color depletion theory', [such that] the theory is not a per se bar to registration of color marks." But, as a result, "if the use of color on the applicant's goods serves a non-trademark purpose that hinders competition, the de jure functionality doctrine precludes trademark protection."]

## NOTES AND QUESTIONS

1. *Color and functionality.* In *Qualitex,* the Supreme Court acknowledged that color per se could be legally functional. The respondent had argued that color per se should not be registrable as a trademark because colors are in limited supply. It claimed that "if one of many competitors can appropriate a particular color for use as a trademark, and each competitor then tries to do the same, the supply of colors will soon be depleted . . . to the point where a competitor's inability to find a suitable color will put that competitor at a significant disadvantage." The Court acknowledged the concern for competition, but did not find it a reason to deny the possibility that some colors per se could be registered because if the color scarcity problem arose, the doctrine of functionality would be available to prevent any anticompetitive consequences.

2. *Relevant market.* The *Wallace* court appears to be concerned with ensuring competition. In what markets is the court analyzing competition? How did it identify the relevant market in which it sought to analyze competition? How would the plaintiff wish to define the relevant market for the court's analysis? The defendant? (Might the parties wish to define the market differently for the purposes of other aspects of trademark analysis?)

3. *Separating the mark and the market.* Functionality doctrine reflects a concern that by ostensibly giving rights in a *mark,* trademark law might afford undue competitive advantages in a discrete *market.* To avoid this problem, trademark rights are denied in the claimed mark. If you are counsel for a producer claiming rights in a mark that may present this problem, what range of arguments might you adopt to persuade a court that granting rights in the mark will not provide a competitive advantage in the market? (Consider what the key variables are in avoiding the problem described.)

4. *Different levels of need.* What level of competitive need (or what competitive effect) must be established to warrant a finding of functionality? According to the *Wallace* court? According to the *Brunswick* court? In what ways is the *Wallace* approach different from the test announced by the *Pagliero* court (and rejected by the *Wallace* court)?

5. *Compatibility and standardization concerns.* Under the *Wallace* and *Brunswick* tests, what is the relevance of color compatibility? That is, if most consumers have purchased complementary goods that have to be a particular color to be compatible, is that relevant to the functionality inquiry? Does it matter whether consumers simply prefer that the goods be a particular color? Should functionality doctrine consider *why* consumers prefer the goods to be a particular color? In *Keene Corp. v. Paraflex Indus., Inc.,* 653 F.2d 822 (3d Cir. 1981), the Court of Appeals for the Third Circuit upheld a trial court's finding that the design of a luminaire was functional because there were only a limited number of configurations or designs for a luminaire that were architecturally

compatible with the structures on which they were placed. Should there be a difference in the analysis of functionality depending on whether the defendant pleads color compatibility, shape compatibility, or style compatibility? What if the reason for compatibility is health related rather than fashion related: should those motivations affect the result? *See Shire US Inc. v. Barr Labs., Inc.*, 329 F.3d 348 (3d Cir. 2003) (finding that the shape and color of plaintiff's drugs were functional because use of the same shape and color by manufacturers of the equivalent generic drug enhanced patient safety and compliance with the prescribed dosing regimen where the drugs in question were frequently dispensed by nonmedical intermediaries such as school secretaries).

**6. *The effect of functionality doctrine on eligible subject matter requirements.*** Functionality doctrine serves to confine trademark rights for the reasons discussed above. But notice how the existence of the functionality doctrine allows courts to be more generous to trademark claimants as they analyze other questions relevant to the availability of trademark rights. In *Qualitex*, the Court rejected respondent's argument that color per se should not be registrable as a trademark because colors are in limited supply, noting:

> This argument is unpersuasive, however, largely because it relies on an occasional problem to justify a blanket prohibition. When a color serves as a mark, normally alternative colors will likely be available for similar use by others. *See, e.g., Owens-Corning,* 774 F.2d, at 1121 (pink insulation). Moreover, if that is not so—if a "color depletion" or "color scarcity" problem does arise—the trademark doctrine of "functionality" normally would seem available to prevent the anticompetitive consequences that Jacobson's argument posits, thereby minimizing that argument's practical force.

**7. *Relation to the genericness doctrine.*** The *Wallace* court comments that it could "perceive no distinction between a claim to exclude all others from use on silverware of basic elements of a decorative style and claims to generic names, basic colors or designs important to a product's utility." Might there be a reason, in certain circumstances, to treat a generic product design differently from a functional product design? *Cf. Kendall Jackson Winery Ltd. v. E&J Gallo*, 150 F.3d 1042, 1050-1051 (9th Cir. 1998) (affirming jury verdict that the trade dress of plaintiff's wine bottles, which represented the "California look," was functional and nondistinctive). Are the interests at stake the same in both instances? *See* Graeme B. Dinwoodie, *Reconceptualizing the Inherent Distinctiveness of Product Design Trade Dress*, N.C. L. Rev. 471, 599-600 (1997).

## C. THE MODERN APPROACH TO FUNCTIONALITY

### 1. THE U.S. SUPREME COURT FRAMEWORK

In recent years, the U.S. Supreme Court has paid increasing attention to the question of functionality. In 1982, in *Inwood Laboratories, Inc. v. Ives Laboratories, Inc.*, 456 U.S. 844 (1982), the Court, in the course of considering the standards for appellate review of a district court's findings in a trademark case, noted in a footnote that "in general terms, a product feature is functional if it is essential to the use or purpose of the article or if it affects the cost or quality of the article." *Id.* at 850, n.10. Thirteen years later, in *Qualitex Co. v. Jacobson Products Co., Inc.*, 514 U.S. 159 (1995), the Court offered more substantial analysis of the functionality doctrine, although again the doctrine was tangential to the main holding of the case. Finally, in 2001 the Court specifically addressed the doctrine, partly in response to disagreements that were brewing in the lower courts regarding its meaning. Central to this disagreement was whether the functionality doctrine was sufficient to effectuate the purposes it claimed to serve. But the debate inevitably also implicated the rationale(s) for the doctrine, the tests for when a claimed trademark was functional, and the evidence relevant to a functionality determination.

### QUALITEX CO. V. JACOBSON PRODS. CO., INC.
### 514 U.S. 159 (1995)

Justice BREYER delivered the opinion of the Court:

[As discussed *supra*, in Chapter 2, in *Qualitex* the U.S. Supreme Court held that color per se could be registered as a trademark under the Lanham Act. In its opinion, however, the Court elaborated on its previous discussions of the functionality doctrine.]

Neither can we find a principled objection to the use of color as a mark in the important "functionality" doctrine of trademark law. The functionality doctrine prevents trademark law, which seeks to promote competition by protecting a firm's reputation, from instead inhibiting legitimate competition by allowing a producer to control a useful product feature. It is the province of patent law, not trademark law, to encourage invention by granting inventors a monopoly over new product designs or functions for a limited time, 35 U.S.C. §§154, 173, after which competitors are free to use the innovation. If a product's functional features could be used as trademarks, however, a monopoly over such features could be obtained without regard to whether they qualify as patents and could be extended forever (because trademarks may be renewed in perpetuity). *See Kellogg Co. v. National Biscuit Co.*, 305 U.S. 111, 119-120 (1938) (Brandeis, J.); *Inwood Laboratories, Inc. v. Ives Laboratories, Inc.*, 456 U.S. 844, 863 (1982) (White, J., concurring in result) ("A functional characteristic is 'an important ingredient in the commercial success of the product,' and, after expiration of a patent, it is no more the property of the originator than the product itself.") (citation omitted). Functionality doctrine therefore would require, to take an imaginary example, that even if customers have come to identify the special illumination-enhancing shape of a new patented light bulb with a particular manufacturer, the manufacturer may not use that shape as a trademark, for doing so, after the patent had expired, would impede competition—not by protecting the reputation of the original bulb maker, but by frustrating competitors' legitimate efforts to produce an equivalent illumination-enhancing bulb. *See, e.g., Kellogg Co., supra*, 305 U.S., at 119-120 (trademark law cannot be used to extend monopoly over "pillow" shape of shredded wheat biscuit after the patent for that shape had expired). This Court consequently has explained that, "[i]n general terms, a product feature is functional," and cannot serve as a trademark, "if it is essential to the use or purpose of the article or if it affects the cost or quality of the article," that is, if exclusive use of the feature would put competitors at a significant non-reputation-related disadvantage. *Inwood Laboratories, Inc., supra*, 456 U.S., at 850, n.10. Although sometimes color plays an important role (unrelated to source identification) in making a product more desirable, sometimes it does not. And, this latter fact — the fact that sometimes color is not essential to a product's use or purpose and does not affect cost or quality — indicates that the doctrine of "functionality" does not create an absolute bar to the use of color alone as a mark. *See Owens-Corning*, 774 F.2d, at 1123 (pink color of insulation in wall "performs no non-trademark function"). . . .

The functionality doctrine, as we have said, forbids the use of a product's feature as a trademark where doing so will put a competitor at a significant disadvantage because the feature is "essential to the use or purpose of the article" or "affects [its] cost or quality." *Inwood Laboratories, Inc.*, 456 U.S. at 850, n.10. The functionality doctrine thus protects competitors against a disadvantage (unrelated to recognition or reputation) that trademark protection might otherwise impose, namely, their inability reasonably to replicate important non-reputation-related product features. For example, this Court has written that competitors might be free to copy the color of a medical pill where that color serves to identify the kind of medication (e.g., a type of blood medicine) in addition to its source. *See id.*, at 853, 858, n.20 ("[S]ome patients commingle medications in a container and rely on color to differentiate one from another"); *see also* J. Ginsburg, D. Goldberg, & A. Greenbaum, *Trademark and Unfair Competition Law* 194-195 (1991) (noting that drug color cases "have more to do with public health policy" regarding generic drug substitution "than with trademark law"). And the federal courts have demonstrated that they can apply this doctrine in a careful and reasoned manner, with sensitivity to the effect on competition. Although we need not comment on the merits of specific cases, we note that lower courts have permitted competitors to copy the green color of farm machinery (because customers wanted their farm equipment to match) and have barred the use of black as a trademark on outboard boat motors (because black has the special functional attributes of decreasing the apparent size of the motor and ensuring compatibility with many different boat colors). *See Deere & Co. v. Farmhand, Inc.*, 560 F. Supp. 85, 98 (SD Iowa 1982), *aff'd*, 721 F.2d 253 (CA8 1983); *Brunswick Corp. v. British Seagull Ltd.*, 35 F.3d 1527, 1532 (CA Fed. 1994); *see also Nor-Am Chemical v. O.M. Scott & Sons Co.*, 4 U.S.P.Q.2d 1316, 1320 (ED Pa. 1987) (blue color of fertilizer held functional because it indicated the presence of nitrogen). The Restatement (Third) of Unfair Competition adds that, if a design's "aesthetic value" lies in its ability to "confe[r] a significant benefit that cannot practically be duplicated by the use of alternative designs," then the design is "functional." Restatement (Third) of Unfair Competition §17, Comment c, pp. 175-176 (1993). The "ultimate test of aesthetic functionality," it explains, "is whether the recognition of trademark rights would significantly hinder competition." *Id.*, at 176.

The upshot is that, where a color serves a significant non-trademark function — whether to distinguish a heart pill from a digestive medicine or to satisfy the "noble instinct for giving the right touch of beauty to common and necessary things," G. Chesterton, *Simplicity and Tolstoy* 61 (1912) — courts will examine whether its use as a mark would permit one competitor (or a group) to interfere with legitimate (non-trademark-related) competition through actual or potential exclusive use of an important product ingredient. That examination should not discourage firms from creating aesthetically pleasing mark designs, for it is open to their competitors to do the same. *See, e.g., W.T. Rogers Co. v. Keene,* 778 F.2d 334, 343 (CA7 1985) (Posner, J.). But, ordinarily, it should prevent the anticompetitive consequences of Jacobson's hypothetical "color depletion" argument, when, and if, the circumstances of a particular case threaten "color depletion."

### TRAFFIX DEVICES, INC. V. MARKETING DISPLAYS, INC.
#### 532 U.S. 23 (2001)

Justice KENNEDY delivered the opinion of the Court:

Temporary road signs with warnings like "Road Work Ahead" or "Left Shoulder Closed" must withstand strong gusts of wind. An inventor named Robert Sarkisian obtained two utility patents for a mechanism built upon two springs (the dual-spring design) to keep these and other outdoor signs upright despite adverse wind conditions. The holder of the now-expired Sarkisian patents, respondent Marketing Displays, Inc. (MDI), established a successful business in the manufacture and sale of sign stands incorporating the patented feature. MDI's stands for road signs were recognizable to buyers and users (it says) because the dual-spring design was visible near the base of the sign.

This litigation followed after the patents expired and a competitor, TrafFix Devices, Inc., sold sign stands with a visible spring mechanism that looked like MDI's. MDI and TrafFix products looked alike because they were. When TrafFix started in business, it sent an MDI product abroad to have it reverse engineered, that is to say copied. Complicating matters, TrafFix marketed its sign stands under a name similar to MDI's. MDI used the name "WindMaster," while TrafFix, its new competitor, used "WindBuster."

MDI brought suit under the Trademark Act of 1946 (Lanham Act), ... against TrafFix for trademark infringement (based on the similar names), trade dress infringement (based on the copied dual-spring design) and unfair competition. TrafFix counterclaimed on antitrust theories. After the United States District Court for the Eastern District of Michigan considered cross-motions for summary judgment, MDI prevailed on its trademark claim for the confusing similarity of names and was held not liable on the antitrust counterclaim; and those two rulings, affirmed by the Court of Appeals, are not before us.

I

We are concerned with the trade dress question. The District Court ruled against MDI on its trade dress claim. After determining that the one element of MDI's trade dress at issue was the dual-spring design, it held that "no reasonable trier of fact could determine that MDI has established secondary meaning" in its alleged trade dress. In other words, consumers did not associate the look of the dual-spring design with MDI. As a second, independent reason to grant summary judgment in favor of TrafFix, the District Court determined the dual-spring design was functional. On this rationale secondary meaning is irrelevant because there can be no trade dress protection in any event. In ruling on the functional aspect of the design, the District Court noted that Sixth Circuit precedent indicated that the burden was on MDI to prove that its trade dress was nonfunctional, and not on TrafFix to show that it was functional (a rule since adopted by Congress, see 15 U.S.C. §1125(a)(3) (1994 ed., Supp. V)), and then went on to consider MDI's arguments that the dual-spring design was subject to trade dress protection. Finding none of MDI's contentions persuasive, the District Court concluded MDI had not "proffered sufficient evidence which would enable a reasonable trier of fact to find that MDI's vertical dual-spring design is non-functional." Summary judgment was entered against MDI on its trade dress claims.

The Court of Appeals for the Sixth Circuit reversed the trade dress ruling. The Court of Appeals held the District Court had erred in ruling MDI failed to show a genuine issue of material fact regarding whether it had secondary meaning in its alleged trade dress, and had erred further in determining that MDI could not prevail in any event because the alleged trade dress was in fact a functional product configuration. The Court of Appeals suggested the District Court committed legal error by looking only to the dual-spring design when evaluating MDI's trade dress. Basic to its reasoning was the Court of Appeals' observation that it took "little imagination to conceive of a hidden dual-spring mechanism or a tri- or quad-spring mechanism that might avoid infringing [MDI's] trade dress." The Court of Appeals explained that "[i]f TrafFix or another competitor chooses to use [MDI's] dual-spring design, then it will have to find *some other way* to set its sign apart to avoid infringing [MDI's] trade dress." It was not sufficient, according to the Court of Appeals, that allowing exclusive use of a particular feature such as the dual-spring design in the guise of trade dress would "hinde[r] competition somewhat." Rather, "[e]xclusive use of a feature must 'put competitors at a *significant* non-reputation-related disadvantage' before trade dress protection is denied on functionality grounds." [*Marketing Displays, Inc. v. TrafFix Devices, Inc.*, 200 F.3d 929, 940 (6th Cir. 1999)] (quoting *Qualitex Co. v. Jacobson Products Co.*, 514 U.S. 159, 165 (1995)). In its criticism of the District Court's ruling on the trade dress question, the Court of Appeals took note of a split among Courts of Appeals in various other Circuits on the issue whether the existence of an expired utility patent forecloses the possibility of the patentee's claiming trade dress protection in the product's design. 200 F.3d, at 939. Compare *Sunbeam Products, Inc. v. West Bend Co.*, 123 F.3d 246 (C.A.5 1997) (holding that trade dress protection is not foreclosed), *Thomas & Betts Corp. v. Panduit Corp.*, 138 F.3d 277 (C.A.7 1998) (same), and *Midwest Industries, Inc. v. Karavan Trailers, Inc.*, 175 F.3d 1356 (C.A. Fed. 1999) (same), with *Vornado Air Circulation Systems, Inc. v. Duracraft Corp.*, 58 F.3d 1498, 1500 (C.A. 10 1995) ("Where a product configuration is a significant inventive component of an invention covered by a utility patent . . . it cannot receive trade dress protection."). To resolve the conflict, we granted certiorari. 530 U.S. 1260 (2000).

II

It is well established that trade dress can be protected under federal law. The design or packaging of a product may acquire a distinctiveness which serves to identify the product with its manufacturer or source; and a design or package which acquires this secondary meaning, assuming other requisites are met, is a trade dress which may not be used in a manner likely to cause confusion as to the origin, sponsorship, or approval of the goods. In these respects protection for trade dress exists to promote competition. As we explained just last Term, *see Wal-Mart Stores, Inc. v. Samara Brothers, Inc.*, 529 U.S. 205 (2000), various Courts of Appeals have allowed claims of trade dress infringement relying on the general provision of the Lanham Act which provides a cause of action to one who is injured when a person uses "any word, term name, symbol, or device, or any combination thereof . . . which is likely to cause confusion . . . as to the origin, sponsorship, or approval of his or her goods." 15 U.S.C. §1125(a)(1)(A). Congress confirmed this statutory protection for trade dress by amending the Lanham Act to recognize the concept. Title 15 U.S.C. §1125(a)(3) (1994 ed., Supp. V) provides: "In a civil action for trade dress infringement under this chapter for trade dress not registered on the principal register, the person who asserts trade dress protection has the burden of proving that the matter sought to be protected is not functional." This burden of proof gives force to the well-established rule that trade dress protection may not be claimed for product features that are functional. *Qualitex, supra,* at 164-165; *Two Pesos, Inc. v. Taco Cabana, Inc.*, 505 U.S. 763, 775 (1992). And in *Wal-Mart, supra,* we were careful to caution against misuse or over-extension of trade dress. We noted that "product design almost invariably serves purposes other than source identification." *Id.*, at 213.

Trade dress protection must subsist with the recognition that in many instances there is no prohibition against copying goods and products. In general, unless an intellectual property right such as a patent or copyright protects an item, it will be subject to copying. As the Court has explained, copying is not always discouraged or disfavored by the laws which preserve our competitive economy. *Bonito Boats, Inc. v. Thunder Craft Boats, Inc.*, 489 U.S. 141, 160 (1989). Allowing competitors to copy will have salutary effects in many instances. "Reverse engineering of chemical and mechanical articles in the public domain often leads to significant advances in technology." *Ibid.*

The principal question in this case is the effect of an expired patent on a claim of trade dress infringement. A prior patent, we conclude, has vital significance in resolving the trade dress claim. A utility patent is strong evidence that the features therein claimed are functional. If trade dress protection is sought for those features the strong evidence of functionality based on the previous patent adds great weight to the statutory presumption that features are deemed functional until proved otherwise by the party seeking trade dress protection. Where the expired patent claimed the features in question, one who seeks to establish trade dress protection must carry the heavy burden of showing that the feature is not functional, for instance by showing that it is merely an ornamental, incidental, or arbitrary aspect of the device.

In the case before us, the central advance claimed in the expired utility patents (the Sarkisian patents) is the dual-spring design; and the dual-spring design is the essential feature of the trade dress MDI now seeks to establish and to protect. The rule we have explained bars the trade dress claim, for MDI did not, and cannot, carry the burden of overcoming the strong evidentiary inference of functionality based on the disclosure of the dual-spring design in the claims of the expired patents.

The dual springs shown in the Sarkisian patents were well apart (at either end of a frame for holding a rectangular sign when one full side is the base) while the dual springs at issue here are close together (in a frame designed to hold a sign by one of its corners). As the District Court recognized, this makes little difference. The point is that the springs are necessary to the operation of the device. The fact that the springs in this very different-looking device fall within the claims of the patents is illustrated by MDI's own position in earlier litigation. In the late 1970's, MDI engaged in a long-running intellectual property battle with a company known as Winn-Proof. Although the precise claims of the Sarkisian patents cover sign stands with springs "spaced apart," U.S. Patent No. 3,646,696, col. 4; U.S. Patent No. 3,662,482, col. 4, the Winn-Proof sign stands (with springs much like the sign stands at issue here) were found to infringe the patents by the United States District Court for the District of Oregon, and the Court of Appeals for the Ninth Circuit affirmed the judgment. *Sarkisian v. Winn-Proof Corp.*, 697 F.2d 1313 (1983). Although the Winn-Proof traffic sign stand (with dual springs close together) did not appear, then, to infringe the literal terms of the patent claims (which called for "spaced apart" springs), the Winn-Proof sign stand was found to infringe the patents under the doctrine of equivalents, which allows a finding of patent infringement even when the accused product does not fall within the literal terms of the claims. [cit.] In light of this past ruling — a ruling procured at MDI's own insistence — it must be concluded the products here at issue would have been covered by the claims of the expired patents.

The rationale for the rule that the disclosure of a feature in the claims of a utility patent constitutes strong evidence of functionality is well illustrated in this case. The dual-spring design serves the important purpose of keeping the sign upright even in heavy wind conditions; and, as confirmed by the statements in the expired patents, it does so in a unique and useful manner. As the specification of one of the patents recites, prior art "devices, in practice, will topple under the force of a strong wind." U.S. Patent No. 3,662,482, col. 1. The dual-spring design allows sign stands to resist toppling in strong winds. Using a dual-spring design rather than a single spring achieves important operational advantages. For example, the specifications of the patents note that the "use of a pair of springs ... as opposed to the use of a single spring to support the frame structure prevents canting or twisting of the sign around a vertical axis," and that, if not prevented, twisting "may cause damage to the spring structure and may result in tipping of the device." U.S. Patent No. 3,646,696, col. 3. In the course of patent prosecution, it was said that "[t]he use of a pair of spring connections as opposed to a single spring connection ... forms an important part of this combination" because it "forc[es] the sign frame to tip along the longitudinal axis of the elongated ground-engaging members."

App. 218. The dual-spring design affects the cost of the device as well; it was acknowledged that the device "could use three springs but this would unnecessarily increase the cost of the device." App. 217. These statements made in the patent applications and in the course of procuring the patents demonstrate the functionality of the design. MDI does not assert that any of these representations are mistaken or inaccurate, and this is further strong evidence of the functionality of the dual-spring design.

### III

In finding for MDI on the trade dress issue the Court of Appeals gave insufficient recognition to the importance of the expired utility patents, and their evidentiary significance, in establishing the functionality of the device. The error likely was caused by its misinterpretation of trade dress principles in other respects. As we have noted, even if there has been no previous utility patent the party asserting trade dress has the burden to establish the nonfunctionality of alleged trade dress features. MDI could not meet this burden. Discussing trademarks, we have said " '[i]n general terms, a product feature is functional,' and cannot serve as a trademark, 'if it is essential to the use or purpose of the article or if it affects the cost or quality of the article.' " *Qualitex*, 514 U.S., at 165 (quoting *Inwood Laboratories, Inc. v. Ives Laboratories, Inc.*, 456 U.S. 844, 850, n.10 (1982)). Expanding upon the meaning of this phrase, we have observed that a functional feature is one the "exclusive use of [which] would put competitors at a significant non-reputation-related disadvantage." 514 U.S., at 165. The Court of Appeals in the instant case seemed to interpret this language to mean that a necessary test for functionality is "whether the particular product configuration is a competitive necessity." 200 F.3d, at 940. *See also Vornado*, 58 F.3d, at 1507 ("Functionality, by contrast, has been defined both by our circuit, and more recently by the Supreme Court, in terms of competitive need."). This was incorrect as a comprehensive definition. As explained in *Qualitex, supra*, and *Inwood, supra*, a feature is also functional when it is essential to the use or purpose of the device or when it affects the cost or quality of the device. The *Qualitex* decision did not purport to displace this traditional rule. Instead, it quoted the rule as *Inwood* had set it forth. It is proper to inquire into a "significant non-reputation-related disadvantage" in cases of aesthetic functionality, the question involved in *Qualitex*. Where the design is functional under the *Inwood* formulation there is no need to proceed further to consider if there is a competitive necessity for the feature. In *Qualitex*, by contrast, aesthetic functionality was the central question, there having been no indication that the green-gold color of the laundry press pad had any bearing on the use or purpose of the product or its cost or quality.

The Court has allowed trade dress protection to certain product features that are inherently distinctive. *Two Pesos*, 505 U.S., at 774. In *Two Pesos*, however, the Court at the outset made the explicit analytic assumption that the trade dress features in question (decorations and other features to evoke a Mexican theme in a restaurant) were not functional. *Id.*, at 767, n.6. The trade dress in those cases did not bar competitors from copying functional product design features. In the instant case, beyond serving the purpose of informing consumers that the sign stands are made by MDI (assuming it does so), the dual-spring design provides a unique and useful mechanism to resist the force of the wind. Functionality having been established, whether MDI's dual-spring design has acquired secondary meaning need not be considered.

There is no need, furthermore, to engage, as did the Court of Appeals, in speculation about other design possibilities, such as using three or four springs which might serve the same purpose. Here, the functionality of the spring design means that competitors need not explore whether other spring juxtapositions might be used. The dual-spring design is not an arbitrary flourish in the configuration of MDI's product; it is the reason the device works. Other designs need not be attempted.

Because the dual-spring design is functional, it is unnecessary for competitors to explore designs to hide the springs, say by using a box or framework to cover them, as suggested by the Court of Appeals. The dual-spring design assures the user the device will work. If buyers are assured the product serves its purpose by seeing the operative mechanism, that in itself serves an important market need. It would be at cross-purposes to those objectives, and something of a paradox, were we to require the manufacturer to conceal the very item the user seeks.

In a case where a manufacturer seeks to protect arbitrary, incidental, or ornamental aspects of features of a product found in the patent claims, such as arbitrary curves in the legs or an ornamental pattern painted on the springs, a different result might obtain. There the manufacturer could perhaps prove that those aspects do not serve a purpose within the terms of the utility patent. The inquiry into whether such features, asserted to be trade dress, are functional by reason of their inclusion in the claims of an expired utility patent could be aided by going beyond the claims and examining the patent and its prosecution history to see if the feature in question is shown as a useful part of the invention. No such claim is made here, however. MDI in essence seeks protection for the dual-spring design alone. The asserted trade dress consists simply of the dual-spring design, four legs, a base, an upright, and a sign. MDI has pointed to nothing arbitrary about the components of its device or the way they are assembled. The Lanham Act does not exist to reward manufacturers for their innovation in creating a particular device; that is the purpose of the patent law and its period of exclusivity. The Lanham Act, furthermore, does not protect trade dress in a functional design simply because an investment has been made to encourage the public to associate a particular functional feature with a single manufacturer or seller. The Court of Appeals erred in viewing MDI as possessing the right to exclude competitors from using a design identical to MDI's and to require those competitors to adopt a different design simply to avoid copying it. MDI cannot gain the exclusive right to produce sign stands using the dual-spring design by asserting that consumers associate it with the look of the invention itself. Whether a utility patent has expired or there has been no utility patent at all, a product design which has a particular appearance may be functional because it is "essential to the use or purpose of the article" or "affects the cost or quality of the article." *Inwood*, 456 U.S., at 850, n.10.

TrafFix and some of its amici argue that the Patent Clause of the Constitution, Art. I, §8, cl. 8, of its own force, prohibits the holder of an expired utility patent from claiming trade dress protection. We need not resolve this question. If, despite the rule that functional features may not be the subject of trade dress protection, a case arises in which trade dress becomes the practical equivalent of an expired utility patent, that will be time enough to consider the matter. The judgment of the Court of Appeals is reversed, and the case is remanded for further proceedings consistent with this opinion.

It is so ordered.

## NOTES AND QUESTIONS

1. *The functionality test after* **TrafFix.** The *TrafFix* opinion speaks to at least two primary issues: first, the test for functionality, upon which the Court had offered passing remarks in *Inwood* and *Qualitex*; and, second, the relevance of an expired utility patent to that analysis. As to the first question, the Court has confirmed that "in general terms, a product feature is functional . . . if it is essential to the use or purpose of the article or if it affects the cost or quality of the article." That is, the Court has endorsed the test for functionality first articulated in a footnote in *Inwood* and approved in *Qualitex*. In what ways is that test different from the tests applied by the courts in the other cases we have read in this chapter? For what reason did the Court conclude that MDI's dual-spring design feature was "essential to the use or purpose of the article in question or affects the cost or quality of the article"?

2. *Evidence.* In applying the *Inwood* test, is there a role for assessing competitive necessity? Is there a role for the number of available alternatives? *See* Graeme B. Dinwoodie, *Product Configuration Marks, Functionality, and the Supreme Court's Opinion in* TrafFix, 7 INT'L INTELL. PROP. L. & POL., Ch. 39 (Hansen ed. 2004). In what ways did the Court of Appeals for the Sixth Circuit err in its functionality analysis?

3. *The relevance of an expired patent.* The second (more particular) question addressed by the Court's opinion was the relevance of an expired utility patent to the functionality question. Here, the Court held that "a utility patent is strong evidence that the features claimed therein are functional." Why is this so? What was the Court's rationale for this rule? *See* Graeme B. Dinwoodie, *Product Configuration Marks, Functionality and the Supreme Court's Opinion in* TrafFix, 7 INT'L INTELL. PROP. L. & POL., Ch. 39 (Hansen ed. 2004) (noting possible explanations for why the Court might have thought utility patent protection relevant to functionality determinations). Was the Court focused on the same concerns as it was when discussing functionality in *Qualitex*?

4. *Trigger for the evidentiary inference.* Does the mere existence of a patent on some part of the product in question trigger this evidentiary inference with respect to all design features embodied in that product? In the case before it, the Court found that there was a "strong evidentiary inference of functionality based upon the disclosure of the dual-spring design in the claim of the expired patents," such design being "the central advance claimed in the expired utility patents" and "the essential feature of the [claimed] trade dress." Which aspect of the Court's description of the dual-spring design

triggered the "strong evidentiary inference of functionality"? In addition to the characteristics noted above, how many other considerations or characteristics can you identify from the opinion that might have been important to the Court's inference of functionality? (Can you determine which of the Court's statements are descriptive of the facts, rather than prescriptive?)

5. *Overcoming the evidentiary inference.* The Court also concluded that the plaintiff in *TrafFix* had failed to overcome the inference of functionality that the expired patent had generated. According to the Court, in what ways can a plaintiff overcome this evidentiary inference of functionality? How easy will it be to overcome this inference? Professor McCarthy has noted that at least one of the Court's hints about the ways in which the inference could be rebutted is somewhat careless in its use of intellectual property concepts. In particular, he has argued that "the Supreme Court confused a patent claim with a patent disclosure." J. THOMAS MCCARTHY, TRADEMARKS AND UNFAIR COMPETITION, §7:89 (2005). Indeed, although the Court observed that in "a case where a manufacturer seeks to protect arbitrary, incidental, or ornamental aspects of features of a product found in the patent claims, such as arbitrary curves in the legs or an ornamental pattern painted on the springs, a different result might obtain," it would be surprising to find such an arbitrary or ornamental feature recited in a utility patent claim (though it may well be that such features would be referenced in the patent's disclosure). However, the Seventh Circuit has since stressed that the language in the *TrafFix* opinion regarding the means by which a plaintiff could overcome the evidentiary inference is merely illustrative (a "for-instance"). *See Eco Mfg. LLC v. Honeywell Int'l Inc.*, 357 F.3d 649 (7th Cir. 2003) (suggesting "technological change" might also be relevant in showing that "what was once functional may . . . later be ornamental"). If the Seventh Circuit is correct, in what other ways might the inference be overcome? Is the "ornamentality" of the feature an appropriate consideration in any event?

6. *The "that is" language from* **Qualitex.** What is the significance of the other language regarding functionality found in the Court's *Qualitex* opinion? Are you persuaded by the Court's interpretation of what was at issue in *Qualitex* or by the Court's analysis of its *Qualitex* opinion? Does the *Inwood* test state the only inquiry that lower courts should make?

7. *Aesthetic functionality.* What is the test for aesthetic functionality after *TrafFix*? Is it the same as the test for functionality generally, or does the Court intend for the functionality of aesthetic features to be assessed differently than utilitarian or mechanical features? Is there a role for an assessment of competitive necessity? Is there a role for the number of available alternatives? Do you think that the Court's approach to aesthetic functionality is more or less generous to trade dress claimants than under the *Pagliero* standard or the *Wallace* opinion?

8. *Terminology and the relationship between the different tests.* The terminology in functionality cases was confusing (and inconsistent) before *TrafFix*. This is likely to continue. Some courts appear to be following the lead of the *TrafFix* court and describing the *Inwood* test as the "traditional" test of functionality, with the additional language from *Qualitex* described variously as constituting an "elaboration" or a "secondary test" or the "competitive

necessity test." The relationship between the two tests is not clear either. The Supreme Court's opinion leaves open at least two ways to approach the "two tests of functionality." First, one could regard the two tests as separate filters, both of which any feature claimed to be nonfunctional must pass through to be protected. Second, one could regard the two tests as applicable to different types of features, *Inwood* to mechanical features and "competitive necessity" to aesthetic features. *See* Graeme B. Dinwoodie, *Report of the United States, in* ADJUNCTS AND ALTERNATIVES TO COPYRIGHT (Besek and Ginsburg eds., 2002) ("while the *TrafFix Devices* opinion remains somewhat enigmatic, under one reading, the Court might be instructing courts to assess claims of functionality based upon mechanical utility primarily under the *Inwood* test (which might be called a test of mechanical necessity), and only claims of aesthetic functionality under a test of competitive necessity"). *See infra* Section 2.C.

9. ***Reconciling past approaches.*** Would Judge Rich (the author of the *Morton-Norwich* opinion) agree with the analysis of the Court in *TrafFix?* In particular, what approach would he take to the term "essential" as that term is used by the *TrafFix* court? Does the *TrafFix* court adhere to the understanding of the relationship between distinctiveness and functionality envisaged by Judge Rich? Would the spray bottle shape in *Morton-Norwich* have passed the *TrafFix* test? To what extent are the *Morton-Norwich* factors relevant after *TrafFix?* Would looking at those factors be consistent with the approach of the Supreme Court in *TrafFix?* If any of them are still relevant, is the weighting of the factors different?

## 2. APPLYING THE MODERN SUPREME COURT FRAMEWORK AFTER *TRAFFIX*

Many of the questions raised in the Notes and Questions following *TrafFix* have of course been addressed in case law since the Supreme Court's decision. But that case law has been anything but consistent. As you read the cases in this section, reconsider the issues raised above and ask yourself whether the lower courts have clarified or modified the approach contained in *TrafFix*. One of the issues we raised above, *see supra* note 8, was whether the Court had established different tests for utilitarian and aesthetic features. In this section, we have divided the lower court case law into cases primarily addressing utilitarian features, on the one hand, and aesthetic features, on the other hand, We do so in order to structure discussion, and do not intend to prejudge the issue that we have raised previously about the relationship between the *TrafFix* tests of functionality.

### (a) Utilitarian Features

VALU ENGINEERING, INC. V. REXNORD CORP.
278 F.3d 1268 (Fed. Cir. 2002)

DYK, Circuit Judge:

Valu Engineering, Inc. ("Valu") appeals a decision of the Trademark Trial and Appeal Board ("Board") sustaining Rexnord Corporation's ("Rexnord") opposition to registration of Valu's cross-sectional designs of conveyor guide rails as trademarks on the Principal Register.... Because the Board correctly concluded that Valu's cross-sectional designs of conveyor guide rails are de jure functional, we affirm the Board's refusal to register Valu's designs....

## Background

On February 25, 1993, Valu filed three applications seeking registration of conveyor guide rail configurations in ROUND, FLAT, and TEE cross-sectional designs as trademarks on the Principal Register. Conveyor guide rails are rails positioned along the length of the sides of a conveyor to keep containers or objects that are traveling on the conveyor from falling off the conveyor. Valu's ROUND, FLAT, and TEE cross-sectional designs are shown below.

 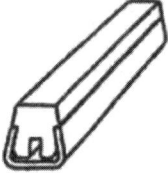 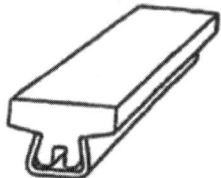

For each cross-sectional design, Valu asserted a claim of acquired distinctiveness under 15 U.S.C. §1052(f). In each application, Valu specified the goods in connection with which Valu uses the marks in commerce as "Conveyor Guide Rails." The Examining Attorney approved the applications. Rexnord timely filed Opposition Nos. 94,922, 94,937, and 94,946, which the Board consolidated.

Rexnord alleged [inter alia] that all three guide rail designs were de jure functional and thus unregistrable.... The focus of the opposition as concerns functionality was on the "wet" areas of bottling and canning plants. Such areas are considered "wet" because the machinery, including conveyor guide rails, is frequently washed with disinfectants containing bactericides, such as chlorine, for sanitation and product spillage. Because these washing solutions are corrosive, the machinery in the wet areas are usually formed of noncorrosive materials, such as stainless steel and plastic.

The Board concluded that Valu's cross-sectional shapes were functional and not registrable, and sustained Rexnord's opposition on May 9, 2000. The Board analyzed the functionality of Valu's guide rail configurations by applying the factors outlined by this court's predecessor in *In re Morton-Norwich Products, Inc.*, 671 F.2d 1332, 1340-41 (CCPA 1982). The Board focused its functionality analysis on the utilitarian advantages of Valu's guide rail configurations as they are used in a particular application, i.e., the so-called "wet areas" of bottling and canning plants, and as they are composed of particular materials, i.e., stainless steel and plastic. The Board determined that all four *Morton-Norwich* factors weighed in favor of a finding of functionality. Specifically, the Board found that: an abandoned utility patent application filed by Valu but rejected under 35 U.S.C. §103 "disclose[d] certain utilitarian advantages of [Valu's] guide rail designs, and that those advantages... result from the shape of the guide rail designs"; Valu's advertising materials "tout the utilitarian advantages of [Valu's] guide rail design[s]"; the "limited number of basic guide rail designs . . . should not be counted as 'alternative designs'" because they are "dictated solely by function"; and Valu's guide rail designs "result[] in a comparatively simple or cheap method of manufacturing." Accordingly, the Board sustained Rexnord's opposition and refused to register Valu's guide rail designs. . . .

The primary issue on appeal is whether the Board erred in confining its functionality analysis to a particular use, rather than considering all potential uses for the marks. . . .

## Discussion

### I. Jurisdiction and Standard of Review

We have jurisdiction over this appeal pursuant to 28 U.S.C. §1295(a)(4)(B) and 15 U.S.C. §1071(a).

Functionality is a question of fact, *Morton-Norwich*, 671 F.2d at 1340, and depends on the totality of the evidence. [cit.] We uphold the Board's factual findings unless they are unsupported by substantial evidence. *Dickinson v. Zurko*, 527 U.S. 150, 165 (1999). [cit.] Legal issues are reviewed without deference. [cit.]

### II. Functionality

Beginning at least with the decisions in *Kellogg Co. v. National Biscuit Co.*, 305 U.S. 111, 119-120 (1938), and *Morton-Norwich*, 671 F.2d at 1336-37, the Supreme Court and this court's predecessor have held that a mark is not registrable if the design described is functional, because "patent law, not trade dress law, is the principal means for providing exclusive rights in useful product features." *Elmer v. ICC Fabricating*, 67 F.3d 1571, 1580 (Fed. Cir. 1995). . . . Commentators share this view: "trademark law cannot properly make an 'end run' around the strict requirements of utility patent law by giving equivalent rights to exclude." J. Thomas McCarthy, 1 *McCarthy on Trademarks and Unfair Competition* §7:64, 7-147 (4th ed. 2001). . . .

Congress explicitly recognized the functionality doctrine in a 1998 amendment to the Lanham Act by making "functionality" a ground for ex parte rejection of a mark. 15 U.S.C. §1052(e)(5) (2000). Under this provision, a mark that comprises "*any matter* that, as a whole, is functional" is not entitled to trademark protection. *Id.* (emphasis added). Although the new statutory basis for refusal of registration does not apply in this case,[3] we note that the 1998 amendment was intended to "make explicit some of the current practices of the Patent and Trademark Office with respect to the trademark protection of matter that is wholly functional," and referred to the amendment as a "mostly technical," "housekeeping" amendment. *See* 105 Cong. Rec. S6572 (daily ed. June 18, 1998) (statement of Sen. Hatch).

---

3. The statute applies only to applications filed after October 30, 1998. Technical Corrections to Trademark Act of 1946, Pub. L. No. 105-330, §201(b), 112 Stat. 3064 (1998). The application in this case was filed on February 25, 1993.

### III. Definition of "Functionality"

To determine whether a particular product design is de jure functional, we have applied the [four] "Morton-Norwich factors." . . .

Because we have an obligation to apply the case law in effect at the time of decision, [cit.], we must determine whether the Supreme Court's recent decision in *TrafFix Devices, Inc. v. Marketing Displays, Inc.*, 532 U.S. 23 (2001) altered the *Morton-Norwich* factors. In order to understand the Supreme Court's decision in *TrafFix*, it is important to understand the background of *TrafFix* and the decisions on which the Court relied, namely *Inwood Laboratories, Inc. v. Ives Laboratories, Inc.*, 456 U.S. 844 (1982), and *Qualitex Co. v. Jacobson Products Co.*, 514 U.S. 159, 165 (1995).

[The Federal Circuit then summarized the Supreme Court's opinions in *Inwood*, *Qualitex*, and *TrafFix*, noting in particular that in *TrafFix*,] the Court . . . reaffirmed the "traditional rule" of *Inwood* that "a product feature is functional if it is essential to the use or purpose of the article or if it affects the cost or quality of the article." *Id.* The Court further held that once a product feature is found to be functional under this "traditional rule," "there is no need to proceed further to consider if there is competitive necessity for the feature," and consequently "[t]here is no need . . . to engage . . . in speculation about other design possibilities. . . . Other designs need not be attempted." *Id.* at 1262.[4]

We do not understand the Supreme Court's decision in *TrafFix* to have altered the *Morton-Norwich* analysis. As noted above, the *Morton-Norwich* factors aid in the determination of whether a particular feature is functional, and the third factor focuses on the availability of "other alternatives." *Morton-Norwich*, 671 F.2d at 1341. We did not in the past under the third factor require that the opposing party establish that there was a "competitive necessity" for the product feature. Nothing in *TrafFix* suggests that consideration of alternative designs is not properly part of the overall mix, and we do not read the Court's observations in *TrafFix* as rendering the availability of alternative designs irrelevant. Rather, we conclude that the Court merely noted that once a product feature is found functional based on other considerations[5] there is no need to consider the availability of alternative designs, because the feature cannot be given trade dress protection merely because there are alternative designs available. But that does not mean that the availability of alternative designs cannot be a legitimate source of evidence to determine whether a feature is functional in the first place. We find it significant that neither party argues that *TrafFix* changed the law of functionality, and

---

4. *TrafFix* suggests that there may be a requirement under *Qualitex* to inquire into a "significant non-reputation-related disadvantage" in aesthetic functionality cases, because aesthetic functionality was "the question involved in *Qualitex*." 121 S. Ct. at 1262. This statement has been criticized because "aesthetic functionality was not the central question in the *Qualitex* case." J. Thomas McCarthy, 1 *McCarthy on Trademarks and Unfair Competition* §7:80, 7-198 (4th ed. 2001). We need not decide what role, if any, the determination of a "significant non-reputation-related disadvantage" plays in aesthetic functionality cases, because aesthetic functionality is not at issue here.

5. For example, a feature may be found functional where the feature "affects the cost or quality of the device." *TrafFix*, 121 S. Ct. at 1263.

that scholarly commentary has reached exactly the same conclusion that we have:

> In the author's view, the observations by the Supreme Court in *TrafFix* do not mean that the availability of alternative designs cannot be a legitimate source of evidence to determine in the first instance if a particular feature is in fact "functional." Rather, the Court merely said that once a design is found to be functional, it cannot be given trade dress status merely because there are alternative designs available. . . .
>
> . . . The existence of actual or potential alternative designs that work equally well strongly suggests that the particular design used by plaintiff is not needed by competitors to effectively compete on the merits.

J. Thomas McCarthy, 1 *McCarthy on Trademarks and Unfair Competition*, §7:75, 7-180-1 (4th ed. 2001). In sum, *TrafFix* does not render the Board's use of the *Morton-Norwich* factors erroneous.

### IV. Analysis Confined to a Single Application

The central question here is whether the Board improperly focused on a single application. Here, in its analysis of the four *Morton-Norwich* factors, the Board focused primarily on the utilitarian advantages of Valu's designs in a particular, competitively significant application, namely, as they are used in the wet areas of bottling and canning plants. [The Federal Circuit concluded that this was proper: "Functionality may be established by a single competitively significant application in the recited identification of goods, even if there is no anticompetitive effect in any other areas of use, since competitors in that single area could be adversely affected." The court decided that this approach aligned with "an important policy underlying the functionality doctrine," namely "the preservation of competition." It was not necessary to show functionality across the entire universe of goods recited in the registration. As applied here, substantial evidence supported the conclusion that the wet areas of bottling and canning plants are "competitively significant," so the Board had not erred in confining its analysis to the application of the asserted trade dress in the wet areas. Moreover, the Board had not erred in its application of the *Morton-Norwich* factors. It was proper, for example, for the Board to consider an abandoned patent application under the first *Morton-Norwich* factor, "because an applied-for utility patent that never issued has evidentiary significance for the statements and claims made in the patent application concerning the utilitarian advantages, just as an issued patent has evidentiary significance. *See TrafFix.*"]

. . .

[*Affirmed.*]

### EPPENDORF-NETHELER-HINZ GMBH v. RITTER GMBH
289 F.3d 351 (5th Cir. 2002)

JONES, Circuit Judge:

[Eppendorf, a German company that manufactured medical and laboratory equipment, sought trade dress protection for a line of disposable pipette tips (so-called combitips) and dispenser syringes capable of accurate and rapid "multiple dispensing" of liquids. After a jury trial finding infringement, the district court permanently enjoined the defendant from selling or marketing in the United States dispenser syringes or syringes of "a confusingly similar design" to Eppendorf's syringes. On appeal, the Court of Appeals for the Fifth Circuit concluded that Eppendorf failed to carry its burden of proving non-functionality and thus reversed the judgment of the district court. The Fifth Circuit offered an analysis of functionality law after *TrafFix*.]

It is clear that functional product features do not qualify for trade dress protection. However, the definition of "functionality" has not enjoyed such clarity. [cit.] In *TrafFix*, the Supreme Court recognized two tests for functionality. First, the Court recognized the "traditional" definition of functionality: "a product feature is functional, and cannot serve as a trademark, 'if it is essential to the use or purpose of the article or if it affects the cost or quality of an article.'" *TrafFix*, 532 U.S. at 32 (citations omitted). Under this traditional definition, if a product feature is "the reason the device works," then the feature is functional. *Id.* at 34. The availability of alternative designs is irrelevant. *Id.* at 33-34.

In addition to the traditional definition, *TrafFix* recognized a second test for functionality: "a functional feature is one the 'exclusive use of which would put competitors at a significant non-reputation-related disadvantage.'" *Id.* at 32 (quoting *Qualitex*, 514 U.S. at 165). This "competitive necessity" test for functionality is an expansion of the traditional test. *Id.* The Court emphasized, however, that the "competitive necessity" test is not "a comprehensive definition" of functionality. *Id.* at 33. The primary test for functionality is the traditional test, and there is no need to consider the "competitive necessity" test where a product feature is functional under the traditional definition. *Id.* at 33-35.

[The Fifth Circuit acknowledged that before *TrafFix*, the Fifth Circuit had adopted a differently stated test of functionality (which the Fifth Circuit had, for several years, rather confusingly called its "utilitarian test" of functionality). That test was, according to the *Eppendorf* court, "virtually identical" to the competitive necessity test discussed in *TrafFix*. Accordingly, the court held that "*TrafFix* supersedes the definition of functionality previously adopted by this court" and that its competitive necessity test, though "still valid as a secondary test, is not a comprehensive definition of functionality. *TrafFix*, 532 U.S. at 32-33. In light of *TrafFix*, the primary test for determining whether a product feature is functional is whether the feature is essential to the use or purpose of the product or whether it affects the cost or quality of the product. *Id.*" The court concluded that the design of the fin features for which plaintiff sought protection was functional because it was undisputed that the fins provided necessary support for the flange (another part of the product).]

The only testimony offered by Eppendorf to prove non-functionality of the fins related to the existence of alternative design possibilities. Eppendorf's functionality expert testified that the appearance and number of fins could be changed without affecting the function of the fins. Eppendorf did not prove, however, that the fins are an arbitrary flourish which serve no purpose in the combitips. Rather, Eppendorf's experts concede that fins of some shape, size or number are necessary to provide support for the flange and to prevent deformation of the product. Thus, the fins are design elements necessary to the operation of the product. Because the fins are essential to the operation of the combitips, they are functional as a matter of law, and it is unnecessary to consider design alternatives available in the marketplace. *TrafFix,* 532 U.S. at 33-34.

Likewise, a careful review of the record demonstrates that Eppendorf failed to prove that the remaining [product] design elements are unnecessary, non-essential design elements. It is undisputed that: (1) The flange is necessary to connect the Combitip to the dispenser syringe; (2) The rings on the plunger head are necessary to lock the plunger into a cylinder in the dispenser syringe; (3) The plunger is necessary to push liquids out of the tip, and the ribs on the plunger stabilize its action; (4) The tips at the lower end of the Combitips are designed to easily fit into test tubes and other receptacles; (5) The size of the Combitip determines the dispensed volume, and size is essential to accurate and efficient dispensing; (6) The color scheme used on the Combitip—clear plastic with black lettering—enables the user easily to see and measure the amount of liquid in the Combitip, and black is standard in the medical industry; and (7) The stumps of the larger Combitips must be angled to separate air bubbles from the liquid and ensure that the full volume of liquid is dispensed. Thus, all eight design elements identified by Eppendorf are essential to the operation of the Combitips.

[The court concluded that although alternative designs are relevant to the test formerly applied by the Fifth Circuit (and now relevant only as a secondary test), "alternative designs are not germane to the traditional test for functionality. Each of the eight design elements identified by Eppendorf is essential to the use or purpose of the Combitips, and is not an arbitrary or ornamental feature. Therefore, no reasonable juror could conclude that Eppendorf carried its burden of proving non-functionality."]

## FUJI KOGYO CO., LTD. v. PACIFIC BAY INT'L, INC.
461 F.3d 675 (6th Cir. 2006)

BOGGS, Chief Judge:

### I

This is a trademark infringement case brought by a Japanese maker of fishing tackle against American distributors of competing goods. The goods at issue are fishing line guides. A line guide, not surprisingly, guides fishing line along the axis of a fishing rod. It consists of a frame and ring. The ring guides the line and the frame holds the ring. The frame has legs that attach to the ring and feet that mount to the rod. Different guides have different fishing uses. For example, lighter guides are used on fly rods or fresh water spinning rods, while heavier guides are used on rods that require little casting or heavier bait. Line guides transmit the force of a caught fish and the weight of the lure to the rod. Strength in several dimensions is as important as flexibility. A line guide should be light, aerodynamic when the rod is in motion, and resist line entanglement.

... [W]ith regard to the products concerned in this case, Fuji has been granted three trademark registrations, four utility patents, and seven design patents within the United States.

Fuji initially protected its innovative product design through United States utility patents. Four patents are here relevant and they are depicted, along with their grant dates, in Figure 1. All of these patents teach a method of manufacture where the line guide is formed from a single piece of sheet metal, hole-punched, and bent into the finished shape. The guides at issue in this case are also made by stamping and forming. Figure 1a illustrates how Fuji's model N line guide is made from forming stamped metal.

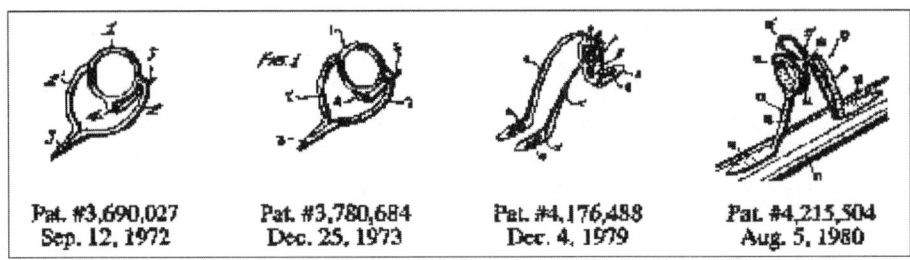

Figure 1

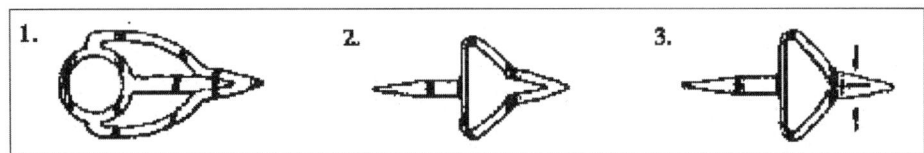

Figure 1a

Next, to achieve further protection from competition, Fuji applied for and was granted seven design patents. These patents, their grant dates, and the models they relate to, if discernible from the record, are illustrated in Figure 2.

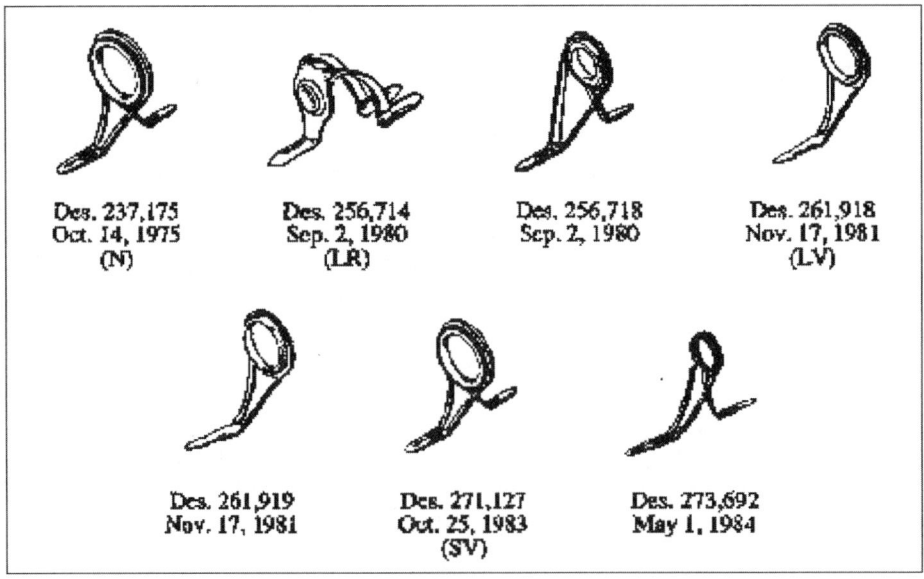

Figure 2

## C. The Modern Approach to Functionality

. . .

As its utility and design patents began to expire, the company learned of a competitor using trademark law to protect its designs. *See, e.g.*, 15 U.S.C. §§1051-1141. So, in 1993, Fuji began to register its product designs as trademarks. [*See* Fig. 3.]

. . .

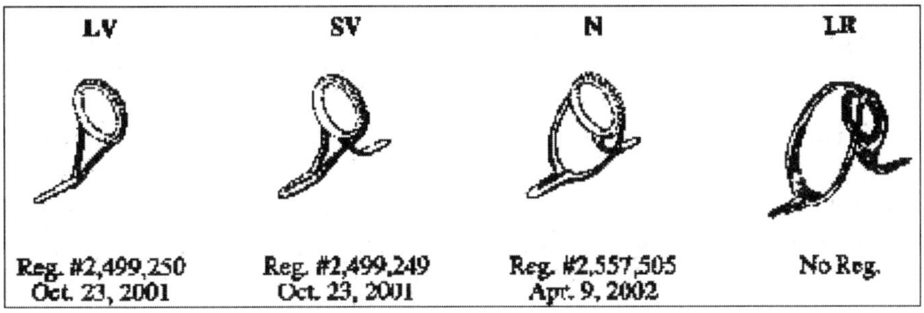

Figure 3

[The defendants import and sell line guides in competition with Fuji. Fuji sued, asserting trade dress infringement. After a bench trial, the trial court ruled for the defendants on the ground that the asserted trade dress was functional. Fuji appealed.]

II

[Part II of the opinion is omitted.]

III

A

. . .

Before considering the district court's findings of fact, we note that Fuji's model N guide is nearly identical to the specification disclosed in the '027 patent as the preferred embodiment of its invention. In this case, Fuji has sought to trademark a patent's disclosed specification for a product that is utilitarian and unadorned. On the strength of this identity, the obvious utility of the design, and the method disclosed for fashioning line guides in the '027 patent, this design must be considered now to be in the public domain. Further, Fuji's LR-type guide is substantially identical to the specification disclosed in the '504 patent. For the same reasons, this design should also be considered in the public domain. When a utility patent expires, "there passes to the public the right to make the machine in the form in which it was constructed during the patent." *Singer Mfg. Co. v. June Mfg. Co.*, 163 U.S. 169, 185 (1896). As an inescapable consequence of this right, a court may not prevent an individual skilled in the art of line guide manufacture from duplicating the specification disclosed in either the '027 or '504 patent and creating guides identical to the N and LR models. *See* 35 U.S.C. §112. Therefore, based solely upon our understanding of patent law, the district court was justified in cancelling Fuji's '505 registration and dismissing its claims based upon its unregistered LR design.

B

If a product's design is functional, that design cannot serve as a trademark. [cit.] . . .

Registration of a trademark gives rise to a rebuttable presumption that the trademark is valid. The burden falls on a challenger to rebut this presumption. [cit.] Under the Lanham Act, the party asserting trade dress protection without registration has the burden of proving that the matter sought to be protected is not functional. 15 U.S.C. §1125(a)(3); *TrafFix Devices, Inc. v. Mktg. Displays, Inc.*, 532 U.S. 23, 29 (2001).

Separate from trademark protection and utility patent, the statute allows for an original ornamental design to be patented. 35 U.S.C. §171. "A design patent is directed to the appearance of an article of manufacture." However, "[i]f the particular design is essential to the use of the article, it can not be the subject of a design patent." *L.A. Gear, Inc. v. Thom McAn Shoe Co.*, 988 F.2d 1117, 1123 (Fed. Cir. 1993) (citations omitted). A design patent, counter to a utility patent, is presumptive evidence of nonfunctionality, evidence that may support a similar trademark claim. [cit.] . . . After fourteen years, the ornamental design contained in a design patent "passes into the public domain." Compare 35 U.S.C. §173 (granting fourteen years for design patents) with 35 U.S.C. §154 (granting twenty years for utility patents).

The design patents in this case do little to help resolve the merits. For example, while the product described in the '714 design patent is almost identical to that in the '488 utility patent, the utility patent presents a presumption of functionality and the design patent presents a presumption of nonfunctionality. Clearly, the variety of intellectual property in this case demonstrates that the issue cannot be decided through evidentiary presumptions. This type of contradiction cannot be resolved without a trial. The district court was correct in evaluating and weighing all the evidence and in not relying on the aggregate of the statutory presumptions. Therefore, it was not error for the district court to fail to make a formal accounting of each of the statutory burdens in its written opinion in a ritualistic manner. [cit.]

The district court held that all three of Fuji's registered trademarks were functional and that its one unregistered mark was functional as well. Although Fuji argues extensively about the presumption of nonfunctionality bestowed upon its asserted marks by statute, it cannot eliminate the fact that Defendants have overcome this presumption through their proofs. In addition to the utility patents on the record, Defendants presented printed materials constituting admissions by Fuji, testimony by lay witnesses regarding the functionality of the designs, and the testimony of expert witnesses as well.

Defendants offered lay witnesses who testified that the curved legs "act as shock absorbers and reduce the occurrences of line entanglement [more] than line guides with straight legs," and experts who opined that "Fuji's curved leg line guide is stronger and more able to withstand shock and torque in the lateral direction than a comparable line guide with straight legs." Fuji's expert countered that the line guide tested with straight legs was stronger than Fuji's trademarked curved configuration and cheaper to manufacture. The credentials and testimony of the opposing experts were impressive. When credited by the district judge, either was enough to rebut a presumption of functionality or non-functionality. The district court was charged with weighing the evidence in this case and making a determination by a preponderance of the evidence. We cannot say that the court's conclusion was erroneous, and certainly not clearly erroneous. We therefore find that Fuji's argument regarding a misplaced burden by the district court is without merit.

C

[The court recited the *TrafFix* standard, and also noted that in *Valu Engineering*, the Federal Circuit "maintains a helpful doctrine of de jure versus de facto functionality," where de jure functionality is assessed using the *Morton-Norwich* factors. The court then reviewed—seemingly with approval—the trial court's analysis of the factors: Fuji owned a utility patent disclosing the advantages of the design; Fuji's advertising materials referred to the functions of the design; and there was expert testimony that alternative designs were not acceptable and that the design affected the cost of manufacture.]

D

Fuji argues that the district court erred when it considered the utility patents as evidence of design functionality without first determining whether Fuji's trademarked product configuration was claimed in any of the patents. Fuji dissects the language of its patents in an attempt to distinguish its claims from similar features in its trademarks. In light of *TrafFix,* we find these arguments unconvincing.

[The court recited the rule from *TrafFix* that a prior patent has "vital significance" in assessing functionality.]

The district court weighed the evidence at trial and concluded that the product designs were functional. Fuji attempted to show that its trademarked legs' shape was "ornamental, incidental, or arbitrary." Mr. Goto testified for Fuji that the trademarked curves "were selected based on aesthetics or an ornamental design," and that "no calculations were conducted regarding the strength" of the legs. Mr. Yamamoto also opined for Fuji that "we did not calculate the strength," the selection criteria was "Mr. Ohmura's preference." In contrast, however, Fuji's own marketing materials claimed that its patented designs were light, strong, shock-absorbent, and flexible. Given the plain language of *TrafFix*, we cannot say that it was error for the district court to give more weight to the utility patents and Fuji's admissions than to its witnesses, including the experts, on the issue of functionality. The district court's weighing of the evidence is plausible [and therefore cannot be clearly erroneous]. [cit.]

To surmount this finding, Fuji argues that the district court did not put enough weight on the Supreme Court's direction that the features must be "claimed" in the utility patent. Fuji maintains that the curvature of the legs in the trademarked designs is outside the scope of its patents. This argument, as a legal argument, is well-taken. However, in this instance, Fuji's reliance upon it is unavailing because the design departure in this case is too slight not to be included by the claims of the utility patents at issue.

The Court in *TrafFix* addressed a similar question. It considered two different designs for a wind-proof sign based upon the double-spring design contained in plaintiff MDI's expired patents. 532 U.S. at 30. In the patented design, the springs were "well apart (at either end of a frame for holding a rectangular sign when one full side is the base)," while in the allegedly infringing design, the springs were close together. *Ibid.* To resolve this difference, the Court looked to evidence from a previous patent infringement lawsuit that MDI had prosecuted against a different competing manufacturer of wind-proof signs with a similar "close together" spring design. In that case, the "stand was found to infringe the patents under the doctrine of equivalents, which allows a finding of patent infringement even when the accused product does not fall within the literal terms of the claims." *Id.* at 31. The Court then concluded that, "In light of this past ruling—a ruling procured at MDI's own insistence—it must be concluded the products here at issue would have been covered by the claims of the expired patents." *Ibid.*

The *TrafFix* Court anticipated the situation where the "heavy burden of showing that the feature is not functional" might not apply because the expired patent did not literally "claim[] the features in question." *Id.* at 30. [In such a case, the *TrafFix* Court suggested that the functionality inquiry "could be aided by going beyond the claims and examining the patent and its prosecution history to see if the feature in question is shown as a useful part of the invention."] *Id.* at 34. This raises two questions. First, did Fuji's patents actually claim the features in question, and two, despite Fuji's literal claims, would their patents still have covered the designs at issue here?

To determine if a patent has been infringed, a court must conduct two separate inquiries. [cit.] First, claim construction, "determining the meaning and scope of the patent claims asserted," is a question of law that is reviewed de novo. [cit.] Second, infringement, "whether literal or under the doctrine of equivalents," that is, "comparing the properly construed claims to the device accused of infringing," is a question of fact. [cit.]

Literal infringement is narrow, restricted to the literal claims of a patent. However, [under the doctrine of equivalents, patent claims may also encompass devices in which equivalent elements have been substituted.] In a simple device like a line guide, where the few functional parts can be slightly relocated or altered in shape, the doctrine of equivalents is easily applied to recognize infringement in a wider variety of duplicates. In determining infringement under the doctrine of equivalents, the operative question is: "Does the accused product or process contain elements identical or equivalent to each claimed element of the patented invention?" *Warner-Jenkinson Co., Inc. v. Hilton Davis Chem. Co.*, 520 U.S. 17, 39-40 (1997). Relevant to this inquiry is "whether the missing element in the accused device 'performs substantially the same function in substantially the same way to obtain the same result.'" [cit.]

If the N and LR guides are held to be literal embodiments of the Fuji '027 and '504 patents, the SV and LV guides can be seen as equivalents under the doctrine of equivalents.[1] The SV design differs from the '027 patent in a minimal way; the attachment point of the dual legs is moved from the midline of the ring (its equator, so to speak) to a point nearer the bottom of the ring (in its southern hemisphere). Nothing is otherwise changed. Each element still "performs substantially the same function in substantially the same way to obtain the same result." The LV design is a closer case because it is missing a rear leg. However, as a device to assist the finding of functionality, it is clear that, given the purpose of the device disclosed in the '027 patent, the patent evidence increases the likelihood of finding that the LV design is also functional.

This likelihood is increased when it is noted that a patent's claims should be considered in light of the other, "intrinsic," evidence inside the patent, including the illustrations and specification. [cit.]

The '027 patent, in its specification, states:

> Although one preferred embodiment of the present invention has been described and shown herein, it is to be understood that the same is illustrative in nature and not to necessarily [sic] limiting upon the scope of the teaching in its broader aspect. Many additional variations within the scope of the appended claims will occur to those skilled in the art.

Integral Guide Device for Fishing Lines, U.S. Patent No. 3,690,027 at 6:20 (filed Dec. 10, 1970) (issued Sept. 12, 1972). *See also* U.S. Patent No. 3,780,684 (issued Dec. 25, 1973). This language makes it more likely that the LV and SV models are equivalent embodiments of the patent and therefore functional designs.

Fuji argues that we must remand this case to the district court so that court can conduct a claim construction analysis in the first instance before we can evaluate the patents under the doctrine of equivalents. This argument fails, not because it is an incorrect statement of the law regarding infringement, but because the district court was never charged with determining the validity of the patents. Rather, it was evaluating and weighing the patent as evidence of functionality. [cit.] The patents in this case were probative evidence, *see* Fed. R. Evid. 401, and the district court, as the trier of fact, could credit or discount the patent evidence by considering the likelihood that various features of the trademarked designs were claimed in any of the patents. Accordingly, we affirm the district court's use of Fuji's patents in its functionality analysis and hold that an evaluation under the doctrine of equivalents is appropriate in the course of this kind of factual finding.

We conclude, in light of the applicable law, that the district court's determination that Fuji's registered and claimed trademarks in its previously patented designs were functional was not clearly erroneous. The court's investigation was properly illuminated by the language of the patents,

---

1. Fuji's threatened actions against its competitors for patent infringement are solidly documented in this record. Between 1982 and 1989, Fuji threatened legal action against any "manufacturers, importers, and/or distributors that show any fishing rods having the infringing line guides at [trade shows]" in the United States. Unfortunately, these designs are not disclosed on the record. Where an inventor has enforced its patent rights against a competitor in the past and subsequently seeks to enforce a trademark right against similar infringing products, it would not be unreasonable for a court to estop the trademark holder from claiming that the previously patented designs are not now functional in a trademark context.

consideration of the doctrine of equivalents, and witness testimony — in short all the evidence considered during the trial.. . . .

[*Affirmed.*]

## NOTES AND QUESTIONS

1. ***Different applications of* Inwood.** Have these courts correctly interpreted the *TrafFix* opinion? Do you discern any differences in the different courts' perceptions of the functionality doctrine post-*TrafFix*? Do you have a good sense of how to apply the *Inwood* test? *See Straumann Co. v. Lifecore Biomedical Inc.*, 278 F. Supp. 2d 130, 135 (D. Mass. 2003) (emphasizing the importance of the disjunctive elements of the *Inwood* test and thus the need to consider whether the design "affects the cost or quality" of the article). In *Eco Mfg. LLC v. Honeywell Int'l Inc.*, 357 F.3d 649 (7th Cir. 2003), the Seventh Circuit suggested three ways in which the round shape of a thermostat could be functional, at least in principle:

> First, rectangular objects may clash with other architectural or decorative choices. . . . Second, round thermostats (and other controls) may reduce injuries, especially to children, caused by running into protruding sharp corners. Third, people with arthritis or other disabilities may find it easier to set the temperature by turning a large dial (or the entire outer casing of the device) than by moving a slider or pushing buttons on boxes. The record does not contain much along any of these lines. . . . Although the three possibilities we have mentioned do not show that roundness is "essential" to a thermostat, that's not required. *TrafFix* rejected an equation of functionality with necessity; it is enough that the design be useful. The Justices told us that a feature is functional if it is essential to the design *or* it affects the article's price or quality.

Do you agree with the Seventh Circuit's reading of *TrafFix*? Under *TrafFix* do you agree that the three possibilities raised by the Court might show functionality? *See also Dippin' Dots, Inc. v. Frosty Bites Distrib.*, 369 F.3d 1197, 1206 (11th Cir. 2004) (finding size of the ice cream beads functional because it contributes to the product's creamy taste, which would be different in a larger "dot"); *cf. General Motors Corp. v. Lanard Toys, Inc.*, 80 U.S.P.Q.2d 1608, 1617 (6th Cir. 2006) (holding that having a function in mind when designing a product does not amount to that design being "essential" to the use or purpose of the article).

2. ***Evidence and the relevance of alternatives.*** How do the *Morton-Norwich* factors contribute to answering the questions at the heart of the *TrafFix* test? Do you agree with the assertions in *Valu* and *Fuji* that the factors are still relevant? To what extent do the post-*TrafFix* courts take different views of the relevance of alternative designs? *See In re Gibson Guitar*, 61 U.S.P.Q.2d 1948, 1951 (TTAB 2002) ("it is not clear, after *TrafFix*, whether the availability of alternatives weighs as a factor in applicant's favor"); *Antioch Co. v. Western Trimming Corp.*, 347 F.3d 150, 157 (6th Cir. 2003) ("[A] court is not *required* to examine alternative designs when applying the traditional test for functionality. . . . The traditional *Inwood* test for functionality is the main rule, and if a product is clearly functional under *Inwood*, a court need not

apply the competitive-necessity test and its related inquiry concerning the availability of alternative designs."). Despite the approach seen in *Eppendorf*, *see also Talking Rain Beverage Co. v. South Beach Beverage Co.*, 349 F.3d 601 (9th Cir. 2003) (the existence of alternative designs does not undermine a finding of functionality reached based upon advertising that touted functionality, the fact that manufacturing considerations influenced the design, and the utilitarian advantages yielded by the design in question), some courts have continued to stress the relevance of alternatives. *See, e.g., Eco. Mfg. LLC v. Honeywell Int'l Inc.*, 357 F.3d 649 (7th Cir. 2003); *Logan Graphic Prods. v. Textus USA, Inc.*, 67 U.S.P.Q.2d 1470 (N.D. Ill. 2003) ("because *TrafFix* dealt with trade dress protection sought for the exact mechanism covered by an expired utility patent, and because the features sought to be protected here are not covered by expired patents, the *TrafFix* decision is not controlling" and thus it was appropriate to consider alternative designs because "functionality has not been established by the existence of expired patents"); *New Colt Holding Corp. v. RJG Holdings of Fla., Inc.*, 312 F. Supp. 2d 195, 214 & 219 (D. Conn. 2004) (noting that "to the extent that Second Circuit law required consideration of design alternatives in all circumstances, that is no longer the law. However, under the present circumstances and given the nature of the product, the existence of design alternatives is helpful for determining whether a particular design is truly necessary to the way the revolver works.").

3. *Functionality in design patent law.* The opinion in *Fuji* alludes briefly to the functionality doctrine in design patent law. We discuss that doctrine in Chapter 5. As we will see, some courts seem to equate functionality in design patents with functionality in trade dress, whereas others suggest that establishing functionality in trade dress calls for a less rigorous showing. Should courts explore the comparison more carefully, in order to define the contours of the *Inwood* trademark test by way of contrast with the design patent system? Or should comparisons be resisted — e.g., on the ground that the two systems serve different purposes?

4. *Focus of analysis.* Whose product — plaintiff's or defendant's — should be analyzed in determining whether a design feature is "essential to the use or purpose of the article or affects its cost or quality"? In *Gateway Inc. v. Companion Prods., Inc.*, 68 U.S.P.Q.2d 1407 (D.S.D. 2003), *aff'd*, 384 F.3d 503 (8th Cir. 2004), the defendant had produced a black-and-white cattle-like design for a product that looked like a cow wrapped around a computer monitor. Gateway claimed that that product infringed its black-and-white cattle-like design mark (which it applied to the packaging of its computers). In concluding that the design was nonfunctional, the lower court noted that there was "no evidence that the defendant's use of black and white spots on a plush cow that wraps around a computer monitor . . . is essential to the use or purpose of a stretch pet [defendant's product]" and that the design was "neither necessary for the defendant to compete effectively in the market nor more economical to manufacture." *Cf. Gibson Guitar Corp. v. Paul Reed Smith Guitars LP*, 311 F. Supp. 2d 690, 720 (M.D. Tenn. 2004) (concluding that the shape of the guitar in which the plaintiff guitar producer claimed rights was not "essential to the [plaintiff's] or any other guitar"), *rev'd on other grounds*, 423 F.3d 539 (6th Cir. 2005). Is this focus on the defendant's product appropriate? Compare the focus

of functionality analysis with that of distinctiveness analysis. If third parties are brought into the picture, which third parties are relevant? Are they the same third parties as are relevant to distinctiveness analysis?

5. *The evidentiary inference and* Inwood. How does the rule articulated by the Supreme Court in *TrafFix* regarding the relevance of utility patents fit into the scheme of functionality tests that lower appellate courts are now articulating?

6. *The evidentiary inference: "central advance"*. In *Leviton Mfg. Co. v. Universal Sec. Instruments, Inc.*, 304 F. Supp. 2d 726 (D. Md. 2004), the plaintiff asserted trade dress rights in the appearance of a ground fault circuit interrupting product that had been disclosed in a prior utility patent. The expired patent was, however, given little weight by the court in considering functionality because the "central advance" of the patent was its "unique switching mechanism and ability to fit into a wall receptacle" rather than the product's appearance. *Id.* at 736 ("*TrafFix* does not dictate a finding of functionality where a patent has been issued. Rather, the Court prohibits affording trade dress protection of the central advance of an existing patent."). If the evidentiary inference is triggered only when the design feature constitutes the "central advance," how are courts to determine the "central advance" in a patent? Is that concept different from a "significant inventive component" as articulated in the *Vornado* case (*see* Section D)?

7. *The evidentiary inference: where to look.* In addition to knowing *what* a court should look for in an expired patent (or an invention) in order to apply *TrafFix*, it is also important to know *where* a court (or competitor) should look to determine whether a product design feature will be subject to the evidentiary inference of functionality. Where in the expired patent should a court look? How does the *Fuji* opinion shed light on the matter? In this regard, think back to the possible purposes underlying the rule the *TrafFix* Court announced. In *Dippin' Dots, Inc. v. Frosty Bites Distrib.*, 369 F.3d 1197, 1206-1207 (11th Cir. 2004), the plaintiff claimed trade dress rights in, inter alia, the shape of its ice cream beads (so-called dippin' dots). In finding the bead shape functional, the court looked at the prosecution history of plaintiff's patent on a method of making such ice cream beads and found a sworn declaration by the plaintiff touting the superior ice cream that resulted from the patented method. The patent did not make reference to the appearance of the ice cream beads that resulted from the process, but this was of little consequence to the court, which stressed that although the disclosure of the appearance in the patent would have been strong evidence of functionality, its absence did not suggest nonfunctionality. Does the *Fuji* court's reliance upon the fact that defendant's design would (hypothetically) have been covered by the doctrine of equivalents had the patent still been extant, provide an alternative standard to whether the feature was a "central advance"? Which, if either, is consistent with *TrafFix*? Does the court's reference to estoppel effectuate a different purpose than that pursued by the Court in *TrafFix*?

8. *The evidentiary inference: who should decide and how.* In the patent context, the Supreme Court has held that judges, not juries, should be responsible for construction of a patent (i.e., deciding what the words in the patent claim mean). Indeed, special procedures have been instituted to establish the

meaning of the claims. *See Markman v. Westview Instruments,* 517 U.S. 370 (1996). In *Fuji*, because of the court's reliance on the scope of the patents, the plaintiff sought a remand to the district court to engage in proper construction of patent claims and equivalents analysis in line with the dictates of patent law. The court rejected that demand on the ground that the "lower court was never charged with determining the validity of the patents," but rather was using the patents merely as probative evidence. If the lower court is relying on an interpretation of the meaning and scope of the patent, should it be forced to follow the procedures patent law has devised for making such determinations? What should be the respective roles for judges and juries in making functionality determinations where an expired patent is involved? *See* Theodore H. Davis, Jr., *Directing* TrafFix: *A Comment on the Construction and Application of Utility Patent Claims in Trade Dress Litigation,* FLA. L. REV. 229, 267-269 (2002). Does this question affect your view on the relative importance of the different devices through which trademark law defines the protection available for product design trade dress? *Cf. Samara Bros. v. Wal-Mart Stores, Inc.,* 165 F.3d 120 (2d Cir. 1998) (Newman J., dissenting), *rev'd,* 529 U.S. 205 (2000).

9. ***Venerable patents.*** Given the reasons behind the "evidentiary inference," what weight would you give to an expired utility patent on a design that had issued over fifty years ago? *See Eco Mfg. LLC v. Honeywell Int'l Inc.,* 357 F.3d 649, 653 (7th Cir. 2003) (noting that "passage of time diminishes a utility patent's significance").

10. ***The relevance of abandoned patent applications.*** In what way is an abandoned utility patent application relevant to the question of functionality, as the Federal Circuit suggests? If it should be relevant, which of the purposes underlying the functionality doctrine is being effectuated? What if the design of the plaintiff's product is "closely related to a potentially patentable . . . process"? *See Incredible Techs. v. Virtual Techs. Inc.,* 284 F. Supp. 2d 1069, 1078 (N.D. Ill. 2003), *aff'd,* 400 F.3d 1007 (7th Cir. 2005). What should be the relevance of the fact that a plaintiff had tried, but failed, to secure a copyright registration on the design? *See Bonazoli v. R.S.V.P. Int'l,* 353 F. Supp. 2d 218 (D.R.I. 2005).

11. ***The relevance of related design and utility patents.*** In *Fuji*, the court noted that a design patent is presumptive evidence of nonfunctionality, but afforded it little weight because of parallel utility patent on the product that created a presumption of functionality. Do you agree with this approach?

12. ***Changes in status.*** Clearly, a design that is at one time distinctive might become functional. Can a design that is once held to be functional become nonfunctional? *Compare Eco Mfg. LLC v. Honeywell Int'l Inc.,* 357 F.3d 649 (7th Cir. 2003); *In re Honeywell, Inc.,* 8 U.S.P.Q.2d 1600, 1604-05 (T.T.A.B. 1988), with *In re Honeywell, Inc.,* 532 F.2d 180, 182-83 (C.C.P.A. 1976). Might that depend upon whether the basis for the functionality determination was the existence of an expired utility patent? *Cf. In re Bose Corp.,* 81 U.S.P.Q.2d 1748 (Fed. Cir. 2007).

13. ***The relevance of procedural context?*** To what extent are the *Valu Engineering* court's conclusions dependent on the procedural posture of its functionality analysis (i.e., in the context of registration, rather than in

infringement proceedings)? Recall that, after an amendment designed to resolve a circuit split on the question of burden of proof, in an infringement action under Section 32 (i.e., where the design is registered as a trademark), the burden to prove functionality rests on the defendant; in an action for infringement of an unregistered design mark (under Section 43), the plaintiff must prove nonfunctionality. *See* 15 U.S.C. §1125(a)(3) (1999 Supp.). If the plaintiff has a registration on the design, should the defendant be able to obtain summary judgment on the question of functionality? *See Tie Tech, Inc. v. Kinedyne Corp.*, 296 F.3d 778 (9th Cir. 2002).

**14. *Cumulation of rights.*** The availability of trade dress protection for potentially patentable subject matter is often justified on the ground that the purposes of trademark law and patent law are different. That is, the different regimes protect different legal interests (rather than one regime extending perpetually the term of protection offered by the other to protect the same interest). To what extent is that true? If, in fact, trademark and patent law effectively protect the same interests, should we restrict cumulation of trademark and patent protection? Should we allow producers to use one intellectual property regime but not the other? *See* Gideon Parchomovsky & Peter Siegelman, *Toward an Integrated Theory of Intellectual Property*, 88 VA. L. REV. 1455 (2002). Others justify cumulative protection on the ground that the scope of rights granted by trademark law is narrower than those afforded under patent law, and thus does not threaten to undermine patent law. (As we discuss the scope of trade dress rights, *see infra* Chapter 4, reconsider the strength of this argument.) When these argument are taken together, some scholars have suggested that because a trade dress claimant must demonstrate use in commerce, distinctiveness, nonfunctionality, and use by the defendant of (typically) a confusingly similar device, and because "none of these showings bears any relationship whatsoever to the prerequisites for utility patent protection, the proposition that an extension of trade dress protection somehow can 'extend' the protection previously afforded by a related utility patent is a non sequitur." Theodore H. Davis, Jr., *Directing* TrafFix: *A Comment on the Construction and Application of Utility Patent Claims in Trade Dress Litigation*, 50 FLA. L. REV. 229, 259 (2002). Are you persuaded that the concern about trade dress rights extending the life of patents is overstated?

### (b) Aesthetic Features

#### ABERCROMBIE & FITCH STORES, INC. V. AMERICAN EAGLE OUTFITTERS
280 F.3d 619 (6th Cir. 2002)

BOGGS, Circuit Judge:

[Abercrombie & Fitch (A&F) brought a trade dress claim against American Eagle Outfitters based on the defendants' alleged copying of, inter alia, the designs of certain articles of clothing, its store setup, and its Quarterly catalog. The district court granted summary judgment in favor of American Eagle (American), reasoning that Abercrombie & Fitch had sought protection for something that did not constitute trade dress at all. The Court of Appeals for the Sixth Circuit affirmed the district court on the alternative grounds that the clothing designs were functional as a matter of law (and the defendant's catalog was not confusingly similar).]

In *TrafFix*, the Court identified two forms of functionality. The first, traditional functionality, deems a feature functional when ' "it is essential to the use or purpose of the device or when it affects the cost or quality of the device.' " [cit.] *Qualitex* "[e]xpand[ed] upon the meaning of this phrase [by] observ[ing] that a functional feature is one the 'exclusive use of which would put competitors at a significant non-reputation-related disadvantage.' " *TrafFix*, 121 S. Ct. at 1261 (quoting *Qualitex*, 514 U.S. at 165). But the competitive disadvantage comment did not displace the traditional functionality standard from *Inwood Laboratories*. Instead it explained the policy underlying the functionality doctrine in a way readily adaptable to the problem of aesthetic functionality, the issue presented in *Qualitex*. See *TrafFix*, 532 U.S. 23. Thus, the "significant non-reputation-related disadvantage" to competitors approach is the second form of trade dress functionality.

None of the design features that Abercrombie claims as its trade dress is essential to the use or purpose of the garments, catalog, and stores they adorn. The design features surely affect the cost and quality of the garments and the design of the catalog affects its cost and aesthetics (which determines, in part, its quality as a device for selling clothing), so a jury question exists as to whether the designs are functional in the traditional sense. However, no reasonable jury could deny the existence of a "significant non-reputation-related disadvantage" that would be imposed on competitors by protecting Abercrombie's claimed trade dress. That form of functionality governs the analysis of this case.[16]

The two most common "tests" of aesthetic functionality under the competition theory prove useful in this case. "The test for 'comparable alternatives' asks whether trade-dress protection of certain features would nevertheless leave a variety of comparable alternative features that competitors may use to compete in the market. If such alternatives do not exist, the feature is functional; but if such alternatives do exist, then the feature is not functional." [Mitchell M. Wong, *The Aesthetic Functionality Doctrine and the Law of Trade Dress Protection,* 83 Cornell L. Rev. 1116, 1144-45 (1998)] (noting that "[t]he comparable alternatives requirement may necessitate more than the mere existence of one alternative, and may instead require a number of alternatives from which competitors may choose") (footnotes omitted).[17] "The 'effective competition' test asks . . . whether trade dress protection for a product's feature would hinder the ability of another manufacturer to compete effectively in the market for the product. If such hindrance is probable, then the feature is

---

16. For quite some time, the circuits have disagreed about the most appropriate theory of functionality to use in aesthetic functionality cases. . . . Because the Supreme Court has . . . repeatedly followed the competition theory's approach in addressing the second form of functionality, *see TrafFix,* 121 S. Ct. at 1261-62 (explaining *Qualitex),* we expressly adopt the competition theory of functionality.

17. The Seventh Circuit described the comparable alternatives problem thus: "a functional feature is one which competitors would have to spend money not to copy but to design around, as they would have to do if they wanted to come up with a nonoval substitute for a football. It is something costly to do without (like the hood [of a car] itself), rather than costly to have (like the statue of Mercury [decorating the hood])." *W.T. Rogers Co. v. Keene 118* F.2d at 339 (7th Cir. 1985).

functional and unsuitable for protection. If the feature is not a likely impediment to market competition, then the feature is nonfunctional and may receive trademark protection." *Id.* at 1149 (footnotes omitted).[18] The same principle applies to trade dress law. *See Two Pesos,* 505 U.S. at 768.

We turn first to Abercrombie's clothing designs.[19] Abercrombie's complaint itself identifies the functions of the design elements it selected: use of the word *performance* "convey[s] the image of an active line of . . . clothing"; use of the words *authentic, genuine brand, trademark,* and *since 1892* "convey the reliability of the . . . brand"; and so on. Use of these elements in combination with one another and with Abercrombie's trademarks on clothing bearing "primary color combinations . . . in connection with solid, plaid and stripe designs" and made from "all natural cotton, wool and twill fabrics" creates reliable rugged and/or athletic casual clothing drawn from a consistent texture, design, and color palette. Were the law to grant Abercrombie protection of these features, the paucity of comparable alternative features that competitors could use to compete in the market for casual clothing would leave competitors at a significant non-reputational competitive disadvantage and would, therefore, prevent effective competition in the market.

Giving Abercrombie a monopoly on the words it claims form part of its trade dress would hamstring any competitor's ability to convey the reliability of its own brand. The English language currently contains a limited list of synonyms for *reliable* and other words that convey a product's integrity. While Abercrombie designers deserve credit for using the company's age as a creative indicator of their products' reliability, few other verbal formulations adequately or efficiently convey this concept. The same is true of using suggestive symbols like lacrosse sticks and the ski patrol cross on clothing to convey the product's athletic nature or capacity to invoke images of athleticism. Producers have a limited range of sports and sporting equipment to

---

18. As the Seventh Circuit explained: "[I]t would . . . be unreasonable to let a manufacturer use trademark law to prevent competitors from making pleasing substitutes for his own brand; yet that would be the effect of allowing him to appropriate the most pleasing way of configuring the product." *W.T. Rogers Co.,* 778 F.2d at 340. In this sense, functionality depends on "whether the feature . . . is something that other producers of the product in question would have to have as part of the product in order to be able to compete effectively in the market—in other words, in order to give consumers the benefits of a competitive market—or whether it is the kind of merely incidental feature which gives the brand some individual distinction but which producers of competing brands can readily do without." *Id.* at 346.

19. For ease of reference, we here reprint the features Abercrombie claims comprise the trade dress of its garment designs: "a) use of the Abercrombie Marks, in particular the A & F trademark in universe bold condensed typeface; b) use of the word *performance* on labels and advertising and promotional material to convey the image of an active line of casual clothing; c) use of such words and phrases as *authentic, genuine brand, trademark,* [and] *since 1892* on labels and advertising and promotional material to convey the reliability of the Abercrombie Brand; d) use of the word *outdoor* on labels and advertising and promotional materials to convey the image of a rugged outdoor line of casual clothing; e) use of design logos, such as the ski patrol cross and lacrosse sticks, and product names for the types of clothing, such as *"field jersey,"* to convey the image of an athletic line of casual clothing; f) use of primary color combinations, such as red, blue, grey, tan and green in connection with solid, plaid and stripe designs, to create a consistent design and color palette, g) use of all natural cotton, wool and twill fabrics to create a consistent texture palette. . . ." Compl. ¶7. The last two features are obviously functional standing alone. And American has not directly copied the first feature, the use of Abercrombie's trademarks; it has used its own. It seems, then, that Abercrombie meant to define its trade dress as including some or many of the features labeled b) through e) in combination with the last two features and the producer's own trademark.

choose from in attempting to convey this idea in this manner on clothing. Producers could go without such images or devise wholly new ways of conveying the athleticism concept in connection with casual clothing, but at present these features are ones that "competitors would have to spend money not to copy but to design around." *W.T. Rogers Co.*, 778 F.2d at 340. The lack of comparable alternatives to pleasing design features means that granting an injunction would deny consumers the benefits of a competitive market. In short, these design features are "something that other producers of the [casual clothing] have to have as part of the product in order to be able to compete effectively in the market . . . [it is not] the kind of merely incidental feature which gives the brand some individual distinction but which producers of competing brands can readily do without." *Id.* at 346.

Finally, Abercrombie is not saved by its characterization of its trade dress as the *combination* of different design features on its clothing: denying American or other producers the right to combine these functional design features with their own trademarks on clothing bearing certain generic designs (unspecified "solid, plaid, and stripe designs," without more, are indisputably generic) made from generic fabrics would undoubtedly force these competitors to spend money to design around Abercrombie's creations. There can be no dispute that preventing other producers from combining these design elements in the way Abercrombie does would prevent them from competing effectively in the market for casual clothing aimed at young people. No reasonable jury could find to the contrary. Remand for further proceedings in the district court on this question would be a waste of judicial resources, not to mention the parties' time and money.

We reach the same conclusion with respect to Abercrombie's claim of trade dress in its in-store display setups and use of college students as sales associates. Forbidding clothiers to use college students to sell garments to or for college-age people indubitably prevents them from effectively competing in the market for casual clothing directed at young people.

Abercrombie's catalog is a different matter entirely.[22] Of course, the Quarterly has certain functions, including "the creation of a cutting edge 'cool' Abercrombie image," and, presumably, selling clothes. But that does not make the catalog's overall design functional. Nor does the presence of many functional elements in the Quarterly's design. Even if the elements Abercrombie identifies were all separately functional, as American argued and the district court held, A&F's arrangement of these features can constitute more than the sum of its non-protectable parts. *See Publications Int'l, Ltd. v. Landoll, Inc.*, 164 F.3d 337, 341-43 (7th Cir. 1998) (holding various elements of a cookbook's design functional but recognizing that their appearance in concert

---

22. Again, for ease of reference, A&F describes its catalog's trade dress thus: "the creation of a cutting edge 'cool' Abercrombie image through photographs and advertising and promotional material . . . which presents the Abercrombie Brand and Trade Dress in a unique manner, namely, it features the Abercrombie Brand and Trade Dress in a 'cutout' or 'clothesline' style and uses color bars to illustrate the available colors of goods, while combining a consistent conceptual theme with a lifestyle editorial content of music, electronics, books, and magazine features and is printed on cougar vellum paper which is unique for a catalog." Compl. ¶7(h).

could garner legal protection "unless it was the only way the product *could* look, consistent with its performing each of the product's functions optimally"). [cit.]

A&F has chosen to print its catalog on an unusual kind of paper, leaving competitors a variety of other paper options. The clothes offered for sale appear in "clothesline" or "cutout" form (the garments appear on the page as if hanging from a clothesline, *i.e.*, not on a model), while many catalogs show garments on a model or display them in other ways. Colorbars are a useful mechanism for communicating the available selection of colors, but the same information can be provided in a handful of other ways. Abercrombie uses grainy images of exceptionally fit and attractive young people in outdoor (often collegiate) settings, alone and in groups, wearing more or less A&F clothing in ways that convey their allegiance to the brand while also seemingly attempting to create a sexual mystique about the wearer. The Quarterlies in the record rarely deviate from this pattern, but clothing retailers have an infinite variety of options for surrounding their clothes with pleasing or desirable imagery that avoids showing scantily clad college students in a grainy photograph. Finally, the record demonstrates that clothing catalogs have included so-called lifestyle editorial content for some time. But mail order retailers can still sell their clothes and create an aura about their products without including such content, although this method seems to have recently become a particularly effective way of creating demand. At the very least, the evidence in the record creates a genuine issue of material fact as to whether protection of the design features chosen by Abercrombie for its catalog leaves open sufficient comparable alternate methods of marketing clothing to young people by mail, such that granting A&F a monopoly on its distinctive configuration would not hinder the ability of another manufacturer to compete effectively in the market. Here, the Seventh Circuit's verbal formulation of the issue seems particularly apt: "whether the [combination of] feature[s] . . . is something that other producers of the product in question would have to have as part of [their catalog] in order to be able to compete effectively in the market . . . or whether it is the kind of merely incidental [configuration] which gives the brand some individual distinction but which producers of competing brands can readily do without." *W.T. Rogers Co.*, 778 F.2d at 346.

Abercrombie claimed three "things" as its trade dress. Its clothing designs and its in-store presentation are not protectable because they are functional, despite their distinctiveness. As to the overall design of the A&F Quarterly, however, we will assume that it satisfies the distinctiveness and non-functionality conditions for protectability because, for purposes of the instant appeal, American conceded secondary meaning and the record evidence raises genuine issues as to the material fact of non-functionality. We therefore proceed to assess whether Abercrombie could prevail on its trade dress infringement claim.

[The court concluded that Abercrombie could not possibly have carried its burden of proving that American's catalog was confusingly similar to what it presumed was the protectable trade dress of Abercrombie's Quarterly.]

### AU-TOMOTIVE GOLD, INC. v. VOLKSWAGEN OF AMERICA, INC.
457 F.3d 1062 (9th Cir. 2006)

McKEOWN, Circuit Judge:

This case centers on the trademarks of two well-known automobile manufacturers—Volkswagen and Audi. The question is whether the Lanham Act prevents a maker of automobile accessories from selling, without a license or other authorization, products bearing exact replicas of the trademarks of these famous car companies. Au-Tomotive Gold, Inc. ("Auto Gold") argues that, as used on its key chains and license plate covers, the logos and marks of Volkswagen and Audi are aesthetic functional elements of the product—that is, they are "the actual benefit that the consumer wishes to purchase"—and are thus unprotected by the trademark laws.

Accepting Auto Gold's position would be the death knell for trademark protection. . . . Taken to its limits, as Auto Gold advocates, this doctrine would permit a competitor to trade on any mark simply because there is some "aesthetic" value to the mark that consumers desire. This approach distorts both basic principles of trademark law and the doctrine of functionality in particular.

Auto Gold's incorporation of Volkswagen and Audi marks in its key chains and license plates appears to be nothing more than naked appropriation of the marks. The doctrine of aesthetic functionality does not provide a defense against actions to enforce the trademarks against such poaching. Consequently, we reverse the district court's grant of summary judgment in favor of Auto Gold on the basis of aesthetic functionality. . . .

#### Background

Volkswagen and Audi are manufacturers of automobiles, parts and accessories that bear well-known trademarks, including the names Volkswagen and Audi, the encircled VW logo, the interlocking circles of the Audi logo, and the names of individual car models. The marks are registered in the United States and have been in use since the 1950s. . . .

Auto Gold produces and sells automobile accessories to complement specific makes of cars, including Cadillac, Ford, Honda, Lexus, Jeep, Toyota, and others. In 1994, Auto Gold began selling license plates, license plate frames and key chains bearing Volkswagen's distinctive trademarks and, in 1997, began selling similar products bearing Audi's distinctive trademarks. . . .

According to Auto Gold, its goods serve a unique market. Consumers want these accessories "to match the chrome on their cars; to put something on the empty space where the front license tag would otherwise go; or because the car is a [Volkswagen or Audi], they want a [Volkswagen or Audi]-logo plate." Both Auto Gold and Volkswagen and Audi serve this market. . . .

[Volkswagen and Audi alleged *inter alia* that Auto Gold's activities constitute trademark infringement, trademark dilution, trademark counterfeiting and unfair competition.] In ruling for Auto Gold, the district court found that "[t]he VW and Audi logos are used not because they signify that the license plate or key ring was manufactured or sold (i.e., as a designation of origin) by Volkswagen or Audi, but because there is a[n] aesthetic quality to the marks that purchasers are interested in having." Concluding that the marks were "protected under the aesthetic functionality doctrine," the district court . . . entered an order declaring that Auto Gold's "license plates, license plate frames and key chains displaying Volkswagen and Audi trademarks . . . are not trademark infringements and/or trademark counterfeiting." [Volkswagen and Audi appealed.]

Analysis

A. Trademark Law and Aesthetic Functionality

[A] functional product feature does not . . . enjoy protection under trademark law. [cit] The Supreme Court has instructed that a feature is functional if it is "essential to the use or purpose of the article [or] affects [its] cost or quality." [The]*Inwood Laboratories* definition is often referred to as "utilitarian" functionality, as it relates to the performance of the product in its intended purpose. Thus, "[t]he functionality doctrine prevents trademark law, which seeks to promote competition by protecting a firm's reputation, from instead inhibiting legitimate competition by allowing a producer to control a useful product feature." *Qualitex*, 514 U.S. at 164.

Extending the functionality doctrine, which aims to protect "useful" product features, to encompass unique logos and insignia is not an easy transition. Famous trademarks have assumed an exalted status of their own in today's consumer culture that cannot neatly be reduced to the historic function of trademark to designate source. Consumers sometimes buy products bearing marks such as the Nike Swoosh, the Playboy bunny ears, the Mercedes tri-point star, the Ferrari stallion, and countless sports franchise logos, for the appeal of the mark itself, without regard to whether it signifies the origin or sponsorship of the product. As demand for these marks has risen, so has litigation over the rights to their use as claimed "functional" aspects of products. [cit]

The results reached in these various aesthetic functionality cases do not easily weave together to produce a coherent jurisprudence, although as a general matter courts have been loathe to declare unique, identifying logos and names as functional. To understand how the concept of functionality applies to the case before us, broad invocations of principle are not particularly helpful. Instead, we find it useful to follow the chronological development and refinement of the doctrine. [The court then traced the development of the doctrine of aesthetic functionality from the 1938 Restatement of Torts, through *Pagliero*, and later Ninth Circuit case law rejecting *Pagliero* that dealt aesthetic functionality "a limiting but not fatal blow"]. . . .

The Supreme Court has yet to address aesthetic functionality as it applies to logos and insignia, in contrast to product features. The Court has, however, outlined the general contours of functionality and aesthetic functionality. . . .

The Court's most recent explication of aesthetic functionality is found in . . . *TrafFix Devices, Inc. v. Marketing Displays, Inc.*, 532 U.S. 23 (2001). . . . [T]he Court clarified *Qualitex*'s emphasis on competitive necessity and the overall test for functionality. . . .

[After quoting the Supreme Court's discussion of the *Inwood* test and the "significant non-reputation-related disadvantage" test, the Ninth Circuit continued.] The Court explained the interplay between these two statements of functionality. If a feature is functional under *Inwood Laboratories* the inquiry ends and the feature cannot be protected under trademark law. As the Court elaborated, "there is no need to proceed further to consider if there is a competitive necessity for the feature." . . .

By contrast, the Court went on to suggest that "[i]t is proper to inquire into a 'significant non-reputation-related disadvantage' in cases of aesthetic functionality, . . .

[W]e read the Court's decision to mean that consideration of competitive necessity may be an appropriate but not necessary element of the functionality analysis. If a design is determined to be functional under the traditional test of *Inwood Laboratories* there is no need to go further to consider indicia of competitive necessity, such as the availability of alternative designs. *Accord Valu Eng'g, Inc. v. Rexnord Corp.*, 278 F.3d 1268, 1275-76 (Fed. Cir. 2002). However, in the context of aesthetic functionality, such considerations may come into play because a "functional feature is one the 'exclusive use of [which] would put competitors at a significant non-reputation related disadvantage.'" [cit.] . . .

### B. Aesthetic Functionality and Auto Gold's Use of Volkswagen and Audi's Products

So where do we stand in the wake of forty years of trademark law scattered with references to aesthetic functionality? After *Qualitex* and *TrafFix* the test for functionality proceeds in two steps. In the first step, courts inquire whether the alleged "significant non-trademark function" satisfies the [*Inwood* definition.] If this is the case, the inquiry is over—the feature is functional and not protected. In the case of a claim of aesthetic functionality, an alternative test inquires whether protection of the feature as a trademark would impose a significant non-reputation-related competitive disadvantage.[1]

We now address the marks at issue in this case. Volkswagen and Audi's trademarks are registered and incontestable, and are thus presumed to be valid, distinctive and non-functional. [cit.] Auto Gold, thus, must show that the marks are functional under the test set forth above. To satisfy this requirement, Auto Gold argues that Volkswagen and Audi trademarks are functional features of its products because "the trademark is the feature of the product which constitutes the actual benefit the consumer wishes to purchase." While that may be so, the fact that a trademark is desirable does not, and should not, render it unprotectable. Auto Gold has not shown that Volkswagen and Audi's marks are functional features of Auto Gold's products. The marks are thus entitled to trademark protection.

---

1. Our long-standing test for functionality largely excluded aesthetic considerations, instead asking: (1) whether the feature delivers any utilitarian advantage, (2) whether alternative designs are possible, (3) whether advertising touts utilitarian benefits of the feature, and (4) whether the feature results in economies in manufacture or use. Following *TrafFix* we reiterated [those] factors as legitimate considerations in determining whether a product feature is functional. *Talking Rain Beverage Co. v. South Beach Beverage Co*, 349 F.3d 601, 603-04 (9th Cir. 2003) (applying the four factors to conclude that a bottle design was utilitarian). We noted that "the existence of alternative designs cannot negate a trademark's functionality," but "may indicate whether the trademark itself embodies functional or merely ornamental aspects of the product."

At the first step, there is no evidence on the record, and Auto Gold does not argue, that Volkswagen and Audi's trademarks are functional under the utilitarian definition in *Inwood Laboratories* as applied in the Ninth Circuit in *Talking Rain*. That is to say, Auto Gold's products would still frame license plates and hold keys just as well without the famed marks. Similarly, use of the marks does not alter the cost structure or add to the quality of the products.

We next ask whether Volkswagen and Audi's marks, as they appear on Auto Gold's products, perform some function such that the "'exclusive use of [the marks] would put competitors at a significant non-reputation-related disadvantage.'" As an initial matter, Auto Gold's proffered rational [sic] — that the trademarks "constitute[] the actual benefit the consumer wishes to purchase" — flies in the face of existing caselaw. We have squarely rejected the notion that "any feature of a product which contributes to the consumer appeal and saleability of the product is, as a matter of law, a functional element of that product." *Vuitton*, 644 F.2d at 773. Such a rule would eviscerate the very competitive policies that functionality seeks to protect. This approach is consistent with the view of our sister circuits. [cit.]

Even viewing Auto Gold's position generously, the rule it advocates injects unwarranted breadth into our caselaw. *Pagliero, Job's Daughters*, and their progeny were careful to prevent "the use of a trademark to monopolize a design feature which, *in itself and apart from its identification of source*, improves the usefulness or appeal of the object it adorns." *Vuitton*, 644 F.2d at 774 (*discussing Pagliero*, 198 F.2d 339) (emphasis added). The concept of an "aesthetic" function that is non-trademark-related has enjoyed only limited application. In practice, aesthetic functionality has been limited to product features that serve an aesthetic purpose wholly independent of any source-identifying function. See *Qualitex*, 514 U.S. at 166 (coloring dry cleaning pads served nontrademark purpose by avoiding visible stains); *Publications Int'l, Ltd. v. Landoll, Inc.*, 164 F.3d 337, 342 (7th Cir. 1998) (coloring edges of cookbook pages served nontrademark purpose by avoiding color "bleeding" between pages); *Brunswick Corp. v. British Seagull Ltd.*, 35 F.3d 1527, 1532 (Fed.Cir. 1994) (color black served nontrademark purpose by reducing the apparent size of outboard boat engine); *Pagliero*, 198 F.2d at 343 (china patterns at issue were attractive and served nontrademark purpose because "one of the essential selling features of hotel china, if, indeed, not the primary, is the design").

It is difficult to extrapolate from cases involving a true aesthetically functional feature, like a box shape or certain uses of color, to cases involving well-known registered logos and company names, which generally have no function apart from their association with the trademark holder. The present case illustrates the point well, as the use of Volkswagen and Audi's marks is neither aesthetic nor independent of source identification. That is to say, there is no evidence that consumers buy Auto Gold's products solely because of their "intrinsic" aesthetic appeal. Instead, the alleged aesthetic function is indistinguishable from and tied to the mark's source-identifying nature.

By Auto Gold's strident admission, consumers want "Audi" and "Volkswagen" accessories, not beautiful accessories. This consumer demand is difficult to quarantine from the source identification and reputation-enhancing value of the trademarks themselves. See *Playboy Enters., Inc. v. Netscape Commc'ns*

*Corp.*, 354 F.3d 1020, 1030-31 (9th Cir. 2004) ("Nothing about the marks used to identify [the trademark holder's] products is a functional part of the design of those products. . . . The fact that the marks make [the junior user's product] more functional is irrelevant."). The demand for Auto Gold's products is inextricably tied to the trademarks themselves. *See Qualitex*, 514 U.S. at 170, (identifying "legitimate (*nontrademark-related*) competition" as the relevant focus in determining functionality) (emphasis added). Any disadvantage Auto Gold claims in not being able to sell Volkswagen or Audi marked goods is tied to the reputation and association with Volkswagen and Audi.

In the end, we take comfort that the doctrine of aesthetic functionality, as we apply it in this case, has simply returned from whence it came. The 1938 Restatement of Torts includes this reminder of the difference between an aesthetic function and a trademark function:

> A feature which merely associates goods with a particular source may be, like a trade-mark or trade name, a substantial factor in increasing the marketability of the goods. But if that is the entire significance of the feature, it is nonfunctional; for its value then lies only in the demand for goods associated with a particular source rather than for goods of a particular design.

Restatement of Torts §742, comment a (1938). Volkswagen and Audi's trademarks undoubtedly increase the marketability of Auto Gold's products. But their "entire significance" lies in the demand for goods bearing those nonfunctional marks. Today, as in 1938, such poaching is not countenanced by the trademark laws.

We hold that Volkswagen and Audi's marks are not functional aspects of Auto Gold's products. These marks, which are registered and have achieved incontestable status, are properly protected under the Lanham Act against infringement, dilution, false designation of source and other misappropriations. . . .

## NOTES AND QUESTIONS

1. ***Focus of analysis.*** What is the central question for a court in determining whether a design is aesthetically functional? *See Malaco Leaf AB v. Promotion in Motion, Inc.*, 287 F. Supp. 2d 355, 366-367 (S.D.N.Y. 2003) (features of fish-shaped gummy candy, such as head, tail, scale pattern, and eye, held to be aesthetically functional and noting that "nearly every third party marketing gummy fish-shaped candy portrays identical features"); *Dippin' Dots, Inc. v. Frosty Bites Distrib.*, 369 F.3d 1197, 1203 (11th Cir. 2004) ("Functional features are by definition likely to be shared by different producers of the same product and therefore are unlikely to identify a single producer."); *Maharashi Hardy Blechman Ltd. v. Abercrombie & Fitch Co.*, 292 F. Supp. 2d 535 (S.D.N.Y. 2003) (denying motion to dismiss on functionality grounds because protecting the design of plaintiff's military-style pants would not prevent defendant from producing a distinguishable line of pants, and thus design not clearly aesthetically functional); *Bonazoli v. R.S.V.P. Int'l*, 353 F. Supp. 2d 218, 227 (D.R.I. 2005) (finding that a design for measuring spoons in which "the bowl of

each spoon was made in the shape of a heart and the handle in the shape of an arrow shaft" was aesthetically functional in that "the appeal" of the heart shape design of plaintiff's measuring spoons "produces demand," and thus to grant trade dress protection would "interfere with legitimate (non-trademark-related) competition through actual or potential exclusive use of an important product ingredient") (quoting *Qualitex*); *cf. Eco Mfg. LLC v. Honeywell Int'l Inc.*, 357 F.3d 649 (7th Cir. 2003) (rejecting the argument that after *TrafFix* a design is functional because "some consumers prefer its look" and commenting that " 'beauty lies in the eye of the beholder' . . . cannot by itself establish functionality of a trade dress"); *Bd of Supervisors of La. State Univ. v. Smack Apparel Co.*, 438 F. Supp. 2d. 653 (E.D. La. 2006) (benefit accruing from trademark value not relevant to aesthetic functionality claim).

**2. Relevant market.** In *New Colt Holding Corp. v. RJG Holdings of Fla., Inc.*, 312 F. Supp. 2d 195, 219 (D. Conn. 2004), the plaintiff sought to protect the shape of its revolvers. The defendant, a replica gun manufacturer whose replicas were much cheaper, argued that the shape of the guns was aesthetically functional because "they and other replica makers would no longer be able to make replicas of the revolvers in question and they would no longer be able to meet the 'consumer need' of those who seek historically accurate revolvers but who cannot afford to purchase plaintiff's revolvers." What is the relevant market with respect to which the functionality analysis should be conducted? Consider this statement from the Eleventh Circuit in *Dippin' Dots, Inc. v. Frosty Bites Distrib.*, 369 F.3d 1197, 1203 n.7 (11th Cir. 2004):

> [T]he color, shape, and size of dippin' dots are "aesthetic functions" that easily satisfy the competitive necessity test because precluding competitors . . . from copying any of these aspects of dippin' dots would eliminate all competitors in the flash-frozen ice cream market, which would be the ultimate non-reputation-related disadvantage. Therefore, [plaintiff's] argument that [the defendant] could still compete in the ice cream market by producing, e.g., soft-serve ice cream, which would not have many of the same functional elements as dippin' dots and thus would not infringe upon [plaintiff's] product trade dress, is unavailing. [Defendant] does not want to compete in the ice cream business; it wants to compete in the flash-frozen ice cream business, which is in a different market from more traditional forms of ice cream. *See* 3 Louis Altman, *Callmann on Unfair Competition, Trademarks and Monopolies* §19:7, at 79 (4th ed. 2003) (stating that "functionality . . . is not to be determined within the broad compass of different but interchangeable products; the doctrine of functionality is intended to preserve competition within the narrow bounds of each *individual* product market").

Does this suggest the answer in *New Colt*? Is *Dippin' Dots* consistent with *TrafFix*?

**3. Evidence.** Though some courts applying *Inwood* have strictly applied the *TrafFix* Court's caution about the relevance of alternatives, courts have been comfortable considering alternative designs in assessing aesthetic functionality. *See, e.g., Yurman Design, Inc. v. Golden Treasure Imports, Inc.*, 275 F. Supp. 2d 506, 512 (S.D.N.Y. 2003) (jewelry designs); *cf. New Colt Holding Corp. v. RJG Holdings of Fla., Inc.*, 312 F. Supp. 2d 195, 214 & 219 (D. Conn. 2004) (noting that "the question of aesthetic functionality explicitly turns on the existence of design alternatives").

**4. *Scope of the application of the functionality doctrine.*** Should the functionality doctrine be applied to trademark subject matter other than color per se, the design or configuration of goods, and packaging? *See Ford Motor Co. v. Lloyd Design Corp.*, 184 F. Supp. 2d 665 (E.D. Mich. 2002). Could a word mark be functional? What about a number mark, such as "23" for basketball uniforms? *Cf. GTFM, Inc. v. Solid Clothing, Inc.*, 215 F. Supp. 2d 273 (S.D.N.Y 2002) (considering whether the mark "05" emblazoned on athletic jerseys is functional).

**5. *Marketing themes and the "look" of humans.*** Abercrombie & Fitch is not alone in seeking to protect the particular "look" of its employees or advertising models from copying by others. There, the look in question ("pleasing or desirable imagery . . . showing scantily clad college students in a grainy photograph") was one feature of the catalogs used to sell Abercrombie & Fitch products. But the Hooters restaurant chain took the argument one step further, and argued that what the court called the "iconic Hooters Girl" (i.e., the waitresses of a somewhat consistent look who wear relatively skimpy tank tops and running shoes and serve food at Hooters restaurants) was part of its trade dress. *See H.I. Ltd. P'ship v. Winghouse of Fla., Inc.*, 347 F. Supp. 2d 1256, 1258 (M.D. Fla. 2004). Should the approach of trademark law differ as between the look of the models in promotional material and the look of employees? In any event, the court denied protection to Hooters, finding that the Hooters Girl was "the very essence of Hooters' business" and thus functional. Does this formulation capture the gist of the functionality inquiry? If not, how else might you deny trade dress protection on these facts? In *Haagen Dazs v. Frusen Gladje, Ltd.*, 493 F. Supp. 73, 75 (S.D.N.Y. 1980), the district court held that a marketing theme cannot constitute trade dress, and thus plaintiff could not obtain exclusive use of a Scandinavian name for its ice cream. Might this be a rule applicable to the trade dress in *HI*? Can you express that rule in terms of a doctrine that we have already discussed? Or do you prefer the apparently simple rule that "a marketing theme cannot constitute trade dress"? How would *Two Pesos* be decided under that rule?

### (c) The Relationship between the Tests

As noted above in the notes following *TrafFix*, the relationship between the two tests of functionality is not clear. We suggested above that the Supreme Court's opinion leaves open at least two ways to approach the two tests. First, they might be separate filters, both of which any feature claimed to be nonfunctional must pass through to be protected. Second, each test may be applicable to different types of features, *Inwood* to mechanical features and "competitive necessity" to aesthetic features.

If the first approach is adopted (i.e., each design feature for which protection is sought must pass both tests), how does this fit with the apparent linking of the "competitive necessity" test and "aesthetic functionality" by the Court in *TrafFix*? Perhaps this linking can be seen merely as an acknowledgment that designs that appear to have no mechanical utility related to the purpose of the article are likely to pass the first, *Inwood*, test and thus stand or fall depending on the competitive necessity test. *Cf. Dippin' Dots, Inc. v. Frosty Bites Distrib.*, 369 F.3d 1197, 1203 (11th Cir. 2004) (noting the "two tests" for functionality and acknowledging that if the terms of the *Inwood* test are satisfied, there is no need to proceed further to consider whether the competitive necessity test, which is "generally applied in cases of aesthetic functionality," is satisfied). *Contra Yurman Design, Inc. v. Golden Treasure Imports, Inc.*, 275 F. Supp. 2d 506, 511 (S.D.N.Y. 2003) ("where trade dress involves an aesthetic feature, that feature is functional" if it violates the competitive necessity test). This treats the use of the adjectives "utilitarian" and "aesthetic" as simply descriptors of the *test* that a feature passes or fails, rather than as ontological classifications of the feature for which protection is sought. This would create a unitary analysis for functionality, *see* Graeme B. Dinwoodie, *The Death of Ontology: A Teleological Approach to Trademark Law*, 84 Iowa L. Rev. 611, 701-721 (1999) (advocating a broad "competitive need" test for aesthetic and utilitarian features alike), albeit one with two hurdles for any design to overcome. Would it make the functionality test easier to apply? Easier or harder for plaintiffs to satisfy? Would it be consistent with *TrafFix* or any of the post-*TrafFix* cases you have read? What issues would remain open?

In considering these questions, note that in *Dippin' Dots*, color was regarded as functional under both the traditional test and the competitive necessity test. *See Dippin' Dots, Inc. v. Frosty Bites Distrib.*, 369 F.3d 1197, 1203-1204 & n.7 (11th Cir. 2004) (holding that the color of ice cream is functional under the traditional test because it indicates flavor—for example, pink signifies strawberry—but would also be aesthetically functional under a competitive necessity test); *see also Gateway Inc. v. Companion Prods., Inc.*, 68 U.S.P.Q.2d 1407 (D.S.D. 2003) (black-and-white cattle-like design for computer products is non-functional under traditional test), *aff'd*, 384 F.3d 503 (8th Cir. 2004).

The second approach, of course, presents problems of formalistic classification. When is a feature utilitarian and when is it aesthetic? *Cf. Baughman Tile Co. v. Plastic Tubing Inc.*, 211 F. Supp. 2d 720, 722 n.2 (E.D.N.C. 2002) (describing the tests that the Supreme Court labeled as "traditional" and an "elaboration," respectively, as tests of "utilitarian functionality" and "aesthetic functionality," and assessing the functionality of the color of plaintiff's tubing under the utilitarian functionality standard because typical consumers of the tubing do not base their purchase decisions on the appearance of the tubing, and thus the court need not inquire into the issue of "significant non-reputation-related disadvantage").

The relationship between *Inwood* and the *Qualitex* "elaboration" is only part of the task of finding doctrinal coherence. There are so many issues raised by *TrafFix*, the interplay between which is unclear. Thus, more generally, courts have not succeeded in articulating coherently the interaction of utility patents with the traditional *Inwood* test, the *Qualitex* "elaboration," the use of alternative designs, the relevance of competitive necessity, and any potential rebuttal of the "evidentiary inference." Nor have they typically even tried. Instead, courts often raise the issues individually or in combinations of two or three. For an ambitious attempt to summarize a complicated analysis, although perhaps with some glosses on the *TrafFix* test, *see ASICS Corp. v. Target Corp.*, 282 F. Supp. 2d 1020 (D. Minn. 2003) (noting that although "ASICS' exclusive use of its Stripe design mark for over 35 years has not stopped competitors from effectively competing," the threshold question before the court is whether the Stripe design is 'essential to the use or purpose of the article or if it *affects the cost of quality"* of shoes. Because ASICS' own utility patents and marketing provide strong evidence that the Stripe design affects the quality of shoes and is not "a mere arbitrary embellishment ... primarily adopted for purposes of identification and individuality," [cit.], and because this evidence has not been effectively rebutted, "there is no need to proceed further to consider if there is a competitive necessity for this feature"); *see also* Graeme B. Dinwoodie, *The Story of* Kellogg v. National Biscuit Company: Breakfast with Brandeis, *in* INTELLECTUAL PROPERTY STORIES (Dreyfuss and Ginsburg eds. 2005) (reviewing recent Supreme Court discussion of the relationship between the right to copy and functionality in the context of the *Kellogg* case).

## NOTES AND QUESTIONS

1. ***Designs "as a whole."*** After *TrafFix*, some commentators expressed concern that the Court's opinion "casts a cloud over the principle that when a decision maker decides whether a product's overall configuration is functional, that configuration should be viewed in its entirety, and not as discrete individual design features." Harold R. Weinberg, *Trademark Law, Functional Design Features and the Trouble with* TrafFix, 9 J. INTELL. PROP. L. 1, 6 (2001). Are those concerns confirmed or alleviated by any of the decisions excerpted above? *Cf. Tie Tech, Inc. v. Kinedyne Corp.*, 296 F.3d 778 (9th Cir. 2002) ("Where the plaintiff offers only evidence that the 'whole is nothing other than the assemblage of functional parts,' our court has already foreclosed this argument, holding that 'it is semantic trickery to say that there is still some sort of separate overall appearance which is non-functional.'"); *Logan Graphic Prods. v. Textus USA, Inc.*, 67 U.S.P.Q.2d 1470 (N.D. Ill. 2003) (appropriate inquiry focuses on the overall trade dress).

2. ***Legislative reform?*** In the wake of *TrafFix*, the Trademark Law Committee of the American Intellectual Property Law Association proposed the following resolutions:

> RESOLVED, that the American Intellectual Property Law Association ("AIPLA") favors, in principle, revision of the Lanham Act §1051, *et seq.*, to provide that the functionality of a product feature for which trade dress protection is sought should be determined by considering the degree to which granting protection would hinder competition.
>
> RESOLVED, that the American Intellectual Property Law Association ("AIPLA") favors amending the Lanham Act to add the following to Section 45, 15 U.S.C. §1127:
>
>> The term "functional" means that the matter sought to be protected under this Act is of such superior design for its utilitarian purpose that to afford it protection under this Act would significantly hinder effective competition. In determining whether matter is functional under this Act, the factors to be considered shall include, but not be limited to—

(1) whether effective alternative designs are available to competitors;
(2) whether the matter yields a significant utilitarian advantage over alternative designs;
(3) whether the matter achieves economies in the manufacture or use of the goods or services, reduces their cost, or enhances their quality;
(4) whether the party seeking to protect the matter has touted its utilitarian advantages; and
(5) whether the matter is or has been claimed in a utility patent or patent application.

Would you support these resolutions?

## 3. FUNCTIONALITY IN THE EUROPEAN UNION

The European Union Directive on Trademark Law, now implemented in the national laws of all the member states of the European Union, contains provisions (in Article 3) that approximate the functionality defense in U.S. law. The Community Trademark Regulation, which provides the basis for EU-wide trademark rights, contains parallel provisions in Article 7. More particularly, Article 3(1)(e) of the Directive provides that a registration will not be granted for "signs which consist exclusively of:

(i) the shape which results from the nature of the goods themselves, or
(ii) the shape of goods which is necessary to obtain a technical result, or
(iii) the shape which gives substantial value to the goods. . . ."

### KONINKLIJKE PHILIPS ELECTRONICS NV v. REMINGTON CONSUMER PRODUCTS LTD
2002 E.T.M.R. 81 (E.C.J. 2002)

JUDGMENT:

#### The Main Proceedings and the Questions Referred

In 1966, Philips developed a new type of three-headed rotary electric shaver. In 1985, Philips filed an application to register a trade mark consisting of a graphic representation of the shape and configuration of the head of such a shaver, comprising three circular heads with rotating blades in the shape of an equilateral triangle. That trade mark was registered on the basis of use under the [UK] Trade Marks Act 1938.

In 1995, Remington, a competing company, began to manufacture and sell in the United Kingdom the DT 55, which is a shaver with three rotating heads forming an equilateral triangle, shaped similarly to that used by Philips.

Philips accordingly sued Remington for infringement of its trade mark. Remington counter-claimed for revocation of the trade mark registered by Philips.

The High Court of England and Wales . . . allowed the counter-claim and ordered revocation of the registration of the Philips trade mark on [distinctiveness grounds]. The High Court also held that the trade mark consisted exclusively of a sign which served in trade to designate the intended purpose of the goods and of a shape which was necessary to obtain a technical result and which gave substantial value to the goods. It went on to hold that, even if the trade mark had been valid, it would not have been infringed.

Philips appealed to the Court of Appeal against that decision of the High Court. [The Court of Appeal decided to refer a number of questions to the European Court of Justice, including questions relating to the functionality provisions in the Directive. More particularly, the Court of Appeal asked as question 4 in its reference:]

> 4. (a) Can the restriction imposed by the words "if it consists exclusively of the shape of goods which is necessary to achieve a technical result" appearing in Article 3(1)(e)(ii) be overcome by establishing that there are other shapes which can obtain the same technical result or
>
> (b) is the shape unregistrable by virtue thereof if it is shown that the essential features of the shape are attributable only to the technical result or
>
> (c) is some other and, if so, what test appropriate for determining whether the restriction applies? . . .

Philips submits that the purpose of [this] provision of the Directive is to prevent the obtaining of a monopoly in a particular technical result by means of trade mark protection. However, the registration of a mark consisting of a shape which has a technical result imposes no unreasonable restraint on industry and innovation if that technical result can be obtained by other shapes which are readily available to competitors. According to Philips, there are many alternatives to the shape constituting the trade mark at issue which would achieve the same technical result in shaving terms at an equivalent cost to that of its products.

According to Remington, the clear meaning of Article 3(1)(e) of the Directive is that a shape that is necessary to achieve a technical result, in the sense that it performs a function in achieving that result but is not necessarily the only shape that can achieve that function, must be excluded from registration. The construction argued for by Philips would render the exclusion so narrow as to be useless and would require a technical evaluation of alternative designs, which would mean that the Directive could not ensure protection of the public interest.

The United Kingdom Government submits that registration must be refused if the essential features of the shape of which the sign consists are attributable only to the technical result.

According to the French Government, the purpose of the exclusion provided for in Article 3(1)(e), second indent, is to prevent the protection of technical creations, which is limited in time, from being circumvented by recourse to the rules on trade marks, the effects of which are potentially longer lasting.

Both the French Government and the United Kingdom Government take the view that the ground for refusal of registration under Article 3(1)(e), second indent, of the Directive cannot be overcome by establishing that there are other shapes capable of achieving the same technical result.

Given the legislative history of Article 3(1)(e), second indent, and the need to construe exceptions narrowly, the Commission is of the view that the relevant criterion is the availability of alternative shapes to achieve the desired technical result.

## Findings of the Court

Article 3(1)(e) thus concerns certain signs which are not such as to constitute trade marks and is a preliminary obstacle liable to prevent a sign consisting exclusively of the shape of a product from being registrable. If any one of the criteria listed in Article 3(1)(e) is satisfied, a sign consisting exclusively of the shape of the product or of a graphic representation of that shape cannot be registered as a trade mark.

The various grounds for refusal of registration listed in Article 3 of the Directive must be interpreted in the light of the public interest underlying each of them. [cit.]

The rationale of the grounds for refusal of registration laid down in Article 3(1)(e) of the Directive is to prevent trade mark protection from granting its proprietor a monopoly on technical solutions or functional characteristics of a product which a user is likely to seek in the products of competitors. Article 3(1)(e) is thus intended to prevent the protection conferred by the trade mark right from being extended, beyond signs which serve to distinguish a product or service from those offered by competitors, so as to form an obstacle preventing competitors from freely offering for sale products incorporating such technical solutions or functional characteristics in competition with the proprietor of the trade mark.

As regards, in particular, signs consisting exclusively of the shape of the product necessary to obtain a technical result, listed in Article 3(1)(e), second indent, of the Directive, that provision is intended to preclude the registration of shapes whose essential characteristics perform a technical function, with the result that the exclusivity inherent in the trade mark right would limit the possibility of competitors supplying a product incorporating such a function or at least limit their freedom of choice in regard to the technical solution they wish to adopt in order to incorporate such a function in their product.

As Article 3(1)(e) of the Directive pursues an aim which is in the public interest, namely that a shape whose essential characteristics perform a technical function and were chosen to fulfil that function may be freely used by all, that provision prevents such signs and indications from being reserved to one undertaking alone because they have been registered as trade marks.

As to the question whether the establishment that there are other shapes which could achieve the same technical result can overcome the ground for refusal or invalidity contained in Article 3(1)(e), second indent, there is nothing in the wording of that provision to allow such a conclusion.

In refusing registration of such signs, Article 3(1)(e), second indent, of the Directive reflects the legitimate aim of not allowing individuals to use registration of a mark in order to acquire or perpetuate exclusive rights relating to technical solutions.

Where the essential functional characteristics of the shape of a product are attributable solely to the technical result, Article 3(1)(e), second indent, precludes registration of a sign consisting of that shape, even if that technical result can be achieved by other shapes. . . .

## CASE C-48/09 P, LEGO JURIS A/S V. OFFICE FOR HARMONISATION IN THE INTERNAL MARKET

2010 ECR _____ (ECJ Advocate-General, January 26, 2010) (EU)

OPINION OF THE ADVOCATE-GENERAL:

[Lego sought to secure a Community Trade Mark for the shape of the well-known LEGO toy brick. The Cancellation Division of OHIM (the EU Trademark Office) had canceled the trade mark upon the petition of a competitor, and the Court of First Instance had affirmed that decision. Lego appealed to the Court of Justice. Article 7(1)(e)(ii) of the Community Trade Mark Regulation denied protection to "signs which consist exclusively of . . . the shape of goods which is necessary to obtain a technical result." The Advocate-General (Mangozzi) commented that the Court had really only addressed the provision in question (or, strictly, its counterpart in the EU Trademark Directive) in one case, *Philips v. Remington*. However, in that case (involving the shape of a three headed shaver), the Court's opinion "emphasised the grounds on which it was appropriate to *refuse* registration of a mark having those characteristics, but it scarcely set out for undertakings the guidelines for *registering* functional signs as trade marks. . . ." He also noted that "in the pleadings lodged by the parties before the Court, United States trade mark law is examined, as a result of which I feel obliged to make reference thereto where this may be useful to the present case."]

[I]t is unanimously accepted that Article 7(1)(e)(ii) [is] based on a twofold premiss: first, that of preventing a monopoly on technical solutions for goods through trade-mark law, in particular where those solutions have previously enjoyed the protection afforded by another industrial property right, and, second, that of keeping separate trade-mark protection and the protection conferred by other forms of intellectual property. . . .

[W]hile [*Philips*] could have adopted a more stringent criterion, restricting the prohibition to signs composed solely of functional characteristics, the judgment in *Philips* preferred a more flexible approach which would include more functional marks within the prohibition, by requiring that the 'essential characteristics' had to perform a technical function. However, by adopting that approach, it introduced an element of vagueness, which is now exacting its price.

The risk that the guidelines developed by the Court may not be treated identically in all the Member States is therefore evident, which is why I consider it appropriate to identify some additional criteria to help develop the case-law which, since *Philips* is the only precedent, is overly focussed on the signs which must be precluded from registration, pursuant to Article 7(1)(e)(ii).

The best method of clarifying the scope of that provision is to identify also those cases in which the trade mark sought deserves to be registered, although it contains some functional characteristics.

First of all, I wish to make clear that the principles laid down by the judgment in *Philips* are valid, that is to say: first, the twofold *rationale*, referred to above, underlying Article 7(1)(e)(ii), comprising the 'anti-monopoly' criterion and the criterion for the strict delineation of the different industrial property rights; second, the fact that the provision at issue precludes the registration of shapes whose *essential characteristics* perform a technical function; and, lastly, the fact that it is established that there are other shapes which could achieve the same technical result cannot overcome the absolute ground for refusal or invalidity contained in that provision.

It is, however, necessary to complete this basis for interpretation by referring to certain methodological guidelines for the application of the provision in question; in my view, *the procedure* when applying Article 7(1)(e)(ii) of Regulation No 40/94 [The Trade Mark Regulation] involves up to three stages.

### a) First Stage

At the outset, the body responsible for examining the absolute ground for refusal or invalidity must identify the most important elements of the shape which has been submitted to it for registration. At this stage the guidelines to be followed assume a fundamental importance.

Since it is not yet a question of determining whether the sign has distinctive character, but merely of identifying its principal characteristics, each of the individual features of the get-up of the mark concerned must be analysed in turn. In contrast to the assessment of distinctive character, it is not necessary to take into account the overall impression, unless, for example, in the case of a simple object all the characteristics comprising its shape are regarded as essential.

It may be inferred from the wording of Article 7(1)(e)(ii) that the essential characteristics of the shape must be ascertained and compared with the technical result in order to assess whether there is a necessary connection between those characteristics and that technical result. In that context, the purpose of ascertaining those essential characteristics is not to determine whether the sign can perform the essential function of a trade mark, that of guaranteeing the origin of the marked goods, but rather to determine its necessary character in relation to the technical result, the features of which must also be precisely defined.

At this initial stage, the point of view of the consumer is therefore irrelevant, because, as *Philips* makes clear, only a *preliminary* requirement, applicable to signs consisting exclusively of the shape of a product, is being assessed, and those signs may be refused registration if that requirement is not fulfilled; whether the signs have distinctive character is not yet being assessed, and that is the stage at which the case-law always regards the opinion of the consumer as being relevant.

Lastly, as part of the first stage, it remains necessary to determine the functionality of each of the essential characteristics that has been identified. Ascertaining such functionality in turn raises methodological issues.

Evidently, this cannot be based on mere conjecture or generalisations based on current experience; as a rule, for those goods which have enjoyed patent or design protection, the explanations included with the certificates of registration for those industrial property rights constitute a simple, yet very powerful, presumption that the essential characteristics of the shape of the object perform a technical function, as the Grand Board of Appeal had already noted, referring to the case-law of the US Supreme Court in the *TrafFix* case. Beyond those cases, the services of an expert may always be used.

The continuation of the *procedure* depends on the result of that assessment of functionality: if, on the one hand (hypothesis A), all the defining characteristics of the shape for which registration is sought perform a technical function, the shape itself is functional and registration must be refused or, if registration has already been granted, it must be cancelled; in that case, the initial stage marks the end of the assessment. However, if, on the other hand (hypothesis B), not all of those characteristics are functional, the second stage is proceeded to.

### b) Second Stage

At the second stage, the body responsible for examining the mark is faced with a shape only some of whose essential characteristics are in part functional. A strict interpretation of *Philips* would preclude Article 7(1)(e)(ii) of Regulation No 40/94 from being applied, since . . . that judgment states that a sign consisting exclusively of the shape of a product is unregistrable, ' . . . if it is established that the essential functional features of that shape are attributable only to the technical result'. However, I believe that once more the judgment in *Philips* focuses too narrowly on the facts of the case.

In fact, considering the two basic premises underlying Article 7(1)(e)(ii) of Regulation No 40/94—that it 'reflects the legitimate aim of [not allowing individuals] . . . to acquire or perpetuate exclusive rights relating to technical solutions' and that a functional shape 'may be freely used by all'—I believe that the provision does have effect in this hybrid situation involving functional and non-functional characteristics.

The examination merely becomes more complex.

The problem arises of determining whether the grant of a trade mark will prevent competitors from using the essential functional characteristics which that mark would protect; for in a situation such as that described, it is not inconceivable that several or many of those functional characteristics are essential for market competitors, for example, to ensure that their own goods are interoperable with those of the proprietor of the functional shape whose registration is being sought. Since such a result contrasts sharply with the premisses of *Philips*, I envisage two alternatives.

The first restricts a trade mark right to the essential and distinctive non-functional elements. Thus, for example, memory sticks are composed of a part which clearly serves to connect to a computer or other device, and another part which, while performing a technical function, may be—and usually is—adorned with a particular shape which is more *aesthetic*. I do not perceive any obstacle to granting trade marks in respect of those USB keys, albeit restricted to the part covered by the design, since the other part always remains functional. However, OHIM would have to adopt a more flexible registration practice. . . . Even though the manufacturers of USB sticks may seek protection for the aesthetic element, without including the connection part in the image in the trade mark application, the trade mark will be less effective, since the consumer might not recognise it as being part of a USB key, thereby reducing the manufacturer's interest in obtaining a trade mark.

That difficulty prompts me to propose a second alternative. Since the purpose of the provision at issue is overwhelmingly to protect competition, the examination of a sign composed in part of functional elements would have to be subject to a requirement that any industrial property right granted must not lead to significant non-reputation-related disadvantage for competitors vis-à-vis their own signs. At this stage, it would be necessary to compare the other compatible market options, as the appellant persistently requests. Without considering that alternative in detail at the present juncture, it should be noted that the alternative shapes would have to be analysed taking into account interoperability and the requirement of availability, which represent the public interest also underlying Article 7(1)(e)(ii) of Regulation No 40/94.

### c) Third Stage

Lastly, once those obstacles have been overcome by means of disclaimers or because it has been established that the shape does not harm competition, the bodies responsible for determining the functionality of a shape of this hybrid type, generally a trade mark office or a court hearing a counterclaim for a declaration of invalidity, begin the third stage, in which it is ascertained whether the mark (shape) has distinctive character. At this point, the overall impression conveyed by the sign, the point of view of the consumer, and the goods or services in respect of which registration has been applied for are now relevant, in accordance with the case-law.

In addition, Article 7(3) of Regulation No 40/94, which prohibits the proprietor of a functional shape from relying on the fact that the latter has become distinctive through use, still pertains. In that connection, first, I believe that the exclusion of functional shapes from the possible benefit conferred by that Article 7(3) caters for the legislature's wish to prevent an object which has enjoyed patent or design protection from benefiting from that possibility. Thus once that other industrial property right has expired, it is probable, particularly in the case of innovative goods, such as Lego, that these already enjoy, in the eyes of the consumer, what would normally be regarded as 'distinctive character', since they have remained unique in their category of goods during the period in which the patent or design right was valid. Second, the Court of Justice has held that the intention of the Community legislature was to grant protection as a Community trade mark only to those marks whose distinctive character had been acquired through use prior to the date of application for registration. Therefore, the proprietor of a trade mark obtained by means of a disclaimer could never rely on the benefit of Article 7(3) of Regulation No 40/94 in order to extend the protection to essential functional characteristics.

[Lego argued that the concept of "essential characteristics" is synonymous with that of "dominant and distinctive elements," which must be assessed from the perspective of the average consumer who is reasonably well informed and reasonably observant and circumspect.]

Lego Juris submits in essence that in the analysis of the essential characteristics account must be taken of the point of view of the consumer, which the Court of First Instance failed to do. . . .

If the interpretation that I propose is followed, it would not be difficult to reject this complaint, since, in accordance with the methodological guidelines set out, the analysis of the distinctive character of functional marks only occurs at the third stage. . . .

However, even if my view is not shared, I believe that the complaint of Lego Juris is unacceptable whichever angle it is approached from. Thus, at paragraph 76 of *Philips*, the Court of Justice observed that the absolute ground for refusal analysed in this case constituted a 'preliminary obstacle'; thus, the examination of that absolute ground for refusal is not subject to the same guidelines as the examination of dominant and distinctive elements, the investigation of which seeks to ascertain whether the sign serves as an indication of origin in the eyes of the consumer, which is a different task from identifying the essential elements of a shape.

In fact, if the argument of Lego Juris were taken to its logical conclusion, the criterion of the average consumer, as he is usually referred to in the case-law of the Court of Justice, would have to be applied also in respect of Article 7(1)(f) of Regulation No 40/94, and the 'accepted principles of morality' or 'public policy' would therefore have to be assessed from the point of view of the consumer.

The absurdity of such a consequence is the result of disregarding the premiss that the different grounds for refusing registration contained in Article 7(1) of Regulation No 40/94 reflect the differing intentions of the legislature, since each ground contains its own normative force as a result of criteria which may be, but do not have to be, identical in all cases of refusal/cancellation of registration. In the present case, since the rationale underlying Article 7(1)(e) is so far removed from the essential function of the trade mark, unlike Article 7(1)(b) (relating to distinctive character), the criterion of the average consumer cannot be accepted.

The appellant is therefore mistaken in seeking to transpose the typical criteria for investigating distinctive character to the essential elements of a shape for the purposes of determining whether it is functional, such elements having to be ascertained objectively, as the Court of First Instance rightly observed in the judgment under appeal.

### BENETTON GROUP SPA v. G-STAR INTERNATIONAL BV
2007 E.C.R. I-07709 (ECJ 2007)

JUDGMENT:

This reference for a preliminary ruling concerns the interpretation of Article 3(1)(e), third indent, of [the Trade Mark Directive].

The reference was made in the course of proceedings between Benetton Group Spa ('Benetton') and G-Star International BV ('G-Star') regarding the marketing by Benetton of an item of clothing which, by virtue of its shape, infringes two shape marks registered by G-Star. . . .

### The Dispute in the Main Proceedings and the Questions Referred for a Preliminary Ruling

G-Star designs, manufactures and markets clothing (in particular jeans) of the trade mark of the same name.

It is the proprietor of two shape marks for goods . . . for clothing. Those two marks were registered on 7 August 1997 and 24 November 1999.

Protection was sought for each of them, respectively, on the basis of the following distinctive elements:

- sloping stitching from hip height to the crotch seam, kneepads, yoke on the seat of the trousers, horizontal stitching at knee height at the rear, band of a contrasting colour or of another material at the bottom of the trousers at the rear, all on one garment;
- seams, stitching and cuts on the kneepad of the trousers, slightly baggy kneepad.

Benetton manages textile trading undertakings. In the Netherlands it sells its products through franchisees.

On 25 May 2000, G-Star brought an action against Benetton before the . . . Amsterdam District Court in order to preclude any manufacture, marketing and/or distribution in the Netherlands of trousers with the mark Benetton. In support of its application, G-Star maintained that Benetton had infringed the trade mark rights attached to its Elwood design trousers by manufacturing and putting on the market, in the summer of 1999, trousers with, inter alia, an oval kneepad and two lines of sloping stitching from hip height to crotch height.

Benetton challenged the application and, as a counterclaim, sought the annulment of the registered marks on the basis . . . that the shapes at issue determined the market value of the goods to a great extent as a result of their beauty or original character.

The first instance court dismissed G-Star's claims based on an infringement of its trade mark rights and Benetton's counterclaim.

Both parties lodged appeals before the Gerechtshof te Amsterdam (Amsterdam Regional Court of Appeal), which allowed G-Star's appeal and dismissed Benetton's application for annulment.

The Gerechtshof held that the Rechtbank was right to find, inter alia, that the Elwood trousers were a great commercial success, that G-Star had conducted intensive advertising campaigns to give those trousers, which have specific characteristics, recognition as a G-Star product, and that, as a result, the reputation of the Elwood trousers was largely attributable not to the aesthetic attractiveness of the shape but to the attractiveness resulting from recognition of the trade mark.

The Gerechtshof pointed out that, through the extensive advertising carried out by G-Star, it had drawn particular attention to the distinctive characteristics of the trousers and the kneepad.

Benetton lodged an appeal in cassation before the Hoge Raad der Nederlanden (Supreme Court of the Netherlands) challenging that analysis by the Gerechtshof.

The Hoge Raad points out that the contested considerations of the Gerechtshof's decision are based on the idea that the prohibition laid down in the third indent of Article 3(1)(e) of the Directive does not have to preclude a lawful trade mark registration where, at a given time prior to the application for registration, the attractiveness of the shape was a consequence of its attractiveness linked to recognition of the shape as a mark.

The Hoge Raad points out that, in its judgment in Case C-229/99 Philips [2002] ECR I-5475, the Court held that, pursuant to Article 3(3) of the Directive, signs which cannot be registered under Article 3(1)(e) thereof cannot acquire a distinctive character through the use made of them.

However, according to the Hoge Raad, the Court has not resolved the question at issue in the main proceedings, which does not relate to the distinctive character of the contested marks.

In those circumstances, the Hoge Raad der Nederlanden decided to stay the proceedings and refer [inter alia] the following question[] to the Court of Justice for a preliminary ruling:

> '(1) Must Article 3(1)(e), third indent, [of the Directive] be interpreted as meaning that the prohibition contained therein permanently precludes the registration of a shape as a trade mark where the nature of the product is such that its appearance and shaping determine its market value entirely or substantially as a result of their beauty or original character, or does the prohibition not apply where, prior to the application for registration, the attractiveness of the relevant shape to the public has been determined predominantly by the recognition of it as a distinctive sign?
>
> . . .

### The Questions Referred for a Preliminary Ruling

By its first question, the national court essentially asks whether the third indent of Article 3(1)(e) of the Directive is to be interpreted as meaning that the shape of a product which gives substantial value to that product can nevertheless constitute a trade mark under Article 3(3) of that Directive where, prior to the application for registration, it acquired attractiveness as a result of recognition of it as a distinctive sign following advertising campaigns presenting the specific characteristics of the product in question.

That question thus relates to a case in which a sign which initially consisted exclusively of a shape giving substantial value to the product subsequently and prior to application for registration acquired recognition following advertising campaigns, that is to say on account of the use made thereof.

In other words, it effectively asks whether the use made of a sign referred to in the third indent of Article 3(1)(e) of the Directive, prior to the application for registration, is capable of enabling it to be registered as a trade mark or of precluding its invalidity where the sign has been registered.

In that regard, it must be stated at the outset that Article 3(3) of the Directive is linked to the concept of 'distinctive character of a sign' for the purposes of Article 2 of the Directive. According to the wording of Article 3(3) of the Directive, the registration or validity of marks referred to in Article 3(1)(b), (c) or (d) is to be allowed by virtue of the use which has been made of them where, on account of that use, the marks have 'acquired a distinctive character'.

Furthermore, it must be stated that Article 3(3) of the Directive does not refer, for the purposes of establishing the extent of the exception laid down therein, to the signs referred to in Article 3(1)(e).

Lastly, it must be borne in mind that in *Philips* the Court has already held that:

- if a shape is refused registration pursuant to Article 3(1)(e) of the Directive, it can in no circumstances be registered by virtue of Article 3(3);
- a sign which is refused registration under Article 3(1)(e) can never acquire a distinctive character for the purposes of Article 3(3) by the use made of it;
- Article 3(1)(e) concerns certain signs which are not such as to constitute trade marks and that it is a preliminary obstacle liable to prevent a sign consisting exclusively of the shape of a product from being registrable with the result that if any one of the criteria listed in Article 3(1)(e) is satisfied, a sign consisting exclusively of the shape of the product cannot be registered as a trade mark.

It follows from this that, in a case such as that described by the national court, the use made by advertising campaigns of a sign referred to in Article 3(1)(e) of the Directive does not make it possible to apply Article 3(3) of the Directive to that sign.

Therefore, the answer to the first question must be that the third indent of Article 3(1)(e) of the Directive is to be interpreted as meaning that the shape of a product which gives substantial value to that product cannot constitute a trade mark under Article 3(3) of that directive where, prior to the application for registration, it acquired attractiveness as a result of its recognition as a distinctive sign following advertising campaigns presenting the specific characteristics of the product in question. . . .

## NOTES AND QUESTIONS

1. ***Comparing* TrafFix *and EU law.*** Does the approach outlined by the Advocate-General in *Lego* comport with your understanding of U.S. law? If so, does his methodological approach go (helpfully) beyond the guidance provided by the Court in *TrafFix*?

2. *A unitary test of functionality?* Earlier in this chapter we explored the relationship between the different tests of functionality. Notice that the European legislation appears to rely on a different provision to exclude protection on the basis of aesthetic functionality, and the language of the exclusion is different. Is such a clear differentiation useful? Review the tests in both U.S. and EU law: to what extent are the exclusions for utilitarian and aesthetic functionality dependent upon the same degree of "necessity"? If you were to establish different approaches to aesthetic and utilitarian functionality, what

would they be? *See* Annette Kur, *Too Pretty to Protect? Trade Mark Law and the Enigma of Aesthetic Functionality*, in TECHNOLOGY AND COMPETITION: ESSAYS IN HONOUR OF HANS ULLRICH (Drexl ed. 2009). In his *Lego* opinion, the Advocate-General concluded that questions of technical necessity cannot depend upon consumer understanding. Would you support having determinations of aesthetic functionality take consumer apprehension into account? *See* Kur, *supra*.

3. *"Substantial value" and trademark protection.* In many respects, the *Benetton* Court ducked the hard question by reading the reference too simply and relying on Article 3(3) of the Directive. It is clear that, *if* the exclusions in Article 3(1)(e) are satisfied, Article 3(3) denies protection notwithstanding acquired distinctiveness. However, to what extent should the development of distinctiveness be relevant to whether the test in the third indent of Article 3(1)(e) is satisfied? *See* Kur, *supra*.

4. *More LEGO cases.* The Canadian Supreme Court has also recently taken a strict line on functional marks. *See Kirkbi AG v. Ritvik Holdings, Inc.*, (2005) 433 C.P.R. (4th) 385 (S.C.C) (Can.) (relying in part on the existence of a prior utility patent to hold LEGO block functional); *see also The LEGO Case: The Supreme Court of Canada Makes It Harder to Protect Product Shapes as Trademarks*, 96 TRADEMARK REP. 596 (2006); Peter Bowal and Christopher Bowal, *What If . . . the Stud Does Not Function?*, 2008 Mich. St. L. Rev. 389 (discussing European and Canadian litigation). Lego has not been much more successful at the national level in Europe, with national courts and offices moving in the same direction as the Court of First Instance and Advocate-General. *See, e.g.*, BGH Case 26 W (Pat.) 80/05 (Ger.) and BGH Case 26 W (Pat.) 82/05 (May 2007) (relying both on functionality exclusion and on the shape of the bricks having become generic).

5. *Slavish imitation.* Several European countries offer protection against misappropriation of a product shape, often via a cause of action for slavish imitation. Both G-Star and Lego have pursued claims under this theory. In January 2010, for example, in litigation in Milan, Italy, G-Star succeeded in showing slavish imitation of the design of its Elwood jeans notwithstanding the lack of any registered trade mark or design right. *See also Jeans I,* BGH Decision of September 15, 2006 (Ger.) (protecting Elwood design under unfair competition laws). Lego's recent efforts to invoke the same doctrine before the Dutch courts have failed, with the courts recognizing that standardization and compatibility concerns should inform the unfair competition analysis that is at the heart of the slavish imitation cause of action. *See* Case LJN BJ6999, *Lego Nederland BV v. Mega Brands Inc.*, Supreme Court of Netherlands, 20 Nov. 2009; *see also Mega Blocks Inc. v. Lego Sys. A/S*, 2008 ETMR 73 (Supreme Court, 2008) (Italy) (marketing products compatible with those of a competitor is not of itself an act of unfair competition).

## D. BEYOND FUNCTIONALITY?

As we have seen, the functionality doctrine is the principal mechanism for policing the boundary between trademark law and other intellectual property regimes, most prominently utility patent law. Combined with other conditions for trademark protection (such as distinctiveness), is functionality sufficient to ensure that trademark protection does not become a vehicle for achieving quasi-patent protection? Is it sufficient to ensure that trademark owners do not assert trademark protection as a surrogate for copyright protection (e.g., in cases where copyright protection was unavailable)?

We take up these questions in this section. One decision of the Court of Appeals for the Tenth Circuit, rendered before *TrafFix Devices*, cast doubt on whether the functionality doctrine addressed all the concerns about overlap between the trademark and utility patent regimes. The decision (*Vornado*) never received much support. For example, the Court of Appeals for the Federal Circuit has noted:

> Other courts of appeals, both before and after *Bonito Boats*, have followed the lead of the Court of Customs and Patent Appeals in holding that a product may be entitled to trade dress protection for distinctive, nonfunctional features, even if the product is, or has been, the subject of a patent. [citing authority] The Tenth Circuit stands alone in holding to the contrary, ruling that trade dress protection is unavailable for a product configuration that is claimed in a patent and is a "described, significant inventive aspect" of the patented invention, even if the configuration is nonfunctional.

*Midwest Indus., Inc. v. Karavan Trailers, Inc.*, 175 F.3d 1356 (Fed. Cir. 1999). Indeed, even though the Supreme Court took up *TrafFix Devices* to address this circuit split, the Court's opinion mentions *Vornado* only in passing. Nevertheless, the question raised in *Vornado* remains intriguing, regardless of one's views on the merits of the *Vornado* court's response to the question.

After the *Vornado* case, we take up a line of cases addressing the trademark-copyright interface, beginning with a discussion of the Supreme Court's *Dastar* decision. As in *Vornado*, the rules articulated in *Dastar* and progeny are not characterized as functionality rules, but the concerns about policing the boundaries between regimes are similar to those expressed in functionality cases. *Dastar* itself is not even a case involving design, but the *Bretford* case, excerpted after the discussion of *Dastar*, addresses whether *Dastar* applies to designs.

## VORNADO AIR CIRCULATION SYS., INC. V. DURACRAFT CORP.
58 F.3d 1498 (10th Cir. 1995), cert. denied, 516 U.S. 1067 (1996)

STEPHEN H. ANDERSON, Circuit Judge:

### Introduction

This case presents an issue of first impression in our circuit concerning the intersection of the Patent Act and the Lanham Trade-Mark Act. We must decide whether a product configuration is entitled to trade dress protection when it is or has been a significant inventive component of an invention covered by a utility patent.

After expiration of any patents or copyrights on an invention, that invention normally passes into the public domain and can be freely copied by anyone. The district court found, however, that because the spiral structure of the household fan grill in question is "nonfunctional," a status largely determined by the availability of enough alternative grill designs so that other fan manufacturers can effectively compete without it, the grill can serve as trade dress. The court held that the grill could be protected under Lanham Act section 43(a) against copying by competitors, because that copying was likely to confuse consumers.

The court's injunction effectively prevents defendant Duracraft Corp. from ever practicing the full invention embodied in the patented fans of plaintiff Vornado Air Circulation Systems, Inc., after Vornado's utility patents expire.[2] For the reasons discussed below, we find this result to be untenable. We hold that although a product configuration must be nonfunctional in order to be protected as trade dress under section 43(a), not every nonfunctional configuration is eligible for that protection. Where a product configuration is a significant inventive component of an invention covered by a utility patent, so that without it the invention cannot fairly be said to be the same invention, patent policy dictates that it enter into the public domain when the utility patents on the fans expire. To ensure that result, it cannot receive trade dress protection under section 43(a). The district court's order is reversed.

## Background
### History of the Spiral Grill Designs

The product configurations at issue in this case are two household fan grills with spiral — or arcuate — vanes, produced by the plaintiff, Vornado, and the defendant, Duracraft.

The idea of using a spiral grill on a fan is not new. An arcuate vane structure for propellers "applicable to ventilators and the like" was reflected in expired U.S. Patent No. 1,062,258, a utility patent issued May 20, 1913, to G.A. Schlotter, and arcuate vanes were incorporated into a household fan guard as early as 1936, as shown by expired U.S. Patent No. 2,110,994, a utility patent issued to J.H. Cohen.

Vornado began selling its fans with spiral grills in November 1988, at a time when it was the only fan company using that type of grill. On January 9, 1989, Vornado's founders, Donald J. Moore and Michael C. Coup, applied for a utility patent on their ducted fan with a spiral grill. They asserted, among other things, that their spiral grill produced an optimum air flow, although their own tests had shown that it performed about the same as the more common straight radial grill, and later tests suggested that some other grills worked better in some respects.

Their patent application claimed a fan with multiple features, including the spiral grill. The inventive aspect of Vornado's spiral grill was that the point of maximum lateral spacing between the curved vanes was moved inboard

---

2. It may also interfere with Duracraft's ability to practice other inventors' earlier spiral-vane inventions covered by previous, expired utility patents. But we need not rest our holding on this further interference, because the conflict with the ability to practice Vornado's invention in the future is clear.

from the grill's outer radius, so that it was at the impeller blade's point of maximum power. Vornado emphasizes that its fan grill was not patentable by itself because a spiral grill per se was already in the public domain as "prior art," a patent law term for what was already known from previous patents or other sources.

On May 22, 1990, Messrs. Moore and Coup were issued a utility patent. They subsequently applied for and on February 22, 1994, were granted a reissue patent expanding their claims, including those that involved the arcuate-shaped grill vane structure.

Vornado advertised its grill as the "Patented AirTensity(tm) Grill," although the company had no separate patent on the grill. Between January 1989 and August 1990, Vornado sold about 135,000 fans. In its advertising, the company touted the grill as a "true achievement in aerodynamic efficiency," "the result of determinant ergonomic design," with "[u]nique AirTensity(tm) vortex action," accomplishing "a high degree of safety and functionality."

In August 1990, Duracraft began offering an inexpensive electric household fan called the Model DT-7 "Turbo Fan." The grill on Duracraft's Turbo Fan incorporated a spiral vane structure that was copied from Vornado's considerably more expensive fan models but was purposely designed not to infringe Vornado's patent. Apart from its look-alike grill and some aspects of the fan blade design, the Turbo Fan differed significantly from Vornado's fans in its overall configuration, its base and duct structure, its center knob, neon colors, packaging, labeling, and price. The box in which the Turbo Fan came had a circle cut out of the front so that the grill design showed through and was emphasized when the fan was displayed in its box.

By November 1992, Duracraft had sold nearly one million Turbo Fans in the United States. The Turbo Fan was the company's second-largest-selling household fan product.

### District Court's Findings

Vornado sued, alleging that Duracraft had intentionally copied Vornado's grill design, but both sides agreed that the Turbo Fan did not infringe Vornado's patents. Vornado argued during the bench trial that the curved vanes in the "Patented AirTensity Grill" were legally nonfunctional, which they had to be in order to be protected as trade dress under section 43(a).

The district court found that the spiral grill was functional in a lay sense but not in a legal sense, based on our definition of trade dress functionality in terms of the competitive need to use a feature. *See Brunswick Corp. v. Spinit Reel Co.*, 832 F.2d 513, 519 (10th Cir. 1987).[3] The district court found that Vornado's grill did in fact perform a unique function in the way that it shaped the flow of air coming from the fan, but the difference in air flow produced by it as compared with other grill designs was not great enough for a customer to

---

3. In *Brunswick*, . . . [our] definition of functionality relied heavily on the existence of a sufficient number of alternatives, or substitutes, for the design in question. *See id.* at 518-20. The question of potential conflict with patent law was not before us in *Brunswick*, however, because the evidence concerning an expired utility patent had not been made part of the record on appeal. *See id.* at 521 n.4.

perceive, so it made no competitive difference. The court also noted that other feasible grill structures could easily do as well on other relevant performance tests, and the spiral grill was not shown to be cheaper to manufacture.

The district court did not find enough evidence to support a finding of aesthetic functionality, a type of functionality based on decorativeness or attractiveness, which we have previously recognized. *Brunswick,* 832 F.2d at 519. Nor did the district court find that Duracraft would suffer a marketing disadvantage if it could not use the spiral grill. The court found that the grill's value lay not in its operational attributes but primarily in its appearance, which the court said suggests something about the fan's performance and creatively suggests Vornado's identity.

The court found that the grill design was nonfunctional and held that trade dress protection of nonfunctional product configurations under the Lanham Act was not incompatible with patent law. The court further found that the grill design was [distinctive]. The court found that consumers were likely to be confused by Duracraft's use of a similar grill, and granted Vornado an injunction but no damages on the section 43(a) claim.

Duracraft contends on appeal that the district court committed legal error [inter alia] in concluding that Vornado's trade dress claim was not barred by federal patent law. . . .

We have considered all of the issues raised by Duracraft, but, finding the patent law argument to be dispositive, we do not decide the other questions.

### Discussion

. . .

### The Conflict before Us

[[T]he Supreme Court [in] *Bonito Boats, Inc. v. Thunder Craft Boats, Inc.,* 489 U.S. 141 (1989), clarified] that patent law creates a federal right to copy and use product features that are in the public domain, whether under an expired patent or for lack of patentability in the first place. *Id.* at 165; *see also Sears, Roebuck & Co. v. Stiffel Co.,* 376 U.S. 225, 229-33 (1964); *Compco Corp. v. Day-Brite Lighting, Inc.,* 376 U.S. 234, 237-39 (1964). Duracraft argues that *Bonito Boats* means that useful product features, which comprise utility patent subject matter, may not be protected as trademarks or trade dress and thereby be permanently monopolized by a single producer.

Vornado replies that there is no problem or inconsistency in its ability to obtain both patent protection for its fan in toto and trade dress protection for its spiral grill. Vornado argues 1) that of the main Supreme Court cases on which Duracraft relies, *Sears, Compco,* and *Bonito Boats* are all distinguishable, and [*Kellogg Co. v. National Biscuit Co.,* 305 U.S. 111 (1938)] predates the Lanham Act; 2) that the Supreme Court and Congress both have said section 43(a) applies to product shapes; and 3) that the functionality doctrine properly reconciles the Patent Act with the Lanham Act, for if a product feature is not necessary to competition, no patent law purpose is served by allowing it to be copied.

We find each of these arguments wanting. At the same time, we need not rule as broadly as Duracraft would have us do either. We need not deal with whether every useful or potentially patentable product configuration is excluded from trade dress protection.[11] Vornado does not argue that its grill was not a significant inventive component of its patented fans. Without that particular grill, the Vornado fan would not be the same invention that it is. We focus, therefore, on the law with regard to product configurations that are patented inventions or significant components thereof, and whether these product configurations can serve as trade dress. . . .

Supreme Court Precedents

When asked to balance the concerns of patent law against those of unfair competition law with respect to the copying of product shapes, the Supreme Court has ruled repeatedly over the years that the right to copy must prevail. See *Bonito Boats*, 489 U.S. at 167-68; *Sears*, 376 U.S. at 232-33; *Compco*, 376 U.S. at 235, 238; *Kellogg*, 305 U.S. at 119-22; *Singer Mfg. Co. v. June Mfg. Co.*, 163 U.S. 169, 185 (1896).

Applying the common law of unfair competition, the Court held in *Kellogg* that it was not unfair competition for Kellogg Co. to copy National Biscuit Co.'s pillow-shaped shredded wheat cereal after invalidation of the design patent for the cereal shape and expiration of the utility patents for the machines to make it, where Kellogg had made reasonable efforts to distinguish its product by using a different carton, label, company name, and biscuit size. See *Kellogg*, 305 U.S. at 119-22. In *Singer,* the Court reached the same conclusion regarding the defendant's copying of Singer sewing machines after their patents had expired. See *Singer*, 163 U.S. at 185-202.

*Sears* and *Compco* pitted patent law's public domain principles against state unfair competition statutes with respect to product copying where patents had been invalidated. In both cases, the Court again held that patent law's public domain concept must prevail over unfair competition concerns about consumer confusion where those concerns arose solely from the product copying. See *Sears*, 376 U.S. at 232; *Compco*, 376 U.S. at 235, 238.

In 1989, in *Bonito Boats,* the Court yet again addressed the copying of product shapes, and, because of the same patent law public domain concerns, struck down another state statute, this one prohibiting the use of the direct-molding process to copy unpatented boat hulls. *Bonito Boats,* 489 U.S. at 167-68.

Vornado would have us ignore these holdings, and we must acknowledge that distinguishing *Sears, Compco,* and/or *Bonito Boats* has become a veritable jurisprudential art form in recent years, in which we as well as many other courts have engaged. [cit.]; Jay Dratler, Jr., *Trademark Protection for Industrial Designs,* 1988 U. ILL. L. REV. 887, 916-24 (discussing courts' use of section 43(a) to make "an end run around Sears/Compco"). It may come as no surprise that we are able to identify distinctions between those cases and the one before us, the most salient, of course, being that in none of the prior cases did the

---

11. Nor do we need to take a position on whether utility patents should be viewed differently than design patents, as some courts have held. See *Kohler Co. v. Moen Inc.*, 12 F.3d 632, 636-43 (7th Cir. 1993); [cit.].

Court apply federal unfair competition law under section 43(a) of the Lanham Act.[14]

To say we find distinctions is not the end of the story, however. Although we may not be strictly bound by the Court's holdings in these cases, we find it impossible to ignore the clear and continuing trend they collectively manifest in favor of the public's right to copy. We turn, then, to the legislative history to see whether Congress has reversed this direction.[15]

### Ambiguous Legislative History

Congress acknowledged and, to some extent, ratified the judicial expansion of section 43(a) in 1988, when it enacted its first comprehensive revision of the Lanham Act. Among other things, Congress broadened the wording of section 43(a), but . . . that wording [which contains no reference to product designs] itself does not help us.

The Senate report accompanying the bill explained that the section was reworded "to codify the interpretation it has been given by the courts. Because Section 43(a) of the Act fills an important gap in federal unfair competition law, the committee expects the courts to continue to interpret the section." S. Rep. No. 515, 100th Cong., 2d Sess. 40 (1988), reprinted in 1988 U.S.C.C.A.N. 5577, 5603.

The district court relied heavily on the Senate report in concluding that Congress intended to grant trademark and trade dress protection to nonfunctional product configurations. That report observed that the courts have applied section 43(a) to cases involving "infringement of unregistered

---

14. We also can distinguish *Singer* because it was decided at a time when the tort of unfair competition was generally perceived to require fraudulent passing off, and unfair competition law has since evolved and expanded, so that it may be violated without active deceit, wherever a product shape has acquired secondary meaning and a likelihood of consumer confusion is found. See [J. Thomas McCarthy, Trademarks and Unfair Competition] §5.02. The force of this particular distinction is reduced, though, by the fact that both the Supreme Court and our own circuit have also preserved defendants' right to copy even where defendants were found to have deliberately palmed off their goods in an effort to deceive consumers. See *Warner & Co. v. Eli Lilly & Co.*, 265 U.S. 526, 531-33 (1924); *Midwest Plastics Corp. v. Protective Closures Co.*, 285 F.2d 747, 750 (10th Cir. 1960) (quoting *Reynolds & Reynolds Co. v. Norick*, 114 F.2d 278, 281 (10th Cir. 1940)).

*Kellogg, Sears,* and *Compco* are distinguishable on the basis that neither secondary meaning nor inherent distinctiveness was found in those cases, whereas in our case the district court found inherent distinctiveness. And, finally, it is possible to distinguish *Bonito Boats* on the grounds that the statute struck down in that case offered broader protection to product shapes than does §43(a). See *Kohler*, 12 F.3d at 641-42.

Duracraft bases its argument on both the Patent Clause, U.S. Const. art. I, §8, cl. 8, and the Patent Act of 1952, codified as amended at Title 35 of the U.S. Code. We do not address the constitutional argument, however, unless this case cannot be resolved as a matter of statutory law. [cit.].

15. Vornado similarly draws too much from the language of two Supreme Court cases it cites. It points to *Two Pesos*, 112 S. Ct. at 2755 n.1, where the Court adopted a definition of trade dress that included product shapes, and to *Bonito Boats*, 489 U.S. at 166, where the Court noted that in §43(a), "Congress has thus given federal recognition to many of the concerns that underlie the state tort of unfair competition, and the application of *Sears* and *Compco* to nonfunctional aspects of a product which have been shown to identify source must take account of competing federal policies in this regard." Although both cases support the notion that §43(a) will protect some nonfunctional configurations, neither requires protection for all such configurations. In determining whether the type of configuration before us should receive trade dress protection, we will follow the Court's instruction and "take account of competing federal policies in this regard."

marks, violations of trade dress and *certain nonfunctional configurations of goods.*" *Id.* (emphasis added). It also stated that in the revised definition of "trademark," the words "symbol or device" were retained "so as not to preclude the registration of colors, *shapes, sounds or configurations where they function as trademarks.*" *Id.* at 44 (1988 U.S.C.C.A.N. at 5607) (emphasis added).

The district court read too much into this report. We cannot conclude that because at the time of the report, "certain nonfunctional configurations of goods" had received trade dress protection, Congress was saying that in the future, all such configurations should.[16] As of 1988, when the Senate report made its observation, we are unaware of any legal precedents upholding protection for those nonfunctional configurations covered by utility patents. But there was case law denying protection to a closely related type of nonfunctional design.

In *In re Shakespeare Co.*, 289 F.2d 506, 508, 48 CCPA 969 (1961), the Court of Customs and Patent Appeals denied trademark registration to a recognizable spiral marking on fishing rods that resulted from the applicant's patented method for making the rods. The court held, as a matter of policy, that even though the spiral mark itself was nonfunctional, protecting it as a trademark would impermissibly interfere with the patent law. Other competitors either would not be able to use the patented manufacturing process after expiration of Shakespeare's patents, or they would have to go to the trouble of removing the marking. *Id.*

The Senate report never even mentioned these patent law concerns, let alone purported to address or resolve them.

### Functionality Doctrine: An Incomplete Answer

To interpret the Senate report as broadly as Vornado would have us do, we would also have to ignore the strong possibility that if Congress thought at all about patent policies in 1988, it assumed that any product qualifying for a utility patent would automatically be functional. It would have been understandable for Congress to assume that a nonfunctionality requirement would eliminate any possible conflicts between the Lanham Act and the Patent Act — at least as to utility patents — given the repeated statements by various courts and commentators that functionality doctrine has precisely that purpose and effect. [cit.] It even appears that at times the Supreme Court may have made the same assumption. *See Qualitex*, 115 S. Ct. at 1304; *Bonito Boats*, 489 U.S. at 166-67; *Inwood*, 456 U.S. at 863 (White, J., concurring in result).

---

16. Vornado similarly draws too much from the language of two Supreme Court cases it cites. It points to Two Pesos, 112 S.Ct. at 2755 n. 1, where the Court adopted a definition of trade dress that included product shapes, and to Bonito Boats, 489 U.S. at 166, where the Court noted that in §43(a), "Congress has thus given federal recognition to many of the concerns that underlie the state tort of unfair competition, and the application of Sears and Compcoto nonfunctional aspects of a product which have been shown to identify source must take account of competing federal policies in this regard." Although both cases support the notion that §43(a) will protect some nonfunctional configurations, neither requires protection for all such configurations. In determining whether the type of configuration before us should receive trade dress protection, we will follow the Court's instruction and "take account of competing federal policies in this regard."

Despite what appears to be a widespread perception that product configurations covered by utility patents are automatically functional for Lanham Act purposes, the district court in our case ably demonstrated that this is not so. Configurations can simultaneously be patentably useful, novel, and nonobvious and also nonfunctional, in trade dress parlance.

This is the case because to meet patent law's usefulness requirement, a product need not be better than other alternatives or essential to competition. [cit.] To obtain a utility patent, an inventor need only show that an invention is 1) useful in the sense of serving some identified, beneficial purpose, and then—much more difficult to prove—that it is 2) novel, i.e., not previously known, and 3) nonobvious, or sufficiently inventive, in light of prior art. [cit.]

Functionality, by contrast, has been defined both by our circuit, and more recently by the Supreme Court, in terms of competitive need. *See Qualitex,* 115 S. Ct. at 1304-07; *Brunswick,* 832 F.2d at 519; *see also* Restatement (Third) of Unfair Competition §17 & cmts. a & b (1995). If competitors need to be able to use a particular configuration in order to make an equally competitive product, it is functional, but if they do not, it may be nonfunctional. The availability of equally satisfactory alternatives for a particular feature, and not its inherent usefulness, is often the fulcrum on which Lanham Act functionality analysis turns.

As some courts have explained the competitive need test, it conceivably could allow one producer to permanently appropriate any distinctive patented invention for exclusive trademark or trade dress use as soon as its patent expired and sufficient alternatives became available to make the invention no longer one of a few superior designs. [cit.]

### Reconciling Two Federal Statutes

Given that the functionality doctrine does not eliminate overlap between the Patent Act and the Lanham Act, we must decide whether Vornado is right that this doctrine nevertheless should be used to limit patent law's public domain.

Except to the extent that Congress has clearly indicated which of two statutes it wishes to prevail in the event of a conflict, we must interpret and apply them in a way that preserves the purposes of both and fosters harmony between them. *See Digital Equip. Corp. v. Desktop Direct, Inc.*, 511 U.S. 863 (1994). [cit.] Where, as here, both cannot apply, we look to their fundamental purposes to choose which one must give way.

### Purposes of the Patent Act

> First, patent law seeks to foster and reward invention; second, it promotes disclosure of inventions to stimulate further innovation and to permit the public to practice the invention once the patent expires; third, the stringent requirements for patent protection seek to assure that ideas in the public domain remain there for the free use of the public.

*Aronson v. Quick Point Pencil Co.*, 440 U.S. 257, 262 (1979). The "centerpiece of federal patent policy" is its "ultimate goal of public disclosure and use." *Bonito Boats,* 489 U.S. at 157. [cit.]

Vornado suggests that no patent law purpose is served by allowing copying of product configurations that are not necessary to competition. We cannot agree. We find no support in the Patent Act itself or its application for the proposition that the patent goals are limited to enhancing competition, at least in the direct sense. To the contrary, patents operate by temporarily reducing competition. They create monopolies to reward inventors who invent "'things which are worth to the public the embarrassment of an exclusive patent.'" *Graham v. John Deere Co.*, 383 U.S. 1, 9 (1966) (quoting Thomas Jefferson, author of the 1793 Patent Act). Although competition ultimately may be enhanced by the increased product supply that results from operation of the patent law, the system's more obvious objective is to give the public the benefits of technological progress.

In this respect, it is significant that the framers of the patent system did not require an inventor to demonstrate an invention's superiority to existing products in order to qualify for a patent. That they did not do so tells us that the patent system seeks not only superior inventions but also a multiplicity of inventions. A variety of choices is more likely to satisfy the desires of a greater number of consumers than is a single set of products deemed "optimal" in some average sense by patent examiners and/or judges. And the ability to intermingle and extrapolate from many inventors' solutions to the same problem is more likely to lead to further technological advances than is a single, linear approach seeking to advance one "superior" line of research and development. We conclude that patent law seeks the invention and the passing into the public domain of even what trade dress law would consider nonfunctional inventions.

Allowing an inventor both patent and trade dress protection in a configuration would not necessarily inhibit invention directly. Quite the opposite, this double benefit would probably increase an inventor's direct incentives to pursue an idea. But the inventor's supply of ideas itself and freedom to experiment with them might diminish if the inventor had to do a competitive market analysis before adopting useful features from others' inventions once their patents expired. *See Bonito Boats*, 489 U.S. at 161-62 (stating that federal patent scheme allows public to ascertain status of intellectual property embodied in a manufacture or design, and "[t]he public may rely upon the lack of notice in exploiting shapes and designs accessible to all").

As to the second patent law objective, encouraging public disclosure of inventions, it is not immediately apparent what effect, if any, the trade dress protection in question would have. But this case clearly shows that trade dress protection can directly interfere with the public's ability to practice patented inventions after the patents have expired, and that it undermines the principle that ideas in the public domain should stay there. We conclude that the inability freely to copy significant features of patented products after the patents expire impinges seriously upon the patent system's core goals, even when those features are not necessary to competition.

### Purposes of Section 43(a) of the Lanham Act

The core concepts of trademark protection are that consumers not be confused, misled, or deceived as to whose product they are buying, that sellers' goodwill—or investment in their reputation for quality—be protected, and that competition thereby be enhanced. *See Park 'N Fly Inc. v. Dollar Park and Fly, Inc.,* 469 U.S. 189 (1985). "[T]he protection of trademarks and trade dress under §43(a) serves the same statutory purpose of preventing deception and unfair competition." *Two Pesos,* 505 U.S. at 773. Because trademarks promote competition and product quality, "Congress determined that 'a sound public policy requires that trademarks should receive nationally the greatest protection that can be given them.'" *Park 'N Fly,* 469 U.S. at 193 (quoting S. Rep. No. 1333, 79th Cong., 2d Sess. 6 (1946), reprinted in 1946 U.S.C.C.S. 1274, 1277); *see also* 15 U.S.C. §1127.

Clearly, any limitation on the use of product designs as protected trade dress will give trade dress less than "the greatest protection that can be given." *Park 'N Fly,* 469 U.S. at 193. But this statement by the Court quotes from the 1946 Senate report, and we cannot assume that Congress in 1946 intended to be as expansive in its protection of product configurations as in its protection of traditional word or picture trademarks. At that time, section 43(a) was not viewed as a broad federal unfair competition provision covering product configurations under the rubric of trade dress; that gloss was added later by judges. *See Two Pesos,* 112 S. Ct. at 2762-63 (Stevens, J., concurring in the judgment).

The degree to which a producer's goodwill will be harmed by the copying of product configurations correlates with the degree of consumer confusion as to source or sponsorship that is likely to result from the copying. We do not doubt that at least some consumers are likely to ignore product labels, names, and packaging and look only to the design of product features to tell one brand from another. These consumers are likely to be confused by similar product designs, and to the degree that this confusion is tolerated, the goals of the Lanham Act will be undermined.

But the Lanham Act, like common law unfair competition law and most state unfair competition statutes, has never provided absolute protection against all consumer confusion as to source or sponsorship. For its first fifteen to twenty years, the act was not even applied to the shapes of products or their containers. [cit.] And even after it was, courts consistently denied protection against that degree of confusion caused by the copying of functional configurations.

As a practical matter, the fate of nonfunctional configurations within patented products has rarely been the subject of legal analysis, because courts often have found such designs to be functional. [cit.]

In two appellate decisions where courts have considered nonfunctional designs that were part of utility-patented products, we find an even split. In *In re Shakespeare,* 289 F.2d at 508, the Court of Customs and Patent Appeals upheld patent law principles and refused trademark registration. In [*Clamp Mfg. Co. v. Enco Mfg. Co.,* 870 F.2d 512, 516-17 (1989)], the Ninth Circuit upheld the district court's finding of trademark status for the nonfunctional design of a "C" clamp. The Ninth Circuit appears to have assumed without discussion that all nonfunctional product configurations can be used as trademarks or trade dress—an assumption which, as noted above, we do not make.

We recognize also that consumer confusion resulting from the copying of product features is, in some measure, a self-fulfilling prophecy. To the degree that useful product configurations are protected as identifiers, consumers will come to rely on them for that purpose, but if copying is allowed, they will depend less on product shapes and more on labels and packaging.

We conclude that protecting against that degree of consumer confusion that may arise from the copying of configurations that are significant parts of patented inventions is, at best, a peripheral concern of section 43(a) of the Lanham Act.

### Conclusion: Balancing Competing Policies

Given, then, that core patent principles will be significantly undermined if we do not allow the copying in question, and peripheral Lanham Act protections will be denied if we do, our answer seems clear. Much has been said in this and other section 43(a) cases about whether a second competitor needs to use a particular product design to compete effectively. But where Lanham Act goals are not the only ones at stake, we must also examine the degree to which a first competitor needs to use a useful product feature instead of something else—a name, a label, a package—to establish its brand identity in the first place.

It would defy logic to assume that there are not almost always many more ways to identify a product than there are ways to make it.[19] *See In re Water Gremlin Co.*, 635 F.2d 841, 844 (C.C.P.A. 1980) ("[A] merchant who wishes to set himself apart has no dearth of means to do so."). And if one of the ways to configure the product itself has been deemed important enough to the advance of technology for the government to grant a utility patent, we must find its value as a product feature to exceed its value as a brand identifier in all but the most unusual cases.

We hold that where a disputed product configuration is part of a claim in a utility patent, and the configuration is a described, significant inventive aspect of the invention, *see* 35 U.S.C. §112, so that without it the invention could not fairly be said to be the same invention, patent law prevents its protection as trade dress, even if the configuration is nonfunctional.[20]

---

19. Although a producer may find efficiencies in combining the brand-identifying function with a product's utilitarian function by using a useful product feature as a trademark or trade dress, we accord this type of efficiency little weight. Although the efficient combining of form and function is at the heart of good industrial design, promoting it is not a Lanham Act objective. For discussion of the repeated, unsuccessful attempts over the years to persuade Congress to pass a general industrial design protection bill, *see Bonito Boats*, 489 U.S. at 167-68; [cit.]

20. We note that our resolution of this issue will avoid any confusion as to the right to copy a patented invention which may arise by virtue of the fact that a feature can switch back and forth between being functional and nonfunctional with the vagaries of the marketplace. *Compare In re Honeywell, Inc.*, 8 U.S.P.Q.2d 1600, 1604-05 (T.T.A.B. 1988), *with In re Honeywell, Inc.*, 532 F.2d 180, 182-83 (C.C.P.A. 1976).

It also avoids potential problem scenarios in which a commercially unimportant but patented configuration is deemed nonfunctional and registered as a trademark, and then later, because of a change in the direction of research and development, inventors wish to use the old technology taught by the expired patent but cannot, because of the trademark. The Fourth Circuit has held that once a trademark becomes incontestable, it may not be cancelled on functionality grounds. *Shakespeare Co. v. Silstar Corp. of America, Inc.*, 9 F.3d 1091, 1099 (4th Cir. 1993), *cert. denied*, 511 U.S. 1127 (1994). *But see* William M. Landes & Richard A. Posner, *The Economics of Trademark Law*, 78 Trademark Rep. 267, 295-96 (1988).

In future cases, the contribution of a particular configuration to the inventiveness of a patented product may not always be clear, and we do not wish to rule out the possibility that a court may appropriately conduct a factual inquiry to supplement its reading of the patent's claims and descriptions.

But in this case, we do not find it necessary to remand for such an inquiry. Vornado included the arcuate grill vane structure as an element of its patent claims and described the configuration as providing "an optimum air flow." Then, after the first patent issued and Vornado subsequently found evidence that other grill structures worked as well as or better than the spiral grill, Vornado did not repudiate or disclaim in any way the grill element of its patent. Instead, Vornado sought and received a reissue patent that expanded its claims with respect to the grill.

Even if we discount entirely Vornado's extensive advertising campaign emphasizing the importance of the "AirTensity Grill," this patent history on its face obviates any need for a remand on the question of inventive significance. We simply take Vornado at its word. Because the "Patented AirTensity Grill" is a significant inventive element of Vornado's patented fans, it cannot be protected as trade dress. The district court's order is REVERSED.

## NOTES AND QUESTIONS

**1. Vornado *in view of* TrafFix.** Justice Kennedy writes that the Court granted certiorari to resolve a conflict between the Tenth Circuit and several other circuits. Did the Court's opinion resolve that conflict? (The Court thinks it did. *See Holmes Group v. Vornado Air Circulation Sys.*, 535 U.S. 826, 829 (2002)). If so, which rule did the Court adopt? Is *Vornado* still good law? In what ways does the *TrafFix* approach differ from the *Vornado* approach? Which (if any) of the issues surrounding functionality doctrine that we have discussed thus far in the chapter remain open after *TrafFix*?

**2. Vornado *in view of* Kellogg.** In *Kellogg Co. v. National Biscuit Co.*, 305 U.S. 111 (1938), excerpted at the beginning of this chapter, the Court made numerous references to the fact that Nabisco's patents had expired, but the Court also noted that "[t]he evidence is persuasive that [the pillow-shaped biscuit form] is functional—that the cost of the biscuit would be increased and its high quality lessened if some other form were substituted for the pillow-shape." Would the *Kellogg* Court's conclusion be sustained under the *Qualitex/Inwood* test of functionality? The *TrafFix* test for functionality? If so, doesn't this undercut the *Vornado* court's conclusion that the functionality doctrine is insufficient to safeguard the "right to copy" the subject matter of expired patents?

**3. *A constitutional right to copy?*** In several of the cases and materials in this book, we have seen references to the so-called right to copy. Does the Constitution guarantee a right to copy? Or are cases such as *Bonito Boats* and the *Sears-Compco* decisions best explained as cases about federal/state preemption? (That is critical in *Vornado,* which presents a putative conflict between two federal regimes, not a conflict between federal and state law.) Would such a right trump the provisions in all federal intellectual property legislation, creating an ironclad public domain? What would be the content of that right (i.e., in what circumstances would it exist)? Recall that *Sears* involved invalidated design and utility patents, *Compco* involved an invalidated design patent (and a rejected utility patent), *Kellogg* involved an invalidated design patent and an expired utility patent, *Singer* involved an expired utility patent, and *Bonito Boats* involved a wholly unpatentable (and never patented) invention. This is a complex matrix. Should the status of the patent affect any constitutional right to copy? Should it matter whether the patent is a design patent or a utility patent? Note that in footnote 11, the *Vornado* court declines to take a position on whether utility patents should be viewed differently from design patents for the purposes of the functionality rule. If Vornado had obtained a design patent on the appearance of its fan, would the arguments advanced by the Tenth Circuit support the articulation of a parallel rule buttressing the functionality doctrine?

4. ***A conditional right to copy?*** Although the *Vornado* court did not rely on the line of Supreme Court cases to find a *constitutional* right to copy, it did use those cases to support the existence of a (nonconstitutional) right to copy. Review the Court's holdings in *Kellogg* (excerpted at the beginning of this chapter) and in *Sears-Compco* and *Bonito Boats* (excerpted in Chapter 1). Does the *Vornado* court accurately capture the holdings in those cases when it concludes simply that they reveal a clear "right to copy"? Might that statement require any conditioning? If so, should those conditions have affected the outcome in *Vornado*?

5. ***Balancing competing purposes.*** After identifying the different purposes of the patent and copyright statutes, and finding the right to copy to be a "core patent principle," the Tenth Circuit had to seek to balance that principle with the concerns of trademark law. Why did the court find that avoiding confusion in this case (which it acknowledged would occur) was "at best, a peripheral concern" of the trademark statute? Did the Tenth Circuit "interpret and apply [the patent and trademark statutes] in a way that preserves the purposes of both and fosters harmony between them"? How else might the court have preserved the purposes of both statutes?

6. ***What is the* Vornado *rule?*** In the "introduction" to the *Vornado* opinion, the court refers to denying trade dress protection where "a product configuration is a significant inventive component of an invention covered by a utility patent, so that without it the invention cannot fairly be said to be the same invention." Is this rule (if it is a rule) different from the rule that the court offers in its conclusion: "We hold that where a disputed product configuration is part of a claim in a utility patent, and the configuration is a described, significant inventive aspect of the invention, *see* 35 U.S.C. §112, so that without it the invention could not fairly be said to be the same invention, patent law prevents its protection as trade dress, even if the configuration is nonfunctional"? In what ways is the new "significant inventive component" or "significant inventive aspect" rule different from the functionality doctrine?

7. ***A patent law source for the* Vornado *rule?*** According to the "conclusion" of the opinion, the *Vornado* standard requires courts to identify anything in a patent that is a "described, significant inventive aspect of the invention," citing 35 U.S.C. §112. Although the court is far from clear, one must presume

that the court was referring to Section 112, paragraph 1 (or possibly paragraph 2). Section 112 of the Patent Act reads as follows:

§112. SPECIFICATION

The specification shall contain a written description of the invention, and of the manner and process of making and using it, in such full, clear, concise, and exact terms as to enable any person skilled in the art to which it pertains, or with which it is most nearly connected, to make and use the same, and shall set forth the best mode contemplated by the inventor of carrying out his invention.

The specification shall conclude with one or more claims particularly pointing out and distinctly claiming the subject matter which the applicant regards as his invention.

What is the relevance of Section 112 to the court's conclusion? Neither Section 112 nor any other provision in U.S. patent law supplies any antecedent for a concept of "significant inventive aspect." Indeed, under U.S. patent law, the claims of a patent define the patent right, and courts have held that in construing and applying patent claims, "there is no legally recognizable or protected 'essential' element, 'gist' or 'heart' of the invention in a combination patent." *Aro Mfg. Co. v. Convertible Top Replacement Co.*, 365 U.S. 336, 345 (1961). *See also Allen Eng. Corp. v. Bartell Indus., Inc.*, 299 F.3d 1336, 1345 (Fed. Cir. 2002) (calling the proposition "well settled"). To the extent that the *Vornado* standard encourages courts to search for the "heart" of a patented invention, the standard works a patent law non sequitur.

**8. *Applying the* Vornado *rule*.** Applying the "significant inventive aspect" test (if that is the correct formulation of the *Vornado* test) is likely to be much more difficult than the *Vornado* court implies. Consider the patent at issue in *Vornado*, U.S. Reissue Patent No. RE 34,551. Was the court saying that the unusual fan grill configuration was a "significant inventive aspect" merely because it was depicted in the patent's drawings? Figs. 3 and 5 of the patent did, indeed, depict one embodiment of a fan grill configuration.

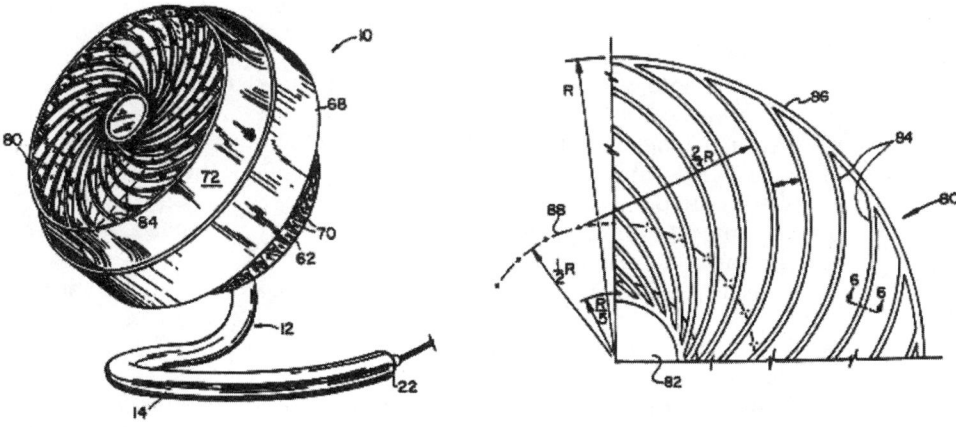

Fig. 3                                                          Fig. 5

However, if the rule is that anything depicted in a patent drawing is "significant," then it is quite possible that all aspects of every embodiment of an invention, down to the very nuts and bolts, will be "significant inventive aspects." We mean this literally. RE 34,551 contains numerous drawing figures, including partial cross-sectional Fig. 8, which shows internal components of an embodiment of the fan. Note bolts 34 and nuts 50.

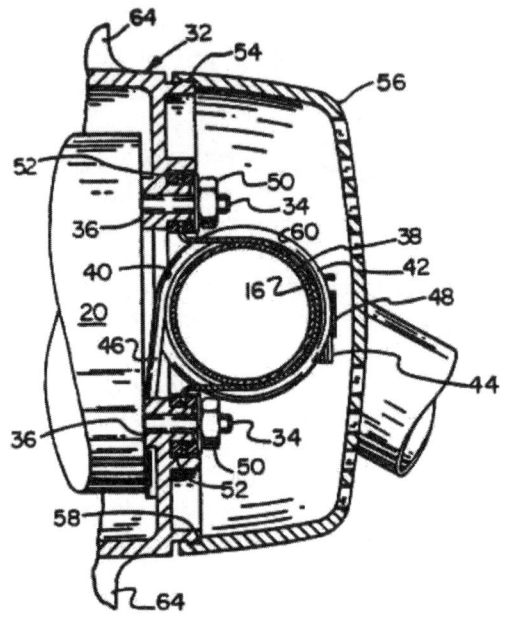

Fig. 8

Was the court instead saying that the fan grill configuration was a significant inventive aspect because it was recited in the claims? Claims 11 and 12 from RE 34,551 do indeed refer to "arcuate shaped ribs":

> 11. A ducted fan comprising:
>    a base member with a motor and bladed impeller attached to the base which blades rotate in one direction;
>    a funnel-shaped duct with its large end facing upstream concentrically positioned upstream of the blades and around the motor and connected thereto;
>    an outer cowling concentrically positioned, connected to the funnel-shaped duct through a series of radial ribs;
>    an inner cowling positioned inside the outer cowling and attached thereto, the inner cowling being circular in lateral cross section and tapered longitudinally in shape from its larger diameter intake end to its lesser diameter discharge end;
>    a circular grill having an outer radius attached to the discharge end of the inner cowling, the grill including a center hub and a series of arcuate shaped ribs extending outwardly from the hub and curving in the opposite direction of rotation from said blades to said outer radius, and each rib

> being equally spaced from each other around the hub, the maximum lateral spacing between the ribs is inboard from said outer radius; and
> 
> a support means pivotally attached to said motor and base member.
> 
> 12. A ducted fan as set forth in claim 11, wherein the lateral spacing between the ribs of the grill is no greater than 0.5 inches.

But these recitations do not require a fan grill identical in appearance to the fan grill depicted in Figs. 3 and 5; the recitations are much broader. Moreover, under this reasoning, the "motor" would be a significant inventive aspect, as would the "base member." Further, RE 34,551 contains twenty-four claims, several of which include no recitations whatsoever directed to the fan grill. For example, claim 21 is silent as to the geometry of the fan grill:

> 21. A ducted fan comprised of a base member including a motor and a bladed propeller operatively attached thereto, an entry duct concentrically positioned upstream of the bladed propeller and connected to said base member, an outer member concentrically positioned relative to and connected to said entry duct so as to be spaced therefrom, duct means for enclosing the bladed propeller and having a portion removably connected to allow access to the interior of said ducted fan.

The claims *do* consistently recite the physical relationship between the entry duct and the outer member or outer cowling. To the extent that Vornado's patent lawyers considered any particular inventive "aspect" of the claims to be "significant," it is far more likely that they considered this physical relationship "significant."

**9. *The nature of relief.*** The *Vornado* court argues that the district court's injunction effectively prevented Duracraft from "ever practicing the full invention embodied in the patented fans of Vornado *after Vornado's utility patents expire*" (our emphasis). If that was the concern underlying the court's rule, what is the relevance of the fact that the Vornado patents had not yet expired? Why did the Tenth Circuit vacate the district court's injunction prior to the expiration of the Vornado utility patents?

**10. *Drawing bright lines.*** The Tenth Circuit suggests that relying on the functionality doctrine to set the parameters of trade dress protection for designs would indirectly inhibit invention (the purpose of the patent laws) because "the inventor's supply of ideas itself and freedom to experiment with them might diminish if the inventor had to do a competitive market analysis before adopting useful features from others' inventions once their patents expired." This concern is not unlike that later expressed by the Supreme Court in *Wal-Mart, supra* Chapter 2, which caused the Court to seek a bright-line rule. Would the rule announced by the Tenth Circuit be easier for competitors to apply than competitive market analysis?

**11. *"Designing around."*** The *Vornado* court notes that "the grill on Duracraft's Turbo Fan incorporated a spiral vane structure that was copied from Vornado's . . . fan models but was purposely designed not to infringe Vornado's patent." "Designing around" existing patents is an important part of competitive innovation strategy. To what extent would that strategy have been undermined if the Tenth Circuit had affirmed the injunction?

12. ***The role of trademark law.*** The *Vornado* court comments that "consumer confusion resulting from the copying of product features is, in some measure, a self-fulfilling prophecy. To the degree that useful product configurations are protected as identifiers, consumers will come to rely on them for that purpose, but if copying is allowed, they will depend less on product shapes and more on labels and packaging." Does this suggest that the *Vornado* court is seeking to influence the ways that consumers identify products? Should rules of trademark law be used in that way?

13. ***Institutional dilemmas.*** Since 1982, regional appellate federal courts have been largely uninvolved in patent litigation. Appeals in patent cases are now heard by the Court of Appeals for the Federal Circuit. Thus, regional appellate courts are not practiced in the art of reading and construing patent documents. Should the Court of Appeals for the Federal Circuit assume exclusive jurisdiction in trademark cases where the availability of trade dress protection will be influenced by patent law? What arguments might support that proposition? *See Midwest Industries, Inc. v. Karavan Trailers, Inc.*, 175 F.3d 1356 (Fed. Cir. 1999) (en banc) (deciding to apply its own law rather than the law of the regional circuit in determining whether patent law conflicted with trade dress rights in product designs); *cf. Holmes Group v. Vornado Air Circulation Sys.*, 535 U.S. 826 (2002) (denying Federal Circuit jurisdiction where patent law claim raised only by counterclaim).

14. ***1998 reforms.*** In footnote 20, the *Vornado* court discusses the extent to which functionality may be asserted as a defense to a trademark whose registration has become "incontestable" through five years of exclusive and continuous use post-registration. (Incontestability is discussed in Chapter 5.) In 1998 Congress amended the Lanham Act to clarify that functionality could be asserted as a defense even in an action for infringement of a mark covered by an incontestable registration, and could be a ground for cancellation of a registration even after the passage of more than five years. *See* Trademark Law Treaty Implementation Act, Pub. L. No. 105-330, §201 (1998); *see also Wilhelm Pudenz, GmbH v. Littlefuse, Inc.*, 177 F.3d 1204 (11th Cir. 1999) (holding that this statutory provision was intended simply to clarify that the *Shakespeare Silstar* decision of the Fourth Circuit was flawed rather than to change the law). The 1998 amendments apply even to registrations that became incontestable prior to the effective date of the amendments. *See Eco Mfg. LLC v. Honeywell Int'l Inc.*, 357 F.3d 649, 653 (7th Cir. 2003).

---

As *Vornado* and the functionality cases in this chapter illustrate, courts regularly express concerns about the overlap between the patent and trademark regimes when deciding whether to grant protection to trade dress, especially product design trade dress. Should courts also be concerned about the potential overlap between the copyright and trademark regimes? In *Dastar Corp. v. Twentieth Century Fox Film Corp.*, 539 U.S. 23 (2003). Fox sued Dastar over Dastar's distribution of a videotape set called "World War II Campaigns in Europe." Dastar had created the set by copying and editing tapes of a television series, "Crusade in Europe," but neither Dastar's packaging nor its screen credits made any reference to the television series. Fox was distributing its own set of videotapes based on the television series, and had owned a copyright in the television series (now expired). Fox sued under Lanham Act Section 43(a), alleging "reverse passing off": defendant's packaging falsely omitted crediting the original television series, thus creating the false impression that Dastar was the origin of the content of the videotapes. Fox also brought a copyright claim based on the copyright in the underlying book from which the television series was made. The Ninth Circuit upheld the Lanham Act claim, but the Supreme Court reversed.

The Court's reversal derived from its interpretation of the term "origin" as used in Section 43(a). According to the Court, origin "refers to the producer of the tangible goods that are offered for sale, and not to the author of any idea, concept, or communication embodied in those goods." *Dastar*, 539 U.S. at 37. A trademark—such as COCA-COLA for a soft drink—signified to consumers that the trademark owner produced the product (or at least "stood behind" the product), but did not necessarily connote that the trademark owner originated the idea for the product. Giving a trademark owner a Section 43(a) claim for omitted attribution in the context of a creative product such as the videotapes would upset the balance between trademark and copyright, the Court reasoned:

> The right to copy, and to copy without attribution, once a copyright has expired, like "the right to make [an article whose patent has expired]—including the right to make it in precisely the shape it carried when patented—passes to the public." *Sears, Roebuck & Co. v. Stiffel Co.*, 376 U.S. 225, 230 (1964); see also *Kellogg Co. v. National Biscuit Co.*, 305 U.S. 111, 121-122 (1938). "In general, unless an intellectual property right such as a patent or copyright protects an item, it will be subject to copying." *TrafFix Devices, Inc. v. Marketing Displays, Inc.*, 532 U.S. 23, 29 (2001). The rights of a patentee or copyright holder are part of a "carefully crafted bargain," *Bonito Boats, Inc. v. Thunder Craft Boats, Inc.*, 489 U.S. 141, 150-151 (1989), under which, once the patent or copyright monopoly has expired, the public may use the invention or work at will and without attribution. Thus, in construing the Lanham Act, we have been "careful to caution against misuse or over-extension" of trademark and related protections into areas traditionally occupied by patent or copyright. *TrafFix*, 532 U.S., at 29. "The Lanham Act," we have said, "does not exist to reward manufacturers for their innovation in creating a particular device; that is the purpose of the patent law and its period of exclusivity." *Id.*, at 34. Federal trademark law "has no necessary relation to invention or discovery," *In re Trade-Mark Cases*, 100 U.S. 82, 94 (1879), but rather, by preventing competitors from copying "a source-identifying mark," "reduce[s] the customer's costs of shopping and making purchasing decisions," and "helps assure a producer that it (and not an imitating competitor) will reap the financial, reputation-related rewards associated with a desirable product," *Qualitex Co. v. Jacobson Products Co.*, 514 U.S. 159, 163-164 (1995) (internal quotation marks and citation omitted). Assuming for the sake of argument that Dastar's representation of itself as the "Producer" of its videos amounted to a representation that it originated the creative work conveyed by the videos, allowing a cause of action under §43(a) for that representation would create a species of mutant copyright law that

> limits the public's "federal right to 'copy and to use'" expired copyrights, *Bonito Boats, supra,* at 165.
>
> When Congress has wished to create such an addition to the law of copyright, it has done so with much more specificity than the Lanham Act's ambiguous use of "origin." The Visual Artists Rights Act of 1990, §603(a), 104 Stat. 5128, provides that the author of an artistic work "shall have the right . . . to claim authorship of that work." 17 U.S.C. §106A(a)(1)(A). That express right of attribution is carefully limited and focused: It attaches only to specified "work[s] of visual art," §101, is personal to the artist, §§106A(b) and (e), and endures only for "the life of the author," at §106A(d)(1). Recognizing in §43(a) a cause of action for misrepresentation of authorship of non-copyrighted works (visual or otherwise) would render these limitations superfluous. A statutory interpretation that renders another statute superfluous is of course to be avoided. [cit.]
>
> Reading "origin" in §43(a) to require attribution of uncopyrighted materials would pose serious practical problems. Without a copyrighted work as the basepoint, the word "origin" has no discernible limits. . . .

*Id.* at 33-35. The Court also concluded that allowing a Section 43(a) claim in *Dastar* would be inconsistent with prior cases, such as *Wal-Mart*:

> Finally, reading §43(a) of the Lanham Act as creating a cause of action for, in effect, plagiarism—the use of otherwise unprotected works and inventions without attribution—would be hard to reconcile with our previous decisions. For example, in *Wal-Mart Stores, Inc. v. Samara Brothers, Inc.,* 529 U.S. 205 (2000), we considered whether product-design trade dress can ever be inherently distinctive. Wal-Mart produced "knockoffs" of children's clothes designed and manufactured by Samara Brothers, containing only "minor modifications" of the original designs. *Id.,* at 208. We concluded that the designs could not be protected under §43(a) without a showing that they had acquired "secondary meaning," *id.,* at 214, so that they "'identify the source of the product rather than the product itself,'" *id.,* at 211. This carefully considered limitation would be entirely pointless if the "original" producer could turn around and pursue a reverse-passing-off claim under exactly the same provision of the Lanham Act. Samara would merely have had to argue that it was the "origin" of the designs that Wal-Mart was selling as its own line. It was not, because "origin of goods" in the Lanham Act referred to the producer of the clothes, and not the producer of the (potentially) copyrightable or patentable designs that the clothes embodied.

*Id.* at 36-37. Should the reasoning of *Dastar* apply to claims of omitted attribution involving trade dress? Should the existence of (potential) copyright protection effectively limit the recognition of trade dress rights? Consider the following case.

### Bretford Mfg., Inc. v. Smith System Mfg. Corp.
419 F.3d 576 (7th Cir. 2005)

Easterbrook, Circuit Judge:

Bretford makes a line of computer tables that it sells under the name Connections TM. Since 1990 many of these tables have featured one rather than two legs on each end. The leg supports a sleeve attached to a V-shaped brace, making it easy to change the table's height while keeping the work surface stable. Although the sleeve and brace together look like a Y, Bretford calls it the V-Design table, and we employ the same usage. This illustration, from Bretford's web site, shows the idea:

Between 1990 and 1997 Bretford was the only seller of computer tables with a V-shaped height-adjustment system. It sold about 200,000 V-Design tables during that period. Smith System, one of Bretford's competitors, decided to copy the sleeve and brace for its own line of computer tables. Smith System made its initial sales of the knockoff product to the Dallas school system in 1997, and this trademark litigation quickly followed.

Invoking §43(a) of the Lanham Act, Bretford contends that the V-shaped design is its product's trade dress, which Smith System has infringed. It also contends that Smith System engaged in "reverse passing off" when it incorporated some Bretford hardware into a sample table that it showed purchasing officials in Dallas. The parties waived their right to a jury trial, and the district court held evidentiary hearings and issued opinions over a number of years. Although at one point the judge found Smith System liable and awarded damages in Bretford's favor, he reversed course in light of *Wal-Mart Stores, Inc. v. Samara Brothers, Inc.*, 529 U.S. 205 (2000), and *Dastar Corp. v. Twentieth Century Fox Film Corp.*, 539 U.S. 23 (2003). The appeal presents two principal questions: whether Smith System is entitled to copy Bretford's design, and, if yes, whether it was nonetheless wrongful for Smith System to use Bretford components in a sample table shown to the Dallas buyers. . . .

The Supreme Court held in *Wal-Mart* that the phrase "word, term, name, symbol, or device, or any combination thereof" [in Section 43(a)] includes distinctive aspects of a product's appearance, commonly known as trade dress. The Court added, however, that a product's physical design cannot be deemed inherently distinctive, so that to prevail under §43(a) the producer must demonstrate "secondary meaning"—in other words, that consumers understand the design elements to signify the goods' origin and not just its attributes. Otherwise, the Court thought, it would be too easy to use the expense and risk of litigation to dissuade rivals from using their right to reverse-engineer and copy products, which they may do down to the last detail unless a feature of the product is protected by patent, copyright, or trademark law. *See, e.g., TrafFix Devices, Inc. v. Marketing Displays, Inc.*, 532 U.S. 23 (2001); *Bonito Boats, Inc. v. Thunder Craft Boats, Inc.*, 489 U.S. 141 (1989); *Sears, Roebuck & Co. v. Stiffel Co.*, 376 U.S. 225 (1964). Trademark law is designed to reduce the costs customers incur in learning who makes the product, and this also helps sellers obtain rewards from producing goods of consistent quality, for consumers will find it easier to find and buy goods with which they have been satisfied in the past. So when trade dress implies the product's origin it is protected as a trademark (unless it also is functional); but when consumers value the feature for its own sake rather than as a badge of origin, it may be copied freely.

The district court found that V-shaped legs do not signal Bretford as a source. The record supports this conclusion; indeed, Bretford has no evidence that the leg design prompts "Bretford" in buyers' minds. There are no surveys and no evidence of actual confusion. Both Bretford and Smith System sell through distributors and field representatives to sophisticated buyers who know exactly where their goods are coming from.

Many buyers ask for tables with V-shaped legs, and Bretford insists that this shows that they want its Connections TM furniture; quite the contrary, this form of specification does more to imply that the leg design is functional than to show that anyone cares who makes the table. In the end, all Bretford has to go on is the fact that it was the only maker of such tables for eight years and spent more than $4 million to promote sales. If that were enough to permit judgment in its favor, new entry would be curtailed unduly by the risk and expense of trademark litigation, for every introducer of a new design could make the same sort of claim. "Consumers should not be deprived of the benefits of competition with regard to the utilitarian and esthetic purposes that product design ordinarily serves by a rule of law that facilitates plausible threats of suit against new entrants based on alleged inherent distinctiveness." *Wal-Mart*, 529 U.S. at 213.

Originators such as Bretford may receive protection via design patents, and strictly aesthetic features of products may be copyrighted. "The availability of these and other protections greatly reduces any harm to the producer that might ensue" from limiting trademark protection to features that have acquired secondary meaning. *Wal-Mart*, 529 U.S. at 214. Bretford did not obtain patent or copyright protection, so it cannot block Smith System's copy-cat tables. Even if the record had evidence of secondary meaning, Bretford likely would lose because the leg design appears to be functional, but we need not explore that issue.

When Smith System decided to copy Bretford's table, it subcontracted the leg assemblies to a specialized metal fabricator, whose initial efforts were unsatisfactory. This left Smith System in a bind when the Dallas school system asked to see a table. Smith System cobbled a sample together by attaching the leg assembly from a Bretford table (which Smith System had repainted) to a top that Smith System had manufactured itself. (Who supplied other components, such as the cable guides and grommets, is disputed but irrelevant.) Dallas was satisfied and placed an order. All of the tables delivered to Dallas included legs manufactured by Smith System's subcontractor. Nonetheless, Bretford contends, by using its leg assemblies on even the one sample, Smith System engaged in reverse passing off and must pay damages.

Passing off or palming off occurs when a firm puts someone else's trademark on its own (usually inferior) goods; reverse passing off or misappropriation is selling someone else's goods under your own mark. [cit.] It is not clear what's wrong with reselling someone else's goods, if you first buy them at retail. If every automobile sold by DeLorean includes the chassis and engine of a Peugeot, with DeLorean supplying only the body shell, Peugeot has received its asking price for each car sold and does not suffer any harm. Still, the Supreme Court said in *Dastar* that "reverse passing off" can violate the Lanham Act if a misdescription of goods' origin causes commercial injury. Our opinion in *Peaceable Planet, Inc. v. Ty, Inc.*, 362 F.3d 986 (7th Cir. 2004), shows how this could occur.

*Dastar* added that the injury must be a trademark loss — which is to say, it must come from a misrepresentation of the goods' origin. Dastar thus had the right (so far as the Lanham Act is concerned) to incorporate into its videos footage taken and edited by others, provided that it manufactured the finished product and did not mislead anyone about who should be held responsible for shortcomings. No one makes a product from scratch, with trees and iron ore entering one end of the plant and a finished consumer product emerging at the other. Ford's cars include Fram oil filters, Goodyear tires, Owens-Corning glass, Bose radios, Pennzoil lubricants, and many other constituents; buyers can see some of the other producers' marks (those on the radio and tires for example) but not others, such as the oil and transmission fluid. Smith System builds tables using wood from one supplier, grommets (including Teflon from du Pont) from another, and vinyl molding and paint and bolts from any of a hundred more sources — the list is extensive even for a simple product such as a table. If Smith System does not tell du Pont how the Teflon is used, and does not inform its consumers which firm supplied the wood, has it violated the Lanham Act? Surely not; the statute does not condemn the way in which all products are made.

Legs are a larger fraction of a table's total value than grommets and screws, but nothing in the statute establishes one rule for "major" components and another for less costly inputs. The right question, *Dastar* holds, is whether the consumer knows who has produced the finished product. In the *Dastar* case that was Dastar itself, even though most of the product's economic value came from elsewhere; just so when Smith System includes components manufactured by others but stands behind the finished product. The portion of §43(a) that addresses reverse passing off is the one that condemns false designations of origin. "Origin" means, *Dastar* holds, "the producer of the tangible product sold in the marketplace". 539 U.S. at 31. As far as Dallas was concerned, the table's "origin" was Smith System, no matter who made any component or subassembly.

Much of Bretford's argument takes the form that it is just "unfair" for Smith System to proceed as it did, making a sale before its subcontractor could turn out acceptable leg assemblies. Businesses often think competition unfair, but federal law encourages wholesale copying, the better to drive down prices. Consumers rather than producers are the objects of the law's solicitude. If Smith System misled Dallas into thinking that it could supply high-quality tables, when its subcontractor could not match Bretford's welds and other attributes of Bretford's V-shaped leg assemblies, then the victim would be the Dallas school system. (As far as we are aware, however, Dallas is happy with the quality of the tables it received; it has not complained about a bait and switch.) As the Court observed in *Dastar*, creators of certain artistic works are entitled (along the lines of the European approach to moral rights) to control how their work is presented or altered by others. *See* 539 U.S. at 34-35, citing 17 U.S.C. §106A. Bretford's table is not a "work of visual art" under §106A (and the definition in 17 U.S.C. §101). Once Bretford sold its goods, it had no control over how customers used their components: the Lanham Act does not include any version of the "derivative work" right in copyright law. *See* 17 U.S.C. §106(2).

. . .

*Affirmed.*

## NOTES AND QUESTIONS

1. *A role for unfair competition?* Bretford endorses, and perhaps even amplifies, *Dastar*'s aversion to a broader unfair competition cause of action. Assuming that *Dastar*'s view of the statute is accurate, should Congress rethink this position? Do the facts in *Bretford* suggest unfairness among competitors that the law should remedy? Or is the court correct in asserting that consumers are the objects of the law's solicitude, such that competition of the sort in *Bretford* should be encouraged? As noted above, in many other countries, unfair competition laws (motivated in large part by impulses against misappropriation) provide protection against simulation of product design. In several jurisdictions, this cause of action is denominated as an action against "slavish imitation." What justifications might exist for such protection? What concerns would it raise?

2. **Peaceable Planet *and the harm from reverse passing off.*** The *Bretford* court cites *Peaceable Planet* for that opinion's explanation of the harm that might flow from reverse passing off. In *Peaceable Planet,* the plaintiff had sold a few thousand plush toy camels under the name NILES, and defendant Ty (a much larger firm, and well known as the maker of BEANIE BABIES), subsequently sold nearly 2 million toy camels under the same name. Peaceable Planet sued. As the court characterized Peaceable Planet's claim:

> In the most common type of suit for trademark infringement, the plaintiff complains that the defendant is passing off his (inferior) product as the

plaintiff's. But here we have the converse case of "reverse passing off," in which the plaintiff complains that the defendant is trying to pass off the plaintiff's product as the defendant's. [cit.] Why would anyone want to do such a thing? One reason might be to obliterate the plaintiff's corporate identity and prevent him from entering new markets, where the defendant, having appropriated the plaintiff's trademark, would claim that the plaintiff was the infringer.

*Peaceable Planet, Inc. v. Ty, Inc.*, 362 F.3d 986, 987-88 (7th Cir. 2004). Is this a plausible theory of harm in general? A plausible theory as applied to the facts of *Bretford*?

# CHAPTER 4
# ENFORCEMENT AND DEFENSES

In Chapters 2 and 3, we discussed the rules for determining whether packaging, design, or other nonverbal indicia can be protected as trade dress under the Lanham Act. In this chapter, we turn to the rules for determining when trade dress rights can be enforced against parties who use that trade dress without authorization. There are two principal enforcement theories under the Lanham Act: confusion-based theories vindicated by causes of action under Lanham Act §§32 or 43(a) (commonly called "infringement" actions) and dilution under Lanham Act §43(c). We cover the former in Section A, and the latter (along with counterfeiting) in Section B.

There are numerous defenses to both the infringement and dilution causes of action. Some defenses are provided for expressly in the Lanham Act, whereas others derive from the common law, as we describe in Section C. We conclude the chapter, in Section D, with a brief look at Lanham Act remedies.

In many other countries, broader theories of unfair competition or misappropriation often provide additional causes of action in design cases. (We briefly mention these causes of action in Chapter 8.) Contemporary American courts have largely rejected these causes of action, although it may be that the misappropriation impulse underlies a number of trade dress decisions in the United States.

## A. TRADE DRESS INFRINGEMENT — LIKELIHOOD OF CONFUSION

The most important vehicles for enforcing rights under the Lanham Act are the confusion-based causes of action codified in Lanham Act §§32 and 43(a). The statutory text is reproduced in relevant part below.

> §1114. (§32) Remedies; infringement; innocent infringement by printers and publishers
> (1) Any person who shall, without the consent of the registrant—

(a) use in commerce any reproduction, counterfeit, copy, or colorable imitation of a registered mark in connection with the sale, offering for sale, distribution, or advertising of any goods or services on or in connection with which such use is likely to cause confusion, or to cause mistake, or to deceive . . .

. . . shall be liable in a civil action by the registrant for the remedies hereinafter provided.

**§1125. (§43) False designations of origin and false descriptions forbidden**
(a) Civil action

(1) Any person who, on or in connection with any goods or services, or any container for goods, uses in commerce any word, term, name, symbol, or device, or any combination thereof, or any false designation of origin, false or misleading description of fact, or false or misleading representation of fact, which—

(A) is likely to cause confusion, or to cause mistake, or to deceive as to the affiliation, connection, or association of such person with another person, or as to the origin, sponsorship, or approval of his or her goods, services, or commercial activities by another person . . .

. . . shall be liable in a civil action by any person who believes that he or she is or is likely to be damaged by such act.

The Section 32 cause of action may be invoked when registered rights are at issue, and is often labeled as an "infringement" cause of action. The Section 43(a) cause of action, as we will describe it in this chapter, is a parallel cause of action that applies to unregistered rights, sometimes labeled as a "false designation of origin" cause of action, but also known as "common law infringement," or even "unfair competition."

As we have discussed in Chapters 2 and 3, for a number of historical and practical reasons, many firms have not registered their trade dress rights, relying instead on common law rights. Accordingly, the section 43(a) cause of action has generally been the vehicle of choice for enforcing trade dress rights. The vast majority of cases discussed in this chapter involve applications of §43(a).

However, in the cases that we will discuss in this chapter, §§32 and 43(a) function similarly. Both include the phrase "likely to cause confusion." All circuits today employ a multifactor test for determining whether a defendant's activities give rise to a likelihood of confusion, using the same test for both §32(a) actions and confusion-based §43(a) actions. A typical recitation of factors can be found in *Polaroid Corp. v. Polarad Elec. Corp.*, 287 F.2d 492, 495 (2d Cir. 1961):

> [Likelihood of confusion] is a function of many variables: the strength of [the] mark, the degree of similarity between the two marks, the proximity of the products, the likelihood that the prior owner will bridge the gap, actual confusion, and the reciprocal of defendant's good faith in adopting its own mark, the quality of the defendant's product, and the sophistication of the buyers. Even this extensive catalogue does not exhaust the possibilities—the court may have to take still other variables into account.

Figure 4-1 on the following pages lists the governing multifactor tests for each circuit. The names of the tests derive from leading cases in the respective jurisdictions. You may find it useful to refer to the chart as you proceed through the cases. Note that the tests all fit the same general pattern. All include as factors (1) the alleged infringer's intent; (2) actual confusion; and (3) a variety of factors that might be lumped together as "market factors." *See* Restatement (Third) of Unfair Competition §§21-23 (1996) (separately articulating rules for market factors, intent, and actual confusion).

The multifactor tests for likelihood of confusion trace back to the Restatement of Torts §731 (1938). When courts began extending trademark liability in cases in which the trademark owner's and alleged infringer's goods or services were not identical, courts needed a test that expressed how the similarity between goods or services would weigh with other potential indicia of confusion. Gradually, courts developed a multifactor test for "unrelated goods" cases.

Eventually, the multifactor test came to be adopted for all trademark infringement cases, whether or not they included "unrelated" goods. Courts also extended the multifactor test to trade dress cases. Notice that in trade dress cases involving product shapes, the goods of the respective parties will be the same in virtually all cases. Ironically, then, the unrelated goods problem that triggered the evolution of the multifactor test probably does not apply to product design trade dress cases, but courts apply the multifactor test to those cases anyway. You may wish to consider whether courts should keep this irony in mind when applying the test to product design cases.

Two other points about the confusion standard bear mentioning here. First, Section 32(1)(a) does not limit confusion to "purchasers." Starting with the original (1946) version of the Lanham Act (the first legislation to adopt explicitly a confusion standard), the Section 32(1)(a) infringement provision required that the trademark owner show that the alleged infringer's use "is likely to cause confusion, or to cause mistake, or to deceive *purchasers* as to the source of origin of such goods or services." In 1962, Congress amended Section 32(1)(a) to eliminate the final clause. To the extent that this change implies that confusion may be assessed at points in time other than the point of purchase, the change is especially important for design cases. Consider, for example, the prospect that a purchaser is not confused by a defendant's product shape at the point of sale, but casual passersby who subsequently see the defendant's product are confused. Consider whether the language of the Lanham Act provides a remedy for such confusion, and whether it should provide a remedy.

Second, Section 32(1)(a) does not limit confusion to confusion about source. Before 1962, Section 32(1)(a) required evidence of confusion as to the "source of origin of such goods or services," but currently the section requires only a showing of a likelihood "to cause confusion, or to cause mistake, or to deceive." This language has been construed to provide a cause of action where the mark owner shows a likelihood of confusion as to affiliation. Since 1988, Section 43(a)(1)(a) has explicitly acknowledged the availability of this cause of action.

## Figure 4-1
## Likelihood of Confusion Factor Tests

| | | | |
|---|---|---|---|
| **1st Circuit**<br>*Boston Athletic Ass'n v. Sullivan*, 867 F.2d 22, 29-34 (1st Cir. 1989); *Keds Corp. v. Renee Int'l Trading Corp.*, 888 F.2d 215, 222 (1st Cir. 1989). | 1. similarity of the marks;<br>2. similarity of the goods;<br>3. relationship between the parties' channels of trade; | 4. the relationship between the parties' advertising;<br>5. the classes of prospective purchasers;<br>6. evidence of actual confusion; | 7. the defendant's intent in adopting the mark; and<br>8. the strength of the plaintiff's mark. |
| **2d Circuit**<br>**"Polaroid" Factors**<br>*Polaroid Corp. v. Polarad Elecs. Corp.*, 287 F.2d 492, 495 (2d Cir. 1961), cert. denied, 368 U.S. 820 (1961); *Playtex Products, Inc. v. Georgia-Pacific Corp.*, 390 F.3d 158, 162 (2d Cir. 2004). | 1. the strength of the senior user's mark;<br>2. the degree of similarity between the two marks;<br>3. the proximity of the products; | 4. the likelihood that the prior owner will bridge the gap;<br>5. actual confusion;<br>6. the junior user's good faith in adopting its own mark; | 7. the quality of defendant's product; and<br>8. the sophistication of buyers. |
| **3d Circuit**<br>**"Lapp" Factors**<br>*Interpace Corp. v. Lapp, Inc.*, 721 F.2d 460, 463 (3d Cir. 1983); *KOS Pharm., Inc. v. Andrx Corp.*, 369 F.3d 700, 709 (3d Cir. 2004). | 1. the degree of similarity between the owner's mark and the alleged infringing mark;<br>2. the strength of the owner's mark;<br>3. the price of the goods and other factors indicative of the care and attention expected of consumers when making a purchase; | 4. the length of time the defendant has used the mark without evidence of actual confusion arising;<br>5. the intent of the defendant in adopting the mark;<br>6. the evidence of actual confusion;<br>7. whether the goods, though not competing, are marketed through the same channels of trade and advertised through the same media; | 8. the extent to which the targets of the parties' sales efforts are the same;<br>9. the relationship of the goods in the minds of consumers because of the similarity of function; and<br>10. other facts suggesting that the consuming public might expect the prior owner to manufacture a product in the defendant's market, or that he is likely to expand into that market. |

| | | | |
|---|---|---|---|
| **4th Circuit**<br>**"Pizzeria Uno" Factors**<br>*Pizzeria Uno Corp. v. Temple*, 747 F.2d 1522, 1527 (4th Cir. 1984); *CareFirst of Maryland, Inc. v. First Care, P.C.*, 434 F.3d 263, 267 (4th Cir. 2006). *Cf. Sara Lee Corp. v. Kayser-Roth Corp.*, 81 F.3d 455, 463-464 (4th Cir. 1996) (suggesting that courts may supplement the *Pizzeria Uno* test with other factors). | 1. the strength or distinctiveness of the mark;<br>2. the similarity of the two marks;<br>3. the similarity of the goods/services the marks identify; | 4. the similarity of the facilities the two parties use in their businesses;<br>5. the similarity of the advertising used by the two parties; | 6. the defendant's intent;<br>7. actual confusion. |
| **5th Circuit**<br>*Roto-Rooter Corp. v. O'Neal*, 513 F.2d 44, 45 (5th Cir. 1975); *Scott Fetzer Co. v. House of Vacuums Inc.*, 381 F.3d 477, 484-485 (5th Cir. 2004). *Cf. Oreck Corp. v. U.S. Floor Sys., Inc.*, 803 F.2d 166, 170 (5th Cir. 1986) (advocating an 8-factor test), *cert. denied*, 481 U.S. 1069 (1987). | 1. the type of mark allegedly infringed;<br>2. the similarity between the two marks;<br>3. the similarity of the products or services; | 4. the identity of the retail outlets and purchasers;<br>5. the identity of the advertising media used; | 6. the defendant's intent; and<br>7. any evidence of actual confusion. |

**Figure 4-1** (continued)

| | | | |
|---|---|---|---|
| **6th Circuit**<br>***"Frisch's" Factors***<br>*Frisch's Rests. v. Elby's Big Boy Inc.*, 670 F.2d 642, 648 (6th Cir. 1982), *cert. denied*, 459 U.S. 916 (1982); *AutoZone, Inc. v. Tandy Corp.*, 373 F.3d 786, 792-793 (6th Cir. 2004). | 1. the strength of the plaintiff's mark;<br>2. the relatedness of the goods or services offered by the parties;<br>3. similarity of the marks; | 4. any evidence of actual confusion;<br>5. the marketing channels used by the parties;<br>6. the probable degree of purchaser care and sophistication; | 7. the defendant's intent; and<br>8. the likelihood of either party expanding its product line using the marks. |
| **7th Circuit**<br>*Helene Curtis Industries, Inc. v. Church & Dwight Co.*, 560 F.2d 1325, 1330 (7th Cir. 1977), *cert. denied*, 434 U.S. 1070 (1978); *Sullivan v. CBS Corp.*, 385 F.3d 772, 776 (7th Cir. 2004). | 1. the degree of similarity between the marks in appearance and suggestion;<br>2. the similarity of the products for which the name is used;<br>3. the area and manner of concurrent use; | 4. the degree of care likely to be exercised by consumers;<br>5. the strength of the complainant's mark; | 6. actual confusion; and<br>7. an intent on the part of the alleged infringer to palm off his products as those of another. |
| **8th Circuit**<br>***"SquirtCo" Factors***<br>*SquirtCo v. Seven-Up Co.*, 628 F.2d 1086, 1091 (8th Cir. 1980); *Frosty Treats, Inc. v. Sony Computer Entm't America Inc.*, 426 F.3d 1001, 1008 (8th Cir. 2005). | 1. the strength of the owner's mark;<br>2. the similarity between the owner's mark and the alleged infringer's mark; | 3. the degree to which the products compete with each other;<br>4. the alleged infringer's intent to "pass off" its goods as those of the trademark owner; | 5. incidents of actual confusion; and<br>6. the type of product, its costs and conditions of purchase. |

A. Trade Dress Infringement—Likelihood of Confusion 217

| | | | |
|---|---|---|---|
| *9th Circuit*<br>*"Sleekcraft" Factors*<br>AMF Inc. v. Sleekcraft Boats, 599 F.2d 341, 348-349 (9th Cir. 1979). | 1. strength of the mark;<br>2. proximity of the goods;<br>3. similarity of the marks; | 4. evidence of actual confusion;<br>5. marketing channels used;<br>6. type of goods and the degree of care likely to be exercised by the purchaser; | 7. defendant's intent in selecting the mark; and<br>8. likelihood of expansion of the product lines. |
| *10th Circuit*<br>Sally Beauty Co. v. Beautyco, Inc., 304 F.3d 964, 972 (10th Cir. 2002); Australian Gold, Inc. v. Hatfield, 436 F.3d 1228, 1239-1240 (10th Cir. 2006). | 1. the degree of similarity between the marks;<br>2. the intent of the alleged infringer in adopting its mark; | 3. evidence of actual confusion;<br>4. the relation in use and the manner of marketing between the goods or services marketed by the competing parties; | 5. the degree of care likely to be exercised by purchasers; and<br>6. the strength or weakness of the marks. |
| *11th Circuit*<br>AmBrit, Inc. v. Kraft, Inc., 812 F.2d 1531, 1538 (11th Cir. 1986); Dippin' Dots, Inc. v. Frosty Bites Distribution, LLC, 369 F.3d 1197, 1207 (11th Cir. 2004). | 1. the strength of the marks;<br>2. the similarity of the marks;<br>3. the similarity of the products; | 4. the similarity of retail outlets and purchasers;<br>5. the similarity of advertising media used; | 6. the defendant's intent; and<br>7. actual confusion. |
| *D.C. Circuit*<br>Partido Revolucionario Dominicano (PRD) Seccional Metropolitana de Washington-DC, Maryland y Virginia v. Partido Revolucionario Dominicano, Seccional de Maryland y Virginia, 312 F. Supp. 2d 1, 14 (D.D.C. 2004). | 1. the strength of the senior user's mark;<br>2. the degree of similarity between the two marks;<br>3. the proximity of the products; | 4. evidence of actual confusion;<br>5. the junior user's good faith in adopting its own mark; | 6. the quality of defendant's product; and<br>7. the sophistication of buyers. |

**Figure 4-1** (continued)

| | | |
|---|---|---|
| **Federal Circuit "DuPont" Factors**<br><br>*In re E. I. DuPont deNemours & Co.*, 476 F.2d 1357, 1361 (C.C.P.A. 1973); *Palm Bay Imports, Inc. v. Veuve Clicquot Ponsardin Maison Fondee En 1772*, 396 F.3d 1369, 1371 (Fed. Cir. 2005). | 1. the similarity or dissimilarity of the marks in their entireties as to appearance, sound, connotation, and commercial impression;<br>2. the similarity or dissimilarity and nature of the goods or services as described in an application or registration or in connection with which a prior mark is in use;<br>3. the similarity or dissimilarity of established, likely-to-continue trade channels;<br>4. the conditions under which and buyers to whom sales are made, i.e., "impulse" vs. careful, sophisticated purchasing; | 5. the fame of the prior mark (sales, advertising, length of use);<br>6. the number and nature of similar marks in use on similar goods;<br>7. the nature and extent of any actual confusion;<br>8. the length of time during and conditions under which there has been concurrent use without evidence of actual confusion;<br>9. the variety of goods on which a mark is or is not used (house mark, "family" mark, product mark); | 10. the market interface between applicant and the owner of a prior mark;<br>11. the extent to which applicant has a right to exclude others from use of its mark on its goods;<br>12. the extent of potential confusion, i.e., whether de minimis or substantial; and<br>13. any other established fact probative of the effect of use. |

## 1. APPLYING THE MULTIFACTOR CONFUSION TEST IN TRADE DRESS CASES

Recall from Chapter 2 that courts apply different distinctiveness rules to product packaging and product design trade dress, respectively. As the following cases show, courts apply the multifactor likelihood of confusion test to both product packaging and product design trade dress. As you read the cases, consider whether courts are applying the multifactor test differently to product packaging than to product design. Should they be?

### a. Product Packaging

#### AMBRIT, INC. v. KRAFT, INC.
812 F.2d 1531 (11th Cir. 1986), *cert. denied*, 107 S. Ct. 1983 (1987)

WISDOM, Senior Circuit Judge:

This appeal presents a variety of questions involving trade dress and trademark rights. The parties are competitors in the ice cream novelty market. The principal question in this controversy is whether the trade dress of Kraft's Polar B'ar infringes the trade dress of Isaly's Klondike bar. The district court answered "Yes" to this question. 619 F. Supp. 983. We affirm, holding that the district court's findings were not clearly erroneous and that the court's conclusions of law were correct.

#### Facts

The parties [Isaly—which later became Ambrit—and Kraft] are competitors in the stickless, five ounce, square, chocolate-covered ice cream bar market. Isaly sells its bar under the trademark "Klondike," and Kraft sells its bar under the trademark "Polar B'ar." The crux of the controversy concerns the packaging of those two products.

Isaly began in the last century as a family-owned dairy business operating in Eastern Ohio and Western Pennsylvania. In 1928 Isaly started making and selling five ounce, chocolate-covered, stickless ice cream bars under the name "Klondike." Isaly now sells three versions of the Klondike bar: plain, crispy, and chocolate/chocolate. The plain Klondike bar has been wrapped in pebbled foil featuring the colors silver, blue, and white since the 1940's. Since at least 1956 the wrapper has featured a 3 × 3 inch panel of silver, white, and blue, the words "Isaly's" and "Klondike," and the figure of a polar bear.

In 1978 Isaly revised the wrapper of the Klondike bar maintaining, however, the impression the original wrapper conveyed. The colors, images, and words on the wrapper remained the same, but "Klondike" was emphasized, "Isaly's" was reduced in size, and the stance of the polar bear was altered. Since 1978, the wrapper has remained the same. The plain Klondike bar is wrapped in pebbled foil presenting a 3 × 3 inch silver panel featuring a white polar bear on all fours before a sunburst design. Both the polar bear and the sunburst are outlined and highlighted with royal blue. Below the bear is the word "Klondike," written in large white letters outlined in royal blue. "Isaly's" appears in small blue letters to the right of the bear. The crispy and chocolate/chocolate wrappers are identical except that those wrappers use the colors yellow and brown respectively in place of the white color used on the plain wrapper.

Isaly began selling the Klondike in a six-pack arrangement in 1963, and between 1963 and 1978 some six-packs were offered in trays overwrapped in clear plastic. Since 1978, all six-packs have been sold in transparently overwrapped trays with a double layer of three bars, presenting the Klondike wrapper three times. The trays are silver and feature a large numeral "6" on the side. The end panels of the Klondike trays display a copy of the appropriate wrapper design depending on the version of the bar contained in the tray. Until 1978, Isaly sold the Klondike bar in a tri-state area composed of Western Pennsylvania, Eastern Ohio, and Northern West Virginia. Isaly advertised in newspapers and in point-of-sales materials in stores, both of which featured the polar bear emblem found on the bar's wrapper. Isaly also advertised on television in a commercial featuring a polar bear and prospector in a supermarket.

In 1978, Isaly began to investigate the possibility of expanding the market for the Klondike bar. Isaly decided to introduce the bar into supermarkets and convenience stores in various expansion markets. To augment the expansion it achieved on its own, Isaly approached Kraft, an international manufacturer and distributor of food products, concerning a distribution arrangement between the two parties. Although Kraft's dairy group produces its own ice cream products, which are principally distributed under the brand names "Sealtest" and "Breyers," since 1970 that group has also distributed ice cream products made by other companies. The parties agreed that Kraft would distribute the Klondike bar in Florida and that Isaly would be responsible for most of the advertising in that market.

The introduction of the Klondike bar into the Florida market in early 1979 was highly successful and Kraft was well satisfied. Kraft had previously been unsuccessful with its ice cream novelty line and viewed the Klondike bar as a way to change that pattern. In October 1979, Kraft informed Isaly that it was interested in purchasing Isaly or having Isaly package its bars for Kraft under the Sealtest name. Isaly rejected these proposals, suggesting instead that Kraft expand its distribution of the Klondike bar. Kraft stated, however, that it was reluctant to expand distribution without a proprietary interest in the product. In late 1979, Kraft began to develop its own five ounce chocolate-covered ice cream bar. Kraft attempted to duplicate the exact size and taste of the Klondike bar. Kraft chose the name "Polar B'ar" after finding that name on a list of unused trademarks. A predecessor of Kraft, Southern Dairies, Inc., had sold an ice cream bar under that trademark from 1929 to 1932, and periodically renewed the trademark registration. Through merger, Kraft acquired it.

Kraft employed two firms to design the packaging for the Polar B'ar product, making clear to these firms that the functional features of the Polar B'ar package were to resemble as closely as possible the Klondike bar package. The bars were to be wrapped in foil and sold in six-pack trays overwrapped in transparent plastic. Kraft supplied these design firms with samples of the Klondike packaging to aid them in their efforts.

The designers presented Kraft with a number of different wrapper designs but ultimately chose the one Isaly now challenges. That wrapper presents a 3 × 3 pebbled silver foil panel with a white polar bear standing on all fours contained within a colored triangle in the bottom right corner. "Polar B'ar" is written in large colored block letters diagonally across the center of the bar. "Sealtest" is written in script in a red box in the upper left corner, and the phrase "made with real milk chocolate" appears in a red circle in the bottom left corner of the panel.

In 1980 Kraft sold Polar B'ars in two forms: plain and "crunchy." The colors of the triangle and block letters on the wrappers varied with each version. Plain wrappers used royal blue and "crunchy" wrappers used red. Later, Kraft introduced four new versions of the bar: chocolate, mint, heavenly hash, and peanut butter, using the colors brown, green, light blue, and golden brown respectively.

As planned, Kraft sold Polar B'ars in a six-pack tray overwrapped in clear plastic. The tray employs a silver background and displays a large numeral "6" between the brand name and the product description. The end panels of Kraft's tray feature a large white polar bear and the words "Polar B'ar" in large block letters against a background colored to correspond with the version of the bar contained in the tray. Kraft promoted the bar with television and newspaper advertising. Its television commercial featured the figure of a bear. Then came a bear's roar when the camera shifted to the polar bar wrapper.

Kraft was the exclusive distributor of the Klondike bar in Florida from 1979 to 1982. In February 1982 Kraft notified Isaly in writing of its intention to terminate its distribution of Klondike as of April 1982. In May 1982 Isaly initiated this suit. Isaly asserted that Kraft's packaging: (1) constituted a false designation of origin under §43(a) of the Lanham Act, (2) infringed Isaly's federal trademarks covering its label and package designs, [and violated various other provisions. The court ruled in favor of Isaly on the trade dress claims, and Kraft appealed that judgment.]

Discussion

I. Trade Dress Infringement

Kraft's first contention on appeal is that the district court erred in finding Kraft guilty of trade dress infringement. Kraft does not contend that the district court applied the wrong test in making this finding, but rather argues that the district court misapplied the proper test.

Section 43(a) of the Lanham Act states in relevant part:

> Any person who shall . . . use in connection with any goods or services, or any container or containers for goods . . . any false description or representation, including words or other symbols tending falsely to describe or represent the same . . . shall be liable to a civil action by . . . any person who believes he is or is likely to be damaged by the use of any such false description or representation.

This Court has held that Section 43(a) creates a federal cause of action for trade dress infringement. [cit.] As we stated in *John Harland Co. v. Clarke Checks, Inc.*,

"'Trade Dress' involves the total image of a product and may include features such as size, shape, color or color combinations, texture, graphics, or even particular sales techniques." [cit.] The trade dress at issue in this controversy is the wrapper and packaging of Isaly's Klondike bar.

As the district court below held, to prevail on a trade dress infringement claim under §43(a), the plaintiff must prove three elements: 1) its trade dress is inherently distinctive or has acquired secondary meaning,* 2) its trade dress is primarily non-functional, and 3) the defendant's trade dress is confusingly similar. [cit.] The district court found that Isaly had established all three elements and therefore ruled in favor of Isaly on the trade dress infringement claim.

[The court's analyses of distinctiveness and functionality are omitted.]

### C. Likelihood of Confusion

"[T]he touchstone test for a violation of §43(a) is the "likelihood of confusion" resulting from the defendant's adoption of a trade dress similar to the plaintiff's." [cit.] In determining whether a likelihood of confusion exists, the fact finder evaluates a number of elements including: the strength of the trade dress, the similarity of design, the similarity of the product, the similarity of retail outlets and purchasers, the similarity of advertising media used, the defendant's intent, and actual confusion. [cit.] The issue of likelihood of confusion is not determined by merely analyzing whether a majority of the subsidiary factors indicates that such a likelihood exists. Rather, a court must evaluate the weight to be accorded the individual factors and then make its ultimate decision. [cit.] The appropriate weight to be given to each of these factors varies with the circumstances of the case.

The district court evaluated these factors, weighed them carefully, and found that Kraft's trade dress creates a likelihood of confusion. . . .

1. Strength of the Trade Dress

The strength of the Klondike trade dress determines the scope of protection it will receive: strong trade dress receives strong protection, and weak trade dress receives weak protection. The strength of a particular trade dress is determined by a number of factors that establish its standing in the marketplace. [cit.] Relying on its finding that the trade dress was [distinctive], the district court concluded that the Klondike trade dress was strong. A more thorough analysis, however, is needed to determine the scope of protection appropriate for the Klondike trade dress. A finding of inherent distinctiveness indicates that the Klondike trade dress will be protected, but the appropriate degree of protection is determined by examining a number of factors that establish the standing of the trade dress in the marketplace: most notably, the type of trade dress and the extent of the third party uses.[36]

---

*[Ed. Note: The case was decided prior to *Wal-Mart*, so the court did not need to engage in a threshold inquiry about whether the trade dress at issue was product design or product packaging trade dress.]

36. [cit.] The strength of the mark analysis is much the same as the inherent distinctiveness analysis. While the latter is concerned with determining whether a threshold level of distinctiveness has been reached, the former is more thorough in that its goal is to determine the degree of distinctiveness of a particular trade dress.

In analyzing the scope of protection a particular trade dress warrants, a court must first consider the type of trade dress involved. As noted above, trade dress may be classified as generic, descriptive, suggestive, or arbitrary, and the scope of protection increases as the trade dress moves toward the arbitrary end of the spectrum. Isaly's trade dress is composed of a number of elements suggesting the coldness of the Klondike bar. The Klondike trade dress is therefore mainly suggestive.... [W]e hold that the mainly suggestive Klondike trade dress merits at least moderate protection.

The second scope-of-protection factor is the extent of third party use. As noted in the discussion of inherent distinctiveness, a number of third parties have used various elements of the Klondike trade dress. The record indicates that, in connection with the sale of frozen desserts, at least eight third parties have used a polar bear image, and that numerous third parties have used silver foil, an arctic sun image, or the royal blue color. Although not as extensive as the third party uses that have led to weak protection in other cases,[38] these uses do require the court to extend less protection to the Klondike wrapper than it would in their absence. Use of isolated elements of the Klondike trade dress that do not convey the same total image does not, however, lead to the Klondike wrapper being stripped of protection. [cit.]

Our review of the evidence leads us to conclude that were we to make the determination as to the strength of Isaly's trade dress *de novo*, we would accord that trade dress moderate, as opposed to either strong or weak, protection.[40] The Klondike trade dress is suggestive, and third parties have used most of the elements of that trade dress. We need not decide, however, whether the district court's finding that the Klondike trade dress warranted strong protection is clearly erroneous. Given that the amalgam of the other likelihood of confusion factors points so strongly in favor of a finding of likelihood of confusion, it does not matter whether the Klondike trade dress is accorded strong or moderate protection, for in either case, the finding of likelihood of confusion is not clearly erroneous.

2. Similarity of Design

The similarity of design test has been described as " 'really nothing more than a subjective eyeball test.' ... The similarity of design is determined by considering the overall impression created by the mark as a whole rather than

---

38. *See Amstar Corp. v. Domino's Pizza, Inc.*, 615 F.2d 252, 259 (5th Cir.) (72 third party uses led to weak protection), *cert. denied*, 449 U.S. 899 (1980); *Sun Banks of Florida, Inc.*, 651 F.2d at 316 (4400 uses in Florida alone led to weak protection). *But see Safeway Stores, Inc.*, 675 F.2d at 1165 ("score" of third party uses did not prevent suggestive mark from being "relatively strong").

40. The district court also found that the Klondike trade dress had acquired secondary meaning. This finding is probative on the strength of the mark issue because it also establishes the mark's standing in the marketplace. [cit.]

The existence of secondary meaning leads to greater protection for the Klondike's trade dress. On the other hand, the Klondike trade dress is protectable mainly because it presents a "distinctive visual impression," not because the elements of that trade dress are arbitrary or unusual. As the Fifth Circuit held in *Falcon Rice Mill, Inc.*, a "distinctive visual impression" normally receives weak protection. 725 F.2d at 346. Nonetheless, a "distinctive visual impression" will be protected. *See Chevron Chemical Co.*, 659 F.2d 695. And indeed, a "distinctive visual impression" composed of suggestive elements will be accorded greater protection than one composed of generic or descriptive elements. *Cf. Falcon Rice Mill, Inc.*, 725 F.2d 336.

simply comparing individual features of the marks." [cit.] Following this approach, the district court stated, "Upon visual inspection, the wrapped bars convey the same overall appearance." Kraft strenuously objects to this finding. Kraft asserts that in making its finding of similarity of design the court disregarded the word marks "Sealtest," "Polar B'ar," "Isaly's," and "Klondike." Kraft also argues that a comparison of the packages reveals many differences including a different overall impression.

Kraft is correct in asserting that the presence of dissimilar word marks lessens the possibility of a finding of similarity of design.[43] Use of distinguishing word marks does not, however, preclude a finding of similarity of design. [cit.] The similarity of design test is an inquiry into the overall similarity of the defendant's trade dress with that of the plaintiff. Therefore, the dissimilar word marks may not be considered separately; rather, they must be considered in the context of the trade dress as a whole.

Even a cursory reading of the district court's order makes clear that in analyzing the overall appearance of the trade dress of the products the district court did not disregard the dissimilar word marks. Indeed, the court even mentioned that each wrapper displayed "the product name printed in large block letters, accompanied by the company name (Sealtest or Isaly's) in much smaller script lettering."

Kraft next argues that the design and color of the trade dress of each product are simply not similar. Kraft points again to the dissimilar word marks and also to the differences between the modern design of the Polar B'ar trade dress and the old-fashioned tone of the Klondike trade dress. In assessing Kraft's contention, it is important to remember that, regardless of the ready accessibility of the exhibits to the reviewing court and the ability of this Court to see as well as the district court, the district court's finding that the designs are similar is still reversible only for clear error.[46]

Viewing the trade dress as a whole, the overall impression conveyed by each is similar. An inspection of the wrappers of the plain Klondike and the plain Polar B'ar reveals that each is the same size, each has a textured silver foil background, each is printed primarily with blue and white inks, each includes the product name in large block letters and the company name in smaller script, and each features a polar bear.[48] Although a close examination of the two wrappers reveals significant differences, a court may not view trade dress in a vacuum. Rather, a court must consider how the trade dress would function in the actual market place. Ice cream novelties are impulse items stored in frosty

---

43. [cit.] That the defendant has placed on its products marks that are different from those employed by the plaintiff is also probative on the intent and actual confusion factors under the likelihood of confusion test.

46. [cit.] Kraft asserts that this court is in as good a position to apply the subjective eyeball test as the lower court. In essence Kraft is asking this court to review the finding of similarity of design de novo. We decline this invitation. . . .

48. Although we have described the elements of the wrappers that are similar, we are not making a comparison of individual elements. Rather, we are explaining why the overall impression of each wrapper is similar. The district court correctly followed this same approach. We note that the manner in which the products are presented to the consumers, in the overwrapped six-pack trays, amplifies the similarity of the trade dress.

freezer cases and sold in busy grocery stores to hurried shoppers. When viewed in this context, the general similarity of the design of the trade dress of the two products is an even stronger indication of the existence of likelihood of confusion.

3. Similarity of the Products

That the products involved are similar is evidence tending to prove the existence of a likelihood of confusion. The district court found and we agree that the products in the instant case are identical. Both are competitively priced, five ounce, stickless, chocolate-covered ice cream bars.

4. Similarity of Retail Outlets and Purchasers

Likelihood of confusion is more probable if the products are sold through the same channels to the same purchasers. The district court found that the products are both sold through the same channels, primarily supermarkets and convenience stores, to the same purchasers. Kraft has not challenged this finding.

5. Similarity of Advertising Media

If the plaintiff and defendant both use the same advertising media, a finding of likelihood of confusion is more probable. The district court found that both parties use the same advertising media, primarily television and radio, and that the advertisements were themselves similar. This finding is clearly correct.

6. Defendant's Intent

Kraft's intent in adopting the Polar B'ar trade dress is a critical factor because a finding that Kraft adopted the trade dress with the intent of deriving benefit from the reputation of Isaly's Klondike may alone be enough to justify the inference that there is confusing similarity. In assessing the intent factor, the district court found that "Kraft intended to emulate if not infringe." Kraft and Isaly have both argued as to the meaning of that phrase and as to whether the evidence supports the position of the other party. After reviewing that phrase and the context in which it is found, we are convinced that the district court's finding was based on solid evidence that Kraft intended to benefit from the goodwill of Isaly. We turn now to examine the evidence supporting that finding.

In early 1979, Kraft began distributing the Klondike bar for Isaly in Florida. The introduction of the Klondike bar in Florida was surprisingly successful. Kraft had been searching for an appropriate ice cream novelty product, and after witnessing the success of the Klondike bar, Kraft approached Isaly with an offer to either buy Isaly or have Isaly pack Klondike bars for Kraft under the Sealtest label. Isaly rejected this offer, proposing instead that Kraft expand its distribution of the Klondike bar. Kraft rejected that offer.

As a result of the distribution relationship, Kraft learned of Isaly's expansion plans for the Klondike bar and of information vital to the successful sale of an ice cream novelty like the Klondike bar. In late 1979, Kraft began developing its own five ounce, stickless, chocolate-covered ice cream bar. Kraft attempted to develop a bar that was, in almost all respects, identical with the highly successful Klondike bar.

Kraft chose to name its new product "Polar B'ar," a name that conveys a double meaning: "polar bear" and "cold bar." At the time it chose the name, Kraft was aware that the Klondike wrapper featured a polar bear. Moreover, prior to the time Kraft selected the name for its product, Isaly had undertaken some promotional and other efforts to develop an association between the polar bear symbol and the Klondike bar.[54]

Kraft retained two design firms to design the packaging for the Polar B'ar. It is undisputed that Kraft requested these firms to copy the functional features of the Klondike packaging, such as the six-pack tray, the dead fold foil wrapper, and the clear plastic overwrap. To help achieve this goal, Kraft supplied the design firms with samples of the Klondike packaging and wrapper. It is also clear that, given the name Kraft had chosen for its product, the use of a polar bear image on the Polar B'ar wrapper was a foregone conclusion.

The design firms offered Kraft a number of wrapper prototypes employing a variety of graphic designs. Kraft chose the design that Isaly is now challenging. The record reveals that Kraft knew of the distinct possibility that the wrapper design it chose infringed the Klondike trade dress. But Kraft never sought an opinion from legal counsel on that issue.[55]

Isaly argues that the unmistakable import of this evidence is that Kraft chose deliberately to come as close to the total image of the Klondike bar as possible. According to Isaly, even though Kraft may have intended to stay within legal bounds, it copied the Klondike bar and functional packaging features exactly and attempted to copy the Klondike trade dress to a sufficient degree that when combined with the other packaging features, Kraft would benefit from the reputation of Isaly's Klondike. Isaly correctly points out that even an intent to come as close as the law will allow is an intent to derive benefit from the other party's reputation and is therefore probative on the likelihood of confusion issue. Indeed, Isaly argues that Kraft even chose its name with the intent of deriving benefit from Isaly's reputation.

Kraft argues, however, that it had no such intent to derive benefit from the reputation of Isaly. Rather, Kraft argues that it copied only those features that it had the right to copy, those that were in the public domain. Kraft asserts that it copied those features not to benefit from Isaly's reputation, but to let the consumers know that they would be getting the same type of product as that offered by Isaly. Kraft points to the word mark "Polar B'ar," which it asserts is clearly not confusing with the "Klondike" word mark, and to the "Sealtest" logo, and argues that if it had been attempting to poach the goodwill of Isaly, it would not have used these distinctive and different marks.

There is no question that Kraft's argument finds support in the evidence — as does Isaly's — but even were we to accept Kraft's position, the district court's finding of intent on the part of Kraft to benefit from Isaly's goodwill would

---

54. In addition to using commercials and a wrapper featuring a polar bear, Isaly had been involved with highly publicized activities such as donating polar bears to the Philadelphia Zoo.

55. Isaly infers that Kraft never sought a legal opinion for fear that such an opinion would confirm the concern expressed by several people involved with the development of the Polar B'ar concept and product: that the Polar B'ar wrapper infringed the Klondike wrapper.

be proper. There is nothing unusual about a finding of intent based on circumstantial evidence. Although Kraft was free to copy the Klondike product and the functional packaging features of that product, the finder of fact may infer from evidence of such actions an intent to derive benefit from Isaly's goodwill. Such a finding is especially fitting when, as here, a review of Kraft's nonfunctional trade dress and that of the plaintiff reveals substantial similarities. Therefore, irrespective of which version of the facts is to be believed, the record supports the district court's finding that Kraft intended to benefit from the goodwill Isaly has built for itself.

7. Actual Confusion

Actual consumer confusion is the best evidence of likelihood of confusion. There is no absolute scale as to how many instances of actual confusion establish the existence of that factor. Rather, the court must evaluate the evidence of actual confusion in the light of the totality of the circumstances involved.

In the instant case, Isaly presented four consumers who testified that they had been confused while making purchases in the market place. Each of the witnesses had notified Isaly of his or her confusion by letter or telephone. Isaly also introduced survey evidence on the actual confusion issue. The district court gave little weight to that survey, but based on the testimony of Isaly's witnesses, the court found that "there is some indication of actual confusion." Kraft argues that the evidence is insufficient to support the finding of actual confusion. Kraft asserts that the number of instances of confusion is quite low given the extensive sales involved, and that those individuals who were confused were careless. Moreover, Kraft argues that the district court erred when it failed to credit the evidence Kraft presented to refute Isaly's actual confusion evidence. Kraft introduced its own survey and also presented several "typical consumers" who testified that they were not confused.

Viewed in the light of the totality of the circumstances, Kraft's protestations are without merit. With respect to Kraft's assertion that the reported instances of confusion are small given the high volume of sales, we note that it takes very little evidence to establish the existence of the actual confusion factor. Moreover, that there were only a few reported instances of actual confusion does not mean that only those individuals were actually confused. As the *Chevron Chemical Co.* court stated: "It would be exceedingly difficult to detect instances of actual confusion when, as here, the goods are relatively inexpensive and their actual properties are exactly identical." It is likely that many consumers who were confused never realized they had been confused and that many of those who did realize they had been confused chose not to spend the time to register a complaint with a faceless corporation about the packaging of an item that retails for approximately $2.50 per six-pack. Given these circumstances, four bona fide instances of actual confusion are sufficient to support the district court's finding of actual confusion. Kraft's argument that the four instances of confusion are inconsequential because these consumers were careless misses the point. Ice cream novelties are an impulse item that consumers purchase without a great deal of care. There is no indication that the four consumers who reported their confusion to Isaly were anything other than typical consumers following normal buying patterns. Finally, the district court properly gave little weight to Kraft's survey and "typical consumer" witnesses.

[Affirmed as to the infringement finding.]

## NOTES AND QUESTIONS

1. *"Market" strength of trade dress.* The court in *Ambrit* assesses the strength of the trade dress as part of its confusion analysis—as expected, given that mark strength is recited as a factor in most multifactor likelihood of confusion tests. The *Ambrit* court considers (1) the level of distinctiveness of the trade dress, and (2) the extent of third-party use. More commonly, courts consider (1) conceptual strength (which probably corresponds to the court's assessment of the level of inherent distinctiveness) and (2) market strength. When courts consider market strength, they typically treat third-party uses as merely one indicator. Would it be correct to conclude that evidence of third-party usage should be given more weight in trade dress cases than in word mark cases? Could such a conclusion be grounded in the proposition that consumers might rely more heavily on word marks than on trade dress in distinguishing among goods? Or should courts apply the same confusion rules to trade dress as they apply to word marks?

2. *"Conceptual" strength of trade dress.* When a court considers conceptual strength in evaluating likelihood of confusion, is the court merely duplicating its distinctiveness analysis? What does the *Ambrit* court say about the potential differences in the analyses? Do you find the court's reasoning persuasive? Would you agree with the proposition that conceptual strength should be eliminated from the confusion analysis? *See* Barton Beebe, *An Empirical Study of the Multifactor Tests for Trademark Infringement*, 94 CAL. L. REV. 1581, 1636-1637, 1647 (2006) (offering this suggestion). What significance, if any, should be given to the distinction between product packaging and product design in evaluating the role of conceptual strength in confusion analysis? Recall that product design cannot qualify as inherently distinctive under the *Wal-Mart* rule, as discussed in Chapter 2. Does this mean that product designs necessarily enter the confusion analysis with impaired strength (low conceptual strength)? Is this good policy? Review this point after you read the next case, *Versa*.

3. *Similarity factor: the overall impression test.* The *Ambrit* court purports to analyze whether the defendant's trade dress is similar to the plaintiff's by viewing the trade dress "as a whole," considering the "overall impression" that the trade dress conveys. But is the court really doing that? Or is the court inevitably led to a comparison of individual features of the respective trade dresses? Consider Justice Holmes's analysis in *Joseph Schlitz Brewing Co. v. Houston Ice & Brewing Co.*, 250 U.S. 28, 29 (1919), a case frequently cited as the basis for the overall impression test. In that case, both parties sold beer in brown bottles with brown labels, but other brewers did too. The prevailing

infringement standards at the time might have been read to suggest that the court should ignore features of the trade dress that were in common use, and consider only whether the defendant had imitated unique features of plaintiff's trade dress. Justice Holmes seemed to reject that approach, remarking that it would be a "fallacy" to break down the trade dress "stick by stick." *Id.* Nevertheless, Justice Holmes's similarity comparison of the trade dress at issue still seemed to revolve around a comparison of individual features:

> The shape of the defendant's label is different from the plaintiff's; the script upon it not only is wholly different from the other in meaning, to one who reads the two, but hardly can be said to resemble it as a picture. The two labels are attached to the bottles in quite unlike modes. The Schlitz [label] is applied in a spiral around the length of the bottle so as to make the ends of the label parallel to the sides of the glass. The defendant's is pasted around the bottom of the bottle in the usual way. This diversity of itself renders mistake unlikely.

*Id.* at 29-30. The tension here between an analysis of overall impression and an analysis of individual features is a common one. We will revisit it in Chapter 6, where we consider the standard for design patent infringement (requiring an analysis of "substantial similarity" and an analysis of whether the defendant appropriated individual "points of novelty" in the patented design). Should courts look to the design patent law to refine the similarity analysis for trade dress infringement?

   4. *Applying the overall impression test.* A wine retailer, Best Cellars, conceived of the idea of marketing wine by various taste categories, rather than the conventional grape types and geographic origins. Best Cellars developed a distinctive interior store decor (including a "wall of wine" on which wines were displayed according to taste categories). Suppose that a competing wine store also decides to market wine by taste categories, and develops a slightly different store decor. In analyzing whether the defendant wine store's decor and Best Cellars' decor evoke a similar overall impression, should the fact finder take into account the similarity in the overall marketing method? Is that properly part of the overall impression? Or must store decor trade dress be limited only to visual elements? *See Best Cellars, Inc. v. Wine Made Simple, Inc.*, 320 F. Supp. 2d 60 (S.D.N.Y. 2003). Is there any general principle underlying the overall impression rule that provides guidance here?

   5. *Side-by-side similarity.* In word mark cases, courts are cautious about relying on simple side-by-side comparisons of marks. Should courts approach trade dress similarity comparisons with similar caution? In *Libman Co. v. Vining Indus., Inc.*, 69 F.3d 1360 (7th Cir. 1995), the trade dress at issue was the contrasting color band on Libman's broom head. Vining sold a competing broom with a contrasting color band. Both firms sold their respective brooms with a plastic wrapper covering the broom head, and in Vining's case, the label affixed to the wrapper was large enough that it partially obscured the contrasting color bristles. Libman's advertising displayed its broom without the wrapper, with the contrasting color band prominently visible, whereas Vining's advertising only displayed a wrapped broom. In assessing similarity, should the court compare the two brooms side by side in their respective

packaging? Side by side without their packaging? Not side by side at all? What additional facts about the marketing (and use) of brooms would help a court formulate a correct similarity comparison? Courts have dealt with these problems, sometimes implicitly, in many cases. For an early example, *see, e.g., Chesebrough Mfg. Co. v. Old Gold Chem. Co.*, 70 F.2d 383, 384 (6th Cir. 1934) (in a case involving infringement of the trade dress of the VASELINE petroleum jelly packaging, concluding that a side-by-side comparison was improper). For a more recent example in a case involving product design, see *Malletier v. Burlington Coat Factory Warehouse Corp.*, 426 F.3d 532 (2d Cir. 2005), discussed *infra* in the notes after the *Versa* case.

6. ***Word-to-picture similarity.*** Hansen makes MONSTER energy drinks, sold in cans as shown below left, while National makes FREEK energy drinks, sold in cans depicting a "Freek Man" figure, as shown below right.

How would you evaluate the argument that the FREEK trade dress is similar to the MONSTER trade dress because the picture of the "Freek Man" evokes the word "monster"? *See Hansen Beverage Co. v. National Beverage Corp.*, 493 F.3d 1074 (9th Cir.), *vacated as moot due to settlement*, 499 F.3d 923 (9th Cir. 2007).

7. ***Effect of labels on trade dress similarity assessments.*** In *Ambrit*, the court concluded that a party's use of distinguishing marks or labeling might affect the similarity analysis, but would not alone preclude confusion. Suppose that Merriam-Webster, publisher of the dictionary shown below on the left, claims that Random House's dictionary, below on the right, infringes Merriam-Webster's trade dress. When analyzing similarity, should the court take into account the fact that Merriam-Webster's dictionary displays the name "Merriam-Webster" and the "bull's-eye" logo, and that Random House's dictionary displays the name "Random House" and the "dwelling" logo? Or would doing so involve the improper dissection of trade dress into its components in violation of the overall impression rule? *See Merriam-Webster, Inc. v. Random House, Inc.*, 35 F.3d 65 (2d Cir. 1994) (involving slightly different trade dress).

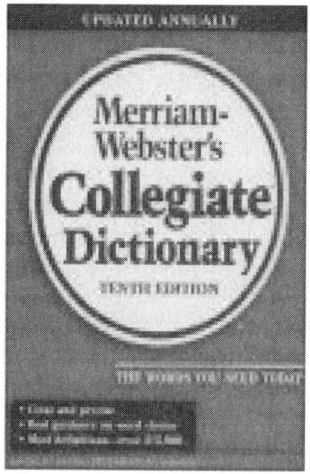

How would you answer the same set of questions regarding the following?

See *Bristol-Myers Squibb Co. v. McNeil-P.P.C., Inc.*, 973 F.2d 1033 (2d Cir. 1992). *Cf. McNeil-P.P.C., Inc. v. Guardian Drug Co.*, 984 F. Supp. 1066 (E.D. Mich. 1997) (distinguishing Bristol-Myers).

8. ***Consumer sophistication and care.*** Likelihood of confusion tests generally include consumer sophistication and/or consumer care as a factor. Should that factor be given special weight in trade dress cases? For example, should courts assume that nonverbal source indicators such as packaging or product design are particularly important to young consumers still learning to read? Non-English speakers? Those of us who do know how to read and speak English but shop in a hurry? For one example involving products marketed to children, see *Tootsie Roll Indus., Inc. v. Sathers, Inc.*, 666 F. Supp. 655 (D. Del. 1987) (TOOTSIE ROLL trade dress).

9. ***Actual confusion as evidence of likely confusion.*** Is actual confusion the "best evidence" of likelihood of confusion, as the *Ambrit* court suggests? Is that pronouncement equally valid for all types of products and services? Does the rule work equally well in both directions? That is, if the existence of actual confusion is strong evidence of likely confusion, is the absence of actual confusion strong evidence of the absence of likely confusion? Consider *Libman Co. v. Vining Indus., Inc.*, 69 F.3d 1360 (7th Cir. 1995), noted above. Judge Posner, writing for the majority, observed that

> Vining sold several hundred thousand of the allegedly infringing brooms, yet there is no evidence that any consumer ever made [an error about which firm

was the source of the product]; if confusion were likely, one would expect at least one person out of this vast multitude to be confused, or more precisely one would expect Libman to have been able to find one such confused person. . . .

*Id.* at 1361. The court continued:

To insist on evidence [that consumers were actually fooled by the appearance of the broom] might seem to be to commit the error of thinking that proof of actual confusion is required in a trademark-infringement case. . . . But our point is only that a finding of likely confusion can no more be based on pure conjecture or a fetching narrative alone than any other finding on an issue on which the proponent bears the burden of proof.

*Id.* at 1363. Is Judge Posner in fact committing the error that he claims to be avoiding? Even if he is not, what is the best response to his assertion that actual confusion evidence is a vital factor in the broom case?

10. *Actual confusion and damages.* Although likelihood of confusion—not actual confusion—is the governing standard for trademark infringement, courts hold that a trademark owner who seeks damages must show actual confusion. *See, e.g., Boosey & Hawkes Music Publishers, Ltd. v. Walt Disney Co.,* 145 F.3d 481 (2d Cir. 1998) (asserting that Second Circuit case law is "well settled" that Lanham Act plaintiffs must prove actual confusion in order to recover damages); *Web Printing Controls Co. v. Oxy-Dry Corp.,* 906 F.2d 1202 (7th Cir. 1990). *See* Section D of this chapter for a brief discussion of the rules governing remedies in trade dress enforcement cases.

11. *Proving actual confusion.* Ambrit introduced survey evidence, along with witness testimony, as evidence of actual confusion. Kraft complained that the evidence revealed only a small number of instances of confusion relative to the large amount of product sales. As a general rule, what percentage of surveyed consumers must be confused before courts should find that actual confusion has been established? For a discussion of relevant precedent on trademark infringement surveys, see, e.g., 5 J. THOMAS MCCARTHY, TRADEMARKS AND UNFAIR COMPETITION, ch. 32 (1996); *see also* Kenneth A. Plevan, *Daubert's Impact on Survey Experts in Lanham Act Litigation,* 95 TRADEMARK REP. 596 (2005); John P. Liefeld, *How Surveys Overestimate the Likelihood of Consumer Confusion,* 93 TRADEMARK REP. 939 (2003). For a discussion of the format of confusion surveys, see, e.g., *Starbucks U.S. Brands LLC v. Ruben,* 78 U.S.P.Q.2d (BNA) 1741, 1753 (TTAB 2006) (discussing the so-called *Ever-Ready* survey format, from *Union Carbide Corp. v. Ever-Ready Inc.,* 531 F.2d 366 (7th Cir.), *cert. denied,* 429 U.S. 830 (1976)).

12. *Intent to simulate and the public domain.* The *Ambrit* court concludes that although Kraft was free to copy unprotected features of the KLONDIKE trade dress, that copying might nonetheless properly give rise to an inference that Kraft intended to trade off Ambrit's goodwill. Does this approach undermine Kraft's freedom to copy those unprotected elements? What should Kraft have done differently to avoid the adverse inference?

13. *Intent to simulate as the basis for presuming actual confusion.* Compare the *Ambrit* court's intent analysis with that of some older trade dress cases that held that where the evidence showed that a defendant

intended to simulate plaintiff's trade dress, *actual* confusion could be presumed. Learned Hand adopted such a view:

> It would be impossible on this record to say that any one who meant to buy the plaintiff's pudding has hitherto been misled into taking the defendants' by mistake in the appearance of the box. Indeed such evidence is usually hard to get even after a trial. . . . The plaintiff has proved no more than that the boxes look a good deal alike, and that confusion may well arise; and were it not for the evidence of the defendants' intent to deceive and so to secure the plaintiff's customers, we should scarcely feel justified in interfering at this stage of the cause. We need not say whether that intent is always a necessary element in such causes of suit. . . . But when it appears, we think that it has an important procedural result; a late comer who deliberately copies the dress of his competitors already in the field, must at least prove that his effort has been futile. . . . [S]uch an intent raises a presumption that customers will be deceived.

*My-T-Fine Corp. v. Samuels*, 69 F.2d 76, 77 (2d Cir. 1934) (Learned Hand); *see also E. Kahn's Sons Co. v. Columbus Packing Co.*, 82 F.2d 897, 900 (6th Cir. 1936) (in a suit between rival sellers of pails of lard, finding that "[t]here was little, if any, evidence of actual deception, but [defendant]'s evident purpose [i.e., to simulate plaintiff's trade dress] raises the presumption that there would be").

Do you agree with this view? Under modern trademark infringement law, a defendant's intent to copy a word mark does not give rise to a presumption of actual confusion. Should there nonetheless be a presumption for trade dress, in accord with Learned Hand's view? Should the application of the presumption depend on whether the trade dress is product packaging or product design?

**14. *Intent and opinions of counsel.*** The court in *Ambrit* notes that Kraft did not secure an opinion of counsel on the issue of whether Kraft's packaging infringed Ambrit's trade dress. Should firms be under a general duty of due care to avoid trade dress infringement—and if so, should securing an opinion of competent counsel (and relying on it) satisfy the duty? Should a firm's failure to secure an opinion of counsel give rise to the inference that the firm intended to trade off the trade dress owner's goodwill? Or should such a failure only be relevant to the extent of damages? For example, should the failure to secure an exculpatory opinion only be relevant to whether the court should award treble damages?

**15. *Remedy.*** The district court had enjoined Kraft from marketing "a five ounce chocolate covered ice cream bar bearing a label, or contained in a tray bearing a label, which features a picture, drawing or other representation of a polar bear" and from marketing "a five ounce chocolate covered ice cream bar in pebbled foil wrappers bearing a label featuring the color royal blue." Does this injunction improperly isolate components of the trade dress (namely the polar bear and the color royal blue) rather than limiting itself to the overall impression created by all of the components collectively?

What if Ambrit were using a fluffy, lovable polar bear and Kraft wanted to adopt a muscular, sinister-looking polar bear (with an evident bad attitude) for use on the ice cream bars at issue? Doesn't the injunction effectively prevent Kraft from using any polar bear representation on its ice cream bar wrappers?

If so, is that consistent with the law of confusion? Do general equitable principles require that it be consistent?

Has the injunction effectively given Ambrit exclusive rights in the royal blue color used in the ice cream bar business? If Isaly had sought to register the color as used in connection with ice cream bars, do you think that the PTO would have issued the registration? (*See* Chapter 2). If not, has Ambrit nonetheless achieved that outcome by asserting that the color is part of its overall wrapper trade dress?

For a related exercise, consider the injunction, entered in favor of the owners of the trade dress for BOUNTY paper towels, in *Procter & Gamble Co. v. McLane Co., Inc.*, Case No. 3:05 CV 0427 (WHR) (S.D. Oh. Feb. 23, 2006). The court's order specified that the defendant's packaging would violate the injunction if it included element "a" below, or an "oval graphic in combination with any three or more of the elements listed in paragraphs 'b' through 'g'":

a. The cornucopia graphic, in equity colors of green, orange, yellow and blue, which is centered on the package—specifically, the use of an identical oval shape using gradients of yellow and magenta to create an orange center, surrounded by a wide green "swoosh" and a blue accent;
b. The overall impression of the equity color being green;
c. The use of gradients of colors;
d. The use of bold, black block lettering to display the brand name within the cornucopia graphic, with an initial capital letter;
e. The upward slope of the brand name, from left to right;
f. The use of a bowtie graphic centered to the lower half of the packaging; or
g. The repeated use of the cornucopia graphic and bowtie graphic on the back of the package.

Is this a remarkably precise, narrow injunction, or is it a surprisingly broad one? Could the defendant easily avoid it? Is this tantamount to converting trade dress to something like a patent claim, and if so, should courts embrace that approach? (*See* Chapters 5 and 6 for a discussion of patent claims in the context of design patents.) How difficult is it for you to translate these verbal recitations into a visual impression?

16. *Avoiding the confusion analysis by imposing a threshold use requirement*. The notes above all focus on the likelihood of confusion analysis (and the relevant remedies). For a time, some courts deciding trademark cases involving online advertising experimented with an alternative doctrinal mechanism, requiring plaintiffs to make a threshold showing that the defendant was using the mark at issue "as a mark." In the United States this experiment may be on the wane. *See Rescuecom v. Google* 562 F.3d 123 (2d Cir. 2009). Outside the United States, litigants have invoked a trademark use requirement in some cases involving trade dress claims. In *Adidas v. Marca Mode*, Adidas owned the registration for figurative trademarks (i.e., logo marks) consisting of three vertical, parallel stripes of equal width used on the side of sports and leisure garments in a color which contrasts with the basic color of the garment. The defendant sought to sell sports and leisure garments adorned with two parallel stripes the color of which contrasted

with the basic color of its garment. The defendant claimed that it was using the stripes as decoration. Should this affect whether or not a court finds infringement? *See* Case C-02/07, *Adidas v. Marca Mode*, [2008] E.T.M.R. 44 (ECJ 2008); *cf. Sebel Furniture Limited v. Acoustic & Felts Pty Limited*, [2009] FCA 6 (2009) (Austl.) (holding that the plaintiff furniture maker failed to prove infringement of its mark in the design of a plastic chair where the defendant rival manufacturer of a similar chair did not use the design "as a mark," and reaching the same result with respect to a parallel passing-off claim). What if the design served both as a decoration and as a signifier? *See Adidas*, 2008 E.T.M.R. 44. To what extent should the need for competitors to use stripes to compete on the market be relevant to an assessment of infringement? *See Adidas*, 2008 E.T.M.R. 44 at ¶30. Is the argument in *Marca Mode* a variant on the failed defense offered in *Au-Tomotive Gold* (Chapter 3)?

### PROBLEM 4-1: LIKELIHOOD OF CONFUSION IN PRIVATE-LABEL GOODS CASES

One court described private-label goods as follows:

Private-label products are typically manufactured by one company for sale to the consuming public under another company's name. Such products are generally made with the same active ingredient as the name-brand or national-brand product with which the private-label product competes. Private-label products are available in a wide range of industries and are often positioned as lower cost alternatives (about 25% less expensive) to national-brand products. As of 2005, private-label sales represented 20% of all U.S. supermarket, drug chain, and mass merchandiser sales and totaled $50 billion.

Store-brand products are a type of private-label product, in which the store or retail chain name is the brand name. Store-brand products have existed in retail chains since 1883, and consumers have become highly aware of them. Indeed, the Private Label Manufacturers Association reported that in 2005, more than 90% of consumers polled were familiar with store brands, and 83% bought them regularly.

Store brands are typically found on store shelves next to the analogous national-brand products. The packaging of store-brand products often includes reference points to invite the consumer to compare them to the national-brand ones. These reference points often include similar product packaging and "compare to" statements on the packaging. Stores also employ tags on store shelves (so-called shelf extenders or shelf talkers) that explicitly invite consumers to compare the store-brand product with the national-brand analog.

Consumers are generally aware of the name of the store in which they are shopping. They are aware that stores have private-label brands that in most cases are merchandised next to the national-brand products. Prices for the products are typically displayed prominently. Consumers can, therefore, see the cost difference between store brands and national brands.

*McNeil Nutritionals, LLC v. Heartland Sweeteners, LLC*, 511 F.3d 350, 353-354 (3d Cir. 2007). The following exercises explore the trade dress infringement issues presented by private label marketing.

(1) In the late 1980s, Conopco developed a new and improved version of its lotion product (VASELINE Intensive Care Lotion, or VICL), and decided to sell

the new version in a new package—a different bottle shape and label from those used previously. Between the fall of 1989 and March of 1990, Conopco spent over $37 million to promote the new version of the product and had succeeded in placing the product with retailers throughout the country.

Ansehl, a private-label manufacturer, became aware of Conopco's new version of VASELINE and developed a competing private-label product, to be labeled with the diagonally striped black-and-white VENTURE logo and sold through Venture stores. Ansehl had previously offered a product that had competed with the old version of Conopco's VICL product for approximately ten years. The photographs accompanying this problem show the old and new versions, respectively, of both Conopco's and Ansehl's products:

COMPARISON OF ORIGINAL VICL AND VENTURE BOTTLES    COMPARISON OF REVISED VICL AND VENTURE BOTTLES

Conopco sued Ansehl for trademark infringement under Section 43(a), claiming trade dress protection in the new VICL bottle shape and label. Assume that validity, ownership, and unauthorized use were all properly established, leaving only the likelihood-of-confusion issue.

The evidence on the likelihood of confusion factors included the above photographs, the bottles themselves, and testimony from a variety of witnesses. The back sides of the respective bottles (not shown in the photographs) were similar, although the Venture bottle contained language in small print at the bottom of the label stating: "This product is manufactured for VENTURE, and is not associated with any national brand product."

Testimony established that Venture stores carried both the VICL product and the Venture private-label product, and that signage invited consumers to "compare and save." Testimony also established that the diagonally striped Venture logo appeared on store signs, on signs in the store's parking lot, on employees' badges, on other private-label products sold by Venture, and in Venture's advertisements.

A consumer, Mrs. Sickles, testified that she purchased a bottle of the private-label product thinking that it was the VICL product. She also testified that she assumed that brand name manufacturers secretly marketed lower-priced private-label brands. There was no evidence from consumers complaining of confusion between the old version of VICL and the old version of the Venture private-label product.

An employee of Ansehl admitted that he was instructed "to make the revised skin care packaging as close as possible to the VICL packaging." Survey evidence showed that approximately 83 percent of survey respondents taken from a national sample recognized the VICL bottle and label, even with all of the text (except the ingredients list) removed.

Analyze likelihood of confusion. What are the best arguments for and against the trademark owner? How would you rule? Analyze the general policy implications of private-label marketing practices, drawing on your own experience as a consumer. Should private-label practices be presumed likely to give rise to confusion, such that case outcomes would rest on private-label manufacturers' ability to rebut the presumption? *See Conopco, Inc. v. May Dept. Stores Co.*, 46 F.3d 1556 (Fed. Cir. 1994). For additional examples of product packaging trade dress cases involving private-label goods, *see Gray v. Meijer, Inc.*, 295 F.3d 641, 648 (6th Cir. 2002); *McKeon Prods. Inc. v. Flents Prods. Co.*, 2003 WL 23100262 (E.D. Mich. 2003); *McNeil-PPC, Inc. v. Guardian Drug Co.*, 984 F. Supp. 1066 (E.D. Mich. 1997).

(2) No-calorie artificial sweeteners contain either saccharin, aspartame, or sucralose. SWEET'N LOW sweetener, a saccharine-based sweetener, uses predominantly red and pink packaging; EQUAL sweetener, which contains aspartame, is sold in predominantly blue packaging. SPLENDA sweetener, the first sucralose-based sweetener, is sold in packaging that features yellow coloring.

All of the sweeteners face competition from private-label products. The private-label products generally have mimicked the predominant packaging colors of the respective sweeteners, and when sold at retail, are typically placed on shelves next to the brand-name sweeteners. Seeking to curtail these practices, McNeil, the manufacturer of SPLENDA sweetener, sued Heartland, the maker of store-brand products for a number of retailers (Ahold, Food Lion, and Safeway), for trade dress infringement. *McNeil Nutritionals, LLC v. Heartland Sweeteners, LLC*, 511 F.3d 350 (3d Cir. 2007).

The appellate court described McNeil's SPLENDA packaging, and the respective store-brand packages, as follows:

> The [SPLENDA] boxes come in 100 and 200-count sizes and are identical except for their size. The boxes are oriented horizontally. The background is yellow, while the lettering on the boxes is primarily blue. The trade name "Splenda" appears at the top-center of the front of the boxes, in italicized blue lettering. The trade name is surrounded by a white, oval-shaped cloud. On the front, lower-right side of the boxes, there is a photograph of a white cup of coffee and saucer, with an individual Splenda packet resting on the saucer. On the front, left side of the boxes, there is a photograph of a glass and pitcher of iced tea. On the bottom-left corner is a circular element that contains the blue all-caps text, "Made from Sugar, Tastes like Sugar."
>
> McNeil also sells granular Splenda in vertically-oriented bags. The front of the Splenda bag is exactly the same as that of the Splenda boxes, except that it displays different physical props: a piece of pie on a plate, behind which are a bowl of cereal and a scoop containing granular Splenda.
>
> The Giant, Stop & Shop, and Tops (collectively, Ahold) store-brand boxes of individual sucralose packets are oriented horizontally. The boxes come in 100 and 200-count sizes and are identical except for their size. The background is

yellow, while the lettering on the boxes is either blue or white. The product name "Sweetener" appears at the top-center of the front of the boxes, in italicized blue font. The product name is outlined in white, but not by a cloud. On the lower-right corner is a photograph of a white cup of coffee and saucer, a glass of lemonade, and several fruits further off to the right side. There is a white rectangular border surrounding the front of the boxes. The store logo (regardless of the store name) appears just above the product name.

The Ahold stores also sell granular sucralose in vertically-oriented bags. The front of the Ahold bags is exactly the same as that of the Ahold boxes, except that it displays different physical props: a slice of cheesecake on a plate, a bowl of cereal with raspberries, and a white cup of coffee and saucer.

The Food Lion store-brand 100-count box of individual sucralose packets is oriented horizontally. The background is yellow, while the lettering on the box is either blue or black. The product name "Sweet Choice" appears on the bottom of the front of the box, in italicized blue font. The product name is not surrounded by a cloud. The front of the box contains a vertical design element that divides it into two portions. The left portion is in a darker yellow than the right, and includes the Food Lion logo (black) and store name (black) at the top. Food Lion uses this vertical design feature in some of its other store-brand packaging. The front-right portion contains a photograph of a white cup of coffee, saucer, and teaspoon, behind which are a pitcher of lemonade, two glasses of lemonade, and sliced lemons.

Food Lion also sells granular sucralose in vertically-oriented bags. The front of the Food Lion bag is exactly the same as that of the Food Lion box, except that it displays different physical props: a loaf of banana nut bread, a container of sucralose with a scoop, and a bowl of mixed berries.

The Safeway store-brand boxes of individual sucralose packets are oriented horizontally. The boxes come in 100 and 200-count sizes and are identical except for their size. The background is yellow, while the lettering on the boxes is mostly blue. The product name "Sucralose" appears on the bottom-left of the front of the boxes, in italicized blue font. Each letter in the product name is surrounded by a white shadow, but not all together by a cloud. The front of the boxes contains a white S-shaped design element that divides it into two portions. The S-shaped element leads to a display of the Safeway name (black) and logo (red) on the bottom-right corner. Safeway uses this S-shaped design feature in some of its other store-brand packaging. To the right of the S-shaped element is a circular element containing the count-size of the box, also found on the Safeway saccharin boxes. To the left of the S-shaped element is a photograph of a white cup of coffee, bowl of strawberries, and packet caddy containing individual packets of "Sucralose."

*Id.* at 355-56. The court also noted that the 100-count box of SPLENDA retails for about $5.00, whereas the store-brand sucralose sweeteners retails for about $4.00 to about $4.60.

In addition, the court noted the following evidence on actual confusion:

In December 2006, Margaret Grossman, a California consumer, mistakenly purchased Safeway's "Sucralose" when she intended to purchase Splenda. At the time, she was "just buzzing through the market." She did not look at pricing, but just grabbed the box and ran. She is a self-described "surgical strike" shopper, intending to shop at a faster pace than others. She is aware that store-brand products exist; however, because she is not a comparison shopper, she is not aware that they are less expensive than national-brand products. Her yearly household income exceeds $300,000, far above the national median. She was not wearing her reading glasses while making the inadvertent purchase. She continued to use the product for three weeks before noticing that it was Safeway's "Sucralose."

Id. at 356.

Analyze likelihood of confusion. Do you reach the same outcome for each of the store-brand products? Do you reach the same outcome that you reached in the VASELINE case above?

(3) The problems above contemplate that the name-brand goods at issue are sold side-by-side with the visually-similar private-label goods. If the sales practices are slightly different, how might your analysis be different? Are there theories other than likely confusion that might be asserted? Suppose that a hypothetical drugstore chain, Fairline, sells FAIRITIN allergy medicine, a private-label alternative to the popular CLARITIN product, in packaging quite similar to that used on CLARITIN. How would the following facts affect your analysis?

- (i) FAIRITIN is sold in Fairline stores, where the Fairline house mark is prominently displayed. Signs on the store shelves direct consumers to "Compare to CLARITIN and save." CLARITIN is shelved nearby, but is placed in a locked case. Consumers must ask a pharmacist to unlock the case in order to access the product.
- (ii) FAIRITIN and CLARITIN are prominently featured in Fairline's print advertisements in newspaper supplements. However, Fairline stores do not actually stock CLARITIN, though they carry abundant inventories of FAIRITIN.

### b. Product Design

### Versa Products Company, Inc. v. Bifold Company (Manufacturing) Ltd.
50 F.3d 189 (3d Cir. 1995)

Becker, Circuit Judge:

#### I. Facts and Procedural History

[Versa and Bifold competed in the market for control valves used in the offshore oil industry. The valves were usually used in connection with a control panel, positioned so that the knobs, buttons, and status indicator actuators of the valves were visible, but the valve bodies were not.

Versa's B-316 valve was a stainless-steel valve having contoured lines and an overall shape that had become associated with Versa. Versa also stamped its name, logo, and a part number on each valve.

Bifold introduced its DOMINO JUNIOR line of valves about eight years after Versa had introduced the B-316 valve line at issue. The knobs, buttons, and status indicator actuators on the DOMINO JUNIOR line were similar to those on the B-316 line, and in various ways, the external visual appearance of the DOMINOR JUNIOR was similar to that of the B-316 line. Apparently, the two valves were not readily interchangeable in the field, however.

Versa sued, alleging trade dress infringement under Section 43(a), and other causes of action. The district court found that Bifold and its contractors had lacked the expertise to design a cast version of the DOMINO JUNIOR, and had examined and "largely copied" the B-316 valve. One of Bifold's contractors had access to B-316 drawings and castings of some B-316 components. The district court also found that Bifold had backdated some documents and had presented misleading testimony aimed at creating the false impression that it had designed the valve independently.]

. . .

### C. Marketing and Sales of the Valves

In order to determine whether Bifold had engaged in unfair competition with Versa, the district court considered whether consumers were likely to confuse the sources of the two companies' valves in light of the ways in which the two valves are marketed and sold. The court found that valves of this sort are not sold off the shelf or selected on sight. Rather, both manufacturers sell their valves based on functional specifications detailed in schematic diagrams, manufacturers' catalogs, or specification sheets and samples available at trade shows and sales presentations. The valves are selected by multi-digit part numbers identifying the particular variation desired. The purchasers and users of the valves are qualified, knowledgeable persons who comprehend the installation and use of the valves. They typically prepare specifications designating which manufacturer's valve they prefer to use in their system before placing the order.

Versa, the more established manufacturer, has sold over 100,000 B-316 valves, and is currently selling over 16,000 per year. This gives it a fifty to fifty-five percent market share of valves sold for use in emergency shutdown systems in the United States. Bifold has only recently begun marketing its Domino Junior valve in the United States, and immediately stopped its efforts to open the United States market pending the outcome of this litigation.

Versa and its B-316 valve have an excellent reputation for producing a high quality product. This quality level is very important in emergency shutdown offshore drilling, for the failure of a valve could cause loss of human life and property as well as severe environmental damage. Versa has therefore subjected its B-316 valve to rigorous quality control tests, and the valve has performed faithfully in the field.

. . .

### II. The District Court's Legal Conclusions

. . .

The district court held that to prevail on a trade dress infringement claim, a plaintiff must demonstrate a likelihood of confusion, but not actual confusion. It held that Versa could do so here if it could show that an appreciable number of buyers are likely to become confused as to the origin of the Domino Junior valve. Importantly, the court further held that the threshold for likelihood of confusion is lower when a newcomer (or "second comer") violates a long-established trade dress.

The district court then seemed to apply the ten factors for likelihood of confusion that this court enumerated in *Scott Paper Co. v. Scott's Liquid Gold, Inc.*, 589 F.2d 1225 (3d Cir. 1978). Under *Scott*, the threshold issue is the question of similarity of product appearances, and the court found that the Domino Junior's appearance was "virtually identical" to the B-316's and hence that there was a likelihood of confusion. The district court reasoned that Bifold's clear designation on the product that it was the manufacturer, while relevant to Bifold's duty to take reasonable steps to prevent deception, was only one factor to be assessed in resolving the confusion issue.

The district court found that "[a]n intent to copy trade dress and/or finding of copying by a junior user is often alone dispositive of a finding of likelihood of confusion," and that since Bifold had copied Versa's design there was a likelihood of confusion. The court also found a likelihood of confusion because of the "competitive proximity" of the goods, which "strongly favors a finding of confusion," since the court found that the Domino Junior can replace the B-316 at the point of conception of the panels.[8]

### III. Discussion

. . .

#### A. "Likelihood" vs. "Possibility" of Confusion

Generally, "the law does not require that a competitor insure against all possible confusion or the likelihood thereof." [cit.] Rather, a plaintiff may prevail in a trade dress infringement action only if it shows that an appreciable number of ordinarily prudent consumers of the type of product in question are likely to be confused as to the source of the goods. [cit.] "The mere possibility that a customer may be misled is not enough." *Surgical Supply Serv., Inc. v. Adler*, 321 F.2d 536, 539 (3d Cir. 1963).

Although this usual formulation of trade dress infringement requires a showing of a likelihood or probability of confusion, this standard has been relaxed in some cases. Where an alleged infringer was new to an area and the plaintiff was well-established, this court has at times replaced the "likelihood of confusion" requirement with a lower "possibility of confusion" standard. These cases have all involved actions for trademark or trade name infringement, not trade dress, and certainly not trade dress alleged in a product configuration. [cit.] We must therefore consider whether the "possibility of confusion" standard should govern product configuration trade dress cases. Since unfair competition law regarding product configurations will diverge substantially in its incidents from the law regarding product packaging, *Duraco*, 40 F.3d at 1439, we begin our consideration by examining the rationale underlying the "possibility of confusion" cases.

---

8. The court additionally considered the "strength" of Versa's trade dress, evidence (albeit slim) of actual confusion, the method in which the valves are sold, and the labeling of Bifold's Domino Junior. Finally, the court also essentially held that New Jersey's Unfair Competition Law, 56 N.J.S.A. §4-1 to -2 (1989), and its common law of unfair competition parallel the unfair competition cause of action under Section 43(a), and hence that Versa prevailed on those causes of action as well.

[That rationale, according to the court, was that a second comer should be compelled to "keep clear" of the marks of a well-established firm.]

We recognize that application of the "keep clear" policy embodied by the trademark "possibility of confusion" standard would not be entirely senseless in the context of alleged infringement of trade dress, even where the dress consists not in a product's packaging but in a *non* functional product configuration. To the extent that product configurations are protectable, a Johnny-come-lately copier arguably creates a greater risk than one who more promptly markets a copy that consumers will be misled by a substantially identical configuration into thinking the newcomer's product to be that of the established business, for there will have been more time for the public to come to associate that configuration with a single source. In and of itself, however, that is no reason to change the measure of confusion (from "probability" to "possibility") required to make out a Lanham Act violation. Rather, it is at most a factor properly taken into account in assessing the likelihood of confusion.

The trademark "possibility of confusion" standard must therefore be supported by other considerations. We believe that the primary reasons for lowering the measure of confusion when a newcomer copies an established trademark are the general lack of legitimate reasons for copying a competitor's mark, *see, e.g., American Chicle Co. v. Topps Chewing Gum, Inc.,* 208 F.2d 560, 562-63 (2d Cir. 1953) ("Why [the defendant] should have chosen a mark that had long been employed by [the plaintiff] and had become known to the trade instead of adopting some other means of identifying its goods is hard to see unless there was a deliberate purpose to obtain some advantage from the trade which [the plaintiff] had built up."), and the high degree of reliance by consumers on trademarks as indicators of the source of products. Whether or not these considerations translate to the realm of product packaging, we think that with respect to product configurations the significance of each of the factors is greatly diminished.

First, the mere copying of product configurations does not suggest that the copier was necessarily trying to capitalize on the good will of the source of the original product. [cit.] A presumption to the contrary would be mandated, if ever, only in the narrow class of cases where both (1) a product configuration is desirable to consumers primarily because of the configuration's inherent or acquired identification with the original source, and (2) the copier adopts affirmatively misleading labeling and/or marketing for the copied product, *cf. Quaker Oats Co. v. General Mills, Inc.,* 134 F.2d 429, 432 (7th Cir. 1943) ("The pirate flies the flag of the one he would loot. The free and honorable non-pirate flies the colors of his own distinctive ensign.").

Second, although a product's trade dress in the form of its configuration could function as an indicator of the product's source, product configurations in general are not reliable as source indicators, for functional configurations are not protected and thus may be freely copied [cit.], and inherently distinctive configurations will be rare, [cit.]. Since substantially identical products are often sold by different manufacturers under different names, consumers are accustomed to relying on product packaging and trademarks to identify product sources. Indeed, if any modification of the likelihood of confusion standard is justified in the product configuration context, the standard might well be heightened, perhaps to a "high probability of confusion." Nevertheless, we see no need to adopt such a standard today, preferring for now merely to reject the "possibility of confusion" standard for product configuration infringement cases, and adhering to the conventional "likelihood of confusion" standard.

### B. The *Scott* Factors in the Product Configuration Context

Having concluded that the appropriate standard in this product configuration trade dress infringement action is a likelihood of confusion, we must determine what that inquiry entails in this context. Although the law of trade dress in product configurations will differ in key respects from the law of trademarks or of trade dress in product packaging, settled law provides the starting point for our analysis.

[The court recited its multifactor test for likelihood of confusion, the *Scott Paper* test: (1) the degree of similarity between the owner's mark and the alleged infringing mark; (2) the strength of [the] owner's mark; (3) the price of the goods and other factors indicative of the care and attention expected of consumers when making a purchase; (4) the length of time [the] defendant has used the mark without evidence of actual confusion arising; (5) the intent of the defendant in adopting the mark; (6) the evidence of actual confusion; (7) whether the goods, though not in competition, are marketed through the same channels of trade and advertised through the same media; (8) the extent to which the targets of the parties' sale efforts are the same; (9) the relationship of the goods in the minds of the public because of the similarity of function; (10) other facts suggesting that the consuming public might expect the prior owner to manufacture a product in the defendant's market. *Scott Paper Co. v. Scott's Liquid Gold, Inc.*, 589 F.2d 1225, 1229 (3d Cir. 1978)]. This test was developed not for product configuration cases but for "cases of alleged trademark infringement and unfair competition by a producer of a non-competing product," *see Fisons Horticulture, Inc. v. Vigoro Indus., Inc.*, 30 F.3d 466, 473 (3d Cir. 1994), and not all of the factors will be appropriate for or function the same way with respect to trade dress inhering in a product configuration, so we consider them in turn.

#### 1. Similarity of Appearance (*Scott* Factor 1)

In trademark infringement cases, the first and primary factor to be considered in the likelihood of confusion inquiry is "the degree of similarity between the owner's mark and the alleged infringing mark." [cit.] In trade dress infringement cases where product packaging is at issue, the corresponding factor is the similarity of the protectable trade dress. Similarity of appearance is properly considered paramount in trademark and product packaging trade dress infringement cases, for unless the allegedly infringing mark or dress is substantially similar to the protectable mark or dress, it is highly unlikely that consumers will confuse the product sources represented by the different marks or trade dresses.

For the same reason, substantial similarity of appearance is necessarily a prerequisite to a finding of likelihood of confusion in product configuration cases. Unlike in trademark or product packaging trade dress cases, however, a finding of substantial similarity of trade dress in a product configuration does not by itself strongly suggest a likelihood of confusion. Consumers have grown accustomed to relying on trademarks as trustworthy indicators of the source of the product: that is the point of a trademark. Perhaps to a somewhat lesser extent, consumers also rely on other aspects of product packaging to identify the manufacturer. Such behavior is rational, for in a trademark or product packaging case, all the consumer usually has to go on to identify the source of the product is the trademark and packaging (and any marketing featuring that mark or packaging).

In a product configuration trade dress infringement case, by contrast, consumers do not have to rely on a potentially distinctive configuration to identify the source of the product; rather, they can generally look to the packaging, trademarks, and advertising used to market the product, which are typically much less ambiguous. Consumers therefore have less need, and so are much less likely, to rely on a product configuration as an indicator of the product's source. Accordingly, they are less likely to be confused as to the sources of two products with substantially similar configurations. Thus, in trade dress infringement suits where the dress inheres in a product configuration, the primary factors to be considered in assessing likelihood of confusion are the product's labeling, packaging, and advertisements. "The most common and effective means of apprising intending purchasers of the source of goods is a prominent disclosure on the container, package, wrapper, or label of the manufacturer's or trader's name . . . [and when] that is done, there is no basis for a charge of unfair competition." [cit.]

Indeed, except where consumers ordinarily exercise virtually no care in selecting a particular type of product (as may be the case with inexpensive disposable or consumable items, [*e.g.,* cookies], clarity of labeling in packaging and advertising will suffice to preclude almost all possibility of consumer confusion as to source stemming from the product's configuration. [cit.]

2. Strength of the Owner's Mark (*Scott* Factor 2)

In trademark cases, the strength of the owner's mark directly affects the likelihood that consumers will be confused as to the sources of products bearing substantially similar marks. Strength includes both "[d]istinctiveness on the scale of trademarks" and "[c]ommercial strength, or marketplace recognition." *Fisons Horticulture, Inc.*, 30 F.3d at 479. A strong trademark is thus one that carries widespread, immediate recognition that one producer (even if unknown) is associated with the mark, and so with the product. If a second comer adopts a mark substantially identical to a strong mark, there is a correspondingly high likelihood that consumers will mistakenly associate the newcomer's product with the owner of the strong mark. The same may be said of a "strong" trade dress consisting of a product's packaging.

But these observations do not translate literally into the product configuration context. [The court first questioned whether the rules of distinctiveness for word marks translate exactly to the context of product configuration. This comment anticipated the Supreme Court's subsequent ruling in *Wal-Mart*. See Chapter 2.] Having rejected the distinctiveness scale in this context, we are left with commercial strength as the measure of trade dress strength in a product configuration. Yet strength of a product configuration must mean more than the *ability* of large numbers of consumers to identify the configuration as coming from a particular producer. This would sanction too much reliance by consumers on product designs that, lacking the protection of a patent, are in large measure copyable at will. *Cf. Duraco*, 40 F.3d at 1447-48 (criticizing the "capable of distinguishing" interpretation of distinctive trade dress).

Rather, "strength" of product configuration as relevant to determining likelihood of confusion on the part of ordinarily careful consumers should be found only if consumers *rely* on the product's configuration to identify the producer of the good. This may perhaps be the case with products purchased largely *because* of their appearance, such as "Carebears," *cf. American Greetings Corp. v. Dan-Dee Imports, Inc.*, 807 F.2d 1136, 1142 (3rd Cir. 1986). Such focus, however, is not generally found in and should not be encouraged in the industrial design context, where product appearance typically plays a lesser role in buyers' selection processes. Hence, to differentiate between these types of product configuration cases, courts should require evidence of actual *reliance* by consumers on a particular product configuration as a source indicator before crediting that configuration's "strength" toward likelihood of confusion.

### 3. Attention Expected of Consumers (*Scott* Factor 3)

The third Scott factor is "the price of the goods and other factors indicative of the care and attention expected of consumers when making a purchase." "The greater the care and attention, the less the likelihood of confusion." *Fisons Horticulture, Inc.*, 30 F.3d at 476 n. 12. We believe that this factor takes on enhanced importance when a claim is made for infringement of trade dress in a product configuration, both as a result of the intersection of the patent laws with the Lanham Act, and as a function of the difference between a trademark and a product configuration.

The penumbra of the federal patent laws restricts the degree to which courts may grant legal recognition of consumer reliance on product configurations as source indicators, for their limited scope of protection impliedly imposes restraint on the workings of Section 43(a). Accordingly, we must bear in mind the Supreme Court's counsel that "mere inability of the public to tell two identical articles apart is not enough to support an injunction against copying . . . that which the federal patent laws permit to be copied." *Sears, Roebuck & Co. v. Stiffel Co.*, 376 U.S. 225, 232 (1964).[12] "[T]he federal policy, found in Art. I, §8, cl. 8, of the Constitution and in the implementing federal statutes, of allowing free access to copy whatever the federal patent and copyright laws leave in the public domain," *Compco Corp. v. Day-Brite Lighting, Inc.*, 376 U.S. 234, 237 (1964), is "an ever-present consideration," Mckenney & Long, *Federal Unfair Competition* §5.03, at 5-25.

---

12. We recognize that we deal here not only with state unfair competition law but also with a federal statute. It is therefore true that the Supremacy Clause does not, as in *Sears, Roebuck & Co.*, 376 U.S. at 225, 84 S. Ct. at 786, and *Compco Corp. v. Day-Brite Lighting, Inc.*, 376 U.S. 234, 84 S. Ct. 779, 11 L. Ed. 2d 669 (1964), operate to bar Section 43(a) from protecting trade dress in the form of the product configuration of Versa's B-316 valve.

Furthermore, one expects a consumer exercising ordinary care to ascertain the source of a product to rely much more on packaging, trademarks, and advertising, which if not deceptive tend to reveal the product's source unambiguously, than on the product configuration, which usually does not contain an explicit statement of the producer's identity. While it might be shown that consumers *in fact rely* on a particular product's configuration to identify its source, such deviation from the normal pattern (i.e., from reliance on trademarks, packaging, and advertising) would be rare. Because clear labeling thus should generally be legally and factually sufficient to remedy confusion where unpatented product configurations are at issue, clarity of labeling (and marketing) must be taken into account in considering whether there is a likelihood that consumers *exercising ordinary care* will be confused as to the sources of substantially identical products.

Much as courts are required to police the boundaries of similarity within which a jury may be permitted to find a likelihood of confusion under the Lanham Act, [cit.], courts must also establish the perimeters of ordinary care that constrain likelihood of confusion. The following non-exhaustive considerations should guide a court's determination of the standard of ordinary care for a particular product. Inexpensive goods require consumers to exercise less care in their selection than expensive ones. The more important the use of a product, the more care that must be exercised in its selection. In addition, "the degree of caution used . . . depends on the relevant buying class. That is, some buyer classes, for example, professional buyers . . . will be held to a higher standard of care than others. Where the buyer class consists of both professional buyers and consumers, . . . the standard of care to be exercised by the reasonably prudent purchaser will be equal to that of the least sophisticated consumer in the class." [cit.]

4. Actual Confusion or Lack Thereof (*Scott* Factors 4 & 6)

The fourth Scott factor is "the length of time defendant has used the mark without evidence of actual confusion arising." While we hold that this factor applies to product configuration cases as well as to trademark and product packaging cases (for it is obviously relevant), we take this opportunity to underscore the role of the "lack of actual confusion" factor. If a defendant's product has been sold for an appreciable period of time without evidence of actual confusion, one can infer that continued marketing will not lead to consumer confusion in the future. The longer the challenged product has been in use, the stronger this inference will be.

"Evidence of actual confusion" (the sixth Scott factor bearing on likelihood of confusion) is similarly relevant: the more evidence of actual confusion that a plaintiff can muster, the stronger the likelihood of confusion in the future, but lack of evidence of actual confusion (at least where the time period that the two products have been in competition is short or "when the particular circumstances [do not] indicate such evidence should have been available," *AMF Inc. v. Sleekcraft Boats*, 599 F.2d 341, 353 (9th Cir. 1979)) does not raise an inference that there is no likelihood of confusion. As the case law makes clear, proof of actual confusion is not required for a successful trade dress infringement action under the Lanham Act. [cit.]

We see no reason that these factors would not also apply to product configuration cases. However, we emphasize again . . . that to make out unfair competition a plaintiff must show a likelihood that a consumer exercising ordinary care to discover the identity of the source would suffer confusion or be mistaken because of the appearance of the allegedly infringing product configuration. Thus, instances of actual confusion may not weigh in favor of a finding of likelihood of confusion unless the confused consumer was acting with the care expected of consumers purchasing the type of good at issue. *See G.D. Searle & Co. v. Hudson Pharmaceutical Corp.*, 715 F.2d 837, 840 & n. 6 (1983) (ignoring testimony of witness who "was not acting as a reasonably prudent consumer of the type of goods in issue when purchasing the product").

### 5. Defendant's Intent (*Scott* Factor 5)

The fifth Scott factor is "the intent of the defendant in adopting the mark." Whatever merit this factor may have in the context of trademark and product packaging trade dress cases, we doubt that it is an appropriate consideration in a trade dress infringement case where the trade dress is alleged in the product configuration itself. In the likelihood of confusion inquiry in trademark cases and product packaging trade dress cases, we do not focus on a defendant's bare *intent to adopt* a mark or product packaging substantially identical to a plaintiff's mark or packaging, since there is little basis in fact or logic for supposing from a defendant's *intent* to copy (without more) that the defendant's *actions* will in fact result in confusion. Thus, what we have held is that a defendant's *intent to confuse or deceive* consumers as to the product's source may be highly probative of likelihood of confusion. [cit.]

The justification for these inferences in a trademark or product packaging case is that there is little or no competitive need to copy another's distinctive symbol or presentation to sell one's product, and that anyone who does so is most likely trying to cash in on the competitor's goodwill attached to the competitor's mark or packaging in order to sell his or her own product. [cit.] This presumption largely duplicates the weight given to the substantial-identity-of-appearance factor (*Scott* factor 1) in the likelihood of confusion inquiry, and the extra weight assigned to the intent to deceive is somewhat punitive. [cit.]

Although these two types of inference from defendant's intent do not directly serve the purpose of preventing consumer confusion or misappropriation of a producer's goodwill—either of which might arise from good faith or bad faith actions—the inferences may serve as a deterrent to infringement. But where product configurations are concerned, we believe there is little room for deterrence if appropriate labeling and marketing are undertaken.

One primary purpose of the Lanham Act is to foster fair competition. [cit.] Indeed, we have said that prevention of unfair competition is the doctrinal basis for trade dress infringement suits under the Act. [cit.] Where product configurations are concerned, we must be especially wary of undermining competition. Competitors have broad rights to copy successful product designs when those designs are not protected by (utility or design) patents. It is not unfair competition for someone to trade off the good will of a *product*, see *Kellogg Co. v. National Biscuit Co.*, 305 U.S. 111 (1938); it is only unfair to deceive consumers as to the origin of one's goods and thereby trade off the good will of a prior *producer*. [cit.]

Unless very narrowly tailored, deterrents to copying of product designs—as opposed to product packaging or trademarks—would inhibit even fair competition, thus distorting the Lanham Act's purpose. We believe that the best way to further Congress's intent is to limit carefully the scope of any possible deterrence of competition. [The court analogized to certain intent standards in utility patent law, noting that they required proof by clear and convincing evidence.]

Accordingly, for all the foregoing reasons, we hold that in the product configuration context, a defendant's intent weighs in favor of a finding of likelihood of confusion only if intent to confuse or deceive is demonstrated by clear and convincing evidence, and only where the product's labeling and marketing are also affirmatively misleading. Of course, a plaintiff might succeed in proving likelihood of confusion without evidence of affirmative deception. We only hold that, to be considered as evidence of a likelihood of confusion in a product configuration case, the defendant's intent must meet the conditions we have set forth.

### 6. Marketing Considerations (*Scott* Factors 7-10)

The remaining factors identified by *Scott* as bearing on the likelihood of confusion address various aspects of the marketing of the products. In the product configuration context, none of these four factors tends to establish a probability of confusion, rather than a mere possibility, and thus we conclude that they should be treated as necessary but insufficient conditions for showing a likelihood of confusion.

The seventh *Scott* factor is "whether the goods, though not competing, are marketed through the same channels of trade and advertised through the same media." We believe that this factor, which is explicitly formulated for application to non-competing products, serves primarily to establish the possibility of confusion and carries little weight toward establishing the probability of confusion; if not shown, it may exonerate a defendant, but if established, it merely allows the plaintiff's case to go forward. Moreover, it will rarely need to be considered in a product configuration trade dress infringement case, for the goods at issue will almost by definition be in competition.

"The extent to which the targets of the parties' sale efforts are the same" is the eighth *Scott* factor. Like the marketing channel inquiry, this factor was developed largely for non-competing products, [cit.], and relates more to the possibility than the probability of confusion. Particularly in a product configuration case, this factor should be considered necessary but not sufficient: If different consumers buy the defendant's product and the plaintiff's product, the defendant will typically win; if substantially overlapping audiences buy the products, the plaintiff does not automatically win, but will usually have the opportunity to further develop its case for likelihood of confusion.

"The relationship of the goods in the minds of the public because of the similarity of function" and "other facts suggesting that the consuming public might expect the prior owner to manufacture a product in the defendant's market" are the ninth and tenth *Scott* factors for determining likelihood of confusion. Bearing in mind that these factors also were developed for noncompeting products, we believe that they are largely superfluous in product configuration cases. The requisite similarity of trade dress *in the product designs themselves* would in most cases presuppose a similarity of function between the products at issue. Hence, some measure of so-called "competitive proximity" will always be present in product configuration trade dress infringement cases and therefore, while a necessary condition for there to be a likelihood of confusion, this factor is not a sufficient condition, nor does it by itself create a strong presumption that confusion is likely to ensue.

### C. The Balance of the Modified *Scott* Factors Here

... For the reasons we explained above, we believe that the district court committed legal error in initially applying a "possibility of confusion" standard, and, applying the (modified) *Scott* factors, we conclude that it clearly erred in inferring from the evidence and testimony that an appreciable number of buyers are likely to be confused as to the origin of Bifold's Domino Junior valve.

...

#### 2. Viability of the District Court's Similarity Fact Finding

The district court correctly identified the similarity of product appearances (*Scott* factor 1) as the threshold inquiry in ascertaining likelihood of confusion. However, it improperly imported the trademark/product packaging standard for the weight to be assigned this factor, holding that "if the overall impression created by the trade dress is essentially the same, it is very probable that the products are confusingly similar." From there, it apparently reasoned that because "[t]he overall appearance of the Versa B-316 valve and the Bifold Domino Junior valve is virtually identical[,] there is a likelihood of confusion."

Despite the appreciable differences between the valves' appearances, we do not hold the district court's finding of similarity of appearance to be clearly erroneous. But in a product configuration case, the similarity of the product designs does not alone give rise to a strong inference of likelihood of confusion, since the greatest weight must be given to the primary means by which consumers identify the products' sources: packaging, trademarks, and advertising. Accordingly, the similar appearance of the two valves' designs allows Versa to argue — but does not establish — a likelihood of confusion. The district court's findings concerning the trade channels and advertising media used by Bifold and Versa (*Scott* factor 7) and Bifold's targeting of the same customer group (*Scott* factor 8) similarly do little to establish likelihood of confusion.

#### 3. Intent, Competitive Proximity, and Likelihood of Confusion

Compounding its error regarding the effect of the similarity of the valves' appearances, the court asserted that "[a]n intent to copy trade dress and/or finding of copying by a junior user is often alone dispositive of a finding of likelihood of confusion." Even as concerns trademarks and product packaging, however, only an *intent to deceive or confuse* consumers can suffice to raise a presumption of likelihood of confusion in this circuit. Moreover, in a product configuration case the defendant's intent (*Scott* factor 5) is not relevant to the issue of likelihood of confusion absent affirmatively misleading labeling and marketing. Here, Bifold's identification of its Domino Junior valves is by no means misleading, and thus Bifold's intent should not be considered.

Similarly, the district court erred in holding that "[w]hen products are used in the same application, such a competitive proximity of goods *strongly* favors a finding of likelihood of confusion" (emphasis supplied). This proposition finds no support in the two decisions of this court cited by the district court, [cit.], and at all events it is not applicable where trade dress consists in a product configuration, as our previous discussion explains.

### 4. Strength of the Trade Dress and Likelihood of Confusion

Turning to the *Scott* factors that are relevant to the likelihood of confusion in this product configuration case, we first note that the "strength" of Versa's trade dress in its B-316 valves' configuration (*Scott* factor 2) may not support a conclusion of likelihood of confusion because there is no evidence that consumers rely on the appearance of the B-316 valve to identify it. To the contrary, all the evidence shows that consumers order valves by multi-digit part and model numbers peculiar to the manufacturer. In selecting the valves buyers do not specify the desired appearance but rather designate functional specifications listed in schematic diagrams, specification sheets, and manufacturers' catalogues. Such precision in ordering is necessary, for Versa offers many variations of its valves. Thus, the "strength" of the B-316's trade dress does not bolster Versa's case for a likelihood of confusion.

### 5. The Evidentiary Role of Actual Confusion

[Reviewing the record, the court found no probative evidence in support of a finding of actual confusion.] Moreover, as the district court found, "[o]nly two Domino Junior valves have been sold to date in the United States and those have been sold to Versa's sales representative so that there has been little, if any, opportunity to develop evidence of further confusion in the United States." Accordingly, evidence of actual confusion or lack thereof does not weigh in favor of or against a finding of likelihood of confusion. We turn to the final relevant *Scott* factor.

### 6. Labeling, Care Expected of Consumers, and Likelihood of Confusion

As noted above, the third *Scott* factor is "the price of the goods and other factors indicative of the care and attention expected of consumers when making a purchase." As we have described, this factor is fundamental in product configuration cases, where the most important facts are the marketing and labeling of the similarly configured products. As we now explain, the district court clearly erred in not finding these factors dispositive in this case.

The district court was technically correct in stating that "[t]he fact that the source of the product is clearly designated on the product does not establish that plaintiff has failed to demonstrate a likelihood of confusion as such an element is simply one factor to be assessed when resolving the confusion issue." However, it failed to appreciate the converse proposition, that a court need not consider all these elements when some are dispositive. [cit.]

Here, as the court properly observed, "[i]n selling a competing valve, Bifold's duty is to take reasonable steps to prevent deception." Under the circumstances, Bifold more than adequately met its duty to take reasonable steps to prevent deception.

a. Bifold's Extensive Labeling Precludes Likelihood of Confusion

Although the configurations of Versa's B-316 and Bifold's Domino Junior valves are quite similar in appearance, we deal here with a product configuration case, and thus the labeling of the products takes on a heightened importance. The facts found by the district court clearly show that Bifold took entirely reasonable and adequate steps to prevent confusion.

The district court found that "[t]he name VERSA and the place of origin, 'N.J., U.S.A.,' are cast into the metal [of the B-316 valve body] to identify Versa as the valve's source." Moreover, "[e]very valve body that Versa sells bears a label displaying the VERSA name, logo and part number." Similarly, the court noted that "Bifold casts its name into the DOMINO JUNIOR valve body, and bolts onto the body a metal label displaying the BIFOLD name."

But this brief recitation fails to convey the adequacy of Bifold's efforts. "In the case of a relatively high-priced, single-purchase article, . . . there is hardly likelihood of confusion or palming off when the name of the manufacturer is clearly displayed." [cit.] Here, the metal label bolted onto the Domino Junior valves does more than "display[] the BIFOLD name." The name appears in a logo of sorts in a font markedly different from that used in the Versa logo. The label also contains Bifold's part number and a valve serial number, the place of origin (Wigan, England), Bifold's telephone number, and its fax number. Moreover, this is not a case where "[t]he items are relatively inexpensive and consumers cannot be expected to examine the labels carefully," *Scott Paper Co.*, 589 F.2d at 1230, and even a quick glance at the permanently affixed label reveals that Bifold is the source of the Domino Junior valve. Thus, Bifold's labeling will suffice to dispel any confusion about the valve's source that the configuration of the Domino Junior valve might otherwise engender in purchasers who exercise ordinary care.

b. The Manner in Which the Valves Are Sold Virtually Precludes Likelihood of Confusion

In addition to the clear labeling, the manner in which the valves are marketed further nullifies any likelihood of confusion. As the district court found:

> The Versa B-316 and Bifold DOMINO JUNIOR valves are not sold on a shelf or selected on sight. Buyers order the valves based on functional specifications as shown on schematic diagrams, manufacturer's catalogs or specification sheets and samples available at trade shows and sales presentations.

Moreover, purchasers cannot buy Versa B-316 or Bifold Domino Junior valves by name only. B-316 valves can be purchased only by specifying a multi-digit part number pursuant to Versa's comprehensive part numbering system. Similarly, Bifold requires the use of its own part numbering system, with the numbers obtainable only by reference to a Bifold specification sheet. Finally, as the district court also found, "[t]he purchasers and users of Versa's B-316 valves are qualified, knowledgeable personnel who understand how the valves are to be installed and operated."

The appearance of these valves simply plays no role in the ordering process, which instead requires the use of detailed technical specifications and lengthy, manufacturer-specific part numbers. Under these circumstances, we find it utterly inconceivable that one of—let alone an appreciable number of—the professional buyers of these valves will be confused, by the appearance of the Domino Junior, as to the valves' manufacturers or the relationship between them.

c. Summary of the Labeling and Care Expected of Consumers

The foregoing evidence must be viewed as virtually precluding any likelihood of confusion. These valves are not bought by children or casual consumers, nor are they purchased solely by name. There is no *likelihood* of confusion—indeed, virtually no possibility that the appearance of the Bifold Domino Junior valve body will mislead purchasers into thinking that they are ordering a Domino Junior valve from Versa or a B-316 valve from Bifold, and the enormous safety concerns surrounding the applications where these valves are used increase the already great care used by purchasers of these valves.[13] Typically, they are found in offshore oil drilling control applications, hazardous and demanding environments where loss of human life, major environmental damage (and consequent liability), and huge property loss may be at stake if a valve does not function properly in an emergency shutdown. Because of the dire consequences of using an improper valve, engineers who design the control panels would be expected to exercise a high degree of caution in selecting valves, and thus would be highly unlikely to mistake a Versa B-316 for a Bifold Domino Junior.

Therefore, in light of the importance of the valves, the process by which they are purchased, the sophistication of the consumers, and the clarity of Bifold's labeling, there is no likelihood (or even a realistic possibility) of consumer confusion as to the source of Versa's or Bifold's valves, and we conclude that the district court's contrary finding was clearly erroneous.

[The court's discussion of the private labeling issue has been omitted.]

## NOTES AND QUESTIONS

1. *Likelihood of confusion v. possibility of confusion.* The court in *Versa* applies the conventional likelihood-of-confusion standard, rejecting the possibility-of-confusion standard. This is not a surprising outcome—it is entirely consistent with the law of word marks.

2. *Similarity factor in product design trade dress cases: the importance of labeling.* The courts in both *Ambrit* and *Versa* concluded that the presence of labeling (in the form of house marks, for example) should be taken into account in evaluating whether product packaging or product designs are similar for

---

13. Although Versa intended its witnesses' testimony to highlight the hazards of confusing a Versa valve with a Bifold valve—which would be product confusion, not *source* confusion as required for a Lanham Act violation—the testimony is nonetheless indicative of the care that ordinarily prudent valve consumers may be expected to use.

likelihood-of-confusion purposes. However, the *Versa* court finds labeling especially crucial in comparing product design trade dress. Do you agree? In some cases but not others? In *Nora Beverages, Inc. v. Perrier Group of Am., Inc.*, 269 F.3d 114 (2d Cir. 2001), plaintiff Nora sold bottled water under the NAYA word mark. Defendant Perrier sold bottled water under various trademarks. Nora claimed trade dress in the shape and overall appearance of the bottle, and sued Perrier for trade dress infringement. The court concluded that differences between the NAYA label and the Perrier labels alone negated a likelihood of confusion and justified affirming a grant of summary judgment of no infringement, because the bottle shape was neither Nora's predominating source indicator, nor its lone source indicator given the presence of the NAYA labeling. Do you agree that courts should assess the relative dominance of the labels and the product design? Is this consistent with the overall impression rule?

For another illustration on the role of labels in assessments of product design similarity, consider the following. Suppose that a water meter producer, Badger, sues its competitor Hersey for trade dress infringement. Hersey shows that its water meters, which are similar in design to the Badger meter, are labeled with Hersey's trademarks. Badger argues that Hersey is known to have entered into private-label arrangements with other manufacturers in which the Hersey label was applied to water meters made by the other manufacturers. Should a court dispense with the usual conclusion about the importance of labels where a consumer might see a Hersey-labeled meter and assume that Hersey had entered into a private-label deal with Badger, especially if the Hersey-labeled meter has the same appearance as the Badger meter? *See Badger Meter, Inc. v. Grinnell Corp.*, 13 F.3d 1145 (7th Cir. 1994).

**3. Side-by-side similarity (again).** In a product design case involving handbags, Judge Calabresi warned that side-by-side similarity comparisons could amount to reversible error. In *Malletier v. Burlington Coat Factory Warehouse Corp.*, 426 F.3d 532 (2d Cir. 2005), plaintiff sold a line of multicolored handbags through its Louis Vuitton stores (and an associated Web site) and at upscale department stores at prices ranging from $400 to $4,000, whereas defendant sold a line of multicolored handbags through its discount stores (and an associated Web site) at about $29.98 per bag. Plaintiff claimed that defendant's trade dress was likely to confuse consumers prior to sale, and after sale (theories that we will study later in this chapter). Viewing the handbags side by side, the district court had concluded that they were dissimilar, and ultimately denied plaintiff's motion for a preliminary injunction. On appeal, the Second Circuit vacated the denial of the motion for injunctive relief and remanded to the district court.

> While a district court's simultaneous comparison of two products is not an inappropriate heuristic means of investigating similarities and differences in their respective designs on the way to an ultimate conclusion as to whether the products are likely to leave similar impressions on consumers, district courts must be careful to maintain a focus on the ultimate issue of the likelihood of consumer confusion. As a result, the Lanham Act requires a court to analyze the similarity of the products in light of the way in which the marks are actually displayed in their purchasing context. [cit.] Whether simultaneous viewing by consumers is likely to result in confusion is not relevant when it is serial viewing that is at issue given the market context or the type of confusion claimed.

In such a case, a district court must ask not whether differences are easily discernable on simultaneous viewing, but whether they are likely to be memorable enough to dispel confusion on serial viewing.

The need for a contextual analysis, rather than a simple focus on whether simultaneous viewing is likely to cause confusion, is grounded in the purpose of the Lanham Act. That Act seeks to eliminate the confusion that is created in the marketplace by the sale of products bearing highly similar marks. [cit.]

Accordingly, a court that seeks to discern confusion without regard to the marketplace frustrates (however unintentionally) Congress's intent. Though two products may be readily differentiated when carefully viewed simultaneously, those same products may still be confusingly similar in the eyes of ordinary consumers encountering the products individually under typical purchasing conditions, and that "real world" confusion is the confusion that the Act seeks to eliminate. As a result, courts must evaluate the likely effect on consumers of the marks' similar and dissimilar features with a focus on market conditions, even if the products appear to be adequately different in a non-marketplace setting.

*Id.* at 538-539.

Here, the parties conceded that the products were not sold side by side, and, in any event, the plaintiff was claiming pre-sale and post-sale confusion, not point-of-sale confusion. Under these circumstances, the district court erred by viewing the handbags simultaneously to assess similarity. *Id.* at 539. Should the approach differ where the products were sold side by side?

**4. *Relatedness of goods/services.*** Multifactor likelihood of confusion tests in the various circuits call for an analysis of the relatedness of the plaintiff's and defendant's respective goods or services. Thus, in a case in which two parties both use the word mark "Domino's," it may be quite important for the court to consider that one party uses DOMINO'S for sugar whereas the other uses DOMINO's for pizza. Does this same analysis translate to product design cases? Should courts develop a special rule for product design cases in which a claim of likely confusion is only plausible if the plaintiff and defendant are using the product design in connection with the same goods? How often would you expect a product design case to involve dissimilar goods?

**5. *Intent to copy.*** In the notes after *Ambrit*, we discussed Learned Hand's view that evidence of a defendant's intent to simulate a plaintiff's trade dress should give rise to a presumption of confusion. The case before Learned Hand appeared to involve product packaging trade dress. Should the same presumption apply in cases involving product design trade dress? Is there anything about the motivations for copying product design that would justify giving the intent factor a greater or lesser role in product design cases than in other cases? *See Sunbeam Prods., Inc. v. West Bend Co.*, 123 F.3d 246, 258 (5th Cir. 1997), *overruled in part on other grounds*, *TrafFix Devices, Inc. v. Mktg. Displays, Inc.*, 532 U.S. 23 (2001) ("the defendant's intent is only one element in the likelihood-of-confusion inquiry, and intent alone is not sufficient to establish trade dress infringement. . . . Nevertheless, it is firmly established that a finding of intent may support an inference of consumer confusion.").

**6. *Remedies in product design trade dress cases.*** As noted above, the *Versa* court, like others, places great emphasis on the defendant's labeling, saying that the labels would go far in dispelling confusion that might be triggered by the similar product shapes. Where a court finds liability for product design trade dress infringement, should the court's injunctive relief also reflect the importance of labels? For example, might a properly drawn injunction permit the infringer to continue using the infringing product design, but require the infringer to add clarifying labels? What other issues may arise when courts attempt to fashion injunctive relief in product design cases? In *Pebble Beach Co. v. Tour 18 I Ltd.*, 155 F.3d 526 (5th Cir. 1998), Tour 18 operated a public golf course in Texas featuring golf holes that were copied from famous golf courses, including Sea Pines, located on Hilton Head Island, South Carolina. One hole on the Sea Pines course is commonly referred to as the "lighthouse hole" because a red-and-white striped lighthouse is visible from the hole. The lighthouse is not actually located on Sea Pines property, but instead is about 100 feet away from the green, across an inlet. Defendant's course likewise included a lighthouse hole, with a replica lighthouse. The trial court found infringement, and enjoined the defendants from "offering in connection with defendant's golf course services a replica, copy, or imitation of" the lighthouse. The court also ordered defendants to remove the replica lighthouses, to place disclaimers in its marketing materials disclaiming any affiliation with the famous courses, and to cease any claims that it used "original" blueprints to construct the replica holes. Evaluate the scope of the injunction in view of the goals of the trademark law. Is the injunction too broad? Too narrow? Both?

7. *Streamlining the confusion analysis in product design cases?* Suppose that, in the name of streamlining the confusion analysis, a judge rests a likelihood-of-confusion analysis in a trade dress case solely on a showing of similarity between the marks and defendant's intent to trade off plaintiff's goodwill. Compare *Jada Toys, Inc. v. Mattel, Inc.*, 518 F.3d 628 (9th Cir. 2008) (error to base a confusion analysis on dissimilarity alone; courts should regularly apply all of the relevant confusion factors) with *Top Tobacco, L.P. v. North Atlantic Operating Co., Inc.*, 509 F.3d 308 (7th Cir. 2007) (concluding that there is no need to consult even a single factor "[i]f we know for sure that consumers are not confused about a product's origin"). Would the quality of decisions suffer if judges adopted such an approach for all product design trade dress cases? Would outcomes be any different? If judges did adopt the streamlined approach, would the infringement analysis differ materially from design patent infringement analysis (*see* Chapter 6)? From the infringement analysis used in connection with sui generis design regimes, such as the European Community design system (discussed in Chapter 8)?

## 2. CONFUSION AWAY FROM THE POINT OF SALE

### Ferrari S.P.A. Esercizio Fabriche Automobili e Corse v. Roberts
944 F.2d 1235 (6th Cir. 1991), *cert. denied*, 505 U.S. 1219 (1992)

Ryan, Circuit Judge:

#### I. The Facts

Ferrari is the world famous designer and manufacturer of racing automobiles and upscale sports cars. Between 1969 and 1973, Ferrari produced the 365 GTB/4 Daytona. Because Ferrari intentionally limits production of its cars in order to create an image of exclusivity, only 1400 Daytonas were built; of these, only 100 were originally built as Spyders, soft-top convertibles. Daytona Spyders currently sell for one to two million dollars. Although Ferrari no longer makes Daytona Spyders, they have continuously produced mechanical parts and body panels, and provided repair service for the cars.

Ferrari began producing a car called the Testarossa in 1984. To date, Ferrari has produced approximately 5000 Testarossas. Production of these cars is also intentionally limited to preserve exclusivity: the entire anticipated production is sold out for the next several years and the waiting period to purchase a Testarossa is approximately five years. A new Testarossa sells for approximately $230,000.

Roberts is engaged in a number of business ventures related to the automobile industry. One enterprise is the manufacture of fiberglass kits that replicate the exterior features of Ferrari's Daytona Spyder and Testarossa automobiles. Roberts' copies are called the Miami Spyder and the Miami Coupe, respectively. The kit is a one-piece body shell molded from reinforced fiberglass. It is usually bolted onto the undercarriage of another automobile such as a Chevrolet Corvette or a Pontiac Fiero, called the donor car. Roberts marketed the Miami Spyder primarily through advertising in kit-car magazines. Most of the replicas were sold as kits for about $8,500, although a fully accessorized "turnkey" version was available for about $50,000.

At the time of trial, Roberts had not yet completed a kit-car version of the Miami Coupe, the replica of Ferrari's Testarossa, although he already has two orders for them. He originally built the Miami Coupe for the producers of the television program "Miami Vice" to be used as a stunt car in place of the more expensive Ferrari Testarossa.

The district court found, and it is not disputed, that Ferrari's automobiles and Roberts' replicas are virtually identical in appearance.

Ferrari brought suit against Roberts in March 1988 alleging trademark infringement, in violation of section 43 (a) of the Lanham Act, and obtained a preliminary injunction enjoining Roberts from manufacturing the replica cars.

[Eventually, Ferrari obtained a permanent injunction.]

### III

To prove a violation of section 43 (a), Ferrari's burden is to show, [inter alia,] that there is a likelihood of confusion based on the similarity of the exterior shape and design of Ferrari's vehicles and Roberts' replicas....

#### B. Likelihood of Confusion

##### 1. District Court's Findings

...

Summarized, the district court's findings on the Frisch "likelihood of confusion" factors are as follows:

| | Factors | Favor |
|---|---|---|
| 1. | Strength of the mark | Ferrari |
| 2. | Relatedness of the goods | Ferrari |
| 3. | Similarity of the marks | Ferrari |

| | | |
|---|---|---|
| 4. | Evidence of actual confusion | No evidence |
| 5. | Marketing channels used | Roberts |
| 6. | Likely degree of purchaser care | Roberts |
| 7. | Roberts' intent in selecting "mark" | Ferrari |
| 8. | Likelihood of expansion of product lines. | No evidence |

[Reviewing the evidence, the appellate court concluded that Ferrari's mark — the exterior design of the vehicle — was "very strong"; that the similarity of the marks was indisputable because the exteriors were indistinguishable from one another, although Roberts sometimes sold vehicles with a "R" insignia added; and Roberts "conceded that his intent in replicating the exterior design of Ferrari's vehicles was to market a product that looked as much as possible like a Ferrari original," although Roberts also hastened to point out that he never represented to his customers that the vehicles were actually Ferraris. This amounted to "strong evidence that the public is likely to be confused by the similarity of the exterior design of Ferrari's vehicles and Roberts' replicas."]

2. Roberts' Objections

Roberts disagrees with the legal significance of the district court's findings of likelihood of confusion. He argues that for purposes of the Lanham Act, the requisite likelihood of confusion must be confusion at the point of sale — purchaser confusion — and not the confusion of nonpurchasing, casual observers. The evidence is clear that Roberts assured purchasers of his replicas that they were not purchasing Ferraris and that his customers were not confused about what they were buying.

. . .

b. Confusion at Point of Sale

Roberts argues that his replicas do not violate the Lanham Act because he informed his purchasers that his significantly cheaper cars and kits were not genuine Ferraris and thus there was no confusion at the point of sale. The Lanham Act, however, was intended to do more than protect consumers at the point of sale. When the Lanham Act was enacted in 1946, its protection was limited to the use of marks "likely to cause confusion or mistake or to deceive purchasers as to the source of origin of such goods or services." In 1962, Congress deleted this language and broadened the Act's protection to include the use of marks "likely to cause confusion or mistake or to deceive." Thus, Congress intended "to regulate commerce within [its control] by making actionable the deceptive and misleading use of marks in such commerce; [and] . . . to protect persons engaged in such commerce against unfair competition. . . ." 15 U.S.C. §1127. Although, as the dissent points out, Congress rejected an antidilution provision when recently amending the Lanham Act, it made no effort to amend or delete this language clearly protecting the confusion of goods *in commerce*. The court in *Rolex Watch* explicitly recognized this concern with regulating commerce:

> The real question before this Court is whether the alleged infringer has placed a product *in commerce* that is "likely to cause confusion, or to cause mistake, or to deceive." . . . The fact that an immediate buyer of a $25 counterfeit watch does

not entertain any notions that it is the real thing has no place in this analysis. Once a product is injected into commerce, there is no bar to confusion, mistake, or deception occurring at some future point in time.

*Rolex Watch*, 645 F. Supp. at 492-93 (emphasis in original). The *Rolex Watch* court noted that this interpretation was necessary to protect against the cheapening and dilution of the genuine product, and to protect the manufacturer's reputation. *Id.* at 495; *see also Mastercrafters*, 221 F.2d at 466. As the court explained:

> Individuals examining the counterfeits, believing them to be genuine Rolex watches, might find themselves unimpressed with the quality of the item and consequently be inhibited from purchasing the real time piece. Others who see the watches bearing the Rolex trademarks on so many wrists might find themselves discouraged from acquiring a genuine because the items have become too common place and no longer possess the prestige once associated with them.

*Rolex Watch*, 645 F. Supp. at 495; *see also Mastercrafters*, 221 F.2d at 466. Such is the damage which could occur here. As the district court explained when deciding whether Roberts' former partner's Ferrari replicas would be confused with Ferrari's cars:

> Ferrari has gained a well-earned reputation for making uniquely designed automobiles of quality and rarity. The DAYTONA SPYDER design is well-known among the relevant public and exclusively and positively associated with Ferrari. If the country is populated with hundreds, if not thousands, of replicas of rare, distinct, and unique vintage cars, obviously they are no longer unique. Even if a person seeing one of these replicas driving down the road is not confused, Ferrari's exclusive association with this design has been diluted and eroded. If the replica Daytona looks cheap or in disrepair, Ferrari's reputation for rarity and quality could be damaged. . . .

*Ferrari*, 11 U.S.P.Q.2d at 1848. The dissent argues that the Lanham Act requires proof of confusion at the point of sale because the eight factor test used to determine likelihood of confusion focuses on the confusion of the purchaser, not the public. The dissent submits that three of the factors, marketing channels used, likely degree of purchaser care and sophistication, and evidence of actual confusion, specifically relate to purchasers. However, evidence of actual confusion is not limited to purchasers. The survey evidence in this case showed that members of the public, but not necessarily purchasers, were actually confused by the similarity of the products. Moreover, the other five factors, strength of the mark, relatedness of the goods, similarity of the marks, defendant's intent in selecting the mark, and likelihood of product expansion, do not limit the likelihood of confusion test to purchasers.

Since Congress intended to protect the reputation of the manufacturer as well as to protect purchasers, the Act's protection is not limited to confusion at the point of sale. Because Ferrari's reputation in the field could be damaged by the marketing of Roberts' replicas, the district court did not err in permitting recovery despite the absence of point of sale confusion. . . .

*Affirmed.*

KENNEDY, Circuit Judge, dissenting:

... The majority first misconstrues the scope of protection afforded by the Lanham Act by misapplying the "likelihood of confusion" test and reading an anti-dilution provision into the language of section 43(a). ...

The majority never clearly defines the target group that is likely to be confused. Although *West Point* counsels that purchasers must be deceived, the majority concludes that the target group is the "public." The majority errs to the extent that its analysis shifts from potential purchasers to the broader more indefinite group of the "public."

The eight-factor test contemplates that the target group is comprised of potential purchasers. For example, the importance of one factor — evidence of actual confusion — is determined by the kinds of persons confused and degree of confusion. "Short-lived confusion or confusion of individuals casually acquainted with a business is worthy of little weight. ..." *Homeowners Group, Inc. v. Home Marketing Specialists, Inc.*, 931 F.2d 1100, 1110 (6th Cir. 1991) (quoting *Safeway Stores, Inc. v. Safeway Discount Drugs, Inc.*, 675 F.2d 1160, 1167 (11th Cir. 1982)). Two other factors obviously refer to potential purchasers: the marketing channels used and the likely degree of purchaser care and sophistication. Thus, three of the eight factors expressly focus on the likelihood of confusion as to potential purchasers. ...

To be sure, some courts have expanded the application of the likelihood of confusion test to include individuals other than point-of-sale purchasers. These courts have included potential purchasers who may contemplate a purchase in the future, reasoning that in the pre-sale context an "observer would identify the [product] with the [original manufacturer], and the [original manufacturer]'s reputation would suffer damage if the [product] appeared to be of poor quality." *Polo Fashions, Inc. v. Craftex, Inc.*, 816 F.2d 145, 148 (4th Cir. 1987); see *Mastercrafters Clock & Radio Co. v. Vacheron & Constantin-Le Coultre Watches, Inc.*, 221 F.2d 464 (2d Cir.), cert. denied, 350 U.S. 832 (1955); *Rolex Watch, U.S.A., Inc. v. Canner*, 645 F. Supp. 484 (S.D. Fla. 1986).

In applying the test in this manner, these courts appear to recognize that the deception of a consumer under these circumstances could dissuade such a consumer from choosing to buy a particular product, thereby foreclosing the possibility of point-of-sale confusion but nevertheless injuring the consumer based on this confusion. The injury stems from the consumer's erroneous conclusion that the "original" product is poor quality based on his perception of a replica that he thinks is the original. These cases protect a potential purchaser against confusion as to the source of a particular product. Hence, even when expanding the scope of this test, these courts did not lose sight of the focus of section 43(a): the potential purchaser. The majority applies the likelihood of confusion test in a manner which departs from this focus.

The cases which have expanded the scope of the target group are distinguishable from the instant case, however. In *Rolex*, the counterfeit watches were labelled "ROLEX" on their face. Similarly, the *Mastercrafters* court found that the clock was labelled in a manner that was not likely to come to the attention of an individual. It is also noteworthy that the Second Circuit has limited *Mastercrafters* "by pointing out that '[i]n that case there was abundant evidence of actual confusion, palming off and an intent to deceive.'" *Bose Corp. v. Linear Design Labs, Inc.*, 467 F.2d 304, 310 n.8 (2d Cir. 1972) (quoting *Norwich Pharmacal Co. v. Sterling Drug, Inc.*, 271 F.2d 569 (2d Cir. 1959), *cert. denied*, 362 U.S. 919 (1960)). No evidence was introduced in the instant case to show actual confusion, palming off or an intent to deceive and, as previously noted, plaintiff does not use any name or logo affiliated with Ferrari on its replicas.

Further, these cases conclude that the proper remedy is to require identification of the source of the replica, not prohibit copying of the product. *See West Point*, 222 F.2d at 589 (stating that under such circumstances "the only obligation of the copier is to identify its product lest the public be mistaken into believing that it was made by the prior patentee"); *see also Coach Leatherware*, 933 F.2d at 173 (Winter, J., dissenting in part) (stating that "[a copier] thus has every right to copy [a product] so long as consumers know they are buying [the copied product]"). Accordingly, even if I were to conclude that plaintiff's copies created confusion in the pre-sale context, I would tailor the remedy to protect only against such confusion; this would best be accomplished through adequate labelling. The majority's remedy goes well beyond protection of consumers against confusion as to a product's source. It protects the design itself from being copied. [cit.]

In sum, the relevant focus of the eight-factor test should be upon potential purchasers in the marketplace. Plaintiff's replicas present no likelihood of confusion because plaintiff provides adequate labelling so as to prevent potential purchasers, whether in the pre-sale or point-of-sale context, from confusing its replicas with Ferrari's automobiles. The majority errs by expanding the target group to include the "public," an expansion unsupported by the language and purpose of the Lanham Act. To the extent that the majority expands the target group, the test increasingly protects the design from replication and the producer from dilution, rather than the potential purchaser from confusion.

## NOTES AND QUESTIONS

1. *Post-sale confusion in the design context.* *Ferrari* is a leading illustration of the post-sale confusion theory — and is especially pertinent to the subject matter of this book, given that the case involves product design. Is it coincidence that the leading post-sale confusion case is a design case? Or is there something about design that makes it peculiarly subject to post-sale confusion theory?

2. *"Secondary" confusion.* The *Mastercrafters* case, cited in *Ferrari*, is a frequently cited early example of the application of a post-sale confusion theory. *Mastercrafters Clock & Radio Co. v. Vacheron & Constatin-Le Coultre Watches, Inc.*, 221 F.2d 464 (2d Cir.), *cert. denied*, 350 U.S. 832 (1955). In *Mastercrafters*, as in some other cases, the court distinguishes between confusion among purchasers and confusion among "secondary" viewers of the mark, which could include members of the public who are potential purchasers. Thus, you may see references in court decisions to "secondary" confusion rather than "post-sale" confusion. *See, e.g., Acad. of Motion Picture Arts & Sciences v. Creative House Promotions, Inc.*, 944 F.2d 1446 (9th Cir. 1991) (statuettes designed to resemble the Oscar award; referring to the likelihood that "secondary" viewers might mistake the award for an original even if the purchaser would not).

3. ***What's the harm?*** According to the *Ferrari* case, how might post-sale confusion harm a trademark owner? The Sixth Circuit supplied a more extensive answer to the question in *Gen. Motors Corp. v. Keystone Automotive Indus., Inc.*, 453 F.3d 351, 358 (6th Cir. 2006):

> Even without point-of-sale confusion, knockoffs can harm the public and the original manufacturer in a number of ways, including: (1) the viewing public, as well as subsequent purchasers, may be deceived if expertise is required to distinguish the original from the counterfeit [cit.]; (2) the purchaser of an original may be harmed if the widespread existence of knockoffs decreases the original's value by making the previously scarce commonplace [cit.]; (3) consumers desiring high quality products may be harmed if the original manufacturer decreases its investment in quality in order to compete more economically with less expensive knockoffs [cit.]; (4) the original manufacturer's reputation for quality may be damaged if individuals mistake an inferior counterfeit for the original [cit.]; (5) the original manufacturer's reputation for rarity may be harmed by the influx of knockoffs onto the market [cit.]; and (6) the original manufacturer may be harmed if sales decline due to the public's fear that what they are purchasing may not be the original [cit.].

The court also took note of the standard countervailing considerations, asserting that the "courts should be wary of overprotecting public domain ideas and works whose exploitation can lead to economic efficiency, greater competition, and lower costs for consumers." *Id.* In the case, defendants produced and distributed replacement grilles for plaintiff's automobiles. Defendant's grilles included a recessed area (a "placeholder") shaped to receive the plaintiff's "bow tie" emblem, long used in connection with plaintiff's Chevrolet vehicles. Defendants did not sell the bow tie emblems. Defendants' packaging included clear markings indicating that the goods were not manufactured by General Motors, and its invoices also included disclaimers. Defendants sold generally to collision shops, which frequently decide which parts to purchase at the direction of insurance companies. On these facts, how would you balance the potential harms of post-sale confusion against the countervailing considerations?

4. ***Post-sale confusion of whom?*** When we speak of point-of-sale confusion, we are speaking of confusion at the point of sale (of course) on the part of the purchaser. When we speak of post-sale confusion, we are speaking of confusion after the point of sale, on the part of . . . whom? Any member of the public who might observe the mark? Any potential purchaser of goods and services of the type who might observe the mark? Does the answer to all of these questions depend on the nature of the goods and services? What if the confused parties are users of the product in a large firm, and under the firm's structure, the users have no influence on the purchase of the products? Judge Kennedy, dissenting in *Ferrari*, is clearly troubled by the problem of expanding the target group beyond prospective purchasers.

In *Lois Sportswear, U.S.A., Inc. v. Levi Strauss & Co.*, 799 F.2d 867 (2d Cir. 1986), Lois Sportswear sold jeans that included a back pocket stitching pattern that was similar to Levi's trademarked stitching pattern. Lois argued that its product tags clearly identified it as the source of the product, dispelling any point-of-sale confusion. The court pointed out that this argument ignored post-sale confusion. Consumers detached the product tags before wearing the jeans, so consumers who saw the jeans "outside of the retail store, perhaps being worn by a passer-by," might associate the jeans with Levi, and that association might influence the consumer's buying decisions. *Id.* at 872-873. Should the case have been decided differently if the evidence showed only that members of the public might associate the jeans with Levi, and not that the association necessarily influenced buying decisions? Compare *Munsingwear Inc. v. Jockey Int'l Inc.*, 31 U.S.P.Q.2d (BNA) 1146 (D. Minn. 1994) (less risk of public exposure, and hence less risk of post-sale confusion, in case involving underwear design as compared to case involving outerwear).

In *Hermes Int. v. Lederer De Paris Fifth Ave.*, 219 F.3d 104 (2d Cir. 2000), defendant Lederer sold knockoffs of plaintiff Hermes handbags. Lederer argued that sophisticated purchasers of Hermes bags would not believe that the Lederer knockoff was a genuine Hermes product, even if members of the general public would likely be unable to distinguish between the two products. The court rejected this argument, concluding that the views of the general public were determinative and finding that Lederer had "encourage[d] consumer confusion in the post-sale context." *Id.* at 107. Do you agree? For another case presenting the question of post-sale confusion in the context of industrial products, *see Dorr-Oliver, Inc. v. Fluid-Quip, Inc.*, 94 F.3d 376 (7th Cir. 1996) ("clamshell" product design for a corn starch washer).

5. **Ferrari *revisited?*** In another kit case, *Gen. Motors Corp. v. Urban Gorilla, LLC*, 500 F.3d 1222 (10th Cir. 2007), the court agreed that post-sale confusion was a viable theory for trade dress infringement cases (citing *Ferrari*), but declined the trade dress owner's motion for a preliminary injunction. At issue was General Motors' trade dress in the appearance of the chassis of the Hummer vehicle. Urban Gorilla sold steel "body kits" to be installed on top of a truck chassis, converting the truck to a military-style vehicle arguably reminiscent of the Hummer. Affirming the denial of a preliminary injunction, the Tenth Circuit panel noted that there was little or no evidence of intentional copying or actual confusion; consumers would exercise sufficient care to avoid confusion "given the high price of the Hummer"; and the channels of trade differed because "the parties were making inherently different kinds of products—a body kit requiring assembly and a finished vehicle." The district court had also seemed to conclude that the Hummer trade dress was not strong, and perhaps not even distinctive at all. Are you persuaded that the analysis in *Urban Gorilla* is both correct and consistent with *Ferrari*?

## Gibson Guitar Corp. v. Paul Reed Smith Guitars, LP
423 F.3d 539 (6th Cir. 2005)

Moore, Circuit Judge:

### I. Background

#### A. Facts

Certain basic facts are not in dispute. Gibson and PRS both manufacture high-quality guitars. Gibson has been in the business of manufacturing musical instruments for over 100 years. PRS founder Paul Reed Smith

("Smith") began manufacturing custom guitars in the mid-1970s and opened a guitar factory in 1985.

Gibson introduced at least one guitar model under the Les Paul (LP) name in 1952. Since that time, Gibson has offered a number of guitar models under the Les Paul name. At least some of these models were solid-body, single-cutaway electric guitars of the type at issue in this litigation.[3] [Eventually, Gibson secured a registration on the silhouette of the Les Paul guitar. When PRS began offering solid-body, single-cutaway electric guitar models, Gibson sued. The district court granted summary judgment on the infringement issue in favor of Gibson, and then enjoined PRS, although other issues remained to be litigated. The Sixth Circuit took the case on interlocutory appeal.]

II. Analysis

. . .

D. Trademark Infringement under the Lanham Act

The district court concluded that, with the exception of actual confusion (factor four) of the Sixth Circuit's multi-factor test, all factors on which it made a finding favored Gibson for summary judgment purposes. Because there was no evidence of point-of-sale confusion, factor four would have favored PRS. [cit.] However, the district court nonetheless concluded that "[g]iven the striking similarity of the PRS Singlecut to Gibson's Les Paul and the instant market recognition of Gibson's Les Paul . . . initial confusion would occur in the marketplace between parties' products as to the 'Singlecut' guitar's source. This factor favors Gibson." [cit.] Having made this substitution of "initial confusion" for actual confusion at the point of sale, the district court went on to determine that summary judgment in favor of Gibson was appropriate on Gibson's claim that the PRS Singlecut infringed the LP Trademark. We disagree with the district court's conclusion that "initial confusion" (or, as discussed below, any of its variants) can apply in this case. Moreover, as Gibson has conceded that no purchaser would be confused at the point of sale, we conclude that there is no theory of confusion upon which Gibson can prevail. In other words, Gibson's concession that there is no point-of-sale confusion

---

3. On appeal, neither party challenges the district court's description of the Les Paul single-cutaway guitar produced by Plaintiff-Appellee Gibson Guitar Corp. ("Gibson"):

> Gibson's Les Paul single cutaway guitar is a traditionally shaped guitar with a portion removed from [the] body of the guitar where the lower section of the fingerboard meets the body of the guitar. The term "cutaway guitar" denotes that portion of the guitar between the neck and its lower [] part, that appears to be missing from the natural, rounded body contour. The removal of this portion forms what is often referred to as the "horn." One aspect of this horn design is that the musician can access higher strings [and] position[s].
>
> As to other parts of a guitar, a pickup selector switch allows the player to change quickly the electromagnetic inputs to any one of three options: the pickup closest to the neck (the "neck pickup"), the one furthest from the neck (the "bridge pickup"), or a combination of both. The combination of volume and tone knobs for each pickup[] allow[s] the player to set the tone and volume of each pickup and[] switching among these pickups can achieve different sounds.

*Gibson Guitar Corp. v. Paul Reed Smith Guitars, LP,* 311 F. Supp. 2d 690, 694-95 (M.D. Tenn. 2004) ("*Gibson I*") (quotation marks, citations, and footnote omitted).

(which goes to the fourth *Frisch* factor, actual confusion) is dispositive of Gibson's claim. Accordingly, it is not necessary for us to discuss the remaining seven *Frisch* factors.

### 1. Gibson's Theories of Purchaser Confusion

Gibson argues that despite the lack of actual confusion at the point of sale, the district court's decision can be affirmed under a theory of either initial-interest confusion (the theory relied on by the district court), post-sale confusion, or some combination of the two. Initial-interest confusion takes place when a manufacturer improperly uses a trademark to create initial customer interest in a product, even if the customer realizes, prior to purchase, that the product was not actually manufactured by the trademark-holder. See *PACCAR Inc. v. TeleScan Techs., L.L.C.*, 319 F.3d 243, 253 (6th Cir. 2003); *see also* J. Thomas McCarthy, *McCarthy on Trademarks and Unfair Competition* §23:6 (4th ed. 1996 & Supp. 2005) ("McCarthy On Trademarks") (collecting cases). Post-sale confusion occurs when use of a trademark leads individuals (other than the purchaser) mistakenly to believe that a product was manufactured by the trademark-holder. See *Esercizio v. Roberts*, 944 F.2d 1235, 1245 (6th Cir. 1991), *cert. denied*, 505 U.S. 1219 (1992); *see also McCarthy on Trademarks* §23:7 (collecting cases). We conclude that neither initial-interest confusion, nor post-sale confusion, nor any combination of two, is applicable in this case.

a. Initial-Interest Confusion

The one case where we arguably have applied initial-interest confusion involved facts strikingly different than those involved in the present dispute. In *PACCAR*, we were faced with a dispute between Telescan, a company operating used-truck-locator web sites, and PACCAR, a truck manufacturer which also operated its own used-truck-locator website. In *PACCAR*, Telescan was using trademarks owned by PACCAR as part of the domain name of some of its used-truck-locator web sites. Noting that "[a]n infringing domain name has the potential to misdirect consumers as they search for web sites associated with the owner of a trademark," we suggested that initial-interest confusion analysis might appropriately be applied. *PACCAR*, 319 F.3d at 253. However, our decision that PACCAR had established a likelihood of success on the merits on the likelihood-of-confusion issue did not rest on initial-interest confusion.[15] Instead, we focused primarily on three other *Frisch* factors that we

---

15. The dissent reads far too much into our discussion of initial-interest confusion in *PACCAR Inc. v. TeleScan Techs., L.L.C.*, 319 F.3d 243, 253 (6th Cir. 2003), which is specifically in reference to a dispute over Internet domain-names. . . .

The three cases we cited in support of the initial-interest-confusion comment in *PACCAR* are also Internet cases. [cit.] Our suggestion that initial-interest-confusion doctrine applies to disputes over Internet domain names does not mean (as the dissent seems suggest) that "initial interest confusion is a recognized theory of relief generally for [all types of] trademark infringements."

To the contrary, the applicability of the initial-interest-confusion doctrine outside of the Internet context is an issue of first impression in our circuit. Although other circuits have applied the initial-interest-confusion doctrine to find trademark infringement based on use of a deliberately deceptive name or logo, [cit.], we are not aware of any circuit that has applied the initial-interest-confusion doctrine to a trademark on a product's shape.

The potential ramifications of applying this judicially created doctrine to product-shape trademarks are different from the ramifications of applying the doctrine to trademarks on a product's name, a company's name, or a company's logo. [cit.] Specifically, there are only a limited number

judged to be particularly important in an Internet-domain-name case. *See id.* at 254-55. As always, our concern was with "whether the defendant's use of the disputed mark is likely to cause confusion among consumers regarding the origin of the goods offered by the parties." *Id.* at 249 (quotations omitted). Other circuits applying the initial-interest confusion doctrine have generally focused on that same issue: whether the consumer might be misled about the source of the relevant product or service.[16]

---

of shapes in which many products can be made. A product may have a shape which is neither functional nor generic (and hence which can be trademarked) but nonetheless is still likely to resemble a competing product when viewed from the far end of a store aisle. Thus, many legitimately competing product shapes are likely to create some initial interest in the competing product due to the competing product's resemblance to the better-known product when viewed from afar. In other words, application of the initial-interest-confusion doctrine to product shapes would allow trademark holders to protect not only the actual product shapes they have trademarked, but also a "penumbra" of more or less similar shapes that would not otherwise qualify for trademark protection.

In response, the dissent suggests that product-shape trademark-holders be required to demonstrate "that its product shape identifies its source when viewed from the vantage point where the confusion is alleged to have occurred" prior to presenting evidence of initial-interest confusion. This strikes us as a needlessly complicated and unworkable inquiry. Particularly when the product is sold by many diverse retailers with varying display styles and store configurations, it would seem to require the district court to conduct an initial hearing as to whether each instance of alleged initial-interest confusion is admissible. As consumers will often observe a product from multiple different locations, it seems difficult to determine in any non-arbitrary manner what observation distances are appropriate when considering whether a given product shape creates initial-interest confusion (e.g., in front of the product shelf, from a store aisle, from the store's front door, etc.).

Finally, our concerns about the effect of extending the initial-interest-confusion doctrine to product-shape trademarks are particularly relevant in the summary-judgment context. To the extent we allow it to do so, evidence of initial-interest confusion comes into the eight-factor *Frisch* test as a substitute for evidence of actual confusion. If our belief that *nearly all* product-shape trademark-holders will be able to show an issue of fact as to whether a competing product creates initial-interest confusion is correct, application of the initial-interest-confusion doctrine in the product-shape context would make it substantially easier for product-shape trademark-holders to survive a defendant's summary-judgment motion than for plaintiffs alleging any other type of trademark infringement. (Contrary to the dissent's view, *see* Dissent at 556 n. 7, product-shape trademark-holders are perfectly capable of protecting their rights without the initial-interest-confusion doctrine: they must simply show, for example, that the marks are sufficiently similar or that purchasers exercise sufficiently little care in choosing a product to show confusion at the point of sale.) Given severe anti-competitive effects such a decision could have, we do not believe it is appropriate to extend the initial-interest-confusion doctrine in this manner.

Given the limited fact situation we have before us, we do *not* go so far as to hold that there is *never* a circumstance in which it would be appropriate to apply the initial-interest-confusion doctrine to a product-shape trademark. However, we are unable to imagine such a situation at this juncture, and we do hold that the doctrine cannot apply on the facts of this case.

16. *See, e.g., Playboy Enters., Inc. v. Netscape Communications Corp.*, 354 F.3d 1020, 1024-26 (9th Cir. 2004) (finding a likelihood of initial-interest confusion when survey results showed that many individuals running Internet searches for trademarked terms would incorrectly believe that banner ads run by competitors were sponsored by or affiliated with the trademark owner); *Elvis Presley Enters., Inc. v. Capece*, 141 F.3d 188, 204 (5th Cir. 1998) (applying initial-interest-confusion analysis to find trademark infringement by nightclub operating under the name, "The Velvet Elvis," because confusion over whether the club was associated with Elvis Presley could "bring[] patrons in the door"); *Mobil Oil Corp. v. Pegasus Petroleum Corp.*, 818 F.2d 254, 259 (2d Cir. 1987) (approving district court finding of actual confusion based on "the likelihood that Pegasus Petroleum would gain crucial credibility in the initial phases of a deal" by using mark confusingly similar to Mobil's flying horse); *Grotrian, Helfferich, Schulz, Th. Steinweg Nachf. v. Steinway & Sons*, 523 F.2d 1331, 1342 (2d Cir. 1975) (concluding that company manufacturing pianos under the name "Grotrian-Steinweg" could be found to be infringing the "Steinway" trademark because of "the likelihood that a consumer, hearing the 'Grotrian-Steinweg' name and thinking it had some connection with 'Steinway,' would consider it on that basis"). *But see Brookfield Communications, Inc. v. West Coast Entm't*

Gibson essentially argues that the shape of the PRS guitar leads consumers standing on the far side of the room in a guitar store to believe they see Gibson guitars and walk over to examine what they soon realize are PRS guitars. *See, e.g.,* J.A. at 1451 (Carter Dep.) ("Just looking at the guitars on the wall, I initially thought I was looking at Les Pauls, and[] on a closer look, I saw I wasn't."). We decline to adopt such a broad reading of the initial-interest-confusion doctrine. Many, if not most, consumer products will tend to appear like their competitors at a sufficient distance. Where product shapes themselves are trademarked, such a theory would prevent competitors from producing even *dissimilar* products which might appear, from the far end of an aisle in a warehouse store, somewhat similar to a trademarked shape. Accordingly, we hold that initial-interest confusion cannot substitute for point-of-sale confusion on the facts of this case.

[The court directed that summary judgment should be granted in favor of PRS.]

KENNEDY, Circuit Judge, concurring in part and dissenting in part:

I agree that the district court erred in granting summary judgment in favor of Gibson and I also agree that Gibson cannot maintain its trademark infringement claim either on a theory of likelihood of confusion at the point-of-sale (for it has disclaimed that a consumer could be confused at the point-of-sale)[1] or on a theory of post-sale confusion.[2] However, because I believe that a product shape trademark holder should be able to present evidence to maintain a trademark infringement claim on the theory of initial-interest confusion, I dissent with respect to this issue.

First, this court has recognized initial-interest confusion as an infringement under the Lanham Act. *See PACCAR Inc., v. Telescan Technologies, L.L.C.*, 319 F.3d 243, 253 (6th Cir. 2003) (citing *Eli Lilly & Co. v. Natural Answers, Inc.*, 233 F.3d 456, 464 (7th Cir. 2000) ("Such confusion, which is actionable as an infringement under the Lanham Act, occurs when a consumer is lured to a product by its similarity to a known mark, even though the consumer realizes the true identity and origin of the product before consummating a

---

*Corp.*, 174 F.3d 1036, 1062 (9th Cir. 1999) (concluding that use of the trademark "MovieBuff" in metatags of a competitor's website resulted in a likelihood of initial-interest confusion even without confusion as to source).

1. The majority states, "Gibson's concession that there is no point-of-sale confusion (which goes to the fourth *Frisch* factor, actual confusion) is dispositive of Gibson's claim." I believe that what is dispositive of any trademark infringement claim brought on a theory of likelihood of confusion at the point-of-sale is not Gibson's concession of the fourth *Frisch* factor, which goes to evidence of actual confusion, but rather Gibson's concession that there is no likelihood of consumer confusion at the point-of-sale, which is the ultimate issue to which the *Frisch* factors are used as a guide to help address when analyzing a trademark infringement claim brought under a theory of likelihood of confusion at the point-of-sale.

2. The last sentence of the post-sale confusion section reads, "[P]ost-sale confusion cannot serve as a substitute for point-of-sale confusion in this case." I view the post-sale confusion theory of relief not, when applicable, as serving as a substitute for point-of-sale confusion, but rather as a distinct theory of relief. When the alleged consumer confusion takes place at the point-of-sale, the ultimate issue is likelihood of confusion at the point-of-sale, in which the plaintiff will introduce evidence of point-of-sale confusion. However, when the alleged consumer confusion takes place in the marketplace (post-sale), then the ultimate issue is likelihood of post-sale confusion, in which the plaintiff introduces evidence of post-sale confusion.

purchase.").³ Second, a product shape can serve as a trademark, i.e., it can identify the source of the product. [cit.] Since a product shape can serve as a trademark, and since initial interest confusion is a recognized theory of relief generally for trademark infringements, I believe that a product shape trademark holder whose product shape does in fact identify the product's source should not be precluded from presenting evidence that a competitor's product shape causes consumers to be attracted to it because of its similarity to a trademark holder's mark.

The majority's reason for rejecting the application of initial interest confusion to product shapes is based upon the concern that since many product shapes within the same category will appear similar when viewed from a sufficient distance, if the initial-interest confusion doctrine were applied to product shapes, a product shape trademark holder could prevent competitors from producing even dissimilar products that appeared from a sufficient distance to be somewhat similar to a trademarked shape. This concern, however, is misplaced. Evidence that a competitor's product shape is similar to a trademark holder's product shape when viewed from afar is irrelevant unless the product shape trademark holder maintains that its product shape identifies its source when viewed from afar. For if a product shape trademark holder does not assert that its product shape identifies its source when viewed from a certain distance, then any alleged confusion between the trademark holder's product shape and a competitor's product shape would not support the trademark holder's claim for infringement. If a product shape trademark holder does assert that its product shape serves to identify the product's source when viewed from a distance where many competitor products appear substantially the same, then this will be evidence that the trademark holder's product shape does not identify its source. If most product shapes in the same product category have similar shapes, a product shape trademark holder will have a difficult time establishing that its trademark identifies the source of its product when viewed from afar, for the further one is away from a product, the more similar products in the same category will look to each other and, thus, the less likely a product shape will identify the source of the product (i.e., serve as a trademark) from that vantage point.⁴ In other words, a product shape trademark holder will not be able to present probative evidence of initial interest confusion unless it first shows that its product shape identifies its

---

3. The majority, in footnote 15, explains that *PACCAR*'s discussion of initial interest confusion was specifically in reference to a dispute over internet-domain names. Obviously, as applied in that case, the doctrine's application related to a company's name trademark as used in an internet-domain name. All trademarks, whether they be a company's name, logo, or a product shape, do the same thing: they identify the source of a good. Since we (and many other circuits) have recognized the doctrine, the majority must explain why this recognized doctrine should not apply to trademarked product shapes. I find the majority's explanation unpersuasive.

4. The majority repeats its concern underlying its rationale for rejecting the application of initial interest confusion to product shapes in footnote 15 by noting that since many competing products will create initial interest due to their resemblance with a trademarked product shape when viewed from afar, a trademark product shape holder would be able to protect a "penumbra" of more or less similar shapes. If there exists a "penumbra" of products in the marketplace with shapes similar to a trademarked product shape when viewed from afar, then the trademarked product shape would likely fail to identify its source. If there does not exist a "penumbra" of products with shapes similar to a trademarked product shape when viewed from afar, and if the product shape does identify its source when viewed from that vantage point, and if the

source when viewed from the vantage point where the confusion is alleged to have occurred.

Thus, this preliminary question (whether a product shape identifies its source when viewed from the point where the confusion is alleged to have occurred), when in dispute, as it is here, must be addressed before determining if there is an issue of fact as to whether a competitor's product shape causes initial interest confusion due to its similarity to a trademark holder's product shape.[5] For if the product shape does not identify its source, then, logically, there can be no confusion as to the source of the product due to the product's shape, since, in such a case, a consumer would not associate the product's shape with its source.

Here, PRS argues that, as there are only a few general shapes in which guitars are made, and since there are numerous single-cutaway style guitars in the market, a consumer would not, and, indeed, could not, identify the source of a guitar on the basis of its shape. Although PRS would likely prevail on this issue, I cannot say, in light of the record as developed, that it has met its burden establishing that there is no genuine issue of material fact as to whether the shape of Gibson's guitar identifies its source.

Since the district court incorrectly analyzed the issue of whether Gibson's trademark served to identify its source from the distance where the confusion was alleged to have occurred, I would remand for consideration of this issue.[6] If it were found that the shape of Gibson's guitar does serve to identify its source from the distance where the confusion is alleged to have occurred, then I

---

functionality doctrine does not prevent the application of the initial interest confusion doctrine when such confusion is alleged, then I believe a product shape trademark holder should be able to maintain a trademark infringement claim on the theory of initial interest confusion.

5. The majority views this inquiry as "needlessly complicated and unworkable." I view it as essential. Since, as noted before, the purpose of every trademark is to identify the source of its good, if a trademark does not identify its source, a trademark holder cannot successfully prosecute a trademark infringement claim. If a product shape trademark holder believes that a competitor's product causes confusion as to its source due to the competitor's products resemblance to the trademark holder's product shape when viewed from a store's aisle or front-door, then the product shape trademark holder will need to establish that its trademark identifies its source when viewed from those perspectives for any evidence of such confusion to support its claim. Thus, the relevant observation distance or location for determining whether the trademark holder's product shape identifies its source is from whatever distance or location the trademark holder alleges confusion occurred.

It is true, of course, that a product shape trademark holder could argue that a competitor's product causes confusion as to its source when viewed from varying perspectives. Assuming the defendant argues that the trademark holder's product shape does not identify its source when viewed from any of those perspectives, the court will need to address this argument. In this case, the only relevant allegation of initial-interest confusion is from Gibson's expert, who claimed that upon entering Gruhn's Guitar store in Nashville, he looked at what he thought was a wall of Gibson Les Paul guitars to discover, upon closer inspection, that the guitars were actually PRS Singlecuts. Since PRS argues that Gibson's guitar shape does not identify its source, Gibson must establish that its shape does identify its source from the perspective where the alleged confusion occurred. Ultimately, Gibson may not be able to succeed in establishing this point, but PRS has not met its burden to be entitled to summary judgment.

6. The district court made two fundamental errors with respect to its analysis of this issue. First, the district court improperly considered factors beyond the shape of Gibson's guitar, such as knob placement and color, in determining that Gibson's trademark identified its source, since Gibson's trademark consists only of the shape of the guitar. And second, the district court improperly concluded that since evidence of widespread use of similar marks "is not sufficient to rebut as a matter of law the presumption" that an incontestable mark identifies its source, such evidence "does not warrant further consideration." 311 F. Supp. 2d 690, 718. Rather, this evidence, which

believe that Gibson should be entitled, just as any other trademark holder would be, to present evidence that a competitor's use of a similar mark causes confusion as to the source of the competitor's product.[7]

Thus, I respectfully dissent.

## NOTES AND QUESTIONS

1. *Initial-interest confusion for nonverbal marks.* Should courts refuse to apply initial-interest confusion to nonverbal marks? Do the majority's arguments remind you of rationales used in *Wal-Mart* (Chapter 2) to eliminate protection for product design trade dress based upon inherent distinctiveness? If there is a connection, should courts refuse to apply initial-interest confusion only to product designs, as opposed to product packaging?

2. *Proving initial-interest confusion for nonverbal marks.* The *Gibson* dissent suggests that proof of instances of initial-interest confusion for product shapes could be established by assessing consumers' perceptions as viewed from the vantage point where the confusion allegedly occurred. In footnote 15, the majority criticizes this approach as "needlessly complicated and unworkable." Is it materially more complicated than surveying consumer perceptions for actual confusion under other confusion theories, such as point-of-sale confusion? If it is, does this argue for eliminating initial-interest confusion for nonverbal marks altogether, as opposed to searching for a more workable methodology for proving instances of initial-interest confusion?

3. *Post-sale confusion.* Gibson also argued that there was a likelihood of post-sale confusion. The court rejected the post-sale confusion theory on the grounds that PRS guitars were not clearly inferior goods as compared to Gibson guitars, citing the *Ferrari* case. Do you agree with the *Gibson* court's view of *Ferrari*?

4. *Smoky-bar confusion?* Gibson also advanced an argument that the court rather skeptically characterized as a "smoky-bar" confusion theory:

> Finally, Gibson argues that, taken together, the initial-interest-confusion and post-sale-confusion doctrines should be extended to include something that we can only describe as a "smoky-bar theory of confusion." . . . In the smoky-bar context, . . . Gibson does not suggest that consumer confusion as to the manufacturer of a PRS guitar would lead a potential purchaser to consider purchasing a PRS, rather than a Gibson, or that Gibson's reputation is harmed

---

goes to the heart of the issue of whether Gibson's shape can identify its source, deserved significant consideration, even if such evidence were found not to be sufficient as a matter of law to establish that Gibson's mark does not identify its source.

7. If the initial interest confusion doctrine were not applicable to product shape trademarks, I believe that product shape trademark holders would be put to a significant disadvantage compared to non-product shape trademark holders since this type of confusion is likely the only type of confusion that could arise with product shapes. It will be the rare case for there to exist a likelihood of confusion with respect to product shape trademarks at the point of sale since any confusion created by a product's similar shape will be dispelled at the point of sale, as most products will have a distinguishing feature that is identifiable from this vantage point, such as its producer's name. Thus, if initial interest confusion were not a viable theory upon which a product shape trademark holder could proceed, a product shape trademark holder may be quite limited, if not foreclosed, from successfully prosecuting a trademark infringement claim.

> by poor-quality PRS guitars. Rather, Gibson argues that this confusion occurs when potential purchasers see a musician playing a PRS guitar and believe it to be a Gibson guitar:
>> In the context of guitar sales, initial interest confusion is of real consequence. Guitar manufacturers know that they can make sales by placing their guitars in the hands of famous musicians. On a distant stage, a smoky bar, wannabe musicians see their heroes playing a guitar they then want.
>
> Gibson Br. at 20-21. As Gibson concedes that PRS produces high-quality guitars, we do not believe such an occurrence could result in confusion harmful to Gibson. If a budding musician sees an individual he or she admires playing a PRS guitar, but believes it to be a Gibson guitar, the logical result would be that the budding musician would go out and purchase a Gibson guitar. Gibson is helped, rather than harmed, by any such confusion.

*Gibson*, 423 F.3d at 552-53. Do you agree with the court's disposal of Gibson's so-called smoky-bar argument? Does it make sense to distinguish between this argument and Gibson's initial-interest confusion argument?

5. *Other theories: reverse confusion.* In a typical confusion allegation, a senior mark owner claims that a junior entrant is using a mark that is confusingly similar to the senior's mark, such that consumers are likely to conclude that the junior's goods or services originate with, or are affiliated with, the senior. This is "forward" confusion. Courts have also recognized a theory of "reverse confusion." In a claim of reverse confusion, a senior mark owner claims that a junior entrant is using a mark that is confusingly similar to the senior's mark, and that the junior entrant is so saturating the market that the junior entrant overwhelms the senior. As a result, consumers are likely to conclude that the *senior* user's goods and services originate from the *junior* entrant — hence, the reference to "reverse" confusion. How should the likelihood of confusion analysis be adapted to fit the reverse-confusion theory? For an excellent discussion, see *A&H Sportswear, Inc. v. Victoria's Secret Stores, Inc.*, 237 F.3d 198 (3d Cir. 2000). Would you expect reverse confusion to arise primarily with regards to word marks, or do you think that it is equally likely to occur with regards to trade dress? One point to consider relates to mark strength. Marks that are conceptually strong (highly distinctive), but commercially weak, are more prone to reverse confusion, at least in theory. After *Wal-Mart*, is it possible for protectable product design trade dress to be conceptually strong and commercially weak? Product packaging trade dress? For an illustration of a reverse-confusion claim in a pre–*Wal-Mart* case involving restaurant decor trade dress, see *Rainforest Café, Inc. v. Amazon, Inc.*, 86 F. Supp. 2d 886 (D. Minn. 1999).

## B. TRADE DRESS DILUTION AND OTHER NON-CONFUSION-BASED THEORIES

The likelihood-of-confusion cause of action is the primary vehicle for vindicating trade dress rights under the Lanham Act. An alternative cause of action, dilution, has been less explored in the area of trade dress, as explained below (Section B.1). Counterfeiting remedies may also be available, as discussed in Section B.2.

## 1. PROTECTION AGAINST DILUTION

Dilution is premised on the assumption that harm can accrue to a trademark owner even in the absence of consumer confusion. The concept is usually traced to an article by Frank I. Schechter, *The Rational Basis of Trademark Protection*, 40 HARV. L. REV. 813 (1927), who in turn relies on German antecedents. Schechter proposed that trademark law provide a remedy preventing the dilution of "unique" marks, which occurred whenever a junior user made use of an identical or very similar mark. Such junior uses, according to Schechter, harmed the mark owner by causing "the gradual whittling away or dispersion of the identity and hold upon the public mind of the mark or name by its use upon non-competing goods." *Id.* at 825.

The examples that Schechter offered, and the examples most commonly surfacing in subsequent legislative debates, involved the use of very famous word marks on goods that were remote from those of the trademark owner. Little has been said about the applicability of the dilution concept to nonverbal marks. The common examples are particularly hard to adapt for cases involving product design trade dress, where the defendant's goods are ordinarily the same as the plaintiff's goods.

Various states adopted antidilution laws, although the laws did not appear to provide protection as robust as the Schechter model envisioned. *See Ringling Bros.-Barnum & Bailey Combined Shows, Inc. v. Utah Div. of Travel Dev.*, 170 F.3d 449 (4th Cir.), *cert. denied*, 528 U.S. 923 (1999) (describing state law antidilution causes of action). In 1995, Congress passed the Federal Trademark Dilution Act, providing a cause of action for dilution in the Lanham Act for the first time. Congress amended the dilution laws in 2006, as detailed below.

LANHAM ACT
Section 43(c) [15 U.S.C. §1125(c)] (2006)

(c) Dilution by Blurring; Dilution by Tarnishment—

(1) INJUNCTIVE RELIEF—Subject to the principles of equity, the owner of a famous mark that is distinctive, inherently or through acquired distinctiveness, shall be entitled to an injunction against another person who, at any time after the owner's mark has become famous, commences use of a mark or trade name in commerce that is likely to cause dilution by blurring or dilution by tarnishment of the famous mark, regardless of the presence or absence of actual or likely confusion, of competition, or of actual economic injury.

(2) DEFINITIONS—

(A) For purposes of paragraph (1), a mark is famous if it is widely recognized by the general consuming public of the United States as a designation of source of the goods or services of the mark's owner. In determining whether a mark possesses the requisite degree of recognition, the court may consider all relevant factors, including the following:

 (i) The duration, extent, and geographic reach of advertising and publicity of the mark, whether advertised or publicized by the owner or third parties.

 (ii) The amount, volume, and geographic extent of sales of goods or services offered under the mark.

 (iii) The extent of actual recognition of the mark.

 (iv) Whether the mark was registered under the Act of March 3, 1881, or the Act of February 20, 1905, or on the principal register.

(B) For purposes of paragraph (1), "dilution by blurring" is association arising from the similarity between a mark or trade name and a famous mark that impairs the distinctiveness of the famous mark. In determining whether a mark or trade name is likely to cause dilution by blurring, the court may consider all relevant factors, including the following:

 (i) The degree of similarity between the mark or trade name and the famous mark.

 (ii) The degree of inherent or acquired distinctiveness of the famous mark.

 (iii) The extent to which the owner of the famous mark is engaging in substantially exclusive use of the mark.

 (iv) The degree of recognition of the famous mark.

 (v) Whether the user of the mark or trade name intended to create an association with the famous mark.

 (vi) Any actual association between the mark or trade name and the famous mark.

(C) For purposes of paragraph (1), "dilution by tarnishment" is association arising from the similarity between a mark or trade name and a famous mark that harms the reputation of the famous mark.

(3) EXCLUSIONS — The following shall not be actionable as dilution by blurring or dilution by tarnishment under this subsection:

(A) Any fair use, including a nominative or descriptive fair use, or facilitation of such fair use, of a famous mark by another person other than as a designation of source for the person's own goods or services, including use in connection with —

 (i) advertising or promotion that permits consumers to compare goods or services; or

 (ii) identifying and parodying, criticizing, or commenting upon the famous mark owner or the goods or services of the famous mark owner.

(B) All forms of news reporting and news commentary.

(C) Any noncommercial use of a mark.

(4) BURDEN OF PROOF — In a civil action for trade dress dilution under this Act for trade dress not registered on the principal register,

the person who asserts trade dress protection has the burden of proving that—

(A) the claimed trade dress, taken as a whole, is not functional and is famous; and

(B) if the claimed trade dress includes any mark or marks registered on the principal register, the unregistered matter, taken as a whole, is famous separate and apart from any fame of such registered marks.

(5) ADDITIONAL REMEDIES—In an action brought under this subsection, the owner of the famous mark shall be entitled to injunctive relief as set forth in section 34. The owner of the famous mark shall also be entitled to the remedies set forth in sections 35(a) and 36, subject to the discretion of the court and the principles of equity if—

(A) the mark or trade name that is likely to cause dilution by blurring or dilution by tarnishment was first used in commerce by the person against whom the injunction is sought after the date of enactment of the Trademark Dilution Revision Act of 2006; and

(B) in a claim arising under this subsection—

(i) by reason of dilution by blurring, the person against whom the injunction is sought willfully intended to trade on the recognition of the famous mark; or

(ii) by reason of dilution by tarnishment, the person against whom the injunction is sought willfully intended to harm the reputation of the famous mark.

(6) OWNERSHIP OF VALID REGISTRATION A COMPLETE BAR TO ACTION—The ownership by a person of a valid registration under the Act of March 3, 1881, or the Act of February 20, 1905, or on the principal register under this Act shall be a complete bar to an action against that person, with respect to that mark, that—

(A) (i) is brought by another person under the common law or a statute of a State; and

(ii) seeks to prevent dilution by blurring or dilution by tarnishment; or

(B) asserts any claim of actual or likely damage or harm to the distinctiveness or reputation of a mark, label, or form of advertisement.

(7) SAVINGS CLAUSE—Nothing in this subsection shall be construed to impair, modify, or supersede the applicability of the patent laws of the United States.

## NOTES AND QUESTIONS

1. *Actual v. likely dilution.* The 1995 version of Section 43(c) provided that the owner of a famous mark was entitled to injunctive relief against another person's commercial use of a mark or trade name if that use "causes dilution of the distinctive quality" of the famous mark. Courts split over whether that language created a likelihood-of-dilution standard or an actual

dilution standard. In *Moseley v. V Secret Catalogue, Inc.*, 537 U.S. 418 (2003), the Supreme Court resolved the split by ruling that Section 43(c) required a showing of actual dilution. Congress's 2006 dilution legislation, the Trademark Dilution Revision Act of 2006 (TDRA), responded to *Moseley*, and attempted to address other concerns. The TDRA provides that dilution liability follows from a showing of likelihood of dilution, thereby abrogating *Moseley*. What are the policy implications of the likelihood of dilution standard? Is the standard too generous to trademark owners, or do other statutory limitations (such as the fame prerequisite of §43(c)(2)(A) and the exclusions in §43(c)(3)) provide an adequate counterweight?

2. *The forms of dilution.* State antidilution law had recognized at least two forms of dilution—dilution by tarnishment and dilution by blurring. The House Report accompanying the 1995 federal legislation stated that the federal dilution cause of action "was designed to encompass all forms of dilution recognized by the courts, including dilution by blurring, by tarnishment and disparagement, and by diminishment." H.R. Rep. No. 104-374 at 2, 104th Cong., 1st Sess. (Nov. 30, 1995). In a case litigated under the 1995 federal legislation, Judge Posner described the theories of dilution by tarnishment and dilution by blurring:

> [The] concern [motivating one form of dilution is] that consumer search costs will rise if a trademark becomes associated with a variety of unrelated products. Suppose an upscale restaurant calls itself "Tiffany." There is little danger that the consuming public will think it's dealing with a branch of the Tiffany jewelry store if it patronizes this restaurant. But when consumers next see the name "Tiffany" they may think about both the restaurant and the jewelry store, and if so the efficacy of the name as an identifier of the store will be diminished. Consumers will have to think harder—incur as it were a higher imagination cost—to recognize the name as the name of the store. *Exxon Corp. v. Exxene Corp.*, 696 F.2d 544, 549-50 (7th Cir. 1982); *cf. Mead Data Central, Inc. v. Toyota Motor Sales, U.S.A., Inc.*, 875 F.2d 1026, 1031 (2d Cir. 1989) ("The [legislative] history [of New York's anti-dilution statute] disclosed a need for legislation to prevent such 'hypothetical anomalies' as 'Dupont shoes, Buick aspirin tablets, Schlitz varnish, Kodak pianos, Bulova gowns'"); [cit.]. So "blurring" is one form of dilution.
>
> Now suppose that the "restaurant" that adopts the name "Tiffany" is actually a striptease joint. Again, and indeed even more certainly than in the previous case, consumers will not think the striptease joint under common ownership with the jewelry store. But because of the inveterate tendency of the human mind to proceed by association, every time they think of the word "Tiffany" their image of the fancy jewelry store will be tarnished by the association of the word with the strip joint. [cit.] So "tarnishment" is a second form of dilution. Analytically it is a subset of blurring, since it reduces the distinctness of the trademark as a signifier of the trademarked product or service.

*Ty Inc. v. Perryman*, 306 F.3d 509, 511 (7th Cir. 2002).

Although it was fairly common for courts to apply tarnishment and blurring theories under the 1995 legislation, courts had not settled on a test for blurring, and in *Moseley*, the Supreme Court expressed skepticism about whether tarnishment was recognized under the federal legislation. Perhaps in response, Congress specifically defined tarnishment and blurring in the 2006 legislation, in Section 43(c)(2)(B). Is the test for blurring largely duplicative of the test for likelihood of confusion? Is this problematic?

3. *Trade dress dilution under the 2006 legislation.* The 1995 federal dilution legislation did not exclude trade dress from the dilution cause of action, but neither did it expressly embrace trade dress dilution. Dilution cases involving trade dress did arise, though not frequently in the reported decisions. *See, e.g., Nabisco, Inc. v. PF Brands, Inc.*, 191 F.3d 208 (2d Cir. 1999) (involving allegation that PF's fish-shaped GOLDFISH cheddar cheese crackers were diluted by Nabisco's cheddar cheese fish-shaped crackers); *cf. Planet Hollywood (Region IV), Inc. v. Hollywood Casino Corp.*, 80 F. Supp. 2d 815, 900 (N.D. Ill. 1999) (concluding that there can be no trade dress dilution as a matter of law, apparently because trade dress was not a "mark" within the meaning of Section 43(c) as it then existed). The 2006 legislation recognized trade dress dilution, but in a backhanded manner, via a provision on the burden of proof:

> (4) BURDEN OF PROOF—In a civil action for trade dress dilution under this Act for trade dress not registered on the principal register, the person who asserts trade dress protection has the burden of proving that—
> (A) the claimed trade dress, taken as a whole, is not functional and is famous; and
> (B) if the claimed trade dress includes any mark or marks registered on the principal register, the unregistered matter, taken as a whole, is famous separate and apart from any fame of such registered marks.

While this language certainly gives a statutory basis (albeit a weak one) for a trade dress dilution claim, is there a good policy basis for recognizing trade dress dilution? Should trade dress dilution apply to both product packaging and product design trade dress?

4. *Trade dress dilution—constitutional implications.* Does the application of Section 43(c) to product design trade dress present constitutional concerns? Might it provide the equivalent of patent protection with unlimited duration, in violation of the "limited times" proviso of Article I, Section 8, Clause 8? The issue was discussed only infrequently in pre-2006 cases. *See, e.g., I.P. Lund Trading ApS v. Kohler Co.*, 163 F.3d 27 (1st Cir. 1998) (discussing but not resolving the issue). What about the application of *state* dilution law to product design trade dress? Under *Bonito Boats* (*see* Chapter 1), would patent law preempt state dilution protection? *See adidas-America, Inc. v. Payless Shoesource, Inc.*, 546 F. Supp. 2d 1029, 1066-1068 (D. Or. 2008) (addressing the issue); *New York Stock Exchange, Inc. v. New York, New York Hotel, LLC*, 293 F.3d 550, 557 (2d Cir. 2002) (discussing state law dilution causes of action and federal dilution under the 1995 legislation). Section 43(c)(7) of the 2006 dilution legislation provides that nothing in the dilution subsection "shall be construed to impair, modify, or supersede the applicability of the patent laws of the United States."

5. *Exclusions.* The first major appellate decision under the TDRA involved claims of both trademark and trade dress dilution, but the court's discussion focused on whether the defendant's activities constituted an effective parody, whether those activities fell within the TRDA's exclusions (particularly

Section 43(c)(3)(A)), and the appropriate analyses of blurring and tarnishment in a case involving parody. *See Louis Vuitton Malletier S.A. v. Haute Diggity Dog, LLC,* 507 F.3d 252 (4th Cir. 2007). We discuss these matters in general below, in Section C.

## 2. PROTECTION AGAINST COUNTERFEITING

U.S. law now contains a broad range of remedies, some quite robust, for trademark counterfeiting. The counterfeiting provisions do not exclude trade dress, and indeed, counterfeiting activities often involve trade dress. The Lanham Act provides for civil remedies against trademark counterfeiting. Lanham Act §32(1)(a), the infringement provision for registered marks, specifically refers to counterfeiting:

> Any person who shall, without the consent of the registrant—use in commerce any reproduction, *counterfeit*, copy, or colorable imitation of a registered mark. . . .

(emphasis supplied). Lanham Act §45, in turn, defines a "counterfeit" as follows:

> A "counterfeit" is a spurious mark which is identical with, or substantially indistinguishable from, a registered mark.

Thus, "counterfeiting" for purposes of Lanham Act liability may be understood as a species of trademark infringement, albeit an especially virulent one in that it involves close copying of a registered mark. In addition, Lanham Act §42 forbids importation of any goods that "copy or simulate" a trademark registered with the PTO, and Lanham Act §43(b) prohibits the importation of goods "marked or labeled in contravention of" Section 43(a) (which covers unregistered marks). *See generally Ross Cosmetics Dist. Ctr. Inc. v. United States,* 34 U.S.P.Q.2d (BNA) 1758 (C.I.T. 1994).

In recognition of the fact that an ordinary civil injunction or damages judgment may be difficult to enforce against a counterfeiter, Lanham Act §34(d) provides that under specified conditions, the trademark owner may obtain an ex parte seizure order against a counterfeiter. Lanham Act §35(b) provides for treble damages and attorneys' fees "in the case of any violation of section 32(1)(a) of this Act . . . that consists of intentionally using a mark or designation, knowing such mark or designation is a counterfeit mark . . . in connection with the sale, offering for sale, or distribution of goods or services." Lanham Act §34(c) provides that as an alternative to actual damages, trademark owners may elect statutory damages in cases "involving the use of a counterfeit mark . . . in connection with the sale, offering for sale, or distribution of goods or services." Section 34(c) specifies statutory damages amounts, ranging from $500 to $1,000,000 per type of good. The extraordinary remedies provided in Sections 34 and 35 against counterfeiters all rely on a slightly tighter definition of "counterfeit," laid out in Section 34(d)(1)(B). This definition conforms to the definition of "counterfeit" used in criminal statutes, as discussed below.

Perhaps in response to the inadequacy of civil remedies against counterfeiting, Congress enacted the Trademark Counterfeiting Act of 1984, creating federal criminal penalties for trademark counterfeiting (now codified in Title 18 U.S.C.). Section 2320 provides criminal penalties for anyone who "intentionally traffics or attempts to traffic in goods or services and knowingly uses a counterfeit mark on or in connection with such goods or services." 18 U.S.C. §2320(a). In *United States v. Foote,* 413 F.3d 1240 (10th Cir. 2005), the court held that this language was not limited to point-of-sale confusion, but extended also to post-sale confusion. Section 2320(e)(1) supplies the applicable definition of "counterfeit," specifying that a counterfeit mark is a spurious mark "the use of which is likely to cause confusion, to cause mistake, or to deceive." 18 U.S.C. §2320(e)(1)(A)(iii). In March 2006, the Stop Counterfeiting in Manufactured Goods Act became law. The Act amended 18 U.S.C. §2320 in various ways, including by the addition of language prohibiting the sale of "labels, patches, stickers, wrappers, badges, emblems, medallions, charms, boxes, containers, cans, cases, hangtags, documentation, or packaging of any type or nature, knowing that a counterfeit mark has been applied thereto."

## C. PERMISSIBLE USE OF ANOTHER'S TRADE DRESS

### HERMAN MILLER, INC. v. A. STUDIO S.R.L.
2006 WL 1307904 (W.D. Mich. 2006)

ROBERT HOLMES BELL, District Judge:

I.

Herman Miller is a manufacturer of home and office furniture. . . . [T]his case involves the lounge chair and ottoman designed by Eames for Herman Miller in 1956. The chair consists of a curved, molded wood shell, a five-legged swivel base, and black leather upholstery. The parties agree that the lounge chair and ottoman is Eames' most well known design and is recognized as one of the most significant furniture designs of the 20th century. By way of illustrating the lounge chair's preeminence, it is part of the Museum of Modern Art's permanent collection. Since the lounge chair was first produced, Herman Miller has sold over 100,000 chairs in the United States. The design of the lounge chair has never been the subject of a patent, however, in 2003, Herman Miller registered the design configuration of the lounge chair with the United States Patent and Trademark Office.

The defendant in this case, Studio, is an Italian furniture company that began operating in 1993. Studio markets furniture reproductions of "modern classic design." . . . Studio manufactures and sells an exact copy of the lounge chair and ottoman designed by Charles Eames and sold by Herman Miller. The lounge chair and ottoman produced by Studio is virtually indistinguishable from the piece manufactured by Herman Miller.

Studio has marketed the lounge chair in both the United States and internationally through various promotional materials, including, since 2000, an internet website[, and catalogues. One such catalogue] includes photographs of the seven furniture pieces originally designed by Eames that Studio has copied and markets for sale, including the lounge chair. The lounge chair is pictured with the name "Charles Eames" in the upper right hand corner and "ALIVAR," Studio's trademark, in the lower left hand corner.

[Herman Miller sued for trade dress infringement, and the Studio asserted that its use of the lounge chair was permissible under the fair use defense.]

### III.

### A. The Fair Use Defense

Section 33(b)(4) of the Lanham Act permits a party in an infringement case to defend on the ground that its use of "the name, term, or device charged to be an infringement is a use, otherwise than as a mark, . . . of a term or device which is descriptive of and used fairly and in good faith only to describe the goods or services of such party, or their geographic origin." 15 U.S.C. §1115(b)(4); *Rock and Roll Hall of Fame and Museum, Inc. v. Gentile Prods.*, 134 F.3d 749, 756 (6th Cir. 1998). This affirmative defense is commonly known as "fair use," and is a complete defense to liability under the Lanham Act, "even if a defendant's conduct would otherwise constitute infringement of another's trademarks." *Cosmetically Sealed Indus., Inc. v. Chesebrough-Pond's USA Co.*, 125 F.3d 28, 30 (2d Cir. 1997).

The fair use defense is a recognition of the fact that trademark protection does not grant the trademark holder a monopoly over the word, image, or device chosen as a trademark, but only grants the holder the exclusive right over the secondary meaning of the mark. *See, e.g., Brother Records, Inc. v. Jardine*, 318 F.3d 900, 906 (9th Cir. 2003) ("[The fair use defense] in essence, forbids a trademark registrant to appropriate a descriptive term for his exclusive use and so prevent others from accurately describing a characteristic of their goods.") (quoting *New Kids on the Block v. News America Publ'g, Inc.*, 971 F.2d 302, 306 (9th Cir. 1992)); *United States Shoe Corp. v. Brown Group, Inc.*, 740 F. Supp. 196, 199 (S.D.N.Y. 1990) ("A user of a descriptive word may acquire the exclusive right to use that descriptive word *as an identifier* of the product or source. This, however, does not justify barring others from using the words in good faith *for descriptive purposes* pertinent to their products.") (emphasis in original); 2 J. Thomas McCarthy, *McCarthy on Trademarks and Unfair Competition* §11:45 (4th ed. 2004) ("McCarthy On Trademarks") ("The only right of exclusion that trademark law creates in a descriptive word is in the secondary, new, 'trademark' meaning of the word that plaintiff has created. The original, descriptive primary meaning is always available for use by others to describe their goods, in the interest of free competition."). Others may always use the word or image in its original, primary descriptive sense to describe their own product. *Palazzetti*, 270 F.3d at 319 ("Under the doctrine of 'fair use,' the holder of a trademark *cannot* prevent others from using the word that forms the trademark in its *primary* or *descriptive* sense.") (emphasis in original); *Car-Freshner Corp. v. S.C. Johnson & Son, Inc.*, 70 F.3d 267, 269 (2d Cir. 1995)

("It is a fundamental principle marking an outer boundary of the trademark monopoly that, although trademark rights may be acquired in a word or image with descriptive qualities, the acquisition of such rights will not prevent others from using the word or image in good faith in its descriptive sense, and not as a trademark."). In evaluating a defendant's fair use defense, the court must consider whether defendant has used the mark: (1) in its descriptive sense; and (2) in good faith. *ETW Corp. v. Jireh Publ'g, Inc.*, 332 F.3d 915, 920 (6th Cir. 2003); *Packman v. Chicago Tribune Co.*, 267 F.3d 628, 639 (7th Cir. 2001); *Review Directories, Inc. v. McLeodusa Publ'g Co.*, 236 F. Supp. 2d 810, 812 (W.D. Mich. 2001) (Enslen, J.). For purposes of this motion, Studio does not dispute that Herman Miller has valid trademark rights in the design configuration of the lounge chair and the name, Charles and Ray Eames.

1. Fair Use of the Lounge Chair

The first issue is whether Studio is using the lounge chair descriptively and "otherwise than as a mark." 15 U.S.C. §1 115(b)(4); *ETW Corp.*, 332 F.3d at 920. Studio uses the lounge chair, Herman Miller's trademark, as a product for sale to the public. This use of an exact copy of another's trademark as a commercial product is unlike any descriptive use in previous cases that have been brought to the attention of the Court. The novelty of this purported fair use is some indication of its validity. In determining whether a defendant's use of a trademark is descriptive, courts often assess "the manner in which the mark is used with respect to the product or service sold by the alleged infringer." *EMI Catalogue P'ship v. Hill, Holliday, Connors, Cosmopulos Inc.*, 228 F.3d 56, 65 (2d Cir. 2000). Such an inquiry is complicated in this case because Studio is not using the trademark "with respect to" or in connection with its own product, it is using an exact replica of Herman Miller's trademark as its product. While Studio has presented evidence regarding it's [sic] non-trademark usage of the lounge chair, it has assiduously avoided explaining the descriptive manner in which it uses Herman Miller's trademark. Such an omission is yet another strong indication of the validity of Studio's position in this case.

Studio makes passing reference to its descriptive use of the lounge chair, explaining that it is the "ultimate example of truly descriptive use." Superlatives aside, no further explanation is given regarding the aspects of Studio's product that the use of the lounge chair describes. *EMI Catalogue P'ship*, 228 F.3d at 65 ("The fair use doctrine permits use of a protected mark by others *to describe certain aspects of the user's own goods*.") (emphasis added). In Studio's reply brief it sheds additional light on its purported descriptive use explaining, "since Miller is claiming the entire configuration . . . of the chair and ottoman as its mark, the design of the chair and ottoman describe the chair and ottoman." Def.'s Reply Br. at 1 n. 3 (Docket # 110) (citation omitted). This too is unsatisfactory and fails to adequately address the purported descriptive use of the lounge chair. It is nothing more than circular logic. Furthermore, if such reasoning were accepted, the fair use exception would swallow the law of trademark in its entirety. In the absence of any showing that Studio is using Herman Miller's trademark to describe Studio's product, the fair use defense cannot apply. *See Palazzetti*, 270 F.3d at 319; *McCarthy on Trademarks* §11:45 ("fair use analysis is appropriate where a defendant has used the plaintiff's mark *only to describe his own product*, and not at all to describe the plaintiff's product") (emphasis added).

Studio's inability to satisfactorily articulate its descriptive use may be attributable to the fact that it is difficult to conceive how the design configuration of the lounge chair can be used descriptively. The design configuration of a product is unlike a word mark which can clearly have both a secondary, trademark meaning as well as an original descriptive sense. A potential infringer can use a word mark in its original descriptive sense but cannot use the term in its secondary, trademark sense. The caselaw is replete with such permissible descriptive uses. *See, e.g., Cosmetically Sealed Indus., Inc.*, 125 F.3d at 30 (holding that defendant's use of the words "Seal it with a Kiss," was a fair use because it described an action "the sellers hope consumers will take, using their product"); *Sunmark, Inc. v. Ocean Spray Cranberries, Inc.*, 64 F.3d 1055 (7th Cir. 1995) (holding that defendant's use of the phrase "sweet-tart" was descriptive of two attributes of defendant's product, a fruit juice drink); *Packman*, 267 F.3d at 641 (noting that "[d]escriptive terms 'impart information directly'" and concluding that defendant's use of the phrase "The joy of six" was descriptive of a newsworthy event and the happiness associated with the Chicago Bulls' sixth NBA championship) (*quoting M.B.H Enter., Inc. v. WOKY, Inc.*, 633 F.2d 50, 54 (7th Cir. 1980); *Sports Authority, Inc. v. Abercrombie & Fitch, Inc.*, 965 F. Supp. 925 (E.D. Mich. 1997) (holding that defendant's use of term "authority" was a fair use because it described defendant's "century-long tradition of outfitting customers for the outdoors," and was not featured prominently); *Wonder Labs, Inc. v. Procter & Gamble Co.*, 728 F. Supp. 1058 (S.D.N.Y. 1990) (usage of the phrase "The dentists' choice for fighting cavities" was a fair use where it described an important aspect of defendant's toothpaste). Unlike the usage of a word mark in its original, descriptive sense, it is unclear how the design configuration of the lounge chair can have a primary, descriptive meaning. Without such descriptive capability, the fair use defense does not apply. *See Car-Freshner Corp.*, 70 F.3d at 269 ("It is true that the [fair use] doctrine can apply only to marks consisting of terms or images with descriptive qualities. That is because only such terms or images are capable of being used by others in their primary descriptive sense."); *Brother Records, Inc.*, 318 F.3d at 905 ("[T]he classic fair use defense . . . applies only to marks that possess both a primary meaning and a secondary meaning — and only when the mark is used in its primary descriptive sense rather than its secondary trademark sense.") (emphasis added); Restatement (Third) Of Unfair Competition §28 cmt. a ("Reasonable use of a descriptive term by another solely to describe the nature or characteristics of its own goods or services will not subject the user to liability for infringement.").

At least one court has extended the defense beyond words or phrases to include such things as shape of a product, that are used in a broader, descriptive sense. *See Car-Freshner Corp. [v. S.C. Johnson & Son, Inc.*, 70 F.3d 267, 270 (2d Cir. 1995)]. A review of the Second Circuit's decision further demonstrates that fair use is not applicable to this case. In *Car-Freshner*, plaintiff, an automotive air-freshener manufacturer, held trademark rights in the pine-tree shape of its product, a cardboard car air freshener. 70 F.3d at 268. Defendant, a home air freshener manufacturer, produced a plastic pine-tree shaped air freshener that plugged into an electrical outlet. *Id.* Plaintiff sued claiming trademark infringement and defendant asserted the fair use defense.

Although the district court granted summary judgment in defendant's favor on the ground of absence of likelihood of confusion, the Second Circuit affirmed based on the fair use defense. After noting that whether plaintiff's own usage of the trademark was descriptive was not a prerequisite for a finding of fair use, and that the focus is on defendant's use of the mark, the court held that defendant's use of the pine tree shape was descriptive. *Id.* at 270. The court explained that fair use permitted "others to use a protected mark to describe aspects of their own goods," so long as the use was in good faith and not as a mark. *Id.* In light of this, the court held that defendant's use was descriptive because it described two aspects of defendant's product: 1) the pine scent of the air freshening agent and 2) the Christmas season, because the pine tree is traditionally associated with the holiday and the product was sold during that season. *Id.* Consequently, the court held that defendant was protected by the fair use defense. *See also Cosmetically Sealed Indus., Inc.*, 125 F.3d at 30 (extending permissible descriptive use to include description of "an action that the sellers hope consumers will take" and holding that defendant's use of the words "Seal it with a Kiss" were within the fair use defense).

In this case, unlike *Car-Freshner* and the other cases cited above, there is no indication that Studio's use of the lounge chair describes an aspect of its product, an action to be taken, or any other broader, descriptive function. In short, Studio has not shown that it is using Herman Miller's trademark in a descriptive sense. While Studio has indicated that it uses the lounge chair in conjunction with its own "Alivar" trademark and uses the lounge chair in the same manner as other furniture reproductions, *see EMI Catalogue P'ship*, 228 F.3d at 64-65 (noting that a relevant factor in determining if a use is descriptive is the "physical nature of the use in terms of size, location, and other characteristics in comparison with the appearance of other descriptive matter or other trademarks.") (quoting Restatement (Third) Of Unfair Competition §28 cmt. c), this evidence does not overcome the absolute dearth of evidence or explanation regarding the descriptive nature of Studio's use. Accordingly, Studio cannot avail itself of the fair use defense because it has failed to show that it is using the lounge chair in a descriptive sense.

[Studio's motion for summary judgment on fair use was denied.]

## NOTES AND QUESTIONS

**1. *The descriptive fair use doctrine.*** As the *Herman Miller* case indicates, the doctrine of "descriptive" or "classic" fair use is well established in the common law, and a form of descriptive fair use doctrine also appears in the Lanham Act. Lanham Act §33(b)(4) provides that one of the preserved defenses, even in cases alleging infringement of marks covered by incontestable registrations, is

> (4) That the use of the name, term, or device charged to be an infringement is a use, otherwise than as a mark, of the party's individual name in his own business, or of the individual name of anyone in privity with such party, or of a

term or device which is descriptive of and used fairly and in good faith only to describe the goods or services of such party, or their geographic origin. . . .

The trademark fair use doctrine should be contrasted with its more well-known namesake, copyright fair use. The copyright fair use doctrine is codified at 17 U.S.C. §107, which provides that "the fair use of a copyrighted work . . . is not an infringement of copyright," and further provides that factors to be considered in determining copyright fair use include "(1) the purpose and character of the use, including whether such is of a commercial nature or is for nonprofit educational purposes; (2) the nature of the copyrighted work; (3) the amount and substantiality of the portion used in relation to the copyrighted work as a whole; and (4) the effect of the use upon the potential market for or value of the copyrighted work." *See* Chapter 7.

**2. *Descriptive fair use and the role of confusion.*** Although courts long ago accepted the descriptive fair use doctrine, a split developed over where to situate fair use relative to the analysis of confusion. The Ninth Circuit held that "the classic fair use defense is not available if there is a likelihood of customer confusion as to the origin of the product." *Cairns v. Franklin Mint Co.*, 292 F.3d 1139, 1151 (9th Cir. 2002); *accord Brother Records, Inc. v. Jardine*, 318 F.3d 900, 907 n.4 (9th Cir. 2003). In other words, if a trademark plaintiff could prove that a defendant's use was likely to cause confusion, the defendant was precluded from asserting that the use was fair. Other courts refused to accept the proposition that the existence of confusion negated a claim of fair use. The Supreme Court took up the question in *KP Permanent Make-Up, Inc. v. Lasting Impression I, Inc.*, 543 U.S. 111, 124 (2004), concluding that "a plaintiff claiming infringement of an incontestable mark must show likelihood of consumer confusion as part of the prima facie case, 15 U.S.C. §1115(b), while the defendant has no independent burden to negate the likelihood of any confusion in raising the affirmative defense that a term is used descriptively, not as a mark, fairly, and in good faith, §1115(b)(4)." On remand in *KP Permanent*, the Ninth Circuit confirmed that "the degree of customer confusion remains a factor in evaluating fair use." *KP Permanent Make-Up, Inc. v. Lasting Impression I, Inc.*, 408 F.3d 596, 598 (9th Cir. 2005). The Ninth Circuit laid out "the relevant factors for consideration by the jury" in determining fair use:

> . . . the degree of likely confusion, the strength of the trademark, the descriptive nature of the term for the product or service being offered by KP and the availability of alternate descriptive terms, the extent of the use of the term prior to the registration of the trademark, and any differences among the times and contexts in which KP has used the term.

*Id.* at 598.

**3. *Good faith.*** What evidence is there (if any) that the Studio in *Herman Miller* was using the chair configuration in good faith, even if it was using that configuration "descriptively"? In *Int'l Stamp Art, Inc. v. U. S. Postal Service*, 456 F.3d 1270, 1274-75 (11th Cir. 2006), the court observed that

> . . . other circuits have concluded that the standard for good faith for fair use is the same as the legal standard for good faith in any other trademark infringement context and that that standard asks whether the alleged infringer

intended to trade on the good will of the trademark owner by creating confusion as to the source of the goods or services. . . . No circuit has used any alternative standard, and we agree that this is the appropriate standard to use.

**4. *Functionality and fair use.*** In *Shakespeare Co. v. Silstar Corp. of America, Inc.*, 110 F.3d 234 (4th Cir. 1997), Shakespeare sold fishing rods and had registered the product's trade dress—specifically, a clear (or "whitish translucent") fiberglass tip and contrasting opaque shaft made of graphite. Silstar began marketing a rod having a similar tip and shaft, and Shakespeare sued. The parties initially battled over whether Shakespeare's registration could be cancelled for functionality, on the ground that clear tip and the opaque shaft constituted nothing more than the natural appearance of the components. The court held that the Lanham Act as it then existed did not allow a functionality challenge to an incontestable registration. (Congress has since amended the Lanham Act, as discussed in Chapter 3). On remand, Silstar transformed its functionality defense into a fair use defense. Silstar argued that it was acting in good faith: it was using a clear tip merely to inform buyers that the tip was made of fiberglass (and that the shaft was made of graphite), a matter of describing the qualities of the rods. Should Silstar prevail on this argument? In general, should a feature's functional characteristics (both de facto and de jure) be taken into account in assessing whether one's use of that feature is a fair use?

**5. *Repair and repackaging.*** Suppose that a party purchases genuine goods that bear trademarks or are subject to trade dress protection, and wants to repackage and resell them. Under what circumstances might the trademark/trade dress owner have a Lanham Act cause of action? In a leading case, *Prestonettes, Inc. v. Coty*, 264 U.S. 359 (1924), Prestonettes purchased Coty's powders and perfumes from authorized sources. As to the perfumes, Prestonettes rebottled and resold them, indicating on the label that Prestonettes was not connected with Coty, that Prestonettes had independently rebottled the product in New York, and that the contents of the bottle were specified Coty products. All of these assertions were true. As to the powders, Prestonettes added binder and subjected the powders to pressure, then sold the resulting product in a metal compact, again indicating on the label that Prestonettes was not affiliated with Coty and that Prestonettes had independently compounded the product from the original Coty product. The label also specified the constituents of the new product and their relative proportions. The Court concluded that a reseller should be entitled to refer "collaterally" to another's trademark using labeling that did not emphasize the other's trademark, but instead gave notice of the repackaging—e.g., by indicating "that the trade-marked product is a constituent in the article now offered as new and changed." *Id.* at 369. Some courts have held that where the resold product contains a latent defect (because the reseller has failed to comport with the original trademark owner's quality control standards), mere notice of the repackaging does not suffice to insulate the reseller from a Lanham Act claim. *Enesco Corp. v. Price/Costco Inc.*, 146 F.3d 1083 (9th Cir. 1998) (discussing relevant case law). Another related line of cases holds that repaired or refurbished goods can be resold under the original trademark as long as the resold goods bear labels giving the consumer some indication that the goods have been refurbished. *Champion Spark Plug Co. v. Sanders*, 331 U.S. 125 (1947). Cases such as *Prestonettes* and *Champion Spark Plug* focused on word marks. Would the presence of protectable trade dress generate a different analysis? Would that analysis be particularly difficult for product design trade dress?

### Mattel Inc. v. Walking Mountain Productions
353 F.3d 792 (9th Cir. 2003)

Pregerson, Circuit Judge:

#### Background

Thomas Forsythe, aka "Walking Mountain Productions," is a self-taught photographer who resides in Kanab, Utah. He produces photographs with social and political overtones. In 1997, Forsythe developed a series of 78 photographs entitled "Food Chain Barbie," in which he depicted Barbie in various absurd and often sexualized positions. Forsythe uses the word "Barbie" in some of the titles of his works. While his works vary, Forsythe generally depicts one or more nude Barbie dolls juxtaposed with vintage kitchen appliances. For example, "Malted Barbie" features a nude Barbie placed on a vintage Hamilton Beach malt machine. "Fondue a la Barbie" depicts Barbie heads in a fondue pot. "Barbie Enchiladas" depicts four Barbie dolls wrapped in tortillas and covered with salsa in a casserole dish in a lit oven.

In his declaration in support of his motion for summary judgment, Forsythe describes the message behind his photographic series as an attempt to "critique [] the objectification of women associated with [Barbie], and [][to] lambast [] the conventional beauty myth and the societal acceptance of women as objects because this is what Barbie embodies." He explains that he chose to parody Barbie in his photographs because he believes that "Barbie is the most enduring of those products that feed on the insecurities of our beauty and perfection-obsessed consumer culture." Forsythe claims that, throughout his series of photographs, he attempts to communicate, through artistic expression, his serious message with an element of humor.

Forsythe's market success was limited. He displayed his works at two art festivals — the Park City Art Festival in Park City, Utah, and the Plaza Art Fair in Kansas City, Missouri.[2] He promoted his works through a postcard, a business card, and a website. Forsythe printed 2000 promotional postcards depicting his work, "Barbie Enchiladas," only 500 of which were ever circulated. Of those that were circulated, some were distributed throughout his hometown of Kanab and some to a feminist scholar who used slides of Forsythe's works in her academic presentations. He also sold 180 of his postcards to a friend who owned a book store in Kanab so she could resell them in her bookstore and sold an additional 22 postcards to two other friends. Prior to this lawsuit, Forsythe

---

2. Additionally, Forsythe's works were chosen for display in various exhibitions, including the Dishman Competition at Lamar University in Texas, and the Through the Looking Glass Art Show in Los Alamos, New Mexico. Some of his "Food Chain Barbie" photographs were also selected for exhibition by the Deputy Director and Chief Curator of the Guggenheim Museum of Modern Art in New York.

received only four or five unsolicited calls inquiring about his work. The "Food Chain Barbie" series earned Forsythe total gross income of $3,659.[3]

Forsythe also produced 1,000 business cards which depicted "Champagne Barbie." His name and self-given title "Artsurdist" were written on the card. He used these cards at fairs and as introductions to gallery owners.

Finally, Forsythe had a website on which he depicted low resolution pictures of his photographs. The website was not configured for online purchasing. "Tom Forsythe's Artsurdist Statement," in which he described his intent to critique and ridicule Barbie, was featured on his website. His website also contained a prominent link to his biography.

[Mattel sued on various theories, including copyright and trademark infringement. The court granted summary judgment against Mattel on the copyright and trademark claims. Mattel appealed.]

## Discussion

### I.

[The court affirmed the grant of summary judgment against Mattel on the copyright claims, on the ground that Walking Mountain's use was a fair use under the copyright statute. See Chapter 7 for this portion of the court's analysis.]

### II.

We now address whether the district court erred in granting summary judgment in favor of Forsythe on Mattel's claims of trademark and trade dress infringement and dilution.

#### A. Trademark[12]

The limited purpose of trademark protections set forth in the Lanham Trade-Mark Act, 15 U.S.C. §1051 *et. seq.*, is to "avoid confusion in the marketplace" by allowing a trademark owner to "prevent[] others from duping consumers into buying a product they mistakenly believe is sponsored by the trademark owner." [*Mattel, Inc. v. MCA Records, Inc.*, 296 F.3d 894, 900 (9th Cir. 2002), *cert. denied*, 537 U.S. 1171 (2003)]. Trademark law aims to protect trademark owners from a false perception that they are associated with or endorse a product. See [*Cairns v. Franklin Mint Co.*, 292 F.3d 1139, 1149-50 (9th Cir. 2002)]. Generally, to assess whether a defendant has infringed on a plaintiff's trademark, we apply a "likelihood of confusion" test that asks whether use of the plaintiff's trademark by the defendant is "likely to cause confusion or to cause mistake, or to deceive as to the affiliation, connection, or association" of the two products. *Id.* at 1149 (quoting 15 U.S.C. §1125(a)(1)(A)).

As we recently recognized in *MCA*, however, when marks "transcend their identifying purpose" and "enter public discourse and become an integral part of our vocabulary," they "assume[] a role outside the bounds of trademark

---

3. Purchases by Mattel investigators comprised at least half of Forsythe's total sales.
12. A trademark is a limited property right in particular word, phrase, or symbol, 15 U.S.C. §1051, that "is used to identify a manufacturer or sponsor of a good or the provider of a service." *MCA*, 296 F.3d at 900.

law." 296 F.3d at 900. Where a mark assumes such cultural significance, First Amendment protections come into play. *Id.* In these situations, "the trademark owner does not have the right to control public discourse whenever the public imbues his mark with a meaning beyond its source-identifying function." *Id. See also New Kids on the Block v. News Am. Publ'g Inc.*, 971 F.2d 302, 307 (9th Cir. 1992).

As we determined in *MCA*, Mattel's "Barbie" mark has taken on such a role in our culture. 296 F.3d at 898-99. In *MCA*, Mattel brought an identical claim against MCA Records, producers of a song entitled "Barbie Girl" that contained lyrics that parodied and mocked Barbie. *Id.* at 894. Recognizing that First Amendment concerns in free expression are particularly present in the realm of artistic works, we rejected Mattel's claim. In doing so, we adopted the Second Circuit's First Amendment balancing test for applying the Lanham Act to titles of artistic works as set forth in *Rogers v. Grimaldi*, 875 F.2d 994, 999 (2d Cir. 1989). *MCA*, 296 F.3d at 902.

The *Rogers* balancing test requires courts to construe the Lanham Act "to apply to artistic works *only* where the public interest in avoiding consumer confusion *outweighs* the public interest in free expression." *Rogers*, 875 F.2d at 999 (emphasis added). Accordingly, the *Rogers* test prohibits application of the Lanham Act to titles of artistic works unless the title "has no artistic relevance to the underlying work whatsoever or, if it has some artistic relevance, unless the title explicitly misleads as to the source or the content of the work." *Id.*

Application of the *Rogers* test here leads to the same result as it did in *MCA*. Forsythe's use of the Barbie mark is clearly relevant to his work. *See MCA*, 296 F.3d at 902 ("[T]he use of Barbie in the song title clearly is relevant to the underlying work, namely, the song itself."). The Barbie mark in the titles of Forsythe's works and on his website accurately describe the subject of the photographs, which in turn, depict Barbie and target the doll with Forsythe's parodic message. *See id.* ("[T]he song is about Barbie and the values [the defendants] claim[] she represents."). The photograph titles do not explicitly mislead as to Mattel's sponsorship of the works. *See id.* ("The song title does not explicitly mislead as to the source of the work; it does not, explicitly or otherwise, suggest that it was produced by Mattel. The *only* indication that Mattel might be associated with the song is the use of Barbie in the title; if this were enough to satisfy this prong of the *Rogers* test, it would render *Rogers* a nullity." (emphasis in original)).

Accordingly, the public interest in free and artistic expression greatly outweighs its interest in potential consumer confusion about Mattel's sponsorship of Forsythe's works.

B. Trade dress

Mattel also claims that Forsythe misappropriated its trade dress in Barbie's appearance, in violation of the Lanham Act, 15 U.S.C. §1125. Mattel claims that it possesses a trade dress in the Superstar Barbie head and the doll's overall appearance. The district court concluded that there was no likelihood that the public would be misled into believing that Mattel endorsed Forsythe's photographs despite Forsythe's use of the Barbie figure.

Arguably, the Barbie trade dress also plays a role in our culture similar to the role played by the Barbie trademark—namely, symbolization of an unattainable ideal of femininity for some women. Forsythe's use of the Barbie trade dress, therefore, presumably would present First Amendment concerns similar to those that made us reluctant to apply the Lanham Act as a bar to the artistic uses of Mattel's Barbie trademark in both *MCA* and this case. But we need not decide how the *MCA/Rogers* First Amendment balancing might apply to Forsythe's use of the Barbie trade dress because we find, on a narrower ground, that it qualifies as nominative fair use.[14]

In the trademark context, we recently held that a defendant's use is classic fair use where "a defendant has used the plaintiff's mark *only* to describe his own product, *and not at all to describe the plaintiff's product.*" *Cairns*, 292 F.3d at 1151 (emphasis in original).[15] In contrast, a defendant's use of a plaintiff's mark is nominative where he or she "used the plaintiff's mark to describe the plaintiff's product, *even if the defendant's ultimate goal is to describe his own product.*" *Id.* (emphasis in original).[16] The goal of a nominative use is

---

14. We have never applied the *Rogers* First Amendment balancing test to trade dress infringement claims. Even if we were to try to balance Mattel's interest in its Barbie trade dress with Forsythe's First Amendment right to use the trade dress in his artistic works, it is not entirely clear whether the *Rogers* balancing test would be apposite. The only Lanham Act claim at issue in *Rogers* was "essentially" a §1125 "false advertising" claim that the defendant's movie *title* "Ginger and Fred" gave "the false impression that the film is about [Ginger] Rogers and [Fred] Astaire." *Rogers*, 875 F.2d at 1002. *Rogers* did not apply its First Amendment balancing test to—much less, even address—*trade dress*; trade dress was not at issue in that case. *See generally id. See also Cliff's Notes, Inc. v. Bantam Doubleday Dell Publ'g Group, Inc.*, 718 F. Supp. 1159, 1163 (S.D.N.Y.) ("*Rogers* did not concern the use of a design, or trade dress, registered pursuant to the Lanham Act, but instead dealt with the specific area of titles of literary works."), *vacated*, 886 F.2d 490 (2d Cir. 1989). There may be something unique about the use of a trademark in the title of a work that makes nontitular uses of trademarks or trade dress incompatible with the *Rogers* test. *Compare Merriam-Webster, Inc. v. Random House, Inc.*, 815 F. Supp. 691, 704 n. 16 (S.D.N.Y. 1993) (stating that the injunction of Random House's use of Merriam-Webster's dictionary jacket trade dress "does not implicate artistic expression in a manner analogous to that in [*Rogers*]"), *vacated on other grounds*, 35 F.3d 65 (2d Cir. 1994), *with Yankee Publ'g*, 809 F. Supp. at 278-82 (applying the *Rogers* balancing test to claim by publishers of *The Old Farmer's Almanac* that publisher of *New York* magazine infringed the *Almanac's* trade dress when *New York* styled its 1990 Christmas Gift issue after the *Almanac*). More importantly, if we were to apply the *Rogers* balancing test, we would have to grapple with First Amendment issues. By instead employing the nominative fair use test—which, incidentally works well in a case like this—we are following the time-honored tradition of avoiding constitutional questions where narrower grounds are available. [cit.] Thus, we leave the applicability of the Second Circuit's *Rogers* balancing test to trade dress infringement claims for another day.

15. In *Cairns*, we cited *In re Dual-Deck Video Cassette Recorder Anti-trust Litig.*, 11 F.3d 1460 (9th Cir. 1993), as a good example of *classic* fair use of another's trademark. *Cairns*, 292 F.3d at 1151 n. 9.

In [*Dual-Deck Video*], the defendant sold receivers to which two videocassette recorders could be attached and labeled the relevant terminals on the backs of its machines "VCR-1" and "VCR-2." We concluded that defendant's use of plaintiff's trademark "VCR-2," a descriptive mark that identified plaintiff's two-deck videocassette recorder, was descriptive of defendant's own product. Because defendant used plaintiff's mark in its primary, descriptive sense and in good faith, defendant's use was not an infringement.

*Brother Records, Inc. v. Jardine*, 318 F.3d 900, 906 (9th Cir. 2003) (citing *Dual-Deck*, 11 F.3d at 1462, 1467).

16. For a good example of *nominative* fair use of another's trademark, see *Cairns*, 292 F.3d at 1152-53. *See also, e.g., Abdul-Jabbar v. Gen. Motors Corp.*, 85 F.3d 407 (9th Cir. 1996) (applying nominative fair use analysis where the defendant automobile manufacture referred to the plaintiff, a basketball star who had won an award three years in a row, in a commercial for a car that also had won an award three years in a row); *Volkswagenwerk Aktiengesellschaft v. Church*, 411 F.2d 350

generally for the "purposes of comparison, criticism [or] point of reference." *New Kids on the Block*, 971 F.2d at 306. These two mutually exclusive forms of fair use are equally applicable here in the trade dress context.[17]

Applying these fair use standards to the trade dress context, we hold that a defendant's use is *classic* fair use where the defendant has used the plaintiff's dress to describe or identify the defendant's own product and not at all to describe or identify the plaintiff's product.[18] Likewise, a defendant's use is *nominative* where he or she used the plaintiff's dress to describe or identify the plaintiff's product, even if the defendant's ultimate goal is to describe or identify his or her own product.

Forsythe's use of the Barbie trade dress is nominative. Forsythe used Mattel's Barbie figure and head in his works to conjure up associations of Mattel, while at the same time to identify his own work, which is a criticism and parody of Barbie. *See Cairns*, 292 F.3d at 1151. Where use of the trade dress or mark is grounded in the defendant's desire to refer to the plaintiff's product as a point of reference for defendant's own work, a use is nominative.

Fair use may be either nominative or classic. *Id.* at 1150. We recognize a fair use defense in claims brought under §1125 where the use of the trademark "does not imply sponsorship or endorsement of the product because the mark is used only to describe the thing, rather than to identify its source." *New Kids on the Block*, 971 F.2d at 306. Thus, we recently reiterated that, in the trademark

---

(applying the nominative fair use analysis where automobile repair business specializing in repair of Volkswagens placed sign in front of premises that read "modern Volkswagen Porsche Service"), *as amended*, 413 F.2d 1126 (9th Cir. 1969).

17. Our *trademark* infringement caselaw is generally applicable to our resolution of Mattel's claim that Forsythe infringed its Barbie *trade dress* because the Supreme Court has clearly stated that trade dress and trademark infringement are very close cousins, both seeking to protect a designation of origin. *Two Pesos*, 505 U.S. at 773 (stating that "§43(a) [of the Lanham Act, *codified at* 15 U.S.C. §1125,] provides no basis for distinguishing between trademark and trade dress. . . . There is no persuasive reason to apply different analysis to the two. . . ."). Our reluctance to apply the Second Circuit's *Rogers* test to Mattel's trade dress claim stems not from the fact that *Rogers* is a trademark case *per se*. Were the nominative fair use test not available and so attractive to this claim, we very well may have had to apply *Rogers*.

18. It is well-established that use of a product feature or trade dress that has become functional will qualify as one form of fair use. *Qualitex Co. v. Jacobson Products Co.*, 514 U.S. 159, 164 (1995) ("The functionality doctrine prevents trademark law, which seeks to promote competition by protecting a firm's reputation, from instead inhibiting legitimate competition by allowing a producer to control a useful product feature.") "A product feature [or trade dress] is functional if it is essential to the use or purpose of the article or if it affects the cost or quality of the article." *Inwood Laboratories, Inc. v. Ives Laboratories, Inc.*, 456 U.S. 844, 851 n. 10 (1982). Because Mattel's Barbie trade dress is not functional, we are concerned with only whether Forsythe's use of it qualifies as either classic or nominative fair use.

A good example of *classic* fair use of another's trade dress is *Car-Freshner Corp. v. S.C. Johnson & Son, Inc.*, 70 F.3d 267 (2d Cir. 1995). In that case, the Second Circuit held that the defendant's sale of a pine-tree-shaped plug-in air freshener was a "fair use" of the pine tree design and did not infringe the plaintiff's rights in its pine tree air freshener design (commonly seen hanging from rear view mirrors). *See id.* at 270. The court held that defendant's use of the pine tree shape for a Christmas season air freshener was intended to call to mind both the scent of the product and the Christmas season. *See id.* According to one of the leading intellectual property commentators, *Car-Freshner* was an "exten[sion] [of] the fair use defense beyond words to the descriptive use of shapes"—*viz.*, trade dress. 2 J. Thomas McCarthy, *McCarthy on Trademarks and Unfair Competition* §11:48, at 11-102 (4th ed. 2003). We believe that extension was prudent and look to it for guidance in the resolution of Mattel's trade dress infringement claim.

context, nominative use becomes nominative *fair use* when a defendant proves three elements:

> First, the plaintiff's product or service in question must be one not readily identifiable without use of the trademark; second, only so much of the mark or marks may be used as is reasonably necessary to identify the plaintiff's product or service; and third, the user must do nothing that would, in conjunction with the mark, suggest sponsorship or endorsement by the trademark holder.

*Cairns*, 292 F.3d at 1151 (quoting *New Kids on the Block*, 971 F.2d at 308).

Forsythe's use easily satisfies the first element; his use of the Barbie figure and head are reasonably necessary in order to conjure up the Barbie product in a photographic medium. *See id.* at 1153 ("[T]here is no substitute for Franklin Mint's use of Princess Diana's likeness on its Diana-related products. . . ."). It would have been extremely difficult for Forsythe to create a photographic parody of Barbie without actually using the doll.

Forsythe also satisfies the second element, which requires that a defendant only use so much of a trademark or trade dress as is reasonably necessary. As we recognized in *Cairns*, "[w]hat is 'reasonably necessary to identify the plaintiff's product' differs from case to case." *Id.* at 1154. Where identification "of the defendant's product depends on the description [or identification] of the plaintiff's product, more use of the plaintiff's trademark" or trade dress is reasonably necessary. *Id.* Given the photographic medium and Forsythe's goal of representing the social implications of Barbie, including issues of sexuality and body image, Forsythe's use of the Barbie torso and head is both reasonable and necessary. It would be very difficult for him to represent and describe his photographic parodies of Barbie without using the Barbie likeness.

Though a "closer call than the first two elements" of the nominative fair use analysis, *id.* at 1155, the final element—that the user do nothing that would, in conjunction with use of the mark or dress, suggest sponsorship or endorsement by the trademark or trade dress holder—is satisfied here and weighs in Forsythe's favor. This element does not require that the defendant make an affirmative statement that their product is not sponsored by the plaintiff. *Id.*

Mattel attempts to argue that Forsythe suggested sponsorship by asserting to potential consumers that one of his photographs "hangs on the wall of the office of Mattel's President of Production," to whom Forsythe referred as "Joe Mattel."[20]

One of the purchasers of Forsythe's work apparently told Forsythe that he had given the work to this Mattel senior executive as a gift. Forsythe repeated this fact in certain letters to galleries and friends. Forsythe claims that he had no intention of suggesting sponsorship and that he meant the statement humorously. In virtually every promotional packet in which Forsythe mentioned "Joe Mattel," he also included a copy of his biography in which he

---

20. The record does not clearly establish whether "Joe Mattel" ever existed. Mattel's assertion, however, that "'Mattel' is not a family name, but a coined word that refers only to Mattel, the company" tends to indicate that "Joe Mattel" is fictitious. In any event, Forsythe claims that he believed that a senior Mattel executive whose first name is "Joe" had one of his works.

identified himself as "someone criticizing Mattel's Barbie and the values for which it stands." The letters in the packets asserted that Forsythe was attempting to "deglamourize[] Barbie," "skewer[] the Barbie myth," and expose an "undercurrent of dissatisfaction with consumer culture." A similar mission statement was prominently featured on his website.

The rest of the materials in these promotional packets sent to galleries reduce the likelihood of any consumer confusion as to Mattel's endorsement of Forsythe's work. Any reasonable consumer would realize the critical nature of this work and its lack of affiliation with Mattel. Critical works are much less likely to have a perceived affiliation with the original work. *New Kids on the Block*, 971 F.2d at 309 (finding no suggested sponsorship in part because a poll in a magazine regarding the popularity of the New Kids asked if the New Kids had become a "turn off").[21] Moreover, even if "Joe Mattel" existed, we question whether possession by a third-party passive recipient of an allegedly infringing work can suggest sponsorship.

We hold that Forsythe's use of Mattel's Barbie qualifies as nominative fair use. All three elements weigh in favor of Forsythe. Barbie would not be readily identifiable in a photographic work without use of the Barbie likeness and figure. Forsythe used only so much as was necessary to make his parodic use of Barbie readily identifiable, and it is highly unlikely that any reasonable consumer would have believed that Mattel sponsored or was affiliated with his work. The district court's grant of summary judgment to Forsythe on Mattel's trade dress infringement claim was, therefore, proper.

### C. Dilution

Mattel also appeals the district court's grant of summary judgment on its trademark and dress dilution claims. The district court found that Forsythe was entitled to summary judgment because his use of the Barbie mark and trade dress was parody and thus "his expression is a non-commercial use."

Dilution may occur where use of a trademark "whittle[s] away . . . the value of a trademark" by "blurring their uniqueness and singularity" or by "tarnishing them with negative associations." *MCA*, 296 F.3d at 903 (internal citations omitted). However, "[t]arnishment caused merely by an editorial or artistic parody which satirizes plaintiff's product or its image is not actionable under an anti-dilution statute because of the free speech protections of the First Amendment. . . ." 4 McCarthy, *supra*, §24:105, at 24-225. A dilution action only applies to purely commercial speech. *MCA*, 296 F.3d at 904. Parody is a form of noncommercial expression if it does more than propose a commercial transaction. *See id.* at 906. Under *MCA*, Forsythe's artistic and parodic work is considered noncommercial speech and, therefore, not subject to a trademark dilution claim.

We reject Mattel's Lanham Act claims and affirm the district court's grant of summary judgment in favor of Forsythe. Mattel cannot use "trademark laws

---

21. We have also found for the defendant on this factor even in situations where there was some amount of ambiguity. *See Cairns*, 292 F.3d at 1154-56 (finding no suggestion of sponsorship despite an assertion by Franklin Mint in their advertisements that all proceeds would go to Diana's charities and its assertion that a Diana porcelain doll is the only *authentic* replica of Diana's famous gown).

to . . . censor all parodies or satires which use [its] name" or dress. *New Kids on the Block*, 971 F.2d at 309.

[*Affirmed.*]

## NOTES AND QUESTIONS

1. *Nominative fair use and speech interests.* The *Walking Mountain* court chooses to use the doctrine of nominative fair use as the vehicle for vindicating defendant Forsythe's speech interests. The case preceded the Supreme Court's *KP Permanent case*, which made clear that a defendant asserting a descriptive (or "classic") fair use defense could not be required to establish a lack of likely confusion as a precondition for invoking descriptive fair use. After *KP Permanent*, some courts have reexamined the nominative fair use doctrine (particularly as set forth in the *New Kids on the Block* test). In particular, in *Century 21 Real Estate Corp. v. Lendingtree, Inc.*, 425 F.3d 211 (3d Cir. 2005), the court held that where a defendant alleges nominative fair use, the court should first apply a revised likelihood of confusion test that focuses on four factors that best fit cases involving alleged nominative fair use: (1) purchaser care and sophistication; (2) length of time that the defendant has used the mark without evidence of actual confusion; (3) the defendant's intent; and (4) the evidence of actual confusion. If the mark owner can show likely confusion under this revised test, the burden shifts to the defendant to show nominative fair use. The court derived its nominative fair use test largely from *New Kids on the Block*, with modification to take account of *KP Permanent*. Specifically, the court's test required the defendant to show (1) that the use of plaintiff's mark is necessary to describe both the plaintiff's product or service and the defendant's product or service; (2) that the defendant uses only so much of the plaintiff's mark as is necessary to describe plaintiff's product; and (3) that the defendant's conduct or language reflect the true and accurate relationship between plaintiff and defendant's products or services. *Century 21*, 425 F.3d at 228. Suppose that the court in *Walking Mountain* had decided to apply the *Century 21* approach to nominative fair use. Same result?

2. *The* **Rogers** *balancing test.* The court in *Walking Mountain* notes that First Amendment concerns arising from Lanham Act claims have been addressed via the balancing test from *Rogers v. Grimaldi*. In the *Rogers* case, the defendant's movie title triggered the Lanham Act claim, and, accordingly, the first step of the *Rogers* test asks a question that is germane particularly to the title of artistic works. Should it follow that the *Rogers* test is only useful in cases involving allegedly infringing titles? Or does the *Rogers* test express a broader First Amendment principle (or a broader trademark principle) that would apply in cases involving all types of marks, including trade dress? *See* E.S.S. Entertainment 2000, Inc. v. Rockstar Video, Inc., 547 F.3d 1095 (9th Cir. 2008). Should courts adapt the *Rogers* test to make clear its applicability to trade dress?

3. *Parody.* In many trademark cases where defendants invoke speech interests, defendants characterize the speech at issue as parody, and thus invoke a "parody" defense. Should courts recognize a separate parody defense in trademark infringement actions? Should they instead rely on fair use

doctrines—or should they hold that an assessment of parody is necessarily part of the confusion analysis (e.g., within the intent factor of that analysis, among others), such that recognizing a parody defense would be duplicative? Should the parody analysis be defined by First Amendment principles—i.e., should the range of protected parody be coextensive with the range of First Amendment protected speech? Or should the protections of the parody defense extend beyond the range of First Amendment speech? Should a parody analysis turn on the commercial vs. noncommercial nature of the defendant's speech? On the distinction between parody (where the defendant's speech targets the mark owner) and satire (where the defendant's speech uses the owner's mark to make a general social commentary)? What about dilution actions?

These issues were raised in a dispute that culminated in an important opinion, *Louis Vuitton Malletier S.A. v. Haute Diggity Dog, LLC*, 507 F.3d 252 (4th Cir. 2007), which ultimately turned largely on the text of the statute. The case involves a dilution claim by the owner of the LOUIS VUITTON mark, interlocking LV logo, and related trade dress for various fashion goods against a firm that sells dog toys under the name "Chewy Vuiton" using an interlocking CV logo and trade dress that arguably mimicked the Louis Vuitton trade dress. The Fourth Circuit defined parody in the trademark context (as involving the juxtaposition of the mark owner's "idealized image" with an irreverent representation of the mark) and analyzed as a threshold matter whether the defendant's use constituted a successful parody. After concluding that it was, the court then considered the trademark infringement and trademark dilution claims, making clear that its analysis of those claims was affected substantially by its conclusion that the defendant's use was parodic. How should a finding of parody affect the analysis—for example, the analysis of the Section 43(c) blurring factors? Specifically, how should the similarity factor (factor (i)) be analyzed in a parody case? What of factor (v) (intent) and factor (vi) (actual association)?

Suppose that the court in *Walking Mountain* had analyzed the case as one about parody, and suppose that the case had arisen under the 2006 TDRA. How would the analysis differ from the analysis in the actual opinion? Note that the TDRA includes a specific exclusion from liability, Section 43(c)(3)(A), applicable to some parodies. Would the exclusion apply in the dispute presented in *Walking Mountain*? The Fourth Circuit discussed the scope of the exclusion in an important portion of the *Louis Vuitton* case, concluding that the exclusion did not apply there.

## D. REMEDIES

The remedies available to a trade dress owner who succeeds in a Lanham Act claim are the same as those available generally to Lanham Act plaintiffs. Section 34 of the Lanham Act provides that in an action for infringement of a registered mark, the courts "shall have the power to grant injunctions, according to the principles of equity and upon such terms as the court may deem reasonable." The same is true in actions for infringement of unregistered marks. Although injunctive relief is indeed an equitable remedy and thus subject to judicial discretion, ordinarily a prevailing plaintiff in a trademark infringement, unfair competition, or false advertising case will be granted injunctive relief. *See* Restatement (Third) of Unfair Competition, §35, cmts. b, h (1995). Damages are normally regarded as inadequate relief in such cases, thus triggering the need for an injunction.

Injunctive relief allows a court equitably to fashion relief that accommodates the interests of both parties to the litigation. Thus, on occasion, a court may decline to issue an injunction absolutely prohibiting the defendant from using the trademark in dispute, but rather grant an order conditioning or limiting the type of use that the defendant can make of the mark. This occurs in particular where the defendant has a limited right to use the mark (for example, because the mark consists of the defendant's personal name, or because the defendant has rights within a remote geographical area) or where likely confusion can be dispelled by narrower remedial measures (such as the addition or display of a disclaimer). *See, e.g., E. & J. Gallo Winery v. Gallo Cattle Co.*, 12 U.S.P.Q.2d (BNA) 1657 (E.D. Cal. 1989), *aff'd*, 967 F.2d 1280 (9th Cir. 1992). For a discussion of the additional circumstances that might warrant the crafting of a limited injunction, see *King-Seeley Thermos Co. v. Aladdin Indus., Inc.*, 321 F.2d 577 (2d Cir. 1963), *later proceeding*, 418 F.2d 31 (2d Cir. 1969); *Forschner Group, Inc., v. Arrow Trading Co.*, 124 F.3d 402 (2d Cir. 1997).

In other areas of intellectual property, particularly patents, absolute prohibitory injunctions have been more common, perhaps reflecting the in-gross nature of the patent property right as compared to the more limited nature of the trademark right. These distinctions are critical to owners of designs who may face an array of choices as to the most appropriate regime for protection, or who may be attempting to secure adequate protection by invoking more than one intellectual property regime. Section 35 of the Lanham Act provides for the award of compensatory damages to the successful Lanham Act plaintiff. Plaintiffs can seek to prove actual damages as the basis for their damages award, or may seek an award of disgorgement of the defendant's profits. *See, e.g., adidas-America, Inc. v. Payless Shoesource, Inc.*, 546 F. Supp. 2d 1029, 1087-1088 (D. Or. 2008) (permitting an accounting of profits in a case in which the jury had awarded adidas-America over $300 million). Courts are split as to whether plaintiffs must demonstrate willful infringement in order to seek a disgorgement remedy. Since 1975, Lanham Act Section 35 has also expressly permitted the award of attorneys' fees to the prevailing party in a case brought under the Act.

# PART III
## DESIGN PATENTS

# CHAPTER 5
# SECURING RIGHTS

In this chapter we discuss the rules for securing design patent rights. In the following chapter, we cover the rules for enforcing issued design patents.

The U.S. patent system encompasses two types of patent regimes: the *utility* patent regime and the *design* patent regime. The utility patent regime is more familiar: since 1790, the U.S. government has granted over 7 million utility patents on an extraordinary array of inventions in many disciplines. By contrast, the design patent regime (the subject of this chapter) is less well-known. Design patent protection has existed in the United States since 1842, but only a relatively modest number of design patents have been granted. United States Design Patent No. 500,000 (to Daimler-Chrysler, for the design of the body of the Chrysler CROSSFIRE convertible) issued in 2005. Moreover, whereas the range of subject matter eligible for utility patent protection extends from machines to compositions to processes and beyond, design patent protection is more targeted. Loosely speaking, "[t]o qualify for [design patent] protection, a design must present an aesthetically pleasing appearance that is not dictated by function alone, and must satisfy the other criteria of patentability." *Bonito Boats, Inc. v. Thunder Craft Boats, Inc.*, 489 U.S. 141, 148 (1989).

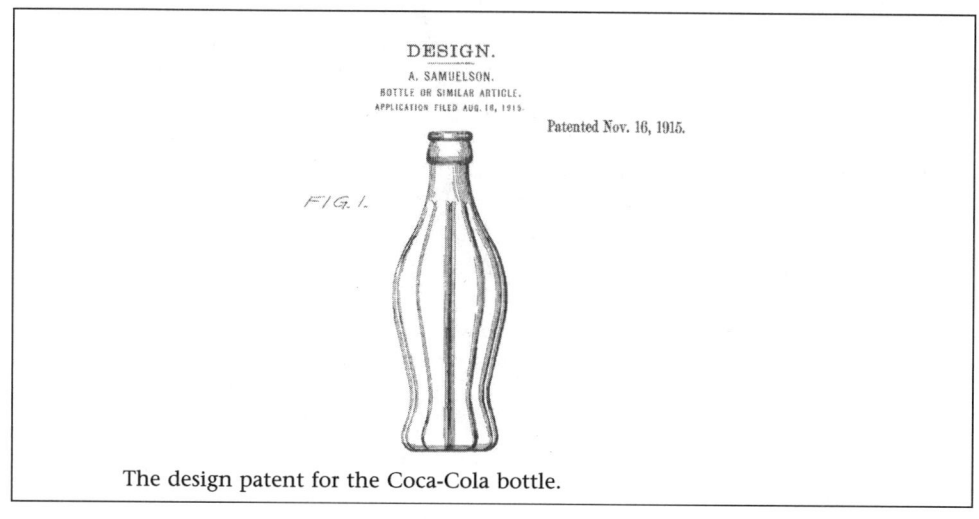

The design patent for the Coca-Cola bottle.

Design patent protection exists in the United States largely because Henry Ellsworth, the first Commissioner of the Patent Office, successfully urged Congress to adopt a regime of protection for the designs of useful articles, pointing out that design protection statutes had existed for some time in England and France. The decision to protect designs through a patent scheme may have had as much to do with the reach of Commissioner Ellsworth's personal influence as with any notion that the patent system was a more suitable system of protection. *See* Thomas B. Hudson, *A Brief History of the Development of Design Patent Protection in the United States*, 30 J. Pat. & Trademark Off. Soc'y 380, 382-83 (1948) (also suggesting that patent protection for designs may have seemed more appropriate because useful articles were more closely connected to the patent system than to the copyright system, and because the copyright system at the time had no centralized system for deposits of protected subject matter, whereas the patent system did). The Supreme Court summed up the purpose of the design patent regime:

> The acts of Congress which authorize the grant of patents for designs were plainly intended to give encouragement to the decorative arts. . . . The law manifestly contemplates that giving certain new and original appearances to a manufactured article may enhance its salable value, may enlarge the demand for it, and may be a meritorious service to the public. It therefore proposes to secure for a limited time to the ingenious producer of those appearances the advantages flowing from them. Manifestly the mode in which those appearances are produced has very little, if anything, to do with giving increased salableness to the article. It is the appearance itself which attracts attention and calls out favor or dislike. It is the appearance itself, therefore, no matter by what agency caused, that constitutes mainly, if not entirely, the contribution to the public which the law deems worthy of recompense. The appearance may be the result of peculiarity of configuration, or of ornament alone, or of both conjointly, but, in whatever way produced, it is the new thing, or product, which the patent law regards.

*Gorham Co. v. White*, 81 U.S. (14 Wall.) 511, 524-525 (1871).

The same institutions that have primary responsibility for overseeing the U.S. utility patent system also have similar responsibility for the design patent system. The U.S. Patent and Trademark Office (PTO) has responsibility for receiving design patent applications, examining them in an ex parte process to determine whether they comply with substantive patentability requirements and other procedural requirements, and issuing them as design patents if they do comply. Design patent protection can only be achieved through a PTO grant; there is no common law design patent akin to a common law trademark, and the PTO's role with respect to design patents is to determine whether to grant protection, not to determine whether preexisting rights qualify to be registered.

The U.S. Court of Appeals for the Federal Circuit is the principal expositor of U.S. patent law, including design patent law. The Federal Circuit has jurisdiction over appeals from PTO decisions on pending patent applications. In addition, the Federal Circuit has appellate jurisdiction over cases arising under the patent laws, including the design patent laws. Accordingly, the Federal Circuit handles appeals from all federal district courts in most cases involving design patent validity, enforceability, or infringement. The selection of cases in this chapter reflects the Federal Circuit's dominant role in design patent law.

The statutory provisions that currently govern design patents in the United States are housed principally in Chapter 16 of the U.S. Patent Act (codified in Title 35 of the U.S. Code):

> **35 U.S.C. §171. Patents for designs**
> Whoever invents any new, original and ornamental design for an article of manufacture may obtain a patent therefor, subject to the conditions and requirements of this title.
>
> The provisions of this title relating to patents for inventions shall apply to patents for designs, except as otherwise provided.
>
> **35 U.S.C. §172. Right of priority**
> The right of priority provided for by subsections (a) through (d) of section 119 of this title and the time specified in section 102(d) shall be six months in the case of designs. The right of priority provided for by section 119(e) shall not apply to designs.
>
> **35 U.S.C. §173. Term of design patent**
> Patents for designs shall be granted for the term of fourteen years from the date of grant.

The Patent Act does contain other important references to design patents. *See, e.g.*, 35 U.S.C. §289 (additional remedy for design patent infringement, discussed *infra* in Chapter 6). As we will see in our study of these statutory provisions, design patent law is a blend of unique concepts (such as Section 171's "ornamentality" criterion) and concepts borrowed from utility patent law (under authority of Section 171's second sentence).

The following excerpt from the PTO's Manual of Patent Examining Procedure (MPEP) identifies some of the principal differences between utility patent and design patents. (The MPEP sets out the PTO's views on relevant statutory and regulatory provisions as guidance for the PTO examining corps. Though it technically does not have the force of law, the MPEP is frequently invoked by the PTO and by patent applicants.)

## PATENT AND TRADEMARK OFFICE MANUAL OF PATENT EXAMINING PROCEDURE
(8th ed., Rev. 4, Oct. 2005)

### Chapter 1500 Design Patents

§1502.01 Distinction between Design and Utility Patents

In general terms, a "utility patent" protects the way an article is used and works (35 U.S.C. §101), while a "design patent" protects the way an article looks (35 U.S.C. §171). The ornamental appearance for an article includes its shape/configuration or surface ornamentation applied to the article, or both. Both design and utility patents may be obtained on an article if invention resides both in its utility and ornamental appearance.

While utility and design patents afford legally separate protection, the utility and ornamentality of an article may not be easily separable. Articles of manufacture may possess both functional and ornamental characteristics.

Some of the more common differences between design and utility patents are summarized below:

(A) The term of a utility patent on an application filed on or after June 8, 1995 is 20 years measured from the U.S. filing date; or if the application contains a specific reference to an earlier application under 35 U.S.C. §120, §121, or §365(c), 20 years from the earliest effective U.S. filing date, while the term of a design patent is 14 years measured from the date of grant (see 35 U.S.C. §173).

(B) Maintenance fees are required for utility patents [cit.], while no maintenance fees are required for design patents.

(C) Design patent applications include only a single claim, while utility patent applications can have multiple claims.

. . .

(E) An international application naming various countries may be filed for utility patents under the Patent Cooperation Treaty (PCT), while no such provision exists for design patents.

(F) Foreign priority under 35 U.S.C. §119(a)-(d) can be obtained for the filing of utility patent applications up to 1 year after the first filing in any country subscribing to the Paris Convention, while this period is only 6 months for design patent applications (see 35 U.S.C. §172).

. . .

(J) Utility patent applications filed on or after November 29, 2000 are subject to application publication . . . whereas design applications are not subject to application publication (see 35 U.S.C. §122(b)(2)).

---

If you are unfamiliar with patent law, you may find the following list of terms and definitions helpful as you study the materials in this and the next chapter:

- Claims: numbered sentences in a patent document that set forth the outer boundaries of the subject matter that the patent protects. Utility patents usually include several claims, while modern design patents include a single claim referring to the design patent drawings.
- Specification: the body of the patent document. In a utility patent, the specification consists primarily of drawings and a written description of the invention. In a design patent, the specification consists almost exclusively of drawings.
- Prior art: information available as proof that a claimed invention is not patentable. "Prior art" is a term of art in patent law and derives from the rules in 35 U.S.C. §§102 and 103.
- Prosecution: the negotiations carried on between a patent applicant and the patent examiner over whether to issue a patent.
- Prosecution history: the record of the prosecution, which is made available to the public when the patent issues.

Design patent documents are less elaborate than utility patent documents, in that design patent documents contain relatively little text, and much of that text is pro forma. In design patents, the drawings are of paramount importance in establishing the scope of protection, as we will discuss. The PTO's regulations provide that the design must be represented by a drawing having "a sufficient number of views to constitute a complete disclosure of the appearance of the design." 37 C.F.R. §1.152. Two sample design patents are reproduced in Appendixes A and B at the end of this chapter.

## A. WHAT IS A "DESIGN FOR AN ARTICLE OF MANUFACTURE"?

Section 171 requires that the subject matter of a design patent be a "design for an article of manufacture." The MPEP defines design as consisting of "the visual characteristics embodied in or applied to an article." MPEP §1502 (8th ed. Rev. 5, Aug. 2006). The following case provides a good starting point for exploring the statutory concepts of a "design" and an "article of manufacture." Although the court frames the issue as one of inventorship, you should concentrate on identifying the subject matter that the respective parties purport to have invented.

Hoop v. Hoop<br/>279 F.3d 1004 (Fed. Cir. 2002)

Mayer, Chief Judge:

Background

In 1998, Jeffrey and Stephen Hoop ("Hoop brothers") conceived of a pair of eagle-shaped motorcycle fairing guards. Fairings are clear glass or plastic structures mounted above motorcycle handlebars to reduce wind drag. The eagle-shaped guards attach to the fairings to prevent damage to the fairings if the motorcycle tips over. The Hoop brothers created sketches of the eagle design. (See figures 1 and 2, below.) Lacking drawing and casting expertise, they hired Lisa Hoop, a graphic designer, and Mark Hoop (their cousin and Lisa's ex-husband), a metal die caster, ("Mark and Lisa") to create detailed drawings and three-dimensional models for a patent application. Mark and Lisa signed non-disclosure agreements and prepared sketches and molds. (See figure 3, below.)

Figure 1    Figure 2    Figure 3

In November of 1999, the Hoop brothers applied for a design patent. After discussions over a manufacturing agreement between the parties failed, in March of 2000, Mark and Lisa also applied for a design patent, using the same drawings they had prepared for the Hoop brothers. The Hoop brothers' patent issued on August 1, 2000, as U.S. Design Patent No. 428,831, and Mark and Lisa's identical patent issued on September 26, 2000, as U.S. Design Patent No. 431,211. [Mark and Lisa sued the Hoop brothers for allegedly infringing the Mark and Lisa patent, and the Hoop brothers counterclaimed, alleging infringement of their patent. The trial court granted a preliminary injunction in favor of the Hoop brothers, and Mark and Lisa appealed, arguing that the Hoop brothers had not shown a likelihood of success on the merits. In particular, Mark and Lisa argued that the Hoop brothers could not establish that they were the inventors of the design depicted in their patent, and that therefore they were not likely to succeed in sustaining the validity of their patent.]

## Discussion

. . .

The question here is whether the refinements made by Mark and Lisa rise to the level of inventorship, so as to displace the Hoop brothers as patentees. Mark and Lisa argue that they are the true inventors because they perfected the original design by adding detail to the design sketches and creating the three-dimensional molds. Accordingly, they assert that the trial court erred in finding the Hoop brothers likely to succeed in sustaining the validity of their patent. We do not agree.

Design patents may be obtained by "[w]hoever invents any new, original and ornamental design for an article of manufacture." 35 U.S.C. §171 (1994). We apply the same standard of inventorship to design patents that we require for utility patents. *In re Rousso*, 222 F.2d 729, 731 (CCPA 1955) (rejecting the assertion that a lesser standard of invention applies to design patents than to mechanical patents). An inventor under the patent laws is the "person or persons who conceived the patented invention." *C.R. Bard, Inc. v. M3 Sys.*, 157 F.3d 1340, 1352 (Fed.Cir. 1998). An inventor may then "use the services, ideas, and aid of others in the process of perfecting his invention without losing his right to a patent." *Ethicon, Inc. v. United States Surgical Corp.*, 135 F.3d 1456, 1460 (Fed. Cir. 1998). The facts are undisputed that the Hoop brothers were the first to conceive of the eagle-shaped fairing guards, and brought the concept to Mark and Lisa for assistance. Thus in the absence of the inventive quality required for a patentable design on the part of Mark and Lisa, the Hoop brothers remain the true inventors.

One may not qualify as a joint inventor, or as here, a new inventor, by "merely assisting the actual inventor *after conception* of the claimed invention." *Ethicon*, 135 F.3d at 1460 (emphasis added). Minor differences between the prior art and the new claim will not suffice. [cit.] The differences here must be substantial and not just superficial; the new design must contain an inventive concept. The ultimate test for design-patent inventorship, like the test for anticipation and infringement, is whether the second asserted invention is "substantially similar" to the first. *Gorham Mfg. Co. v. White*, 81 U.S. (14 Wall.) 511, 528 (1871). . . .

The district court found that Mark and Lisa's drawing lacked an "independent," which we read as inventive, concept. The court summarized its improvements over the Hoop brothers' sketch as increased detailed feathering and an overall less triangular shape. Noting the strong similarity between the drawings, the court reasoned that Mark and Lisa merely refined and perfected the Hoop brothers' concept. Therefore, the two designs were not separate inventions. Mark and Lisa did remove the suggestion of the eagle's tail, see figure 2, but the two eagles have the same proportions, body size, orientation, three rows of feathers, head and beak shape, and eye placement. We agree that the trial court could permissibly conclude at the preliminary injunction stage that the second design was likely to be found to be merely a more refined version of the first. However, final resolution of this factual question must await a trial on the merits. The court's determination that the Hoop brothers are likely to be found to be the true inventors and that they are likely to succeed in sustaining the validity of their patent is sustained.

[*Affirmed.*]

LOURIE, Circuit Judge, dissenting:

I respectfully dissent. I would reverse the district court's grant of a preliminary injunction on the ground that the district court applied the wrong legal standard in determining inventorship of a design patent and that the court's determination that the Hoop brothers had proved a likelihood of success on the question of validity was therefore flawed. I would remand for a redetermination of the likelihood of success under the proper standard.

. . . The district court determined that the Hoop brothers were the inventors of the patented fairing design and that Mark and Lisa were infringing the brothers' patent. The court relied on its conclusion that the original drawings made by the brothers and that made by Mark and Lisa do not "evidence an independent concept," and that the brothers hired Mark and Lisa to refine what was their drawing. The majority has affirmed that determination. I disagree.

The undisputed facts are that the Hoop brothers made a sketch of an eagle fairing design and asked Mark and Lisa to make three-dimensional drawings and models of that design. In doing so, Mark and Lisa made a different design, one that differed from the original design of the brothers in several respects. Both parties then filed patent applications and obtained the grant of patents on the design of Mark and Lisa. The majority opinion does not note that the design that accompanied the brothers' patent application and constituted its claim, which is illustrated in Figure 3 of the majority opinion, was Mark and Lisa's design.

When one party conceives an invention and then asks a second party to reduce it to practice, the second party is not normally an inventor, or co-inventor, unless the second party has made significant changes in the original proposal necessary to carry out the conception. [cit.] The second party's work may constitute a separate invention if it is different in respects that render it nonobvious and the first party did not conceive of those aspects. If the parties worked together, they may be co-inventors, *id.*, but that does not appear to be the case here. What does appear to be the case here is that the second party may have made an invention that is distinct from, and possibly separately patentable from, that of the first party's original design.

Design patents do not claim concepts. They claim specific designs set forth in their claims, which invariably refer to the appearance of what is illustrated in the patent's drawings. 37 C.F.R. §1.153(a) (2001). Contrary to the conclusion of the district court, as the invention is not the concept of an eagle design, but only the specific claimed representation of that eagle, the "concept" of the design is not what one must look at in determining whether the inventions are one and the same or separate. [cit.] One must look at the differences between the overall appearance of the eagles to determine inventorship of the specific design. [cit.] When a design is changed, the result may be a new design. *See In re Mann,* 861 F.2d 1581, 1582 (Fed. Cir. 1988) ("[I]f the design is changed, the result is a new and different design; the original design remains just what it was. Design patents have almost no scope.").

It is undisputed that both patents claim the same design, a design consisting of the specific appearance of the eagle shown in the patents, which is different from that in the sketch made by the Hoop brothers and identical to that made by Mark and Lisa, i.e., Figure 3—not Figures 1 and 2. Quite possibly, one could reasonably conclude that the changes are significant enough to constitute a new design. The brothers' design has little detail in the eyes and wings, has a fairly straight beak, and has humps in the wings near the head. In contrast, the patented design of Mark and Lisa has substantial eye and wing detail, a curved beak, and nearly straight wings adjacent the head. Without recognizing the specifics of each design, one cannot evaluate the identity or separate patentability of the designs. [cit.]

The principal question in determining the validity of the Hoop brothers' patent is whether the design claimed in that patent, which is the design Mark and Lisa made and claimed, is the same as or patentably indistinct from the sketch the brothers made and gave to Mark and Lisa, i.e., whether it is the brothers' invention. Contrary to what seemed to impress the district court, it does not matter how much or how little experience the respective parties had in the field of motorcycle fairings. Nor does it matter that the brothers may have hired Mark and Lisa to make a design, or whether, through contract or operation of law, the brothers were entitled to ownership of any invention Mark and Lisa may have made. . . . What matters in determining whether the brothers are the inventors of the claimed design is whether, from the standpoint of an ordinary designer, the claimed design is the same as or different and patentably distinct from the brothers' original design. Because we are not designers of ordinary skill, we cannot make the conclusive factual evaluations necessary to determine whether the original brothers' design and Mark and Lisa's design are patentably distinct [and hence whether the Hoop brothers are likely to succeed in defending their inventorship.]

## NOTES AND QUESTIONS

1. *What is a design?* Did the majority in *Hoop* effectively recognize protection for a design concept as opposed to a design, as Judge Lourie's dissenting opinion argues? In view of the purposes of design patent protection, should the term "design" in 35 U.S.C. §171 ("Whoever invents any new, original and ornamental design for an article of manufacture may obtain a patent therefor . . . .") be interpreted to encompass design concepts? The Court in

*Gorham Co. v. White*, 81 U.S. 511, 524-525 (1871), analyzing a predecessor to Section 171, asserted that the predecessor statute contemplated "not an abstract impression, or picture, but an aspect" given to articles of manufacture as then specified in the governing provision. Does this history illuminate the meaning of "design" in the modern statute? *See also OddzOn Prods., Inc. v. Just Toys, Inc.*, 122 F.3d 1396, 1405 (Fed. Cir. 1997) (analyzing a design for a football having stabilizer fins attached at one end; distinguishing between the claimed design's "overall ornamental visual impression" and "the broader general design concept of a rocket-like tossing ball"). Is trademark law more sensitive to concerns about protecting design concepts? *See* Chapter 2 (discussion of the *Dyson* judgment of the ECJ).

2. *Defining the designs under the single claim rule.* As the *Hoop* case illustrates, identifying the protected design in any given case may be difficult. The analysis begins with the patent's claims. Utility patents typically include numerous claims in the form of numbered sentences at the end of the patent document that set forth the metes and bounds of the protected invention. Frequently, utility patents include claims of varying scope—claims broad enough to encompass all of the disclosed embodiments, as well as claims more narrowly directed to each individual embodiment. Design patents, by contrast, include only a single, pro forma claim, which in turn refers to the drawings: "The ornamental design for a _____, as shown and described." *See, e.g.*, the sample design patents reproduced in the appendixes to this chapter; *see also* 37 C.F.R. §1.153(a) ("The claim shall be in formal terms to the ornamental design for the article (specifying name) as shown, or as shown and described. More than one claim is neither required nor permitted."). Hence, though the claims technically define the protected subject matter in a design patent, the drawings are crucial.

The single claim rule provides another perspective on the design vs. design concept issue explored in note 1. Suppose that (as in *Hoop*) a designer develops the *concept* of a motorcycle fairing in the shape of a bird of prey. Suppose further that the designer draws up three embodiments of the concepts—a drawing of a bald eagle fairing, of a falcon fairing, and of a red-tailed hawk fairing, and includes them all in a single design patent application, along with a claim that encompasses all three embodiments, e.g., "an ornamental design for a motorcycle fairing as shown." Is this an improper attempt to use design patent protection to cover an entire design concept? What if the applicant filed three separate design patent applications on the same day, directed to each of the respective embodiments—would this also be disallowed as an improper effort to gain exclusive rights in a design concept? For a general discussion, *see* Andrew J. Patch, *Plural Embodiments in Design Patent: Two Pitfalls and a Solution*, 73 J. Pat. & Trademark Off. Soc'y 70 (1991).

3. *What is an "article of manufacture" for design patent purposes?* Section 171 specifies that the design patent right may attach to any new, original and ornamental design "for an article of manufacture." In a classic test of the scope of this language, the applicant in *In re Hruby*, 373 F.2d 997 (C.C.P.A. 1967), claimed the following ornamental design for a water fountain:

**306** Chapter 5 Securing Rights

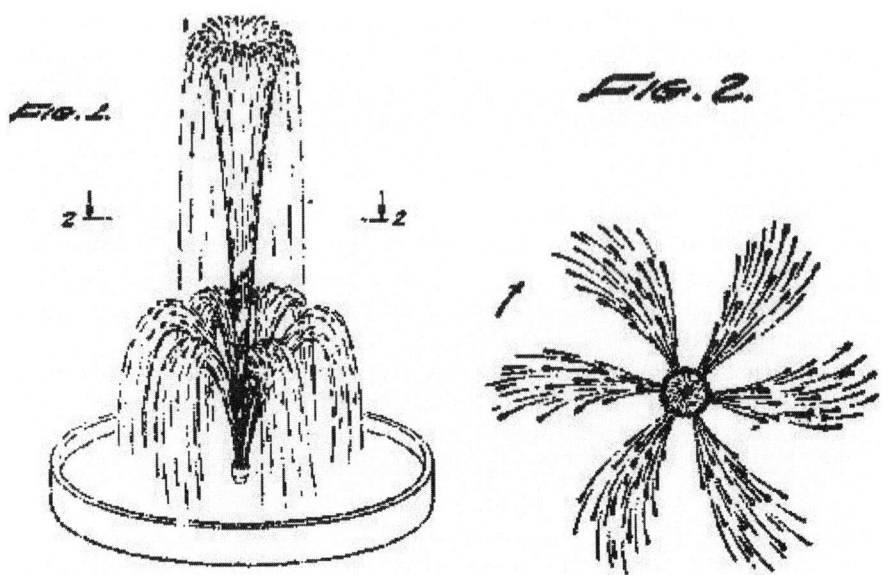

The court's analysis centered around the permanence of the claimed design. Judge Rich, writing for the court, took the view that

> ... the permanence of any design is a function of the materials in which it is embodied and the effects of the environment thereon. Considering the fact that the Romans and the French built now famous fountains hundreds of years ago which still produce the same water designs today, the notion that a fountain is "fleeting" is not one which will "hold water."

*Id.* at 999. Droplets might be "fleeting," but the fountain in its entirety "presents a product of constant appearance." *Id.* Moreover, it was of no moment that the visual appearance of the fountain might depend on factors outside the fountain itself:

> We do not see that the dependence of the existence of a design on something outside itself is a reason for holding it is not a design "for an article of manufacture." Many such designs depend upon outside factors for the production of the appearance which the beholder observes. The design of a lampshade may not be apparent unless the lamp is lighted. The design of a woman's hosiery is not apparent unless it is in place on her legs. The designs of inflated articles such as toy balloons, water toys, air mattresses, and now even buildings are not apparent in the absence of the compressed air which gives them form, as the water pressure here gives shape to the fountain. Even the design of wall paper is not always fully apparent in the commodity as it is sold and requires a wall and the services of a paperhanger to put it into condition for enjoyment by the beholder, which is the ultimate purpose of all ornamental design.

*Id.* at 1001. Judge Worley rejected these conclusions:

> It is inconceivable that Congress could possibly have intended Sec. 171, in letter or spirit, to allow an individual to remove from the public domain and

monopolize mere sprays of water. To do so, one must necessarily rely on strained semantics at the expense of common sense. The instant sprays, so evanescent and fugitive in nature, presumably subject to the whims of wind and weather, incapable of existing in and of themselves, are merely the effect flowing from articles of manufacture, but certainly are no more articles of manufacture per se than are the vapor trails of jets, wakes of ships or steam from engines.

*Id.* at 1002 (Worley, J., dissenting) (footnote omitted). Would you have voted with Judge Rich or Judge Worley? Or with neither?

**4.** ***Design "for" an article or design "on" an article?*** Section 171 extends to any qualifying design "for" an article of manufacture, but what of designs *on* articles of manufacture? Consider the following design for a "floor diamond border pattern":

*See* U.S. Design Patent D445,513, issued July 24, 2001. Should mere surface ornamentation qualify as a Section 171–eligible "design for an article of manufacture"? *See* Manual of Patent Examining Procedure (MPEP) §1504.01 (8th ed., Rev. 5, Aug. 2006).

**5.** ***Design for part of an article of manufacture.*** Does Section 171 require that a design be a design for a complete article? In *In re Zahn*, 617 F.2d 261 (C.C.P.A. 1980), the applicant claimed an "ornamental design for a Drill tool or the like as shown and described," accompanied by the following drawings:

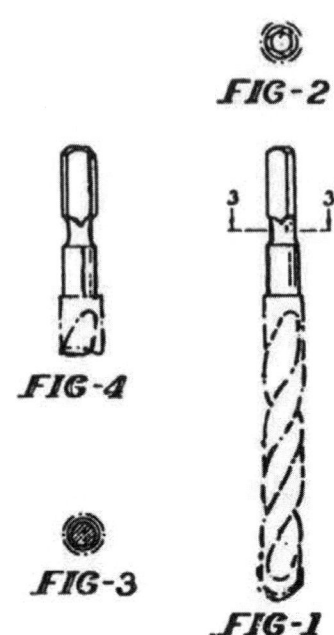

The applicant also included an explanatory note about the drawings:

> The phantom representation of the cutting portion of the drill bit is made in the drawings merely for the purpose of illustrating the environment in which the shank of this invention is used. The structure shown in broken lines is not part of the design sought to be patented.

*Id.* at 263. Should the application be rejected on the ground that it does not conform to Section 171's "article of manufacture" requirement? On some other ground?

**6. *Trade dress protection concurrent with design patent protection.*** In the *Hoop* case, would Mark and Lisa (or the Hoop brothers) have been better-off to claim trade dress protection? Do you think that the subject matter is likely to be protectable as trade dress under the rules discussed in Chapters 2 and 3? If Mark and Lisa had succeeded in establishing trade dress protection, would that preclude them from concurrently asserting design patent protection?

This last question is a common one in intellectual property law. On the surface, design patent eligibility is an exercise in applying the statutory language, asking whether subject matter constitutes a "design" and whether it is a design "for an article of manufacture." Below the surface, design patent eligibility analysis (like most eligibility inquiries in intellectual property law) is frequently about defining interfaces between intellectual property regimes, and about considering whether to allow subject matter to be protected under more than one regime concurrently, or whether to channel subject matter toward one intellectual property regime or another. The interface between the design patent and trade dress regimes is a good example. Suppose that Mark and Lisa from the *Hoop* case can show secondary meaning in a particular fairing design, and thus assert trade dress protection in addition to design patent protection. Are you troubled by the fact that design patents expire fourteen years after grant, whereas trade dress protection may extend indefinitely? Should Mark and Lisa be required to elect between design patent and trade dress protection? Are the purposes of the design patent and trade dress regimes the same, and if so, does this mean that the protections are duplicative? *See In re Mogen David Wine Corp.*, 328 F.2d 925 (C.C.P.A. 1964); MPEP §1512 (8th ed., Rev. 5, Aug. 2006). Would an approach that allows concurrent protection be consistent with the *Sears* and *Compco* decisions discussed in Chapter 1? Are those decisions even relevant? *See In re Mogen David Wine Corp.*, 372 F.2d 539 (C.C.P.A. 1967). *See also* Tracy-Gene G. Durkin & Julie D. Shirk, *Design Patents and Trade Dress Protection: Are the Two Mutually Exclusive?*, 87 J. Pat. & Trademark Off. Soc'y 770 (2005) (concluding that they are probably not); David S. Welkowitz, *Trade Dress and Patent — The Dilemma of Confusion*, 30 Rutgers L.J. 289 (1999) (analyzing the problem prior to the Supreme Court's decisions in *Wal-Mart* and *TrafFix Devices*). For a legislative proposal to allow designers to secure design patent protection, then later surrender that protection in favor of trade dress protection at a time when the requisites of trade dress protection can be demonstrated, *see* Takashi Saito, *Dressing Design Patent: A Proposal for Amending the Design Patent Law in Light of Trade Dress*, 89 J. Pat. & Trademark Off. Soc'y 682 (2007).

The above design patent, for the American Legion emblem, has had its term extended by special legislation. Such a design patent arguably functions as a quasi-trademark.

**7. *Copyright protection concurrent with design patent protection.*** Is Mark and Lisa's design in the *Hoop* case a copyrightable work? (We discuss copyright protection in Chapter 7). Does your answer depend on whether Mark and Lisa have valid design patent protection? Some of the same questions that we posed in the preceding note would be pertinent here as well. *See Mazer v. Stein*, 347 U.S. 201 (1954) (discussing whether patentability bars copyright protection); *In re Yardley*, 493 F.2d 1389 (C.C.P.A. 1974) (discussing whether an applicant should be required to elect between design patent and copyright protection).

**LIBERTY ENLIGHTENING THE WORLD.**

Auguste Bartholdi secured this design patent for the Statue of Liberty—subject matter that may seem more amenable to copyright protection.

8. *Utility patent protection concurrent with design patent protection: the double patenting doctrine.* Should an inventor be allowed to secure a utility patent and a design patent that cover the same commercial product? Consider a simple example: an inventor creates an athletic shoe having an inflatable bladder to surround and protect the wearer's foot. The inventor secures a utility patent claiming the shoe with the novel inflatable bladder. Surely this should not preclude the inventor from seeking design patent protection on the external appearance of the shoe. The claimed subject matter of the design patent is distinct from that of the utility patent. This is true even if the same drawings that appear in the design patent (and define the scope of that patent) also appear as part of the text of the utility patent, because the words of the utility patent's claims, not the utility patent's drawings, define the scope of the utility patent.

What if the subject matter claimed in the utility patent is not so clearly distinct from the subject matter claimed in the design patent? In rare cases, the later of the design or utility patent may be subject to attack under the doctrine of "obviousness-type" double patenting. The premise of the doctrine is that an inventor should not be allowed effectively to prolong patent life by claiming subject matter in one patent that is an obvious variation of subject matter that the same inventor has claimed in another patent. Obviousness as used here is a patent law term of art, a topic that we take up later in the chapter. Under the obviousness-type double patenting test as applied in the utility patent/design patent situation, the court must conduct a two-way analysis, asking whether the subject matter claimed in the design patent would have been obvious in view of the subject matter claimed in the utility patent, and vice versa. *See, e.g., Carman Indus., Inc. v. Wahl,* 724 F.2d 932, 939-940 (Fed. Cir. 1983); *In re Thorington,* 418 F.2d 528 (C.C.P.A. 1969); *see also* MPEP 1504.06 (8th ed. Rev. 5, Aug. 2006) (guidelines for applying double patenting rejections to design patents). Generally, an inventor can overcome an obviousness-type double patenting problem by filing a "terminal disclaimer"—i.e., by voluntarily giving up the portion of the patent term of the later-expiring patent that would extend beyond the expiration of the earlier-expiring patent.

9. *Applying utility patent rules to design patents.* Throughout this chapter, we will encounter many cases in which courts must attempt to extend utility patent rules to design patents. Indeed, the statute specifies that except as otherwise provided in the relatively few provisions devoted specifically to design patents, the provisions of Title 35 "relating to patents for inventions shall apply to patents for designs." 35 U.S.C. §171. In *Hoop,* the court seeks to apply the utility patent rules for determining who qualifies as an inventor. Is the subject matter of a design patent so different from the subject matter of a utility patent that different rules of inventorship should apply? More generally, as you read the cases in this chapter, consider which utility patent rules translate well to the design patent context, and which do not.

10. *The design patent "rocket docket."* PTO regulations provide that an applicant for a design patent may request expedited examination, if the applicant conducts a preexamination search of the prior art and so certifies to the PTO, and if the applicant satisfies other formal requirements. 37 C.F.R.

§1.155 (2008); MPEP 1504.30 (8th Ed. Rev. 7 July 2008). Expedited examination is a streamlined process in which the PTO takes up the application "out of turn" and gives the application priority throughout the examination process. Suppose that by opting for expedited examination, a typical applicant can secure design patent protection in about a year from the application filing date. How should this pendency time fit into an intellectual property strategy? That is, if you were advising a client on the options for intellectual property protection for designs, would you view the prospect of expedited examination as providing a significant incentive to make design patents the centerpiece of your intellectual property strategy?

### PROBLEM 5-1: COMPUTER-GENERATED ICONS

Professor Janis's Brother Billy got interested in computers, and eventually sold his bass boat and became a full-time software developer. He designed the following graphic icon to serve as the control for the "task finished" function in personal organization software:

Concerned about copying by his competitors, Brother Billy filed a design patent application claiming "an ornamental design for a computer-generated icon as shown," using the drawing depicted above. Does the claimed invention define a Section 171–eligible "design for an article of manufacture"? Would your analysis be different if Brother Billy had claimed "an ornamental design for a computer display panel including a computer-generated icon as shown"?

## B. ORNAMENTALITY AND FUNCTIONALITY

### IN RE WEBB
916 F.2d 1553 (Fed. Cir. 1990)

CLEVENGER, Circuit Judge:

This is an appeal from a decision of the U.S. Patent and Trademark Office Board of Patent Appeals and Interferences ("Board") affirming the final rejection of the sole claim of appellants' ("Webb") U.S. Design Patent Application Serial No. 833,470. The claim for "[t]he ornamental design for a grooved femoral hip stem prosthesis as shown and described," was "rejected as being unpatentable under 35 U.S.C. §171 as being directed to non-statutory subject matter."

The design can be appreciated from Figure 2 of the application reproduced below.

. . .

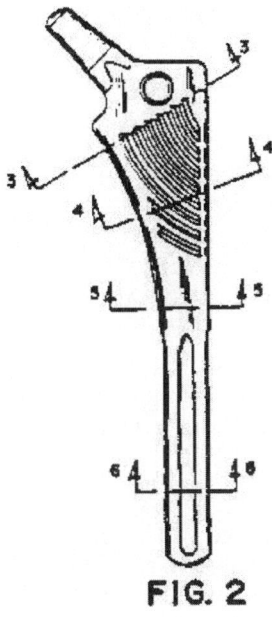

FIG. 2

I

Hip stem prostheses of the design invented by Webb are metallic implants that are generally used by orthopedic surgeons to supplant the functioning of a diseased or broken femur, near the hip, where the femur is joined to the pelvis. According to Webb, and not disputed by the Patent and Trademark Office ("PTO"), surgeons are made aware of differing brands and types of prostheses through advertisements in professional journals and through trade shows, where the prostheses themselves are displayed. Advertisements that were put in the record prominently and visually display the features of the prostheses. Furthermore, the applicant's agent submitted that "an implant's appearance is observed by potential and actual purchasers, surgeons, nurses, operating room staff, and other hospital personnel." After purchase, the prosthesis is surgically implanted into a patient's body where the implant is to remain indefinitely. Neither party disputes that, after implantation, the prosthesis is no longer visible to the naked eye.

II

[The Examiner had rejected the claim under 35 U.S.C. §171 for lack of ornamentality (and for functionality, a topic that we take up *infra*). According to the Examiner, the claimed subject matter lacked ornamentality because it was hidden during normal use. Webb responded that subject matter was not hidden in normal use because the "visual appearance can certainly draw attention to a particular implant at a trade show or in advertising." The Examiner maintained the rejection, asserting that advertising uses were not "normal uses." For design patent purposes, normal uses should be limited to incidents in an article's life which are integral to its purpose, according to the Examiner. Because articles are not designed for repair, service, or display, those activities should not count as normal uses. The Board of Appeals affirmed.]

. . .

### IV

The issuance of design patents is limited by statute to designs that are ornamental. 35 U.S.C. §171 (1988). Our predecessor court has affirmed the rejection of design applications that cannot be perceived in their normal and intended uses. For instance, the Court of Customs and Patent Appeals affirmed the rejection of a design claim for a vent tube placed in the wall of a frame house, stating that "[i]t is well-settled that patentability of a design cannot be based on elements which are concealed in the normal use of the device to which the design is applied." *In re Cornwall*, 230 F.2d 457, 459 (1956). Even earlier, that court affirmed the rejection of a design claim for a vacuum cleaner brush. *In re Stevens*, 173 F.2d 1015 (1949). There the court noted:

> [A]rticles which are concealed or obscure are not proper subjects for design patents, since their appearance cannot be a matter of concern. . . . Almost every article is visible when it is made and while it is being applied to the position in which it is to be used. Those special circumstances, however, do not justify the granting of a design patent on an *article such as here under consideration* which is always concealed in its normal and intended use.

*Id.* at 1016 (emphasis added).

We read those cases to establish a reasonable general rule that presumes the absence of ornamentality when an article may not be observed. This is a sound rule of thumb, but it is not dispositive. [cit.] In each case, the inquiry must extend to whether at some point in the life of the article an occasion (or occasions) arises when the appearance of the article becomes a "matter of concern."

Here, we read the Board's decision to have established a *per se* rule under §171 that if an article is hidden from the human eye when it arrives at the final use of its functional life, a design upon that article cannot be ornamental. The rule in *Stevens* does not compel the Board's decision. Instead, *Stevens* instructs us to decide whether the "article such as here under consideration"—a hip stem implant—"is always concealed in its normal and intended use." The issue before us, then, is whether "normal and intended use" of these prosthetic devices is confined to their final use.

### V

Although we agree that "normal and intended use" excludes the time during which the article is manufactured or assembled, it does not follow that evidence that an article is visible at other times is legally irrelevant to ascertaining whether the article is ornamental for purposes of §171. Contrary to the reasoning of the Examiner in this case, articles *are* designed for sale and display, and such occasions are normal uses of an article for purposes of §171. The likelihood that articles would be observed during occasions of display or sale could have a substantial influence on the design or ornamentality of the article. "The law manifestly contemplates that giving certain new and original appearances to a manufactured article may enhance its salable value. . . ." *Gorham Co. v. White*, 81 U.S. (14 Wall.) 511, 525, (1871).

In short, we construe the "normal and intended use" of an article to be a period in the article's life, beginning after completion of manufacture or assembly and ending with the ultimate destruction, loss, or disappearance of the article. Although the period includes all commercial uses of the article prior to its ultimate destination, only the facts of specific cases will establish whether during that period the article's design can be observed in such a manner as to demonstrate its ornamentality.

It is possible, as in *Stevens*, that although an article may be sold as a replacement item, its appearance might not be of any concern to the purchaser during the process of sale. Indeed, many replacement items, including vacuum cleaner brushes, are sold by replacement or order number, or they are noticed during sale only to assess functionality. In such circumstances, the PTO may properly conclude that an application provides no evidence that there is a period in the commercial life of a particular design when its ornamentality may be a matter of concern. However, in other cases, the applicant may be able to prove to the PTO that the article's design is a "matter of concern" because of the nature of its visibility at some point between its manufacture or assembly and its ultimate use. Many commercial items, such as colorful and representational vitamin tablets, or caskets, have designs clearly intended to be noticed during the process of sale and equally clearly intended to be completely hidden from view in the final use. Here, for example, there was ample evidence that the features of the device were displayed in advertisements and in displays at trade shows. That evidence was disregarded by the Board because, in its view, doctors should select implants solely for their functional characteristics, not their design. It is not the task of the Board to make such presumptions.

The decision of the Board is
*Reversed* and the case is *Remanded*.

## NOTES AND QUESTIONS

1. *C.C.P.A. precedent and the "matter of concern" inquiry for assessing ornamentality.* In *Webb*, the Federal Circuit cites cases from its predecessor court (the Court of Customs and Patent Appeals, or C.C.P.A.), establishing the "matter of concern" inquiry for assessing compliance with the statutory requirement of ornamentality. What is the inquiry? The Federal Circuit purports to refine the inquiry—how? Is the Federal Circuit following the C.C.P.A.'s test, or skillfully circumventing it? In *South Corp. v. United States*, 690 F.2d 1368 (Fed. Cir. 1982), the Federal Circuit's first decision, the Federal Circuit agreed to accept C.C.P.A. decisions as binding precedent.

2. *"Matter of concern" to whom?* Answering the matter of concern inquiry may require first addressing some critical subsidiary questions. One such question concerns the perspective from which the matter of concern analysis is undertaken. To whom must the article's appearance be a matter

of concern — the vendor of the article, or those who might observe the article? Is the inquiry objective? If so, is it to be conducted through the eyes of the hypothetical "ordinary observer"? The observer trained in industrial design? The ordinary vendor of goods of the type? Some other objective lens? Or should the subjective intentions of the vendor control? Which formulation better serves the goals of the design patent system? In view of your answers, what types of evidence would you seek to assemble in order to prove that the appearance of an article was a matter of concern?

**3.** *"Matter of concern" as of when?* Under its formulation of the matter of concern inquiry, the Federal Circuit asks whether the article at issue is concealed during its normal and intended use. How does the court define the time period of "normal and intended use"? Does the court's definition merely respond to the facts of *Webb*? Or has the court crafted a workable general definition of the relevant time frame, one that comports with the goals of the design patent system, as embodied in Section 171?

**4.** *Is ornamentality synonymous with beauty?* Consider the "Brute" — a dolly for transporting trash cans, as depicted below. Is the design for the "Brute" ornamental?

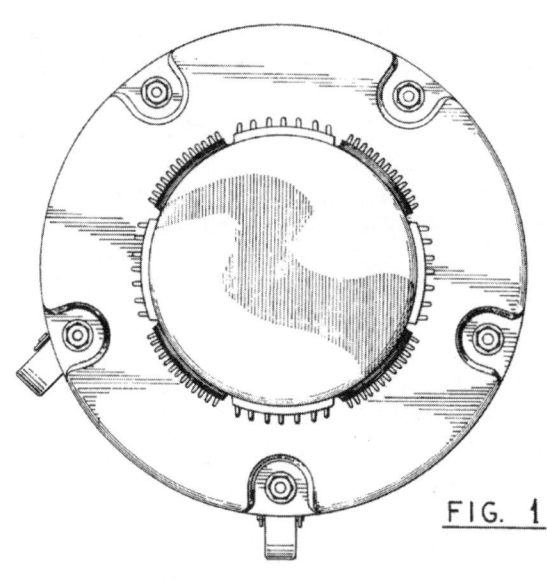

FIG. 1

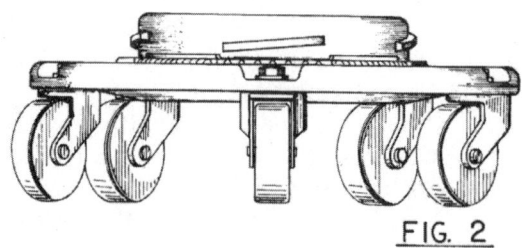

FIG. 2

The Eighth Circuit reasoned that

> ... design patents are concerned with the industrial arts, not the fine arts. The statute refers to "*any* . . . ornamental design for an article of manufacture." 35 U.S.C. §171 (emphasis supplied). Perhaps it is too much to expect that a trash-can dolly be beautiful. It is enough for present purposes that it is not ugly, especially when compared to prior designs.

*Contico Int'l, Inc. v. Rubbermaid Commercial Prods., Inc.*, 665 F.2d 820, 825 (8th Cir. 1981). Do you agree with the Eighth Circuit's conclusion? Do you agree with the Eighth Circuit's general approach to ornamentality—that a design is ornamental if it is "not ugly" relative to other prior designs? Does that standard avoid subjective judgments of aesthetic taste? Or does it invite such judgments? Should the court have chosen a standard of absolute not-ugliness, as contrasted to relative not-ugliness? As you ponder the appropriate standard, consider the following design for a pitcher:

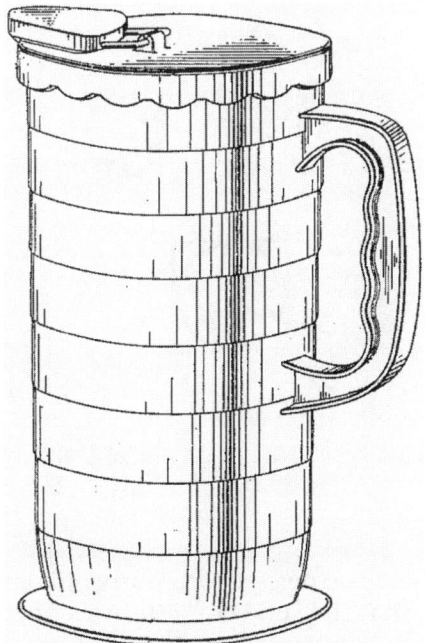

Is the design ornamental under the "not ugly" standard? In *Blisscraft of Hollywood v. United Plastics Co.*, 294 F.2d 694 (2d Cir. 1961), the court applied a stricter standard, asserting that ornamentality requires that the design

> be the product of aesthetic skill and artistic conception. [cit.] Plaintiff's pitcher has no particularly aesthetic appeal in line, form, color, or otherwise. It contained no dominant artistic motif either in detail or in its overall conception. Its lid, body, handle and base retain merely their individual characteristics when used in conjunction with each other without producing any

combined artistic effect. The reaction which the pitcher inspires is simply that of the usual, useful and not unattractive piece of kitchenware.

*Id.* at 696 (concluding that the design lacked ornamentality). Is the Second Circuit's approach to ornamentality any more reliable than the Eighth Circuit's? Can you formulate a standard that gives meaning to the statutory requirement of ornamentality, while also minimizing the need for courts and examiners to make aesthetic judgments?

5. ***Ornamentality vs. distinctiveness.*** Recall from Chapter 2 that one of the chief elements of protectability in trademark law is distinctiveness — the ability of a symbol, shape, or overall image to indicate the source of the goods or services with which it is connected. In *Rowe v. Blodgett & Clapp Co.*, 112 F. 61 (2d Cir. 1901), the court rejected the proposition that evidence of distinctiveness could be sufficient to satisfy the requirements for design patentability. Rowe owned a design patent on a design for a horseshoe "calk" — i.e., an extension or spike on a horseshoe that minimizes slipping, as shown below:

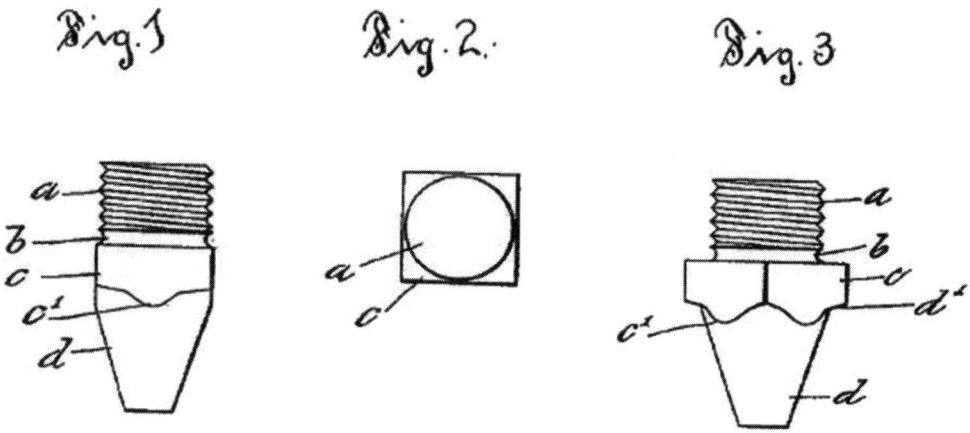

The lower court had held the design patent invalid, and Rowe appealed. The Second Circuit agreed that the subject matter was not patentable:

> There is nothing in the record to indicate that there is anything attractive about the appearance of the complainant's calk, or that the downward projecting curved lines appeal in any way to the eye, or serve to commend the article to purchasers, except for the suggestion that, seeing those lines, they will know the calk on which they appear is the product of the patentee, and not of some other maker. But the designers of articles of manufacture not otherwise entitled to receive design patents cannot justify the issuance of such patents on any theory that the design is a trade-mark.

*Id.* at 62-63 (critiquing the Patent Office's design patent examination practices as "'not only liberal, but lax'"). So understood, the ornamentality requirement performs a policing function, channeling some subject matter away from the design patent regime and toward other regimes, such as the trademark system. Is this an important function? Does the comparison to trademark distinctiveness help elucidate the meaning of design patent ornamentality? As we will see, cases on the doctrine of design patent functionality frequently refer to the doctrine as policing the boundary between design patents and utility patents.

**6. *The origin of ornamentality.*** The modern ornamentality language first appeared in the design patent statute in 1902. Section 4929, Revised Statutes, May 9, 1902. Prior statutes, tracing back to the original design patent statute (the Act of 1842) included neither an overarching ornamentality requirement nor an overall limitation to articles of manufacture. Instead, the 1842 Act designated categories of eligible subject matter in some detail. Specifically, the 1842 Act offered protection to

(1) [Any new and original design for a] manufacture, whether of metal or other material;

(2) Any new and original design for the printing of woolen, silk, cotton, or other fabrics;

(3) Any new and original design for a bust, statue, bas-relief, composition in alto or basso-relievo;

(4) Any new and original impression or ornament to be placed on any article of manufacture, the same being formed in marble or other material;

(5) Any new and useful pattern, print or picture, to be either worked into or worked on, or printed, painted, cast or otherwise fixed on any article of manufacture;

(6) Any new and original shape or configuration of any article of manufacture.

5 Stat. 543, Section 3, (Act of August 29, 1842). In addition to predictable arguments over the boundaries of the respective categories (e.g., whether category (5) encompassed everything included in category (2)), there was significant controversy over the extent to which the subject matter of a design patent needed to be useful (a requirement appearing in express terms only in category (5)). *See* Thomas B. Hudson, *A Brief History of the Development of Design Patent Protection in the United States*, 30 J. PAT. & TRADEMARK OFF. SOC'Y 380, 383-388 (1948). In 1901, the Patent Commissioner proposed that the statute be amended to delete the term "useful" along with the subject matter categories, and to substitute the term "artistic," along with a generic reference to articles of manufacture. Congress accepted these suggestions, except that it changed the term "artistic" to "ornamental." *Id*. at 388-391.

Does this discussion affect your views as to the appropriate interpretation of the ornamentality requirement in the modern statute? After you read the following cases and materials on functionality, consider how this historical discussion bears on your understanding of that requirement.

---

Section 171 contains an ornamentality requirement, but does not contain any express reference to non-functionality. Nonetheless, it is well settled that non-functionality is an element of design patentability, as the following cases illustrate.

## BEST LOCK CORP. v. ILCO UNICAN CORP.
### 94 F.3d 1563 (Fed. Cir. 1996)

LOURIE, Circuit Judge:

### Background

This case involves a design patent for a key "blade." A typical key consists of a bow, which allows the user to turn the key in a corresponding lock, and a blade, which is the portion of the key inserted into the lock's keyway. When a key is manufactured, the key blade is "blank," *i.e.*, the blade has not been cut or "bitted" with the combination required to operate the corresponding lock. Although a blank key blade will not operate the lock, the profile of the key blade is manufactured to fit into the corresponding lock's keyway. Subsequently, the blank key blade is cut to match the corresponding lock's combination.

In the replacement key market, a locksmith or a retail store with a key duplicating facility stocks blank key blades with various key profiles. The locksmith or retailer makes a replacement key by first selecting the appropriate blank key blade. This is done by matching the key blade profile with the corresponding lock keyway. Then, the locksmith or retailer cuts the blade of the key blank with the combination required to operate the lock.

Best Lock manufactures and sells locks and keys used to maintain security at industrial, commercial, and institutional facilities. At these facilities, it is often feared that the keys used in their locks may readily be duplicated. Consequently, key and lock manufacturers, including Best Lock, have attempted to restrict unauthorized access to duplicate key blanks by obtaining utility or design patent protection on the keys. By obtaining patent protection, a company hopes to control the market for duplicate key blanks during the life of the patent.[1]

[Best Lock's design patent in suit, U.S. Design Patent 327,636, entitled "Portion of a Key Blade Blank," claimed the ornamental design for the operative portion of a key blade blank.] In addition to the '636 design patent, Best Lock is the assignee of 33 other design patents on key blade designs. It also is the assignee of 34 design patents directed to keyways designed to mate with the key blades claimed in Best Lock's 34 key blade design patents. The '636 patent is the only design patent at issue on appeal.

---

1. Key and lock manufacturers also use other methods to restrict access to duplicate key blanks. For example, some manufacturers limit the sale of a particular type of lock and key to a single customer or particular geographic region, thereby making consumer demand for replacement keys for that particular lock design so small that replacement key manufacturers have no incentive to manufacture duplicate key blanks.

Figures 1-5 of the '636 design patent are shown below:

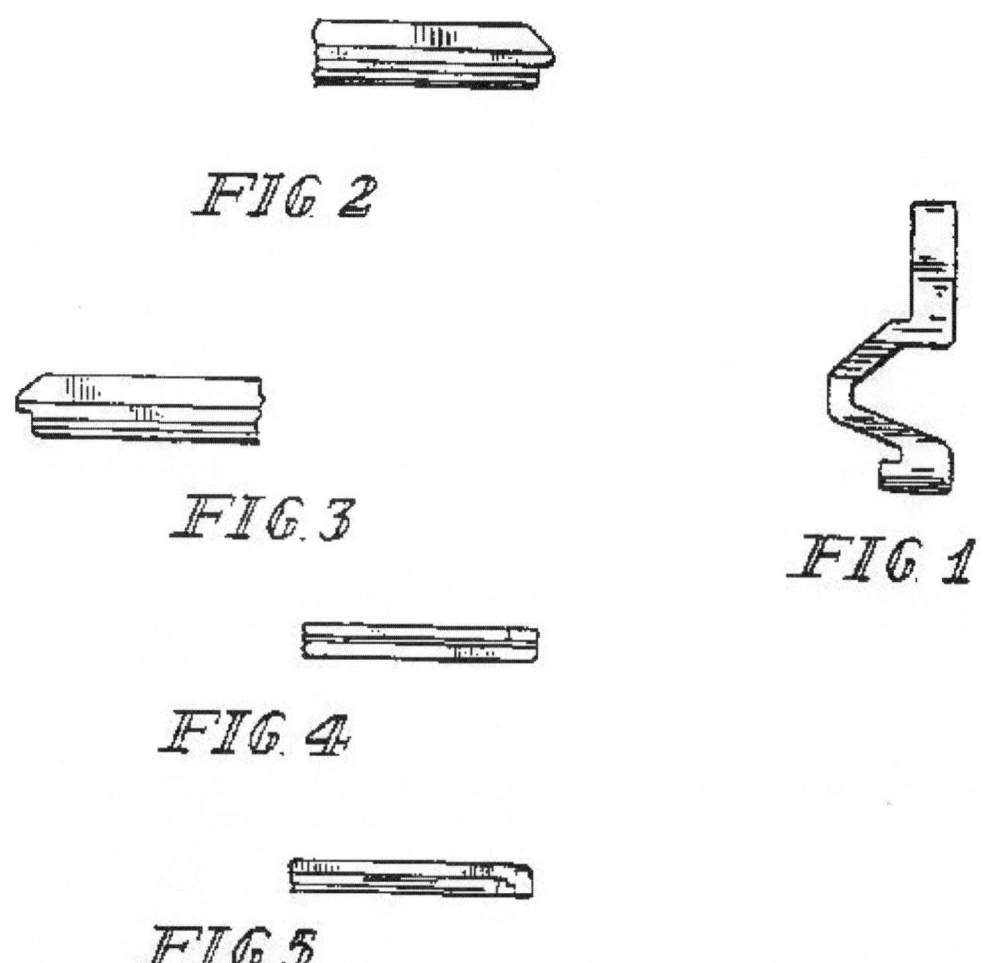

Ilco manufactures duplicate and replacement key blanks for existing locks. It sells its replacement key blanks to locksmiths and replacement key retailers. In 1993, Ilco copied the design of a Best Lock key, which had a key blade shaped like the design shown in the '636 patent. It subsequently distributed key blanks with that key blade shape at the annual convention of the Associated Locksmiths of America. [Best Lock sued, alleging, *inter alia*, infringement of the '636 design patent. The trial court invalidated the '636 patent on the grounds that the subject matter was "not a matter of ornamental concern to the purchaser or the user" and the shape of the key blade blank was dictated by function. Best Lock appealed.]

. . .

Discussion

Under 35 U.S.C. §171, a design patent may be granted for a "new, original and ornamental design for an article of manufacture." However, if the design claimed in a design patent is dictated solely by the function of the article of manufacture, the patent is invalid because the design is not ornamental. *See Bonito Boats, Inc. v. Thunder Craft Boats, Inc.*, 489 U.S. 141, 148 (1989) ("To qualify for protection, a design must present an aesthetically pleasing appearance that is not dictated by function alone, and must satisfy the other criteria of patentability."); *see also In re Carletti*, 328 F.2d 1020, 1022 (1964) ("[I]t has long been settled that when a configuration is the result of functional considerations only, the resulting design is not patentable as an ornamental design for the simple reason that it is not 'ornamental'—was not created for the purpose of ornamenting."). A design is not dictated solely by its function when alternative designs for the article of manufacture are available. *See L.A. Gear, Inc. v. Thom McAn Shoe Co.*, 988 F.2d 1117, 1123 (Fed. Cir.), *cert. denied*, 510 U.S. 908 (1993). We review for clear error the district court's determination that the design claimed in the '636 patent is functional. [cit.]

On appeal, Best Lock argues that the court erred in holding the '636 design patent invalid as being directed solely to a functional design. As support, it asserts that although a particular key and its corresponding lock must mate to operate the lock, an unlimited number of key blade and corresponding keyway designs are available. Choice of any particular design is arbitrary. Thus, Best Lock maintains that the key blade blank may have any number of different shapes and is therefore not dictated solely by functional concerns.

We disagree. The design shown in the claim of the '636 patent is limited to a blank key blade as shown in Figures 1-5 of the patent. Best Lock did not claim a design for the entire key.[2] *See* 37 C.F.R. §1.153 (1995) (The claim of a design patent "shall be in formal terms to the ornamental design for the article . . . *as shown, or as shown and described.*") (emphasis added). The parties do not dispute that the key blade must be designed as shown in order to perform its intended function—to fit into its corresponding lock's keyway. An attempt to create a key blade with a different design would necessarily fail because no alternative blank key blade would fit the corresponding lock. In fact, Best Lock admitted that no other shaped key blade would fit into the corresponding keyway, and it presented no evidence to the contrary. Therefore, we find no clear error in the court's finding that the claimed key blade design was dictated solely by the key blade's function. Any aesthetic appeal of the key blade design shown in the '636 patent is the inevitable result of having a shape that is dictated solely by functional concerns.

Further, Best Lock's assertion that a variety of possible shapes of interfaces between keys and locks exists does not compel a different result. Clearly,

---

2. As our predecessor court previously held, "a design for an article of manufacture may be embodied in less than all of an article of manufacture. . . ." *In re Zahn*, 617 F.2d 261, 267 (CCPA 1980).

different interfaces between key blades and corresponding lock keyways can be designed to permit the combination to function as a lock and key set. However, Best Lock's patent does not claim the combination of a lock and corresponding key. Instead, the claim in the '636 design patent is limited to a key blade, which must be designed as shown in the '636 patent in order to perform its intended function.

Moreover, the fact that Best Lock also has a design patent on the keyway that mates with the key blade shown in the '636 patent does not alter our analysis. The existence of a separate patent on the keyway is irrelevant to the construction of the '636 patent claim and to the ultimate determination that the claimed design is dictated solely by function. [cit.] The validity of a patent must be evaluated based on what it claims rather than on the totality of the claims of multiple patents.

For the foregoing reasons, the district court's finding that the claimed design is solely governed by functional concerns is not clearly erroneous. Consequently, we affirm its resulting conclusion that the '636 patent is invalid under 35 U.S.C. §171 for failure to satisfy the statute's ornamentality requirement.

*Affirmed.*

PAULINE NEWMAN, Circuit Judge, dissenting:

I respectfully dissent. The design of this key blade profile meets the statutory criteria of design patent subject matter. . . .

Whether the design of the D'636 patent is otherwise patentable, for example on the criteria of originality or non-obviousness, was not reached by the district court and is not before us. However, the panel majority has misapplied 35 U.S.C. §171 in holding that the arbitrary design of the key profile is "functional" because it mates with its matching keyway.

The design of the key profile is not removed from access to the design statute because the key fits a matching keyway. That two articles are designed in harmony does not deprive the design of access to the design patent law. The design of the key profile is not determined by the function of the key to fit the lock. In the case at bar there are said to be "thousands" of alternative key blade profiles.

The district court concluded that the design of the D'636 patent was not "a matter of ornamental concern to the purchaser or the user," and thus held that the design was functional. The statute requires that the subject of a design patent be an ornamental design of a useful object. However, "ornamental" does not always mean artistic or pleasing to the eye. The Court of Customs and Patent Appeals early recognized that "the beauty and ornamentation requisite in design patents is not confined to such as may be found in the 'aesthetic or fine arts.'" *In re Koehring*, 37 F.2d 421, 422 (1930).

Recognizing that ornamentation is in the eye of the beholder, the courts have sought a more objective standard in the general rule that a design is "ornamental" for purposes of 35 U.S.C. §171 when it is not primarily functional. [cit.] However, the article itself must have a utility in order for its design features to be patentable under 35 U.S.C. §171. [cit.]

If the design is dictated by the function performed by the article of manufacture, the design is not patentable. [cit.] A design is "not dictated by function alone" when there are alternative designs or configurations available for the article of manufacture, as in the case before us.

. . .

A review of patentable designs in general illustrates the mixture of functional and non-functional features embraced in the patented design. *See, e.g., Winner Int'l Corp. v. Wolo Mfg. Corp.*, 905 F.2d 375 (Fed. Cir. 1990) (design of steering wheel lock); *Lee v. Dayton-Hudson Corp.*, 838 F.2d 1186 (Fed. Cir. 1988) (design patent for massage device); *FMC Corp. v. Hennessy Indus., Inc.*, 836 F.2d 521 (Fed. Cir. 1987) (design patent for changer for tubeless tires); *Unette Corp. v. Unit Pack Co.*, 785 F.2d 1026 (Fed. Cir. 1986) (container for dispensing liquids); *In re Igarashi*, 228 USPQ 463 (Bd. Pat. App. & Interf. 1985) (tire tread design); *Trans-World Mfg. Corp. v. Al Nyman & Sons, Inc.*, 750 F.2d 1552 (Fed. Cir. 1984) (design for eyeglass display rack).

An effective design patent law must recognize the distinction between functionality of the article and of the particular design of the article or features thereof. *See L.A. Gear, supra,* (the sneaker tongue, moustache, delta wing, and side mesh, were useful parts of the sneaker, but the overall design of these features and the shoe was not dictated by function alone). This interaction of form and function does not remove the design from the statutory scope of the design patent law, or defeat the statutory patentability of a primarily non-functional design—although it is not always easy to draw a bright line between the functionality of an article and its design, as discussed by J.H. Reichman, *Design Protection and the New Technologies: The United States Experience in a Transnational Perspective*, 19 BALT. L. REV. 6 (1989), for design patents often appear on quite mundane articles of manufacture. *See, e.g., Tone Bros., Inc. v. Sysco Corp.*, 28 F.3d 1192 (Fed. Cir. 1994) (bottle for spices); *In re Klein*, 987 F.2d 1569 (Fed. Cir. 1993) (roof or siding shingle); *KeyStone Retaining Wall Sys., Inc. v. Westrock, Inc.*, 997 F.2d 1444 (Fed. Cir. 1993) (concrete block for retaining wall); *In re Webb*, 916 F.2d 1553 (Fed. Cir. 1990) (femoral hip stem prosthesis); *In re Cho*, 813 F.2d 378 (Fed. Cir. 1987) (bottle cap); *Pacific Furniture Mfg. Co. v. Preview Furniture Corp.*, 800 F.2d 1111 (Fed. Cir. 1986) (upholstered armchair); *Litton Sys., Inc. v. Whirlpool Corp.*, 728 F.2d 1423 (Fed. Cir. 1984) (microwave oven); *In re Koehring*, 37 F.2d 421 (1930) (concrete mixing truck).

The design of the key blade profile is primarily non-functional, as the Patent and Trademark Office recognized in granting the patent in suit. The Manual of Patent Examining Procedure defines "design" as follows for purposes of §171:

> The design of an object consists of the visual characteristics or aspects displayed by the object. It is the appearance presented by the object which creates a visual impact upon the mind of the observer.
>
> Since a design is manifested in appearance, the subject matter of a design patent application may relate to the configuration or shape of an object, to the surface ornamentation on an object, or both.

> Design is inseparable from the object to which it is applied and cannot exist alone merely as a scheme of surface ornamentation. It must be a definite, preconceived thing, capable of reproduction and not merely the chance result of a method.

MPEP §1502 (6th ed. 1995). . . .

The parties to this litigation agree that there are myriad possible designs of key profiles. All keys require, of course, mating keyways. In holding that because the key must fit a keyway, the abstract design of the key profile is converted to one solely of function, the court creates an exception to design patent subject matter. An arbitrary design of a useful article is not statutorily excluded from §171 simply because in use it interacts with an article of complementary design. Although precedent is sparse, it is contrary to this holding. In *Motorola Inc. v. Alexander Mfg. Co.*, 786 F. Supp. 808 (N.D. Iowa 1991), the only United States case on this point of which we are aware, the court considered a design patent for a battery housing intended for use in a portable phone. Since the battery housing had to fit into the phone and a battery charger, the accused infringer argued that this function dictated the design. The court disagreed:

> The design of the battery housing was not dictated by the design of the battery charger because the charger did not exist when the housing was designed. The design of the phone was done concurrently with the battery housing. Therefore, the design of the battery housing cannot fairly be said to have been "dictated" by the design of the phone.

*Id.* at 812. This reasoning is equally apt in this case. The design of the key profile was not dictated by the design of the keyway, and indeed the two share the same arbitrary design.

In sum, the fact that the key blade is the mate of a keyway does not convert the arbitrary key profile into a primarily functional design. It is not the design of the key profile that is functional, but the key itself. Thus I must, respectfully, dissent from the ruling of the panel majority that the design of the key blade profile is not patentable because the key blade requires a mating keyway.

## PHG Technologies, LLC v. St. John Companies, Inc.
### 469 F.3d 1361 (Fed. Cir. 2006)

Prost, Circuit Judge:

. . .

PHG and its predecessors have been in the business of selling certain medical patient identification labels as well as identification labeling software in the United States since 1995. PHG owns the two design patents at issue in this case: United States Patent Nos. D496,405 (the "'405 patent") and D503,197 (the "'197 patent"). The '405 patent claims "[t]he ornamental design for the medical label sheet, as shown." The '197 patent claims "[t]he ornamental design for a label pattern for a medical label sheet, as shown."

Figure 1 from the '405 patent and figure 1 from the '197 patent appear below, respectively:

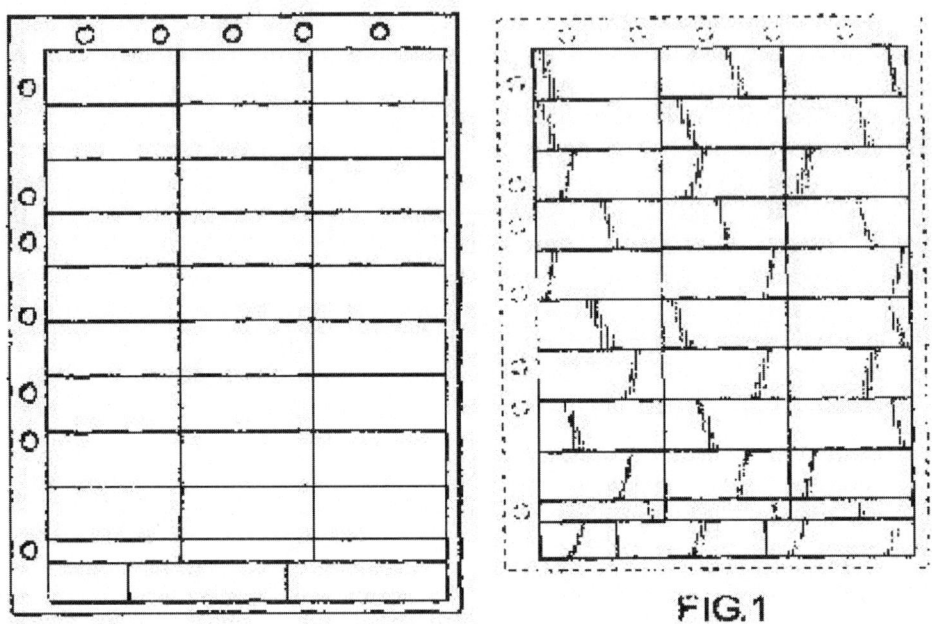

As can be seen, both designs include eleven rows of labels, with each row containing three labels. The first nine rows are depicted to contain three labels of equal size, the size being consistent with a standard medical chart label. The tenth and eleventh row each contain differently-sized labels which apparently correspond to the size of a pediatric and adult patient wristband respectively. The difference between the two patents is that the border is part of the design claimed in the '405 patent but not part of the design claimed in the '197 patent. The '405 and '197 patents depend from a utility patent application, No. 09/952,425 (the "'425 utility application"), which is still pending at the United States Patent and Trademark Office.

[PHG sued a rival, St John, for design patent infringement, and moved for a preliminary injunction. The court granted the preliminary injunction. On ornamentality and functionality, the court concluded that the design was not dictated by function, that there are other ways to arrange different sized labels on an $8\frac{1}{2}"\times 11"$ sheet, and that the inventors of the design chose the design from among other alternatives because they thought that it had the "best flow and look."

St. John appealed.]

## II. Discussion

[The court noted that in order to prevail on its motion for preliminary injunction, PHG had to show that it was likely to succeed on the merits.

The court's discussion of the likelihood of success factor focused on whether there was a substantial question about validity.]

St. John asserts that the district court erred in finding that the patented designs are primarily ornamental rather than merely a byproduct of functional considerations. In support of its assertion of functionality, St. John points to various statements made by PHG in the prosecution of the '425 utility application and to statements made by Mr. Press [St. John's CEO] in an affidavit submitted to the court. St. John argues that the statements made during prosecution and those submitted by Mr. Press constitute a clear and convincing showing of functionality. Further, St. John asserts that because PHG presented no evidence to rebut St. John's showing of invalidity, the district court clearly erred in finding that the patented designs are primarily ornamental.

PHG responds that the district court correctly determined that St. John failed to raise a substantial question regarding the functionality of the designs because the patented designs were not dictated by the use or purpose of the article of manufacture—a medical label sheet. PHG concedes that the design has functional features but argues that the arrangement of the different sizes of labels on the sheet is primarily ornamental because, as found by the district court, "there are a multitude of ways to arrange different sizes of labels on an $8\frac{1}{2}$" × 11" sheet." Further, PHG accuses St. John of focusing solely on the individual features of the claimed designs rather than analyzing the overall appearance to determine if the designs were dictated by functional considerations.

The district court determined that St. John failed to carry its burden of raising a substantial question of validity of PHG's design patents to defeat PHG's motion for preliminary injunction. The district court's sole finding with regard to St. John's assertion of invalidity was that the design was not dictated by its function because "[t]he testimony revealed [that] there are a multitude of ways to arrange different sizes of labels on an $8\frac{1}{2}$" × 11" sheet." In support, the district court noted that "Brian Moyer testified that PHG considered various arrangements for medical label sheets and settled on the design ultimately patented because it had 'the best flow and look.'" In sum, the district court concluded that "[t]he different sizes of labels and the arrangement of those labels on PHG's Medical Label Sheet are primarily ornamental because there are other ways to arrange different sizes of labels on an $8\frac{1}{2}$" × 11" sheet."

"Whoever invents any new, original and ornamental design for an article of manufacture may obtain a patent therefor, subject to the conditions and requirements of this title." 35 U.S.C. §171 (2006). As the statute indicates, a design patent is directed to the appearance of an article of manufacture. *L.A. Gear, Inc. v. Thom McAn Shoe Co.*, 988 F.2d 1117, 1123 (Fed. Cir. 1993). "If the patented design is primarily functional rather than ornamental, the patent is invalid." *Power Controls Corp. v. Hybrinetics, Inc.*, 806 F.2d 234, 238 (Fed. Cir. 1986). The design of a useful article is deemed to be functional when "the appearance of the claimed design is 'dictated by' the use or purpose of the article." *L.A. Gear*, 988 F.2d at 1123; *see also Rosco, Inc. v. Mirror Lite Co.*, 304 F.3d 1373, 1378 (Fed. Cir. 2002).

"[T]he determination of whether the patented design is dictated by the function of the article of manufacture must ultimately rest on an analysis of its overall appearance." *Berry Sterling Corp. v. Pescor Plastics, Inc.*, 122 F.3d 1452,

1455 (Fed. Cir. 1997). Our cases reveal a "list of . . . considerations for assessing whether the patented design as a whole — its overall appearance — was dictated by functional considerations," including:

> whether the protected design represents the best design; *whether alternative designs would adversely affect the utility of the specified article*; whether there are any concomitant utility patents; whether the advertising touts particular features of the design as having specific utility; and whether there are any elements in the design or an overall appearance clearly not dictated by function.

*Id.* at 1456 (emphasis added). In particular, we have noted that "[t]he presence of alternative designs may or may not assist in determining whether the challenged design can overcome a functionality challenge. Consideration of alternative designs, if present, is a useful tool that may allow a court to conclude that a challenged design is not invalid for functionality." *Id.* "When there are several ways to achieve the function of an article of manufacture, the design of the article is more likely to serve a primarily ornamental purpose." *Rosco*, 304 F.3d at 1378.

Our case law makes clear that a full inquiry with respect to alleged alternative designs includes a determination as to whether the alleged "alternative designs would adversely affect the utility of the specified article," such that they are not truly "alternatives" within the meaning of our case law. *Id.* In this case, while the district court relied exclusively on its finding that there were a multitude of alternative designs, the court did not make any findings with respect to whether any of the alternatives would adversely affect the utility of the medical label sheet. One might presume that the district court's findings with respect to alternatives implicitly include the additional finding that the alternatives did not adversely affect the utility of the medical label sheet. The difficulty in doing so in this case, however, is that the district court makes no reference to St. John's evidence that the overall arrangement of the labels on the medical label sheet was dictated by the use and purpose of the medical label sheet and that alternative designs lacking that arrangement would adversely affect the utility of the sheet. Specifically, St. John presented Mr. Press's affidavit, in which he stated:

> The labels for use on the wristbands themselves are located on the bottom two rows of the sheet as these are usually the first labels used when a patient is admitted to a medical facility. The lower right hand corner is the easiest location for a right-handed user to remove the label as it is flush to an edge and unencumbered by a file or binder clip along the top or left hand margins. By placing the labels for the wristbands at the bottom of the page, the subsequent removal of additional labels adjacent to the removed label is facilitated.

Mr. Press's affidavit constitutes evidence that alternative designs, which do not include the "novel feature" of PHG's design — the placement of various sizes of medical labels at the bottom of the sheet — would adversely affect the utility of the medical label sheet. It articulates a clear functional reason why the use and purpose of the article of manufacture dictated that the "wristband" labels be located at the bottom of the sheet. Additionally, PHG's statements during prosecution of the '425 utility application indicate that there were functional reasons for each of the other features of the medical label sheet, including: for creating one sheet containing labels of different sizes; for the particular sizes of each differently-sized label; for the size of the sheet itself; and for including holes along the side and top of the sheet.

While a district court's determination as to whether a design is primarily ornamental is reviewed for clear error, in this case there is no explicit finding by the court on whether the alleged alternatives are in fact functionally equivalent (i.e., that the alternatives do not adversely affect the utility of the medical label sheet), or any mention or finding whatsoever with respect to the evidence presented in Mr. Press's affidavit. The evidence presented by St. John, in our view, was sufficient to raise a substantial question of invalidity. The only evidence presented by PHG and relied upon by the district court was [inventor] Mr. Moyer's testimony that he and his co-inventor chose the patented designs because they had "the best flow and look." PHG did not offer testimony refuting the assertions made in Mr. Press's affidavit—that functional considerations dictated the medical label design, specifically the "novel feature" of the differently-sized labels being placed at the bottom of the sheet. In fact, on cross-examination Mr. Moyer testified that the original intent in designing a medical label sheet with differently-sized labels was "functional." Therefore, this case is clearly distinguishable from *L.A. Gear*, in which the patentee introduced evidence indicating that "a myriad of athletic shoe designs" could achieve the same functions that were achieved by the patented designs and "[i]t was not disputed that there were other ways of designing athletic shoes to perform the functions of the elements of the [patented] design." 988 F.2d at 1123.

Further, we reject PHG's assertion that St. John's analysis focuses solely on the individual features of the designs rather than their overall appearance. The evidence presented by St. John not only addresses the individual features of the designs, but also their overall appearance.[2] Mr. Press's statements directly pertain to the overall arrangement of the designs as a whole and indicate that the use and purpose of the medical label sheet dictate that the wristband-sized labels be located at the bottom of the sheet. *See supra.* His statements reasonably indicate that once the location of the wristband-sized labels has been dictated by the use and purpose of the medical label sheet, the location of

---

2. Although our case law recognizes that the relevant inquiry with respect to a design patent is the overall appearance of the design, this court invariably also considers whether the elements of the design are themselves dictated by the purpose or use of the article of manufacture. *See Power Controls*, 806 F.2d at 240 ("In determining whether a design is primarily functional, the purposes of the particular elements of the design necessarily must be considered."); *see also L.A. Gear*, 988 F.2d at 1123 (noting that the record showed "the existence of a myriad of athletic shoe designs in which each of the functions identified by [the alleged infringer] as performed by the [patented] design elements was achieved in a way other than by the design of the . . . patent" (emphasis added)). Therefore, St. John's evidence that the particular elements of PHG's designs were dictated by the use or purpose of the medical label sheet "necessarily must be considered." St. John's evidence in this regard includes PHG's statements during prosecution of the '425 utility application indicating that the particular elements of the designs are dictated by the use or purpose of the medical label sheet. While PHG argues that a utility application may be drawn to different features of the same product, a statement with which we whole-heartedly agree, PHG has not done so in this case. Its statements in prosecution are directed to the same features of the medical label sheet as the design. For example, the medical label sheet itself is ideally of standard-size, $8\frac{1}{2}" \times 11"$, and the three different label sizes are all standard-sized as well, one size being standard for medical charts and record books, another for adult patient wristbands, and a third for pediatric patient wristbands. Therefore, PHG's statements during prosecution are relevant to whether the elements of the design are primarily ornamental, and as discussed infra, are also relevant to whether the designs' overall appearance was "dictated by" its use and purpose.

the remaining labels is necessarily dictated as well. This is because the remaining labels, as well as the medical label sheet itself, are of standard size. Therefore, in order to maximize the efficient use of space on the sheet, the location and number of the medical chart and record labels is dictated by the placement of the wristband-sized labels at the bottom of the sheet. St. John's evidence thus directly pertains to, and is sufficient to raise a substantial question with respect to, whether the overall appearance of the patented designs is "dictated by" the medical label sheet's use and purpose. Because St. John has satisfied its burden of raising a substantial question of invalidity, the district court's finding that PHG was likely to show that the patented designs were primarily ornamental is clearly erroneous.

We also note that, contrary to PHG's assertion, the facts in this case are distinguishable from those presented in *Rosco*. In *Rosco*, this court reversed the district court's finding of invalidity based on functionality because the record indicated that other mirror designs "that have non-oval shapes also offer that particular field of view . . . and the record shows that other non-oval shaped mirrors have the same aerodynamic effect." 304 F.3d at 1378. In this case, however, the evidence of record at this preliminary stage indicates that other medical label designs would adversely affect the utility of the medical label sheet, and the district court made no findings to the contrary.

. . .

Accordingly, we vacate the district court's grant of a preliminary injunction.

## NOTES AND QUESTIONS

1. ***The statutory basis for functionality.*** Section 171 does not include an express non-functionality requirement. It does require that designs be "ornamental," and, as the *Best Lock* and *PHG* cases illustrate, courts have concluded that designs that are functional do not qualify as "ornamental." Does functionality capture just one type of scenario where ornamentality is lacking? Or is functionality the flip side of ornamentality—i.e., is functionality always established when there is a lack of ornamentality? Recall that in *Webb*, the court set out the rule that for the design of an object to be ornamental, the appearance of the object had to be a "matter of concern" sometime during the life of the object. Does it follow that the test for functionality is likewise the "matter of concern" test? (Indeed, was the *Webb* case really about functionality?) Why don't the *Best Lock* and *PHG* cases rely on that test to determine functionality?

2. ***"Dictated by" functional considerations.*** In *PHG*, the court quotes the following rule on functionality: "If the patented design is primarily functional rather than ornamental, the patent is invalid." (citing *Power Controls Corp. v. Hybrinetics, Inc.*, 806 F.2d 234, 238 (Fed. Cir. 1986)). In the next sentence, the court asserts that "[t]he design of a useful article is deemed to be functional when 'the appearance of the claimed design is 'dictated by' the use or purpose of the article.'" (citing *L.A. Gear, Inc. v. Thom McAn Shoe Co.*, 988 F.2d 1117, 1123 (Fed. Cir.), *cert. denied*, 510 U.S. 908 (1993)). Are these two statements consistent? Should it be more difficult to establish functionality under a "dictated by" standard than under a "primarily functional" standard? *Rosco, Inc. v. Mirror Lite Co.*, 304 F.3d 1373, 1378 (Fed. Cir. 2002) (reciting the "dictated by" standard and characterizing it as "stringent").

3. *"Dictated by" and evidence of alternative designs.* In *Best Lock*, the court stated that a design is not "dictated by" functional considerations "when alternative designs for the article of manufacture are available." A number of other Federal Circuit decisions likewise emphasize the alternative designs criterion. *See, e.g., L.A. Gear, Inc. v. Thom McAn Shoe Co.*, 988 F.2d 1117, 1123 (Fed. Cir. 1993), *cert. denied*, 510 U.S. 908 (1993) ("When there are several ways to achieve the function of an article of manufacture, the design of the article is more likely to serve a primarily ornamental purpose."); *Rosco, Inc. v. Mirror Lite Co.*, 304 F.3d 1373, 1378 (Fed. Cir. 2002) ("[I]f other designs could produce the same or similar functional capabilities, the design of the article in question is likely ornamental, not functional."); *Seiko Epson Corp. v. Nu-Kote Int'l, Inc.*, 190 F.3d 1360, 1368 (Fed. Cir. 1999) ("[T]he design must not be governed solely by function, *i.e.*, that this is not the only possible form of the article that could perform its function."). In *PHG*, the court states that, among other factors, it will consider "whether alternative designs would adversely affect the utility of the specified article," citing *Berry Sterling Corp. v. Pescor Plastics, Inc.*, 122 F.3d 1452, 1456 (Fed. Cir. 1997). Is the *PHG/Berry Sterling* alternative design criterion different from that recited in other cases, like *Best Lock*? Suppose that the design at issue is an oval mirror and the evidence shows that a commercial embodiment of the claimed design exhibits a superior field of view. In order to escape a conclusion of functionality, must the patentee show not only that alternative designs exist, but that those alternative designs have an equally satisfactory field of view? Is the relevant function to provide a generally satisfactory field of view, or is it to provide a superior field of view? *See Rosco, Inc. v. Mirror Lite Co.*, 304 F.3d 1373 (Fed. Cir. 2002). Suppose that the design at issue is a mold for producing a simulated rock walkway. Would it be sufficient to show that there were alternative designs that also had the same general use (producing a simulated rock walkway)? *See Hupp v. Siroflex of America, Inc.*, 122 F.3d 1456, 1460-1461 (Fed. Cir. 1997). Does *PHG* affect your answers to these questions?

4. *Functionality factors: design patent functionality vs. trade dress functionality.* In *Berry Sterling Corp. v. Pescor Plastics, Inc.*, 122 F.3d 1452, 1456 (Fed. Cir. 1997), cited with approval in *PHG*, the Federal Circuit opined that in determining whether a patented design was dictated by functional considerations, the court should consider a number of factors:

> Other appropriate considerations might include: whether the protected design represents the best design; whether alternative designs would adversely affect the utility of the specified article; whether there are any concomitant utility patents; whether the advertising touts particular features of the design as having specific utility; and whether there are any elements in the design or an overall appearance clearly not dictated by function.

This is a restatement of the *Morton-Norwich* factors, which long guided the C.C.P.A. and Federal Circuit in assessing functionality of trade dress. *See* Chapter 3. Do you support equating trade dress functionality with design patent functionality? Why or why not?

Recall from Chapter 3 that the Supreme Court articulated a trade dress functionality standard in *TrafFix Devices*, citing its *Inwood* decision. Also recall that the *TrafFix Devices* court cast some doubt on the continuing vitality of the "alternative designs" factor of the *Morton-Norwich* test. Should design patent law move in the same direction? One panel opinion of the Federal Circuit may suggest that it should. In *Amini Innovation Corp. v. Anthony California, Inc.*, 439 F.3d 1365, 1370-1371 (Fed. Cir. 2006), the court opined that a feature of a patented design is functional for design patent purposes "if it is essential to the use or purpose of the article or if it affects the cost or quality of the article," citing *Inwood Labs., Inc. v. Ives Labs., Inc.*, 456 U.S. 844, 851 (1982). Is the *Amini* court's formulation consistent with *Best Lock*? With *Berry Sterling*? If not, is it nevertheless preferable, in view of the goals of the design patent system? Also recall that the Court in *TrafFix Devices* said that in determining aesthetic functionality in trade dress cases, it was proper to inquire into whether giving one party exclusive rights in the trade dress would put others at a "significant non-reputation-related disadvantage." Should courts recognize an analogous doctrine of aesthetic functionality for design patents?

5. *Functionality of the claimed design vs. functionality of the commercial embodiment of the claimed design.* In utility patent law, the court routinely faults parties for analyzing substantive patent issues such as infringement and validity in reference to the patentee's commercial embodiment, when those issues instead must be analyzed in reference to the patentee's claimed invention. In *Berry Sterling Corp. v. Pescor Plastics, Inc.*, 122 F.3d 1452, 1456 (Fed. Cir. 1997), the Federal Circuit determined that the trial court erroneously analyzed design patent functionality by examining the patentee's commercial embodiment (a Coke-to-go program cup suitable for an automobile cup holder), instead of the patentee's claimed design, shown below in one of the drawings from the patent-in-suit:

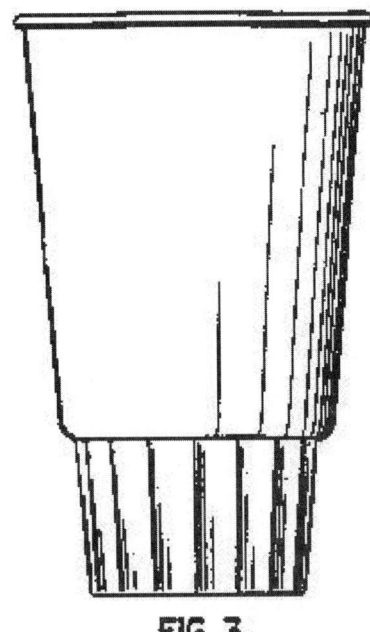

FIG. 3

The commercial embodiment was designed to fit into a majority of cup holders, to fit underneath the valve of a soda fountain, and to hold thirty-two ounces of soft drink while still being reasonably resistant to tipping. These were the manufacturing specifications of the Coke-to-go program cup, but none of these limitations were properly considered in the functionality analysis because the claimed design did not require them for its overall visual appearance as shown in the drawings, according to the Federal Circuit.

Do you agree with the Federal Circuit's approach? Did the Federal Circuit follow its own warning in *Best Lock* and *PHG*? In general, is it possible to assess the functioning of features in an article by reference only to the drawings, and not to an embodiment of the article itself?

**6. *Functionality of design features vs. functionality of overall design*.** In many of its functionality opinions, the Federal Circuit distinguishes between functionality of individual design features and functionality of the design as a whole. The Federal Circuit has held that the functionality assessment must be directed to the overall design:

> [T]he court erred in its analysis by failing to return to the overall appearance after purportedly analyzing each of the elements of the design. While analyzing elements of the design may be appropriate in some circumstances, the determination of whether the patented design is dictated by the function of the article of manufacture must ultimately rest on an analysis of its overall appearance [citing *L.A. Gear, Inc. v. Thom McAn Shoe Co.*, 988 F.2d 1117, 1123 (Fed. Cir. 1993)].

*Berry Sterling Corp. v. Pescor Plastics, Inc.*, 122 F.3d 1452, 1456 (Fed. Cir. 1997). What does the court mean when it says that an analysis of individual features may be appropriate "in some circumstances"? Which circumstances, and for which purposes? Did the Federal Circuit assess the functionality of the design as a whole in *Best Lock*?

Of course, a determination that a design as a whole is functional is not equivalent to a determination that the design as a whole, in fact, does something. The adoption of this latter standard — a standard of de facto functionality as it was called in *Morton-Norwich* — would arguably be fatal to design patent protection. *See Avia Group Int'l, Inc. v. L.A. Gear California, Inc.*, 853 F.2d 1557, 1563 (Fed. Cir. 1988) (theorizing that under such a standard, "it would not be possible to obtain a design patent on a utilitarian article of manufacture").

This tension between analyzing a design's features and analyzing the design as a whole permeates design patent law, as several of the remaining cases in the chapter reflect.

**7. *Burden of proof on functionality*.** In general, on the issue of whether the design claimed in an issued patent is functional, who bears the burden of proof? If the issue arises in connection with a preliminary injunction motion, who bears the burden? As to the second question, the Federal Circuit's utility patent law specifies that a patentee's showing of likelihood of success on the merits must include not only a showing that the plaintiff is likely to succeed in showing infringement, but also evidence that the plaintiff is likely to defeat any challenges to validity. Why, then, does the court in *PHG* say that St. John bears the burden there of raising a substantial question as to functionality?

**8. *Functionality v. claim construction*.** The Federal Circuit has stated that claim construction necessarily precedes any functionality analysis.

*See Berry Sterling Corp. v. Pescor Plastics, Inc.*, 122 F.3d 1452, 1456 (Fed. Cir. 1997); *but cf. Egyptian Goddess*, excerpted in Chapter 6 (discouraging courts from rendering any *verbal* claim construction at all). If claim construction entails eliciting from the overall design the visual appearance of the ornamental features, doesn't claim construction necessarily require an embedded functionality analysis? Under those circumstances, how could a court do a claim construction first, and then do a functionality analysis? We discuss claim construction in more depth later in this chapter.

**9. Best Lock** *and the significance of the claims.* In *Best Lock*, the majority notes that Best Lock did not claim a design "for the entire key." What difference would that have made to the functionality analysis? Why do you suppose that Best Lock claimed a key blade *blank* rather than a finished (bitted) key? Likewise, the majority points out that Best Lock did not claim the *combination* of "a lock and corresponding key." What difference would this have made?

Best Lock had also acquired design patents on other key blade blanks, and separate design patents on the keyways corresponding to each of the key blade blanks. For example, U.S. Design Pat. No. 328,414 issued Aug. 4, 1992, claimed the keyway design ("front face of a key plug") corresponding to the blade profile design of the design patent-in-suit in *Best Lock*.

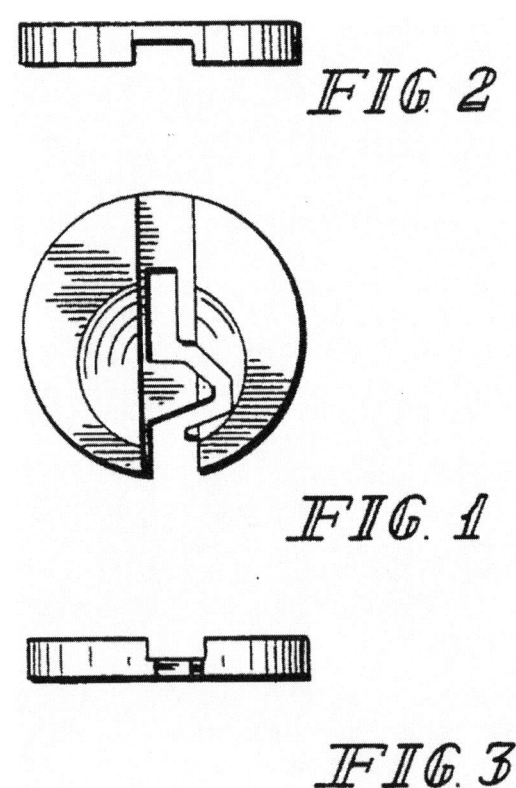

Why is the existence of separate design patent on the keyways "irrelevant" to whether the claimed key blade blank is functional, as the majority asserts?

## C. NOVELTY AND NONOBVIOUSNESS

As we have seen, Section 171 requires that the subject matter of a design patent be a "new, original and ornamental design for an article of manufacture," and that it satisfy the other provisions of Title 35 applicable to utility patents (except as displaced by design patent provisions). Two important provisions of Title 35 that apply to both utility and design patents are Sections 102 and 103, which together establish the framework for analyzing whether claimed subject matter is patentable over the "prior art." More specifically, Section 102 defines the evidence that may qualify as patent-defeating prior art, and incorporates the requirement that claimed subject matter not be "anticipated" by that prior art (also known as the "novelty" requirement), whereas Section 103 provides that novel claimed subject matter must also be nonobvious in view of the prior art. In utility patent law, novelty and nonobviousness are the central aspects of nearly all patentability determinations, having occupied the courts and the PTO in hundreds of cases. The many subsidiary doctrines developed in those cases, and the policy determinations that underlie those doctrines, have been motivated by the need to fine-tune the utility patent system to serve its constitutional purpose of promoting "progress in the useful arts."

What happens when the rules of novelty and nonobviousness are transplanted to the design patent context, where the underlying policy balancing may be different? The cases and materials in this section reflect the struggle to bend novelty and nonobviousness doctrines to the unique needs of the design patent system.

### Door-Master Corp. v. Yorktowne, Inc.
256 F.3d 1308 (Fed. Cir. 2001)

Rader, Circuit Judge:

### I.

There are two basic ways to mount a cabinet door on the surrounding cabinet frame: inset mounting and overlay mounting. With inset mounting, the door fits within the frame and does not cover any of the frame's front surface. The front surface of an inset-mounted door is typically flush with the front surface of the surrounding frame. With overlay mounting, the door covers some or all of the frame's front surface. The rear surface of an overlay-mounted door abuts the front surface of the frame and the front surface of the door is offset from the front surface of the frame. During mounting, inset-mounted doors are more difficult to align with the surrounding frame, but they generally have a more desirable appearance than overlay-mounted doors.

The '718 patent [U.S. Patent No. Des. 338,718] covers a design for an "integrated door and frame." As the name suggests, while the article shown in the '718 patent is a single door, its front view appears like an inset door and frame combination. Accordingly, the door has the desirable look of an inset-mounted door without the difficulty of inset mounting. As a design patent, the '718 patent includes a single claim. That claim reads, "An ornamental

**336** Chapter 5 Securing Rights

design for an integrated door and frame as shown and described." The '718 patent includes four figures:

FIG. 1 is a front elevation of the integrated door and frame of the present invention, the broken lines showing a door pull are for illustrative purposes only and form no part of the claim design;

FIG. 2 is a rear view of an integrated door and frame of FIG. 1;

FIG. 3 is a side elevation, both sides being identical, of an integrated door and frame of FIG. 1; and,

FIG. 4 is a section taken through 4-4 of FIG. 1, showing the tongue and groove construction of an integrated door and frame of FIG. 1.

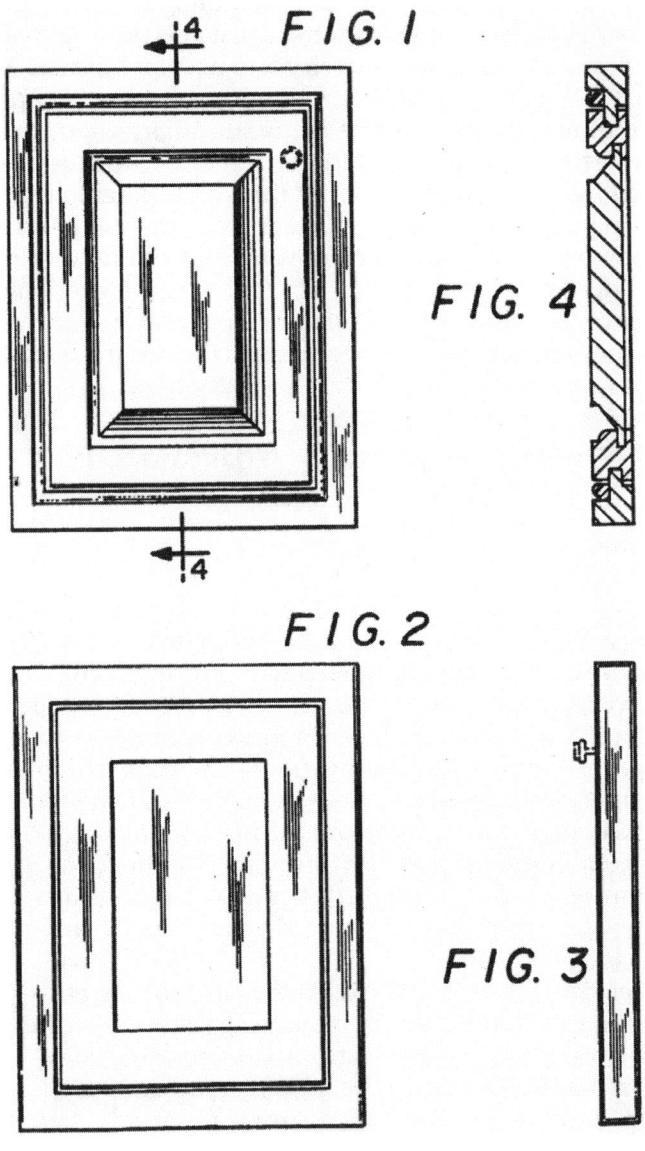

Conestoga manufactures the accused door, known as the "Richland" door, for Yorktowne. Yorktowne markets and resells the Richland door for cabinets. Like the '718 patent design, the front view of the Richland door looks like an inset door and frame combination.

During trial, Conestoga and Yorktowne asserted Conestoga's CRP-10 door and a corresponding CRP-10 end panel as prior art against the '718 patent. Cabinet dealers have inset mounted the CRP-10 door within a beaded cabinet frame. When the inset-mounted CRP-10 door is closed, the front view of the combined door and frame looks very similar to the front view of the '718 patent design shown in FIG. 1 above, except that the hinges of the CRP-10 are visible from the front. When the CRP-10 door is opened, the rear of the door becomes visible. The rear of the CRP-10 door lacks the outer border of the rear of the '718 patent design, as shown in FIG. 2.

The front of the CRP-10 end panel looks like FIG. 1 of the '718 patent. The rear of the end panel is fixed to a substrate at the end of a cabinet to simulate a door and frame that matches the adjacent doors and frames. Because the end panel is fixed to a substrate, it does not have a rear view that corresponds to the rear view shown in FIG. 2 of the '718 patent.

[The jury determined that the '718 patent was not anticipated by the prior art and was infringed. Yorktowne and Conestoga appealed.]

II.

As with a utility patent, design patent anticipation requires a showing that a single prior art reference is "identical in all material respects" to the claimed invention. *Hupp v. Siroflex of Am., Inc.*, 122 F.3d 1456, 1461 (Fed. Cir. 1997). Because "[t]hat which infringes, if later, would anticipate, if earlier," [cit.], the design patent infringement test also applies to design patent anticipation. That test requires the court to first construe the claimed design, if appropriate, and then to compare the claimed design to the article. *OddzOn Prods., Inc. v. Just Toys, Inc.*, 122 F.3d 1396, 1404 (Fed. Cir. 1997).

In construing the claimed design, this court first notes that only "the nonfunctional aspects of an ornamental design as shown in a patent" are proper bases for design patent protection. *KeyStone Retaining Wall Sys., Inc. v. Westrock, Inc.*, 997 F.2d 1444, 1450 (Fed. Cir. 1993). In addition, "generally concealed features are not proper bases for design patent protection because their appearance cannot be a 'matter of concern.'" *Id.* at 1451 (quoting *In re Stevens*, 173 F.2d 1015, 1016 (1949)). The parties appear to agree that the front view of FIG. 1 (and the portions of FIG. 4 that show more detail of the front features) is part of the claimed design and its features are proper bases for design patent protection. Moreover, the parties do not appear to dispute that the internal connecting features of FIG. 4 are generally concealed and thus are not protected by the design patent.

However, Yorktowne and Conestoga urge this court to construe the claims so that the rear features shown in FIG. 2 and part of FIG. 4 of the '718 patent are not part of the protected design. They assert that the rear features only appear in the patent to fully show the article of manufacture, as required by the regulations in effect when the '718 patent issued. *See* 37 C.F.R. §1.152 (1993) (requiring design patent drawings to "contain a sufficient number of views to constitute a complete disclosure of the appearance of the article"). While a patented design may be embodied in less than an entire article of manufacture, [cit.], a "patented design is defined by the drawings in the patent." *KeyStone*, 997 F.2d at 1450. Nothing in the '718 patent indicates that the rear features are not part of the claimed design. Indeed, the '718 patent claims "[a]n ornamental design for an integrated door and frame, as shown and described." Then FIG. 2 and part of FIG. 4 show the rear features.

Furthermore, §1.152 may have required the drawings to disclose the appearance of the entire article of manufacture, but it did not require those drawings to claim the design embodied in the entire article of manufacture. This is clear from the '718 patent itself. The drawings show a door pull in broken lines and the description of FIG. 1 excludes that door pull from the claimed design by stating, "the broken lines showing the door pull are for illustrative purposes only and form no part of the claimed design." Similarly, the patentee could have shown the rear features in broken lines to comply with §1.152 while excluding those features from the claimed design. Rather than doing so, the patentee included the rear features in the claimed design. In addition, the rear features are not generally concealed. After the door has been installed, the rear features may be temporarily hidden from view when the door is closed. The rear features are visible, however, before the door is installed and when the door is open during use. Accordingly, the rear features are not "hidden" and their appearance is a "matter of concern." *See KeyStone*, 997 F.2d at 1451 (holding that "there is no hidden portion" of a patented block even though "it ceases to be visible as a block when incorporated in a wall" because "[a]s a block, all parts of it are visible").

Finally, the rear features are not functional. Many different configurations of those features (oval, triangular, etc.) could perform the same functions of an integrated door and frame. *See L.A. Gear, Inc. v. Thom McAn Shoe Co.*, 988 F.2d 1117, 1123 (Fed. Cir. 1993). . . . Therefore, the rear features are proper bases for design protection in the '718 patent.

In the second step of the test for infringement or anticipation, the court compares the claim to the accused or allegedly anticipating article. For infringement or anticipation to be found the two designs must be substantially the same. *Gorham Mfg. Co. v. White*, 81 U.S. 511, 528 (1871). Two designs are substantially the same if their resemblance is deceptive to the extent that it would induce an ordinary observer, giving such attention as a purchaser usually gives, to purchase an article having one design supposing it to be the other. *Id.* In making this comparison, the court must focus on the protected features of the design, and determine whether those common features would deceive the ordinary observer. *OddzOn Prods.*, 122 F.3d at 1405.

The front of the CRP-10 end panel and the front of the CRP-10 inset door and frame look very similar to the design features shown in FIG. 1 of the '718 patent. However, the CRP-10 door is mounted on hinges that are visible from the front when the door is closed. The '718 patent shows no such hinges. Moreover, the rear view of the prior art both the end panel and the CRP-10 inset door looks substantially different from the rear features of the '718 patent shown in FIG. 2 and part of FIG. 4. On the CRP-10 inset door, the entire outer border is missing. The back of the CRP-10 end panel does not have any visible features similar to the rear features shown in FIG. 2 and part of FIG. 4 of the '718 patent because it is secured to a substrate that covers the rear of the panel. In light of these differences between the design of the '718 patent and the prior art, a reasonable jury could have concluded that Yorktowne and Conestoga did not meet their burden of showing anticipation by clear and convincing evidence.

Yorktowne and Conestoga argue that the jury's finding that the CRP-10 door and end panel did not anticipate the '718 patent is inconsistent with its finding that the Richland door infringed it. Although the Richland door has an appearance similar to the prior art, the similarity arises in comparison of the front view of the accused door and the prior art. As noted before, however, the CRP-10 door has visible hinges in the front view, while neither the Richland door nor the '718 patent design has such hinges. Additionally, many of the differences between the prior art and the claimed design appear on the back panel. On the Richland door, unlike the prior art, the back panel is identical to the claimed design. Thus, not only are the front features of the Richland door similar to the '718 patent, but the rear features are also similar. Accordingly, a reasonable jury could have consistently concluded that the Richland door infringed the '718 patent and that the CRP-10 door and end panel did not anticipate it. The jury could have found no anticipation because of the differences in the rear panels of the prior art and the claimed designs. Then, the jury could have found infringement because the Richland door has a rear design strikingly similar to the claimed design.

[*Affirmed.*]

## NOTES AND QUESTIONS

1. ***An overview of Section 102: establishing that evidence qualifies as "prior art."*** Although we need not delve into all the nuances of Section 102, a brief overview will be useful. Oversimplifying, Section 102 creates two classes of prior art, sometimes referred to as "prior invention" and "statutory bar" prior art, respectively. Sections 102(a) and (b) are illustrative:

> 35 U.S.C. §102 Conditions for patentability; Novelty and loss of right to patent.
> A person shall be entitled to a patent unless—
> (a) the invention was known or used by others in this country, or patented or described in a printed publication in this or a foreign country, before the invention thereof by the applicant for patent, or
> (b) the invention was patented or described in a printed publication in this or a foreign country or in public use or on sale in this country, more than one year prior to the date of the application for patent in the United States. . . .

Section 102(b) is the principal statutory bar (or "loss of right") provision, and is probably the major source of prior art in the patent system. In a statutory bar provision, prior art is defined by reference to the patent application filing date. Under Section 102(b), for example, a publication dated more than a year before the applicant's filing date qualifies as Section 102(b) prior art against the applicant's claims, even if the publication is authored by the applicant herself. Effectively, the applicant has one year after publication within which to file a U.S. patent application. This is conventionally referred to as the one-year "grace period."

Section 102(a) is an illustrative "prior invention" provision. Prior art under Section 102(a) is defined by reference to the applicant's date of invention. For example, a third party's publication dated before the applicant's invention date qualifies as prior art against the applicant's claims. However, the applicant's own publication cannot qualify as Section 102(a) prior art. The applicant's publication signifies the applicant's act of invention, and so cannot be prior to the applicant's invention date. Because of the practical difficulties of establishing a date of invention, Section 102(a) and (other prior invention provisions) tend to be less frequently invoked in debates over patent validity.

In *Door-Master*, the asserted prior art evidence is the Conestoga CRP-10 door and its end panel. The application date of the patent-in-suit is February 15, 1991. Assuming that the CRP-10 door and end panel were available in the marketplace by March 1989, would it qualify as Section 102(b) prior art? Section 102(a) prior art? Both?

2. *Claim interpretation as a predicate for the anticipation analysis.* In *Door-Master*, whether the evidence qualified as prior art was apparently not an issue on appeal. Instead, the court's opinion focused on whether the qualifying prior art anticipated the claimed design. The anticipation analysis requires a comparison between the prior art and the claims, and so the court (or the PTO) must properly interpret the claims before it can conduct an anticipation analysis. In utility patents, claim interpretation involves understanding the meaning of claim terms by considering the terms themselves, other portions of the patent document and prosecution history, and (possibly) evidence extrinsic to the patent documents. *See Phillips v. AWH Corp.*, 415 F.3d 1303 (Fed. Cir. 2005) (en banc). In design patents, the claims merely reference the drawings, so design patent claim interpretation starts with the drawings. What steps did the *Door-Master* court take in its claim interpretation? Did the *Door-Master* court improperly conflate claim interpretation with other design patent doctrines?

3. *Section 102 and the strict-identity rule for anticipation.* In utility patent law, as the *Door-Master* opinion points out, anticipation exists where a single prior art reference discloses each element of a given patent claim. (Section 102 does not articulate the strict-identity rule in express terms, but its subsections do refer to the "invention," which is understood to mean the precise invention as claimed.) In design patent law, the relevant comparison for anticipation is between the disclosures of the prior art reference and the properly interpreted design patent drawings. According to the *Door-Master* court, does that comparison involve matching the prior art disclosures with the design patent drawings under a rule of strict identity? If not, what is the relevant rule for comparison? Why does the *Door-Master* court refer to infringement rules when explaining the rules for anticipation? Is it sensible to insist on symmetry between the anticipation rules and the infringement rules? Symmetry was an important consideration in *International Seaway*, excerpted below.

4. *Color and the patentability of designs.* Suppose that a design patent claims a design for a microwave oven having two stripes in contrasting colors

around the border of the oven's door. A prior art reference discloses a microwave oven having two stripes of the same color around the border of the door. May color be considered in distinguishing the claimed design from the prior art? *See In re Haruna*, 249 F.3d 1327, 1336 (Fed. Cir. 2001).

5. *"New" and "original."* Section 171 specifies that in order to be patentable, designs must be "new" and "original," in addition to satisfying other "provisions of this title relating to patents for inventions." Given that those other provisions include Sections 102 and 103, which include detailed rules about the extent of newness and inventiveness, should the term "new" in Section 171 be accorded any independent significance? Note that 35 U.S.C. §101 also specifies that the subject matter of utility patents must be "new." What about the term "original" in Section 171? Should it be treated as a separate patentability requirement, or should it be treated as subsumed by Sections 102 and 103?

---

In utility patent law, the infringement analysis is connected to the validity analysis. The next case explores the implications of that interconnection for design patents. In 2008, as we discuss in Chapter 6, the Court of Appeals for the Federal Circuit decided a major case, *Egyptian Goddess*, on the standard for design patent infringement. Given the connection between infringement and validity standards, it was not surprising that the Federal Circuit subsequently confronted arguments about whether the *Egyptian Goddess* infringement standard affected the standard for anticipation. In the following case, the Federal Circuit overrules, in part, its *Door-Master* opinion. Although the case is about anticipation in design patents, and thus belongs at this point in the book, you may find that the discussion in the case is more meaningful after you have studied the materials on design patent infringement in Chapter 6.

### INTERNATIONAL SEAWAY TRADING CORP. v. WALGREENS CORP.
589 F.3d 1233 (Fed. Cir. 2009)

DYK, Circuit Judge:

. . .

#### Background

Plaintiff-Appellant Seaway is an Ohio corporation that acts as a buyer's agent and/or importer of footwear to mass merchandise retailers, as well as to footwear, apparel, and sporting goods stores. Seaway also creates its own shoe and boot designs and pursues design patents for them. Defendant-Appellee Walgreens is an Illinois corporation with retail drug stores across the country that sell footwear, among other products. Defendant-Appellee Touchsport is a California corporation that, like Seaway, serves as a buyer's agent and/or importer of footwear to retailers, including Walgreens.

[Seaway's patents-in-suit included D529,263, among others. The patents-in-suit claimed designs for clogs—which the court described as "casual, lightweight footwear."]

A single Patent Office Examiner examined and allowed each of the three patents-in-suit. During prosecution of the '263 patent application, the examiner considered and found the '263 patent design patentable over: (a) four pages from the website of Crocs that depicted various models of Crocs clogs, including the Beach model clog; (b) five pages of photographs of the Crocs Beach model clog; and (c) a December 2002 archival version of the Crocs website, depicting various views of a Crocs clog. In the examination of the '263 patent application, the examiner did not have the benefit of the Crocs '789 patent [D517,789], which depicted the Crocs Beach model clog, even though the '789 patent issued before the examination was concluded. . . .

[Seaway sued on the patents-in-suit.] Seaway asserted that Touchsport had imported and continued to import shoes that infringed the Seaway patents and that Walgreens had sold and continued to sell the allegedly infringing shoes. Walgreens and Touchsport filed a motion for summary judgment on June 24, 2008, contending that Seaway's patents were invalid as anticipated under 35 U.S.C. §102(a) & (e) by the Crocs Beach and Cayman model clogs and/or the Crocs '789 patent, or as obvious under 35 U.S.C. §103 in view of the Crocs Beach and Cayman model clogs and/or the Crocs '789 patent. [Figure 1] depicting the design in the '789 patent, and [Figure 2 from the] '263 patent . . . are set forth below.

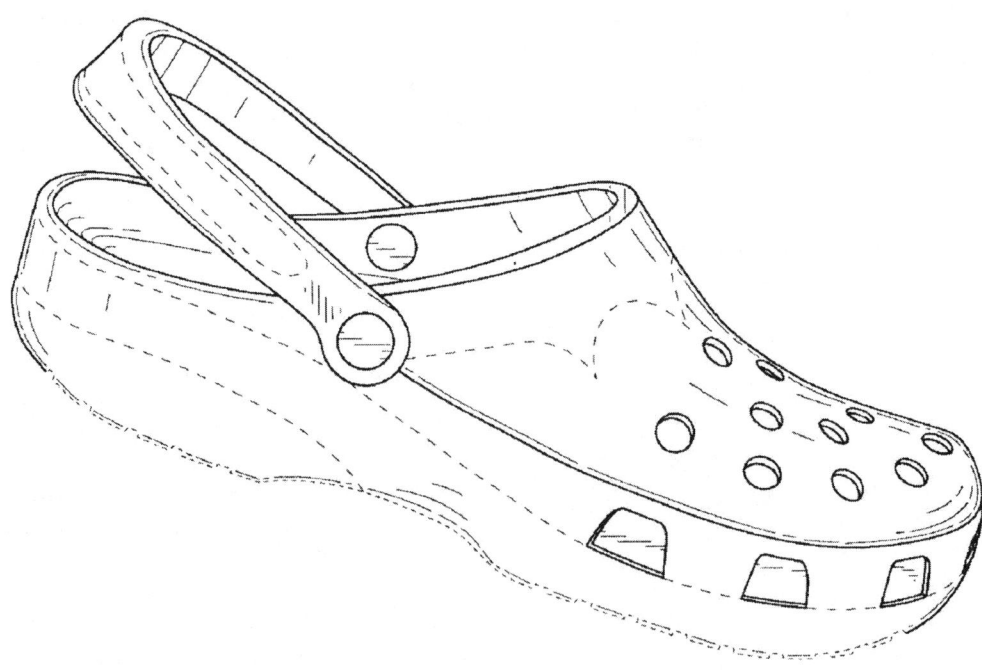

FIG.1

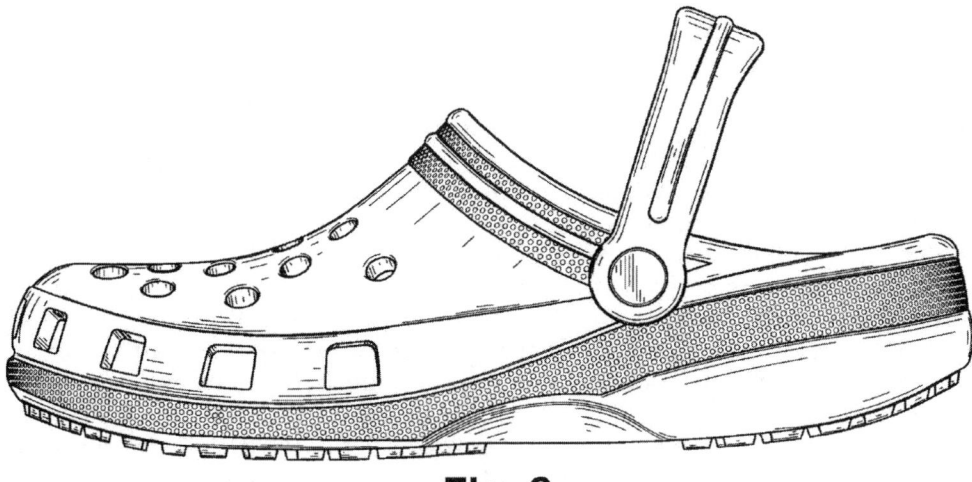

**Fig. 2**

[The district court granted summary judgment on anticipation, and Seaway appealed.]

. . .

### Discussion

#### I

Seaway first contends that the district court should have applied the point of novelty test in addition to the ordinary observer test during its anticipation analysis. Our decision in *Egyptian Goddess, Inc. v. Swisa, Inc.*, 543 F.3d 665 (Fed. Cir. 2008) (en banc), changed the test for infringement. In doing so, we held "that the 'point of novelty' test should no longer be used in the analysis of a claim of design patent infringement" and that "the 'ordinary observer' test should be the sole test for determining whether a design patent has been infringed." The issue remains whether *Egyptian Goddess* also requires a similar change in the test for invalidity. We reserved this question in *Egyptian Goddess* and more recently in *Titan Tire Corp. v. Case New Holland, Inc.*, 566 F.3d 1372, 1384 (Fed. Cir. 2009). After careful consideration, we have concluded that the district court was correct in concluding that *Egyptian Goddess* necessarily requires a change in the standard for anticipation.

Section 171 of Title 35 provides the criteria for obtaining a design patent. It provides that: "Whoever invents any new, original and ornamental design for an article of manufacture may obtain a patent therefor, subject to the conditions and requirements of this title." 35 U.S.C. §171. . . . Section 171 requires that the "conditions and requirements of this title" be applied to design patents, thus requiring application of the provisions of sections 102 (anticipation) and 103 (invalidity). Our cases have recognized that in the past we have applied a dual test for anticipation identical to the then-applicable test for infringement, namely the ordinary observer and point of novelty tests. *See Bernhardt, L.L.C. v. Collezione Europa USA, Inc.*, 386 F.3d 1371, 1383 (Fed. Cir. 2004).[2] But the application of those tests in the context of infringement and anticipation was necessarily different.

---

2. *See also Contessa Food Prods., Inc. v. Conagra, Inc.*, 282 F.3d 1370, 1377 (Fed. Cir. 2002); [cit].

In the case of infringement, in applying the ordinary observer test, we compared the patented design with the accused design. *Contessa,* 282 F.3d at 1377. In the case of anticipation, we compared the patented design with the alleged anticipatory reference. *Door-Master Corp. v. Yorktowne, Inc.,* 256 F.3d 1308, 1313 (Fed. Cir. 2001).

In applying the point of novelty test in the case of infringement, we looked at whether the accused design appropriated the points of novelty of the patented design. *Litton Sys., Inc. v. Whirlpool Corp.,* 728 F.2d 1423, 1444 (Fed. Cir. 1984) ("For a design patent to be infringed . . . no matter how similar two items look, 'the accused device must appropriate the novelty in the patented device which distinguishes it from the prior art.'" (internal citations omitted)). The points of novelty for the patented design were determined by comparing the patented design to the prior art designs. *Bernhardt,* 386 F.3d at 1382. In the case of anticipation, we compared the patented design with the alleged anticipatory reference to see if it appropriated the points of novelty of the prior art reference. The points of novelty of the prior art reference were determined by looking to earlier prior art to determine the points of novelty in the anticipatory reference. The ordinary observer and point of novelty tests were applied in much the same manner for obviousness as for anticipation,[3] except that in the case of obviousness the features of the prior art could be combined to create a single anticipatory reference or an earlier single reference could be modified based on the knowledge of a skilled artisan. *See, e.g., Durling v. Spectrum Furniture Co.,* 101 F.3d 100, 103 (Fed. Cir. 1996).

While our cases have utilized the point of novelty test for infringement and anticipation, as we pointed out in *Egyptian Goddess,* 543 F.3d at 672, this test was not mandated by *Smith v. Whitman Saddle Co.,* 148 U.S. 674 (1893), or precedent from other courts. In *Whitman,* the Supreme Court utilized only the ordinary observer test for determining infringement and invalidity, as did at least one later circuit case following *Whitman (Bevin Bros. Mfg. Co. v. Starr Bros. Bell Co.,* 114 F. 362, 362 (C.C.D. Conn. 1902)).

Moreover, it has been well established for over a century that the same test must be used for both infringement and anticipation. This general rule derives from the Supreme Court's proclamation 120 years ago in the context of utility patents: "[t]hat which infringes, if later, would anticipate, if earlier." *Peters v. Active Mfg. Co.,* 129 U.S. 530, 537 (1889). The same rule applies for design patents. *See Bernhardt,* 386 F.3d at 1378 (explaining that the test for determining anticipation of a design patent is the same as the test for infringement); *Door-Master,* 256 F.3d at 1312 (stating that the test for infringement is the same as the test for anticipation in the design patent context); *Litton,* 728 F.2d at 1440.

In *Egyptian Goddess,* we abandoned the point of novelty test for design patent infringement and held that the ordinary observer test should serve as

---

3. *See Bernhardt,* 386 F.3d at 1384 (noting that the point of novelty determination "is not especially different from the factual determinations that district courts routinely undertake" in their obviousness analysis); *cf. Goodyear Tire & Rubber Co. v. Hercules Tire & Rubber Co.,* 162 F.3d 1113, 1119 (Fed. Cir. 1998) (noting that the district court had "adopted the same points of novelty that it had relied on in determining that the '080 patent was not invalid for obviousness" and affirming the district court's decision); *Litton,* 728 F.2d at 1444 (applying the results of the obviousness analysis when determining the point of novelty of the claimed design).

the sole test for design patent infringement. 543 F.3d at 678. The ordinary observer test originated in 1871 when the Supreme Court held

> that if, in the eye of an ordinary observer, giving such attention as a purchaser usually gives, two designs are substantially the same, if the resemblance is such as to deceive such an observer, inducing him to purchase one supposing it to be the other, the first one patented is infringed by the other.

*Gorham Mfg. Co. v. White,* 81 U.S. 511, 528 (1871). In *Egyptian Goddess,* we also refined the ordinary observer test by characterizing the ordinary observer as being "deemed to view the differences between the patented design and the accused product in the context of the prior art." 543 F.3d at 676. . . . We further determined that the point of novelty test, as a second and free-standing requirement for proof of design patent infringement, was inconsistent with the ordinary observer test laid down in *Gorham* and was not mandated by Supreme Court cases or other precedent. *Id.* at 672.*

In light of Supreme Court precedent and our precedent holding that the same tests must be applied to infringement and anticipation, and our holding in *Egyptian Goddess* that the ordinary observer test is the sole test for infringement, we now conclude that the ordinary observer test must logically be the sole test for anticipation as well. In doing so, we will prevent an inconsistency from developing between the infringement and anticipation analyses, and we will continue our well-established practice of maintaining identical tests for infringement and anticipation.

We note as well that the problems inherent in the point of novelty test in the infringement context also exist in the anticipation context. The test is just as difficult to apply in the context of anticipation as in the context of infringement, encouraging the focus on minor differences between the allegedly anticipatory reference and the patented design. So too, applying the point of novelty test in the context of anticipation, as in the context of infringement, creates the need to canvass the entire prior art to identify the points of novelty. In addition, eliminating the point of novelty test for anticipation "has the advantage of avoiding the debate over the extent to which a combination of old design features can serve as a point of novelty under the point of novelty test." *Id.* at 677. Just as the problems deriving from the point of novelty test exist in both the infringement and anticipation contexts, the benefits of applying the refined ordinary observer test are identical in both.

Seaway's arguments to preserve the point of novelty test for invalidity are unconvincing. Seaway argues that adopting the ordinary observer test for anticipation will blur the distinction between the tests for obviousness under §103 and for anticipation under §102, resulting in jury confusion. According to Seaway, the test for invalidity due to obviousness is whether a designer of ordinary skill in the art would have found the patented design, as a whole, obvious in light of the prior art. *Litton,* 728 F.2d at 1443. The test for invalidity due to anticipation, on the other hand, requires the jury to consider the perspective of the ordinary consumer. There is in fact no potential for confusion. For design patents, the role of one skilled in the art in the

---

*Ed. note: We discuss *Gorham* and *Egyptian Goddess* in detail in Chapter 6.

obviousness context lies only in determining whether to combine earlier references to arrive at a single piece of art for comparison with the potential design or to modify a single prior art reference.[5] Once that piece of prior art has been constructed, obviousness, like anticipation, requires application of the ordinary observer test, not the view of one skilled in the art. And, as noted by Seaway, "[b]oth the ordinary observer test, whether applied for infringement or invalidity, and the obviousness test, applied for invalidity under Section 103, focus on the *overall* designs." Appellant's Br. 28 (citing *OddzOn*, 122 F.3d at 1405, and *Litton*, 728 F.2d at 1443). Under these circumstances, we see no potential for jury confusion.

In summary, the district court did not err in concluding that the ordinary observer test is the sole test for design patent invalidity under §102.

II

A

Seaway's second contention is that, even if the ordinary observer test is found to be the sole and proper test for anticipation under §102, the district court misapplied the ordinary observer test by failing to compare the entirety of the patented designs, including the clogs' insoles, with the Crocs '789 patent. The district court, relying on *Contessa*, held "that the law requires a court to consider only those portions of the product that are visible during normal use, regardless of whether those portions are visible during the point of sale." *Int'l Seaway Trading Corp.*, 599 F. Supp.2d at 1315. The court did "not consider any aspects of the insoles of the shoes" because the insoles are "hidden by the user's foot." *Id.* We conclude that the district court erred, and we vacate and remand for a determination of whether the differences between the insole patterns in the patents-in-suit and in the prior Crocs art bar a finding of anticipation or obviousness.

In *Contessa*, we considered the issue of infringement with regard to a shrimp serving tray. The district court held that "any reasonable fact finder would conclude that the competing designs are substantially similar despite the minor differences in tray structure." *Contessa*, 282 F.3d at 1377. The district court did not consider the undersides of the trays because they were not visible at the time of sale. *Id.* at 1377-78. On appeal, we stated: "Our precedent makes clear that all of the ornamental features illustrated in the figures must be considered in evaluating design patent infringement." *Id.* at 1378. We found that the district court in *Contessa* erred by limiting its infringement inquiry to those features visible at the time of sale, rather than to those features visible at any time in the "normal use" lifetime of the accused product. *Id.* at 1379. We explained that "normal use" in the design patent context extends from the completion of manufacture or assembly until the ultimate destruction, loss, or disappearance of the article. *Id.* at 1379-80 (citing *In re Webb*, 916 F.2d 1553, 1557-58 (Fed. Cir. 1990)). The same test necessarily applies to anticipation.

The district court here misconstrued *Contessa* as requiring that the normal use of a clog be limited to the time when it is worn. *Contessa* did not exclude

---

5. That combination or modification would not necessarily yield a single piece of prior art identical to a patented design since there may be no motivation to change the prior art to achieve such identity.

the point of sale from the normal use of a product. Rather, it emphasized that normal use should not be limited to only one phase or portion of the normal use lifetime of an accused product. *Id.* at 1380 (citing *KeyStone Retaining Wall Sys., Inc. v. Westrock, Inc.*, 997 F.2d 1444, 1450 (Fed. Cir. 1993)). The sale of a clog occurs after it has been manufactured and before it is ultimately destroyed. Thus, the point of sale for a clog clearly occurs during its normal use lifetime. At the point of sale, the insole is visible to potential purchasers when the clog is displayed on a shelf or rack and when the clog is picked up for examination. Similarly, removing a clog from a wearer's foot also occurs after manufacture and before destruction of the clog, so it also falls squarely within the clog's normal use lifetime. The wearer may remove the clog temporarily to stretch out his or her toes, leave the clogs on the beach to go for a swim, or engage in countless other activities that would leave the insole exposed.

Walgreens and Touchsport acknowledge that the district court misinterpreted *Contessa* but argue that it was harmless error. They assert that it was a harmless error because insoles have an insignificant effect on the overall visual appearance of the clogs. They claim there is a "universal truth that consumers buy shoes primarily for their exterior appearance. The insole therefore contributes little to the overall appearance of the shoe to an ordinary observer with knowledge of the prior art." Appellees' Br. 51. We reject this argument. The burden is on an accused infringer to show by clear and convincing evidence facts supporting the conclusion that the patent is invalid. [cit.] Hence, Walgreens and Touchsport had the burden to establish by clear and convincing evidence that consumers do not consider the insoles of shoes to be significant. The appellees failed to present any evidence in support of this argument.

Walgreens and Touchsport also argue that the district court's error was harmless because the asserted differences between the insoles of the patents-in-suit and the prior art "were at most slight variations of design elements already present in the Crocs prior art." Appellees' Br. 51. We disagree. The insole pattern for the patents-in-suit is distinctly different than the Crocs insole pattern.

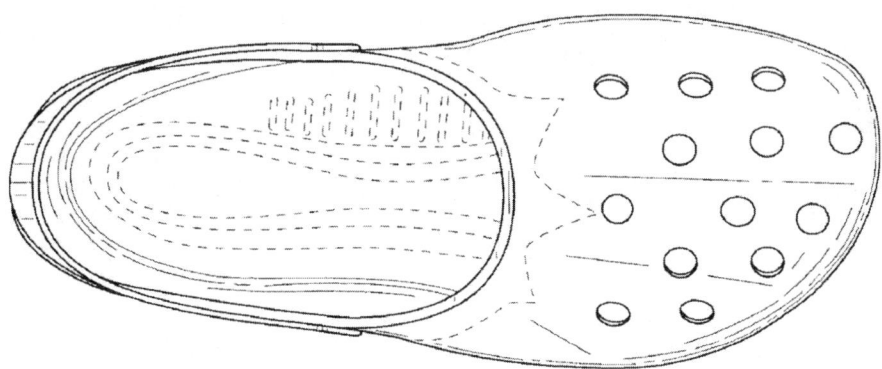

FIG.6

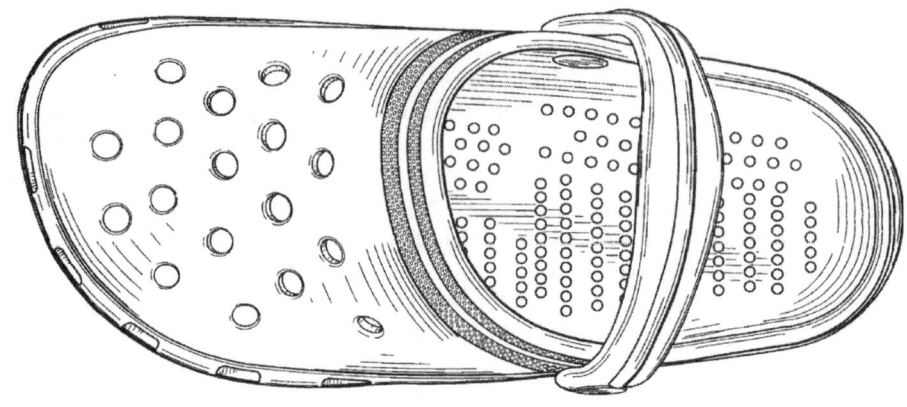

**Fig. 6**

The Crocs '789 patent, as shown above in [the top figure], contains a long, U-shaped dimpling pattern on the insole. In contrast, the patents-in-suit, as demonstrated above in the [bottom] figure, have a dimpling pattern that includes multiple short rows of dimples. Because we cannot say that these differences are insignificant as a matter of law, a genuine issue of material fact exists as to whether the designs would be viewed as substantially similar in the eyes of the ordinary observer armed with the knowledge of the prior art.

Beyond the insole features of its patented designs, Seaway argues that a genuine issue of material fact exists as to whether the exterior features of its designs preclude a finding of anticipation. It claims that four exterior features differ from the prior art to the degree necessary to preclude summary judgment: (1) the number and arrangement of the circular openings on the upper of the clog; (2) the number and position of the rectangular cut-outs in the lower portion of the upper of the clog; (3) the shape of the toe portion of the clog; and (4) the raised pattern of the outsole of the clog. These features are identical in all three of Seaway's patents-in-suit. With regard to these alleged dissimilarities, the district court stated:

> Slight variations on the number and position of the circular holes on the top of the shoe, the rectangular holes on the toe of the shoe as well as the design of different shaped rectangles on the sole of the shoe would not convince a reasonable jury, or an ordinary observer with knowledge of the prior art, that the limitations were not inherently disclosed in the '789 patent. This conclusion does not change merely because plaintiff slightly changed the arrangement of the textured portions on the top and around the bottom portion of the sides of the shoe.

*Int'l Seaway Trading Corp.*, 599 F. Supp.2d at 1318. We agree with the district court that these minor variations in the shoe are insufficient to preclude a finding of anticipation because they do not change the overall visual impression of the shoe. Although the ordinary observer test requires consideration of the design as a whole, *Egyptian Goddess,* 543 F.3d at 675; *Contessa,* 282 F.3d at 1378; *Braun, Inc. v. Dynamics Corp. of Am.,* 975 F.2d 815, 820 (Fed. Cir. 1992), this does not prevent the district court on summary judgment from determining that individual features of the design are insignificant from the point of view of the ordinary observer and should not be considered as part of the overall comparison. The mandated overall comparison is a comparison taking into account significant differences between the two designs, not minor or trivial differences that necessarily exist between any two designs that are not exact copies of one another. Just as "minor differences between a patented design and an accused article's design cannot, and shall not, prevent a finding of infringement," *Litton,* 728 F.2d at 1444, so too minor differences cannot prevent a finding of anticipation.

. . .

## Conclusion

In summary, we conclude that the district court correctly held that the ordinary observer test is the sole test of invalidity. The district court erred, however, in failing to compare the insole patterns in Seaway's patented designs to the prior art as part of an overall comparison of the designs. We vacate and remand for further proceedings on the limited issue of whether the differences in the insole patterns between the prior (Crocs) art and the patented designs bar a finding of anticipation or obviousness.

[*Affirmed-in-part, vacated-in-part, and remanded.*]

CLEVENGER, Circuit Judge, dissenting in part:

I part company with the court on only one issue, which is the scope of the district court's further action on remand.

The majority concludes that the district court was correct as a matter of law in holding that the ordinary observer must find anticipation when comparing the four different exterior design elements of the patented designs with the Crocs design patent. However, with regard to the comparable insole designs, the majority ascertains a sufficient difference to preclude anticipation as a matter of law. The majority thus concludes that the law permits dissection of a design as a whole into its component pieces. With laser-like focus, the fact finder is permitted to decide that the changes on the top of the clogs are trivial enough to sustain anticipation. The same holds for changed design elements on the lower portions of the clogs, the shape of the toe portions and the raised pattern of the outsoles. Because the majority is not satisfied that the same can be said of the changed insole design, which the district court erroneously refused to assess, the insole design is carved out of the overall design and independently remanded for further proceedings.

As recognized by the majority, the ordinary observer test requires assessment of the designs as a whole. *See Egyptian Goddess v. Swisa, Inc.,* 543 F.3d 665, 675 (Fed. Cir. 2008) (en banc); *Contessa Food Prods., Inc. v. Conagra, Inc.,* 282 F.3d 1370, 1378 (Fed. Cir. 2002); *Oddzon Prods., Inc. v. Just Toys, Inc.,* 122 F.3d 1396, 1405 (Fed. Cir. 1997). I agree that the differences in the inner sole designs are to be assessed as part of the anticipation inquiry. But the differences in the inner sole designs must be appreciated in conjunction with all of the design differences. This is so especially with regard to the differing number and arrangement of the circular openings on the upper of the clogs.

When the two designs are observed from above . . . the distinctions in the different number and location of the circular openings on the upper of the clogs are apparent, in addition to the different insole designs. And when the differing insoles are sorted in the mind of the ordinary observer along with the four external differences of the clogs, the ordinary observer surely reaches a different conclusion about the designs as a whole than when the ordinary observer only looks at the differences in the insoles.

The effect of the majority bifurcation of the insole design differences from the exterior design differences, and the piecemeal adjudication of the exterior design differences, is to treat the patents on remand as without any exterior design. The fact finder will only assess anticipation on the basis of design differences on the insoles. I think this violates the rule for anticipation that the designs have to be compared as a whole. The effect of the summation of all the design differences is what counts, not the comparison of differences one by one, isolated from each other. Such an approach invites the problems we sought to eliminate by rejecting the "point of novelty" test. As the court stated in *Egyptian Goddess,* when there are several different alleged points of novelty, "[t]he attention of the court may therefore be focused on whether the accused design has appropriated a single specified feature of the claimed design, rather than on the proper inquiry, i.e., whether the accused design has appropriated the claimed design as a whole." 543 F.3d at 667. Remanding for adjudication of anticipation solely on the insole inappropriately focuses the fact finder on a single specified feature of the claimed design.

The majority has forged a new rule for design patent anticipation, if not for infringement as well. The new rule is that the "design as a whole" rule

> does not prevent the district court on summary judgment from determining that individual features of the design are insignificant from the point of view of the ordinary observer and should not be considered as part of the overall comparison. The mandated overall comparison is a comparison taking into account significant differences between the two designs, not minor or trivial differences that necessarily exist between any two designs that are not exact copies of one another. Just as "minor differences between a patented design and an accused article's design cannot, and shall not, prevent a finding of infringement," *Litton,* 728 F.2d 1444, so too minor differences cannot prevent a finding of anticipation.

Maj. Op. at 16, lines 1-12.

The majority's reliance on *Litton Systems, Inc. v. Whirlpool Corp.*, 728 F.2d 1423 (Fed. Cir. 1984), to support its new rule is misplaced. The quotation from the *Litton* opinion is in the context of that court's faithful application of the "design as a whole" rule. Minor differences between one design taken as a whole and another design likewise appreciated (the "mandated overall comparison"), of course, cannot fool the ordinary observer. So the court in *Litton,* after earlier quoting verbatim from *Gorham Co. v. White,* was correct in stating "that minor differences between *a patented design* and *an accused article's design* cannot, and shall not, prevent a finding of infringement." 728 F.2d at 1444 (emphasis added). The majority would have us believe that the *Litton* decision authorizes dissection of designs into component parts for purposes of partial summary judgments of anticipation or infringement. That is not correct and runs counter to precedent.[1]

The district court should be directed on remand to evaluate the differences in the designs as a whole. Partial judgments of anticipation on segments of a design prohibit assessment of designs as a whole, in violation of long-standing law, starting with *Gorham*.

## NOTES AND QUESTIONS

1. ***An inevitable ruling?*** In cases such as *Door-Master*, the Federal Circuit's dual test for anticipation appeared to require courts to consider (1) whether the claimed design was substantially similar to the alleged anticipatory design as viewed by the ordinary observer, and (2) whether the claimed design included the points of novelty disclosed in the allegedly anticipatory design. *International Seaway* eliminates the second prong, just as *Egyptian Goddess* eliminated the second prong of the infringement analysis. Was this ruling inevitable given the maxim that literal infringement is connected to anticipation? Even if so, should the court adhere to that maxim for design patents? In thinking about this issue, you might consider whether *Egyptian Goddess* was actually about literal infringement, a matter that you will be better equipped to contemplate when you have studied Chapter 6.

2. ***The significance of insignificance, and the ordinary observer.*** Under the majority's rule, for purposes of the anticipation analysis, the ordinary observer is to ignore design features that are insignificant (in that they do not affect the overall appearance of the article). Judge Clevenger criticizes this approach. Who has the better argument? Do you predict that design patent validity litigation will become a war over the significance (or lack thereof) of individual design features? Does the majority's approach mangle the concept of the ordinary observer?

3. ***Three-way comparison?*** In utility patent law, infringement analysis involves comparison between the claimed invention and the accused device, whereas patentability (or validity) analysis involves a comparison between the claimed invention and the prior art. In design patent law, as we will see, infringement analysis after *Egyptian Goddess* may involve a three-way comparison between the claimed design, the accused design, and the prior art. Validity analysis would therefore involve a comparison between the claimed design, the prior art, and . . . what? Is there a corresponding three-way analysis for design patent validity, or does the symmetry break down?

4. ***Distinguishing between anticipation and obviousness.*** Anticipation is not the only doctrine of patentability over the prior art. As the *Durling* case

---

1. *See, e.g., Braun Inc. v. Dynamics Corp. of Am.*, 975 F.2d 815, 820 (Fed. Cir. 1992) ("In evaluating a claim of design patent infringement, a trier of fact must consider the ornamental aspects of the design as a whole and not merely isolated portions of the patented design.") (citing *In re Salmon*, 705 F.2d 1579, 1582 (Fed. Cir. 1983)); *In re Rubinfield*, 270 F.2d 391, 395 (CCPA 1959) ("It has been consistently held for many years that it is the appearance of a design as a whole which is controlling in determining questions of patentability and infringement."), *cert. denied*, 362 U.S. 903 (1960).

(below) indicates, a claimed design that is not anticipated by the prior art may nevertheless be unpatentable if it would have been obvious in view of the prior art. After you read *Durling*, consider whether there are significant differences between the anticipation analysis expressed in *International Seaway* and the obviousness analysis expressed in *Durling*. If not, is that a problem? In an omitted part of the majority opinion in *International Seaway*, the court concluded that "for the same reasons that the district court's failure to compare the insoles of the patented designs to the prior art designs precludes a finding of anticipation, it also precludes a finding of obviousness." Does this suggest overlap between the anticipation and obviousness analyses?

### PROBLEM 5-2: THE MIDDLE FINGER DESIGN

Professor Janis's Cousin Clem, never known for his refined taste, designed what he referred to as the "Up Yours" keychain — a novelty keychain having a miniature replica human hand, clenched in a fist, with the middle finger extended. Cousin Clem subsequently filed a patent application claiming the design. Should the examiner reject the application on Section 171 grounds? What specific language in Section 171 would support a rejection? If the examiner believes that the design is offensive or obscene, does Section 171 give the examiner any authority to reject the application on that ground? *See Durdin v. Kuryakyn Holdings, Inc.*, 440 F. Supp.2d 921 (W.D. Wis. 2006) (discussing patentability of design for a motorcycle brake in the form of a naked woman).

### PROBLEM 5-3: EXPERIMENTING WITH DESIGNS

*Background.* The utility patent statute provides that subject matter qualifies as potentially patent-defeating prior art if the subject matter is put into "public use," or is put "on sale," in the United States more than a year before the patent application filing date.

The §102(b) public use and on-sale bars have been the subject of extensive litigation in utility patent cases. The public use bar has generally been given an expansive reach, reflecting a desire that inventors diligently seek patent protection for their inventions, and that they avoid creating public expectations that an invention is free for use. Accordingly, even a single, nonconfidential use that is not readily visible to the public may trigger the public use bar. *See Egbert v. Lippmann*, 104 U.S. 333 (1881).

The on-sale bar likewise reaches far, encompassing completed sales transactions as well as mere offers for sale, and applies even to confidential sales. Under the test enunciated in *Pfaff v. Wells Electronics, Inc.*, 525 U.S. 55 (1998), subject matter is "on sale" in the sense of §102(b) if (1) the subject matter has been the subject of a commercial offer for sale, and (2) the subject matter is "ready for patenting," meaning that it either has been reduced to practice or that it is embodied in drawings that are sufficiently specific to enable a person skilled in the relevant art to practice the invention.

In applying the §102(b) public use and on-sale bars, courts have long recognized that inventors may need to experiment with inventions to determine whether they operate for their intended purposes. Under some circumstances, it may be reasonable — or even imperative — to carry out these experiments publicly (e.g., in testing a paving composition for wear) or to imbue the experiments with some commercial character (e.g., by selling prototypes at cost to a third party to induce the third party to cooperate in the experimentation). Courts have long recognized an "experimental use" doctrine, holding that evidence of an inventor's experimentation negates a showing that a use is "public," *City of Elizabeth v. American Nicholson Pavement Co.*, 97 U.S. 126 (1877), or negates a showing that an offer for sale is "commercial." *EZ Dock, Inc., v. Schafer Sys. Inc.*, 276 F.3d 1347 (Fed. Cir. 2002).

***Problem Statement.*** P Corp. sells highly successful plastic containers for spices. P Corp. has a U.S. design patent on one of its container designs, as shown below:

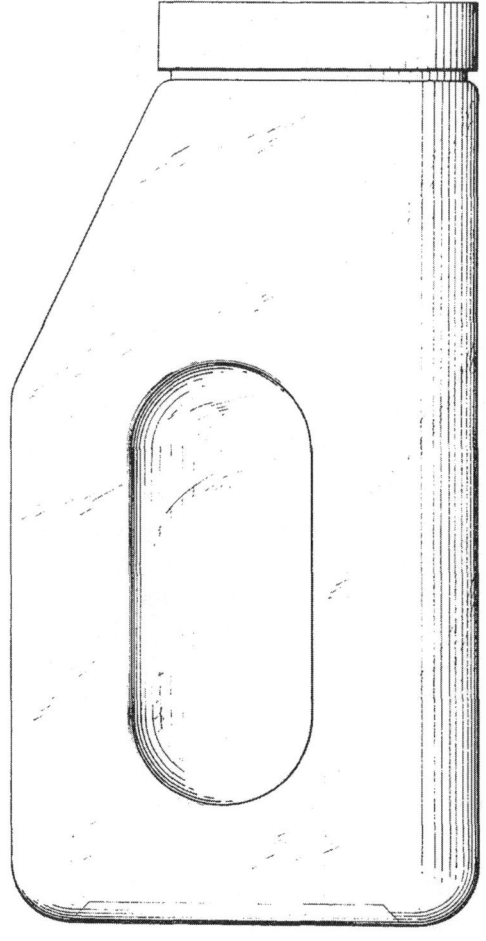

The patent has an effective filing date of June 1, 2002, and issued on August 15, 2004.

D Corp. competes with P Corp. After D Corp. introduced a new line of containers, P Corp. sued, alleging infringement of its design patent.

D Corp. defended on the ground that the patent was invalid, alleging that P Corp. had put the identical subject matter disclosed and claimed in the design patent into public use, and on sale, more than a year before the June 1, 2002, application filing date, in violation of 35 U.S.C. §102(b).

On March 7, 2000, P Corp. conducted a study (the "UNI study") at the University of Northeastern Iowa dietetics department. According to P Corp.'s documents, the purpose of the study was to evaluate the "feel" of the containers—e.g., whether they were comfortable and easy to grip, and whether the grip felt comfortable when the user was shaking the contents out of the container. Dietetics students participated in the study, and P's personnel documented the results of the study, which included students' general reactions, as well as more specific comments about particular design problems or suggested improvements.

On September 15, 2000, P Corp. displayed the patented containers at a trade show. The personnel at P's trade show booth replicated the UNI study, asking trade show attendees the same questions that were directed to the UNI students, and recording the responses.

P Corp. argues that neither the UNI study nor the trade show study should constitute §102(b) bars because in both cases, evidence of public use or sale is negated by evidence that P was conducting legitimate experimentation. P Corp. asserts that the experiments addressed the functional features of the patented design, and that the applicable rule should be that experimentation directed solely to the functional features of a patented design can negate evidence of public use of the design for 102(b) purposes. D Corp. argues that there should be a per se rule that the experimental use doctrine should not apply to design patents at all.

Assess the respective positions of the parties and develop a set of rules to guide future disputes in this area.

---

Even where a single prior art reference does not identically disclose the subject matter of a patent, the subject matter may differ so little that sound patent policy would suggest that no patent rights be granted. Reacting to this impulse, courts long ago developed a doctrine of patentability requiring that the claimed subject matter evidence some inventive variation over the prior art. In 1952, Congress brought Section 103, the doctrine of nonobviousness, into the statute.

**35 U.S.C. §103 Conditions for patentability: Non-obvious subject matter**
(a) A patent may not be obtained though the invention is not identically disclosed or described as set forth in section 102 of this title, if the differences between the subject matter sought to be patented and the prior art are such that the subject matter as a whole would have been obvious at the time the invention was made to a person having ordinary skill in the art to which said

subject matter pertains. Patentability shall not be negatived by the manner in which the invention was made.

Nonobviousness is one of the most subtle doctrines in utility patent law. It may be even more challenging to apply in design patent law, as the following cases and materials suggest.

### DURLING V. SPECTRUM FURNITURE CO., INC.
101 F.3d 100 (Fed. Cir. 1996)

CLEVENGER, Circuit Judge:

I

Since 1989, Durling has served as a freelance furniture designer in Tupelo, Mississippi. In the spring of 1991, the president of Global Furniture Company (Global) requested that Durling prepare a design for a low-cost sectional sofa group with a corner table and integral end tables. Durling conceived of the design shown in the '243 patent (reproduced below), the embodiment of which Global sold until it went out of business in the spring of 1992. At that time, one of Global's customers had sufficient interest in the product that it asked Spectrum Furniture Co., Inc. (Spectrum) to make furniture embodying the design. Spectrum contacted the former president of Global and received his approval to supply the product to Global's former customer.

In August 1992, Durling submitted an application for a patent on the furniture design he had provided to Global. This application matured into the '243 patent, which issued in September 1993. Shortly thereafter, Durling sued Spectrum for infringement of his patent.

At trial, Spectrum argued that the sole claim of the '243 patent was invalid as obvious in view of several prior art designs that were not considered by the examiner. Of these several references, the district court emphasized the design of a sectional group manufactured by Schweiger Furniture Industries, Inc. (the Schweiger model), reproduced below.

Relying heavily on Durling's concession that the Schweiger model is the "closest prior art to the design that's involved in this case," the district court found that the differences between the prior art and the '243 patent are insignificant. Based on its further finding that Durling had not established commercial success related to the patented design, the district court concluded that the sole claim of the '243 patent is invalid as obvious under 35 U.S.C. §103 (1994). Durling appeals. . . .

### II

Pursuant to 35 U.S.C. §171 (1994), one may obtain a design patent for "any new, original and ornamental design for an article of manufacture." To obtain such a patent, however, one must satisfy the patentability requirement of 35 U.S.C. §103 (1994). *In re Borden*, 90 F.3d 1570, 1574 (Fed. Cir. 1996); *see* 35 U.S.C. §171 (1994). In the design patent context, the ultimate inquiry under section 103 is whether the claimed design would have been obvious to a designer of ordinary skill who designs articles of the type involved. *In re Rosen*, 673 F.2d 388, 390 (C.C.P.A. 1982). More specifically, the inquiry is whether one of ordinary skill would have combined teachings of the prior art to create the same overall visual appearance as the claimed design. *See In re Borden*, 90 F.3d at 1574.

Before one can begin to combine prior art designs, however, one must find a single reference, "a something in existence, the design characteristics of which are basically the same as the claimed design." *In re Rosen*, 673 F.2d at 391. Once this primary reference is found, other references may be used to modify it to create a design that has the same overall visual appearance as the claimed design. *See In re Harvey*, 12 F.3d 1061, 1063 (Fed. Cir. 1993). These secondary references may only be used to modify the primary reference if they are "so related [to the primary reference] that the appearance of certain ornamental features in one would suggest the application of those features to the other." *In re Borden*, 90 F.3d at 1575.

### III

Durling contends that the district court's invalidity decision is erroneous because no primary reference exists in the present case. Durling explains that although the prior art cited by Spectrum has the same basic design concept as his claimed design (i.e., a sofa sectional with integrated end tables), each of those prior art designs create a different visual impression than his design. We agree.

As explained above, the first step in an obviousness analysis for a design patent requires a search of the prior art for a primary reference. This requires the trial court to: (1) discern the correct visual impression created by the patented design as a whole; and (2) determine whether there is a single reference that creates "basically the same" visual impression. In comparing the patented design to a prior art reference, the trial court judge may determine almost instinctively whether the two designs create basically the same visual impression. Nonetheless, the judge must communicate the reasoning behind the decision. This explanation affords the parties a basis upon which to challenge, and also aids the appellate court in reviewing, the judge's ultimate decision. [cit.]

In the design patent context, however, the judge's explanation of the decision is more complicated because it involves an additional level of abstraction not required when comprehending the matter claimed in a utility patent. Unlike the readily available verbal description of the invention and of the prior art that exists in a utility patent case, a design patent case presents the judge only with visual descriptions. Given the lack of a visual language, the trial court must first translate these visual descriptions into words—i.e., into a common medium of communication. From this translation, the parties and appellate courts can discern the internal reasoning employed by the trial court to reach its decision as to whether or not a prior art design is basically the same as the claimed design.

In the present case, the district court's opinion demonstrates that it misinterpreted the visual impression created by Durling's claimed design. The district court described Durling's design as follows: "The look that the patent-in-suit presented is a sectional sofa with double rolls of upholstery under the seating area which curve arcuately upward under the end tables. The end tables have the appearance of little vertical support." The district court had earlier defined "vertical support" to mean "the extent to which the base extends under the end tables."

Based on this verbal description of Durling's claimed design, it comes as no surprise that the district court determined that the prior art, especially the Schweiger model, had "looks that are similar to the patent-in-suit." Like Durling's design, the Schweiger model has integral end tables and a continuous front rail that curves upwardly to support the end tables. According to the district court, the main difference between Durling's design and the Schweiger model is that Durling's design has somewhat less vertical support.

The error in the district court's approach is that it construed Durling's claimed design too broadly. The district court's verbal description of Durling's claimed design does not evoke a visual image consonant with the claimed design. Instead, the district court's description merely represents the general concept of a sectional sofa with integrated end tables. As we have explained in the past, however, the focus in a design patent obviousness inquiry should be on visual appearances rather than design concepts. *See In re Harvey*, 12 F.3d 1061, 1064 (Fed. Cir. 1993). By focusing on the design concept of Durling's design rather than its visual appearance, the district court erred.

A proper interpretation of Durling's claimed design focuses on the visual impression it creates. This visual appearance is that of a contiguous three-piece sectional sofa group containing two sofa sections at approximately right angles to each other with a triangular corner table at their juncture. On the sides away from the corner table, each sofa section has rounded corners and includes a bolster pillow as an armrest. In addition, each sofa section has a double front rail that begins at the end adjacent to the corner table, follows along the bottom of the sofa towards the other end, and curves upwardly (*i.e.*, sweeps upward) through a 90° angle to truncate at a horizontal plane upon which the end table rests.

The visual appearance created by the Schweiger model is that of a three-piece contiguous sofa sectional group. Two linear sofa sections are placed at approximately right angles to each other, as in Durling's design. Instead of having a triangular corner table at their juncture, however, the Schweiger model contains a third, curved sofa section that lies between the other two sofa sections. When the three sofa sections are joined, the appearance is that of a rounded right angle. As in Durling's design, the Schweiger model has rounded ends, bolster pillows, and a double front rail. In the Schweiger model, however, the double front rail curves upward slightly, and then curves outward in a horizontal direction to wrap around the end tables.

From these two verbal descriptions, it is readily apparent that the Schweiger model does not create the same visual impression as does Durling's claimed design. The Schweiger model does not have a corner table, as does Durling's design. More significantly, the front rail in the Schweiger model curves upward and then around the end table. In contrast, the front rail in Durling's claimed design simply curves upwardly until it is truncated at a horizontal plane. If not for the truncating, the front rail in Durling's design would continue vertically; that in the Schweiger model would continue horizontally. Because of these significant differences, the Schweiger model does not create basically the same visual impression as does Durling's design, and therefore cannot suffice as a primary reference.

IV

In conclusion, the district court's verbal description reveals that it improperly interpreted Durling's claimed design in terms of design concepts rather than its visual appearance as a whole. The record contains no prior art design that creates basically the same visual impression as does Durling's claimed design. No primary reference has been shown to exist. Without such a primary reference, it is improper to invalidate a design patent on grounds of obviousness. The judgment of the district court must be *Reversed*.

## NOTES AND QUESTIONS

1. *Obviousness as the ultimate condition of design patentability?* Obviousness performs a critical role in the utility patent system, earning it a designation as the "ultimate condition" of patentability. In utility patent law, anticipation operates under a strict identity standard, and competent patent attorneys who know about particular prior art references can frequently draft claim language that avoids anticipation by those references. Would you expect obviousness to be equally important in the design patent system? To the extent that the design patent law features a more flexible anticipation analysis (*see Door-Master, supra*), is the obviousness doctrine less important? Redundant?

2. *How can visual appearance be "obvious"?* Though the notion of obvious variation may make some sense in connection with, say, mechanical inventions, does it translate well into design patent law, where the variation that is purportedly obvious relates to visual appearance? Legendary patent Judge Giles Rich, who was also a drafter of the 1952 recodification of the patent statute, explained that the drafters were well aware of the conceptual difficulties of applying the obviousness criterion to designs, but decided to attack the problem after the massive recodification effort was finished. According to Judge Rich:

> Thus it was that the patentability of designs came to be subject to the new §103 which was written with an eye to the kinds of inventions encompassed by §101 with no thought at all of how it might affect designs. Therefore, the design protection problem was in no way made better; perhaps it was made worse.

*In re Nalbandian*, 661 F.2d 1214, 1219 (C.C.P.A. 1981) (Rich, J., concurring). However, obviousness nonetheless remained a part of design patent law. Recounting efforts dating back to 1954 to enact comprehensive design protection legislation, Judge Rich argued that

> [i]t is time to pass [design protection legislation] and get the impossible issue of obviousness in design patentability cases off the backs of the courts and the Patent and Trademark Office, giving some sense of certainty to the business world of what designs can be protected and how.
> ... The bar would do well to devote its energies to backing this effort of the PTO rather than pursuing appeals such as these which may sometimes result in patents to "extraordinary" designers whose patents . . . may then suffer a 70% mortality rate in the courts at the hands of judges reviewing the 103 unobviousness of the designs.

*Id.* As we discuss in Chapter 8, European countries have accepted Judge Rich's advice, but the United States has not. Even in the absence of comprehensive design protection legislation, should the United States eliminate the obviousness requirement from its design patent law?

3. *The* Graham v. John Deere *framework for obviousness analysis.* In *Graham v. John Deere Co.*, 383 U.S. 1 (1966), the Court laid out the doctrinal framework for analyzing the obviousness provision in the context of utility

patents. According to the Court, obviousness should be assessed by undertaking a series of primary inquiries into:

(1) scope and content of the prior art;
(2) differences between the prior art and the claims at issue; and
(3) level of ordinary skill in the pertinent art.

The Court also noted that inquiries into certain "secondary" considerations might be appropriate. The Federal Circuit has held that the *Graham* factors analysis also applies to design patent. *L.A. Gear, Inc. v. Thom McAn Shoe Co.*, 988 F.2d 1117, 1124 (Fed. Cir. 1993). The *Durling* court's analysis, which focuses on the combinability of prior art references, may be understood as an application of *Graham* factor #1, for example. The following notes explore how the *Graham* factors may apply in the design patent setting.

**4. *Combining prior art references and the focus on the primary reference* (Graham *factor #1*).** Unlike proof of anticipation, which must rest on the disclosures from only a single reference source, obviousness can be proved based on a combination of multiple references, taken in view of the background knowledge of the person of ordinary skill in the art, where that evidence together teaches or suggests the claimed subject matter. The Federal Circuit, and its predecessors have occasionally advised courts to organize such an obviousness analysis by identifying a primary reference that contains many of the elements of the claimed subject matter, and then combine that reference with "teaching" references (or other evidence) that disclose or suggest the remaining elements of the claimed subject matter. (This exercise may be understood as falling within the inquiry into the scope and content of the prior art as called for in *Graham* factor #1.) In the utility patent law, identifying primary and teaching references is considered an orderly and prudent way to proceed with an obviousness analysis. In the law of design patents, the Federal Circuit seems to have elevated this mode of analysis into a legal requirement, as exemplified by the court's remarks in *Durling*. Is there something about the nature of design patents that justifies the Federal Circuit's insistence on formalizing the steps of identifying and applying primary and secondary references?

**5. *Combinability and the teaching/suggestion/motivation test* (Graham *factor #1*).** A major problem with obviousness analysis in utility patent law is that many inventions look simple in hindsight. With the benefit of hindsight, judges and patent examiners may be tempted to hunt through the prior art references, extracting relevant teachings and hypothesizing that a person of ordinary skill in the art would have combined them to achieve the claimed invention. Spurred in part by this concern over hindsight bias, the Federal Circuit elaborated a requirement that the obviousness proponent prove not only that the relevant disclosures existed in the various references, but also that there existed some teaching, suggestion, or motivation for combining those disclosures. *See, e.g., Al-Site Corp. v. VSI Int'l, Inc.*, 174 F.3d 1308, 1323-1324 (Fed. Cir. 1999). The Federal Circuit extended the teaching/suggestion/motivation test to design patents:

> If the basic reference alone does not render the claimed design unpatentable, design elements from other references in the prior art can be considered in

determining whether the claimed design would have been obvious to one of skill in the art. In order for secondary references to be considered, however, there must be some suggestion in the prior art to modify the basic design with features from the secondary references. [cit.] That is, the teachings of prior art designs may be combined only when the designs are "so related that the appearance of certain ornamental features in one would suggest the application of those features to the other." [cit.]

*In re Borden*, 90 F.3d 1570, 1574-1575 (Fed. Cir. 1996). In *KSR Int'l Co. v. Teleflex Inc.*, 127 S. Ct. 1727 (2007), a utility patent case, the Court reversed the Federal Circuit's application of the teaching/suggestion/motivation test, and warned that to the extent that the test had become a "[r]igid preventative rule" that "den[ied] fact finders recourse to common sense," it was an inappropriate response to fears of hindsight bias, and inconsistent with the law of obviousness. According to the Court, the Federal Circuit had committed two errors in applying its test: (1) focusing only on the problem that the inventor was attempting to solve, rather than considering any need or problem known to those of skill in the pertinent art; and (2) assuming that a person of ordinary skill seeking to solve a problem would be led only to those elements of the prior art directed at solving the same problem. Are these errors likely to arise in an analysis of design patent obviousness? Does invention in the design arts lend itself to being characterized as a "solution" to some discrete "problem," as may be the case in the mechanical arts? (If not, should *KSR* apply to design patents at all?) Should the Federal Circuit retain the teaching/suggestion/motivation test for design patents, unaltered by the skepticism expressed in *KSR*? *See Titan Tire Corp. v. Case New Holland, Inc.*, 566 F.3d 1372 (Fed. Cir. 2009) (raising but not resolving the questions).

6. *Applying* **Graham** *factor #1: analogous art.* In utility patent law, courts have developed a rather weak rule of "non-analogous" art. The rule holds that a prior art reference should be disqualified for use in an obviousness analysis (i.e., should be deemed to fall outside the scope and content of the prior art) where it is neither (1) within the patentee's field of endeavor, nor (2) reasonably pertinent to the problem that the patentee seeks to solve. *In re Clay*, 966 F.2d 656 (Fed. Cir. 1992). The idea is that a hypothetical person of ordinary skill in a particular art would not be expected to explore nonanalogous arts in seeking to solve a particular technological problem. A tractor mechanic designing a mechanical arm for a corn planter, for example, might not be expected to look at grappling arms used to lift satellites into the cargo bays of space ships.

Should the doctrine of nonanalogous art apply to design patents? In *Hupp v. Siroflex of America, Inc.*, 122 F.3d 1456, 1462 (Fed. Cir. 1997), the Federal Circuit seemed to imply that it did, asserting that "[t]he scope of the prior art is not the universe of abstract design and artistic creativity, but designs of the same article of manufacture or of articles sufficiently similar that a person of ordinary skill would look to such articles for their designs." However, older cases, including some C.C.P.A. decisions, took a contrary view, seeming to support

> the rejection of a design application on a combination of references from arts which would be considered nonanalogous from a mechanical standpoint.

Thus in the *Jabour* case, it was held to be proper to combine features from a tank and a microphone.

*In re Glavas*, 230 F.2d 447, 450 (C.C.P.A. 1956) (emphasis added) (referring to *In re Jabour*, 182 F.2d 213 (C.C.P.A. 1950)). *See also Black & Decker Inc. v. Pittway Corp.*, 636 F. Supp. 1193, 1196 (N.D. Ill. 1986) (citing *Glavas* with approval). How would you resolve this apparent conflict among authorities?

7. *Applying* **Graham** *factor #2: obviousness of overall appearance, or obviousness of features?* The Federal Circuit takes the view that the obviousness inquiry

> focuses on the visual impression of the claimed design as a whole and not on selected individual features. . . . A finding of obviousness cannot be based on selecting features from the prior art and assembling them to form an article similar in appearance to the claimed design.

*In re Borden*, 90 F.3d 1570, 1574 (Fed. Cir. 1996). Is the court placing undue restrictions on the proof of obviousness, or is the court's approach another good strategy for avoiding hindsight obviousness analysis?

8. *Level of ordinary skill* (**Graham** *factor #3*). The obviousness provision, 35 U.S.C. §103(a), specifies that patent protection will not be awarded where the claimed subject matter would have been obvious "to a person having ordinary skill in the art to which said subject matter pertains." In *Durling*, the Federal Circuit translates the obviousness standard for design patent purposes: the inquiry is whether the claimed design would have been obvious "to a designer of ordinary skill who designs articles of the type involved." Should the court instead be assessing obviousness in view of the ordinary lay observer? Consider the following argument: assessing obviousness from the perspective of the ordinary designer would thwart progress in the design arts because it would deny protection in all but the most extraordinary cases. Do you agree? *See In re Nalbandian*, 661 F.2d 1214 (C.C.P.A. 1981).

Review the court's analysis of novelty in *Door-Master*. Does the court undertake the analysis from the perspective of the "ordinary designer" or the layperson—i.e., the "ordinary observer"? Should the analyses be undertaken from the same perspective? Why or why not? What is meant by claim construction in design patents? Are the "claims" (meaning, necessarily, the drawings) construed from the perspective of the ordinary designer, or the ordinary observer? Recall that claim construction is the threshold step in nearly all substantive patent law analyses, including novelty and nonobviousness. Should the claims be construed from differing perspectives depending on the type of substantive analysis in which the court is engaging?

9. *Secondary considerations for design patent obviousness.* In addition to articulating a set of three primary considerations for adjudicating obviousness, the Court in *Graham v. John Deere* also suggested that courts were free to consider additional considerations that might bear on obviousness, including such considerations as the commercial success of the claimed invention, evidence of long-felt but unmet need, and evidence of skepticism followed by acceptance among those skilled in the art. *Graham v. John Deere Co.*, 383 U.S. 1, 17-18 (1966). These so-called secondary considerations are widely used

in modern obviousness law. Indeed, the Federal Circuit has held that secondary considerations, when in evidence, must be taken into account in a court's obviousness determination, though there must be evidence of a nexus between any given secondary consideration and the features of the claimed invention. *See Hybritech Inc. v. Monoclonal Antibodies, Inc.*, 802 F.2d 1367 (Fed. Cir. 1986). Should the secondary considerations be used in adjudicating design patent obviousness? Some but not all?

10. *Effects of* **International Seaway** *and* **Egyptian Goddess**. In *International Seaway*, as we have seen, the Federal Circuit applied infringement concepts (from the *Egyptian Goddess* case) to the anticipation analysis. One consequence is to elevate the importance of the "ordinary observer" in the anticipation inquiry. Obviousness, at least under *Durling*, is to be assessed from the perspective of the "ordinary designer." Should (must?) the court overrule this aspect of *Durling*, and assess obviousness from the perspective of the ordinary observer? Should the court assess the combinability of prior art references from the perspective of the ordinary designer, and then compare overall visual appearance from the perspective of the ordinary observer? How do you think this approach would affect case outcomes in general? *See Yokohama Rubber Co. v. Stamford Tyres International PTE Ltd.*, No. SACV 07-00010-CJC(MGLx) (C.D. Cal. Jan. 19, 2010) (grappling with these ideas).

### PROBLEM 5-4: THE FOOTBALL HELMET BIRDHOUSE

Consider the following design:

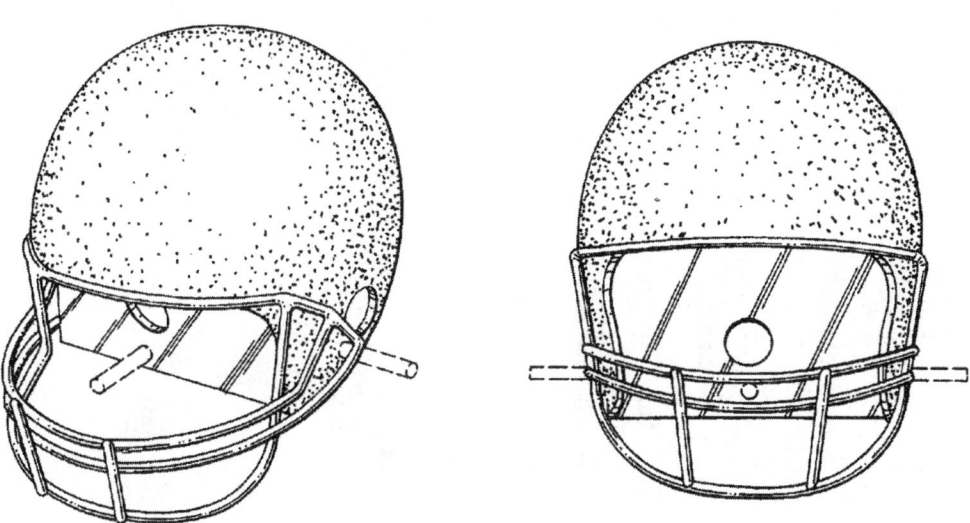

Assume that one prior art reference discloses a football helmet that is identical in appearance to the one depicted above, and assume that another prior art reference discloses a birdhouse, likewise identical to the illustrated birdhouse. Evaluate whether the claimed subject matter would have been obvious under 35 U.S.C. §103.

## PROBLEM 5-5: PRIORITY

The patent statute has a number of provisions that are designed to ensure that the utility patent applicant provides an adequate disclosure of the claimed invention. These are predominantly housed in 35 U.S.C. §112. The first paragraph of §112 provides that:

> The specification shall contain a written description of the invention, and of the manner and process of making and using it, in such full, clear, concise, and exact terms as to enable any person skilled in the art to which it pertains, or with which it is most nearly connected, to make and use the same, and shall set forth the best mode contemplated by the inventor of carrying out his invention.

Should the requirements of §112, 1st paragraph carry over directly to design patents? Suppose that Professor Janis's Cousin Clem, acting on behalf of his client, Brother Billy, filed a first design patent application claiming the following design for a "leecher" (which, we're told by Brother Billy, is a device for trapping leeches):

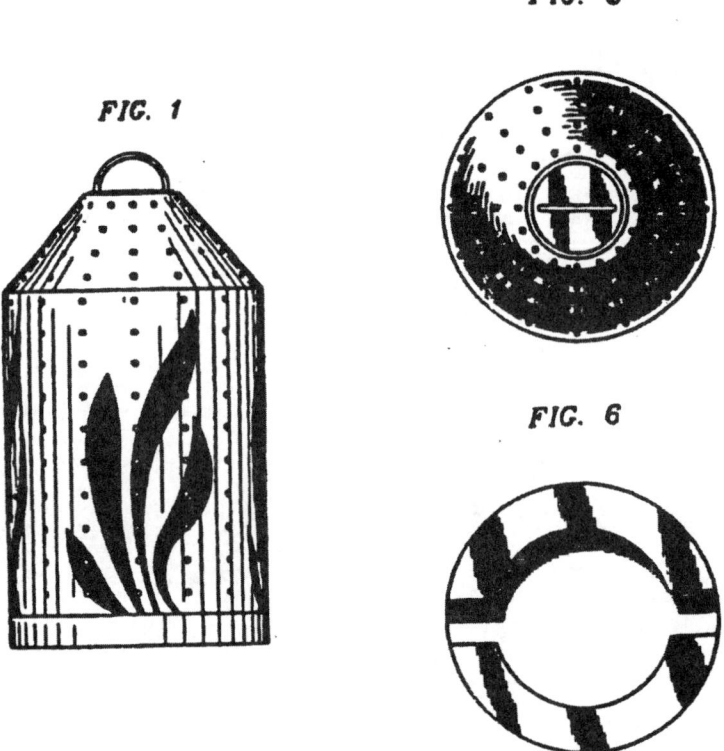

Unfortunately, Brother Billy subsequently had a dispute with Cousin Clem involving a load of leeches and Brother Billy's girlfriend. Brother Billy hired a new attorney, who immediately recognized that the leaf pattern shown in Fig. 1 of the drawings was an unnecessary limitation on the claims. The new attorney filed a second application showing the leecher design without the leaf pattern:

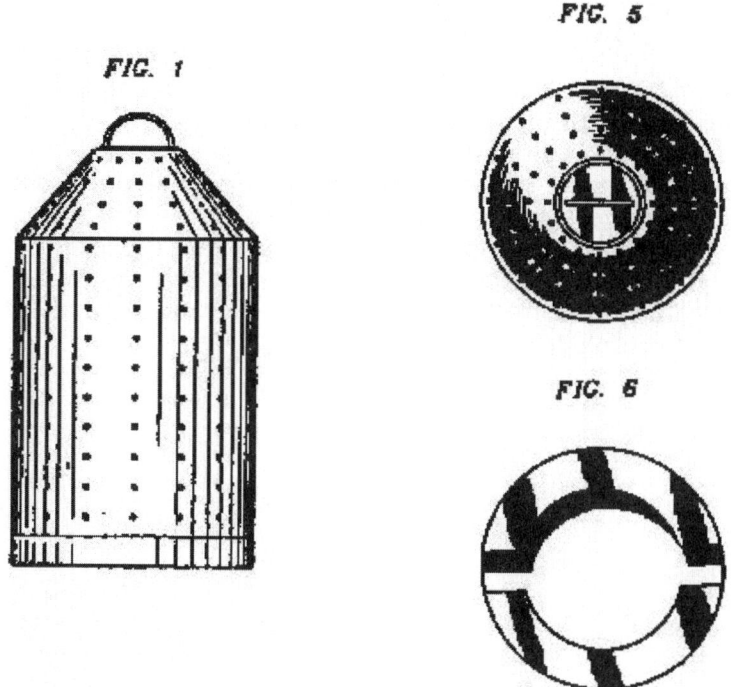

The new application claimed to be a "continuation" of the first application under 35 U.S.C. §120. Under that provision, as it has been applied in the context of utility patents, an applicant who has a first application on a given subject matter pending before the PTO, may file a second patent application directed to the same subject matter and have the second patent application treated as if it were filed on the filing date of the first application — i.e., the second application may claim "priority" to the first application. A claim of priority to an earlier application under §120 is allowable if the subject matter that is disclosed in the first application is adequate to support anything that is claimed in the second application. This requires a comparison between the disclosure in the first application and the claims in the second application, applying the rules for adequacy of disclosure in 35 U.S.C. §112, 1st paragraph. One of those rules, the §112, 1st paragraph "written description" requirement (the only one relevant to this Problem) considers whether the inventor disclosed enough in the first application to demonstrate that he or she had possession of the invention later claimed in the second application.

Consider the following questions:

(1) Should §120 apply in the design patent context, given that design patent claims incorporate by reference the design patent's disclosure (its drawings)?
(2) Should §112, 1st paragraph's written description requirement apply in the design patent context, given that the design patent's drawings must necessarily constitute the entirety of the written description?
(3) Should courts rule that any change to a design patent drawing defeats a claim of §120 priority as a matter of law, on the ground that a design is to be viewed as a unitary whole? Should it matter that some designs consist of features that are physically separable one from another? What about designs consisting of some features that are conceptually separable one from another? If we can say that the leaf pattern in the design at issue is conceptually separable from the rest of the design, is that concept helpful in determining whether the claim to §120 priority should be upheld?

## APPENDIX A:
## U.S. DESIGN PATENT NO. 543,681

US00D543681S

(12) **United States Design Patent**  (10) Patent No.: **US D543,681 S**
McCarthy                                (45) Date of Patent: ** **Jun. 5, 2007**

| | | | | | |
|---|---|---|---|---|---|
| (54) | **FOOTWEAR UPPER** | | EP | 0 802 041 A2 | 10/1997 |
| | | | EP | 0 884 005 A1 | 12/1998 |
| (75) | Inventor: | **Kevin McCarthy**, Sammamish, WA (US) | FR | 2 595 213 | 9/1987 |
| | | | GB | 2322286 | 8/1998 |
| | | | WO | WO 2004/105531 A1 | 12/2004 |
| (73) | Assignee: | **Crocs, Inc.**, Niwot, CO (US) | WO | WO 2004/105534 A3 | 12/2004 |
| | | | WO | WO 2004/105534 A2 | 12/2004 |
| (**) | Term: | **14 Years** | | | |

OTHER PUBLICATIONS

(21) Appl. No.: **29/228,428**

(22) Filed: **Apr. 22, 2005**

(51) LOC (8) Cl. .................................................. **02-99**
(52) U.S. Cl. .................................................. **D2/969**
(58) Field of Classification Search ................ D2/902, D2/905–908, 943, 944, 969, 972–974, 903, D2/916–919, 926, 932; 36/45, 50.1, 77 M, 36/77 R, 83, 88, 113, 114, 126–131
See application file for complete search history.

(56) **References Cited**

U.S. PATENT DOCUMENTS

| | | | |
|---|---|---|---|
| 1,392,350 A | 10/1921 | O'Brien |
| D66,083 S | 11/1924 | Johnson |
| 2,180,924 A | 11/1939 | Dunbar |

(Continued)

FOREIGN PATENT DOCUMENTS

| | | |
|---|---|---|
| CA | 2199084 | 10/1997 |
| CA | 2233842 | 12/1998 |
| CA | 2375957 | 9/2002 |
| EM | 000061122-0001 | 11/2003 |
| EM | 000257001-0001 | 2/2005 |
| EM | 000257001-0002 | 2/2005 |
| EM | 000257001-0003 | 2/2005 |
| EM | 000308903-0001 | 5/2005 |
| EM | 000308903-0002 | 5/2005 |
| EM | 000308903-0003 | 5/2005 |
| EM | 000308903-0004 | 5/2005 |
| EM | 000408745-0001 | 12/2005 |
| EM | 000408745-0002 | 12/2005 |
| EP | 0 802 039 A2 | 10/1997 |
| EP | 0 802 040 A2 | 10/1997 |

*Birkenstock®, Spring & Summer 2003 Catalog*, Birkenstock Orthopudie GMbh, Germany (82 pages).
*Comfortable Walking*, Italian Technology, Oct. 1999, n. 3, p. 168 (abstract, 1 page).
COMPLAINT, *Holey Soles Holdings LTDv. Foam Creations, Inc. and CROCS, Inc.* (05CV6893 (MBM) (AJP) S.D.N.Y. filed Aug. 2, 2005) (including Appendices A–D, 59 pages).
Cindy MacDonald, *The Entrepreneurs: they're billingual, multicultural and talented. Distance and language present no barriers to Quebec plastics processors and mold makers as the province's plastics industry continues to increase its level of exports and welcome new companies*, Canadian Plastics, O'99, v. 57(10), p. 35–50 (9 pages). dices A–C, 236 pages).

(Continued)

*Primary Examiner*—Dominic Simone
(74) *Attorney, Agent, or Firm*—Faegre & Benson LLP

(57)                    **CLAIM**

The ornamental design for footwear upper, as shown and described.

**DESCRIPTION**

FIG. 1 is a front perspective view.
FIG. 2 is a front view.
FIG. 3 is a rear view.
FIG. 4 is an inner side view.
FIG. 5 is an outer side view.
FIG. 6 is a top view; and,
FIG. 7 is a bottom view.

**1 Claim, 4 Drawing Sheets**

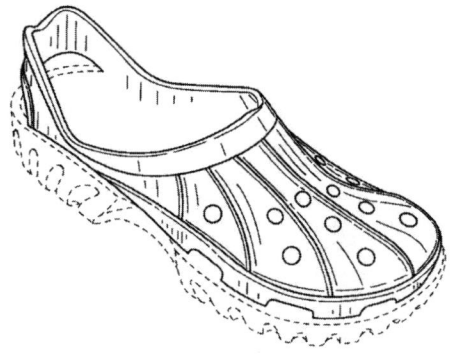

**US D543,681 S**
Page 2

### U.S. PATENT DOCUMENTS

| | | | |
|---|---|---|---|
| D151,304 S | 10/1948 | Walsh | |
| 2,470,089 A | 5/1949 | Booth | |
| D155,956 S | 11/1949 | Wood | |
| 2,897,566 A | 8/1959 | Albiniano | |
| 3,407,517 A | * 10/1968 | Gessner | 36/11.5 |
| 3,698,107 A | 10/1972 | Fukuoka | |
| 4,032,611 A | 6/1977 | Fukuoka | |
| D247,136 S | 2/1978 | Mizoguchi | |
| 4,100,685 A | 7/1978 | Dassler | |
| D251,158 S | 2/1979 | Edmonds | |
| 4,408,401 A | 10/1983 | Seidel et al. | |
| 4,476,600 A | 10/1984 | Seidel et al. | |
| 4,888,887 A | 12/1989 | Solow | |
| 4,967,750 A | 11/1990 | Cherniak | |
| D345,245 S | 3/1994 | McDonald | |
| D350,021 S | * 8/1994 | Stein | D2/969 |
| D350,223 S | 9/1994 | Buckner | |
| 5,369,895 A | 12/1994 | Hammerschmidt | |
| D355,526 S | 2/1995 | Duclos | |
| 5,438,767 A | 8/1995 | Stein | |
| D368,797 S | 4/1996 | Brooks et al. | |
| 5,528,841 A | 6/1996 | Pozzobon | |
| 5,561,919 A | 10/1996 | Gill | |
| 5,615,496 A | 4/1997 | Sharpstein | |
| 5,651,195 A | 7/1997 | Clancy | |
| D381,794 S | 8/1997 | Gelli | |
| 5,736,167 A | 4/1998 | Chang | |
| 5,814,254 A | 9/1998 | Bisconti | |
| D415,606 S | 10/1999 | Bray, Jr. et al. | |
| D416,667 S | 11/1999 | Lamstein | |
| D418,281 S | 1/2000 | Bray, Jr. et al. | |
| D422,780 S | 4/2000 | Aguerre | |
| 6,052,920 A | 4/2000 | Bathum | |
| D428,239 S | 7/2000 | Plamondon | |
| D431,346 S | 10/2000 | Birkenstock | |
| 6,237,249 B1 | 5/2001 | Aguerre | |
| 6,237,250 B1 | 5/2001 | Aguerre | |
| 6,256,906 B1 | 7/2001 | Matis et al. | |
| D448,918 S | 10/2001 | Hoyt et al. | |
| D452,366 S | 12/2001 | Wilson | |
| 6,416,610 B1 | 7/2002 | Matis et al. | |
| 6,439,536 B1 | 8/2002 | Piccolo | |
| D467,065 S | 12/2002 | Chen | |
| D473,040 S | * 4/2003 | Hawker et al. | D2/932 |
| 6,560,900 B2 | 5/2003 | Bray, Jr. et al. | |
| D476,797 S | 7/2003 | Schenone | |
| D479,034 S | * 9/2003 | Tzenos | D2/926 |
| D479,906 S | * 9/2003 | Hawker et al. | D2/969 |
| 6,625,904 B1 | 9/2003 | Frederiksen et al. | |
| 6,640,464 B2 | 11/2003 | Hsin et al. | |
| D483,929 S | 12/2003 | Tzenos | |
| D490,219 S | 5/2004 | Lu | |
| D492,095 S | 6/2004 | Sanchez et al. | |
| D492,096 S | 6/2004 | Sanchez et al. | |
| D492,841 S | 7/2004 | Magro | |
| D493,611 S | 8/2004 | Chen | |
| D494,345 S | 8/2004 | Werman | |
| 6,772,539 B1 | 8/2004 | Tai | |
| D498,901 S | 11/2004 | Hawker et al. | |
| D499,234 S | * 12/2004 | Dal Magro et al. | D2/916 |
| 6,860,035 B2 | 3/2005 | Girard | |
| D517,789 S | * 3/2006 | Seamans | D2/969 |
| D525,419 S | * 7/2006 | Seamans | D2/972 |
| 2001/0001350 A1 | 5/2001 | Aguerre | |
| 2002/0124434 A1 | 9/2002 | Hsin et al. | |
| 2003/0009909 A1 | 1/2003 | Chen | |
| 2003/0074806 A1 | 4/2003 | Urie et al. | |
| 2004/0231189 A1 | 11/2004 | Seamans | |
| 2004/0231190 A1 | 11/2004 | Seamans | |
| 2004/0231191 A1 | 11/2004 | Seamans | |

### OTHER PUBLICATIONS

*Defendant's Response to Request for Particulars, Foam Creations Inc.* vs. *Holey Soles Holdings Ltd.*, Ontario, Canada Federal Court, Court File No. T–161–05, Apr. 22, 2005, Oyen Wiggs Green & Mutala LLP (including Appen *Defendant's Statement of Defence, Foam Creations Inc.* vs. *Holey Soles Holdings Ltd.*, (Ontario, Canada Federal Court, Court File No. T–161–05, Mar. 10, 2005, Oyen Wiggs Green & Mutala LLP (9 pages).

*The Elastomers Times: Engage Adds Comfort to Sporting Components*, Chemical Business New Base: The Elastomers Times, Dec. 1, 2000 (2 pages).

*Engage® polyolefin elastomers, the critical ingredient for Success*, DuPont Dow Elastomers, Copyright© 2000, DuPont Dow Elastomers, www.dupont-dow.com/engage (12 pages).

*FinProject Brews an Extralight* (*Evasol Plastics and Finproject signed a joint venture agreement to introduce a range of new–block and net–fit soles for shoes*), Footwear News, World Week, Aug. 4, 1997, v. 53, N. 31, p. 8 93 pages).

*Inject Eva*, Macplas International, Aug. 1999, n. 10, p. 90 (abstract, 1 page).

http://web.archive.org/web/19980420230857/www.birkenstock.com/featprof.htm (3 pages).

Luisa Zargani, *One Fine Year; Anton Magnani's Quirky Dry–Shod Designs have Gained the Italian Designer Respect, Recognition and a Deal with Comme Des Garcons*, Footwear News, Aug. 2, 1999, p. 102 (2 pages).

*Plaintiff's Statement of Claim, Foam Creations Inc.* vs. *Holey Soles Holdings Ltd.*, Ontario, Canada Federal Court, Jan. 28, 2005, Ridout & Maybee LLP (8 pages).

*Plaintiff's Request for Particulars of Defence, Foam Creations Inc.* vs. *Holey Soles Holdings Ltd.*, Ontario, Canada Federal Court, Court File No. T–161–05, May 1, 2005, Ridout & Maybee (5 pages).

*Plaintiff's Further Request for Particulars, Foam Creations Inc.* vs. *Holey Soles Holdings Ltd.*, Ontario, Canada Federal Court, Court File No. T–161–05, May 12, 2005, Ridout & Maybee (including Schedule A, 6 pages).

*Plaintiff's Reply, Foam Creations Inc.* vs. *Holey Soles Holdings Ltd.*, Ontario, Canada Federal Court, Court File No. T–161–05, Ridout & Maybee (7 pages).

Rhoda Miel, *Snowshoe Walks Away with Best Design*, Plastics News, Apr. 22, 2002, v. 14, n. 8, p. 4 (2 pages).

*Trade Name Record*, Official Gazette of the US Patents and Trademarks Office, Mar. 24, 1998, 1208, n. 4, p. 73, (abstract, 1 page).

waldenstore.com, *Footwear Waldies*, Aug. 4, 2003, http://www.waldenstore.com/waldies.html, (1 page).

*Walking on Modified Eva*, Italian Technology, May 1999, n. 2, p. 121, (abstract, 1 page).

* cited by examiner

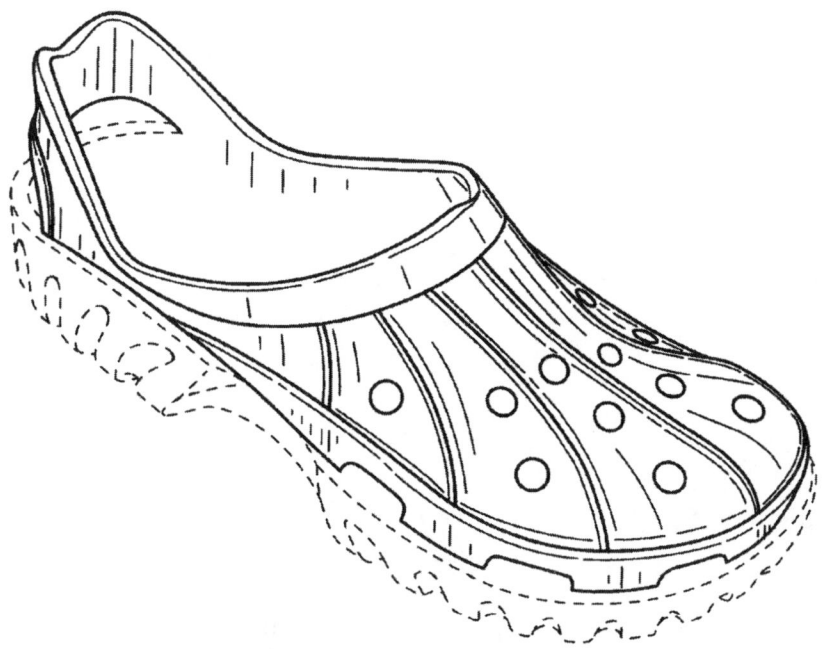

FIG.1

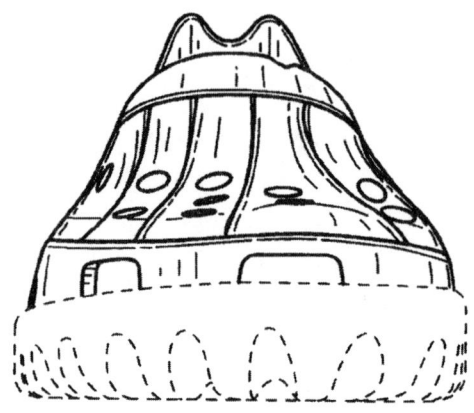

FIG.2

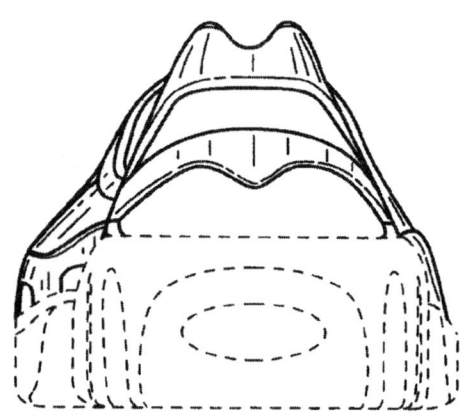

FIG.3

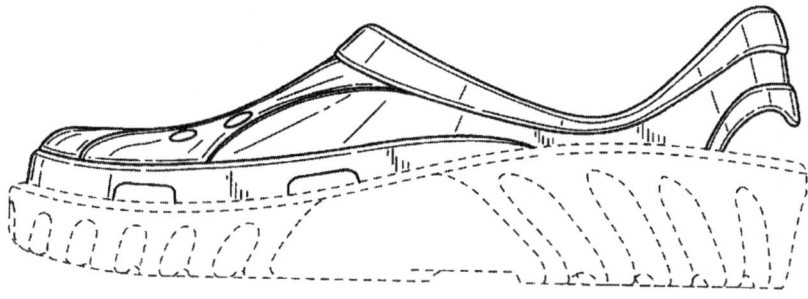

FIG.4

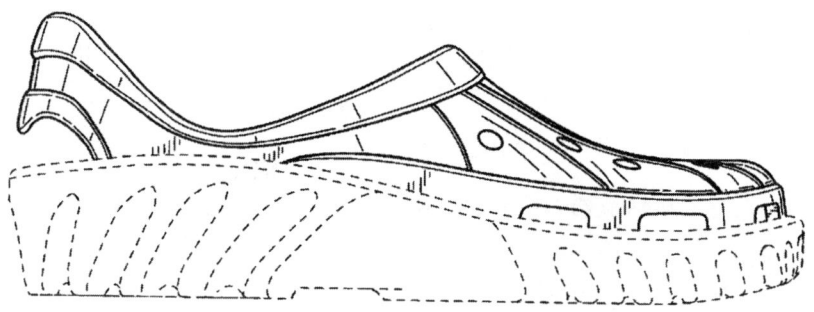

FIG.5

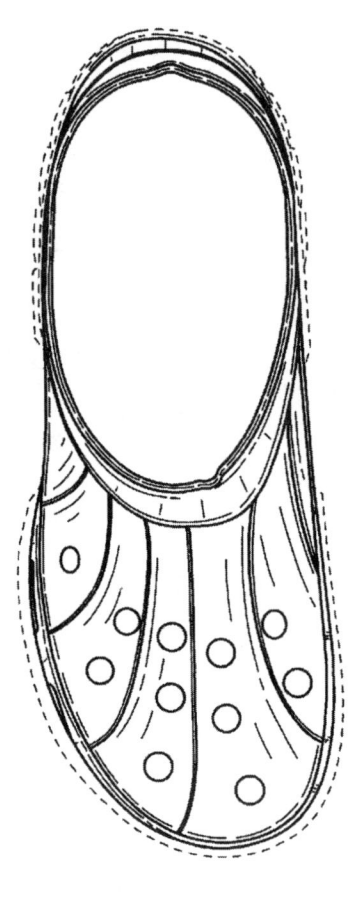

FIG.6

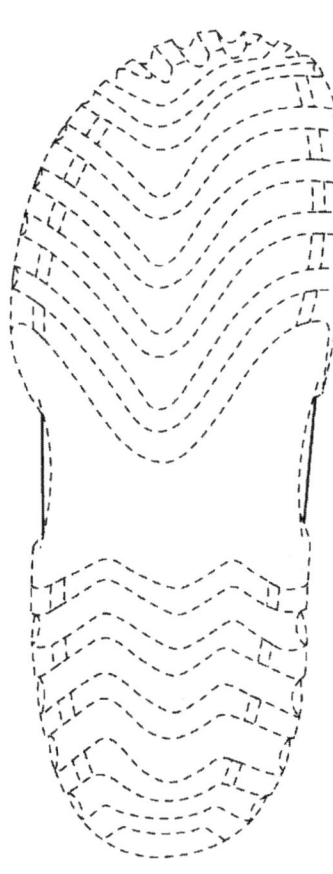

FIG.7

## APPENDIX B:
## U.S. DESIGN PATENT NO. 367,440

**United States Patent** [19]

**Mays**

[11] Patent Number: **Des. 367,440**

[45] Date of Patent: **\*\*Feb. 27, 1996**

[54] **AUTOMOBILE**

[75] Inventor: **Jay C. Mays**, Woodland Hills, Calif.

[73] Assignee: **Volkswagen AG**, Wolfsburg, Germany

[\*\*] Term: **14 Years**

[21] Appl. No.: **23,405**

[22] Filed: **May 24, 1994**

[52] **U.S. Cl.** ............................................................ **D12/90**

[58] **Field of Search** .................... D12/82–100; 296/185

[56] **References Cited**

U.S. PATENT DOCUMENTS

| D. 172,249 | 5/1954 | Rivolta | D12/90 |
| D. 273,098 | 3/1984 | Ohhashi | D12/90 |
| D. 336,868 | 6/1993 | Dehner et al. | **D12/92** |
| D. 352,482 | 11/1994 | Cannara et al. | D12/90 |

OTHER PUBLICATIONS

Modern Plastics Meinkel Car, top of page, Mar. 1960.
Design News Ford Concept Car Shusher, Sep. 7, 1981.

*Primary Examiner*—M. H. Tung
*Attorney, Agent, or Firm*—Watson, Cole, Grindle & Watson

[57] **CLAIM**

The ornamental design for an automobile, as shown and described.

**DESCRIPTION**

FIG. **1** is a front, left perspective view of an automobile according to the present invention;

FIG. **2** is a rear, left perspective view;

FIG. **3** is a front elevational view;

FIG. **4** is a top plan view thereof, on a reduced scale;

FIG. **5** is a rear elevational view;

FIG. **6** is a left side elevational view, on a reduced scale, the right side is a mirror image.

The broken line drawings of wheels in FIGS. **1–3** and **5–6** are for illustrative purposes only and form no part of the claim design.

**1 Claim, 6 Drawing Sheets**

**374** Chapter 5 Securing Rights

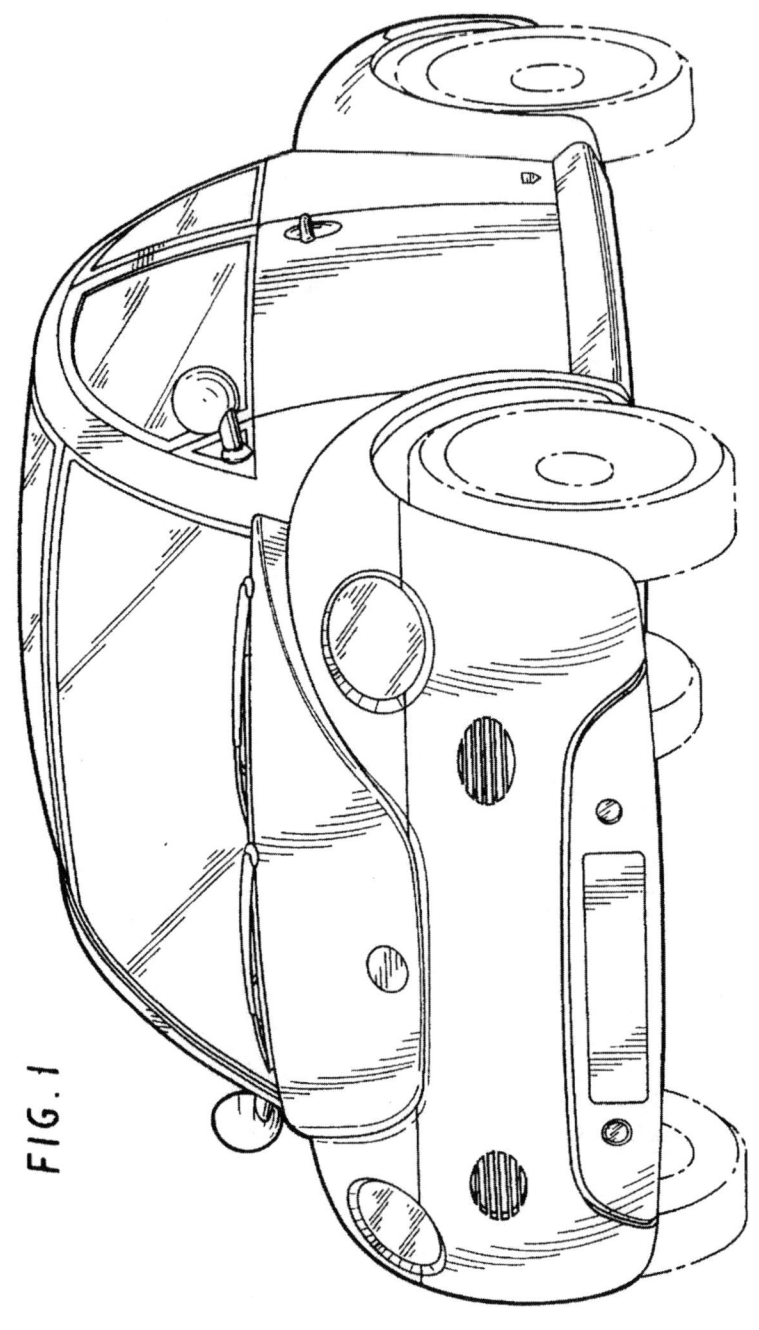

U.S. Patent     Feb. 27, 1996     Sheet 1 of 6     Des. 367,440

FIG. 1

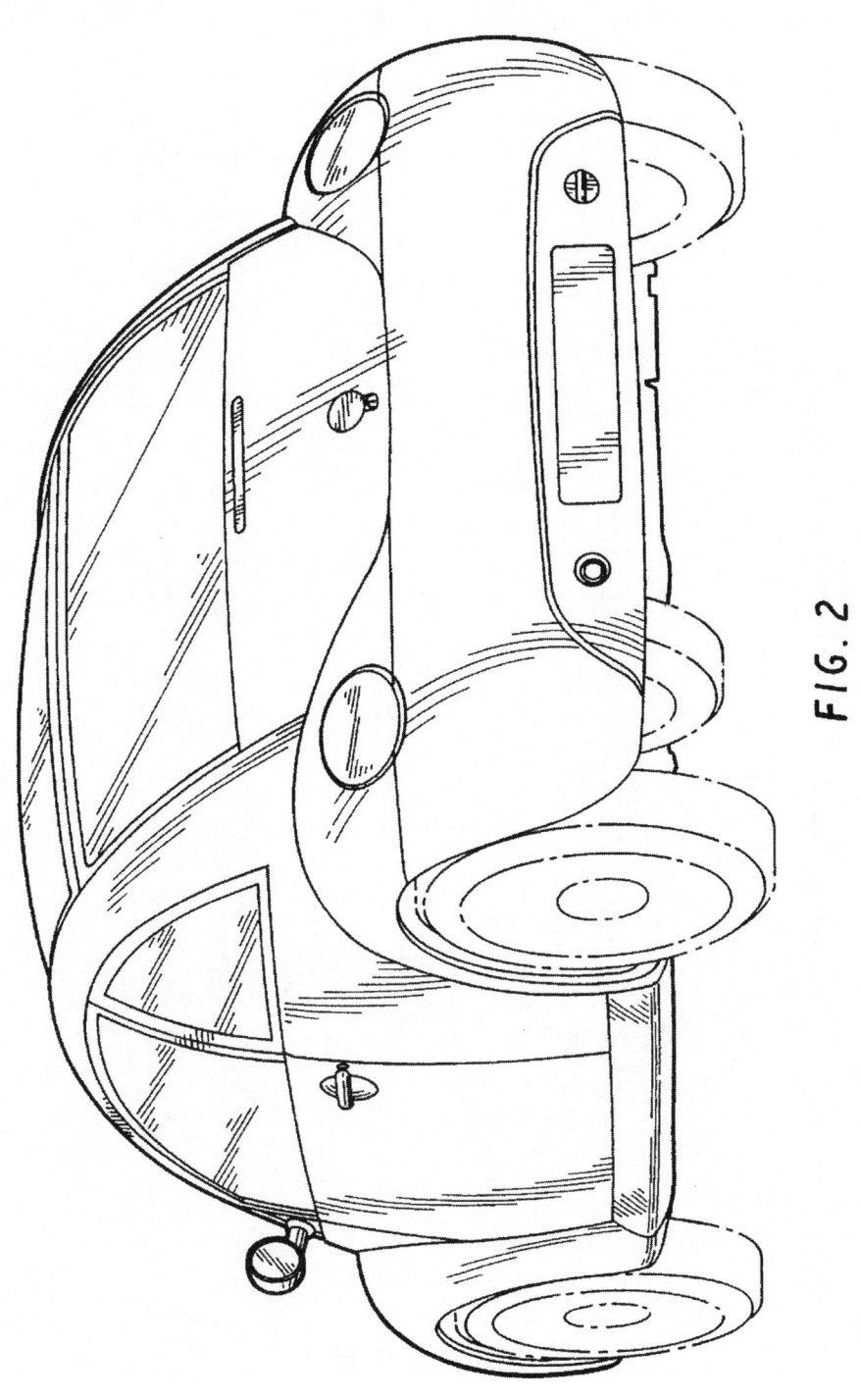

FIG. 2

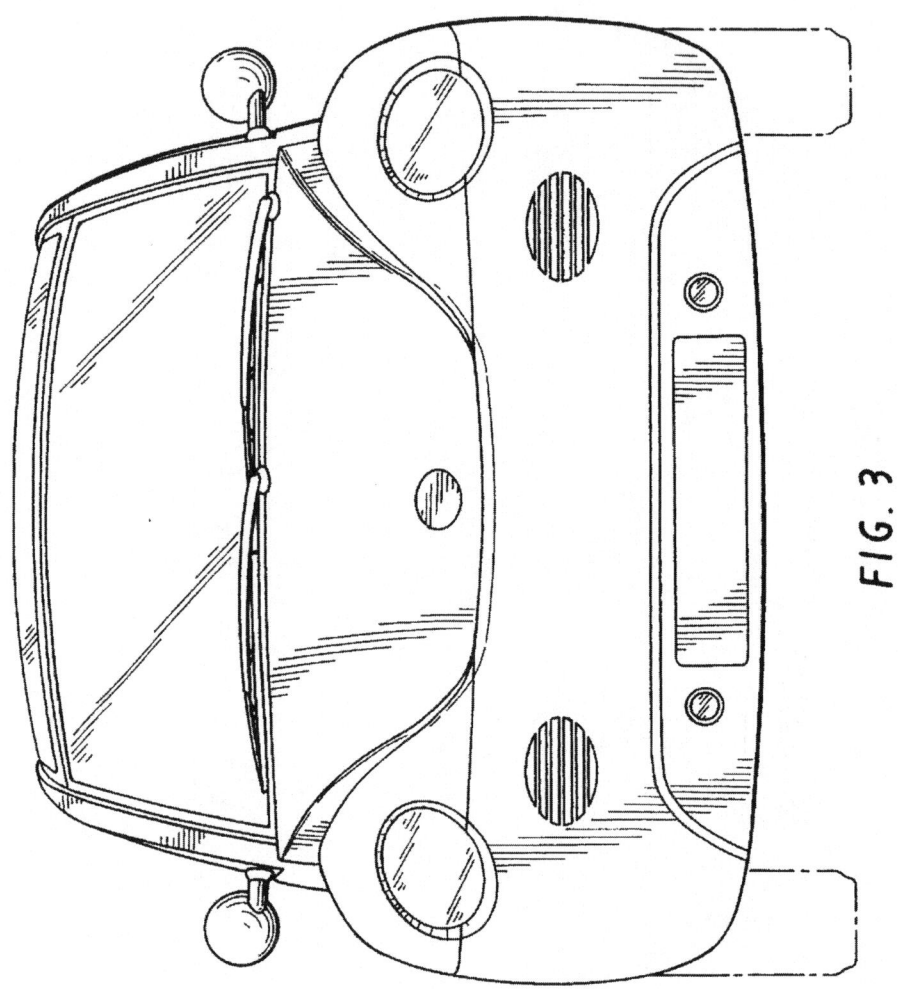

FIG. 3

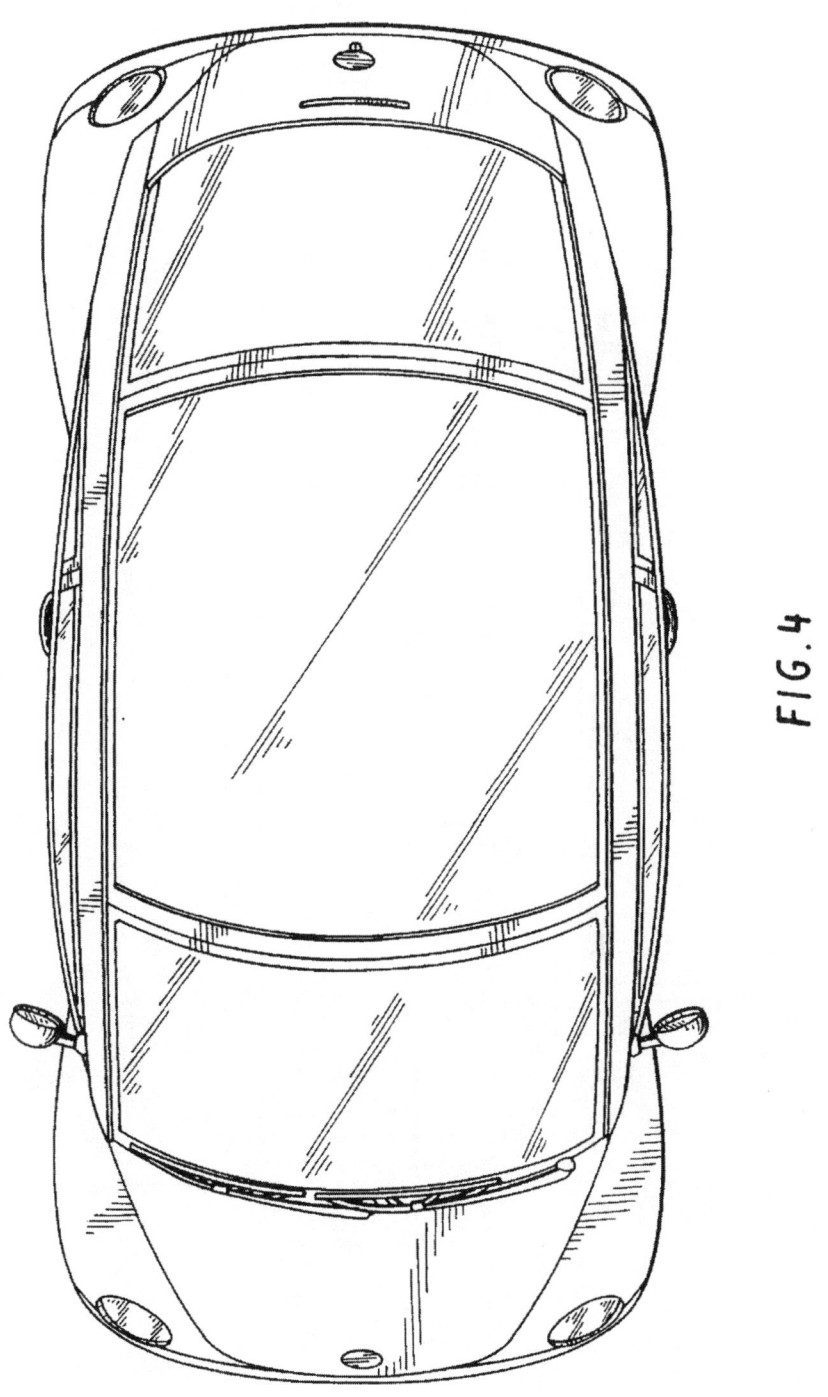

FIG. 4

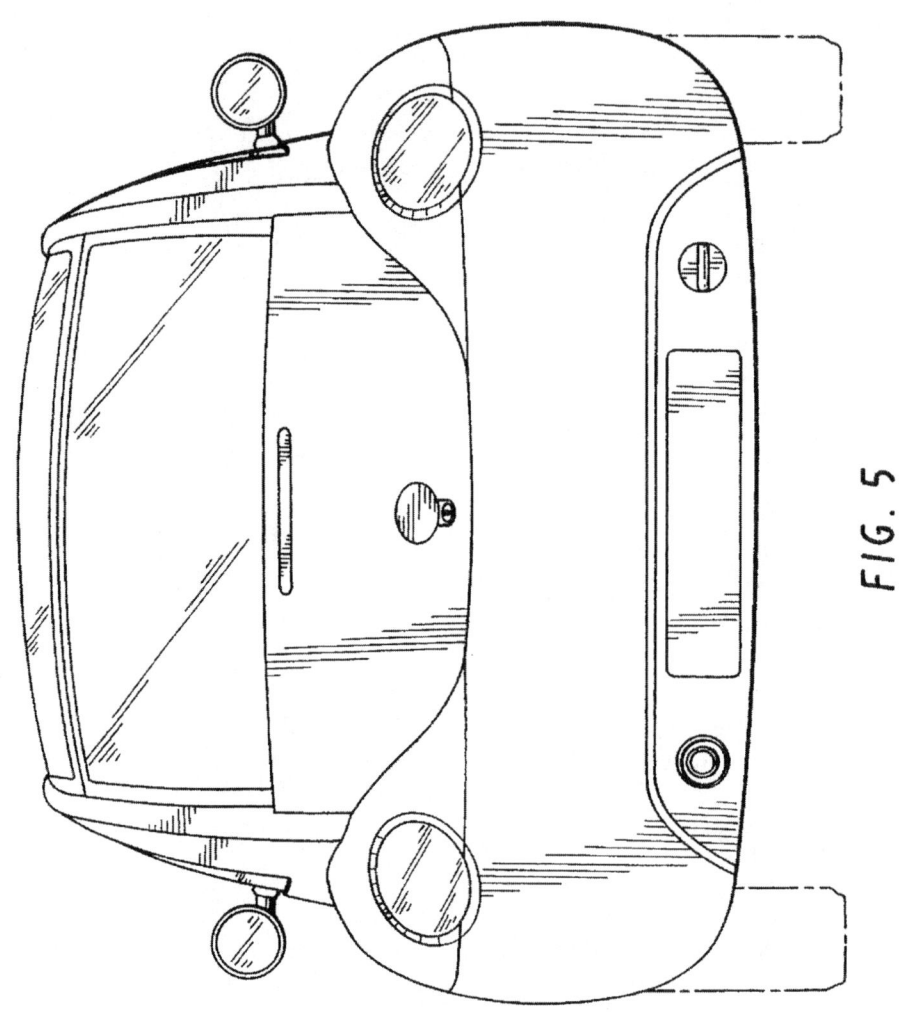

C. Novelty and Nonobviousness 379

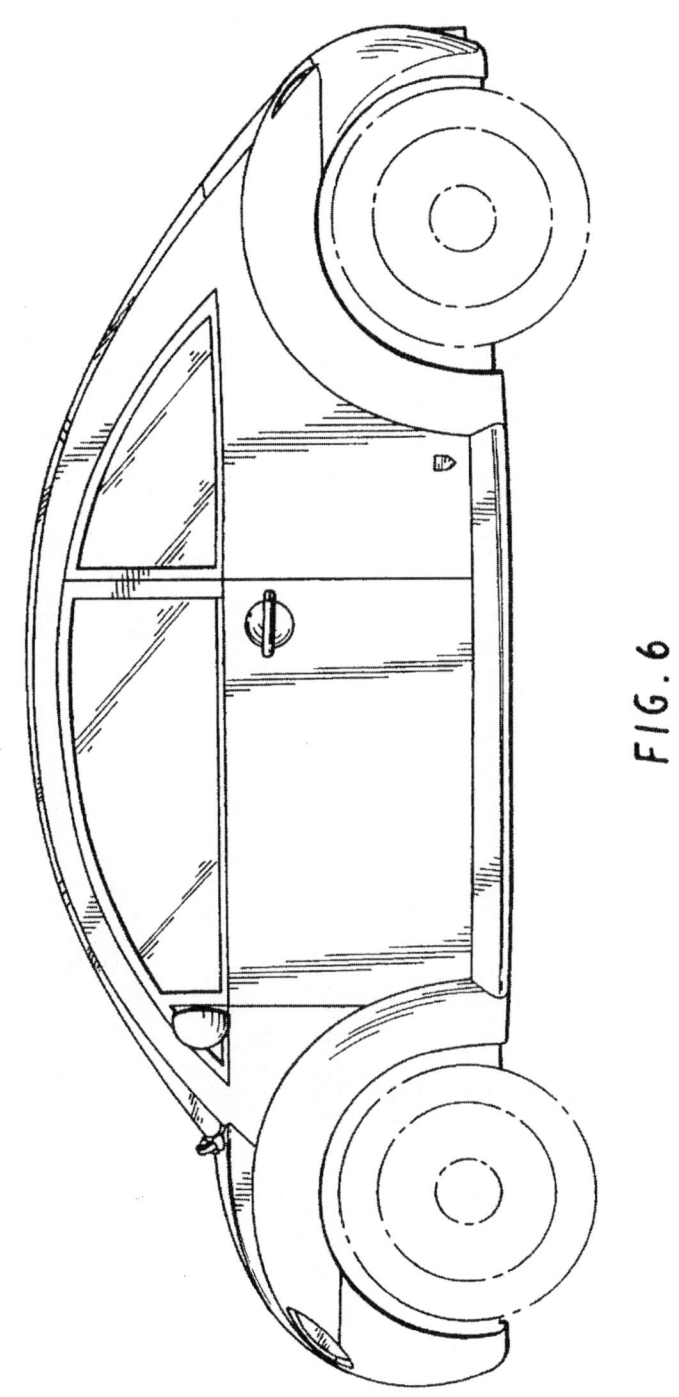

FIG. 6

# CHAPTER 6
# ENFORCING RIGHTS

In Chapter 5, we discussed the rules that govern issues of the patentability of design patent claims. We turn now to the rules that govern enforcement issues. The bulk of the chapter is devoted to the infringement analysis (Section A). Section B covers remedies.

## A. THE INFRINGEMENT ANALYSIS

For both utility and design patents, patent infringement occurs most commonly when a party makes, uses, sells, or offers to sell a patented invention in the United States, or imports a patented invention into the United States, without the patent owner's permission during the term of the patent. 35 U.S.C. §271(a). The patent statute also defines certain other acts as infringing acts (e.g., in §§271(b), (c), (f), and (g)), but these provisions have rarely, if ever, been at issue in design patent litigation. The patent statute also includes a remedies provision specific to design patents which incidentally recites the kinds of acts that could trigger liability under the infringement provision. *See* 35 U.S.C. §289 ("Whoever during the term of a patent for a design, without license of the owner, (1) applies the patented design, or any colorable imitation thereof, to any article of manufacture for the purpose of sale, or (2) sells or exposes for sale any article of manufacture to which such design or colorable imitation has been applied shall be liable. . . ."). Note that these acts align closely with those defined in 35 U.S.C. §271(a).

Because the statute defines acts of infringement so broadly, most disputes in patent infringement cases revolve around the scope of rights—i.e., whether the alleged infringer's acts in fact involve the claimed invention. In utility patent law, the fact-finder makes this determination by comparing an individual patent claim to the accused infringing device under a theory of literal infringement (strict identity between the recitations of the claim and the features of the accused device) or a theory of infringement under the doctrine of equivalents (strict identity or at least equivalent substitutes between claim recitations and the features of the accused device). In design patent law, a quite different comparison governs. The cases in this section reflect the relevant rules: the basic "substantial similarity" test enunciated in the *Gorham* case, and the modern two-part framework of which the *Gorham* test is one part.

## 1. THE *GORHAM* "SUBSTANTIAL SIMILARITY" TEST

### GORHAM CO. v. WHITE
81 U.S. 511 (1871)

Mr. Justice STRONG delivered the opinion of the Court:

[In 1861, Gorham received a design patent on its popular silverware pattern called the "cottage pattern" (shown on the left in the diagram below). Defendant White sold forks and spoons in the patterns labeled "White, 1867" and "White, 1868" in the diagram. Gorham sued for infringement. At trial, both sides put on extensive opinion testimony from tradesman. The witnesses substantially agreed that experts would be able to discern differences between the designs. For example, one of White's experts identified fifteen differences, such as:

> In the Gorham design the stem of the handle, between the shoulders and the bowl, has a second thread upon it, which is parallel with and inside of the boundary thread. No such second thread is found in White's.

Gorham's witnesses, however, opined that the designs were substantially similar when viewed by an ordinary purchaser, who would be expected to examine the designs casually.

The lower court found no infringement. The court considered the designs to be composed of two elements, "the outline which the handle presents to the eye when its broader face is looked at, and the ornamentation on such face." The court concluded that the Gorham design was similar in outline, but different in ornamentation, from the White 1867 design, and that the Gorham design was different in both outline and ornamentation from the White 1868 design. In a detailed analysis, the lower court rejected the argument that the proper test for design patent infringement should be a test of substantial similarity from the viewpoint of the ordinary observer. Instead, the comparison should be made by reference to experts. Applying this approach, the lower court concluded that ordinary purchasers might be deceived, but experts would be able to identify substantial differences between the designs, and accordingly held for White. Gorham appealed.

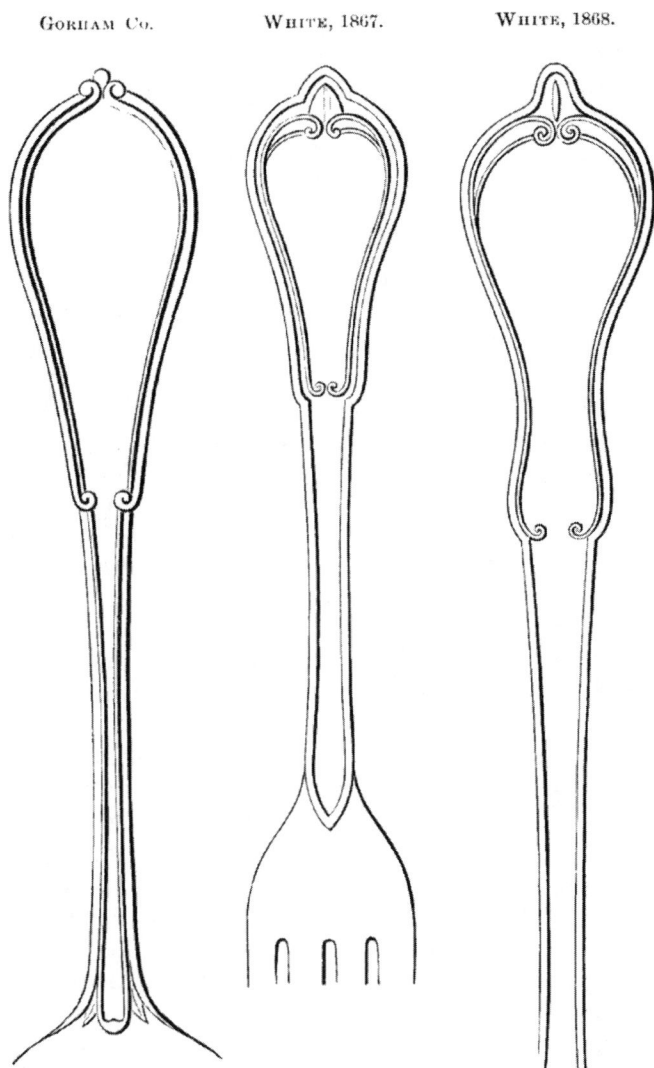

GORHAM CO.  WHITE, 1867.  WHITE, 1868.

The sole question is one of fact. Has there been an infringement? Are the designs used by the defendant substantially the same as that owned by the complainants? To answer these questions correctly, it is indispensable to understand what constitutes identity of design, and what amounts to infringement?

...

We are now prepared to inquire what is the true test of identity of design. Plainly, it must be sameness of appearance, and mere difference of lines in the drawing or sketch, a greater or smaller number of lines, or slight variances in configuration, if sufficient to change the effect upon the eye, will not destroy the substantial identity. An engraving which has many lines may present to the eye the same picture, and to the mind the same idea or conception as another with much fewer lines. The design, however, would be the same. So a pattern for a carpet, or a print may be made up of wreaths of flowers arranged in a particular manner. Another carpet may have similar wreaths, arranged in a like manner, so that none but very acute observers could detect a difference. Yet in the wreaths upon one there may be fewer flowers, and the wreaths may be placed at wider distances from each other. Surely in such a case the designs are alike. The same conception was in the mind of the designer, and to that conception he gave expression.

If, then, identity of appearance, or . . . sameness of effect upon the eye, is the main test of substantial identity of design, the only remaining question upon this part of the case is, whether it is essential that the appearance should be the same to the eye of an expert. The court below was of opinion that the test of a patent for a design is not the eye of an ordinary observer. The learned judge thought there could be no infringement unless there was "substantial identity" "in view of the observation of a person versed in designs in the particular trade in question — of a person engaged in the manufacture or sale of articles containing such designs — of a person accustomed to compare such designs one with another, and who sees and examines the articles containing them side by side." There must, he thought, be a comparison of the features which make up the two designs. With this we cannot concur. Such a test would destroy all the protection which the act of Congress intended to give. There never could be piracy of a patented design, for human ingenuity has never yet produced a design, in all its details, exactly like another, so like, that an expert could not distinguish them. No counterfeit bank note is so identical in appearance with the true that an experienced artist cannot discern a difference. It is said an engraver distinguishes impressions made by the same plate. Experts, therefore, are not the persons to be deceived. Much less than that which would be substantial identity in their eyes would be undistinguishable in the eyes of men generally, of observers of ordinary acuteness, bringing to the examination of the article upon which the design has been placed that degree of observation which men of ordinary intelligence give. It is persons of the latter class who are the principal purchasers of the articles to which designs have given novel appearances, and if they are misled, and induced to purchase what is not the article they supposed it to be, if, for example, they are led to purchase forks or spoons, deceived by an apparent resemblance into the belief that they bear the "cottage" design, and, therefore, are the production of the holders of the Gorham, Thurber, and Dexter patent, when in fact they are not, the patentees are injured, and that advantage of a market which the patent was granted to secure is destroyed. The purpose of the law must be effected if possible; but, plainly, it cannot be if, while the general appearance of the design is preserved, minor differences of detail in the manner in which the appearance is produced, observable by experts, but not noticed by ordinary observers, by those who buy and use, are sufficient to relieve an imitating design from condemnation as an infringement.

We hold, therefore, that if, in the eye of an ordinary observer, giving such attention as a purchaser usually gives, two designs are substantially the same, if the resemblance is such as to deceive such an observer, inducing him to purchase one supposing it to be the other, the first one patented is infringed by the other.

Applying this rule to the facts of the present case, there is very little difficulty in coming to a satisfactory conclusion. The Gorham design, and the two designs sold by the defendant, which were patented to White, one in 1867, and the other in 1868, are alike the result of peculiarities of outline, or configuration, and of ornamentation. These make up whatever is distinctive in appearance, and of these, the outline or configuration is most impressive to the eye. Comparing the figure or outline of the plaintiffs' design with that of the White design of 1867, it is apparent there is no substantial difference. This is in the main conceded. Even the minor differences are so minute as to escape observation unless observation is stimulated by a suspicion that there may be diversity. And there are the same resemblances between the plaintiffs' design and the White design of 1868, and, with a single addition, the minor differences are the same. That additional one consists in this. At the upper part of the handle, immediately above the point where the broader part widens from the stem with a rounded shoulder, while the external lines of both designs are first concave, and then gradually become convex, the degree of concavity is greater in the White design. How much effect this variance has must be determined by the evidence. . . . No doubt to the eye of an expert [the differences] are all real. Still, though variances in the ornament are discoverable, the question remains, is the effect of the whole design substantially the same? Is the adornment in the White design used instrumentally to produce an appearance, a distinct device, or does it work the same result in the same way, and is it, therefore, a colorable evasion of the prior patent, amounting at most to a mere equivalent? In regard to this we have little doubt, in view of the evidence. Both the White designs we think are proved to be infringements of the Gorham patent. A large number of witnesses, familiar with designs, and most of them engaged in the trade, testify that, in their opinion, there is no substantial difference in the three designs, and that ordinary purchasers would be likely to mistake the White designs for the "cottage" (viz., that of the plaintiffs). This opinion is repeated in many forms of expression, as, that they are the same pattern; that the essential features are the same; that seven out of ten customers who buy silverware would consider them the same; that manufacturers as well as customers would consider them the same; that the trade generally would so consider them; that, though there are differences, they would not be noticed without a critical examination; that they are one and the same pattern, &c., &c. This is the testimony of men who, if there were a substantial difference in the appearance, or in the effect, would most readily appreciate it. Some think the White designs were intended to imitate the other, and they all agree that they are so nearly identical that ordinary purchasers of silverware would mistake one for the other. On the other hand a large number of witnesses have testified on behalf of the defendant that the designs are substantially unlike, but when they attempt to define the dissimilarity they specify only the minor differences in the ornamentation, of which we have heretofore spoken. Not one of them denies that the appearance of the designs is substantially the same, or asserts that the effect upon the eye of an observer is different, or that ordinary purchasers, or even persons in the trade, would not be led by their similarity to mistake one for another. Their idea of what constitutes identity of design seems to be that it is the possibility of being struck from the same die, which, of course, cannot be if there exists the slightest variation in a single line. They give little importance to configuration, and none to general aspect. Such evidence is not an answer to the complainants' case. It leaves undisputed the facts that whatever differences there may be between the plaintiffs' design and those of the defendant in details of ornament, they are still the same in general appearance and effect, so much alike that in the market and with purchasers they would pass for the same thing — so much alike that even persons in the trade would be in danger of being deceived.

Unless, therefore, the patent is to receive such a construction that the act of Congress will afford no protection to a designer against imitations of his invention, we must hold that the sale by the defendant of spoons and forks bearing the designs patented to White in 1867 and 1868 is an infringement of the complainants' rights.

*Decree reversed* and the cause remitted with instructions to enter a decree in *accordance with this opinion.*

[Justices MILLER, FIELD, and BRADLEY *dissented.*]

## NOTES AND QUESTIONS

1. *Statutory basis for the substantial similarity test.* The Court in *Gorham* does not cite any statutory basis for the "substantial similarity" test. Re-read the language of §289 quoted above (before the *Gorham* case). Is there a statutory foundation for the *Gorham* test in the modern design patent provisions? Note that the scheme of two alternative infringement theories in utility patent law (literal infringement and infringement under the doctrine of equivalents) does not emanate from any express statutory provision.

2. *The relevant comparison in the substantial similarity test.* Suppose that a court conducts a substantial similarity analysis by viewing the design patentee's commercial product and the alleged infringer's product side by side. Such a comparison would be deemed legally erroneous in most circumstances. *See Unette Corp. v. Unit Pack Co., Inc.*, 785 F.2d 1026, 1028 (Fed. Cir. 1986); *cf. Lee v. Dayton-Hudson Corp.*, 838 F.2d 1186 (Fed. Cir. 1988) (not erroneous when the claimed design and the patentee's product are substantially the same). What is the basis for objecting to a side-by-side comparison of actual products?

(1) Would such a comparison be consistent with the rule espoused in *Gorham*? In applying the substantial similarity test in *Gorham*, did the Court compare the patentee's commercial product with the defendant's accused product?

(2) Would such a comparison be problematic because it fails to conform with utility patent law? In utility patent law, it is well established that patent infringement involves a comparison between the claimed subject matter and

the accused subject matter. What is the rationale for such a rule? Would the rationale apply equally well to design patents? Consider *Payless Shoesource, Inc. v. Reebok Int'l Ltd.*, 998 F.2d 985, 990 (Fed. Cir. 1993), in which Payless sued for a declaration that its shoes did not infringe two of Reebok's design patents, the '353 and '809 patents. One of the shoe models that Reebok sold under the '353 patent included a PUMP logo on the tongues of the shoe, but the logo did not appear in the '353 patent drawings. Does this illustrate the problem?

(3) Would a side-by-side comparison be problematic because it might not reflect the way ordinary observers encounter the respective goods of the plaintiff and defendant? *See, e.g., Sanson Hosiery Mills v. S.H. Kress & Co.*, 109 F. Supp. 383, 384 (M.D. N.C. 1952), *aff'd*, 202 F.2d 395 (3d Cir. 1953); *Ashley v. Weeks-Numan Co.*, 220 F. 899, 902 (2d Cir. 1915); *but cf. Braun Inc. v. Dynamics Corp. of Am.*, 975 F.2d 815, 820 (Fed. Cir. 1992) (stating that "[d]esign patent infringement does not concern itself with the broad issue of consumer behavior in the marketplace," and upholding a jury verdict on design patent infringement while reversing a verdict on trade dress infringement). How is the issue of the propriety of side-by-side comparison handled in the context of the similarity of marks factor in the likelihood of confusion analysis for trademark infringement? Recall Judge Posner's views in *Libman, supra*, Chapter 4.

**3. *Likelihood of confusion and substantial similarity*.** The preceding note raises a broader question: is there a connection between trademark infringement (assessed via the likelihood of confusion multifactor test) and design patent infringement (assessed, in part, via the substantial similarity test)? In some cases, the Federal Circuit has emphasized the differences between the two. *See, e.g., L.A. Gear, Inc. v. Thom McAn Shoe Co.*, 988 F.2d 1117, 1126 (Fed. Cir. 1993) ("Design patent infringement relates solely to the patented design, and does not require proof of unfair competition in the marketplace. . . ."); *Unette Corp. v. Unit Pack Co., Inc.*, 785 F.2d 1026, 1029 (Fed. Cir. 1986) ("Likelihood of confusion as to the source of the goods is not a necessary or appropriate factor for determining infringement of a design patent. The holder of a valid design patent need not have progressed to the manufacture and distribution of a 'purchasable' product for its design patent to be infringed by another's product. . . ."). In other cases, the Federal Circuit has been less definitive. *See, e.g., OddzOn Prods., Inc. v. Just Toys, Inc.*, 122 F.3d 1396, 1406-07 (Fed. Cir. 1997) (actual confusion evidence was "clearly relevant" to substantial similarity, but exclusion of that evidence was harmless error); *Hupp v. Siroflex of America, Inc.*, 122 F.3d 1456, 1464-65 (Fed. Cir. 1997) (appearing to accept the relevance of confusion evidence, while upholding a jury verdict that there was no substantial similarity in spite of the confusion evidence). Is there language in *Gorham* that supports the conclusion that confusion evidence is highly relevant to the substantial similarity assessment?

**4. *Substantial similarity in copyright infringement*.** A substantial similarity test also appears in most judicial formulations of the copyright infringement standard. When you study the materials on copyright protection of designs in Chapter 7, consider whether the substantial similarity standard in copyright is substantially similar to the substantial similarity standard in

*Gorham*, and (if not), whether courts should attempt to harmonize the concepts.

**5. *Proving substantial similarity: point-of-sale, or any time during the product's life?*** Consider the following design for a serving tray for shrimp:

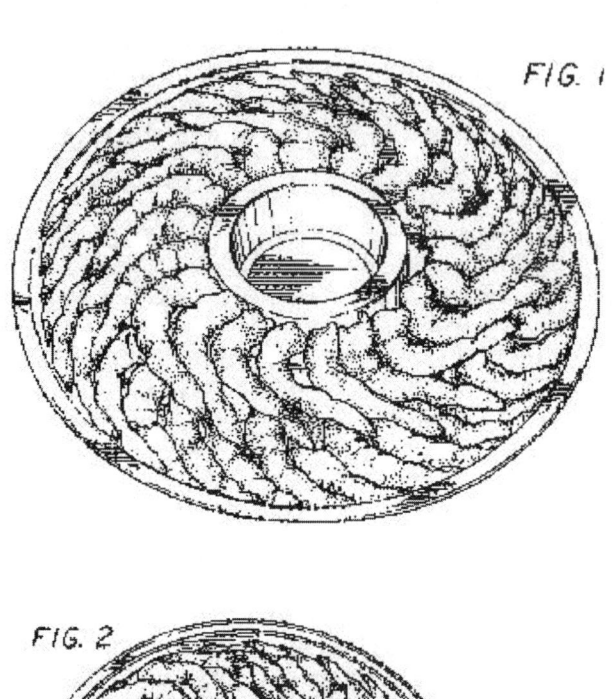

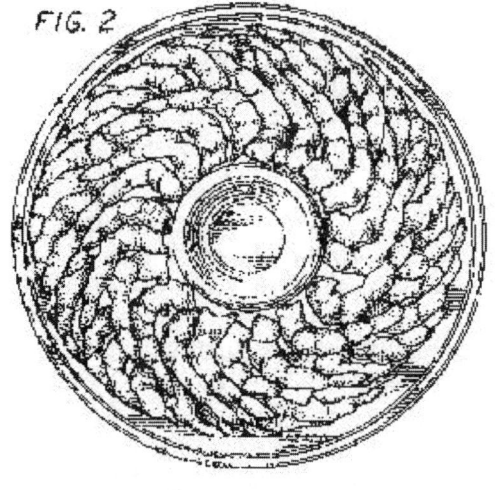

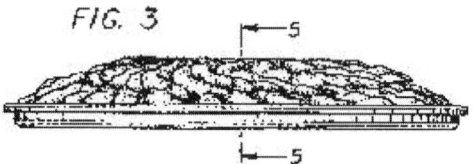

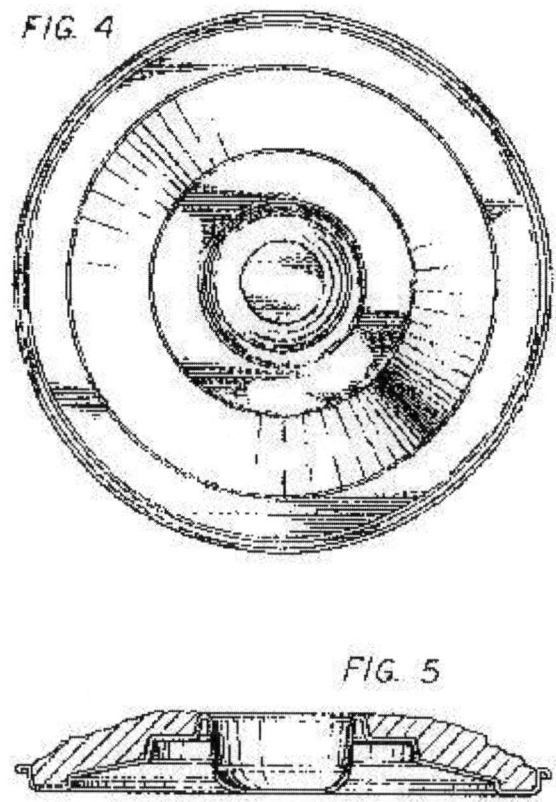

FIG. 4

FIG. 5

For purposes of the substantial similarity analysis, does the claimed design include only features that the ordinary observer would discern *at the point of purchase*? In that regard, consider the underside of the tray as depicted in Fig. 4. Is the underside of the tray part of the claimed design if the ordinary observer would not see it, at least not at the point of purchase? Is *In re Webb* (see Chapter 5) relevant to the answer? What about the arrangement of shrimp shown in Figs. 1-3 — must it be included in the substantial similarity analysis? Could a competitor sell an identical tray with a different shrimp arrangement, and thereby avoid infringement? *See generally Contessa Food Prods., Inc. v. Conagra, Inc.*, 282 F.3d 1370 (Fed. Cir. 2002) (litigation involving the depicted shrimp tray). Recall that in the law of trademark infringement, the Lanham Act has been construed to extend beyond point-of-sale confusion, to pre- and post-sale confusion. Should that matter here?

6. ***Proving substantial similarity: who is the relevant "ordinary observer"?*** The questions in the preceding note might be addressed in a different way: by asking whether the "ordinary observer" is the ultimate

consumer, or some other intermediate purchaser. For example, suppose that the design is for a block used in retaining walls, as shown below:

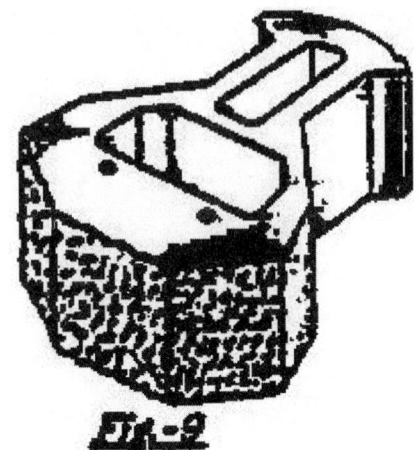

Is the relevant ordinary observer the purchaser of the individual blocks (e.g., a landscaper) or the purchaser of a completed wall (e.g., the property owner)? What additional evidence would you need, if any, in order to resolve the issue? *See KeyStone Retaining Wall Systems, Inc. v. Westrock, Inc.*, 997 F.2d 1444, 1451 (Fed. Cir. 1993); *Spotless Enters. v. A&E Prods. Group L.P.*, 294 F. Supp. 2d 322 (E.D.N.Y. 2003). Suppose that the design at issue is the hip prosthesis design of *In re Webb*. Who is the ordinary observer in such a case—the surgeon who implants the prosthesis? The patient? Someone else (e.g., a purchasing agent for the hospital)? Could someone who might be considered an "expert" also be considered an "ordinary observer," or is this proposition at odds with *Gorham*?

7. ***Proving substantial similarity: expert testimony; survey evidence?*** Where the design at issue is a consumer product sold through ordinary retail channels, as was presumably the case in *Gorham*, is proof of substantial similarity merely a matter of putting the design patent and a sample of the accused design into evidence, and arguing similarity? That is, in such a case, is the fact finder (say, a jury) capable of adopting the perspective of the relevant ordinary observer? *See Catalina Lighting, Inc. v. Lamps Plus, Inc.*, 295 F.3d 1277, 1287 (Fed. Cir. 2002) (upholding jury's determination of overall similarity under *Gorham* in a case involving a lamp design). Should design patent plaintiffs in such a case supplement their proofs with expert testimony? Should design patent plaintiffs be required to produce survey evidence in support of claims of substantial similarity? Strongly encouraged, if not required?

8. ***Proving substantial similarity: relevance of the defendant's patents.*** In *Gorham*, defendant White held design patents, issued in 1867 and 1868, that covered the accused designs. The White patents did not affect the validity of Gorham's patent because the White patents did qualify as prior art against Gorham's patent. Why not? Should the existence of the White patents have affected the court's conclusions as to substantial similarity? If so, how? *See, e.g., Sanson Hosiery Mills v. S.H. Kress & Co.*, 202 F.2d 395, 397 (3d Cir. 1953).

## 2. SUBSTANTIAL SIMILARITY UNDER *EGYPTIAN GODDESS*

As courts began to apply the *Gorham* substantial similarity test, they began to confront questions about the nature of the "ordinary observer." For example, in *Applied Arts Corp. v. Grand Rapids Metalcraft Corp.*, 67 F.2d 428 (6th Cir. 1933), the court wondered what the hypothetical ordinary observer knew of the prior art. *Gorham* had distinguished the ordinary observer from the expert, yet surely the ordinary observer familiar with articles in the marketplace should be charged with at least some knowledge of the prior art. Accordingly, in *Applied Arts*, the Sixth Circuit panel concluded that some of the visually notable similarities between the plaintiff's and defendant's designs were also found in the prior art. When the scope of the patent was limited in view of this prior art, the scope was insufficient to encompass the defendant's designs. Courts eventually restated the *Applied Arts* formulation as a two-part analysis:

> The test of whether one design infringes another depends primarily upon whether the appearance of the two designs is substantially the same. The application of this test involves two considerations: first, to infringe, the identity of appearance, or sameness of effect as a whole upon the eye of an ordinary purchaser must be such as to deceive him, inducing him to purchase one, supposing it to be the other, *Gorham Mfg. Company v. White*, 81 U.S. 511; [cit.] and, second, to infringe, the accused device must appropriate the novelty in the patented device which distinguishes it from the prior art. *Applied Arts Corp. v. Grand Rapids Metalcraft Corp.*, 6 Cir., 67 F.2d 428, 429, 430; [cit.]

*Sears, Roebuck & Co. v. Talge*, 140 F.2d 395, 396 (8th Cir. 1944). The Federal Circuit adopted this two-part analysis in *Litton Sys., Inc. v. Whirlpool Corp.*, 728 F.2d 1423, 1444 (Fed. Cir. 1984) (citing both *Sears* and *Applied Arts*). The Federal Circuit applied this analysis in numerous cases, frequently concluding that the accused design did not appropriate the points of novelty and thus did not infringe. Complaints about the point of novelty concept, and the Federal Circuit's effort to implement that concept, multiplied. *See, e.g.*, Perry J. Saidman, *The Crisis in the Law of Designs*, 89 J. Pat. TM. Off. Soc'y 301 (2007). Eventually, divisions became apparent at the Federal Circuit. For example, in *Lawman Armor Corp. v. Winner Int'l L.L.C.*, 437 F.3d 1383 (Fed. Cir.), *pet. on rehearing en banc denied*, 449 F.3d 1190 (Fed. Cir. 2006) (supplemental and dissenting opinions), the Federal Circuit split over whether a design's overall visual impression could itself constitute a separate point of novelty. In *Egyptian Goddess, Inc. v. Swisa, Inc.*, 498 F.3d 1354 (Fed. Cir. 2007), a Federal Circuit panel held that to prove a point of novelty, a patentee needed to show both that a feature was novel over the prior art, and that the feature was a nontrivial advance over the prior art. The Federal Circuit vacated that ruling and granted a petition for en banc rehearing. In the resulting en banc decision, reproduced below, the Federal Circuit revisited all aspects of the design patent infringement standard.

## Egyptian Goddess, Inc. v. Swisa, Inc.
543 F.3d 665 (Fed. Cir. 2008) (en banc)

Bryson, Circuit Judge:

We granted rehearing en banc in this design patent case to address the appropriate legal standard to be used in assessing claims of design patent infringement.

Appellant Egyptian Goddess, Inc., ("EGI") brought this action in the United States District Court for the Northern District of Texas, alleging that Swisa, Inc., and Dror Swisa (collectively, "Swisa") had infringed EGI's U.S. Design Patent No. 467,389 ("the '389 patent"). The patent claimed a design for a nail buffer, consisting of a rectangular, hollow tube having a generally square cross-section and featuring buffer surfaces on three of its four sides. Swisa's accused product consists of a rectangular, hollow tube having a square cross-section, but featuring buffer surfaces on all four of its sides.

The district court first issued an order construing the claim of the '389 patent. In so doing, the district court sought to describe in words the design set forth in Figure 1 of the patent, which is depicted below:

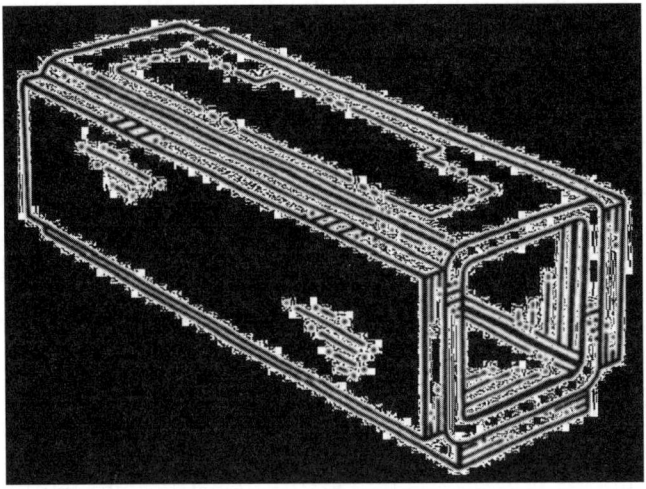

Upon study of the claimed design, the court described it as follows:

A hollow tubular frame of generally square cross section, where the square has sides of length S, the frame has a length of approximately 3S, and the frame has a thickness of approximately T = 0.1S; the corners of the cross section are rounded, with the outer corner of the cross section rounded on a 90 degree radius of approximately 1.25T, and the inner corner of the cross section rounded on a 90 degree radius of approximately 0.25T; and with rectangular abrasive pads of thickness T affixed to three of the sides of the frame, covering the flat portion of the sides while leaving the curved radius uncovered, with the fourth side of the frame bare.

. . .

Swisa then moved for summary judgment of noninfringement. The district court granted the motion. Citing precedent of this court, the district court stated that the plaintiff in a design patent case must prove both (1) that the accused device is "substantially similar" to the claimed design under what is referred to as the "ordinary observer" test, and (2) that the accused device contains "substantially the same points of novelty that distinguished the patented design from the prior art." [cit.] After comparing the claimed design and the accused product, the court held that Swisa's allegedly infringing product did not incorporate the "point of novelty" of the '389 patent, which the court identified as "a fourth, bare side to the buffer."

The district court noted that the parties disagreed as to the points of novelty in the '389 patent. EGI identified four elements in its design, and for each element it identified prior art that did not embody that element. EGI therefore contended that the point of novelty of the '389 patent is the combination of those four elements. The district court, however, declined to address the question whether the point of novelty could be found in the combination of elements not present in various prior art references, because the court found that a single prior art reference, United States Design Patent No. 416,648 ("the Nailco patent"), contained all but one of the elements of the '389 design. The court described the Nailco Patent as disclosing "a nail buffer with an open and hollow body, raised rectangular pads, and open corners." The only element of the '389 patent design that was not present in the Nailco patent, according to the district court, was "the addition of the fourth side without a pad, thereby transforming the equilateral triangular cross-section into a square." Because the Swisa product does not incorporate the point of novelty of the '389 patent—a fourth side without a pad—the court concluded that there was no infringement.

EGI appealed, and a panel of this court affirmed. The panel agreed with the district court that there was no issue of material fact as to whether the accused Swisa buffer "appropriates the point of novelty of the claimed design." *Egyptian Goddess, Inc. v. Swisa, Inc.*, 498 F.3d 1354, 1355 (Fed. Cir. 2007). In reaching that conclusion, the panel stated that the point of novelty in a patented design "can be either a single novel design element or a combination of elements that are individually known in the prior art." *Id.* at 1357. The panel added, however, that in order for a combination of individually known design elements to constitute a point of novelty, "the combination must be a nontrivial advance over the prior art." *Id.*

The panel noted that EGI's asserted point of novelty was a combination of four of the claimed design's elements: (1) an open and hollow body, (2) a square cross-section, (3) raised rectangular buffer pads, and (4) exposed corners. The panel agreed with the district court's observation that the Nailco prior art patent contained each of those elements except that the body was triangular, rather than square, in cross-section. 498 F.3d at 1358. In light of the prior art, the panel determined that "no reasonable juror could conclude that EGI's asserted point of novelty constituted a non-trivial advance over the prior art." *Id.*

The panel further observed that the various design elements of the claimed design "were each individually disclosed in the prior art." 498 F.3d at 1358.

The Swisa buffers, the panel noted, have raised, abrasive pads on all four sides, not just on three of the four sides, as in the claimed design, in which the fourth side is bare. The panel then concluded that "[w]hen considering the prior art in the nail buffer field, this difference between the accused design and the patented design cannot be considered minor." *Id.* The panel therefore concluded that summary judgment was appropriate.

The dissenting judge would not have adopted the "non-trivial advance" test as a way of ascertaining whether a particular feature of the claimed design constituted a point of novelty for infringement purposes. In the view of the dissenting judge, the "nontrivial advance" test was inconsistent with and unsupported by prior precedent; it conflated the criteria for infringement and obviousness; it applied only to designs that involved combinations of design elements; and it improperly focused on the obviousness of each point of novelty, rather than the obviousness of the overall design. 498 F.3d at 1359-60 (Dyk, J., dissenting).

This court granted rehearing en banc and asked the parties to address several questions, including whether the "point of novelty" test should continue to be used as a test for infringement of a design patent; whether the court should adopt the "non-trivial advance test" as a means of determining whether a particular design feature qualifies as a point of novelty; how the point of novelty test should be administered, particularly when numerous features of the design differ from certain prior art designs; and whether district courts should perform formal claim construction in design patent cases.

I

The starting point for any discussion of the law of design patents is the Supreme Court's decision in *Gorham Co. v. White*, 81 U.S. 511 (1871). [The court summarized the *Gorham* opinion.]

Since the decision in *Gorham*, the test articulated by the Court in that case has been referred to as the "ordinary observer" test and has been recognized by lower courts, including both of this court's predecessors, as the proper standard for determining design patent infringement. [cit.] However, in a series of cases tracing their origins to *Litton Systems, Inc. v. Whirlpool Corp.*, 728 F.2d 1423 (Fed. Cir. 1984), this court has held that proof of similarity under the ordinary observer test is not enough to establish design patent infringement. Rather, the court has stated that the accused design must also appropriate the novelty of the claimed design in order to be deemed infringing. The court in *Litton Systems* wrote as follows:

> For a design patent to be infringed . . . no matter how similar two items look, "the accused device must appropriate the novelty in the patented device which distinguishes it from the prior art." That is, even though the court compares two items through the eyes of the ordinary observer, it must nevertheless, to find infringement, attribute their similarity to the novelty which distinguishes the patented device from the prior art.

*Litton Systems*, 728 F.2d at 1444 (citations omitted). After identifying the combination of features in the design that it considered novel, the court in *Litton*

*Systems* held that the accused design had none of those features and therefore did not infringe. *Id.*

In a number of cases decided after *Litton Systems,* this court has interpreted the language quoted above to require that the test for design patent infringement consider both the perspective of the ordinary observer and the particular novelty in the claimed design. *See, e.g., Bernhardt, L.L.C. v. Collezione Europa USA, Inc.,* 386 F.3d 1371, 1383 (Fed. Cir. 2004); *Contessa Food Prods., Inc. v. Conagra, Inc.,* 282 F.3d 1370, 1377 (Fed. Cir. 2002); *Unidynamics Corp. v. Automatic Prods. Int'l, Inc.,* 157 F.3d 1311, 1323-24 (Fed. Cir. 1998); *Oakley, Inc. v. Int'l Tropic-Cal., Inc.,* 923 F.2d 167, 169 (Fed. Cir. 1991); *Avia Group Int'l, Inc. v. L.A. Gear Cal., Inc.,* 853 F.2d 1557, 1565 (Fed. Cir. 1988).

The extent to which the point of novelty test has been a separate test has not always been clear in this court's case law. In cases decided shortly after *Litton,* the court described the ordinary observer test and the point of novelty test as "conjunctive." *See L.A. Gear, Inc. v. Thom McAn Shoe Co.,* 988 F.2d 1117, 1125 (Fed. Cir. 1993); *Shelcore, Inc. v. Durham Indus., Inc.,* 745 F.2d 621, 628 n. 16 (Fed. Cir. 1984). It has not been until much more recently that this court has described the ordinary observer and point of novelty tests as "two distinct tests" and has stated that "[t]he merger of the point of novelty test and the ordinary observer test is legal error." *Unidynamics Corp.,* 157 F.3d at 1323-24; *see also Lawman Armor Corp. v. Winner Int'l, LLC,* 437 F.3d 1383, 1384 (Fed. Cir. 2006); *Contessa Food Prods., Inc.,* 282 F.3d at 1377; *Sun Hill Indus., Inc. v. Easter Unlimited, Inc.,* 48 F.3d 1193, 1197 (Fed. Cir. 1995).

Regardless of the differences in the way it has been characterized, the point of novelty test has proved reasonably easy to apply in simple cases in which the claimed design is based on a single prior art reference and departs from that reference in a single respect. In such cases, it is a simple matter to identify the point of novelty and to determine whether the accused design has appropriated the point of novelty, as opposed to copying those aspects of the claimed design that were already in the prior art. However, the point of novelty test has proved more difficult to apply where the claimed design has numerous features that can be considered points of novelty, or where multiple prior art references are in issue and the claimed design consists of a combination of features, each of which could be found in one or more of the prior art designs. In particular, applying the point of novelty test where multiple features and multiple prior art references are in play has led to disagreement over whether combinations of features, or the overall appearance of a design, can constitute the point of novelty of the claimed design. *Compare Lawman Armor Corp. v. Winner Int'l, LLC,* 449 F.3d 1190 (Fed. Cir. 2006) (supplemental opinion on petition for rehearing), *with Lawman Armor Corp. v. Winner Int'l, LLC,* 449 F.3d 1192 (Fed. Cir. 2006) (Newman, J., dissenting from denial of rehearing en banc). In light of the questions surrounding the status and application of the point of novelty test, we use this case as a vehicle for reconsidering the place of the point of novelty test in design patent law generally.

## II

EGI argues that this court should no longer recognize the point of novelty test as a second part of the test for design patent infringement, distinct from the ordinary observer test established in *Gorham*. Instead of requiring the fact-finder to identify one or more points of novelty in the patented design and then determining whether the accused design has appropriated some or all of those points of novelty, EGI contends that the ordinary observer test can fulfill the purposes for which the point of novelty test was designed, but with less risk of confusion. As long as the ordinary observer test focuses on the "appearance that distinguishes the patented design from the prior art," EGI contends that it will enable the fact-finder to address the proper inquiry, i.e., whether an ordinary observer, familiar with the prior art, would be deceived into thinking that the accused design was the same as the patented design. Relatedly, EGI argues that if the ordinary observer test is performed from the perspective of an ordinary observer who is familiar with the prior art, there is no need for a separate "non-trivial advance" test, because the attention of an ordinary observer familiar with prior art designs will naturally be drawn to the features of the claimed and accused designs that render them distinct from the prior art.

Several of the amici make essentially the same point, referring to the proper approach as calling for a three-way visual comparison between the patented design, the accused design, and the closest prior art. The amici point out that courts, including this one, have on occasion applied that approach in design patent cases, without identifying it as a separate test. [cit.]

Swisa counters that this court may not, and should not, abandon the point of novelty test. According to Swisa, the point of novelty test was adopted by the Supreme Court in *Smith v. Whitman Saddle Co.*, 148 U.S. 674 (1893). Swisa interprets that case as dictating the use of the point of novelty test as a second and distinct test for design patent infringement, separate from the ordinary observer test set forth in *Gorham*. Swisa contends that the subsequent decisions of this court and others applying the point of novelty test are soundly based on *Whitman Saddle*, and that we cannot depart from that test without disregarding that governing Supreme Court precedent as well as intervening precedent from other courts of appeals.

We disagree with Swisa's submission. A close reading of *Whitman Saddle* and subsequent authorities indicates that the Supreme Court did not adopt a separate point of novelty test for design patent infringement cases. In fact, a study of the development of design patent law in the years after *Gorham* shows that the point of novelty test, in its current form, is of quite recent vintage. After a review of those authorities, which we examine in some detail below, we conclude that the point of novelty test, as a second and free-standing requirement for proof of design patent infringement, is inconsistent with the ordinary observer test laid down in *Gorham*, is not mandated by *Whitman Saddle* or precedent from other courts, and is not needed to protect against unduly broad assertions of design patent rights.

*Whitman Saddle* involved a patent on a design for a saddle. The Court began by reciting the requirements for obtaining patent protection for a design. The Court emphasized the importance of "invention" to the patentability of a design. It stated, "Mere mechanical skill is insufficient. There must be something akin to genius, an effort of the brain as well as the hand. The adaptation of old devices or forms to new purposes, however convenient, useful, or beautiful they may be in their new role, is not invention." 148 U.S. at 679. The Court then explained (*id.*):

> The exercise of the inventive or originative faculty is required, and a person cannot be permitted to select an existing form, and simply put it to a new use, any more than he can be permitted to take a patent for the mere double use of a machine. If, however, the selection and adaptation of an existing form is more than the exercise of the imitative faculty, and the result is in effect a new creation, the design may be patentable.

In the case before it, the Court characterized the patented saddle design as a combination of elements from two saddle designs that were well known in the art. The Court explained that the patented design consisted of a combination of the front half of the so-called Granger saddle and the back end of the so-called Jenifer saddle. The design differed from a simple combination of the two known saddles, according to the Court, only in that the front end of the design had "a nearly perpendicular drop of some inches at the rear of the pommel," unlike in the Granger saddle. *Id.* at 680.

Although the trial court, sitting in equity, concluded that the design was patentable, the Supreme Court disagreed. The Court wrote, "Nothing more was done in this instance (except as hereafter noted) than to put the two halves of these saddles together in the exercise of the ordinary skill of workmen of the trade, and in the way and manner ordinarily done." 148 U.S. at 681. The Court noted that there was a difference between the pommel of the designed saddle and the pommel of the Granger saddle, and it added that the "shape of the front end being old, the sharp drop of the pommel at the rear seems to constitute what was new and to be material." *Id.* at 682. That feature, however, was not present in the defendants' saddle. The Court then concluded with the following remarks (*id.*):

> If, therefore, this drop were material to the design, and rendered it patentable as a complete and integral whole, there was no infringement. As before said, the design of the patent had two features of difference as compared with the Granger saddle, one the cantle, the other the drop; and unless there was infringement as to the latter there was none at all, since the saddle design of the patent does not otherwise differ from the old saddle with the old cantle added, an addition frequently made. Moreover, that difference was so marked that in our judgment the defendant's saddle could not be mistaken for the saddle of the complainant.

Because *Whitman Saddle* was an action in equity, the Court did not distinguish sharply between its analysis of patentability and its discussion of infringement. Within the same passage, the Court moved from stating that it could not agree with the trial court that the design in issue was patentable to the conclusion that if the design were patentable because of the drop at the rear of the pommel, there was no infringement. Nothing in the Court's opinion suggested that it was fashioning a separate point of novelty test for infringement. The point the Court was making was that, viewed in light of the similarities between the prior art and the patented design, the accused design did not contain the single feature that would have made it appear distinctively similar to the patented design rather than like the numerous prior art designs. For that reason, the Court held, the accused design did not infringe.

Subsequent cases applied that principle, interpreting the ordinary observer test of *Gorham* to require that the perspective of the ordinary observer be informed by a comparison of the patented design and the accused design in light of the prior art, so as to enable the fact-finder to determine whether the accused design had appropriated the inventiveness of the patented design. For example, two cases decided in the wake of *Whitman Saddle* shed light on the Supreme Court's analysis in *Whitman Saddle* and illustrate the application of the ordinary observer test in light of the prior art.

In the first of those cases, *Bevin Brothers Manufacturing Co. v. Starr Brothers Bell Co.*, 114 F. 362 (C.C.D. Conn. 1902), the patent drawing showed an oblate spheroid and neck, and the claim covered "a bell as herein shown and described." Sitting in equity, the court addressed both validity and infringement, noting that the test of identity on both issues "is the eye of the ordinary observer." *Id.* at 363. After noting that the patented form was commonly found in a variety of prior art structures, the court held that the "defense of want of patentable novelty is sustained." *Id.* As for infringement, the court again consulted particular objects in the prior art having a similar shape, including a door knob, and concluded that "[t]he shape of the defendant's bell differs from plaintiff's more widely than plaintiff's differs from the door knob, and therefore defendants' construction does not infringe the patent." *Id.* Thus, the court's approach, like that of the Supreme Court in *Whitman Saddle*, did not employ a point of novelty test, but invoked the ordinary observer test in which the observer was comparing the patented and accused designs in the context of similar designs found in the prior art.

The second case, *Zidell v. Dexter*, 262 F. 145 (9th Cir. 1920), cited *Whitman Saddle* for the proposition that under the ordinary observer standard, a patented design that consists "only of bringing together old elements with slight modifications of form" is not infringed by "another who uses the same elements with his own variations of form . . . if his design is distinguishable by the ordinary observer from the patented design." *Id.* at 146. The court emphasized the importance of similar prior art designs to the determination of infringement under the ordinary observer test:

> The evidence shows that at and prior to the conception of this design there were in use and on sale very many similar garments, with variations in design so slight as to leave to the ordinary observer the impression of a very general resemblance, and we must assume that to womankind, who are the purchasers in the main of this class of garment, these various coincident forms of garments were known, and whether such purchasers would be deceived into taking the garments which are alleged to infringe for a garment of the patented design would necessarily depend largely upon that general knowledge.

*Id.* at 147.

Some years later, the Sixth Circuit addressed a similar issue in a case involving a design patent on a combination ash tray and electric lighter. *Applied Arts Corp. v. Grand Rapids Metalcraft Corp.*, 67 F.2d 428 (6th Cir. 1933). The district court found infringement by two of the defendant's designs upon finding that the resemblance between the patented design and the accused design was such as to deceive the ordinary observer. In analyzing the case, the court addressed the question whether the ordinary observer test of *Gorham* was in conflict with the principle that "similitude of appearance is to be judged by the scope of the patent in relation to the prior art." *Id.* at 429.

The court explained that the ordinary observer of the *Gorham* test was not one "who has never seen an ash tray or a cigar lighter, but one who, though not an expert, has reasonable familiarity with such objects," and is capable of assessing the similarity of the patented and accused designs in light of the similar objects in the prior art. 67 F.2d at 430. Viewing the ordinary observer test in that manner, the court stated:

> [W]hile there is some similarity between the patented and alleged infringing designs, which without consideration of the prior art might seem important, yet such similarity as is due to common external configuration is no greater, if as great, between the patented and challenged designs as between the former and the designs of the prior art.

*Id.* After noting the similarities between the patented design and the prior art designs, the court concluded that the differences between the two "are no greater than those that exist between the patented design and the alleged infringing designs." Accordingly, the court concluded, assuming the patent to be valid "it is quite clear it is entitled to a very limited interpretation and that so limited the defendant's designs do not infringe." *Id.* The court ruled that while it was aware that similarity "is not to be determined by making too close an analysis of detail," nonetheless, "where in a crowded art the composite of differences presents a different impression to the eye of the average observer (as above defined), infringement will not be found." *Id.*

That precedent was followed by the Eighth Circuit in *Sears, Roebuck & Co. v. Talge*, 140 F.2d 395 (8th Cir. 1944). The district court in that case held that the defendant's home fruit juicer infringed the plaintiff's patents on fruit juicer designs. The court stated that the test for design patent infringement involves two elements: (1) "the identity of appearance, or sameness of effect as a whole upon the eye of an ordinary purchaser must be such as to deceive him, inducing him to purchase one, supposing it to be the other" and (2) "the accused device must appropriate the novelty in the patented device which distinguishes it from the prior art." *Id.* at 395-96. To make the latter determination, the court explained, "requires a comparison of the features of the patented designs with the prior art and with the accused design." *Id.* at 396. By examining the prior art fruit juicers, the court was able to identify the "novel elements embodied in the [patented] design." The court then determined that there was no identity of appearance with respect to those elements between the claimed designs and the accused products. *Id.*

The *Sears, Roebuck* and *Applied Arts* cases, in turn, became the principal precedents relied upon by this court in the seminal *Litton Systems* case to which this court's precedents dealing with the point of novelty test trace their origin. In Litton *Systems*, as in *Sears, Roebuck*, the court identified the *Gorham* ordinary observer test as the starting point for design patent infringement. Quoting from *Sears, Roebuck*, the Litton court added, however, that "no matter how similar two items look, 'the accused device must appropriate the novelty in the patented device which distinguishes it from the prior art.'" 728 F.2d at 1444. That is, the court added, after comparing two items through the eyes of the ordinary observer, the court must, to find infringement, "attribute their similarity to the novelty which distinguishes the patented device from the prior art." *Id.* The court then referred to that second test as the point of novelty approach, and that tag has been applied to the second part of the design patent infringement test ever since.

In analyzing the claim of infringement, the court in *Litton Systems* focused on what it characterized as the novelty of the patent in suit, i.e., "the combination on a microwave oven's exterior of a three-stripe door frame, a door without a handle, and a latch release lever on the control panel." Significantly, however, the court quoted from the *Applied Arts* case and stated that the degree of similarity between the accused design and the patented design had to be assessed in light of the designs in the prior art. The court noted that where, as in the case before it, "a field is crowded with many references relating to the design of the same type of appliance, we must construe the range of equivalents very narrowly." 728 F.2d at 1444. Accordingly, the court held that the scope of protection of the patent in that case was limited to "a narrow range" that did not include the accused design. *Id.*

As noted, this court has cited *Litton Systems* for the proposition that the point of novelty test is separate from the ordinary observer test and requires the patentee to point out the point of novelty in the claimed design that has been appropriated by the accused design. We think, however, that *Litton* and the predecessor cases on which it relied are more properly read as applying a version of the ordinary observer test in which the ordinary observer is deemed to view the differences between the patented design and the accused product in the context of the prior art. When the differences between the claimed and accused design are viewed in light of the prior art, the attention of the hypothetical ordinary observer will be drawn to those aspects of the claimed design that differ from the prior art. And when the claimed design is close to the prior art designs, small differences between the accused design and the claimed design are likely to be important to the eye of the hypothetical ordinary observer. It was for that reason that the Supreme Court in *Whitman Saddle* focused on the one feature of the patented saddle design that departed from the prior art—the sharp drop at the rear of the pommel. To an observer familiar with the multitude of prior art saddle designs, including the design incorporating the Granger pommel and the Jenifer cantle, "an addition frequently made," 148 U.S. at 682, the sharp drop at the rear of the pommel would be important to the overall appearance of the design and would serve to distinguish the accused design, which did not possess that feature, from the claimed design.

The same can be said of the courts' analysis in *Bevin Brothers*, *Zidell*, *Applied Arts*, and *Sears, Roebuck*. In *Bevin Brothers* and *Zidell*, the courts emphasized that the defendant's product would appear different from the plaintiff's protected design to an ordinary observer aware of the great number of closely similar prior art designs. In *Applied Arts*, the accused ash tray would not appear to be the same as the claimed ash tray as long as "similitude of appearance is . . .

judged by the scope of the patent in relation to the prior art." 67 F.2d at 429. And in *Sears, Roebuck*, the court concluded that the accused fruit juicer would not appear similar to the claimed design if the fact-finder performed the required "comparison of the features of the patented designs with the prior art and with the accused design." 140 F.2d at 396.

Not only is this approach consistent with the precedents discussed above, but it makes sense as a matter of logic as well. Particularly in close cases, it can be difficult to answer the question whether one thing is like another without being given a frame of reference. The context in which the claimed and accused designs are compared, i.e., the background prior art, provides such a frame of reference and is therefore often useful in the process of comparison. Where the frame of reference consists of numerous similar prior art designs, those designs can highlight the distinctions between the claimed design and the accused design as viewed by the ordinary observer.

Applying the ordinary observer test with reference to prior art designs also avoids some of the problems created by the separate point of novelty test. One such problem is that the point of novelty test has proved difficult to apply in cases in which there are several different features that can be argued to be points of novelty in the claimed design. In such cases, the outcome of the case can turn on which of the several candidate points of novelty the court or fact-finder focuses on. The attention of the court may therefore be focused on whether the accused design has appropriated a single specified feature of the claimed design, rather than on the proper inquiry, i.e., whether the accused design has appropriated the claimed design as a whole. *See Amini Innovation Corp. v. Anthony Cal., Inc.*, 439 F.3d 1365, 1370-71 (Fed. Cir. 2006); *Keystone Retaining Wall Sys., Inc. v. Westrock, Inc.*, 997 F.2d 1444, 1450 (Fed. Cir. 1993); *Braun Inc.*, 975 F.2d at 820.

In addition, the more novel the design, and the more points of novelty that are identified, the more opportunities there are for a defendant to argue that its design does not infringe because it does not copy all of the points of novelty, even though it may copy most of them and even though it may give the overall appearance of being identical to the claimed design. In such cases, a test that asks how an ordinary observer with knowledge of the prior art designs would view the differences between the claimed and accused designs is likely to produce results more in line with the purposes of design patent protection.

This court has characterized the purpose of the point of novelty test as being "to focus on those aspects of a design which render the design different from prior art designs." *Sun Hill Indus., Inc.*, 48 F.3d at 1197, quoting *Winner Int'l Corp. v. Wolo Mfg. Corp.*, 905 F.2d 375, 376 (Fed. Cir. 1990). That purpose can be equally well served, however, by applying the ordinary observer test through the eyes of an observer familiar with the prior art. If the accused design has copied a particular feature of the claimed design that departs conspicuously from the prior art, the accused design is naturally more likely to be regarded as deceptively similar to the claimed design, and thus infringing. At the same time, unlike the point of novelty test, the ordinary observer test does not present the risk of assigning exaggerated importance to small differences between the claimed and accused designs relating to an insignificant feature simply because that feature can be characterized as a point of novelty.

This approach also has the advantage of avoiding the debate over the extent to which a combination of old design features can serve as a point of novelty under the point of novelty test. An ordinary observer, comparing the claimed and accused designs in light of the prior art, will attach importance to differences between the claimed design and the prior art depending on the overall effect of those differences on the design. If the claimed design consists of a combination of old features that creates an appearance deceptively similar to the accused design, even to an observer familiar with similar prior art designs, a finding of infringement would be justified. Otherwise, infringement would not be found.

One function that has been served by the point of novelty test, according to Swisa and its supporting amici, is to cabin unduly broad assertions of design patent scope by ensuring that a design that merely embodies or is substantially similar to prior art designs is not found to infringe. Again, however, we believe that the preferable way to achieve that purpose is to do so directly, by relying on the ordinary observer test, conducted in light of the prior art. Our rejection of the point of novelty test does not mean, of course, that the differences between the claimed design and prior art designs are irrelevant. To the contrary, examining the novel features of the claimed design can be an important component of the comparison of the claimed design with the accused design and the prior art. But the comparison of the designs, including the examination of any novel features, must be conducted as part of the ordinary observer test, not as part of a separate test focusing on particular points of novelty that are designated only in the course of litigation.

On the basis of the foregoing analysis, we hold that the "point of novelty" test should no longer be used in the analysis of a claim of design patent infringement. Because we reject the "point of novelty" test, we also do not adopt the "non-trivial advance" test, which is a refinement of the "point of novelty" test. Instead, in accordance with *Gorham* and subsequent decisions, we hold that the "ordinary observer" test should be the sole test for determining whether a design patent has been infringed. Under that test, as this court has sometimes described it, infringement will not be found unless the accused article "embod[ies] the patented design or any colorable imitation thereof." *Goodyear Tire & Rubber Co.*, 162 F.3d at 1116-17; *see also Arminiak & Assocs., Inc. v. Saint-Gobain Calmar, Inc.*, 501 F.3d 1314, 1319 (Fed. Cir. 2007).

In some instances, the claimed design and the accused design will be sufficiently distinct that it will be clear without more that the patentee has not met its burden of proving the two designs would appear "substantially the same" to the ordinary observer, as required by *Gorham*. In other instances, when the claimed and accused designs are not plainly dissimilar, resolution of the question whether the ordinary observer would consider the two designs to be substantially the same will benefit from a comparison of the claimed and accused designs with the prior art, as in many of the cases discussed above and in the case at bar. Where there are many examples of similar prior art designs, as in a case such as *Whitman Saddle*, differences between the claimed and accused designs that might not be noticeable in the abstract can become significant to the hypothetical ordinary observer who is conversant with the prior art.

We emphasize that although the approach we adopt will frequently involve comparisons between the claimed design and the prior art, it is not a test for determining validity, but is designed solely as a test of infringement. Thus, as is always the case, the burden of proof as to infringement remains on the patentee. However, if the accused infringer elects to rely on the comparison prior art as part of its defense against the claim of infringement, the burden of production of that prior art is on the accused infringer. To be sure, we have stated that the burden to introduce prior art under the point of novelty test falls on the patentee. *See Bernhardt*, 386 F.3d at 1384. Under the ordinary observer test, however, it makes sense to impose the burden of production as to any comparison prior art on the accused infringer. The accused infringer is the party with the motivation to point out close prior art, and in particular to call to the court's attention the prior art that an ordinary observer is most likely to regard as highlighting the differences between the claimed and accused design. Regardless of whether the accused infringer elects to present prior art that it considers pertinent to the comparison between the claimed and accused design, however, the patentee bears the ultimate burden of proof to demonstrate infringement by a preponderance of the evidence. As in our recent decision in *In re Seagate Technology, LLC*, we "leave it to future cases to further develop the application of this standard." 497 F.3d 1360, 1371 (Fed. Cir. 2007) (en banc).

III

One of the issues raised by this court in its order granting en banc review was whether trial courts should conduct claim construction in design patent cases. While this court has held that trial courts have a duty to conduct claim construction in design patent cases, as in utility patent cases, *see Elmer*, 67 F.3d at 1577, the court has not prescribed any particular form that the claim construction must take. To the contrary, the court has recognized that design patents "typically are claimed as shown in drawings," and that claim construction "is adapted accordingly." *Arminiak & Assocs., Inc.*, 501 F.3d at 1319; *see also Goodyear Tire & Rubber Co.*, 162 F.3d at 1116. For that reason, this court has not required that the trial court attempt to provide a detailed verbal description of the claimed design, as is typically done in the case of utility patents. *See Contessa Food Prods., Inc.*, 282 F.3d at 1377 (approving district court's construction of the asserted claim as meaning "a tray of a certain design as shown in Figures 1-3").[1]

As the Supreme Court has recognized, a design is better represented by an illustration "than it could be by any description and a description would probably not be intelligible without the illustration." *Dobson v. Dornan*, 118 U.S. 10, 14 (1886). The Patent and Trademark Office has made the same observation. *Manual of Patent Examining Procedure* §1503.01 (8th ed. 2006)

---

1. This court has required that in determining obviousness, a district court must attempt to "translate [the] visual descriptions into words" in order to communicate the reasoning behind the court's decision and to enable "the parties and appellate courts . . . to discern the internal reasoning employed by the trial court." *Durling v. Spectrum Furniture Co.*, 101 F.3d 100, 102 (Fed. Cir. 1996). Requiring such an explanation of a legal ruling as to invalidity is quite different from requiring an elaborate verbal claim construction to guide the finder of fact in conducting the infringement inquiry.

("[A]s a rule the illustration in the drawing views is its own best description."). Given the recognized difficulties entailed in trying to describe a design in words, the preferable course ordinarily will be for a district court not to attempt to "construe" a design patent claim by providing a detailed verbal description of the claimed design.

With that said, it is important to emphasize that a district court's decision regarding the level of detail to be used in describing the claimed design is a matter within the court's discretion, and absent a showing of prejudice, the court's decision to issue a relatively detailed claim construction will not be reversible error. At the same time, it should be clear that the court is not obligated to issue a detailed verbal description of the design if it does not regard verbal elaboration as necessary or helpful. In addition, in deciding whether to attempt a verbal description of the claimed design, the court should recognize the risks entailed in such a description, such as the risk of placing undue emphasis on particular features of the design and the risk that a finder of fact will focus on each individual described feature in the verbal description rather than on the design as a whole. In this case, for example, the district court came up with a detailed verbal description of the claimed design. We see no inaccuracy in the court's description, and neither party has pointed to any prejudice resulting from the court's interpretation. Yet it is not clear that the considerable effort needed to fashion the verbal description contributed enough to the process of analyzing the case to justify the effort.

While it may be unwise to attempt a full description of the claimed design, a court may find it helpful to point out, either for a jury or in the case of a bench trial by way of describing the court's own analysis, various features of the claimed design as they relate to the accused design and the prior art. In a case such as this one, for example, there would be nothing wrong with the court pointing out to a jury that in the patented design only three sides have buffers attached, while in the accused product (and in the three-sided Nailco patent), all of the sides have buffers attached. It would similarly be permissible for the court to point out that, for example, although the Falley Buffer Block has four sides, it is not hollow, unlike the design of the '389 patent, the Nailco patent, and the accused Swisa product.

Apart from attempting to provide a verbal description of the design, a trial court can usefully guide the finder of fact by addressing a number of other issues that bear on the scope of the claim. Those include such matters as describing the role of particular conventions in design patent drafting, such as the role of broken lines, *see* 37 C.F.R. §1.152; assessing and describing the effect of any representations that may have been made in the course of the prosecution history, *see Goodyear Tire & Rubber Co.*, 162 F.3d at 1116; and distinguishing between those features of the claimed design that are ornamental and those that are purely functional, *see OddzOn Prods., Inc. v. Just Toys, Inc.*, 122 F.3d 1396, 1405 (Fed. Cir. 1997) ("Where a design contains both functional and non-functional elements, the scope of the claim must be construed in order to identify the non-functional aspects of the design as shown in the patent.").

Providing an appropriate measure of guidance to a jury without crossing the line and unduly invading the jury's fact-finding process is a task that trial courts are very much accustomed to, and any attempt by an appellate court to guide that process in detail is likely to do more harm than good. We therefore leave the question of verbal characterization of the claimed designs to the discretion of trial judges, with the proviso that as a general matter, those courts should not treat the process of claim construction as requiring a detailed verbal description of the claimed design, as would typically be true in the case of utility patents.

## IV

We now turn to the facts of this case. It is agreed that the general shape of the accused nail buffer at issue in this case is the same as that of the patented buffer design. The difference between the two is that the accused buffer has raised buffing pads on all four sides, while the patented buffer has buffing pads on only three sides. The two closest prior art nail buffers before the court were the Falley nail buffer, which has a solid, rectangular cross section with slightly raised buffers on all sides, and the Nailco patent, which shows a nail buffer design having a triangular shape and a hollow cross section, and in which raised buffing pads are located on all three sides. The four nail buffers are pictured below:

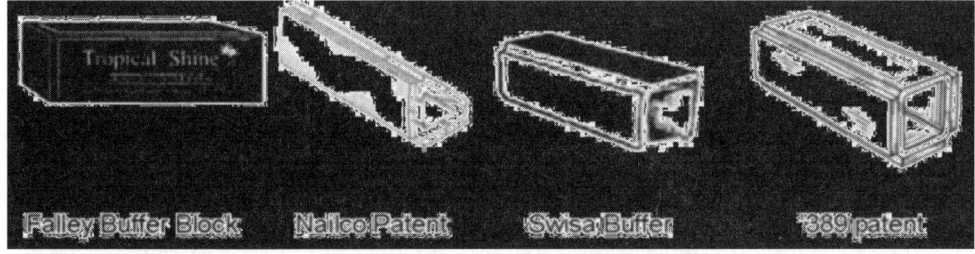

Falley Buffer Block    Nailco Patent    Swisa Buffer    '389 patent

The question before this court under the standard we have set forth above is whether an ordinary observer, familiar with the prior art Falley and Nailco designs, would be deceived into believing the Swisa buffer is the same as the patented buffer. EGI argues that such an observer would notice a difference between the prior art and the '389 patent, consisting of "the hollow tube that is square in cross section and that has raised pads with exposed gaps at the corners." To support that contention, EGI invokes the declaration of its expert witness, Kathleen Eaton. After viewing the patented, accused, and Nailco buffers, Ms. Eaton concluded that the patented and accused designs would "confuse an ordinary observer into purchasing the accused buffer thinking it to be the patented buffer design." She reached that conclusion, she explained, because "the substantially similar appearance [between the accused and patented designs] results from both designs having a hollow tube, square in cross section and rectangular in length, with multiple raised rectangular pads mounted on the sides, and that do not cover the corners of the tube." While recognizing that the accused buffer has pads on all four sides and that the claimed design has buffer pads on only three sides, she stated that "I do not believe that, to an ordinary observer and purchaser of nail buffers, the presence of one more buffer pad[s] greatly alters the ornamental effect and appearance of the whole design as compared to the whole patented design."

Swisa counters that the '389 patent closely tracks the design of the Nailco nail buffer, except that it "add[s] a fourth side without an abrasive pad, resulting in square ends." In light of the close prior art buffers, including a number having square cross-sections, Swisa argues that an ordinary observer would notice the difference between the claimed and accused designs. To support that contention, Swisa cites the declaration of its expert, Steve Falley. Mr. Falley addressed the differences among the prior art designs, the accused design, and patented design, and he concluded that

> you could simply add to the Nailco Buffer a fourth side without an abrasive on it. This merely takes the Nailco Buffer to the block shape of the original Falley Buffer Block, while keeping the hollow aspect of the Nailco Buffer. As there had already been on the market for a long time 3-way buffer blocks that had no abrasive on one side, it was also obvious after the Nailco Buffer that you could have a three way hollow buffer that had four sides but with no abrasive on one side.

Mr. Falley added that "four-way" nail buffers having four different abrasive surfaces have been made since 1985, and that four-sided "buffer blocks" have been on the market since 1987. He pointed to catalogs showing three-sided and four-sided buffer blocks that have been offered for sale since at least 1994, and in light of his knowledge of the industry, he stated that the "number of sides with abrasive surface on them would be important to purchasers because it determines whether a buffer is a 'three way buffer' or a 'four way buffer.'" Accordingly, he concluded:

> The difference between a buffer with abrasive on three sides — a "three-way buffer" — and a buffer with abrasive on four sides — a "four-way buffer" — is immediately apparent to any consumer used to buying nail buffers. Even if such a consumer did not have a preference for either three-way or four-way buffers (although they almost always do), they would at a glance be able to tell that a buffer with abrasive on only three sides had abrasive on three sides, and was a three-way buffer, while a buffer with abrasive on four sides had abrasive on all four sides, and was a four-way buffer. I cannot imagine consumers would buy buffers with abrasive on four sides thinking that they were buying buffers with abrasive on three sides.

The problem with Ms. Eaton's declaration is that she characterized the accused and patented designs as similar because they both have square cross sections and "multiple" raised buffer pads, without directly acknowledging that the patented design has three pads while the accused design has four, one on each side. She also failed to address the fact that the design of the Nailco patent is identical to the accused device except that the Nailco design has three sides rather than four. Thus, she could as easily have said that the Nailco buffer design "is like the accused design because both designs have a hollow tube, have multiple rectangular sides with raised rectangular pads mounted on each side that do not cover the corners of the tube," in which case the Nailco prior art buffer would be seen to closely resemble the accused design. Nothing about Ms. Eaton's declaration explains why an ordinary observer would regard the accused design as being closer to the claimed design than to the Nailco prior art patent. In fact, Ms. Eaton's reference to the prior art buffers is limited to the single, and conclusory, comment that an ordinary observer and purchaser of nail buffers would consider the patented design and the accused buffer to be substantially similar, "particularly in light of other nail buffers, such as a solid block buffer and the hollow triangular Nailco buffer."

In light of the similarity of the prior art buffers to the accused buffer, we conclude that no reasonable fact-finder could find that EGI met its burden of showing, by a preponderance of the evidence, that an ordinary observer, taking into account the prior art, would believe the accused design to be the same as the patented design. In concluding that a reasonable fact-finder could not find infringement in this case, we reach the same conclusion that the district court reached, and for many of the same reasons. Although we do so by using the ordinary observer test as informed by the prior art, rather than by applying the point of novelty test, our analysis largely tracks that of the district court. After analyzing the Nailco patent and the claimed design, as they related to the accused design, the district court concluded that "in the context of nail buffers, a fourth side without a pad is not substantially the same as a fourth side with a pad." While the district court focused on the differences in the particular feature at issue rather than the effect of those differences on the appearance of the design as a whole, we are satisfied that the difference on which the district court focused is important, viewed in the context of the prior art.

Finally, although we do not adopt the "non-trivial advance" test employed by the panel in this case, we note that our analysis under the ordinary observer test is parallel to the panel's approach in an essential respect. The panel focused on viewing the difference between the claimed and accused designs in light of the prior art, as we do. The panel wrote: "The Swisa buffers have raised, abrasive pads on *all four* sides. When considering the prior art in the nail buffer field, this difference between the accused design and the patented design cannot be considered minor." 498 F.3d at 1358. That point captures the essence of the rationale of our decision today, even though the panel decision employed a different analytical approach. For the foregoing reasons, we sustain the district court's entry of summary judgment of no infringement, but we do so under the ordinary observer test in the form that we have adopted, and without using the point of novelty test that we have disapproved. In the language used by the Supreme Court in *Gorham*, 81 U.S. at 528, we hold that the accused design could not reasonably be viewed as so similar to the claimed design that a purchaser familiar with the prior art would be deceived by the similarity between the claimed and accused designs, "inducing him to purchase one supposing it to be the other."

*Affirmed.*

## NOTES AND QUESTIONS

1. *Discarding the "point of novelty" test — or not?* In *Egyptian Goddess*, the Federal Circuit declared that the point of novelty test should no longer be used as a second step in the infringement analysis. But the court also noted that in applying the *Gorham* substantial similarity test to designs that are not "plainly dissimilar," courts might benefit from comparing the claimed and accused

designs with the prior art. Did the court really discard the point of novelty test, or merely merge it with the *Gorham* substantial similarity test? One way to address this question concretely is to review infringement cases that preceded *Egyptian Goddess* and analyze whether the outcome on the infringement issue would be the same after *Egyptian Goddess*. Problem 6-1 below poses that question. An additional way is to consider how the Federal Circuit applies its analysis to the facts of *Egyptian Goddess* itself. How significant is it that the Federal Circuit affirms the district court's grant of summary judgment of non-infringement? How significant is it that the Federal Circuit en banc declares that the vacated Federal Circuit panel opinion "capture[d] the essence of the rationale of our decision today, even though the panel decision employed a different analytical approach"?

2. ***How does* Egyptian Goddess *affect design patent scope in general?*** Judge Rich once opined that "[d]esign patents have almost no scope." *In re Mann*, 861 F.2d 1581, 1582 (Fed. Cir. 1988). Is this still true after *Egyptian Goddess*? The simple answer might be no, because *Egyptian Goddess* eliminated the point-of-novelty test. But there are a few reasons to doubt the simple answer. First, as the above note explores, although the court discarded the point-of-novelty test in *Egyptian Goddess*, it did not discard consideration of the prior art as part of the infringement analysis. Second, the impact of the prior art in a design patent infringement analysis will not necessarily be uniform across cases. The prior art might have the effect of diminishing patent scope by highlighting differences between the patented and accused designs, as the *Egyptian Goddess* opinion points out: "Where there are many examples of similar prior art designs . . . differences between the claimed and accused designs that might not be noticeable in the abstract can become significant to the hypothetical ordinary observer who is conversant with the prior art." But might the prior art also have the effect of enhancing patent scope by highlighting the similarities between the patented and accused designs?

3. ***Proving substantial similarity after* Egyptian Goddess**. Review the notes and questions following the *Gorham* case. Does *Egyptian Goddess* answer any of those questions about proving substantial similarity? To the extent that it does, are any of the answers different than they would have been prior to *Egyptian Goddess*?

4. ***Design patents and claim interpretation methodology.*** In *Egyptian Goddess*, the Federal Circuit also instructed courts on the methodology for interpreting the claims of design patents. The law of utility patents would seem to provide a natural starting point; after all, claim interpretation is a threshold matter in most utility patent issues. For example, the modern infringement analysis for utility patents involves the following steps: (1) the patent claim at issue is interpreted (a question of law); and (2) the claim at issue is compared to the accused infringing activity (a question of fact) under the rules for literal infringement or, alternatively, infringement under the doctrine of equivalents. *See Markman v. Westview Instruments, Inc.*, 52 F.3d 967 (Fed. Cir. 1995) (en banc), *aff'd*, 517 U.S. 370 (1996) (designating claim interpretation a question of law). Prior to *Egyptian Goddess*, the Federal Circuit had extended this framework to design patent infringement, albeit without specifying how a court should carry out claim interpretation of a design patent claim. *See, e.g., Contessa Food Prods., Inc. v. Conagra, Inc.*, 282 F.3d 1370, 1376

(Fed. Cir. 2002); *Elmer v. ICC Fabricating, Inc.*, 67 F.3d 1571, 1577 (Fed. Cir. 1995). As we have seen, a design patent claim merely incorporates the design patent drawings, so interpreting such a claim would have involved translating the drawings into a verbal description. As commentators pointed out, that exercise might deprive design patents of meaningful scope. *See* Perry J. Saidman & Allison Singh, *The Death of Gorham Co. v. White: Killing It Softly with Markman*, 86 J. Pat. & Trademark Off. Soc'y 792 (2004) (arguing that *Markman* determinations should not be made in design patent cases, at least not to the extent that they require the claims to be verbalized). In *Egyptian Goddess*, the Federal Circuit acknowledged that it might be problematic to purport to require courts to "interpret" the claims of design patents. What alternative approach did the Federal Circuit suggest? Is the Federal Circuit's approach superior to the claim interpretation analysis that it displaced? For an illustration of claim construction in a design patent case after *Egyptian Goddess*, see *Arc'teryx Equip., Inc. v. Westcomb Outerwear, Inc.*, 2008 WL 4838141 (D. Utah Nov. 4, 2008).

**5. *Claim interpretation: discrete elements v. overall impression.*** When a court attempts to interpret a design patent claim, is there a danger that the court will become enmeshed in an analysis of discrete features of the design, and lose sight (literally and metaphorically) of the overall visual impression of the design? For a Federal Circuit critique of a lower court's design patent infringement analysis on the ground that the analysis focused too narrowly on isolated ornamental features, *see Amini Innovation Corp. v. Anthony California, Inc.*, 439 F.3d 1365, 1371 (Fed. Cir. 2006) (asserting that the patent drawings on a design for a bed frame "affirm that it is the overall 'bed frame' that is patented—not just the details of its ornamentation"); *see also Durling* (excerpted in Chapter 5) ("A proper interpretation of [the patentee's] claimed design focuses on the visual impression it creates."). These critiques were offered prior to *Egyptian Goddess*. If courts follow the guidance in *Egyptian Goddess*, are they more likely to maintain a correct focus on a design's overall impression?

**6. *Claim interpretation and related products.*** Suppose that a claim is directed to "tire tread," and the patent drawings show the claimed tread on a tire with the tire sidewall depicted in broken lines to indicate that the sidewall "forms no part of the design claimed." If the patentee's commercial embodiment was a truck tire should the properly construed design patent claim extend beyond truck tires? Would it have been proper for the court to construe the claim as extending beyond tires altogether? Suppose that a firm sells beer mugs that have been etched with the identical tire tread pattern, or earrings that have been engraved with the tire tread pattern? Is it conceivable that these products could fall within the scope of the design claim?

**7. *Doctrine of equivalents for designs?*** Should the doctrine of equivalents theory be recognized for design patents? In cases like the beer mug hypothetical in the note above? Under utility patent law, a claim is infringed under the doctrine of equivalents if the patentee shows that the accused device includes at least equivalent substitutes for all of the limitations of the claim. Equivalency has often been assessed by determining whether the accused device performs substantially the same function, in substantially the same way, to achieve substantially the same result as the claimed invention. The Federal Circuit has held that the doctrine of equivalents applies to design patents. *See Lee v. Dayton-Hudson Corp.*, 838 F.2d 1186, 1190 (Fed. Cir. 1988). What should the test be for the doctrine of equivalents for design patents? Does "substantial" in the *Gorham* substantial similarity test invoke an equivalency notion, such that no separate equivalency theory may be invoked? Prior to *Egyptian Goddess*, courts raised concerns about how the doctrine of equivalents might coexist with the "point of novelty" test. In *Sun Hill Indus., Inc. v. Easter Unlimited, Inc.*, 48 F.3d 1193, 1199 (Fed. Cir. 1995), the Federal Circuit acknowledged the existence of the doctrine of equivalents, but specified that it required a showing that the accused product include features at least equivalent to the *novel* features of the claimed design. Otherwise, a patentee could invoke the doctrine of equivalents to eviscerate the purpose of the point of novelty prong. *Id.* (concluding that where the accused device had not appropriated any of the features that made up the design's point of novelty, there could be no infringement under the doctrine of equivalents). Is this still a concern after *Egyptian Goddess*?

8. ***Spare parts.*** Should design patent laws—or other types of design protection regimes—protect spare parts, such as automobile replacement parts? The issue has arisen in many contexts worldwide. It drew particular attention in Europe, as discussed in Chapter 8. The question is especially thorny because spare parts generally must match the appearance of the original component part in order to be viable in the marketplace. In *In re Certain Automotive Parts*, 2007 WL 2021234 (ITC 2007), the International Trade Commission prohibited an importer from importing replacement parts for Ford trucks because those parts infringed Ford's design patents. In early 2008, legislation was introduced in the House of Representative proposing to add the following exemption to the main infringement provision of the patent statute, 35 U.S.C. §271:

> (j) It shall not be an act of infringement to make, use, offer to sell, or sell within the United States or import into the United States any article of manufacture that itself constitutes a component part of another article of manufacture, if the sole purpose of the component part is for the repair of the article of manufacture of which it is a part so as to restore its original appearance.

Does this provision advance the aims of the patent system? Note that the provision is not expressly limited to design patents. Is that a problem?

### Crocs, Inc. v. International Trade Commission
—F.3d—, 2010 WL 638272 (Fed. Cir., Feb. 24, 2010)

Rader, Circuit Judge:

[Crocs, a Colorado firm, sued numerous firms for importing foam footwear (specifically, the Holey Soles, Gen-X, Collective, Effervescent, and Double Diamond products) allegedly in violation of several patents, including U.S. Patent No. D517,789 (the "'789 patent"). Crocs brought its complaint before the United States International Trade Commission ("ITC" or "Commission") under 19 U.S.C. §1337, which prohibits infringing imports that would injure domestic industry. The ITC found no infringement of the '789 patent, and Crocs appealed to the Federal Circuit.]

## I.

... The '789 patent, entitled "Footwear," issued on March 28, 2006, based on a filing in 2004. The '789 patent has one claim and seven figures. It claims an ornamental footwear design as depicted in the figures:

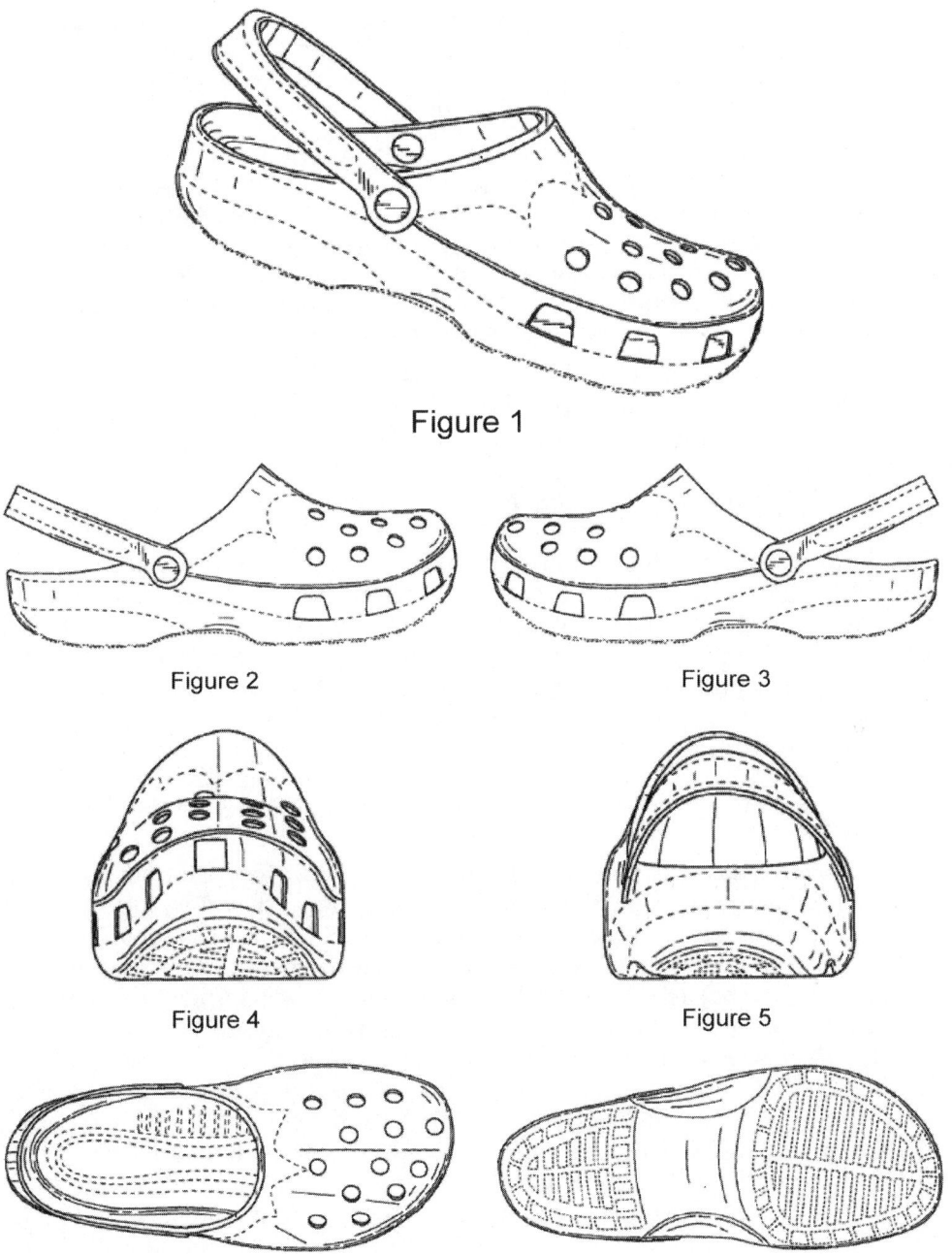

Figure 1

Figure 2

Figure 3

Figure 4

Figure 5

Figure 6

Figure 7

## II.

. . .

With respect to the design patent, the '789 patent, the administrative judge provided a detailed verbal claim construction:

> In summary, when the '789 patent is considered as a whole, the visual impression created by the claimed design includes: footwear having a foot opening with a strap that may or may not include any patterning, is attached to the body of the footwear by two round connectors, is of uniform width between the two round connectors, has a wrench-head like shape at the point of attachment, and extends to the heel of the shoe; with round holes on the roof of the upper placed in a systematic pattern; with trapezoid-shaped holes evenly spaced around the sidewall of the upper including the front portion; with a relatively flat sole (except for upward curvature in the toe and heel) that may or may not contain tread on the upper and lower portions of the sole, but if tread exists, does not cover the entire sole, and scalloped indentations that extend from the side of the sole in the middle portion that curve toward each other.

Based on this description, the administrative judge found the Holey Soles and Gen-X accused products did not infringe because their strap is not of uniform thickness and does not extend to the heel of the shoe. The same reasoning excused the Collective and Effervescent accused products from infringement but the administrative judge added the further explanation that these imports did not have round holes in the upper portion. He found that the Double Diamond accused products did not infringe because each of the accused products has at least one of the following: a strap that does not have uniform thickness and does not extend to the heel of the shoe; holes in the upper that are not round; holes in the upper that are placed in a web-shaped, not systematic, pattern; or a tread pattern that covers the entire sole.

## III.

. . .

### A.

This court has cautioned, and continues to caution, trial courts about excessive reliance on a detailed verbal description in a design infringement case. *See, e.g., Egyptian Goddess, Inc. v. Swisa, Inc.*, 543 F.3d 665, 679 (Fed. Cir. 2008) (en banc). In *Egyptian Goddess*, this court warned that misplaced reliance on a detailed verbal description of the claimed design risks undue emphasis on particular features of the design rather than examination of the design as a whole. *Id.* at 679-80. In many cases, the considerable effort in fashioning a detailed verbal description does not contribute enough to the infringement analysis to justify the endeavor. *See id.* at 680. Depictions of the claimed design in words can easily distract from the proper infringement analysis of the ornamental patterns and drawings.

Design patents are typically claimed as shown in drawings, and claim construction must be adapted to a pictorial setting. *See, e.g., Contessa Food Prods., Inc. v. Conagra, Inc.*, 282 F.3d 1370, 1377 (Fed. Cir. 2002) (construing a design patent claim as meaning "a tray of a certain design as shown in Figures 1-3"). Thus an illustration depicts a design better "than it could be by any description and a description would probably not be intelligible without the illustration." *Dobson v. Dornan,* 118 U.S. 10, 14 (1886). "[A]s a rule, the illustration in the drawing views is its own best description." *Manual of Patent Examining Procedure* §1503.01 (8th ed. 2006).

This case shows the dangers of reliance on a detailed verbal claim construction. The claim construction focused on particular features of the '789 patent design and led the administrative judge and the Commission away from consideration of the design as a whole. This error is apparent in the Commission's explicit reference to two details required by the written claim construction but not by the '789 drawings: (1) a strap of uniform width, and (2) holes evenly spaced around the sidewall of the upper. As shown in Figure 1 of the '789 patent, the strap bulges to a greater width at the middle of the strap on the far left of the figure. Thus, the design figure does not require a strap of uniform width between the two round connectors. Also, as shown in Figure 4 of the '789 patent, the holes are not evenly spaced. Figure 4 shows a gap in the spacing (particularly towards the big toe). Nonetheless, the written claim description required uniform strap width and uniform hole spacing-contrary to the claimed invention. This error distorts the infringement analysis by the ordinary observer viewing the design as a whole. The administrative judge and the Commission needed to apply the ordinary observer test to "the design shown in Figures 1-7."

B.

In determining whether an accused product infringes a patented design, this court applies the "ordinary observer" test, without any "point of novelty" perspective. *Egyptian Goddess,* 543 F.3d at 678. To show infringement under the proper test, an ordinary observer, familiar with the prior art designs, would be deceived into believing that the accused product is the same as the patented design. *See id.* at 681. When the differences between the claimed and accused designs are viewed in light of the prior art, the attention of the hypothetical ordinary observer may be drawn to those aspects of the claimed design that differ from the prior art. *Id.* If the claimed design is close to the prior art designs, small differences between the accused design and the claimed design assume more importance to the eye of the hypothetical ordinary observer. *Id.* The ordinary observer, however, will likely attach importance to those differences depending on the overall effect of those differences on the design. *Id.* Even if the claimed design simply combines old features in the prior art, it may still create an overall appearance deceptively similar to the accused design. In that case, this court will uphold a finding of infringement. *Id.* at 677-78. In other words, "the deception that arises is a result of the similarities in the overall design, not of similarities in ornamental features in isolation." *Amini Innovation,* 439 F.3d at 1371. The ordinary observer test applies to the patented design in its entirety, as it is claimed. *See Braun, Inc. v. Dynamics Corp. of Am.*, 975 F.2d 815, 820 (Fed. Cir. 1992). "[M]inor differences between a patented design and an accused article's design cannot, and shall not, prevent a finding of infringement." *Payless Shoesource,* 998 F.2d at 991 (quoting *Litton Sys., Inc. v. Whirlpool,* 728 F.2d 1423, 1444 (Fed. Cir. 1984)).

Turning to this case, the Commission placed undue emphasis on particular details of its written description of the patented design. Those details became a mistaken checklist for infringement. Without a view to the design as a whole, the Commission used minor differences between the patented design and the accused products to prevent a finding of infringement. In other words, the concentration on small differences in isolation distracted from the overall impression of the claimed ornamental features.

The proper comparison requires a side-by-side view of the drawings of the '789 patent design and the accused products. The depiction below shows the '789 patent (on the left) and the Double Diamond Revised Beach DAWGS™ (on the right).

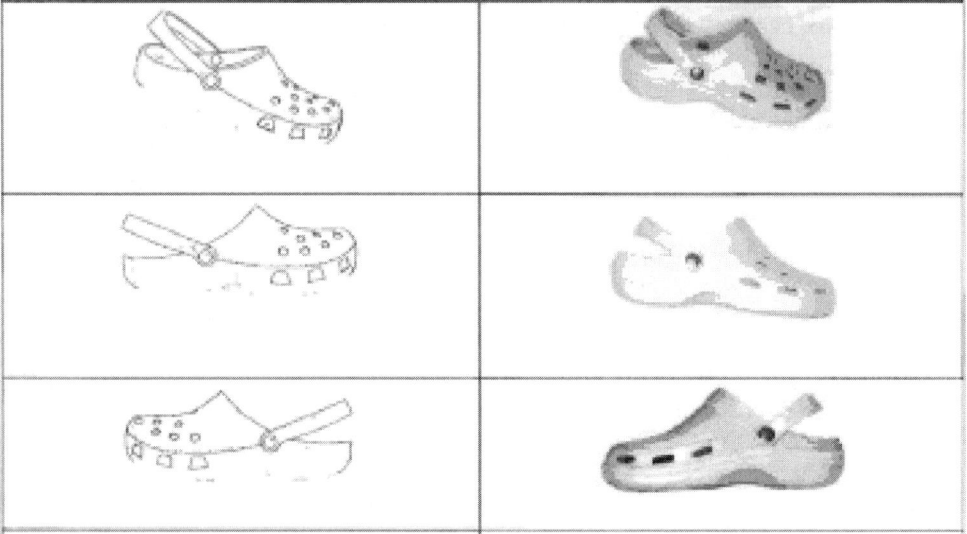

The depiction below compares the '789 patent (on the left), the Groovy DAWGS™ shoes (in the center), and Big DAWGS™ shoes (on the right).

A. The Infringement Analysis    415

The comparison below shows the '789 patent (on the left) and the Double Diamond Original Beach DAWGS™ shoes (on the right).

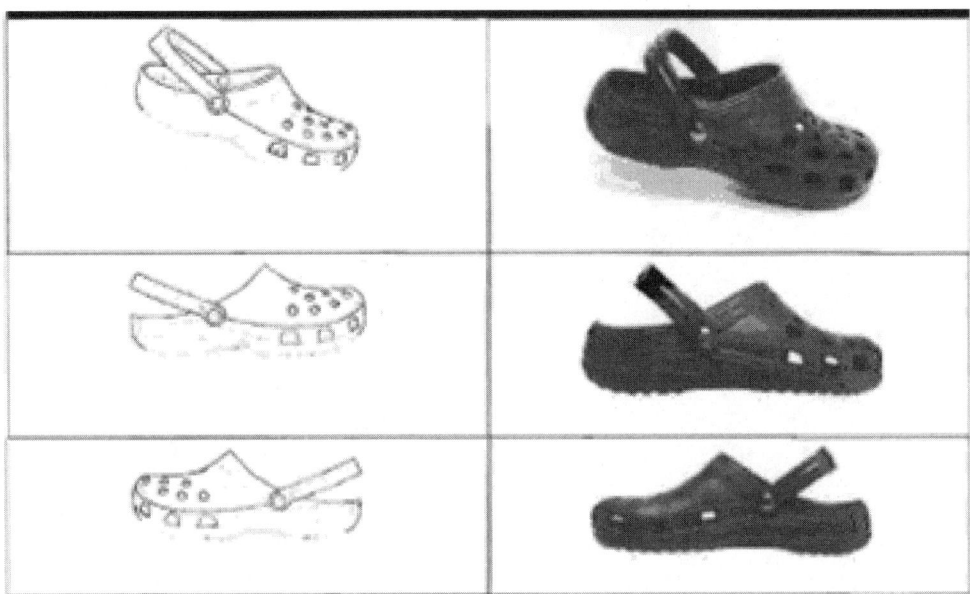

The depiction below compares the '789 patent (on the left), the Holey Soles Explorer shoes (in the center), and Holey Soles Cricket shoes (on the right).

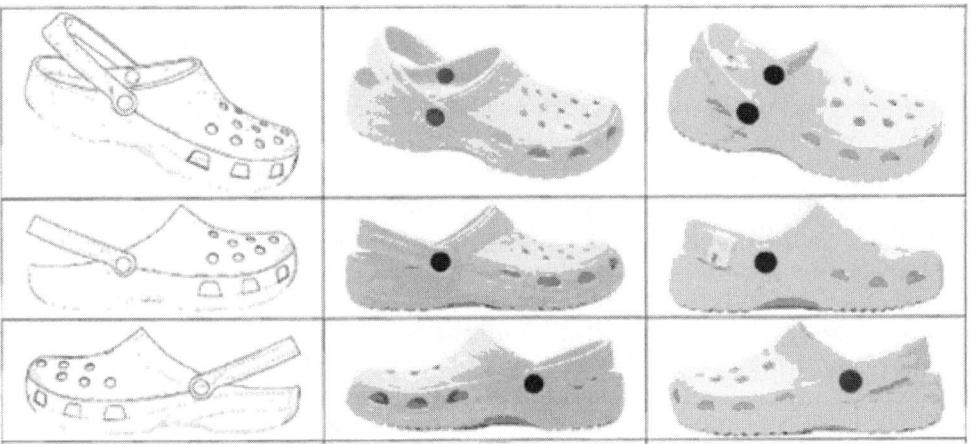

A final comparison places the '789 patent on the left and the Effervescent Waldies AT shoe on the right.

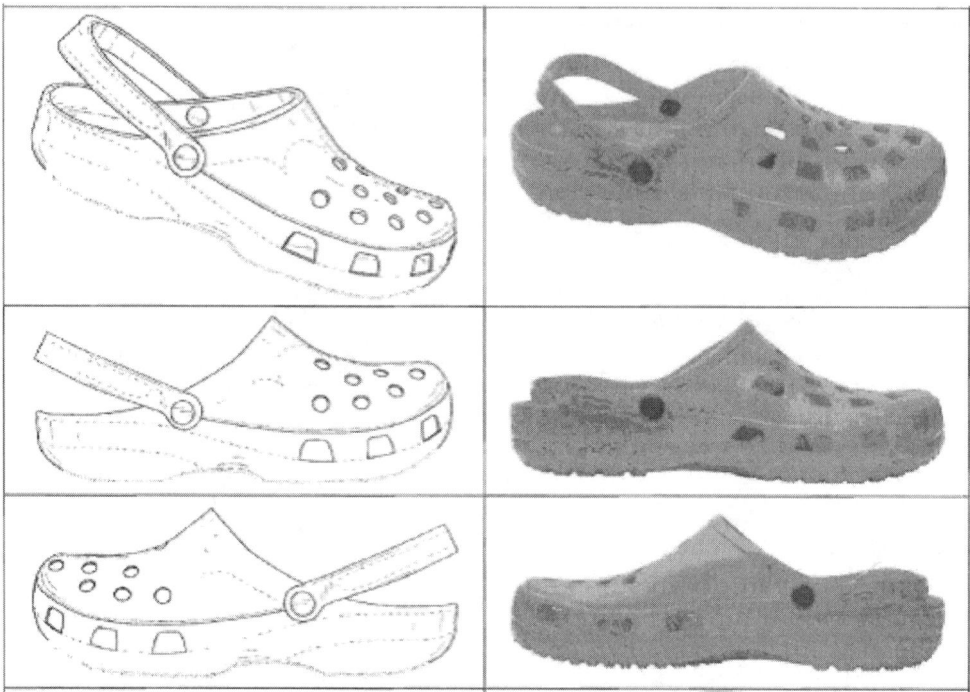

These side-by-side comparisons of the '789 patent design and the accused products suggest that an ordinary observer, familiar with the prior art designs, would be deceived into believing the accused products are the same as the patented design. In one comparison after another, the shoes appear nearly identical. If the claimed design and the accused designs were arrayed in matching colors and mixed up randomly, this court is not confident that an ordinary observer could properly restore them to their original order without very careful and prolonged effort.

One of the overall effects of the design is the interaction between the strap assembly portion and the base portion of the shoes where the strap is attached to the base. Multiple major design lines and curves converge at that point creating a focal point attracting the eye of the ordinary observer when viewing the overall effect of the design. Another overall effect of the design is a visual theme of rounded curves and ellipses throughout the design, including the strap forming a sort of continuation of the sidewall of the base to create a visually continuous ring encircling the entire shoe. Other examples of rounded curves or ellipses in the design are the ellipses formed by the strap and the foot opening in the base. Both the claimed design and the accused designs have these overall effects.

In any event, this court perceives that the accused products embody the overall effect of the '789 design in sufficient detail and clarity to cause market confusion. Thus, the accused products infringe the '789 design.

C.

[The court determined that Crocs' products were the same as Crocs' patented designs, such that Crocs satisfied the technical prong of the domestic industry requirement.]

[Reversed and remanded.]

## RICHARDSON v. STANLEY WORKS, INC.
—F.3d—, 2010 WL 774334 (Fed. Cir., March 9, 2010)

LOURIE, Circuit Judge:

### Background

Richardson owns the '167 patent, a design patent that claims the design for a multi-function carpentry tool that combines a conventional hammer with a stud climbing tool and a crowbar. The tool is known as the "Stepclaw." The only claim of the '167 patent claims the ornamental design of the tool as depicted in figures 1 and 2 of the patent:

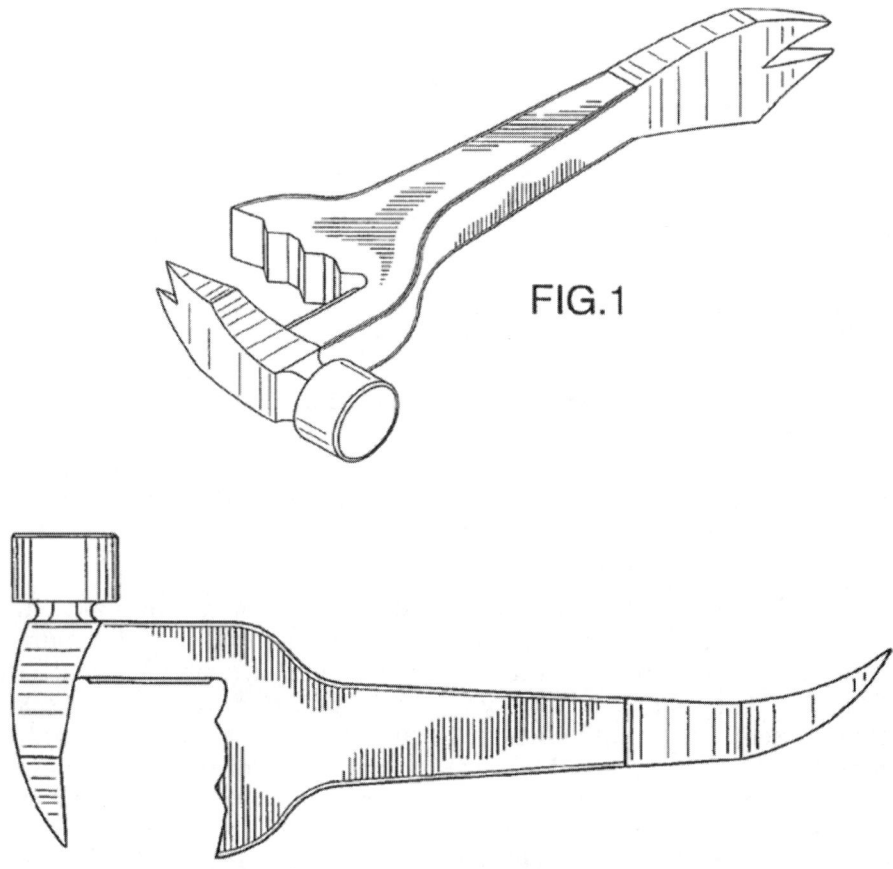

Stanley manufactures and sells construction tools. In 2005, Stanley introduced into the U.S. market a product line of tools by the series name "Fubar." The Fubar is sold in five different versions and is useful in carpentry, demolition, and construction work. Stanley successfully applied for and obtained U.S. Patent D562,101 ("the '101 patent") on the basic Fubar design. All five versions of the tool are built around that same basic Fubar design. Figures 1 and 5 of the '101 patent are illustrative of the Fubar design:

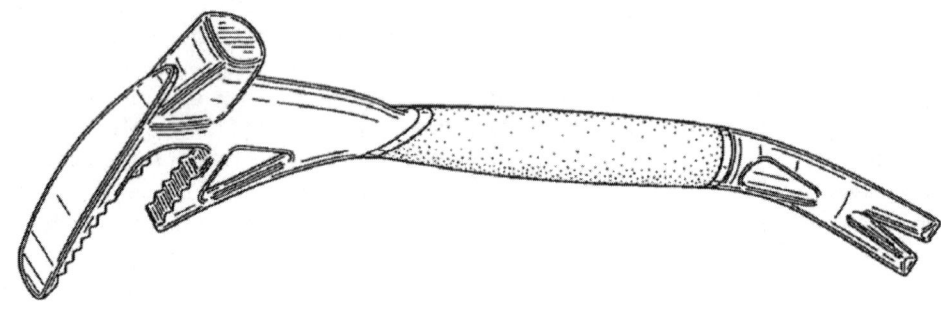

**Figure 1**

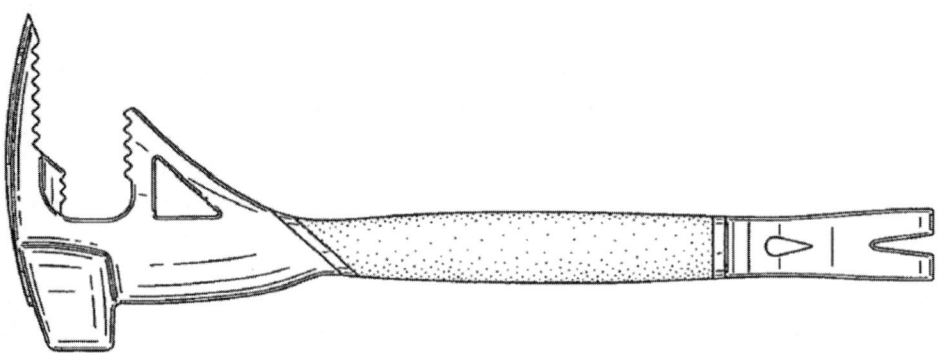

**Figure 5**

[Richardson sued, alleging design patent infringement, inter alia. In the district court's order on the design patent infringement claim], the court first distinguished, as part of its claim construction, the ornamental aspects from the functional aspects of Richardson's design and then determined that an ordinary observer, after discounting the functional elements of Richardson's design, would not be deceived into thinking that any of the Fubar tools were the same as Richardson's Stepclaw. The court therefore concluded that the overall visual effect of the Fubar was not substantially similar to that of the Stepclaw, and that the '167 patent had not been infringed. Richardson timely appealed the court's rulings. . . .

Discussion

A. Claim Construction

Richardson argues that the district court's approach to evaluating infringement of a design patent was incorrect. Richardson primarily argues that the district court erred in its claim construction by separating the functional aspects of the design from the ornamental ones, rather than considering the design as a whole. Richardson argues that our *Egyptian Goddess* decision requires that the patented design be compared in its entirety with the accused design, and that the comparison be made from the perspective of an ordinary observer. *See Egyptian Goddess, Inc. v.. Swisa, Inc.*, 543 F.3d 665 (Fed. Cir. 2008) (en banc). A claim construction such as the one performed by the district court, Richardson argues, is necessary only for designs that contain "purely functional" elements. According to Richardson, a design element is purely functional only when the function encompassed by that element cannot be performed by any other design. Richardson contends that the overall design of the '167 patent is not dictated by the useful elements found in the tool, and that the functional parts of its design remain relevant to the scope of the patented claim.

We review claim construction *de novo* on appeal. [cit.] We disagree with Richardson that the district court erred in its claim construction by separating the functional and ornamental aspects of the '167 patent design. In *OddzOn*, we affirmed a district court's claim construction wherein the court had carefully distinguished the ornamental features of the patented design from the overall "rocket-like" appearance of the design of a football-shaped foam ball with a tail and fin structure. *OddzOn Prods., Inc. v. Just Toys, Inc.*, 122 F.3d 1396, 1405 (Fed. Cir. 1997). We held that "[w]here a design contains both functional and non-functional elements, the scope of the claim must be construed in order to identify the non-functional aspects of the design as shown in the patent." *Id.*

The issue before us is not very different from that in *OddzOn*, and we are not persuaded by Richardson's argument that our holding in *Egyptian Goddess* mandates a different result here. In *Egyptian Goddess*, we abandoned the point of novelty test for design patent infringement and held that the ordinary observer test should serve as the sole test for infringement. [cit.] Although we proposed that the preferable course ordinarily will be for a district court not to attempt to construe a design patent claim, *id.*, we also emphasized that there are a number of claim scope issues on which a court's guidance would be useful to the fact finder. [cit.] Among them, we specifically noted, is the distinction between the functional and ornamental aspects of a design. *Id.* (citing *OddzOn*, 122 F.3d at 1405).

The district court here properly factored out the functional aspects of Richardson's design as part of its claim construction. By definition, the patented design is for a multi-function tool that has several functional components, and we have made clear that a design patent, unlike a utility patent, limits protection to the ornamental design of the article. *Lee v. Dayton-Hudson Corp.*, 838 F.2d 1186, 1188 (Fed. Cir. 1988) (citing 35 U.S.C. §171). If the patented design is primarily functional rather than ornamental, the patent is invalid. *Id.* However, when the design also contains ornamental aspects, it is entitled to a design patent whose scope is limited to those aspects alone and does not extend to any functional elements of the claimed article. *See L.A. Gear, Inc. v. Thom McAn Shoe Co.*, 988 F.2d 1117, 1123 (Fed. Cir. 1993) ("The elements of the design may indeed serve a utilitarian purpose, but it is the ornamental aspect that is the basis of the design patent.").

Richardson's multi-function tool comprises several elements that are driven purely by utility. As the district court noted, elements such as the handle, the hammerhead, the jaw, and the crowbar are dictated by their functional purpose. The jaw, for example, has to be located on the opposite end of the hammer head such that the tool can be used as a step. The crowbar, by definition, needs to be on the end of the longer handle such that it can reach into narrow spaces. The handle has to be the longest arm of the tool to allow for maximum leverage. The hammer-head has to be flat on its end to effectively deliver force to the object being struck. As demonstrated by the prior art, those are purely functional elements whose utility has been known and used in the art for well over a century.

Richardson's argument that the court erred in separating out functional aspects of his design essentially is an argument for a claim scope that includes the utilitarian elements of his multi-function tool. We agree with the district court that it would indeed be improper to allow Richardson to do so. The '167 patent specifically claims "the ornamental design" for the multi-function tool shown in the drawings. *See* '167 patent, Cl. 1. A claim to a design containing numerous functional elements, such as here, necessarily mandates a narrow construction. Nothing in our *en banc Egyptian Goddess* opinion compels a different outcome.

We also reject Richardson's argument that the court did not include drawings from the patent in its claim construction. Richardson argues that it is the ordinary observer's perception of those drawings that is the controlling consideration under the Supreme Court's opinion in *Gorham Manufacturing Company v. White.* . . . We agree with Richardson on the decisive importance of drawings in a design patent. We have recently stated that design patents are typically claimed according to their drawings, and claim construction must be adapted to a pictorial setting. *Crocs, Inc. v. Int'l Trade Comm'n,* [2010 WL 638272] (Fed. Cir., Feb. 24, 2010). However, we do not agree that the district court's claim construction necessarily excluded drawings of the '167 patent. The court's entire construction was based on what was "shown and described in the '167 patent." The court concluded its discussion by noting that the purpose of the claim construction was simply to highlight the ornamental aspects of Richardson's design. Richardson fails to explain how a court could effectively construe design claims, where necessary, in a way other than by describing the features shown in the drawings. Richardson's proposition that the claim construction should comprise nothing more than the drawings is simply another way of arguing that the court erred by identifying the functional elements of the patented article, and is therefore unavailing. We find no error in the court's claim construction.

B. Infringement

Richardson argues that the district court failed to analyze infringement of the '167 patent by Stanley's tools under an ordinary observer test. According to Richardson, had the court conducted a three-way comparison between the prior art, the patented design and the accused products, it would have found the accused product design to be substantially the same as the patented one.

Stanley responds that, having identified the ornamental aspects of Richardson's patented design, the court properly found that the only similarities between the patented Stepclaw and the accused Fubar tools were those of unprotectable functional elements. Stanley argues that when those utilitarian aspects are ignored, none of the accused Fubar products looks even remotely like Richardson's patented design.

We agree with the court's finding of noninfringement. Design patent infringement is a question of fact, which a patentee must prove by a preponderance of the evidence. *L.A. Gear,* 988 F.2d at 1124. In *Egyptian Goddess,* we held that "the 'ordinary observer' test should be the sole test for determining whether a design patent has been infringed." [cit.] The patentee must establish that an ordinary observer, familiar with the prior art designs, would be deceived into believing that the accused product is the same as the patented design. [cit.] In our recent *Crocs* decision, we set out in detail how an ordinary observer analysis could be conducted to determine infringement. [cit.] In analyzing whether a design patent on footwear was infringed, noting the various differences that could be found between the two pieces of footwear in question, we compared their overall effect on the designs. [cit.] We looked to ornamental elements such as the curves in the design, the strap assembly, and the base portion of the footwear. *Id.* We concluded that both the claimed design and the accused designs contained those overall ornamental effects, thereby allowing for market confusion. [cit.]

The ordinary observer test similarly applies in cases where the patented design incorporates numerous functional elements. *See Amini Innovation Corp. v. Anthony Cal., Inc.,* 439 F.3d 1365, 1372 (Fed. Cir. 2006) (holding that while it is proper to factor out the functional aspects of various design elements, that discounting of functional elements must not convert the overall infringement test to an element-by-element comparison). In evaluating infringement, we determine whether "the deception that arises is a result of the similarities in the overall design, not of similarities in ornamental features in isolation." *Amini Innovation,* 439 F.3d at 1371.

We do not agree with Richardson that the district court failed to apply the ordinary observer test in finding no infringement. The court specifically concluded that "[f]rom the perspective of an ordinary observer familiar with the prior art, the overall visual effect of the Fubar is significantly different from the Stepclaw." It recited the significant differences between the ornamental features of the two designs but, in determining infringement, it mainly focused on whether an ordinary observer would be deceived into thinking that any of the Fubar designs were the same as Richardson's patented design. We therefore find no error in the district court's approach. *See Egyptian Goddess,* 543 F.3d at 681 ("An ordinary observer, comparing the claimed and accused designs in light of the prior art, will attach importance to differences between the claimed design and the prior art depending on the overall effect of those differences on the design."); *see also Int'l Seaway Trading Corp. v. Walgreens Corp.*, 589 F.3d 1233, 1243 (Fed. Cir. 2009) ("The mandated overall comparison is a comparison taking into account significant differences between the two designs, not minor or trivial differences that necessarily exist between any two designs that are not exact copies of one another.").

We also agree that, ignoring the functional elements of the tools, the two designs are indeed different. Each of the Fubar tools has a streamlined visual theme that runs throughout the design including elements such as a tapered hammer-head, a streamlined crow-bar, a triangular neck with rounded surfaces, and a smoothly contoured handle. In a side-by-side comparison with the '167 patent design, the overall effect of this streamlined theme makes the Fubar tools significantly different from Richardson's design. Overall, the accused products clearly have a more rounded appearance and fewer blunt edges than the patented design. The court therefore was not clearly erroneous in concluding that the accused products embody an overall effect that cannot be found in the '167 patent design and hence cannot cause market confusion. *See Egyptian Goddess*, 543 F.3d at 681 (infringement cannot be found unless the accused product creates an appearance deceptively similar to the claimed design).

[Affirmed.]

### PROBLEM 6-1: APPLYING *EGYPTIAN GODDESS*: THE GIANT STUFF-A-PUMPKIN

Sun Hill owned a design patent, U.S. D310,023, claiming the following design for a bag:

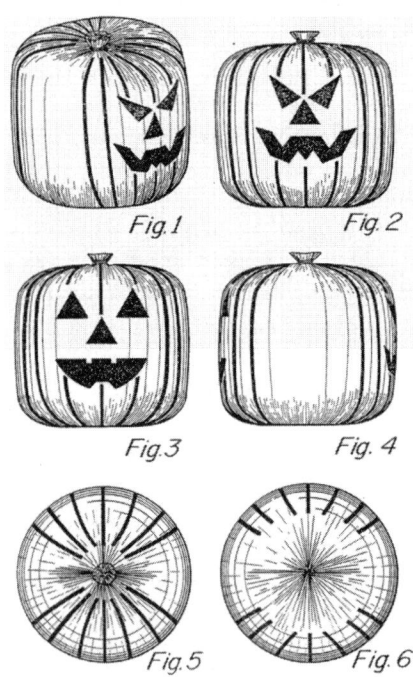

Sun Hill marketed an embodiment of the claimed design as the GIANT STUFF-A-PUMPKIN, a large, orange plastic lawn bag having jack-o'-lantern faces on both sides. The bag could be filled with leaves or other debris to take on the appearance of a pumpkin.

Other firms had previously marketed smaller trick-or-treat bags decorated to look like pumpkins. For example, one prior art reference, the Noteworthy publication, disclosed the following trick-or-treat bag:

The publication indicated that the bag could be stuffed and tied at the top.

We (Professors Dinwoodie and Janis) have been advised not to celebrate Halloween, on the ground that we already scare people enough under ordinary circumstances. But we know a good source of supplemental income when we see it, and when we saw the Sun Hill bag, our first impulse was to copy it and start our own firm, Big Fun Bags, to sell it. Our second impulse was to make some variations. So, on our bags, there is only a jack-o'-lantern face on one side, and there are no vertical stripes. We also copied the jack-o'-lantern faces from a prior art Halloween book. But our bags are large and orange, and intended to look like a pumpkin when filled.

Does our bag infringe Sun Hill's patent? What other intellectual property regimes, in addition to design patent protection, might Sun Hill employ in order to protect its design?

## PROBLEM 6-2: DESIGN PATENTS AND THE REPAIR/RECONSTRUCTION DISTINCTION

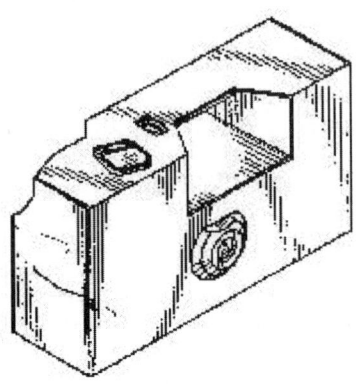

FIG. 1

Suppose that a camera manufacturer owns a design patent claiming the following design for the exterior appearance of a camera:

> The camera manufacturer sells single-use cameras under the patent — cameras that are designed to be used once and then turned in for film processing.

Suppose that another firm, without the manufacturer's permission, recovers used camera bodies and loads new film into them, and then resells them. Should a court find design patent infringement? There is no issue here under the infringement standard (the defendant's cameras are substantially similar — indeed, identical in appearance). There is also an unauthorized sale, as required under §289. The question is whether the court should recognize an exception from the infringement statute where the articles at issue were the subject of an authorized purchase (even though they were subsequently reconditioned and resold). In utility patent law, courts apply such an exception when the article at issue has been "repaired," but refuse to recognize an exception where the article has been "reconstructed." Should the same rule apply to design patents? Would you find repair or reconstruction here? *See Jazz Photo Corp. v. Int'l Trade Comm'n*, 264 F.3d 1094, 1110 (Fed. Cir. 2001). Would you support legislation that would create an exemption from design patent infringement for making, using, selling, offering to sell, or importing a component of an article of manufacture if the "sole purpose of the component part is for the repair of the article of manufacture so as to restore its original appearance"? *See* H.R. 3059, 111th Cong. 1st Sess. (introduced June 25, 2009).

## B. REMEDIES

Three provisions in the patent statute govern most questions concerning remedies in design patent cases:

> 35 U.S.C. §283
>
> The several courts having jurisdiction of cases under this title may grant injunctions in accordance with the principles of equity to prevent the violation of any right secured by patent, on such terms as the court deems reasonable.
>
> 35 U.S.C. §284
>
> Upon finding for the claimant the court shall award the claimant damages adequate to compensate for the infringement, but in no event less than a reasonable royalty for the use made of the invention by the infringer, together with interest and costs as fixed by the court.
>
> When the damages are not found by a jury, the court shall assess them. In either event the court may increase the damages up to three times the amount found or assessed. . . .
>
> 35 U.S.C. §289
>
> Whoever during the term of a patent for a design, without license of the owner, (1) applies the patented design, or any colorable imitation thereof, to any article of manufacture for the purpose of sale, or (2) sells or exposes for sale any article of manufacture to which such design or colorable imitation has been applied shall be liable to the owner to the extent of his total profit, but not less than $250, recoverable in any United States district court having jurisdiction of the parties.

In addition, 35 U.S.C. §286 provides a six-year time limitation on damages: no recovery may be had for acts of infringement committed more than six years before the patentee files its complaint. Finally, as discussed in the case below, 35 U.S.C. §287(a) imposes a patent marking requirement and a damages limitation for violations of that requirement.

### NIKE, INC. v. WAL-MART STORES, INC.
138 F.3d 1437 (Fed. Cir. 1998)

PAULINE NEWMAN, Circuit Judge:

#### Background

The D'765 patent is for Nike's "Air Mada Mid" model athletic shoe design, illustrated as:

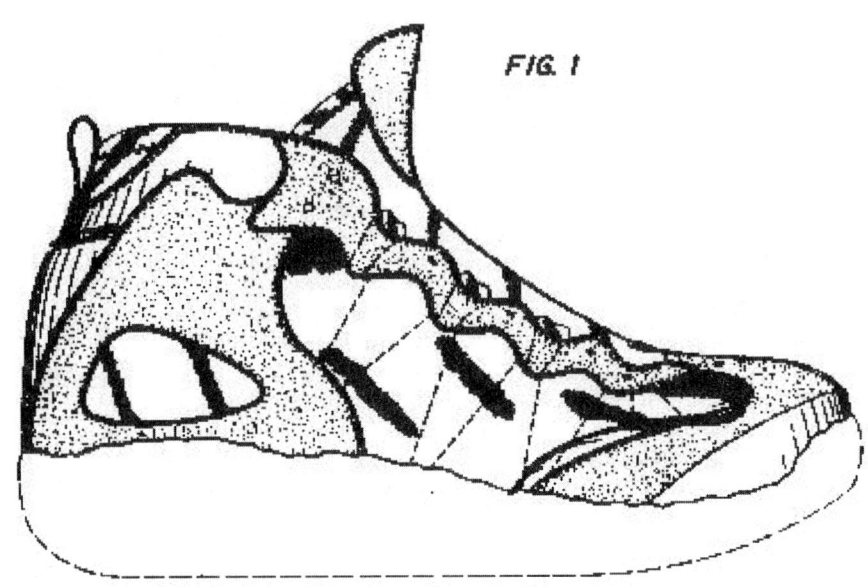

[Nike sued Hawe Yue and Wal-Mart for importing and selling copies of the Air Mada Mid design. The defendants argued that Nike had failed to mark a number of the shoes with a patent marking, thus precluding Nike from recovering damages prior to the filing of the lawsuit under 35 U.S.C. §287(a):

> Patentees may give notice to the public that the same is patented, either by fixing thereon the word "patent" or the abbreviation "pat.," together with the number of the patent. . . . In the event of a failure to so mark, no damages shall be recovered by the patentee in any action for infringement, except on proof that the infringer was notified of the infringement and continued to infringe thereafter, in which event damages may be recovered only for infringement occurring after such notice. Filing of an action for infringement shall constitute such notice.

The district court held that the marking statute applies when the requested remedy is "damages" under the general damages provision, 35 U.S.C. §284, but does not limit the recovery of profits under the alternative remedy provision, 35 U.S.C. §289, for design patents. The defendants appealed.]

I. Marking

. . .

A. Damages and Profits

The first [U.S.] patent statutes [tracing to 1790] reflect the separation of law and equity, carried over from the English common law of patents . . . [Subsequent decisions established that the Patent Act of 1870] provided for the recovery of damages in equity, but it did not allow for recovery of the infringer's profit as such in an action at law.

Because both the patentee's losses and the infringer's profits could be obtained in equity, whereas only the patentee's losses were recoverable at law, after 1870 a patentee had incentive to invoke equity jurisdiction even when injunctive relief was not important. However, even when the patentee prevailed in the equity court, computation of the amount of the patentee's recovery, whether measured as the infringer's profits or the patentee's losses, often presented a difficult problem of proof, for the Court had meanwhile held that the patentee could recover only the proportionate amounts that were proven to be attributable to the patented feature. *E.g., Garretson v. Clark*, 111 U.S. 120, 121 (1884) (the patentee "must, in every case, give evidence tending to separate or apportion the defendant's profits and the patentee's damages between the patented feature and the unpatented features").

Apportionment presented particularly difficult problems of proof for design patentees, for the patentee was required to show what portion of the infringer's profit, or of his own lost profit, was due to the design and what portion was due to the article itself. A series of cases involving carpet designs brought matters to a head, leading to the separate remedy for design patent infringement. The cases involved the Dobson brothers, who were found to have infringed patented designs for carpets. The Supreme Court held that the Dobsons were liable for no more than "nominal damages" of six cents because the patentees could not show what portion of their losses or the infringers' profits was due to the patented design and what portion was due to the unpatented carpet. *See Dobson v. Dornan*, 118 U.S. 10 (1886); *Dobson v. Hartford Carpet Co.*, 114 U.S. 439 (1885); *Dobson v. Bigelow Carpet Co.*, 114 U.S. 439 (1885).

Legislative remedy, specific to design patents, soon followed. Referring to the *Dobson* decisions, Congress reported that:

> It now appears that the design patent laws provide no effectual money recovery for infringement. This is the result of the statute, as applied to the peculiar character of property involved, in a test case decided April last by the Supreme Court of the United States. Since that decision the receipts of the Patent Office in the design department have fallen off upwards of 50 per cent, and the average weekly issue of design patents has also fallen off just one half.

H.R. Rep. No. 1966 at 1 (1886), *reprinted in* 18 Cong. Rec. 834 (1887). The Report explained that "[i]t is expedient that the infringer's entire profit on the article should be recoverable," for "it is not apportionable," and "it is the design that sells the article." *Id.* at 2-3. The Report drew analogy to trademark law, and "the good will the design has in the market." *Id.* at 3. The Act of 1887, specific to design patents, removed the apportionment requirement when recovery of the infringer's profit was sought:

> §1. Hereafter, during the term of letters patent for a design, it shall be unlawful for any person other than the owner of said letters patent, without the license of such owner, to apply the design secured by such letters patent, or any colorable imitation thereof, to any article of manufacture for the purpose of sale, or to sell or expose for sale any article of manufacture to which such design or colorable imitation shall, without the license of the owner, have been applied, knowing that the same has been so applied. Any person violating the provisions, or either of them, of this section, shall be liable in the amount of two hundred and fifty dollars, he shall be further liable for the excess of such profit

over and above [that sum, the full amount recoverable] either by action at law or upon a bill in equity for an injunction to restrain such infringement.

§2. That nothing in this Act contained shall prevent, lessen, impeach, or avoid any remedy at law or in equity which any owner of letters patent for a design, aggrieved by the infringement of the same might have had if this act had not been passed; but such owner shall not twice recover the profit made from the infringement.

Act of 1887, 24 Stat. 387. The Act of 1887 thus authorized recovery by the patentee of the infringer's profit when the infringer appropriated the patented design "knowing that the same has been so applied." *Id.*

[In 1952, the general damages provision was codified at 35 U.S.C. §284, and the 1887 provisions regarding the recovery of infringers' profits for design patent infringement were separately codified at §289.]

. . . Relevant to the marking issue, the phrase "knowing that the same has been so applied" of the 1887 Act was omitted from §289. . . .

Thus the statutory record shows the origins in law and equity of remedy for patent infringement, initially and until 1887 without distinction between utility and design patents. Recovery of the infringer's profit was available for both utility and design patent infringement. The additional remedy created in 1887 for design patents was enacted to overcome the allocation problem for designs, and did not deplete the remedies available for either utility or design patent infringement. Further, the general damages statutes, which authorized recovery of the infringer's profits as well as the patentee's losses, continued in effect for both utility and design patents. . . .

This statutory context must be compared with the statutes concerning patent marking, for the marking statutes underwent an independent evolution leading to the anomaly we today observe, where the word "damages" has different meanings in different provisions of Title 35.

### B. The Marking Statutes

The marking statute serves three related purposes: 1) helping to avoid innocent infringement, [cit.]; 2) encouraging patentees to give notice to the public that the article is patented, [cit.]; and 3) aiding the public to identify whether an article is patented, [cit.].

The early patent statutes contained no marking requirement [on the theory that patents were public records and the public was on notice of them. The Patent Act of 1842 imposed a marking requirement. It was modified in 1861, and has not been changed substantially since then.]

These [marking] provisions remained constant through the various changes in remedy for patent infringement . . . including the consolidations of legal and equitable relief, the provision for recovery in the same action of the infringer's profits and the patentee's losses, the 1887 special remedy for design patent infringement, and the 1952 codification.

. . .

The conclusion that the marking statute with its use of the word "damages" applies broadly to include recovery of the infringer's profits under the special provision for design patent infringement is strongly reinforced by historical expressions of congressional concern about notice for design patent infringement. The Act of 1887 was accompanied by assurances that the infringer would not be liable if he did not know that the design was patented. The statute imposed liability only upon a person who acts "knowing that the [design] has been so applied" without authority. Act of 1887, 24 Stat. 387-88. The House Report explained that "an innocent dealer or user is not affected." H.R. Rep. No. 1966 at 4 (1886). The floor debate in 1887 was to similar effect. *See* 18 Cong. Rec. 835 (1887) (statement of Rep. Butterworth: "[N]o man will suffer either penalty or damage unless he willfully appropriates the property of another.") In *Dunlap v. Schofield*, 152 U.S. 244 (1894) the Court reversed an award of the statutory penalty of $250 because the owner of the design patent failed to prove that the design was copied by the alleged infringer "knowing that the same has been so applied." The Court held that the phrase "knowing that the same has been so applied" in the Act of 1887 was "equivalent to saying 'with a knowledge of the patent and of his infringement.'" *Id.* at 248-50.

With such steady emphasis on knowledge of or notice of the patent, as a matter of fairness, we doubt that both actual and constructive notice were silently abandoned, either by Congress or the courts, as applied to §289 and design patents. Although in the 1952 codification the phrase "knowing that the same has been so applied" was omitted in writing §289, that omission is explicable only on the ground of redundancy with the marking statute codified at §287. To view it otherwise would be to accept that a major substantive change was made in silence or by implication. Congress and the draftsmen of the 1952 Act can not have intended to eliminate both actual and constructive notice from liability under §289, after a century of legislative concern about notice. . . .

. . . Should this court now limit the word "damages" in the marking statute to a compensatory recovery at law, we ignore the history of marking as applied to recovery of profits in equity, and negate the purpose of the marking statute, i.e., to give notice and thus to prevent innocent infringement, [cit]. Indeed, a general principle of the common law is that although there may be liability without actual or constructive notice of adverse rights, damages therefor are rarely greater than nominal. Statute and precedent have shown concern for the principles of fairness that underlie this principle.

Upon review of statute, legislative history, policy, and precedent, we conclude that the marking requirement, §287(a), applies to design patents whether remedy for infringement is sought under §284 or §289.

[The court remanded for a determination of whether Nike had complied with the marking requirement.]

## NOTES AND QUESTIONS

1. *No willfulness requirement.* The current remedies provision pertaining to design patents, 35 U.S.C. §289, allows for recovery of the infringer's total profit from the infringement. The predecessor provision, Section 1 of the 1887 Act (quoted and discussed above in the *Nike* case), recognized an infringement remedy only for "knowing" acts of infringement—leading courts at the time to impose a "willfulness" requirement. Section 289 includes no willfulness

requirement, and the Federal Circuit has declined to interpret the statute as requiring such a requirement. *See Catalina Lighting, Inc. v. Lamps Plus, Inc.*, 295 F.3d 1277, 1290 (Fed. Cir. 2002). As a policy matter, should design patent infringement be limited as under the 1887 Act?

2. **Enhanced damages for willfulness.** Although willfulness is not a prerequisite to collecting profits under §289, suppose that a design patentee succeeds in showing willful infringement. Could a court award profits under §289 and then treble those damages in view of the willfulness finding? *See Braun, Inc. v. Dynamics Corp.*, 975 F.2d 815 (Fed. Cir. 1992). Under the law of remedies for *utility* patents, the court must award damages at least equal to a reasonable royalty for the use made of the invention by the infringer, and the court "may increase the damages up to three times the amount found or assessed," 35 U.S.C. §284; *In re Seagate Technology L.L.C.*, 497 F.3d 1360 (Fed. Cir. 2007) (en banc) (where infringement is shown to be willful, court may enhance damages under §284).

3. **Remedy for combined infringement.** Suppose that a firm owns a utility patent claiming a lamp (say, a lamp that features a unique mechanism for attaching the light source to the lamp post) and a design patent covering the design of the lamp. Suppose that a competitor sells lamps that infringe both the utility patent and the design patent. If the court determines that the reasonable royalty on sales of the lamp amounts to $600,000, and that the infringer's profit on the sale of the lamp amounts to $700,000, what is the proper measure of damages? *See Catalina Lighting, Inc. v. Lamps Plus, Inc.*, 295 F.3d 1277, 1291 (Fed. Cir. 2002).

4. **Injunctive relief and eBay.** Under Federal Circuit practice, the grant of a permanent injunction against future infringement was virtually automatic in utility patent cases — or, at least, Federal Circuit cases could easily be read to support that conclusion. In *eBay Inc. v. MercExchange, L.L.C.*, 126 S. Ct. 1837 (2006), the Supreme Court reminded the Federal Circuit that injunction grants were always a matter of equity, and directed courts in utility patent cases to adopt a "traditional" four-factor test for determining whether to grant a permanent injunction after a finding of infringement, under which the plaintiff must show "(1) that it has suffered an irreparable injury; (2) that remedies available at law, such as monetary damages, are inadequate to compensate for that injury; (3) that, considering the balance of hardships between the plaintiff and defendant, a remedy in equity is warranted; and (4) that the public interest would not be disserved by a permanent injunction." Should this test also apply to design patent infringement? If it is justifiable to afford a different damages remedy to design patents, as evidenced by §289, is it justifiable to apply a different approach to injunctive relief? Would your analysis be affected by the approach that courts have taken toward *eBay* in the context of trade dress cases? *See, e.g., North American Medical Corp. v. Axiom Worldwide, Inc.*, 522 F.3d 1211 (11th Cir. 2008) (cautiously suggesting that "a strong case can be made that *eBay*'s holding necessarily extends to the grant of preliminary injunctions under the Lanham Act").

# PART IV
# COPYRIGHT

# CHAPTER 7
# COPYRIGHT

In this chapter, we consider the use of copyright law as a vehicle for protecting designs. As in other parts of the book, we define designs broadly, to encompass industrial design embodied in mass-produced articles, in addition to those designs embodied in "artistic works" more traditionally understood.

The 1976 Copyright Act, as amended at various times in the past decades and codified at 17 U.S.C. §101 et seq., governs U.S. copyright law. Copyright subsists from the time an original work of authorship is fixed in a tangible medium of expression. Formally, the Copyright Office reviews registration applications for compliance with the requirements of the Act but rarely rejects applications on substantive grounds. Registration serves jurisdictional and evidentiary purposes in copyright infringement litigation, and affects the remedies available for infringement. Copyrightability determinations are essentially left to the courts. Copyright endures for the life of the author plus seventy years for many works, although copyrights in works-made-for-hire last for fixed terms (95 years from publication or 120 years from publication, whichever expires first).

Our study of copyright in this chapter covers copyrightability thresholds in general (Section A), rules regarding copyrightable subject matter of particular importance in design (Sections B–D), and the scope of copyright protection for designs (Section E).

## A. COPYRIGHTABILITY IN GENERAL

Under the Copyright Act, copyrightability in general involves three inquiries: (1) whether the work at issue is original under 17 U.S.C. §102(a) (stating that "[c]opyright protection subsists . . . in original works of authorship . . ."); (2) whether the subject matter for which protection is sought is excluded from protection under 17 U.S.C. §102(b) (stating that "[i]n no case does copyright protection for an original work of authorship extend to any idea, procedure, process, system, method of operation, concept, principle, or discovery, regardless of the form in which it is described, explained, illustrated, or embodied in such work"); and (3) whether the subject matter falls into a category of protectable "works of authorship" under 17 U.S.C. §102(a) for which special restrictions apply. In this section, we consider the first inquiry, originality, and the second, distinguishing between protectable "expression" and unprotectable "ideas."

## 1. ORIGINALITY

In *Feist Publ., Inc. v. Rural Telephone Service,* 499 U.S. 340 (1991), the Court characterized originality as a "constitutional requirement" and as "[t]he *sine qua non* of copyright." Under the standard articulated by the Court, originality has two components: "the work was independently created by the author (as opposed to copied from other works)" and the work "possesses at least some minimal degree of creativity." The requirement for creativity is truly minimal; most works meet it easily, but it is frequently at issue in design cases.

### YURMAN STUDIO, INC. V. CASTANEDA
### 591 F. Supp.2d 471 (S.D.N.Y. 2008)

SCHEINDLIN, J.:

. . .

#### II. Background
#### A. Facts

Since 2004, defendants, through their website http://www.overstockjeweler.com ("Overstock website"), have been offering for sale and selling "designer knock-off Jewelry" and "reproductions or replicas of popular designs." Plaintiffs [including Yurman] are designers and suppliers of high-end jewelry and luxury watches. Numerous jewelry items and watches offered for sale on the Overstock website are advertised as replicas of, or inspired by, the jewelry designs of Yurman. . . .

. . . Yurman owns twelve copyright registrations, covering both individual jewelry designs and jewelry collections, that form the basis of its claims against defendants. In addition, Yurman owns a patent in an ornamental design for a watch bracelet. . . . [Defendants moved for summary judgment on the ground, inter alia, that some of plaintiff's copyright registrations were invalid.]

. . .

#### III. Applicable Law

. . .

The validity of a copyright depends upon its originality. [*See Yurman Design, Inc. v. PAJ, Inc.* ("*PAJ, Inc.*"), 262 F.3d 101, 109 (2d Cir. 2001) (citing *Feist Publ., Inc. v. Rural Telephone Service,* 499 U.S. 340, 345-47 (1991).] The Supreme Court held that originality "does not signify novelty" and indeed, "a work may be original even though it closely resembles other works so long as the similarity is fortuitous, not the result of copying." [*Feist*, 499 U.S. at 345.] Rather, originality "means only that the work was independently created by the author (as opposed to copied from other works), and that it possesses at least some minimal degree of creativity." [*Id.* (citation omitted).] This level of creativity is "extremely low," with "the vast majority of works mak[ing] the grade quite easily" as long as they possess "some creative spark, no matter how crude, humble or obvious." [*Id.* (quotation marks omitted).] "Copyright law may protect a combination of elements that are unoriginal in themselves." [*PAJ, Inc.*, 262 F.3d at 109-110.] With respect to compilations of facts, for example, protection extends to choices of "selection and arrangement, so long as they are made independently by the compiler and entail a minimal degree of creativity." [*Feist,* 499 U.S. at 348.] This Court has previously observed that "in cases involving design, [] it is difficult to discern when a combination of unoriginal component parts is itself original so as to merit copyright protection."[*Diamond Direct, LLC v. Star Diamond Group, Inc.*, 116 F. Supp. 2d 525, 529 (S.D.N.Y. 2000).]

. . .

## IV. Discussion

. . .

Defendants argue that [Yurman's] designs existed in the public domain in substantially the same form prior to Yurman's registrations, and therefore they lack sufficient originality to be protected by copyright. Plaintiffs contend that defendants have failed to provide any evidence in support of their defense of lack of originality in Yurman's designs.

The bar for originality is extremely low; a work must possess merely "some minimal degree of creativity." [*Feist,* 499 U.S. at 345.] Further, copyright law protects the combination of elements that are not original in themselves. [*See id.*] Protection extends to choices of "selection and arrangement, so long as they are made independently by the compiler and entail a minimal degree of creativity."[*Feist,* 499 U.S. at 348.] Yurman concedes that it does not own each and every design element used in its creations, but rather claims it owns the unique combination of elements which "work together to make an overall design that is new, fresh, and distinct from anything else. . . ."

To rebut the presumption that Yurman's designs are original, defendants claim that the elements found in Yurman's products, such as twisted cable, the combination of gold and silver, and gemstones, are in the public domain and have been used in jewelry design for hundreds of years. With respect to most of Yurman's designs, "this showing misses the point, however: the originality in Yurman's . . . designs inheres in the ways Yurman has recast and arranged those constituent elements." [*PAJ, Inc.*, 262 F.3d at 109 (holding that Yurman designs were sufficiently original).]

With respect to two copyrighted designs, however, the submissions by defendants raise fact issues regarding the originality of the combination of specific elements. First, a bracelet in Yurman's "Albion" collection, which consists of a thick twisted cable capped by a large gemstone that is attached to the cable with a contrasting metal sleeve on either side, is strikingly similar to an Egyptian "Bracelet with a Sardonyx" dated from the Third Century.

Specifically, the Egyptian bracelet combines the elements of twisted cable, a single large gemstone, and metal sleeves connecting the gemstone to the cable in the same way as the Yurman bracelet. Similarly, the single chain bracelets and necklaces in Yurman's "Linked Renaissance" collection use a very similar combination of elements — a single link of twisted cable alternated with a single small gemstone—as a chain identified in defendants' submissions as an 1880s-1890s bracelet.

Scholars disagree, and the Second Circuit has not decided, as to whether a defendant challenging the originality of a plaintiff's copyrighted work must provide evidence of actual copying, or if copying may be inferred through plaintiff's access to designs in the public domain and the substantial similarity of the works to those designs. At the summary judgment stage, drawing all inferences in favor of the non-moving party, Yurman's access to these historical jewelry designs in the public domain must be inferred.

Because defendants' submissions raise fact issues regarding the originality of the two designs, summary judgment is denied on defendants' counterclaim as to the Albion collection bracelet and the Linked Renaissance single chain jewelry. However, with respect to all other Yurman copyrighted designs, after careful review of the images of preexisting jewelry produced by defendants, I conclude that Yurman's designs are sufficiently original as a matter of law and Yurman is entitled to summary judgment on the claims for cancellation of those designs.

## NOTES AND QUESTIONS

1. ***Works of design as "compilations."*** The court notes that the component parts of a work might themselves be unoriginal, but their combination might be original, satisfying the low threshold established in *Feist*. Section 103(a) of the Copyright Act specifies that compilations are included within the subject matter of copyright. Section 101, defining "compilation," also explains how compilations could qualify as original: a compilation is defined as "a work formed by the collection and assembling of preexisting materials or of data that are selected, coordinated, or arranged in such a way that the resulting work as a whole constitutes an original work of authorship." Designs frequently will include many visual elements. Even if those elements individually are unoriginal, would you expect that (as in *Yurman*) there will usually be a basis for arguing that the designer exercised creative judgment in the selection, coordination, or arrangement of visual elements? *See also Glasscraft Door I, L.P. v. Seybro Door & Weathership Co., Inc.*, 2009 WL 3460372 (S.D. Tex. 2009) (originality of copyrighted door designs having wrought iron geometric patterns worked into glass panels); *Montwillo v. Tull*, 632 F. Supp. 2d 917 (N.D. Cal. 2008) ("drag queen" and "trailer trash" dolls original). In *Feist* itself, the work at issue was a telephone directory, and originality was lacking both in the listings themselves and in the alphabetical selection and arrangement of those listings.

2. ***Total concept and feel.*** In *Roth Greeting Cards v. United Card Co.*, 429 F.2d 1106 (9th Cir. 1970), the plaintiff had produced a series of greeting cards featuring commonplace phrases and fairly simple artwork. The phrases alone were not original, but according to the court, "proper analysis of the problem requires that all elements of each card, including text, arrangement of text, art work, and association between art work and text, be considered as a whole." In assessing the "total concept and feel" of plaintiff's cards, the court considered the characters depicted in the drawings, "the mood they portrayed," the

combination of particular artwork with a particular message, the appearance of the lettering, and "the arrangement of the words on the greeting card." Is this approach to originality too generous? *See also Apple Computer, Inc. v. Microsoft Corp.*, 779 F. Supp. 133 (N.D. Cal. 1991) (discussing total concept and feel in the context of graphical user interfaces for software). Similar considerations of the total concept and feel arise in the context of the substantial similarity analysis for determining copyright infringement, as we discuss below in Section C. How does the total concept and feel approach to protectability compare to doctrines of trade dress protection or design patent protection discussed in previous chapters?

## 2. THE SECTION 102(B) EXCLUSIONS

Section 102(b) of the Copyright Act denies protection to pure concepts or ideas, instead permitting protection only for the expression of those concepts or ideas. It also contains additional exclusions. *See generally* Pamela Samuelson, *Why Copyright Law Excludes Systems and Processes from the Scope of Its Protection*, 85 Tex. L. Rev. 1921 (2007) (explaining that the exclusions in Section 102(b) go beyond the exclusion of ideas). The idea/expression inquiry may be understood as a copyrightability doctrine, but it also frequently implicates copyright scope. For example, in the following case, consider whether the plaintiff is attempting to claim rights in the idea of a jewel-encrusted bee pin, rather than asserting a more modest claim to a particular implementation of that idea.

### Herbert Rosenthal Jewelry Corp. v. Kalpakian
446 F.2d 738 (9th Cir. 1971)

Browning, Circuit Judge:

Plaintiff and defendants are engaged in the design, manufacture, and sale of fine jewelry.

Plaintiff charged defendants with infringing plaintiff's copyright registration of a pin in the shape of a bee formed of gold encrusted with jewels. A consent decree was entered, reciting that the parties had agreed to a settlement of the action and entry of the decree. It provided that plaintiff's copyright of the jeweled bee was "good and valid in law," that defendants had manufactured a jeweled bee "alleged to be similar," and that defendants were enjoined from infringing plaintiff's copyright and from manufacturing or selling copies of plaintiff's jeweled bee pin.

Later plaintiff filed a motion for an order holding defendants in contempt of the consent decree. The district court, after an evidentiary hearing, found that while defendants had manufactured and sold a line of jeweled bee pins, they designed their pins themselves after a study of bees in nature and in published works and did not copy plaintiff's copyrighted bee. The court further found that defendants' jeweled bees were "not substantially similar" to plaintiff's bees, except that both "do look like bees." The court concluded that defendants had neither infringed plaintiff's copyright nor violated the consent decree, and entered a judgment order denying plaintiff's motion. We affirm.

. . .

II

Plaintiff contends that its copyright registration of a jeweled bee entitles it to protection from the manufacture and sale by others of any object that to the ordinary observer is substantially similar in appearance. The breadth of this claim is evident. For example, while a photograph of the copyrighted bee pin attached to the complaint depicts a bee with nineteen small white jewels on its back, plaintiff argues that its copyright is infringed by defendants' entire line of a score or more jeweled bees in three sizes decorated with from nine to thirty jewels of various sizes, kinds, and colors.

Although plaintiff's counsel asserted that the originality of plaintiff's bee pin lay in a particular arrangement of jewels on the top of the pin, the elements of this arrangement were never identified. Defendants' witnesses testified that the "arrangement" was simply a function of the size and form of the bee pin and the size of the jewels used. Plaintiff's counsel, repeatedly pressed by the district judge, was unable to suggest how jewels might be placed on the back of a pin in the shape of a bee without infringing plaintiff's copyright. He eventually conceded, "not being a jeweler, I can't conceive of how he might rearrange the design so it is dissimilar."

If plaintiff's understanding of its rights were correct, its copyright would effectively prevent others from engaging in the business of manufacturing and selling jeweled bees. We think plaintiff confuses the balance Congress struck between protection and competition under the Patent Act and the Copyright Act.

The owner of a patent is granted the exclusive right to exploit for a period of seventeen years (a maximum of fourteen years for design patents) the conception that is the subject matter of the patent. 35 U.S.C. §§154, 173. The grant of this monopoly, however, is carefully circumscribed by substantive and procedural protections. To be patentable the subject matter must be new and useful, and represent a nonobvious advance — one requiring "more ingenuity and skill than that possessed by an ordinary mechanic acquainted with the business"; an advance that would not be obvious to a hypothetical person skilled in the art and charged with knowledge of all relevant developments publicly known to that point in time. [cit.] A patent is granted only after an independent administrative inquiry and determination that these substantive standards have been met. [cit.] This determination is subject to both administrative and court review. [cit.]

Copyright registration, on the other hand, confers no right at all to the conception reflected in the registered subject matter. "Unlike a patent, a copyright gives no exclusive right to the art disclosed; protection is given only to the expression of the idea — not the idea itself." *Mazer v. Stein*, 347 U.S. 201, 217 (1954). Accordingly, the prerequisites for copyright registration are minimal. The work offered for registration need only be the product of the registrant. So long as it is not a plagiarized copy of another's effort, there is no requirement that the work differ substantially from prior works or that it contribute anything of value. "The copyright protects originality rather than novelty or invention." *Id.* at 218. . . . [R]egistration is accomplished simply by filing a claim and depositing copies of the work with the Register of Copyrights, 17 U.S.C. §§11, 13. There is no administrative investigation or determination of the validity of the claim. A certificate is refused only if the object falls outside the broad category of matter subject to copyright registration. 17 U.S.C. §§4-5. A copyright affords little protection. It confers "only 'the sole right of multiplying copies.' Absent copying there can be no infringement of copyright." *Mazer v. Stein, supra,* 347 U.S. at 218. Because the registrant's protection is limited and the social cost therefore small, the life of the copyright is long. . . .

Obviously a copyright must not be treated as equivalent to a patent lest long continuing private monopolies be conferred over areas of gainful activity without first satisfying the substantive and procedural prerequisites to the grant of such privileges.

Because copyright bars only copying, perhaps this case could be disposed of on the district court's finding that defendants did not copy plaintiff's bee pin. [The court concluded that there was substantial evidence in support of the finding that defendant had independently created its pin, but also noted that copying can be subconscious, and found it unrealistic to suppose that defendants could have closed their minds to plaintiff's highly successful jeweled bee pin as they designed their own.]

A finding that defendants "copied" plaintiff's pin in this sense, however, would not necessarily justify judgment against them. A copyright, we have seen, bars use of the particular "expression" of an idea in a copyrighted work but does not bar use of the "idea" itself. Others are free to utilize the "idea" so long as they do not plagiarize its "expression." As the court said in *Trifari, Krussman & Fishel, Inc. v. B. Steinberg-Kaslo Co.*, 144 F. Supp. 577, 580 (S.D.N.Y. 1956), where the copyrighted work was a jeweled pin representing a hansom cab, "though an alleged infringer gets the idea of a hansom cab pin from a copyrighted article there can be no infringement unless the article itself has been copied. The idea of a hansom cab cannot be copyrighted. Nevertheless plaintiff's expression of that idea, as embodied in its pin, can be copyrighted." Or as Judge Hand put it in *Sheldon v. Metro-Goldwyn Pictures Corp.*, 81 F.2d 49, 54 (2d Cir. 1936), "defendants were entitled to use, not only all that had gone before, but even the plaintiffs' contribution itself, if they drew from it only the more general patterns; that is, if they kept clear of its 'expression.'"

The critical distinction between "idea" and "expression" is difficult to draw. As Judge Hand candidly wrote, "Obviously, no principle can be stated as to when an imitator has gone beyond copying the 'idea,' and has borrowed its 'expression.'" *Peter Pan Fabrics, Inc. v. Martin Weiner Corp.*, 274 F.2d 487, 489 (2d Cir. 1960). At least in close cases, one may suspect, the classification the court selects may simply state the result reached rather than the reason for it. In our view, the difference is really one of degree as Judge Hand suggested in his striking "abstraction" formulation in *Nichols v. Universal Pictures Corp.*, 45 F.2d 119, 121 (2d Cir. 1930). The guiding consideration in drawing the line is the preservation of the balance between competition and protection reflected in the patent and copyright laws.

What is basically at stake is the extent of the copyright owner's monopoly — from how large an area of activity did Congress intend to allow the copyright owner to exclude others? We think the production of jeweled bee pins is a larger private preserve than Congress intended to be set aside in the public market without a patent. A jeweled bee pin is therefore an "idea" that defendants were free to copy. Plaintiff seems to agree, for it disavows any claim that defendants cannot manufacture and sell jeweled bee pins and concedes that only plaintiff's particular design or "expression" of the jeweled bee pin "idea" is protected under its copyright. The difficulty, as we have noted, is that on this record the "idea" and its "expression" appear to be indistinguishable. There is no greater similarity between the pins of plaintiff and defendants than is inevitable from the use of jewel-encrusted bee forms in both.

When the "idea" and its "expression" are thus inseparable, copying the "expression" will not be barred, since protecting the "expression" in such circumstances would confer a monopoly of the "idea" upon the copyright owner free of the conditions and limitations imposed by the patent law. [cit.].

*Affirmed.*

## NOTES AND QUESTIONS

1. *Idea/Expression and functionality.* As we have seen, functionality doctrine operates to channel certain types of subject matter away from trademark and design patent regimes, and toward the utility patent regime. The idea/expression inquiry performs a similar function, channeling certain subject matter away from copyright toward utility patent. (In the best known articulation of the idea/expression dichotomy, *Baker v. Selden*, 101 U.S. 99 (1879), the Court speaks at length about the need to separate the copyright and patent regimes.) Is that as far as the comparison goes, based on what you have read above about the idea/expression inquiry, and in previous chapters about functionality? Or should the idea/expression case law in copyright inform the functionality case law in trade dress and design patent, and vice versa?

2. *Other manifestations of the idea/expression divide?* Most of the designs with which we are concerned in this book are designs incorporated into useful articles. Thus, the idea/expression divide is particularly important for protecting designs. As you consider the specialized rules for various types of subject matter in the following sections, ask whether those rules are largely derivative of the core notion of separating idea from expression.

## B. "PICTORIAL, GRAPHIC AND SCULPTURAL WORKS": USEFUL ARTICLES AND THE SEPARABILITY DOCTRINE

Section 102(5) of the 1976 Copyright Act extends copyright protection to pictorial, graphic, and sculptural works ("PGS" works), and Section 101 of the Act defines PGS works. Traditional art forms have presented little controversy under these provisions. For example, the figure of Professor Janis as Hercules, rendered in concrete statuary and displayed (discreetly, of course) in his formal rose garden, is unquestionably a "sculptural work" eligible for copyright. However, at one point it was not so clear that mass-produced works

## B. "Pictorial, Graphic and Sculptural Works": Useful Articles and the Separability Doctrine

incorporated sculptural design should be deemed eligible for copyright protection. The Supreme Court addressed the issue in *Mazer* (under a prior incarnation of the statute).

### 1. COPYRIGHT PROTECTION FOR USEFUL ARTICLES

MAZER V. STEIN
347 U.S. 201 (1954)

REED, J. delivered the opinion of the Court:
This case involves the validity of copyrights obtained by respondents for statuettes of male and female dancing figures made of semivitreous china. The controversy centers around the fact that although copyrighted as "works of art," the statuettes were intended for use and used as bases for table lamps, with electric wiring, sockets and lamp shades attached.

[Stein registered the statuettes with the Copyright Office, then incorporated the statuettes into lamps and sold them. Mazer copied the statuettes and sold competing lamps. Stein sued, losing at the District Court but winning on appeal. Mazer persuaded the Supreme Court to grant certiorari on the following question: "Can statuettes be protected in the United States by copyright when the copyright applicant intended primarily to use the statuettes in the form of lamp bases to be made and sold in quantity and carried the intentions into effect?" Mazer argued that when an otherwise copyrightable work is mass produced, there can be no valid copyright in the work; instead, the originator of the work must seek a design patent.]

In answering [the certiorari question], a review of the development of copyright coverage will make clear the purpose of the Congress in its copyright legislation. In 1790 the First Congress conferred a copyright on "authors of any map, chart, book or books already printed". Later, designing, engraving and etching were included; in 1831 musical composition; dramatic compositions in 1856; and photographs and negatives thereof in 1865.

The Act of 1870 defined copyrightable subject matter as [ ]

> ... any book, map, chart, dramatic or musical composition, engraving, cut, print, or photograph or negative thereof, or of a painting, drawing, chromo, statute, statuary, and of models or designs intended to be perfected as works of the fine arts. (Emphasis supplied.)

The italicized part added three-dimensional work of art to what had been protected previously. In 1909 Congress again enlarged the scope of the copyright statute. The new Act provided in §4. "That the works for which copyright may be secured under this Act shall include all the writings of an author." Some writers interpret this section as being coextensive with the constitutional grant, but the House Report, while inconclusive, indicates that it was "declaratory of existing law" only. Section 5 relating to classes of writings in 1909 read as shown in the margin with subsequent additions not material to this decision.[19] Significant for our purposes was the deletion of the

---

19. "The application for registration shall specify to which of the following classes the work in which copyright is claimed belongs: (a) Books, including composite and cyclopaedic works,

fine-arts clause of the 1870 Act. Verbal distinctions between purely aesthetic articles and useful works of art ended insofar as the statutory copyright language is concerned.

[The Court then reviewed the pertinent Copyright Office regulations, concluding that the Office had long construed the statute to allow registration for articles of the type at issue.]

... It is clear Congress intended the scope of the copyright statute to include more than the traditional fine arts. Herbert Putnam, Esq., then Librarian of Congress and active in the movement to amend the copyright laws, told the joint meeting of the House and Senate Committees:

> The term "works of art" is deliberately intended as a broader specification than "works of the fine arts" in the present statute with the idea that there is subject-matter (for instance, of applied design, not yet within the province of design patents), which may properly be entitled to protection under the copyright law. [cit.]

The successive acts, the legislative history of the 1909 Act and the practice of the Copyright Office unite to show that "works of art" and "reproductions of works of art" are terms that were intended by Congress to include the authority to copyright these statuettes. Individual perception of the beautiful is too varied a power to permit a narrow or rigid concept of art. As a standard we can hardly do better than the words of the present Regulation, §202.8 . . . naming the things that appertain to the arts. They must be original, that is, the author's tangible expression of his ideas. Compare *Burrow-Giles Lithographic Co. v. Sarony*, [cit.]. Such expression, whether meticulously delineating the model or mental image or conveying the meaning by modernistic form or color, is copyrightable. What cases there are confirm this coverage of the statute.

The conclusion that the statues here in issue may be copyrighted goes far to solve the question whether their intended reproduction as lamp stands bars or invalidates their registration. This depends solely on statutory interpretation [because copyright is a creature of statute]. . . .

But petitioners assert that congressional enactment of the design patent laws should be interpreted as denying protection to artistic articles embodied or reproduced in manufactured articles.[33] They say: "Fundamentally and

---

directories, gazetteers, and other compilations; (b) Periodicals, including newspapers; (c) Lectures, sermons, addresses, prepared for oral delivery; (d) Dramatic or dramatico-musical compositions; (e) Musical compositions; (f) Maps; (g) Works of art; models or designs for works of art; (h) Reproductions of a work of art; (i) Drawings or plastic works of a scientific or technical character; (j) Photographs; (k) Prints and pictorial illustrations: Provided, nevertheless, That the above specifications shall not be held to limit the subject-matter of copyright as defined in section four of this Act, nor shall any error in classification invalidate or impair the copyright protection secured under this Act." 35 Stat. 1076. Subsection (k) was amended by the addition of the words "including prints or labels used for articles of merchandise" in 1939. 53 Stat. 1142. . . . Two more classes "(l) Motion-picture photoplays" and "(m) Motion pictures other than photoplays" were added in 1912. 37 Stat. 488.

33. Two cases are relied upon to support the position of the petitioners. *Taylor Instrument Companies v. Fawley-Brost Co.*, 7 Cir., 139 F.2d 98, and *Brown Instrument Co. v. Warner*, 82 U.S. App. D.C. 232, 161 F.2d 910. These cases hold that the Mechanical Patent Law and Copyright Laws are mutually exclusive. As to overlapping of Design Patent and Copyright Laws, however, a different answer has been given by the courts. *Louis De Jonge & Co. v. Breuker & Kessler Co.*, C.C., 182 F. 150, affirmed on other grounds in 3 Cir., 191 F. 35, and 235 U.S. 33. . . .

historically, the Copyright Office is the repository of what each claimant considers to be a cultural treasure, whereas the Patent Office is the repository of what each applicant considers to be evidence of the advance in industrial and technological fields." Their argument is that design patents require the critical examination given patents to protect the public against monopoly. Attention is called to *Gorham Mfg. Co. v. White*, [cit.], interpreting the design patent law of 1842, 5 Stat. 544, granting a patent to anyone who by "their own industry, genius, efforts, and expense, may have invented or produced any new and original design for a manufacture...." A pattern for flat silver was there upheld. [Under the current design patent law,] "[w]hoever invents any new, original and ornamental design for an article of manufacture may obtain a patent therefor, ..." subject generally to the provisions concerning patents for invention. [35 U.S.C. §171]. As petitioner sees the effect of the design patent law: "If an industrial designer can not satisfy the novelty requirements of the design patent laws, then his design as used on articles of manufacture can be copied by anyone." Petitioner has furnished the Court a booklet of numerous design patents for statuettes, bases for table lamps and similar articles for manufacture, quite indistinguishable in type from the copyrighted statuettes here in issue.[35] Petitioner urges that overlapping of patent and copyright legislation so as to give an author or inventor a choice between patents and copyrights should not be permitted. We assume petitioner takes the position that protection for a statuette for industrial use can only be obtained by patent, if any protection can be given.

As we have held the statuettes here involved copyrightable, we need not decide the question of their patentability. Though other courts have passed upon the issue as to whether allowance by the election of the author or patentee of one bars a grant of the other, we do not. [cit.] We do hold that the patentability of the statuettes, fitted as lamps or unfitted, does not bar copyright as works of art. Neither the Copyright Statute nor any other says that because a thing is patentable it may not be copyrighted. We should not so hold. [cit.]

Unlike a patent, a copyright gives no exclusive right to the art disclosed; protection is given only to the expression of the idea — not the idea itself. Thus, in *Baker v. Selden*, 101 U.S. 99, the Court held that a copyrighted book on a peculiar system of bookkeeping was not infringed by a similar book using a similar plan which achieved similar results where the alleged infringer made a different arrangement of the columns and used different headings. The distinction is illustrated in *Fred Fisher, Inc. v. Dillingham*, D.C., 298 F. 145, 151, when the court speaks of two men, each a perfectionist, independently making maps of the same territory. Though the maps are identical each may obtain the exclusive right to make copies of his own particular map, and yet neither will infringe the other's copyright. Likewise a copyrighted directory is not infringed by a similar directory which is the product of independent work. The copyright protects originality rather than novelty or invention — conferring only "the sole right of multiplying copies." Absent copying there

---

35. E.g., Design Patent 170,445 Base for table lamps, a fanciful statuette of a girl standing in front of a high rock in bathing costume.

can be no infringement of copyright. Thus, respondents may not exclude others from using statuettes of human figures in table lamps; they may only prevent use of copies of their statuettes as such or as incorporated in some other article. Regulation §202.8 . . . makes clear that artistic articles are protected in "form but not their mechanical or utilitarian aspects." *See Stein v. Rosenthal*, D.C., 103 F. Supp. 227, 231. The dichotomy of protection for the aesthetic is not beauty and utility but art for the copyright and the invention of original and ornamental design for design patents. We find nothing in the copyright statute to support the argument that the intended use or use in industry of an article eligible for copyright bars or invalidates its registration. We do not read such a limitation into the copyright law.

Nor do we think the subsequent registration of a work of art published as an element in a manufactured article, is a misuse of the copyright. This is not different from the registration of a statuette and its later embodiment in an industrial article.

"The copyright law, like the patent statutes, makes reward to the owner a secondary consideration." *United States v. Paramount Pictures*, 334 U.S. 131, 158. However, it is "intended definitely to grant valuable, enforceable rights to authors, publishers, etc., without burdensome requirements; 'to afford greater encouragement to the production of literary (or artistic) works of lasting benefit to the world.'" *Washingtonian Pub. Co. v. Pearson*, 306 U.S. 30, 36.

The economic philosophy behind the clause empowering Congress to grant patents and copyrights is the conviction that encouragement of individual effort by personal gain is the best way to advance public welfare through the talents of authors and inventors in "Science and useful Arts." Sacrificial days devoted to such creative activities deserve rewards commensurate with the services rendered.

*Affirmed.*

## NOTES AND QUESTIONS

1. ***Constitutional issues.*** Justices Douglas and Black, concurring, questioned whether the grant of copyright protection for the statuettes fell within Congress' constitutional authority as set forth in Art. I, Sec. 8, Cl. 8. According to Justice Douglas, the Court had never determined whether a sculptor was a "writer" and a statue was a "writing" in the constitutional sense. Douglas thought that the question deserved "much research," and would have allowed reargument on the point, observing that:

> [t]he interests involved in the category of 'works of art,' as used in the copyright law, are considerable. The Copyright Office has supplied us with a long list of such articles which have been copyrighted-statuettes, book ends, clocks, lamps, door knockers, candlesticks, inkstands, chandeliers, piggy banks, sundials, salt and pepper shakers, fish bowls, casseroles, and ash trays. Perhaps these are all 'writings' in the constitutional sense. But to me, at least, they are not obviously so. It is time that we came to the problem full face. I would accordingly put the case down for reargument.

*Id.* at 221. The majority opinion contained a lengthy footnote asserting that the constitutional question was not properly before the Court. *Id.* at 206 n. 5.

Suppose that the Court had reached the question. What policy goals would be served by denying copyright protection here? What goals would be undermined?

**2. *Requirement for election?*** The lamp design at issue in *Mazer* is the type of subject matter that might qualify for design patent protection, but that fact alone does not disqualify the lamp design from copyright protection, the Court holds in *Mazer*. Should the securing of a design patent preclude copyright protection, on the ground that a designer must elect between the forms of protection? *See In re Yardley*, 493 F.2d 1389 (C.C.P.A. 1974) (discussing election).

**3. *A radical change?*** Writing some twenty years after *Mazer*, the Register of Copyrights (Barbara Ringer) characterized *Mazer* as effecting a "radical change in the legal status of original designs in the United States." Draft, Second Supplementary Report of the Register of Copyrights on the General Revision of the U.S. Copyright Law, Chapter VII (1975). Before *Mazer*, it was generally believed that design patent protection was the only available means for securing rights in designs of useful articles, but design patents were believed "inadequate as a practical form of protection." *Id.* (citing reasons for the inadequacy, including judicial hostility, high cost, and delay resulting from the patent examination process). Nearly fifty design protection bills had been introduced; none were enacted. *See id. Mazer* was decided against this backdrop. We will look more closely at *sui generis* design protection legislation in Chapter 8. Based on your study of modern design patent law, does copyright protection of the sort contemplated in *Mazer* still have a role to play in compensating for the inadequacies of design patent protection? Or has design patent protection overcome those inadequacies?

**4. *The "unity of art" thesis.*** The Court in *Mazer* was by no means the first to grapple with the idea that works of applied art might warrant copyright protection alongside works of "fine" art. In nineteenth century France, a view emerged that distinguishing between types of design was futile, and that copyright protection should extend to designs whatever their merit or purpose. On the basis of this "unity of art" theory, France amended its copyright law in 1902 to extend copyright protection to designs of useful articles. *See* J. H. Reichman, *Design Protection in Domestic and Foreign Copyright Law: From the Berne Revision of 1948 to the Copyright Act of 1976*, 1983 DUKE L.J. 1143, 1153-58 (1983). Does the unity of art theory still resonate today? Is it consonant with modern notions of design? Does it (or should it) reflect the current legal landscape? Or are there good reasons why copyright should withdraw to its more traditional domain in the "fine" arts?

## 2. THE SEPARABILITY DOCTRINE UNDER THE 1976 ACT

Section 101 of the Copyright Act defines pictorial, graphic, and sculptural works:

> "Pictorial, graphic, and sculptural works" include two-dimensional and three-dimensional works of fine, graphic, and applied art, photographs, prints and art reproductions, maps, globes, charts, diagrams, models, and technical

drawings, including architectural plans. Such works shall include works of artistic craftsmanship insofar as their form but not their mechanical or utilitarian aspects are concerned; the design of a useful article, as defined in this section, shall be considered a pictorial, graphic, or sculptural work only if, and only to the extent that, such design incorporates pictorial, graphic, or sculptural features that can be identified separately from, and are capable of existing independently of, the utilitarian aspects of the article.

As the next case illustrates, the task of identifying pictorial, graphic, or sculptural features separately of utilitarian features has proven to be challenging.

### Pivot Point Int'l, Inc. v. Charlene Products, Inc.
372 F.3d 913 (7th Cir. 2004)

Ripple, Circuit Judge:

## I. Background

Pivot Point develops and markets educational techniques and tools for the hair design industry. It was founded in 1965 by Leo Passage, an internationally renowned hair designer. One aspect of Pivot Point's business is the design and development of mannequin heads, "slip-ons" (facial forms that slip over a mannequin head) and component hair pieces.

In the mid-1980s, Passage desired to develop a mannequin that would imitate the "hungry look" of high-fashion, runway models. Passage believed that such a mannequin could be marketed as a premium item to cutting-edge hair-stylists and to stylists involved in hair design competitions. Passage then worked with a German artist named Horst Heerlein to create an original sculpture of a female human head. Although Passage discussed his vision with Heerlein, Passage did not give Heerlein any specific dimensional requirements. From Passage's description, Heerlein created a sculpture in plaster entitled "Mara."

Wax molds of Mara were made and sent to Pivot Point's manufacturer in Hong Kong. The manufacturer created exact reproductions of Mara in polyvinyl chloride ("PVC"). The manufacturer filled the PVC form with a liquid that expands and hardens into foam. The process of creating the Mara sculpture and of developing the mannequin based on the sculpture took approximately eighteen months.

In February of 1988, when Pivot Point first inspected the PVC forms of Mara, it discovered that the mannequin's hairline had been etched too high on the forehead. The manufacturer corrected the mistake by adding a second, lower hairline. Although the first, higher hairline was visible upon inspection, it was covered with implanted hair. The early PVC reproductions of Mara, and Pivot Point's first shipment of the mannequins in May of 1988, possessed the double hairlines.

About the same time that it received its first shipment of mannequins, Pivot Point obtained a copyright registration for the design of Mara, specifically the bareheaded female human head with no makeup or hair. Heerlein assigned all of his rights in the Mara sculpture to Pivot Point. Pivot Point displayed the copyright notice in the name of Pivot Point on each mannequin.

Pivot Point enjoyed great success with its new mannequin. To respond to customer demand, Pivot Point began marketing the Mara mannequin with different types and lengths of hair, different skin tones and variations in makeup; however, no alterations were made to the facial features of the mannequin. For customer ease in identification, Pivot Point changed the name of the mannequin based on its hair and skin color; for instance, a Mara mannequin implanted with yak hair was called "Sonja," and the Mara mannequin implanted with blonde hair was called "Karin."

At a trade show in 1989, Charlene, a wholesaler of beauty products founded by Mr. Yau [a former employee of Pivot Point], displayed its own "Liza" mannequin, which was very close in appearance to Pivot Point's Mara. In addition to the strikingly similar facial features, Liza also exhibited a double hairline that the early Mara mannequins possessed. [Pivot Point sued, and the district court granted summary judgment in favor of Charlene. Pivot Point appealed.]

## II. Analysis

. . .

### B. Copyrightability

The central issue in this case is whether the Mara mannequin is subject to copyright protection. This issue presents, at bottom, a question of statutory interpretation. We therefore begin our analysis with the language of the statute. Two provisions contained in 17 U.S.C. §101 are at the center of our inquiry. The first of these is the description of pictorial, graphic and sculptural works:

> "Pictorial, graphic, and sculptural works" include two-dimensional and three-dimensional works of fine, graphic, and applied art, photographs, prints and art reproductions, maps, globes, charts, diagrams, models, and technical drawings, including architectural plans. Such works shall include works of artistic craftsmanship insofar as their form but not their mechanical or utilitarian aspects are concerned; the design of a *useful article*, as defined in this section, shall be considered a pictorial, graphic, or sculptural work *only if, and only to the extent that*, such design incorporates pictorial, graphic, or sculptural features that can be identified separately from, and are capable of existing independently of, the utilitarian aspects of the article.

The definition section further provides that "[a] 'useful article' is an article having an intrinsic utilitarian function that is not merely to portray the appearance of the article or to convey information. An article that is normally a part of a useful article is considered a 'useful article.'" 17 U.S.C. §101. As is clear from the definition of pictorial, graphic and sculptural work, only "useful article[s]," as the term is further defined, are subject to the limitation contained in the emphasized language above. If an article is not "useful" as the term is defined in §101, then it is a pictorial, graphic and sculptural work entitled to copyright protection (assuming the other requirements of the statute are met).

### 1. Usefulness

Pivot Point submits that the Mara mannequin is not a "useful article" for purposes of §101 because its "inherent nature is to portray the appearance of runway models. Its value," continues Pivot Point, "resides in how well it portrays the appearance of runway models, just as the value of a bust—depicting Cleopatra, for example, . . . —would be in how well it approximates what one imagines the subject looked like." Pivot Point relies upon the decisions of the Fourth Circuit in *Superior Form Builders* and of the Second Circuit in *Hart* for the proposition that mannequins, albeit in those cases animal and fish mannequins, are not useful articles. Specifically, the Fourth Circuit explained that

> [a] mannequin provides the creative form and expression of the ultimate animal display. . . . Even though covered with a skin, the mannequin is not invisible but conspicuous in the final display. The angle of the animal's head, the juxtaposition of its body parts, and the shape of the body parts in the final display is little more than the portrayal of the underlying mannequin. Indeed, the mannequin can even portray the intensity of flexed body parts, or it can reveal the grace of relaxed ones. None of these expressive aspects of a mannequin is lost by covering the mannequin with a skin. Thus, any utilitarian aspect of the mannequin exists "merely to portray the appearance" of the animal.

[*Superior Form Builders, Inc. v. Dan Chase Taxidermy Supply Co., Inc.*, 74 F.3d 488, 494 (4th Cir. 1996); *see also* [*Hart v. Dan Chase Taxidermy Supply Co., Inc.*, 86 F.3d 320, 323 (2d Cir. 1996)] ("The function of the fish form is to portray its own appearance, and that fact is enough to bring it within the scope of the Copyright Act."). Consequently, in Pivot Point's view, because the Mara mannequin performs functions similar to those of animal and fish mannequins, it is not a useful article and is therefore entitled to full copyright protection.

Charlene presents us with a different view. It suggests that, unlike the animal mannequins at issue in *Superior Form Builders* and in *Hart,* the Mara mannequin does have a useful function other than portraying an image of a high-fashion runway model. According to Charlene, Mara also is marketed and used for practicing the art of makeup application. Charlene points to various places in the record that establish that Mara is used for this purpose and is, therefore, a useful article subject to the limiting language of §101.

Pivot Point strongly disputes that the record establishes such a use and argues that the district court's reliance on Charlene's alleged proof improperly resolves an issue of fact against the non-moving party in contravention of Federal Rule of Civil Procedure 56. Indeed, our own review of the record leads us to believe that many of the documents cited by Charlene are susceptible to more than one interpretation.

Nevertheless, we shall assume that the district court correctly ruled that Mara is a useful article and proceed to examine whether, despite that usefulness, it is amenable to copyright protection.

### 2. Separability

We return to the statutory language. A useful article falls within the definition of pictorial, graphic or sculptural works "*only if, and only to the extent that, such design incorporates pictorial, graphic, or sculptural features that can be identified separately from, and are capable of existing independently of, the utilitarian aspects of the article.*" 17 U.S.C. §101.[6] It is common ground between the parties and, indeed, among the courts that have examined the issue, that this language, added by the 1976 Act, was intended to distinguish creative works that enjoy protection from elements of industrial design that do not. *See* H.R. Rep. No. 94-1476, at 55 (1976), *reprinted in* 1976 U.S.C.C.A.N. 5659, 5668 (stating that the purpose behind this language was "to draw as clear a line as possible between copyrightable works of applied art and uncopyrighted works of industrial design"). Although the Congressional goal was evident, application of this language has presented the courts with significant difficulty. Indeed, one scholar has noted: "Of the many fine lines that run through the Copyright Act, none is more troublesome than the line between protectible pictorial, graphic and sculptural works and unprotectible utilitarian elements of industrial design." Paul Goldstein, 1 *Copyright* §2.5.3, at 2:56 (2d ed. 2004).

The difficulty in the application of this language would not have come, in all likelihood, as a surprise to the Congressional drafters. The language employed by Congress is not the language of a bright-line rule of universal application. Indeed, the circuits that have addressed the interpretative problem now before us uniformly have recognized that the wording of the statute does not supply categorical direction, but rather requires the Copyright Office and the courts "to continue their efforts to distinguish applied art and industrial design." Robert C. Denicola, *Applied Art & Industrial Design: A Suggested Approach to Copyright in Useful Articles*, 67 MINN. L. REV. 707, 730 (1983). In short, no doubt well-aware of the myriad of factual scenarios to which its policy guidance would have to be applied, Congress wisely chose to provide only general policy guidance to be implemented on a case-by-case basis through the Copyright Office and the courts.

Even though the words of the statute do not yield a definitive answer, we believe that the statutory language nevertheless provides significant guidance in our task. We therefore shall examine in more detail what that language has to tell us, and we return to the necessary starting point of our task, §101.

The statutory language provides that "the design of a useful article . . . shall be considered a pictorial, graphic, or sculptural work only if, and only

---

6. Prior to the addition of this language in the 1976 Act, Congress had not explicitly authorized the Copyright Office to register "useful articles." Indeed, when Congress first extended copyright protection to three-dimensional works of art in 1870, copyright protection was limited to objects of fine art; objects of applied art still were not protected. *See* Paul Goldstein, 1 *Copyright* §2.5.3 at 2:58 (2d ed. 2004). This changed with the adoption of the Copyright Act of 1909 ("1909 Act"); Professor Goldstein explains:

> The 1909 Act, which continued protection for three-dimensional works of art, dropped the requirement that they constitute fine art and thus opened the door to protection of useful works of art. In 1948, the Copyright Office broadened the scope of protection for three-dimensional works of art to cover "works of artistic craftsmanship insofar as their form but not their utilitarian aspects are concerned." The United States Supreme Court upheld this interpretation in *Mazer v. Stein,* . . . holding that the fact that statuettes in issue were intended for use in articles of manufacture — electric lamp bases — did not bar them from copyright. Five years later, in 1959, the Copyright Office promulgated a rule that if "the sole intrinsic function of an article is its utility, the fact that the work is unique and attractively shaped will not qualify it as a work of art." The regulation did, however, permit registration of features of a utilitarian article that "can be identified separately and are capable of existing independently as a work of art."

*Id.* (quoting 37 C.F.R. §207.8(a) (1949) and 37 C.F.R. §202.10(c) (1959); footnotes omitted).

to the extent that, such design incorporates pictorial, graphic, or sculptural features *that can be identified separately from and are capable of existing independently of, the utilitarian* aspects of the article." Although the italicized clause contains two operative phrases—"*can be identified separately from*" and "*are capable of existing independently of*"—we believe, as have the other courts that have grappled with this issue, that Congress, in amending the statute, intended these two phrases to state a single, integrated standard to determine when there is sufficient separateness between the utilitarian and artistic aspects of a work to justify copyright protection.

Certainly, one approach to determine whether material can be "identified separately," and the most obvious, is to rely on the capacity of the artistic material to be severed physically from the industrial design. *See Mazer v. Stein*, 347 U.S. 201 (1954). . . . When a three-dimensional article is the focus of the inquiry, reliance on physical separability can no doubt be a helpful tool in ascertaining whether the artistic material in question can be separated from the industrial design. As Professor Denicola points out, however, such an approach really is not of much use when the item in question is two-dimensional. *See* Denicola, *supra,* at 744. Indeed, because this provision, by its very words, was intended to apply to two-dimensional material, it is clear that a physical separability test cannot be the exclusive test for determining copyrightability.

It seems to be common ground between the parties and, indeed, among the courts and commentators, that the protection of the copyright statute also can be secured when a conceptual separability exists between the material sought to be copyrighted and the utilitarian design in which that material is incorporated.[8]

---

8. Although the district court was skeptical that the statutory language encompassed both physical and conceptual separability, circuits have been almost unanimous in interpreting the language of §101 to include both types of separability. *See Superior Form Builders, Inc. v. Dan Chase Taxidermy Supply Co., Inc.*, 74 F.3d 488, 494 (4th Cir. 1996) (asking whether functional aspects of animal mannequins are "conceptually separable from the works' sculptural features"); *Brandir Int'l, Inc. v. Cascade Pac. Lumber Co.*, 834 F.2d 1142, 1144 (2d Cir. 1987) (stating that "'[c]onceptual separability' is alive and well"); *Carol Barnhart Inc. v. Econ. Cover Corp.*, 773 F.2d 411, 418 (2d Cir. 1985) (judging copyrightability of mannequin torsos based on whether "forms possess aesthetic or artistic features that are physically or conceptually separable from the forms' use as utilitarian objects to display clothes"); *Norris Indus., Inc. v. Int'l Tel. & Tel. Corp.*, 696 F.2d 918, 923 (11th Cir. 1983) ("Both case law and legislative history indicate that separability encompasses works of art that are either physically severable from the utilitarian article or conceptually severable."); *Kieselstein-Cord v. Accessories by Pearl, Inc.*, 632 F.2d 989, 993 (2d Cir. 1980) (applying test of conceptual separability).

Only one appellate court has rejected the idea of conceptual separability. *See Esquire, Inc. v. Ringer*, 591 F.2d 796 (D.C. Cir. 1978). In that case, arising under the 1909 Act, the Copyright Office had refused to register a design for outdoor lighting fixtures. The district court, however, believed the fixtures were copyrightable and issued a writ of mandamus that the copyright issue. However, the D.C. Circuit reversed.

The precise question before the court was whether the regulation implementing the 1909 Act mandated that the Copyright Office register a copyright for the lighting fixtures. The regulation at issue provided:

(c) If the sole intrinsic function of an article is its utility, the fact that the article is unique and attractively shaped will not qualify it as a work of art. However, if the shape of a utilitarian article incorporates features, such as artistic sculpture, carving, or pictorial representation, which can be identified separately and are capable of existing independently as a work of art, such features will be eligible for registration.

## B. "Pictorial, Graphic and Sculptural Works": Useful Articles and the Separability Doctrine

As is evident from the passages set forth above, the issue addressed by the D.C. Circuit in *Esquire* arose in a much different procedural and legal environment than the issue in the present case. The court's focus in *Esquire* was a regulation adopted pursuant to the former law and its obligation to defer to the agency's interpretation of the law embodied in that regulation. Furthermore, the court acknowledged that the 1976 Act was "not applicable to the case before" it. *Id.* at 803. Given these differences, we do not believe that the D.C. Circuit would conclude that its decision in *Esquire* disposed of the issue of conceptual separability presently before this court.

The difficulty lies not in the acceptance of that proposition, which the statutory language clearly contemplates, but in its application. As noted by Pivot Point, the following tests have been suggested for determining when the artistic and utilitarian aspects of useful articles are conceptually separable: 1) the artistic features are "primary" and the utilitarian features "subsidiary," *Kieselstein-Cord,* 632 F.2d at 993; 2) the useful article "would still be marketable to some significant segment of the community simply because of its aesthetic qualities," Melville B. Nimmer & David Nimmer, 1 *Nimmer on Copyright* §2.08[B][3], at 2-101 (2004); 3) the article "stimulate[s] in the mind of the beholder a concept that is separate from the concept evoked by its utilitarian function," *Carol Barnhart,* 773 F.2d at 422 (Newman, J., dissenting); 4) the artistic design was not significantly influenced by functional considerations, *see Brandir Int'l,* 834 F.2d at 1145 (adopting the test forwarded in Denicola, *supra,* at 741); 5) the artistic features "can stand alone as a work of art traditionally conceived, and . . . the useful article in which it is embodied would be equally useful without it," Goldstein, 1 *Copyright* §2.5.3, at 2:67; and 6) the artistic features are not utilitarian, *see* William F. Patry, 1 *Copyright Law & Practice* 285 (1994).

Pivot Point submits that "the test for conceptual separability should reflect the focus of copyright law — the artistic, not the marketability, design process,

---

*Id.* at 800 (quoting 37 C.F.R. §202.10(b) (1976)). The Copyright Office took the position that the regulation barred "copyright registration for the overall shape or configuration of a utilitarian article, no matter how aesthetically pleasing that shape or configuration may be." *Id.* In determining whether to accept or reject the proffered interpretation, the court noted that "[c]onsiderable weight is to be given to an agency's interpretation of its regulations," especially when "an administrative interpretation relates to a matter within the field of administrative expertise." *Id.* at 801. The court concluded that the Copyright Office had adopted a "reasonable and well-supported interpretation of §202.10(c)." *Id.* at 800. In the court's view, the interpretation was grounded in "the principle that industrial designs are not eligible for copyright." *Id.* The court also believed that the interpretation found support in the legislative history of the newly enacted 1976 Act. The court acknowledged, however, that the legislative history was not "free from ambiguity"; it explained:

> Esquire could arguably draw some support from the statement that a protectable element of a utilitarian article must be separable "physically *or conceptually*" from the utilitarian aspects of the design. But any possible ambiguity raised by this isolated reference disappears when the excerpt is considered in its entirety. The underscored passages indicate unequivocally that the overall design or configuration of a utilitarian object, even if it is determined by aesthetic as well as functional considerations, is not eligible for copyright. Thus the legislative history, taken as congressional understanding of existing law, reinforces the Register's position.

*Id.* at 803-04.

or usefulness." According to Pivot Point, the central inquiry is whether the article is a " 'work of art.' " Pivot Point further explains:

> Conceptual separability would inhere in a "work of art" integrated into a useful article, or a "work of art" put to unexpected use, since the independent concepts of art and utility coexist. Conceptual separability would not exist in a useful article rendered simply aesthetically pleasing, since the independent concept of art does not exist, only the "artistic" embellishment to its utility, so that such "artistic" features are actually utilitarian. Should the "artistic" embellishment of utility reach the level of a "work of art," however, conceptual separability may exist.

*Id.* at 26-27. This test, Pivot Point suggests, has the additional benefit of "satisf[ying] most, if not all, of the current definitions of conceptual separability." *Id.* at 27.

Charlene, by contrast, lauds the district court's adoption of Professor Goldstein's test. "Under Goldstein's test," Charlene asserts, " 'a pictorial, graphic or sculptural feature incorporated in the design of a useful article is conceptually separable if it can stand on its own as a work of art traditionally conceived, and if the useful article in which it is embodied would be *equally* useful without it.' " Charlene contends that this approach mirrors that adopted by the majority in *Carol Barnhart Inc. v. Economy Cover Corp.*, 773 F.2d 411 (2d Cir. 1985), "the most closely related precedent to the case at bar."

Although both sides present thoughtful explanations for their proposed tests, we perceive shortcomings in the parties' choices. With respect to Pivot Point's focus on the article as a "work of art," it is certainly correct that Congress, in enacting §101, attempted to separate the artistic from the utilitarian. However, this approach necessarily involves judges in a qualitative evaluation of artistic endeavors — a function for which judicial office is hardly a qualifier. With respect to the Charlene's approach, we believe that the test, at least when applied alone, is tied too closely to physical separability and, consequently, does not give a sufficiently wide berth to Congress' determination that artistic material conceptually separate from the utilitarian design can satisfy the statutory mandate.

In articulating a meaningful approach to conceptual separability, we note that we are not the first court of appeals to deal with this problem. The work of our colleagues in the other circuits provides significant insights into our understanding of Congressional intent. Indeed, even when those judges have disagreed on the appropriate application of the Congressional mandate to the case before them, their insights yield a bountiful harvest for those of us who now walk the same interpretative path.

Among the circuits, the Court of Appeals for the Second Circuit has had occasion to wrestle most comprehensively with the notion of "conceptual separability." Its case law represents, we believe, an intellectual journey that has explored the key aspects of the problem. We therefore turn to a study of the key stages of doctrinal development in its case law.

a.

The Second Circuit first grappled with the issue of conceptual separability in *Kieselstein-Cord v. Accessories by Pearl, Inc.*, 632 F.2d 989 (2d Cir. 1980). In that case, Kieselstein-Cord, a jewelry designer, had created a line of decorative and jeweled belt buckles inspired by works of art; he obtained copyright registrations for his designs. When the line was successful, Accessories by Pearl, Inc., ("Pearl") copied the designs and marketed its own, less-expensive versions of the belt buckles. Kieselstein-Cord then sued Pearl for copyright infringement; however, Pearl claimed that the belt buckles were not copyrightable because they were "'useful articles' with no 'pictorial, graphic, or sculptural features that can be identified separately from, and are capable of existing independently of, the utilitarian aspects' of the buckles." *Id.* at 991-92. The Second Circuit disagreed. Although it did not articulate a specific test for evaluating conceptual separability, it focused on the "primary" and "subsidiary" elements of the article and concluded:

> We see in appellant's belt buckles conceptually separable sculptural elements, as apparently have the buckles' wearers who have used them as ornamentation for parts of the body other than the waist. The primary ornamental aspect of the Vaquero and Winchester buckles is conceptually separable from their subsidiary utilitarian function. This conclusion is not at variance with the expressed congressional intent to distinguish copyrightable applied art and uncopyrightable industrial design. Pieces of applied art, these buckles may be considered jewelry, the form of which is subject to copyright protection.

*Id.* at 993 (internal citations omitted).

b.

The Second Circuit revisited the issue of conceptual separability in *Carol Barnhart Inc. v. Economy Cover Corp.*, 773 F.2d 411 (2d Cir. 1985). In that case, Carol Barnhart, a provider of retail display items, developed four mannequins consisting of human torsos for the display of shirts and jackets. It obtained copyright registrations for each of the forms.[10] When a competitor, Economy Cover, copied the designs, Carol Barnhart claimed infringement of that copyright. The Second Circuit held that the designs were not copyrightable. It explained:

> [W]hile copyright protection has increasingly been extended to cover articles having a utilitarian dimension, Congress has explicitly refused copyright protection for works of applied art or industrial design which have aesthetic or artistic features that cannot be identified separately from the useful article. Such works are not copyrightable regardless of the fact that they may be "aesthetically satisfying and valuable."
>
> Applying these principles, we are persuaded that since the aesthetic and artistic features of the Barnhart forms are inseparable from the forms' use as utilitarian articles the forms are not copyrightable. . . . [Barnhart] stresses that the forms have been responded to as sculptural forms, and have been used for purposes other than modeling clothes, e.g., as decorating props and signs without any clothing or accessories. While this may indicate that the forms are "aesthetically satisfying and valuable," it is insufficient to show that the forms possess aesthetic or artistic features that are physically or conceptually separable from the forms' use as utilitarian objects to display clothes. On the contrary, to the extent the forms possess aesthetically pleasing features, even

---

10. There were a total of four mannequins at issue, two male and two female. Of those four, two of the mannequin forms were unclothed, and two were formed with one layer of clothing and were meant specifically for the display of outerwear.

when these features are considered in the aggregate, they cannot be conceptualized as existing independently of their utilitarian function.

*Id.* at 418 (internal citations omitted). The court also rejected the argument that *Kieselstein-Cord* was controlling. The majority explained that what distinguished the Kieselstein-Cord buckles from the Barnhart forms was "that the ornamented surfaces of the buckles were not in any respect required by their functions; the artistic and aesthetic features would thus be conceived as having been added to, or superimposed upon, an otherwise utilitarian article." *Id.* at 419.

Perhaps the most theoretical and comprehensive discussion of "conceptual separability," as opposed to physical separability, can be found in the dissenting opinion of Judge Newman in *Carol Barnhart,* 773 F.2d at 419. After reviewing the possible ways to determine conceptual separability, Judge Newman set forth his choice and rationale:

> How, then, is "conceptual separateness" to be determined? In my view, the answer derives from the word "conceptual." For the design features to be "conceptually separate" from the utilitarian aspects of the useful article that embodies the design, the article must stimulate in the mind of the beholder a concept that is separate from the concept evoked by its utilitarian function. The test turns on what may reasonably be understood to be occurring in the mind of the beholder or, as some might say, in the "mind's eye" of the beholder. . . .
>
> . . .
>
> The "separateness" of the utilitarian and non-utilitarian concepts engendered by an article's design is itself a perplexing concept. I think the requisite "separateness" exists whenever the design creates in the mind of the ordinary observer two different concepts that are not inevitably entertained simultaneously. Again, the example of the artistically designed chair displayed in a museum may be helpful. The ordinary observer can be expected to apprehend the design of a chair whenever the object is viewed. He may, in addition, entertain the concept of a work of art, but, if this second concept is engendered in the observer's mind simultaneously with the concept of the article's utilitarian function, the requisite "separateness" does not exist. The test is not whether the observer fails to recognize the object as a chair but only whether the concept of the utilitarian function can be displaced in the mind by some other concept. That does not occur, at least for the ordinary observer, when viewing even the most artistically designed chair. It may occur, however, when viewing some other object if the utilitarian function of the object is not perceived at all; it may also occur, even when the utilitarian function is perceived by observation, perhaps aided by explanation, if the concept of the utilitarian function can be displaced in the observer's mind while he entertains the separate concept of some non-utilitarian function. The separate concept will normally be that of a work of art.

*Id.* at 422-23.

c.

The Second Circuit soon addressed conceptual separability again in *Brandir International, Inc. v. Cascade Pacific Lumber Co.*, 834 F.2d 1142 (2d Cir. 1987). That case involved the work of an artist, David Levine; specifically, Levine had created a sculpture of thick, interwoven wire. A cyclist friend of Levine's realized that the sculpture could, with modification, function as a bicycle rack and thereafter put Levine in touch with Brandir International, Inc. ("Brandir"). The artist and the Brandir engineers then worked to modify the sculpture to

## B. "Pictorial, Graphic and Sculptural Works": Useful Articles and the Separability Doctrine

produce a workable and marketable bicycle rack. Their work culminated in the "Ribbon Rack," which Brandir began marketing in 1979. Shortly thereafter, Cascade Pacific Lumber Co. ("Cascade") began selling a similar product, and, in response, Brandir applied for copyright protection and began placing copyright notices on its racks. The Copyright Office, however, rejected the registration on the ground that the rack did not contain any element that was "capable of independent existence as a copyrightable pictorial, graphic or sculptural work apart from the shape of the useful article." *Id.* at 1146.

The court first considered the possible tests for conceptual separability in light of its past decisions and, notably, attempted to reconcile its earlier attempts:

> Perhaps the differences between the majority and the dissent in *Carol Barnhart* might have been resolved had they had before them the Denicola article on *Applied Art and Industrial Design: A Suggested Approach to Copyright in Useful Articles,* [67 MINN. L. REV. 707 (1983)]. . . . Denicola argues that "the statutory directive requires a distinction between works of industrial design and works whose origins lie outside the design process, despite the utilitarian environment in which they appear." He views the statutory limitation of copyrightability as "an attempt to identify elements whose form and appearance reflect the unconstrained perspective of the artist," such features not being the product of industrial design. *Id.* at 742. "Copyrightability, therefore, should turn on the relationship between the proffered work and the process of industrial design." *Id.* at 741. He suggests that "the dominant characteristic of industrial design is the influence of nonaesthetic, utilitarian concerns" and hence concludes that copyrightability "ultimately should depend on the extent to which the work reflects artistic expression uninhibited by functional considerations." *Id.* To state the Denicola test in the language of conceptual separability, if design elements reflect a merger of aesthetic and functional considerations, the artistic aspects of a work cannot be said to be conceptually separable from the utilitarian elements. Conversely, where design elements can be identified as reflecting the designer's artistic judgment exercised independently of functional influences, conceptual separability exists.
>
> We believe that Professor Denicola's approach provides the best test for conceptual separability and, accordingly, adopt it here for several reasons. First, the approach is consistent with the holdings of our previous cases. In *Kieselstein-Cord,* for example, the artistic aspects of the belt buckles reflected purely aesthetic choices, independent of the buckles' function, while in *Carol Barnhart* the distinctive features of the torsos — the accurate anatomical design and the sculpted shirts and collars — showed clearly the influence of functional concerns. . . . Second, the test's emphasis on the influence of utilitarian concerns in the design process may help . . . "alleviate the de facto discrimination against nonrepresentational art that has regrettably accompanied much of the current analysis." *Id.* at 745.

*Id.* at 1145 (footnotes omitted).

Applying Professor Denicola's test to the Ribbon Rack, the court found that the rack was not copyrightable. The court stated that, "[h]ad Brandir merely adopted one of the existing sculptures as a bicycle rack, neither the application to a utilitarian end nor commercialization of that use would have caused the object to forfeit its copyrighted status." *Id.* at 1147. However, when the Ribbon Rack was compared to earlier sculptures, continued the court, it was "in its final form essentially a product of industrial design." *Id.*

> In creating the RIBBON Rack, the designer . . . clearly adapted the original aesthetic elements to accommodate and further a utilitarian purpose. These altered design features of the RIBBON Rack, including the space-saving, open design achieved by widening the upper loops . . . , the straightened vertical elements that allow in—and above—ground installation of the rack, the ability to fit all types of bicycles and mopeds, and the heavy-gauged tubular construction of rustproof galvanized steel, are all features that combine to make for a safe, secure, and maintenance-free system of parking bicycles and mopeds.
> . . .
> . . . While the RIBBON Rack may be worthy of admiration for its aesthetic qualities alone, it remains nonetheless the product of industrial design. Form and function are inextricably intertwined in the rack, its ultimate design being as much the result of utilitarian pressures as aesthetic choices. . . . Thus there remains no artistic element of the RIBBON Rack that can be identified as separate and "capable of existing independently, of, the utilitarian aspects of the article."

*Id.* at 1146-47.

d.

We believe that the experience of the Second Circuit is also reflected in the more recent encounter of the Fourth Circuit with the same problem. In *Superior Form Builders, Inc. v. Dan Chase Taxidermy Supply Co., Inc.*, 74 F.3d 488 (4th Cir. 1996), the court considered whether animal mannequins qualified for copyright protection. The Fourth Circuit first considered whether the mannequins were useful articles as defined by §101 and concluded that they were not:

> A mannequin provides the creative form and expression of the ultimate animal display. . . . Even though covered with a skin, the mannequin is not invisible but conspicuous in the final display. The angle of the animal's head, the juxtaposition of its body parts, and the shape of the body parts in the final display is little more than the portrayal of the underlying mannequin. . . . None of these expressive aspects of a mannequin is lost by covering the mannequin with a skin. Thus, any utilitarian aspect of the mannequin exists "merely to portray the appearance" of the animal. *See* 17 U.S.C. §101.
> . . . It is the portrayal of the animal's body expression given by the mannequin that is thus protectable under the Copyright Act. We therefore agree with the district court in this case because "the usefulness of the forms is their portrayal of the appearance of animals." The mannequin forms "by definition are not useful articles."

*Id.* at 494 (quoting *Superior Form Builders v. Dan Chase Taxidermy Supply Co., Inc.*, 851 F. Supp. 222, 223 (E.D. Va. 1994)).

The court, however, also considered whether, if useful, the utilitarian and aesthetic aspects of the mannequin were separable:

> To the extent that an argument can be made that the mannequins in this case perform a utilitarian function—other than portraying themselves—by supporting the mounted skins, we believe the function to be conceptually separable from the works' sculptural features. *See Brandir Int'l, Inc. v. Cascade Pac. Lumber Co.*, 834 F.2d 1142, 1145 (2d Cir. 1987) ("Where design elements can be identified as reflecting the designer's artistic judgment exercised

independently of functional influences, conceptual separability exists."); *Kieselstein-Cord v. Accessories by Pearl, Inc.*, 632 F.2d 989, 993 (2d Cir. 1980) (finding sculptural element of belt buckle conceptually separable from utilitarian function).

*Id.* Thus, without specifically adopting one of the tests of conceptual separability, the Fourth Circuit determined that artistic work put into the design of the animal frame was copyrightable; the fact that a skin was placed on the model and that the model, therefore, was useful in the display of the skin did not negate the artistic elements of the design.[11]

e.

There is one final Second Circuit case that bears comment. In *Mattel, Inc. v. Goldberger Doll Manufacturing Co.*, 365 F.3d 133 (2d Cir. 2004), the Second Circuit rejected the idea that a particular expression of features on a doll's face was not subject to copyright protection. The case arose out of the alleged copying of the facial features of Mattel's Barbie dolls by Goldberger Doll Manufacturing when creating its "Rockettes 2000" doll. On Goldberger's motion for summary judgment, the district court held that "copyright protection did not extend to Barbie's eyes, nose, and mouth. . . ." *Id.* at 134. The Second Circuit reversed. Although it did not speak specifically in terms of

---

11. Notably, in *Hart v. Dan Chase Taxidermy Supply Co.*, 86 F.3d 320 (2d Cir. 1996), the Second Circuit shortly thereafter addressed the question whether a fish mannequin was copyrightable. Although the court did not address specifically the issue before us today, its analysis is nevertheless helpful. Referring to its decision in *Carol Barnhart,* the Second Circuit posed the question rather simplistically: "Is taxidermy different [for purposes of copyright protection]?" *Id.* at 321. The Second Circuit resolved that it is:

> We do not agree that *Barnhart* mandates a finding that fish mannequins are "useful articles" undeserving of copyright protection. . . . [W]e do not believe that the *Barnhart* torsos can be analogized to the fish in this case. In *Barnhart,* the headless, armless, backless styrene torsos were little more than glorified coat-racks used to display clothing in stores. The torsos were designed to present the clothing, not their own forms. In taxidermy, by contrast, people look for more than a fish skin; they wish to see a complete "fish." The superficial characteristics of the fish, such as its color and texture, are admittedly conveyed by the skin, but the shape, volume, and movement of the animal are depicted by the underlying mannequin. Whether the fish is shown as resting, jumping, wiggling its tail, or preparing to munch on some plankton, is dictated by the mannequin and by its particular form, not by the skin.
> 
> In short, the fish mannequin is designed to be looked at. That the fish mannequin is meant to be viewed clothed by a fish skin, rather than naked and on its own, makes no difference. The function of the fish form is to portray its own appearance, and that fact is enough to bring it within the scope of the Copyright Act. 17 U.S.C. §101; *accord Superior Form Builders v. Dan Chase Taxidermy Supply Co.*, 74 F.3d 488 (4th Cir. 1996) (distinguishing *Barnhart* and holding that mammal taxidermy mannequins are "sculptural works" rather than "useful articles" because their utilitarian aspects serve "merely to portray the appearance" of the animal). . . .
> 
> We conclude that fish mannequins even if considered "useful articles," are useful insofar as they "portray the[ir] appearance." 17 U.S.C. §101. That makes them copyrightable.

*Id.* at 323 (internal citation omitted). Thus, the Second Circuit distinguished fish mannequins from human mannequins; however, it did so on the basis that the fish mannequins were not "useful articles" as that term is defined in §101, not on the basis that, although useful, the artistic aspects were physically or conceptually separable from the useful aspects of the article.

conceptual separability, the court's reasoning is nevertheless instructive; it stated:

> The proposition that standard or common features are not protected is inconsistent with copyright law. To merit protection from copying, a work need not be particularly novel or unusual. It need only have been "independently created" by the author and possess "some minimal degree of creativity." *Feist Publ'ns, Inc. v. Rural Tel. Serv. Co.*, 499 U.S. 340, 345 (1991). . . . There are innumerable ways of making upturned noses, bow lips, and widely spaced eyes. Even if the record had shown that many dolls possess upturned noses, bow lips, and wide-spread eyes, it would not follow that each such doll—assuming it was independently created and not copied from others—would not enjoy protection from copying.

*Id.* at 135 (footnotes and parallel citations omitted). Additionally, the court noted the scope of the copyright protection that the Barbie dolls enjoyed:

> The copyright does not protect ideas; it protects only the author's particularized expression of the idea. Thus, Mattel's copyright in a doll visage with an upturned nose, bow lips, and widely spaced eyes will not prevent a competitor from making dolls with upturned noses, bow lips, and widely spaced eyes, even if the competitor has taken the idea from Mattel's example, so long as the competitor has not copied Mattel's particularized expression. An upturned nose, bow lips, and wide eyes are the "idea" of a certain type of doll face. That idea belongs not to Mattel but to the public domain. But Mattel's copyright will protect its own particularized expression of that idea and bar a competitor from copying Mattel's realization of the Barbie features.

*Id.* at 136 (citations omitted).

### C. Application

Each of these cases differs in the object at issue and the method by which the court evaluated whether the object was entitled to copyright protection. Yet, each court attempted to give effect to "the expressed congressional intent to distinguish copyrightable applied art and uncopyrightable industrial design." *Kieselstein-Cord*, 632 F.2d at 993; *see also Carol Barnhart*, 773 F.2d at 417-18 (reviewing legislative history in detail and concluding that, although "copyright protection has increasingly been extended to cover articles having a utilitarian dimension," Congress did not intend all useful articles that are "aesthetically satisfying or valuable" to be copyrightable); *Brandir Int'l*, 834 F.2d at 1145 (adopting Professor Denicola's test that makes copyrightability dependent upon "the extent to which the work reflects artistic expression uninhibited by functional considerations" (internal quotation marks and citations omitted)); *Superior Form Builders*, 74 F.3d at 494 (distinguishing the animal mannequins at issue from "aesthetically pleasing articles of industrial design").

The Second Circuit cases exhibit a progressive attempt to forge a workable judicial approach capable of giving meaning to the basic Congressional policy decision to distinguish applied art from uncopyrightable industrial art or design. In *Kieselstein-Cord*, the Second Circuit attempted to distinguish artistic expression from industrial design by focusing on the present use of the item, i.e., the "primary ornamental aspect" versus the "subsidiary utilitarian function" of the object at issue. 632 F.2d at 993. In *Carol Barnhart,* the Second Circuit moved closer to a process-oriented approach:

> What distinguishes those [Kieselstein-Cord] buckles from the Barnhart forms is that the ornamented surfaces of the buckles were not in any respect required by their utilitarian functions; the artistic and aesthetic features could thus be conceived of as having been added to, or superimposed upon, an otherwise utilitarian article. The unique artistic design was wholly unnecessary to performance of the utilitarian function. In the case of the Barnhart forms, on the other hand, the features claimed to be aesthetic or artistic, e.g., the life-size configuration of the breasts and the width of the shoulders, are inextricably intertwined with the utilitarian feature, the display of clothes. Whereas a model of a human torso, in order to serve its utilitarian function, must have some configuration of the chest and some width of shoulders, a belt buckle can serve its function satisfactorily without any ornamentation of the type that renders the Kieselstein-Cord buckles distinctive.

773 F.2d at 419. Thus, it was the fact that the creator of the torsos was driven by utilitarian concerns, such as how display clothes would fit on the end product, that deprived the human torsos of copyright protection.

This process-oriented approach for conceptual separability—focusing on the process of creating the object to determine whether it is entitled to copyright protection—is more fully articulated in *Brandir* and indeed reconciles the earlier case law pertaining to conceptual separability.

> [T]he approach is consistent with the holdings of our previous cases. In *Kieselstein-Cord,* for example, the artistic aspects of the belt buckles reflected purely aesthetic choices, independent of the buckles' function, while in *Carol Barnhart* the distinctive features of the torsos—the accurate anatomical design and the sculpted shirts and collars—showed clearly the influence of functional concerns. Though the torsos bore artistic features, it was evident the designer incorporated those features to further the usefulness of the torsos as mannequins.

*Brandir,* 834 F.2d at 1145.

Furthermore, *Brandir* is not inconsistent with the more theoretical rendition of Judge Newman in his *Carol Barnhart* dissent—that "the requisite 'separateness' exists whenever the design creates in the mind of an ordinary observer two different concepts that are not inevitably entertained simultaneously." 773 F.2d at 422. When a product has reached its final form as a result of predominantly functional or utilitarian considerations, it necessarily will be more difficult for the observer to entertain simultaneously two different concepts—the artistic object and the utilitarian object. In such circumstances, *Brandir* has the added benefit of providing a more workable judicial methodology by articulating the driving principle behind conceptual separability—the influence of industrial design. When the ultimate form of the object in question is "as much the result of utilitarian pressures as aesthetic choices," "[f]orm and function are inextricably intertwined," and the artistic aspects of the object cannot be separated from its utilitarian aspects for purposes of copyright protection. *Brandir,* 834 F.2d at 1147.

Conceptual separability exists, therefore, when the artistic aspects of an article can be "conceptualized as existing independently of their utilitarian function." *Carol Barnhart*, 773 F.2d at 418. This independence is necessarily informed by "whether the design elements can be identified as reflecting the designer's artistic judgment exercised independently of functional influences." *Brandir*, 834 F.2d at 1145. If the elements do reflect the independent, artistic judgment of the designer, conceptual separability exists. Conversely, when the design of a useful article is "as much the result of utilitarian pressures as aesthetic choices," *id.* at 1147, the useful and aesthetic elements are not conceptually separable.

Applying this test to the Mara mannequin, we must conclude that the Mara face is subject to copyright protection. It certainly is not difficult to conceptualize a human face, independent of all of Mara's specific facial features, i.e., the shape of the eye, the upturned nose, the angular cheek and jaw structure, that would serve the utilitarian functions of a hair stand and, if proven, of a makeup model. Indeed, one is not only able to conceive of a different face than that portrayed on the Mara mannequin, but one easily can conceive of another visage that portrays the "hungry look" on a high-fashion runway model. Just as Mattel is entitled to protection for "its own particularized expression" of an "upturned nose[], bow lips, and widely spaced eyes," *Mattel*, 365 F.3d at 136, so too is Heerlein (and, therefore, Pivot Point as assignee of the copyright registration) entitled to have his expression of the "hungry look" protected from copying.

Mara can be conceptualized as existing independent from its use in hair display or make-up training because it is the product of Heerlein's artistic judgment. When Passage approached Heerlein about creating the Mara sculpture, Passage did not provide Heerlein with specific dimensions or measurements; indeed, there is no evidence that Heerlein's artistic judgment was constrained by functional considerations. Passage did not require, for instance, that the sculpture's eyes be a certain width to accommodate standard-sized eyelashes, that the brow be arched at a certain angle to facilitate easy make-up application or that the sculpture as a whole not exceed certain dimensional limits so as to fit within Pivot Point's existing packaging system. Such considerations, had they been present, would weigh against a determination that Mara was purely the product of an artistic effort. By contrast, after Passage met with Heerlein to discuss Passage's idea for a "hungry-look" model, Heerlein had carte blanche to implement that vision as he saw fit. Consequently, this is not a situation, such as was presented to the Second Circuit in *Carol Barnhart*, in which certain features ("accurate anatomical design and the sculpted shirts and collars") were included in the design for purely functional reasons. *Brandir*, 834 F.2d at 1145. Furthermore, unlike "the headless, armless, backless styrene torsos" which "were little more than glorified coat-racks used to display clothing in stores," *Hart*, 86 F.3d at 323, the creative aspects of the Mara sculpture were meant to be seen and admired. Thus, because Mara was the product of a creative process unfettered by functional concerns, its sculptural features "can be identified separately from, and are capable of existing independently of," its utilitarian aspects. It therefore meets the requirements for conceptual separability and is subject to copyright protection.

## B. "Pictorial, Graphic and Sculptural Works": Useful Articles and the Separability Doctrine

Conclusion

The Mara mannequin is subject to copyright protection. We therefore must reverse the summary judgment in favor of Charlene Products and Mr. Yau; the case is remanded for a trial on Pivot Point's infringement claim. Furthermore, because Charlene Products and Mr. Yau have not prevailed on the merits at this point, the judgment of the district court with respect to attorneys' fees must be vacated. The cross-appeal with respect to attorneys' fees is moot. Pivot Point may recover its costs in this court.

[*Reversed and remanded.*]

KANNE, Circuit Judge, dissenting:

Writing for the majority, Judge Ripple has applied his usual thorough and scholarly approach to this difficult intellectual property problem; however, I cannot join the majority opinion because I am not persuaded that the "Mara" mannequin is copyrightable. All functional items have aesthetic qualities. If copyright provided protection for functional items simply because of their aesthetic qualities, Congress's policy choice that gives less protection in patent than copyright would be undermined. [cit.]

[Judge Kanne asserted that regardless of whether Section 101's useful article provision called for physical separability, conceptual separability, or both, Mara was uncopyrightable.]

Taking physical separability first, the district court used examples from case law to illustrate that the sculptural features in many useful items can be physically removed from the object and sold separately without affecting the functionality of the useful article. *See, e.g., Mazer v. Stein*, 347 U.S. 201 (1954) (holding that a sculpture of a dancer carved into the base of a lamp may be copyrighted); *Kieselstein-Cord v. Accessories by Pearl, Inc.*, 632 F.2d 989 (2d Cir. 1980) (holding that decorative belt buckles could be copyrighted as separate objects sold not to hold up one's pants).

Mara, on the other hand, has only functional attributes. Thus, any physical separation of a portion of her would not be independent of her utilitarian aspects. She is sold to beauty schools as a teaching device; students style her hair and apply makeup as realistic training for such pursuits on live subjects. A mannequin head without a neck, or with different eyes and musculature, would not serve the utilitarian purpose of applying makeup or teaching the art of matching hair styles to facial features. As the district court explained: "Beauty students style hair to flatter the face, not to be worn on featureless ovoids. The use of a mannequin head in training students of beauty schools *lies in its aesthetic qualities.*" There is nothing in Mara that we could physically remove that would not be part of Mara's utility as a teaching aid. Like mannequins of human torsos, *Carol Barnhart Inc. v. Economy Cover Corp.*, 773 F.2d 411, 418-19 (2d Cir. 1985), mannequins of human faces are not physically separable from their functional purpose and are therefore not copyrightable.

[As for conceptual separability, Judge Kanne concluded that Mara failed the Goldstein conceptual separability test.] Mara has no conceptually separable features to which copyright protection could be granted. Her features are incapable of being identified separately from the utilitarian use of those features. Without features, the mannequin's head and neck would be little more than an egg on a stick, useless for its intended purpose. . . .

. . .

Problematically, the majority's test for conceptual separability seems to bear little resemblance to the statute. The statute asks two questions: Does the useful article incorporate "sculptural features that can be identified separately from the utilitarian aspects" of the article? And are these features "capable of existing independently" from the utilitarian aspects? The copyright statute is concerned with protecting only non-utilitarian features of the useful article. To be copyrightable, the statute requires that the useful article's functionality remain intact once the copyrightable material is separated. In other words, Pivot Point needs to show that Mara's face is not a utilitarian "aspect" of the product "Mara," but rather a separate non-utilitarian "feature." The majority, by looking only to whether the features could also "be conceptualized as existing independently of *their utilitarian function*" and ignoring the more important question of whether the features themselves are utilitarian *aspects* of the useful article, mistakenly presupposes that utilitarian aspects of a useful article can be copyrighted. If we took away Mara's facial features, her functionality would be greatly diminished or eliminated, thus proving that her features cannot be copyrighted.

Moreover, the "process-oriented approach" advocated by the majority drifts even further away from the statute. The statute looks to the useful article as it exists, not to how it was created. I believe it simply is irrelevant to inquire into the origins of Mara's eyes, cheekbones, and neck. If such features have been fully incorporated as functional aspects of the mannequin, then copyright does not provide protection. Even if we were to look at the "process" that led to the creation of Mara, it is undeniable that, from the beginning, Pivot Point intended Mara to serve a functional purpose and commissioned her creation to fulfill that purpose (not to create a work of art for aesthetic beauty).

The majority, as evidenced by its emphasis on the fact that Charlene Products apparently copied Mara with its doll, "Liza," seems unduly concerned in this context with Charlene's questionable business practices. This is immaterial to the determination of whether the Mara doll is protected by copyright law. Importantly, other possible legal protections for Pivot Point's intellectual property—design patent, trademark, trade dress, and state unfair competition law—are available to address the majority's concerns. Copyright does not protect functional products. Charlene is free, under its own brand name, to copy and sell copies of useful articles that do not have patent protection. *See, e.g.,* [*TrafFix Devices; Bonito Boats*; and *Sears, Roebuck & Co. v. Stiffel*]. I fear that the majority's opinion grants copyright protection to functional aspects of a useful article. I would, therefore, affirm the district court's grant of summary judgment in favor of Charlene Products and Mr. Yau.

## NOTES AND QUESTIONS

1. ***The concept of the "useful article."*** At Halloween, and other times when the mood strikes us, the two of us (Dinwoodie and Janis) wander around

campus dressed in various types of "buddy" costumes (for example, the Men in Black; Ernie and Bert of Muppets fame; the Blues Brothers; two sausage mascots from the sausage races at Milwaukee Brewers baseball games; and Ted Kennedy and Newt Gingrich). You can find pictures on Professor Dinwoodie's Facebook page. (Actually not.) Last week, we appeared as superheros—Janis as Batman, Dinwoodie as Spiderman. The Batman costume consisted of a bat mask and a bat jumpsuit (with belt, gloves, boots, and of course, cape). Is the Batman costume a "useful article"? Or is its only function to portray itself—such that it is effectively a cloth sculpture not subject to the separability requirement? Does your answer depend on our subjective purposes for using the costumes? Would you reach one result for the mask and a different result for the rest of the costume? *See* the Copyright Office's Policy Decision on the Registrability of Costume Designs, 56 Fed. Reg. 56530 (Nov. 5, 1991) (distinguishing between masks and costumes); *see also Masquerade Novelty, Inc. v. Unique Indus.*, 912 F.2d 663 (3d Cir. 1990) (regarding nose masks); *Whimsicality, Inc. v. Rubie's Costume Co.*, 891 F.2d 452 (2d Cir. 1989) (regarding costumes). If you distinguish between the mask and the rest of the costume, how would you apply that approach to Dinwoodie's Spiderman outfit, which is a one-piece thing covering him from head to toe? What are the implications for copyright protection of more conventional fashion designs? Recall the *Wal-Mart* decision discussed in Chapter 2; consider how you would analyze the copyrightability of the designs at issue there. For another example involving unusual subject matter, see *Spinmaster Ltd. v. Overbreak, LLC*, 404 F. Supp. 2d 1097 (N.D. Ill. 2005) (remote-controlled flying saucer toy not a useful article).

2. ***The separability doctrine and channeling.*** Legislative proposals leading to the 1976 Copyright Act had included a separate title (Title II) devoted to design protection. In that scheme, the separability doctrine operated as a channeling mechanism, policing the boundary between design protection under Title II and traditional copyright protection. Ultimately, Congress dropped Title II but retained the separability doctrine. Should the doctrine be interpreted in light of this history? If so, how would the doctrine differ from the current approach (or approaches)?

3. ***Separability: a further example.*** How would you apply the separability analysis from *Pivot Point* to a design for measuring spoons in which the bowl of each spoon is shaped like a heart, and the handle is shaped like the feathers and shaft of an arrow? *See Bonazoli v. R.S.V.P. Int'l, Inc.*, 353 F. Supp. 2d 218 (D.R.I. 2005). The issue arises in design cases involving many industries. *See, e.g., Universal Furniture v. Collezione Europe USA*, 2007 WL 2712926 (M.D.N.C. 2007) (furniture); *Eliya v. Kohls Dept. Stores*, 2006 WL 2645196 (S.D.N.Y. 2006) (shoes); *Conwest Resources v. Playtime Novelties*, 2006 WL 3346226 (N.D. Cal. 2006) (adult novelty items).

4. ***Scope of rights in PGS works.*** As we will discuss in Section C below, section 106 of the Copyright Act defines the copyright owner's exclusive rights, but Section 113 elaborates on those rights for PGS works. Section 113(a) states that "[s]ubject to the provisions of subsections (b) and (c) of this section, the exclusive right to reproduce a copyrighted pictorial, graphic, or sculptural work in copies under section 106, includes the right to

reproduce the work in or on any kind of article, whether useful or otherwise." The last clause, referencing articles "useful or otherwise," is intended to incorporate the rule from *Mazer v. Stein*. See H.R. Rep. 94-1476, 94th Cong. 2d Sess. (1976).

    5. *The Section 113(b) limitation.* Suppose that Prof. Janis makes detailed technical drawings depicting a luxury sports car (with convertible top). Prof. Dinwoodie begins building cars identical to the one depicted in the drawings. Has Prof. Dinwoodie infringed the copyright in Prof. Janis's drawings? *See* 17 U.S.C. §113(b); *see also* H.R. 94-1476, 94th Cong. 2d Sess. (1976). For a comparative reference, see *British Leyland v. Armstrong Patents*, 1986 All E.R. 850 (H.L.), *overruled legislatively*, Copyright, Designs, and Patents Act 1988 §§51-52.

    6. *Copyright protection for typefaces.* Consider the design of the typeface of this book—or the many font designs available in a typical word-processing program. Should those designs be copyrightable? The answer has been no. *See Eltra Corp. v. Ringer*, 579 F.2d 294 (4th Cir. 1978) (typeface not a copyrightable work under 1909 Copyright Act); *see also* H.R. Rep. 94-1476, 94th Cong. 2d Sess. (1976) (stating that the House Committee "does not regard the design of typeface . . . to be a copyrightable 'pictorial, graphic, or sculptural work' within the meaning of [the 1976 Act]"). But *cf. Adobe Sys. Inc. v. Southern Software Inc.*, 45 U.S.P.Q.2d (BNA) 1827 (N.D. Cal. 1998) (software code generating typeface is copyrightable). Is this a sensible approach to the copyrightability of typeface design?

## C. SCOPE OF COPYRIGHT PROTECTION

In this section, we turn to matters of copyright scope—in particular, the rules of copyright infringement, and defenses to infringement. Many of the rules of infringement, and the rules pertaining to the major defense (fair use), have been developed through the case law. However, it will be useful to keep in mind a few relevant statutory provisions:

> **17 U.S.C. §106** defines the copyright owner's exclusive rights of reproduction, adaptation, distribution, public performance, public display, and digital performance. The Section 106(1) right to exclude others from reproducing the work in copies is, of course, the core right among the copyright owner's bundle of rights.
>
> **17 U.S.C. §501(a)** states that anyone who violates any one of the exclusive rights enumerated in Section 106 is an infringer.
>
> **17 U.S.C. §107** codifies the fair use defense and establishes four factors for courts to consider in assessing claims of fair use.
>
> **17 U.S.C. §§108-122** establish numerous limitations on and exemptions to the copyright owner's exclusive rights. Most pertinent for our purposes are the limitations on the scope of rights in PGS works (Section 113) and in architectural works (Section 120), which we will study later in this chapter.

## 1. COPYRIGHT INFRINGEMENT

We now turn to the law of copyright infringement. To demonstrate infringement, the owner of a valid copyright must show (1) that the defendant copied the protected work and (2) that the copying constitutes an improper appropriation. The first prong, copying, can be shown by direct evidence or, more typically, by circumstantial evidence—in particular, evidence that defendant had access to the work and that the defendant's work is similar enough to the copyrighted work to negate an inference of independent creation. This latter element is sometimes referred to as "probative" similarity to connote a level of similarity sufficient to be probative of copying.

The second prong, improper appropriation, also calls for evidence of similarity and is sometimes called a requirement of "substantial similarity." Here, the copyright owner must show that the defendant appropriated enough of the protectable elements of the copyrighted work to justify a conclusion that the works are substantially similar. Where the defendant has copied verbatim from the plaintiff's work, there is no mystery in assessing substantial similarity. Where the defendant has not copied verbatim, the similarity analysis can be difficult. As we have seen, visual comparisons of designs frequently challenge the courts. In the *Peter Pan Fabrics* case below, Learned Hand offers his views on the standard for conducting such a visual comparison.

### PETER PAN FABRICS, INC. v. MARTIN WEINER CORP.
274 F.2d 487 (2d Cir. 1960)

HAND, Circuit Judge:

This is an appeal from a preliminary injunction . . . forbidding the defendant to copy an ornamental design, printed upon cloth. [Plaintiff and defendant] are both "converters" of textiles, used in the manufacture of women's dresses. A "converter" buys uncolored cloth upon which he prints ornamental designs, and which he then sells to dressmakers. The plaintiffs bought from a Parisian designer a design, known as "Byzantium," which it registered [in the U.S. Copyright Office]. This design they print upon uncolored cloth, sold in bolts to dressmakers. [The court turned to the issue of whether defendant infringed plaintiff's copyright.]

The test for infringement of a copyright is of necessity vague. In the case of verbal "works" it is well settled that although the "proprietor's" monopoly extends beyond an exact reproduction of the words, there can be no copyright in the "ideas" disclosed but only in their "expression." Obviously, no principle can be stated as to when an imitator has gone beyond copying the "idea," and has borrowed its "expression." Decisions must therefore inevitably be ad hoc. In the case of designs, which are addressed to the aesthetic sensibilities of an observer, the test is, if possible, even more intangible. No one disputes that the copyright extends beyond a photographic reproduction of the design, but one cannot say how far an imitator must depart from an undeviating reproduction to escape infringement. In deciding that question one should consider the uses for which the design is intended, especially the scrutiny that observers will give to it as used. In the case at bar we must try to estimate how far its overall appearance will determine its aesthetic appeal when the cloth is made into a garment. Both designs have the same general color, and the arches, scrolls, rows of symbols, etc. on one resemble those on the other though they are not identical. Moreover, the patterns in which these figures are distributed to make up the design as a whole are not identical. However, the ordinary observer, unless he set out to detect the disparities, would be disposed to overlook them, and regard their aesthetic appeal as the same. That is enough; and indeed, it is all that can be said, unless protection against infringement is to be denied because of variants irrelevant to the purpose for which the design is intended. . . .

[*Affirmed.*]

---

The *Ty* case, excerpted below, explores the first prong of the infringement analysis in a dispute involving a PGS work. In particular, *Ty* deals with the relationship between access and similarity, the two components of a typical circumstantial showing of copying.

### TY, INC. v. GMA ACCESSORIES, INC.
132 F.3d 1167 (7th Cir. 1997)

POSNER, Chief Judge:

Ty, the manufacturer of the popular "Beanie Babies" line of stuffed animals, has obtained a preliminary injunction under the Copyright Act against the sale by GMA (and also a retailer, but we can disregard that aspect of the injunction) of "Preston the Pig" and "Louie the Cow." These are bean-bag animals manufactured by GMA that Ty contends are copies of its copyrighted pig ("Squealer") and cow ("Daisy"). Ty began selling the "Beanie Babies" line, including Squealer, in 1993, and it was the popularity of the line that induced GMA to bring out its own line of bean-bag stuffed animals three years later. GMA does not contest the part of the injunction that enjoins the sale of Louie, but asks us on a variety of grounds to vacate the other part, the part that enjoins it from selling Preston.

[The appellate record includes five pictures.] The first shows Squealer (the darker pig, actually pink) and Preston (white). The second is a picture of two real pigs. The third and fourth are different views of the design for Preston that Janet Salmon submitted to GMA several months before Preston went into production. The fifth is a picture of the two bean-bag cows; they are nearly identical. A glance at the first picture shows a striking similarity between the two bean-bag pigs as well. The photograph was supplied by GMA and actually understates the similarity (the animals themselves are part of the record). The "real" Preston is the same length as Squealer and has a virtually identical snout. The difference in the lengths of the two animals in the picture is a trick of the camera. The difference in snouts results from the fact that the pictured Preston was a manufacturing botch. And GMA put a ribbon around the neck of the Preston in the picture, but the Preston that it sells doesn't have a ribbon.

The two pigs are so nearly identical that if the second is a copy of the first, the second clearly infringes Ty's copyright. But identity is not infringement. The Copyright Act forbids only copying; if independent creation results in an identical work, the creator of that work is free to sell it. *Selle v. Gibb,* 741 F.2d 896, 901 (7th Cir. 1984); *Grubb v. KMS Patriots, L.P.,* 88 F.3d 1, 3 (1st Cir. 1996). The practical basis for this rule is that unlike the case of patents and trademarks, the creator of an expressive work—an author or sculptor or composer—cannot canvass the entire universe of copyrighted works to discover whether his poem or song or, as in this case, "soft sculpture" is identical to some work in which copyright subsists, especially since unpublished, unregistered works are copyrightable. [cit.] But identity can be powerful evidence of copying. [cit.] The more a work is both like an already copyrighted work *and*—for this is equally important—unlike anything that is in the public domain, the less likely it is to be an independent creation. As is generally true in the law, circumstantial evidence—evidence merely probabilistic rather than certain—can confer sufficient confidence on an inference, here of copying, to warrant a legal finding.

The issue of copying can be broken down into two subissues. The first is whether the alleged copier had access to the work that he is claimed to have copied; the second is whether, if so, he used his access to copy. *CMM Cable Rep, Inc. v. Ocean Coast Properties, Inc.,* 97 F.3d 1504, 1513 (1st Cir. 1996); *Fisher-Price, Inc. v. Well-Made Toy Mfg. Corp.,* 25 F.3d 119, 123 (2d Cir. 1994). It might seem that access could not be an issue where, as in this case, the allegedly copied work is a mass-produced consumer product purchasable for $5. But we shall see that GMA has attempted to make an issue of access.

Obviously, access does not entail copying. An eyewitness might have seen the defendant buy the copyrighted work; this would be proof of access, but not of copying. But copying entails access. If, therefore, two works are so similar as to make it highly probable that the later one is a copy of the earlier one, the issue of access need not be addressed separately, since if the later work was a copy its creator must have had access to the original. *Selle v. Gibb, supra,* 741 F.2d at 901; [cit.]. Of course the inference of access, and hence of copying, could be rebutted by proof that the creator of the later work could not have seen the earlier one or (an alternative mode of access) a copy of the earlier one. But unlike the court in *Towler v. Sayles,* 76 F.3d 579, 584-85 (4th Cir. 1996), and the authors of 4 *Nimmer on Copyright* §13.02[B], pp. 13-24 to 13-25 (1997), we do not read our decision in *Selle* to hold or imply, in conflict with the *Gaste* decision [*Gaste v. Kaiseiman,* 863 F.2d 1061 (2d Cir. 1988)], that no matter how closely the works resemble each other, the plaintiff must produce some (other) evidence of access. He must produce evidence of access, all right—but, as we have just said, and as is explicit in *Selle* itself, *see* 741 F.2d at 901, a similarity that is so close as to be highly unlikely to have been an accident of independent creation *is* evidence of access.

What troubled us in *Selle* but is not a factor here is that two works may be strikingly similar—may in fact be identical—not because one is copied from the other but because both are copies of the same thing in the public domain. In such a case—imagine two people photographing Niagara Falls from the same place at the same time of the day and year and in identical weather—there is no inference of access to anything but the public domain, and, equally, no inference of copying from a copyrighted work. *Id.* at 904; [cit.]. A similarity may be striking without being suspicious.

But here it is both. GMA's pig is strikingly similar to Ty's pig but not to anything in the public domain—a real pig, for example. The parties' bean-bag pigs bear little resemblance to real pigs even if we overlook the striking anatomical anomaly of Preston—he has three toes, whereas real pigs have cloven hooves. We can imagine an argument that the technology of manufacturing bean-bag animals somehow prevents the manufacturer from imitating a real pig. But anyone even slightly familiar with stuffed animals knows that there are many lifelike stuffed pigs on the market, and whether they are stuffed with beans or other materials does not significantly affect their verisimilitude—though here we must emphasize that any factual assertions in this opinion should be treated as tentative, since the case is before us on an appeal from the abbreviated record of a preliminary-injunction proceeding and a full trial may cast the facts in a different light.

Real pigs are not the only pigs in the public domain. But GMA has not pointed to any fictional pig in the public domain that Preston resembles. Preston resembles only Squealer, and resembles him so closely as to warrant an inference that GMA copied Squealer. In rebuttal all that GMA presented was the affidavit of the designer, Salmon, who swears, we must assume truthfully, that she never looked at a Squealer before submitting her design. But it is not her design drawing that is alleged to infringe the copyright on Squealer; it is the manufactured Preston, the soft sculpture itself, which, as a comparison of the first with the third and fourth pictures . . . reveals, is much more like Squealer than Salmon's drawing is. And remember that the manufactured Preston *in the photograph* is a sport, with its stubby snout and its ribbon. Interestingly, these are features of Salmon's drawing but not of the production-model Preston, suggesting design intervention between Salmon's submission and actual production.

It is true that only a few months elapsed between Salmon's submission of the drawing to GMA and the production of Preston. But the record is silent on how long it would have taken to modify her design to make it more like Squealer. For all we know, it might have been done in hours—by someone who had bought a Squealer. The Beanie Babies are immensely popular. They are also, it is true, sometimes hard to find (though not this Christmas, in Chicago at any rate). Ty's practice, apparently, is to create a shortage (that is, to price its bean-bag animals below the market-clearing price) in order to excite the market. But it is unbelievable that a substantial company like GMA which is in the same line of business as Ty could not have located and purchased a Squealer if it wanted to copy it. A glance at the last picture . . . shows an identity between Louie the Cow and Ty's Daisy that is so complete (and also not explainable by reference to resemblance to a real cow or other public domain figure) as to compel an inference of copying. If GMA thus must have had access to Daisy, it is probable, quite apart from any inference from the evidence of similarity, that it had access to Squealer as well.

This discussion shows how the tension between *Gaste* and *Selle* can be resolved and the true relation between similarity and access expressed. Access (and copying) may be inferred when two works are so similar to each other and not to anything in the public domain that it is likely that the creator of the second work copied the first, but the inference can be rebutted by disproving access or otherwise showing independent creation — and in this connection GMA complains that the district judge refused to conduct an evidentiary hearing at which it might have presented evidence of independent creation. If genuine issues of material fact are created by the response to a motion for a preliminary injunction, an evidentiary hearing is indeed required. [cit.] But as in any case in which a party seeks an evidentiary hearing, he must be able to persuade the court that the issue is indeed genuine and material and so a hearing would be productive — he must show in other words that he has and intends to introduce evidence that if believed will so weaken the moving party's case as to affect the judge's decision on whether to issue an injunction. Here is where GMA falters. The only evidence that it seeks to present is the designer's oral testimony in support of the claim of independent creation. Her testimony would presumably have duplicated her affidavit, which was already in evidence; at least, GMA has not indicated what her testimony would add to her affidavit. Affidavits are ordinarily inadmissible at trials but they are fully admissible in summary proceedings, including preliminary-injunction proceedings. [cit.] So the evidence that GMA wants to put before the district judge was before him when he ruled.

Even if fully credited, the affidavit does not establish the independent creation of Preston but merely the independent creation of a drawing that resembles Squealer much less than the production model of Preston does. This is not to deny that the affidavit is *some* evidence of independent creation of Preston, so it was relevant evidence. No one doubts that; and since it was already part of the evidentiary record, having its contents repeated orally would not have assisted the district judge.

But this is on the assumption that the judge credited the affidavit. If he did not even though it was not contradicted — if, for example, he was laboring under the misapprehension that affidavits are inadmissible in preliminary-injunction proceedings — he would have committed an error that would have been cured by his allowing Salmon to testify in person, and his not allowing her to do so would therefore be a ground for appeal. But there is no basis for imputing such an error to the district judge. As we read his opinion, he credited Salmon's affidavit and merely concluded, as do we, that it was only weak evidence of independent creation. Silence can be pregnant; the absence of any evidence of how the designer's drawing was translated into the Squealer-resembling production model, combined with the similarity of that model to Squealer (and to nothing in the public domain) and with GMA's obviously having copied Ty's cow, overbore the weak evidence of the affidavit.

So, on the record compiled in the preliminary-injunction proceedings, Ty has indeed a strong case. But that is not the end of our inquiry. . . . [The court proceeded to analyze irreparable harm.]

. . .

We find no error of law, no clear error of fact, and no abuse of discretion in the grant of the preliminary injunction to Ty. The judgment of the district court is therefore

*Affirmed.*

We now move from cuddly pig dolls to mildly repulsive human dolls. In the next case, the court also addresses a similarity issue in connection with a PGS work. As you read the case, consider whether the court is addressing similarity as part of the first prong of the infringement analysis, the second prong of the infringement analysis, or a bit of both simultaneously.

## JCW Investments, Inc. v. Novelty, Inc.
482 F.3d 910 (7th Cir. 2007)

Wood, Circuit Judge:

Meet Pull My Finger® Fred. He is a white, middle-aged, overweight man with black hair and a receding hairline, sitting in an armchair wearing a white tank top and blue pants. Fred is a plush doll and when one squeezes Fred's extended finger on his right hand, he farts. He also makes somewhat crude, somewhat funny statements about the bodily noises he emits, such as "Did somebody step on a duck?" or "Silent but deadly."

Fartman could be Fred's twin. Fartman, also a plush doll, is a white, middle-aged, overweight man with black hair and a receding hairline, sitting in an armchair wearing a white tank top and blue pants. Fartman (as his name suggests) also farts when one squeezes his extended finger; he too cracks jokes about the bodily function. Two of Fartman's seven jokes are the same as two of the 10 spoken by Fred. Needless to say, Tekky Toys, which manufactures Fred, was not happy when Novelty, Inc., began producing Fartman, nor about Novelty's production of a farting Santa doll sold under the name Pull-My-Finger Santa.

Tekky sued for copyright infringement, trademark infringement, and unfair competition and eventually won on all claims. [Novelty appealed.]

I

Somewhat to our surprise, it turns out that there is a niche market for farting dolls, and it is quite lucrative. Tekky Toys, an Illinois corporation, designs and sells a whole line of them. Fred was just the beginning. Fred's creators, Jamie Wirt and Geoff Bevington, began working on Fred in 1997, and had a finished doll in 1999. They applied for a copyright registration on Fred as a "plush toy with sound," and received a certificate of copyright on February 5, 2001; later, they assigned the certificate to Tekky. In the meantime, Tekky sent out its first Fred dolls to distributors in 1999. By the time this case arose, in addition to Fred, Tekky's line of farting plush toys had expanded to Pull My Finger® Frankie (Fred's blonde, motorcycle-riding cousin), Santa, Freddy Jr., Count Fartula (purple, like the Count on Sesame Street), and Fat Bastard (character licensed from New Line Cinema's "Austin Powers" movies), among others. By March 2004, Tekky had sold more than 400,000 farting dolls.

Novelty, a privately held Indiana corporation, is owned by Todd Green, its president. Green testified in his deposition, "any time we'd create an item, okay, we try to copy—or try to think of some relevant ideas." Novelty personnel go to trade shows and take pictures of other companies' products, seeking "ideas" for their own. In early 2001, Green visited the Hong Kong showroom of TL Toys, a manufacturer of Tekky's Fred doll, and he spotted

Fred. In his deposition, Green testified that he might have photographed Fred since "[i]t wouldn't be unusual for us to photograph everything we see." Green admits that his idea for Fartman was based on Fred and that he described his idea to Mary Burkhart, Novelty's art director, who prepared a drawing based on Green's description. According to Burkhart, Green wanted "a plush doll that would . . . fart and shake. . . . And make a sound . . . a hillbilly-type guy, sitting in a chair that would fart and be activated by actually pulling his finger." Typically, Novelty would assign the job of drawing a new product to an artist, such as Burkhart, and the artist would then take her drawing to Green for his approval. That was the procedure it followed for Fartman. Novelty began to manufacture plush farting dolls around October 8, 2001; the first doll it released was the one it called Pull-My-Finger Santa. Fartman hit the stores one month later, on November 5, 2001.

[Tekky won a jury verdict and an award of damages and attorney's fees.]

## II

### A

To establish copyright infringement, one must prove two elements: "(1) ownership of a valid copyright, and (2) copying of constituent elements of the work that are original." *Feist Publications, Inc. v. Rural Telephone Service Co., Inc.*, 499 U.S. 340, 361 (1991). What is required for copyright protection is "some minimal degree of creativity," or "the existence of . . . intellectual production, of thought, and conception." *Id.* at 362 (quoting *Burrow-Giles Lithographic Co. v. Sarony*, 111 U.S. 53, 59-60 (1884)). Generally, copyright protection begins at the moment of creation of "original works of authorship fixed in any tangible medium of expression," including "pictorial, graphic, and sculptural" works and sound recordings. 17 U.S.C. §102(a). . . .

Once it is established that a party has a valid copyright, whether registered or not, the next question is whether another person has copied the protected work. Copying may be proven by direct evidence, but that is often hard to come by. In the alternative, copying may be inferred "where the defendant had access to the copyrighted work and the accused work is substantially similar to the copyrighted work." [cit.]; *see also Ty, Inc. v. GMA Accessories, Inc.*, 132 F.3d 1167, 1169-70 (7th Cir. 1997). It is not essential to prove access, however. If the "two works are so similar as to make it highly probable that the later one is a copy of the earlier one, the issue of access need not be addressed separately, since if the later work was a copy its creator must have had access to the original." *Ty, Inc.*, 132 F.3d at 1170. "The more a work is both like an already copyrighted work *and*—for this is equally important—unlike anything that is in the public domain, the less likely it is to be an independent creation." *Id.* at 1169 (emphasis in original). If the inference of copying is drawn from proof of access and substantial similarity, it can be rebutted if the alleged copier can show that she instead "independently created" the allegedly infringing work. *Susan Wakeen Doll Co.*, 272 F.3d at 450. "A defendant independently created a work if it created its own work without copying anything or if it copied something other than the plaintiff's copyrighted work." *Id.* (citing 3 Melville B. Nimmer & David Nimmer, *Nimmer on Copyright* §12.11[D], at 12-175 (2001)).

Novelty contends that the district court protected too much of Tekky's toy—not just the expression but the idea or common elements known as scènes à faire, which we defined in *Atari* as "incidents, characters or settings which are as a practical matter indispensable or at least standard, in the treatment of a given topic." [*Atari, Inc. v. N. Am. Philips Consumer Elecs. Corp.*, 672 F.2d 607, 616 (7th Cir. 1982).] Novelty also takes issue with the district court's finding that it had access to Fred, that Burkhart copied rather than independently created Fartman, and that Fred and Fartman were substantially similar. As we explain below, we are unpersuaded. Tekky had a valid copyright in Fred, Novelty (the company) indisputably did have access to Fred, and the two dolls are so similar that the inference of copying even without access is irresistible.

Novelty does not argue that Tekky lacks a valid copyright in Fred or that Fred is so lacking in creativity that a copyright could not attach. Indeed, Fred is a far cry from a noncreative compilation of facts such as the telephone book in *Feist*. Here, we have a creative doll and a valid copyright registration. There is no doubt that there is a valid copyright. How much creativity Fred reflects and what ideas he embodies (as opposed to the way he expresses those ideas) merely help us to decide whether we can infer copying from substantial similarity.

It is notable that Green, Novelty's president, admits that he saw and perhaps photographed Fred, and that Fred gave him the idea for Fartman. While Burkhart denies having seen Fred or even a picture of him, she drew the model for Fartman at Green's direction. Moreover, Fred was already on the market in the United States at the time Fartman was created. In *Moore v. Columbia Pictures Industries, Inc.*, 972 F.2d 939, 942 (8th Cir. 1992), the Eighth Circuit found that a "reasonable possibility of access can be established under the 'corporate receipt doctrine,'" under which:

> if the defendant is a corporation, the fact that one employee of the corporation has possession of plaintiff's work should warrant a finding that another employee (who composed defendant's work) had access to plaintiff's work, where by reason of the physical propinquity between the employees the latter has the opportunity to view the work in the possession of the former.

*Id.* (quoting 3 *Nimmer on Copyright* §13.02[A]). In this case, Novelty's president saw Fred, directed that the artist draw a figure that looks like Fred, and from that drawing approved the manufacture of Fartman. On those facts, the corporate receipt doctrine may just be icing on the cake; the fact that Green directed Burkhart as she created the drawing, rather than taking pencil in hand and sketching it himself, is immaterial. Novelty plainly had access to Fred and used that access in the manufacture of Fartman.

Even if access existed, Tekky had to show substantial similarity between the two items in order to support an inference of copying. The test for substantial similarity is an objective one. *See Incredible Technologies, Inc. v. Virtual Technologies, Inc.*, 400 F.3d 1007, 1011 (7th Cir. 2005) (noting that we look at "whether the accused work is so similar to the plaintiff's work that an ordinary reasonable person would conclude that the defendant unlawfully appropriated the plaintiff's protectable expression by taking material of substance and value"). We look at the dolls themselves to determine substantial similarity; to give the reader some idea of what the dispute is about, we have attached as an Appendix to this opinion a photograph from the record that depicts Fred, Fartman, and Fartboy. [The Appendix has been omitted.] The pictures show that the similarities between Fred and Fartman go far beyond the fact that both are plush dolls of middle-aged men sitting in armchairs that fart and tell jokes. Both have crooked smiles that show their teeth, balding heads with a fringe of black hair, a rather large protruding nose, blue pants that are identical colors, and white tank tops. On the other hand, Fartman has his name emblazoned in red across his chest, his shoes are a different color from Fred's, as is his chair, and Fartman wears a hat. In the end, despite the small cosmetic differences, the two dolls give off more than a similar air. The problem is not that both Fred and Fartman have black hair or white tank tops or any other single detail; the problem is that the execution and combination of features on both dolls would lead an objective observer to think they were the same. [cit.] We conclude that no objective person would find these dolls to be more than minimally distinguishable. To the contrary, they are substantially similar. That, in combination with Green's access, compels an inference of copying. Indeed, the dolls are so similar that an inference of copying could be drawn even without the evidence of access. [cit.]

Novelty contends that rather than copy, it merely made a similar doll based on the same comic archetype, that of "a typical man wearing jeans and a T-shirt in a chair doing the 'pull my finger' joke." That, Novelty argues, is the idea, not the expression, and the reason that the two dolls are similar is they are both based on that idea. The district court found that Novelty tried to shoehorn too much into the "idea" and that the only idea here is that of a "plush doll that makes a farting sound and articulates jokes when its finger is activated." As the district court put it:

> Fred—a smiling, black-haired balding Caucasian male, wearing a white tank top and blue pants, reclining in a green armchair, who makes a farting sound, vibrates and utters phrases such as "Did somebody step on a duck?" and "Silent but deadly" after the protruding finger on his right hand is pinched—is plaintiff's expression of that idea.

It is, of course, a fundamental tenet of copyright law that the idea is not protected, but the original expression of the idea is. *See Feist*, 499 U.S. at 348-49. Although it is not always easy to distinguish idea from expression, by the same token the task is not always hard. Novelty urges that the similarity of the two dolls reflects the fact that Fred himself is only minimally creative, representing a combination of elements that were in the public domain or were scènes à faire. The problem with this argument is that the very combination of these elements as well as the expression that is Fred himself are creative.

Novelty wants us to take the entity that is Fred, subtract each element that it contends is common, and then consider whether Novelty copied whatever leftover components are creative. But this ignores the fact that the details— such as the appearance of Fred's face or even his chair—represent creative expression. It is not the idea of a farting, crude man that is protected, but this particular embodiment of that concept. Novelty could have created another plush doll of a middle-aged farting man that would seem nothing like Fred. He could, for example, have a blond mullet and wear flannel, have a nose that is drawn on rather than protruding substantially from the rest of the head, be standing rather than ensconced in an armchair, and be wearing shorts rather than blue pants. To see how easy this would be, one need look no further than Tekky's Frankie doll, which is also a plush doll, but differs in numerous details: he is not sitting, and he has blond hair, a tattoo, and a red-and-white striped tank. Frankie is not a copy of Fred. Fartman is. We have no trouble concluding that the district court properly granted partial summary judgment to Tekky on the issue of liability for copyright infringement.

[*Affirmed.*]

"Pull My Finger" Fred.

## NOTES AND QUESTIONS

1. ***Inferring access.*** In *Ty*, Judge Posner sketches out the circumstances under which access may be inferred in a copyright infringement analysis. Why should access ever be inferred? When the similarity analysis comes to dominate the copyright infringement analysis, does that analysis begin to resemble a patent infringement analysis? A trademark infringement analysis? Would that be problematic? *See also Mag Jewelry Co., Inc. v. Cherokee, Inc.*, 496 F.3d 108 (1st Cir. 2007) (declining to find access).

2. ***How ordinary is the ordinary observer?*** In *Peter Pan*, Learned Hand adopts an "ordinary observer" test for substantial similarity, and makes

some suppositions about features that an ordinary observer might overlook. Does this approach present a risk of overbroad copyright protection? Should the court adopt a "more discerning ordinary observer" test, relying on this ordinary observer's extraordinary discernment to minimize or filter out the public domain elements from the analysis? *See, e.g., Odegard, Inc. v. Safavieh Carpets, Inc.*, 398 F. Supp. 2d 275 (S.D.N.Y. 2005) (discussing such a test). Does this debate remind you of the efforts to construct an "ordinary observer" for purposes of the design patent infringement analysis? *See* Chapter 6.

3. *Pigs in the public domain.* Judge Posner's analysis contemplates a three-way comparison between the plaintiff's pig, the defendant's pig, and pigs of the public domain. Does this analysis resemble the design patent infringement standard announced in *Egyptian Goddess* (Chapter 6)? Should it? The design patent infringement standard relies on an analysis of the prior art, as defined by patent rules. Is the prior art the same as the "public domain"? *Cf. Boisson v. Banian, Ltd.*, 273 F.3d 262 (2d Cir. 2001) (assessing the "concept and feel" of a work, but requiring a "discerning scrutiny" of the public domain aspects of the work as part of that analysis).

4. *The public display right.* Many copyright infringement cases involve alleged violations of the reproduction right, as the excerpted cases illustrate. Suppose that someone—a shop owner, for example—does not duplicate a copyrighted design, but simply displays it without the copyright owner's authorization. Is this a violation of the display right of 17 U.S.C. §106(5)? Does 17 U.S.C. §109 provide a defense? What if a passerby takes a photograph of the displayed item. Does this constitute copyright infringement? For a comparative view, see *Re Marcio X*, 2008 ECC 19 (Sup. Ct. France, Criminal Chamber 2008); *Peek & Cloppenburg v. Cassina*, 2009 ECDR 9 (ECJ 2008) (showing furniture in the window of a menswear store might constitute a form of distribution of the work to the public).

5. *Secondary liability.* Professor Janis's brother Billy frequently sells his wares at the flea markets of southern Indiana. Suppose that Brother Billy made many knockoff "Pull My Finger" Fred dolls and sold them at a flea market—all without the copyright owner's permission, of course. Could the copyright owner succeed in an infringement suit against the flea market operator for facilitating Brother Billy's copyright infringement? Under what circumstances? *See Fonovisa, Inc. v. Cherry Auction, Inc.*, 76 F.3d 259 (9th Cir. 1996).

## 2. FAIR USE

### MATTEL INC. v. WALKING MOUNTAIN PRODUCTIONS
353 F.3d 792 (9th Cir. 2003)

PREGERSON, Circuit Judge:

[For a discussion of the factual background and the court's analysis of the trade dress claims, see Chapter 4.]

Discussion

I

We first address the question whether the Los Angeles federal district court erred in granting Forsythe's motion for summary judgment on Mattel's claim of copyright infringement. . . .

Mattel owns the copyright to the unadorned Superstar Barbie head[6] and parts of the figure including revisions to the hands, feet, neck, shoulder and buttocks. Because Forsythe photographed the Barbie figure and reproduced those photographs, Mattel has established a prima facie case of copyright infringement [under the pertinent part of 17 U.S.C. §106].

Consistent with its policy goals, however, the Copyright Act recognizes certain statutory exceptions to protections on copyrights. At its core, the Act seeks to promote the progress of science and art by protecting artistic and scientific works while encouraging the development and evolution of new works. *See Campbell v. Acuff-Rose Music, Inc.*, 510 U.S. 569, 575-76 (1994). Recognizing that science and art generally rely on works that came before them and rarely spring forth in a vacuum, the Act limits the rights of a copyright owner regarding works that build upon, reinterpret, and reconceive existing works. *See id.* at 575-77 ("[F]ew, if any, things . . . are strictly new and original throughout. Every book in literature, science and art, borrows, and must necessarily borrow. . . .") (quoting *Emerson v. Davies*, 8 F. Cas. 615, 619 (C.C.D. Mass. 1845) (No. 4,436)). The fair use exception excludes from copyright restrictions certain works, such as those that criticize and comment on another work. 17 U.S.C. §107. *See also Dr. Seuss Enters., L.P. v. Penguin Books USA, Inc.*, 109 F.3d 1394, 1399 (9th Cir.) (holding that fair use "permits courts to avoid rigid application of the copyright statute when, on occasion, it would stifle the very creativity which that law is designed to foster"), *cert. dismissed*, 521 U.S. 1146 (1997).

To determine whether a work constitutes fair use, we engage in a case-by-case analysis and a flexible balancing of relevant factors. *Campbell*, 510 U.S. at 577-78. The factors are "to be explored, and the results weighed together, in light of the purposes of copyright." *Id.* at 578. Depending on the particular facts, some factors may weigh more heavily than others. *Id.* at 577-79. [The court recited the four fair use factors from Section 107.]

The district court concluded that Forsythe's reproduction of Mattel's copyrighted Barbie was fair use. The district court reasoned that a trier of fact could only conclude that Forsythe's works were fair use because: (1) his use was parody meant to criticize Barbie, (2) he only copied what was necessary for his purpose, and (3) his photographs could not affect the market demand for Mattel's products or those of its licensees.

. . .

Because we agree with the district court that no triable issues of fact exist on whether Forsythe's use of Mattel's Barbie constitutes fair use, we weigh the four §107 fair use factors on appeal. . . .

---

6. "Unadorned" includes only the facial structure without hair, eyebrows, eye color, eye lashes, lip color, and painted teeth.

A. Purpose and Character of Use

The "purpose and character of use" factor in the fair use inquiry asks "to what extent the new work is transformative" and does not simply "supplant []" the original work and whether the work's purpose was for- or not-for-profit. *Campbell,* 510 U.S. at 579, 584.

A work must add "something new, with a further purpose or different character, altering the first with new expression, meaning, or message." *Id.* at 579. The Supreme Court has recognized that parodic works, like other works that comment and criticize, are by their nature often sufficiently transformative to fit clearly under the fair use exception. *Id.* (recognizing that parody "has an obvious claim to transformative value"). In our circuit, a "parodist is permitted a fair use of a copyrighted work if it takes no more than is necessary to 'recall' or 'conjure up' the object of his parody." *Dr. Seuss,* 109 F.3d at 1400. A parodic work, however, like other potential fair uses, has to "work its way through the relevant factors, and be judged case by case, in light of the ends of copyright law." *Campbell,* 510 U.S. at 581.

"[T]he threshold question [in the analysis of this first factor] . . . is whether a parodic character may reasonably be perceived." *Id.* at 582. [cit.] Mattel argues that the district court erred in finding parody because a reasonable jury could conclude that Forsythe's works do not parody Mattel's Barbie. In support of this argument, Mattel offered into evidence a survey in which they presented individuals from the general public in a shopping mall with color photocopies of Forsythe's photographs and asked them what meaning they perceived. Relying on this survey, Mattel asserts that only some individuals may perceive parodic character.

The issue of whether a work is a parody is a question of law, not a matter of public majority opinion. *See Campbell,* 510 U.S. at 582-83; *Dr. Seuss,* 109 F.3d at 1400-01 ("[U]nless the plaintiff's copyrighted work is at least in part the target of the defendant's satire, then the defendant's work is not a 'parody' in the *legal sense.* . . ." (emphasis added)). Forsythe correctly points out that Mattel presents no case law in support of its contention that the parodic nature of a defendant's work should be assessed using surveys and opinion testimony. Forsythe is further correct that every court to address the issue whether a defendant's work qualifies as a parody has treated this question as one of law to be decided by the court. *E.g., Campbell,* 510 U.S. at 582-83; [cit.].

We decline to consider Mattel's survey in assessing whether Forsythe's work can be reasonably perceived as a parody. Parody is an objectively defined rhetorical device. Further, because parody is "a form of social and literary criticism," it has "socially significant value as free speech under the First Amendment." *Dr. Seuss,* 109 F.3d at 1400. While individuals may disagree on the success or extent of a parody, parodic elements in a work will often justify fair use protection. *See, e.g., Yankee Publ'g, Inc. v. News Am. Publ'g, Inc.,* 809 F. Supp. 267, 280 (S.D.N.Y. 1992) ("First Amendment protections do not apply only to those who speak clearly, whose jokes are funny, and whose parodies succeed."). Use of surveys in assessing parody would allow majorities to determine the parodic nature of a work and possibly silence artistic creativity. Allowing majorities to determine whether a work is a parody would be greatly at odds with the purpose of the fair use exception and the Copyright Act. *See generally Campbell,* 510 U.S. at 583.

A parody is a "literary or artistic work that imitates the characteristic style of an author or a work for comic effect or ridicule." *Id.* at 580 (quoting AMERICAN HERITAGE DICTIONARY 1317 (3d. 1992)). For the purposes of copyright law, a parodist may claim fair use where he or she uses some of the "elements of a prior author's composition to create a new one that, at least in part, comments on that author's works." *Id.* The original work need not be the sole subject of the parody; the parody "may loosely target an original" as long as the parody "reasonably could be perceived as commenting on the original or criticizing it, to some degree." *Id.* at 580-81, 583. That a parody is in bad taste is not relevant to whether it constitutes fair use; "it would be a dangerous undertaking for persons trained only to the law to constitute themselves final judges of the worth of [a work]." *Id.* at 582-83 (quoting *Bleistein v. Donaldson Lithographing Co.,* 188 U.S. 239, 251 (1903)).

In assessing whether Forsythe's photographs parody Barbie, Mattel urges us to ignore context—both the social context of Forsythe's work and the actual context in which Mattel's copyrighted works are placed in Forsythe's photographs. However, "[i]n parody, as in news reporting, context is everything." *Id.* at 588 (citations omitted). We conclude that Forsythe's work may reasonably be perceived as a parody of Barbie.

Mattel, through impressive marketing, has established Barbie as "the ideal American woman" and a "symbol of American girlhood" for many. [cit.] As abundantly evidenced in the record, Mattel's advertisements show these plastic dolls dressed in various outfits, leading glamorous lifestyles and engaged in exciting activities. To sell its product, Mattel uses associations of beauty, wealth, and glamour.

Forsythe turns this image on its head, so to speak, by displaying carefully positioned, nude, and sometimes frazzled looking Barbies in often ridiculous and apparently dangerous situations. His lighting, background, props, and camera angles all serve to create a context for Mattel's copyrighted work that transform Barbie's meaning. Forsythe presents the viewer with a different set of associations and a different context for this plastic figure. In some of Forsythe's photos, Barbie is about to be destroyed or harmed by domestic life in the form of kitchen appliances, yet continues displaying her well known smile, disturbingly oblivious to her predicament. As portrayed in some of Forsythe's photographs, the appliances are substantial and overwhelming, while Barbie looks defenseless. In other photographs, Forsythe conveys a sexualized perspective of Barbie by showing the nude doll in sexually suggestive contexts. It is not difficult to see the commentary that Forsythe intended or the harm that he perceived in Barbie's influence on gender roles and the position of women in society.

However one may feel about his message—whether he is wrong or right, whether his methods are powerful or banal—his photographs parody Barbie and everything Mattel's doll has come to signify. Undoubtedly, one could make similar statements through other means about society, gender roles, sexuality, and perhaps even social class. But Barbie, and all the associations she has acquired through Mattel's impressive marketing success, conveys these messages in a particular way that is ripe for social comment.[7]

Parody emerges from this "joinder of reference and ridicule." *Campbell,* 510 U.S. at 583; *cf. Dr. Seuss,* 109 F.3d at 1401 (holding that defendants who wrote a poem titled "Cat NOT in the HAT" about the O.J. Simpson trial were not parodying Dr. Seuss' original work because the stanzas had "no critical bearing on the substance or style of" the original). By developing and transforming associations with Mattel's Barbie doll, Forsythe has created the sort of social criticism and parodic speech protected by the First Amendment and promoted by the Copyright Act. We find that this factor weighs heavily in favor of Forsythe.

Another element of the first factor analysis is whether the work's "purpose" was commercial or had a non-profit aim. *Campbell,* 510 U.S. at 584. Clearly, Forsythe had a commercial expectation and presumably hoped to find a market for his art. However, as the Supreme Court noted in *Campbell,* even works involving comment and criticism "are generally conducted for profit in this country." *Id.* (quoting *Harper & Row,* 471 U.S. at 592). On balance, Forsythe's commercial expectation does not weigh much against him. Given the extremely transformative nature and parodic quality of Forsythe's work, its commercial qualities become less important. *Id.* at 579 (recognizing that the more "transformative the new work, the less will be the significance of the other factors").

### B. Nature of the Copyrighted Work

The second factor in the fair use analysis "recognizes that creative works are 'closer to the core of intended copyright protection' than informational and functional works." *Dr. Seuss,* 109 F.3d at 1402 (quoting *Campbell,* 510 U.S. at 586). Mattel's copyrighted Barbie figure and face can fairly be said to be a creative work. However, the creativity of Mattel's copyrighted Barbie is typical of cases where there are infringing parodies. *Campbell,* 510 U.S. at 586 ("[P]arodies almost invariably copy publicly known, expressive works."). As we have recognized in the past, "this [nature of the copyrighted work] factor typically has not been terribly significant in the overall fair use balancing." *Dr. Seuss,* 109 F.3d at 1402. In any event, it may weigh slightly against Forsythe.

### C. Amount and Substantiality of the Portion Used

The third factor in the fair use analysis asks whether "'the amount and substantiality of the portion used in relation to the copyrighted work as a whole,' are reasonable in relation to the purpose of copying." *Id.* (quoting

---

7. Mattel strongly argues that Forsythe's work is not parody because he could have made his statements about consumerism, gender roles, and sexuality without using Barbie. Acceptance of this argument would severely and unacceptably limit the definition of parody. We do not make judgments about what objects an artist should choose for their art. For example, in *Campbell,* the Supreme Court found that hip-hop band 2-Live Crew's rendition of "Pretty Woman" was a parody because it targeted the original song and commented "on the naivete of the original of an earlier day, as a rejection of its sentiment that ignores the ugliness of street life and the debasement that it signifies." 510 U.S. at 583. No doubt, 2-Live Crew could have chosen another song to make such a statement. Parody only requires that "the plaintiff's copyrighted work is at least in part the target of the defendant's satire," not that the plaintiff's work be the irreplaceable object for its form of social commentary. *Dr. Seuss,* 109 F.3d at 1400.

17 U.S.C. §107(3)). We assess the "persuasiveness of a parodist's justification for the particular copying done," recognizing that the "extent of permissible copying varies with the purpose and character of the use." *Campbell,* 510 U.S. at 586-87.

Mattel argues that Forsythe used the entirety of its copyrighted work and that this factor weighs against him. Mattel contends that Forsythe could have used less of the Barbie figure by, for example, limiting his photos to the Barbie heads.

First, Forsythe did not simply copy the work "verbatim" with "little added or changed." *Id.* at 587-88.[8] A verbatim copy of Barbie would be an exact three dimensional reproduction of the doll. Forsythe did not display the entire Barbie head and body in his photographs. Parts of the Barbie figure are obscured or omitted depending on the angle at which the photos were taken and whether other objects obstructed a view of the Barbie figure.

Second, Mattel's argument that Forsythe could have taken a lesser portion of its work attempts to benefit from the somewhat unique nature of the copyrighted work in this case. Copyright infringement actions generally involve songs, video, or written works. [cit.] Because parts of these works are naturally severable, the new work can easily choose portions of the original work and add to it. Here because the copyrighted material is a doll design and the infringing work is a photograph containing that doll, Forsythe, short of severing the doll, must add to it by creating a context around it and capturing that context in a photograph. For our purposes, Forsythe's use is no different from that of a parodist taking a basic melody and adding elements that transform the work. *See Campbell,* 510 U.S. at 589 (noting that 2 Live Crew's rendition of "Pretty Woman" did not approach verbatim copying because, even though 2 Live Crew may have taken the most recognizable portion of the work, it had added "scraper" noises and overlays to the music). In both Forsythe's use of the entire doll and his use of dismembered parts of the doll, portions of the old work are incorporated into the new work but emerge imbued with a different character.

Moreover, Forsythe was justified in the amount of Mattel's copyrighted work that he used in his photographs. Mattel's argument that Forsythe could have used a lesser portion of the Barbie doll is completely without merit and would lead to absurd results. We do not require parodic works to take the absolute minimum amount of the copyrighted work possible. As the Supreme Court stated in *Campbell,* "[o]nce enough has been taken to assure identification, how much more is reasonable will depend, say, on the extent to which the [work's] overriding purpose and character is to parody the original or, in contrast, the likelihood that the parody may serve as a market substitute for the original." *Id.* at 587. We conclude that the extent of Forsythe's copying of the Barbie figure and head was justifiable in light of his parodic purpose and medium used. This factor also weighs in his favor.

---

8. We have, however, held that entire verbatim reproductions are justifiable where the purpose of the work differs from the original. *Kelly,* 336 F.3d at 821("This factor neither weighs for nor against either party because, although [the defendant] did copy each of [the plaintiff's] images as a whole, it was reasonable to do so in light of [the defendant's] use of the images.").

D. Effect of the Use upon Potential Market

The fourth factor asks whether actual market harm resulted from the defendant's use of plaintiff's protected material and whether "unrestricted and widespread conduct of the sort engaged in by the defendant . . . would result in a substantially adverse impact on the potential market" for the original or its derivatives. *Id.* at 590 (quoting 3 Melville B. Nimmer & David Nimmer, *Nimmer on Copyright* §13.05[A](4), at 13-102.61 (1993)). This inquiry attempts to strike a balance between

> the benefit the public will derive if the use is permitted and the personal gain the copyright owner will receive if the use is denied. The less adverse effect that an alleged infringing use has on the copyright owner's expectation of gain, the less public benefit need be shown to justify the use.

*Dr. Seuss,* 109 F.3d at 1403 (quoting *MCA, Inc. v. Wilson,* 677 F.2d 180, 183 (2d Cir. 1981)).

Mattel argues that Forsythe's work could lead to market harm by impairing the value of Barbie itself, Barbie derivatives,[9] and licenses for use of the Barbie name and/or likeness to non-Mattel entities.[10] Because of the parodic nature of Forsythe's work, however, it is highly unlikely that it will substitute for products in Mattel's markets or the markets of Mattel's licensees. In *Campbell,* the Court clearly stated, "as to parody pure and simple, it is more likely that the new work will not affect the market for the original in a way cognizable under this factor." *Campbell,* 510 U.S. at 591. Nor is it likely that Mattel would license an artist to create a work that is so critical of Barbie. "[T]he unlikelihood that creators of imaginative works will license critical reviews or lampoons of their own productions removes such uses from the very notion of a potential licensing market." *Id.* at 592.

As to Mattel's claim that Forsythe has impaired Barbie's value, this fourth factor does not recognize a decrease in value of a copyrighted work that may result from a particularly powerful critical work. *Id.* at 593 ("The fact that a parody may impair the market for derivative uses by the very effectiveness of its critical commentary is no more relevant under copyright than the like threat to the original market. . . ."). We recognize, however, that critical works may have another dimension beyond their critical aspects that may have effects on potential markets for the copyrighted work. *Id.* at 592 (recognizing that the new work "may have a more complex character, with effects not only in the arena of criticism but also in protectable markets for derivative works"). Thus, we look more generally, not only to the critical aspects of a work, but to the type of work itself in determining market harm. *Id.* at 593 (looking beyond the critical aspect of 2 Live Crew's rap rendition of "Pretty Woman" to the derivative market for rap music). Given the nature of Forsythe's photographs, we decline Mattel's invitation to look to the licensing market for art in general.

---

9. By "derivatives," we refer to the numerous other Mattel products in the Barbie line, such as the "Ken" doll (Barbie's boyfriend); the "Kira," "Skipper," and "Teresa" dolls (Barbie's friends); the "Splash Cycle" (a three-wheeled amphibious cycle on which Barbie can sit); and the "Barbie Dream House" (a battery operated two-story Victorian-style dollhouse).

10. We address only potential harm because the actual harm to works of Mattel's licensees was non-existent.

Forsythe's photographs depict nude and often sexualized figures, a category of artistic photography that Mattel is highly unlikely to license. "The existence of this potential market cannot be presumed." [cit.]

In a case almost identical to this one, *Mattel, Inc. v. Pitt* ("*Pitt*"), 229 F. Supp. 2d 315, 321-22 (S.D.N.Y. 2002), the Southern District Court of New York found no danger of potential market harm to derivative uses. In *Pitt*, Mattel brought a copyright infringement suit against Susanne Pitt, an artist who sold and designed a line of figures called "Dungeon Dolls." These dolls were essentially Barbie dolls, physically altered, clothed in sado-masochistic attire, and placed in contexts with like themes. *Id.* Having found the works sufficiently transformative, the *Pitt* court concluded that potential market harm was improbable because Mattel was unlikely to develop or license others to develop a product in the "adult" doll market. *Id.* at 324.

Forsythe's work could only reasonably substitute for a work in the market for adult-oriented artistic photographs of Barbie. We think it safe to assume that Mattel will not enter such a market or license others to do so. As the Court noted in *Campbell*, "the market for potential derivative uses includes only those that creators of original works would in general develop or license others to develop." 510 U.S. at 592.

Finally, the public benefit in allowing artistic creativity and social criticism to flourish is great. The fair use exception recognizes this important limitation on the rights of the owners of copyrights. No doubt, Mattel would be less likely to grant a license to an artist that intends to create art that criticizes and reflects negatively on Barbie's image. It is not in the public's interest to allow Mattel complete control over the kinds of artistic works that use Barbie as a reference for criticism and comment.

Having balanced the four §107 fair use factors, we hold that Forsythe's work constitutes fair use under §107's exception. His work is a parody of Barbie and highly transformative. The amount of Mattel's figure that he used was justified. His infringement had no discernable impact on Mattel's market for derivative uses. Finally, the benefits to the public in allowing such use—allowing artistic freedom and expression and criticism of a cultural icon—are great. Allowing Forsythe's use serves the aims of the Copyright Act by encouraging the very creativity and criticism that the Act protects. *Kelly*, 336 F.3d at 819-20. We affirm the district court on its grant of summary judgment on Mattel's copyright infringement claims.

## NOTES AND QUESTIONS

1. ***Transformative use.*** Review the court's discussion of fair use factor (1), and in particular, the concept of a transformative use. How would you describe the concept as applied to a literary work? Would that same description fit for designs? Or does the concept need to be adapted? Discarded altogether? Does the concept work well in *Mattel*?

2. ***Amount and substantiality.*** Where the subject matter is a design, will the alleged infringer's use usually involve the entirety of the plaintiff's work? How much weight should courts give to this factor in assessing fair use in cases involving designs?

## D. ARCHITECTURAL WORKS

For copyright purposes, should architectural works be treated as another species of pictorial graphic, and sculptural work? Or should they be singled out for special treatment? U.S. law has adopted the latter approach, as we detail in the following materials.

### T-Peg, Inc. v. Vermont Timber Works, Inc.
459 F.3d 97 (1st Cir. 2006)

Lynch, Circuit Judge:

This case is the first occasion for us to address a copyright infringement suit under the [1990] Architectural Works Copyright Protection Act ("AWCPA") . . . (codified in scattered sections of 17 U.S.C.), which created a new category of copyrightable subject matter for "architectural works." 17 U.S.C. §102(a)(8).

The plaintiffs, T-Peg, Inc. and Timberpeg East, Inc. (collectively, "Timberpeg"), sell both architectural designs and the associated packages of material for the construction of timberframed homes. [A timberframe is a house frame using wooden posts and beams which remain visible inside the building, as contrasted with the more common "stick built" home.] Timberpeg created architectural plans for a home for Stanley Isbitski in Salisbury, New Hampshire. The central feature of those plans was the timberframed main house, although the plans did not show a completed final architectural design for the actual timberframe. [Timberpeg had created a first set of preliminary plans for Isbitski in December 1999, but he was dissatisfied with them, and so Timberpeg created a second set in April 2001.] The plaintiffs registered their second set of preliminary plans as an architectural work with the Copyright Office, and maintained ownership over the copyright in the work embodied in the plans.

[The second set of preliminary plans contained elevations and floor plans. The plans showed a two-floor main house connected via a covered breezeway to a three-car garage with a lofted space above it. The first floor of the main house was nine feet tall; the second floor was eight feet tall. The main house consisted, broadly speaking, of two major portions. One portion — the portion which would be timberframed — was backwards-L-shaped. A great room (with two-floor ceilings on the northern end of the house), kitchen, breakfast room, and dining room were on the first floor, and a den was on the lofted second floor (which occupied only the southern portion of the house). The plans for this portion of the house did not contain a complete design of the timberframe, but the floor plans did show where the vertical posts would connect to the foundation and the location of at least some of the internal horizontal beams. The timberframing in this portion of the house used a particular style featuring common rafters with principal purlins (horizontal timbers supporting the rafters). The roof in this portion was oriented north-to-south, with a particular pitch (roof angle) referred to as a "twelve-by-twelve" pitch.

The exact dimensions of the timberframed portion of the main house were 44 feet by 28 feet, with a 14-foot-by-8-foot section cut out in the northwest corner to form the L shape, where a screen porch would be located. There was also a "bump-out" in the kitchen on the western side of the house—an approximately eight-foot portion of the western wall containing windows that jutted out one foot beyond the rest of the wall. The timberframed portion of the house also featured a central switchback staircase located in the center of the timberframed portion of the home. In addition to labels denoting the various rooms, the floor plan showed the location of various fixtures, including a kitchen sink (located at the "bump-out"), a stove, and a fireplace.

The second major component of the main house—containing bedrooms, bathrooms, and the foyer—was connected to the eastern side of the timber-framed portion, and was to be stick-built. The roof in this portion of the house was oriented east-to-west, and had a pitch of nine-by-twelve. There was a covered porch on the northern part of this portion, which connected to the covered breezeway and the three-car garage.]

Isbitski, however, never purchased a construction materials package and final plans from Timberpeg. He did file the registered plans with the Town of Salisbury in order to get a building permit. Isbitski hired defendant, Vermont Timber Works, Inc. ("VTW"), to erect a timberframe for his home. [Isbitski approached VTW in December 2000. VTW began the drawings at the end of 2000. Isbitski provided VTW with a copy of the first set of preliminary plans from Timberpeg, but VTW asserted that it did not rely on those plans because Isbitski stated that he was unhappy with them. VTW also claimed that Isbitski had frequently injected himself into the drafting process, specifying details such as the appearance of the stairway, the placement of various posts, and the precise pitch of the roof. In March 2002, Isbitski agreed to purchase the VTW timberframe.] VTW erected its timberframe, but Isbitski never completed his home. A later owner bought the property and completed the home.

[Timberpeg sued Isbitski and VTW for infringing the registered copyright in the architectural work embodied in the second set of plans. Isbitski could not be found and was never served. The district court granted summary judgment of non-infringement in favor of VTW; Timberpeg appealed.]

. . .

III.

Before turning to the specific arguments on appeal, we discuss the governing framework of copyright law and the AWCPA. The AWCPA extended copyright protection to a class of works called "architectural works," 17 U.S.C. §102(a)(8), which are defined as

> the design of a building as embodied in any tangible medium of expression, including a building, architectural plans, or drawings. The work includes the overall form as well as the arrangement and composition of spaces and elements in the design, but does not include individual standard features.

17 U.S.C. §101. Timberpeg argues that this definition is broad, and that VTW's timberframe (as reflected in the shop drawings and as constructed) infringes

Timberpeg's copyright in the architectural work as embodied in its second, registered preliminary plans and including a particular configuration of elements which together form the work.

We first briefly lay out the requirements of a claim of copyright infringement.

### A. Copyright Infringement

[The court explained that under the copyright infringement standard, Timberpeg needed to show, inter alia, that VTW had copied constituent elements of the work that were protectable. In order to apply the standard, the court had to identify the protectable elements of the architectural work.]

### B. The Architectural Works Copyright Protection Act

Historically, copyright law provided limited protection to works of architecture. Architectural plans, while not explicitly mentioned in the Copyright Act of 1976, were covered under a provision affording protection to "pictorial, graphic, and sculptural works." 17 U.S.C. §102(a)(5); [cit.] But architectural structures themselves were afforded virtually no protection. [cit.]

This began to change with the accession of the United States to the Berne Convention for the Protection of Literary and Artistic Works, Sept. 9, 1886, as last revised July 24, 1971, and amended Sept. 28, 1979, S. Treaty Doc. No. 99-27, 1161 U.N.T.S. 30. The Berne Convention requires protection for "works of ... architecture" as distinct from "illustrations, maps, plans, sketches and three-dimensional works relative to ... architecture." *Id.* art. 2. The United States joined the Berne Convention with the passage of the Berne Convention Implementation Act of 1988 ("BCIA"), Pub. L. No. 100-568, 102 Stat. 2853 (1988). While the BCIA amended the definition of "pictorial, graphic, and sculptural works" to explicitly include "architectural plans," *id.* §4 (codified at 17 U.S.C. §101), it did not explicitly extend protection to "architectural works," as distinct from architectural plans.

To ensure United States' compliance with the requirements of the Berne Convention, the AWCPA was signed into law on December 1, 1990. Pub. L. No. 101-650, §§701-706, 104 Stat. 5089, 5133-34 (codified in scattered sections of 17 U.S.C.); *see also* H.R. Rep. No. 101-735 (1990), reprinted in 1990 U.S.C.C.A.N. 6935. The AWCPA added "architectural works" as a new category of copyrightable works. 17 U.S.C. §102(a)(8). The legislative history makes it clear that "[p]rotection for architectural plans, drawings, and models as pictorial, graphic, or sculptural works under section 102(a)(5) ... is unaffected by" the AWCPA. H.R. Rep. No. 101-735, reprinted in 1990 U.S.C.C.A.N. at 6950.

The definition of an "architectural work," 17 U.S.C. §101, quoted in full above, has three main components. First, an "architectural work" is the "design of a building as embodied in any tangible medium of expression." *Id.* The definition provides three exemplars of such a tangible medium of expression—"a building, architectural plans, or drawings"—although these are not the only possible media of expression. *Id.* As originally drafted, the bill only referred to architectural works as embodied in buildings. H.R. Rep. No. 101-735, reprinted in 1990 U.S.C.C.A.N. at 6950. According to the legislative history for the AWCPA, "there was concern that a defendant with access to the plans or drawings could construct an identical building but escape liability so long as the plans or drawings were not copied." *Id.* To close this potential gap, the bill was reworded to expand the definition of an architectural work to encompass a building design "as embodied in any tangible medium of expression." *Id.*

This more expansive definition means that the holder of a copyright in an architectural plan (such as Timberpeg) has two forms of protection, one under the provision for an "architectural work" under 17 U.S.C. §102(a)(8), and another under the provision for a "pictorial, graphical, or sculptural work" under 17 U.S.C. §102(a)(5). The legislative history confirms this point. *See* H.R. Rep. No. 101-735, reprinted in 1990 U.S.C.C.A.N. at 6950 ("An individual creating an architectural work by depicting that work in plans or drawing will have two separate copyrights, one in the architectural work (section 102(a)(8)), the other in the plans or drawings (section 102(a)(5))."). The two avenues of protection are slightly different in scope, as discussed below. As Timberpeg made clear in its motion for reconsideration before the district court, its "central theory" is based on the protection afforded architectural works under §102(a)(8) rather than the protection afforded architectural plans under §102(a)(5).

The second component of the definition is that an architectural work "includes the overall form as well as the arrangement and composition of spaces and elements in the design." 17 U.S.C. §101. According to the legislative history,

> [t]he phrase "arrangement and composition of spaces and elements" recognizes that: (1) creativity in architecture frequently takes the form of a selection, coordination, or arrangement of unprotectible elements into an original, protectible whole; (2) an architect may incorporate new, protectible design elements into otherwise standard, unprotectible building features; and (3) interior architecture may be protected.

H.R. Rep. No. 101-735, *reprinted in* 1990 U.S.C.C.A.N. at 6949.

Finally, the definition excludes from the protectable "architectural work" "individual standard features." 17 U.S.C. §101. The legislative history provides examples of such individual standard features: "common windows, doors, and other staple building components." H.R. Rep. No. 101-735, reprinted in 1990 U.S.C.C.A.N. at 6949. Non-standard individual features reflecting some amount of originality are not necessarily excluded from copyright protection. *Id.* Furthermore, while individual standard features may not be individually copyrightable, as the quoted legislative history above confirms, the combination of such standard features may be copyrightable. *Id.*

Under the Copyright Act, architectural works are, in at least one sense, "subject to a standard of copyrightability more generous than that accorded pictorial, graphic or sculptural works." Ginsburg, *supra*, at 491. Under 17 U.S.C. §101,

> pictorial, graphic, and sculptural works . . . include works of artistic craftsmanship insofar as their form *but not their mechanical or utilitarian aspects are concerned*; the design of a useful article, as defined in this section, shall be considered a pictorial, graphic, or sculptural work only if, and only to the extent that, such design incorporates pictorial, graphic, or sculptural features that can be identified separately from, and are capable of existing independently of, the utilitarian aspects of the article.

*Id.* (emphasis added). The requirement that the protectable elements of a pictorial, graphic, or sculptural work be separated from the "utilitarian aspects" of the work under 17 U.S.C. §102(a)(5) is known as the "separability test." By contrast, there is no separability test for an architectural work. In the AWCPA, Congress purposely did not impose such a separability test for determining the copyrightability of architectural works. *See* H.R. Rep. No. 101-735, reprinted in 1990 U.S.C.C.A.N. at 6951 ("[T]he copyrightability of architectural works shall not be evaluated under the separability test applicable to pictorial, graphic, or sculptural works.").

## IV.

. . .

On appeal, the arguments center around whether there is a genuine issue of material fact as to substantial similarity [of protectable expression] . . .

### A. Actual Copying

[The court found that Timberpeg had raised at least a fact issue as to actual copying, the first prong of the infringement analysis.]

### B. Substantial Similarity

[The court then turned to the second prong of the infringement analysis, substantial similarity of protectable expression.]

The record shows the following similarities between VTW's shop drawings and Timberpeg's registered plans:

1. VTW's shop drawings and the frame as constructed had a backwards-L-shaped footprint with exactly the same dimensions as the timber-framed portion of the main house in Timberpeg's plans.
2. VTW's shop drawings and the constructed frame had a kitchen "bump-out" along the western wall, although the VTW bump-out was about two feet wider than the one in Timberpeg's plans.
3. VTW's shop drawings showed a central switchback staircase in precisely the same location as the staircase in Timberpeg's plans, and the constructed frame included the posts used to define the stair bay.
4. VTW's frame showed a lofted second floor in the same location and with the same dimensions as in Timberpeg's plans.
5. VTW's frame had the same roof pitch and dimensions as in Timberpeg's plans.

6. The plate (wall) height was the same in both Timberpeg's plans and VTW's shop drawings.
7. VTW's shop drawings appeared to contemplate a further wing attached to the eastern wall of the timberframe; the shop drawings showed the location of exterior wall panels (which VTW would not erect but were nonetheless reflected in the drawings), and there were no such panels along the eastern side. The Timberpeg plans showed a separate stick-built wing attached to the eastern side of the timberframed portion of the home.

VTW and the district court pointed to a number of differences shown in the record between VTW's shop drawings and Timberpeg's registered plans:

1. VTW asserts that its frame was able to support any number of designs, depending on how the panels and walls were applied to the frame, while the Timberpeg design showed a particular internal floor plan and external features. Timberpeg acknowledges that the frame was not determinative, but points out that VTW's frame could accommodate Timberpeg's whole house design (if one chose to do so).
2. Timberpeg's registered plans did not show a complete timberframe design, while VTW's shop drawings showed only a timberframe, and VTW only erected a timberframe.
3. The frame components that were shown in Timberpeg's second, registered preliminary plans reflected a certain framing style with common rafters and principal purlins, while VTW's shop drawings and frame were in a bent style.
4. While Timberpeg's plans and VTW's frame both had 27 posts, there are differences. There were two posts in the VTW shop drawings without any corresponding equivalents in the Timberpeg design. Of the twenty-five equivalent posts, only two were identical in size, orientation, notching, and location.

VTW argues that these differences "preclude[] the existence of a material dispute on whether there was 'substantial similarity.'" Timberpeg argues that all of these differences are minimal, and are insufficient to overcome the similarities such that summary judgment for VTW is warranted.

Keeping in mind the definition of an "architectural work" as "includ[ing] the overall form as well as the arrangement and composition of spaces and elements in the design," 17 U.S.C. §101, we conclude that there are genuine issues of material fact as to substantial similarity.

The district court erred in failing to consider those similarities that went to the "overall form" of the building as well as the "arrangement and composition of spaces and elements." The district court found that the only similarities were in "the idea of a twenty-eight by forty-four foot part of a house, with a stair bay located in a particular position"[8] and so found that no reasonable jury could

---

8. The district court referred to the "idea/expression" dichotomy in copyright law. "It is axiomatic that, while 'no author may copyright his ideas or the facts he narrates,' an author may copyright the expression of those ideas." *John G. Danielson, Inc. v. Winchester-Conant Props., Inc.*,

conclude that VTW's shop drawings were substantially similar to Timberpeg's registered plans.

In fact, the relevant similarities here go beyond those recognized by the district court. At issue here is a particular combination of elements in Timberpeg's architectural work: a portion of a home featuring a timberframe with a backwards-L-shaped footprint, with a particular arrangement of posts, with certain dimensions and a bump-out along the western wall, featuring a central switchback staircase, with a lofted second floor of a certain floor area and in a certain location, with a certain roof pitch with certain dimensions, and certain wall heights. A reasonable jury, properly considering this combination of elements, could conclude that VTW's frame was substantially similar to Timberpeg's registered plans.

. . .

As to VTW's claim that it is a dispositive difference that the VTW frame could accommodate any number of internal layouts and external features other than those reflected in the architectural plans created by Timberpeg, this too stems from a misunderstanding of Timberpeg's claim. Copyright protection exists not only in the architectural work taken as a whole (which includes a particular floor plan and arrangement of external features), but also in protectable portions of the work. Timberpeg bases its claims here on a combination of elements, which, taken together, are protectable under the definition of an architectural work in 17 U.S.C. §101. As the legislative history for the AWCPA states, "[t]he phrase 'arrangement and composition of spaces and elements' recognizes that . . . creativity in architecture frequently takes the form of a selection, coordination, or arrangement of unprotectible elements into an original, protectible whole." H.R. Rep. No. 101-735, reprinted in 1990 U.S.C.C.A.N. at 6949. A jury could reasonably conclude that VTW's frame is substantially similar to these protectable elements of Timberpeg's architectural work. The fact that VTW's frame might not necessarily result in other elements being taken from Timberpeg's architectural work is not dispositive.

VTW also considers the differences in the posts between Timberpeg's plan and VTW's frame to be dispositive. This is an argument that can be addressed to the jury, but is not itself dispositive on summary judgment. Timberpeg argues that differences in almost all of the posts are measured on the scale of inches rather than feet. VTW has not argued that Timberpeg is wrong on this point, and has not demonstrated that no reasonable jury would find the differences insignificant. VTW makes general statements that certain posts have a different size, orientation, or notching, but the actual measure of the

---

322 F.3d 26, 42 (1st Cir. 2003) (quoting *Harper & Row Publishers, Inc. v. Nation Enters.*, 471 U.S. 539 (1985)). Drawing the line between an idea and the expression of that idea can be difficult. As Judge Learned Hand recognized, "Obviously, no principle can be stated as to when an imitator has gone beyond copying the 'idea,' and has borrowed its 'expression.' Decisions must therefore inevitably be ad hoc." *Peter Pan Fabrics, Inc. v. Martin Weiner Corp.*, 274 F.2d 487, 489 (2d Cir. 1960). Regardless of whether a house of certain dimensions with a central staircase might be regarded as an idea, the combination of elements at issue here go beyond an idea into the realm of expression.

differences is important to evaluating substantial similarity; a difference of a few feet obviously weighs more strongly against substantial similarity than a difference of a few inches. Both the magnitude and significance of any differences present disputed issues of material fact that cannot be resolved on summary judgment.

VTW also relies on the difference in the size of the kitchen bump-out and the fact that Timberpeg's second preliminary plan contemplated a common rafter style, whereas the VTW frame featured a bent style. While these differences may also weigh against a finding of substantial similarity by the fact finder, this is evidence for the jury to weigh.

. . .

[*Reversed.*]

## NOTES AND QUESTIONS

1. *Tailoring copyright protection to fit particular types of works?* The Copyright Act singles out architectural works for treatment separate from other artistic works. Do architectural works differ from other types of copyrightable works? In ways that justify different treatment under the copyright law? Is there a broader principle in operation here—should the copyright law offer specialized protection for other types of subject matter? Or should "one size fits all" be the guiding principle? As we discuss in Chapter 8, copyright law also offers specialized protection for designs of vessel hulls, a federal legislative response to the Supreme Court's *Bonito Boats* decision striking down a Florida law. Similar proposals to provide special protection for fashion designs have surfaced in recent years. Do the architectural works cases provide lessons for these other areas?

2. *Separating out standard-building features.* It may not be very easy for courts to distinguish between protectable architectural elements and unprotectable standard-building features. Indeed, this inquiry may not be much of an improvement over the separability analysis. The *T-Peg* case provides a hint of the difficulties, evident from its cataloguing of apparently protectable features of the plaintiff's design. How does the court know that those features are not standard-building features? Would the sizes and placement of rooms, windows, and doors ordinarily be "standard" or protectable? Or must that question be answered on a case-by-case basis after detailed analysis? *See, e.g., Richmond Homes Mgmt., Inc. v. Raintree, Inc.*, 862 F. Supp. 1517 (W.D. Va. 1994) (analyzing the copyrightability of several interior and exterior features of a home).

3. *What is a "building"?* When the two of us (Dinwoodie and Janis) travel on tour, we generally ride in the Dinwoodie & Janis Cruisemobile, a luxurious bus/recreational vehicle modified by our personal architects. Is the Cruisemobile a "building" in accord with the Section 101 definition of an "architectural work" (defining such a work as "the design of a building as embodied in any tangible medium of expression . . .")? What about Professor Janis' ice-fishing shelter, a 6' × 6' shack which he constructs on a lake in northern Iowa each winter when the ice thickens, and occupies for three hours each Sunday, generally during NFL broadcasts?

## Leicester v. Warner Brothers
232 F.3d 1212 (9th Cir. 2000)

Rymer, Circuit Judge:

In 1994, the 801 Tower in downtown Los Angeles and four towers that form its streetwall on the south side of the building became the Second Bank of Gotham in *Batman Forever*. Andrew Leicester, an artist known for large scale public art, claims copyright protection for these towers along with other artistic works he created in a courtyard space called the Zanja Madre. He registered the whole of Zanja Madre as a "sculptural work" and sued Warner Brothers for infringement. Following a bench trial, the district court found that the streetwall towers (even though they have artistic elements) are part of the "architectural work." As such, the court concluded, pictures taken of the streetwall towers along with the 801 Tower are not infringing pursuant to the exemption for pictorial representations of buildings in the Architectural Works Copyright Protection Act of 1990. 17 U.S.C. §120(a). Leicester argues that the court erred by refusing to consider the Zanja Madre as a unitary sculptural work, and by construing the 1990 Act so as to eliminate separate protection for sculptural works attached to buildings. We disagree that the court erred in either respect (or in any other), and affirm.

I

. . .

The artistic development consists of separate artistic works intended by Leicester to tell an allegorical story of the history of Los Angeles. In the courtyard proper, there is a fountain consisting of a rock split by an arrowhead from which water flows through a channel representing the "Mother Ditch," or Zanja Madre, which brought water to Los Angeles in its early history. Also inside the perimeter of the courtyard are two sets of two towers representing the city — two building towers and two towers with drill bits on top. The fountain area and garden, which has benches for public use, represents a mountainous area around Los Angeles that is a source of the city's water.

Five more towers and gates are aligned along the Figueroa Street side of the courtyard, forming a wall and the entrance to the courtyard and the 801 Tower. This is the "streetwall" portion of the artwork. Of the five towers comprising the streetwall, the two closest to the building (the "smoke towers") are topped by a brass metalwork design illustrating smoke flattening out under an inversion layer. The two tallest towers (the "lantern towers") have a lantern topped with grillwork. The lanterns are at the same height and recall those affixed to the building; the tower bases likewise recall the pilasters of the building. The lantern towers are lit at night (like the lanterns on the building). The grillwork assembly consists of concentric rings that symbolize 1930s-era radio waves and modern telecommunications signals. Between the two lantern towers is a fifth, shorter tower which is capped by a vampire figure and to which the main gates are attached. When closed, the gates represent a vampire bat derived from William Mulholland's statement that Los Angeles is a "water vampire." There is also a streetwall consisting of three additional smoke towers (identical to those on perimeter of the courtyard) that extends westerly from the building to the property line on Eighth Street. This streetwall is not part of Zanja Madre or of Leicester's copyright claim.

In the 1991 contract between Leicester and R & T, Leicester gave R & T a "perpetual irrevocable license to make reproductions" of Zanja Madre "including but not limited to reproductions used in advertising, brochures, media, publicity, and catalogs or other similar publications." Leicester also agreed that he would "not make any duplicate, three-dimensional reproductions" of the Zanja Madre or grant permission to others to do so.

In July 1994, Warner Bros. obtained written permission from R & T to use the premises of the 801 Tower for filming *Batman Forever*. Leicester and the architect were not consulted, nor was the Zanja Madre mentioned in the agreement although the parties understood that Warner Bros. would film the property line along Figueroa. The 801 Tower and the two lantern towers and two smoke towers in the streetwall appear briefly as background in a few scenes in the movie. The building is the Gotham City bank where nefarious deeds occur before Batman comes to the rescue. The balance of Zanja Madre — the vampire tower and the courtyard portion — do not appear in the film. In addition, Warner Bros. built a miniature model of the 801 Tower that included a miniature of the Zanja Madre for a special effects shot, and the two lantern towers and two smoke towers along with the building were shown in the videotape taken from the movie as well as in some promotional items.

Leicester registered the Zanja Madre for copyright as a sculptural work in 1995 and brought this suit against Warner Bros. for copyright infringement, unfair competition, and interference with prospective business relations. The parties agreed to a bifurcated trial in which the court was first to decide in a non-jury phase whether §120(a) applies to Warner Bros.'s use of the Zanja Madre; whether the use was permissible under a valid license or otherwise; whether Leicester is the sole author of Zanja Madre or any portion used by Warner Bros.; and whether Leicester owns a copyright to the Zanja Madre, or any portion used by Warner Bros., and its scope. Remaining issues were to be tried in a second phase to a jury.

After trial on Phase I, including a site visit, the court found that R & T had an exclusive license to sublicense three-dimensional reproductions to Warner Bros. and did so,[1] but that it did not have the right to sublicense Warner Bros. to make photographic or other pictorial copies of Zanja Madre. However, the court found that the two lantern towers and the two smoke towers have functional aspects designed to be part of the building plan and from their appearance are designed to match up with the architecture of the building; it also found that the artistic work at the tops are incorporated into the tower structure and design, and are therefore an integrated part of the "architectural work." Consequently, the court held that Warner Bros. did not infringe Leicester's copyright because 17 U.S.C. §120(a) exempts pictorial representations of architectural works from copyright infringement. It declined to construe the 1990 amendments as Leicester urged, to leave intact the previously authorized protection for sculptural works that were "conceptually separable" from the building of which they are a part, concluding instead that the intent of

---

1. The court thus held that the special effects miniature of the Zanja Madre was duly licensed.

Congress was to substitute the new protection afforded architectural works for the previous protection sometimes provided under the conceptual separability test for non-utilitarian sculptures (such as gargoyles and stained glass windows) incorporated into a work of architecture. Accordingly, the court entered judgment for Warner Bros. Leicester has timely appealed.

. . .

### III

Leicester argues that the Zanja Madre is a unitary sculptural work that the district court effectively mutilated by severing four of its eight towers and treating them as part of the building. He points out that any three-dimensional, non-utilitarian, original, creative work qualifies as a "sculptural work," relying on *Kamar Int'l, Inc. v. Russ Berrie & Company,* 657 F.2d 1059, 1061 (9th Cir. 1981). The Zanja Madre is obviously three-dimensional, original and creative, and in his view, it is "non-utilitarian" because it is not humanly habitable, it is not a building, and it can't become "functional" simply because it is physically or aesthetically oriented to the 801 Tower. In any event, Leicester contends, the towers are conceptually separate from the building and are protectable as a sculptural work after the 1990 Act as they were before.

### A

Title 17 U.S.C. §102(a) defines eight categories of original works of authorship that are afforded copyright protection. Section 102(a)(8) protects "architectural works" and §102(a)(5) protects "pictorial, graphic, and sculptural works" (PGS works). Classification of the Zanja Madre as an architectural work is critical because unlike PGS works, architectural works are afforded a more limited copyright protection:

> The copyright in an architectural work that has been constructed does not include the right to prevent the making, distributing, or public display of pictures, paintings, photographs, or other pictorial representations of the work, if the building in which the work is embodied is located in or ordinarily visible from a public place.

17 U.S.C. §120(a); [cit.].

Prior to 1990, the Copyright Act afforded no protection to architectural works. Buildings were considered to be "useful articles," not protected by the Copyright Act. [cit.] Although buildings were not protected prior to 1990, an architect's plans and drawings were protected as a PGS work. Title 17 U.S.C. §101 defines PGS works as follows:

> "Pictorial, graphic, and sculptural works" include two-dimensional and three-dimensional works of fine, graphic, and applied art, photographs, prints and art reproductions, maps, globes, charts, diagrams, models, and technical drawings, including architectural plans.

17 U.S.C. §101.

On March 1, 1989, the United States joined the Berne Convention for the Protection of Literary and Artistic Works. To comply with this treaty obligation, Congress passed the Architectural Works Copyright Protection Act of

1990 (AWCPA), establishing a new category of copyright protection for works of architecture. *See* H.R. Rep. 101-735, at 4-10.

As defined in 17 U.S.C. §101, an

> "architectural work" is the design of a building as embodied in any tangible medium of expression, including a building, architectural plans, or drawings. The work includes the overall form as well as the arrangement and composition of spaces and elements in the design, but does not include individual standard features.

17 U.S.C. §101. Congress did not afford architectural works full copyright protection; rather, it exempted the making of pictorial representations of architectural works from copyright infringement. The House Report notes that "[a]rchitecture plays a central role in our daily lives, not only as a form of shelter or as an investment, but also as a work of art. It is an art form that performs a very public, social purpose." H.R. Report 101-735, at 12. The Report explains the reason for exempting pictorial representations of architectural works from copyright infringement:

> Architecture is a public art form and is enjoyed as such. Millions of people visit our cities every year and take back home photographs, posters, and other pictorial representations of prominent works of architecture as a memory of their trip. Additionally, numerous scholarly books on architecture are based on the ability to use photographs of architectural works.
>
> These uses do not interfere with the normal exploitation of architectural works. Given the important public purpose served by these uses and the lack of harm to the copyright owner's market, the Committee chose to provide an exemption, rather than rely on the doctrine of fair use, which requires ad hoc determinations.

H.R. Rep. 101-735, at 22.

B

Against this backdrop, the district court found that the lantern towers and the smoke towers, including the decorative elements at the top, are part of the 801 Tower as a whole. As it explained, each tower appears to be an integrated concept which includes both architectural and artistic portions. The court rejected Leicester's assumption that the decorative portion should be looked at alone as conceptually separate, artistic embellishments of the whole; rather, it found, the artistic and architectural impression is one created by the towers as a whole, complementing the pilasters and continuing the theme of the third floor lanterns of the building. Thus, it concluded, the four towers are part of the design plan of the building.

These findings are well supported in the record. The four towers form a streetwall that extends the building to the property line. The streetwall was not a creative aspect of Leicester's work; it was an architectural element mandated by the CRA, which required a structure with sufficient mass to establish the street edge and be no higher than three stories. Thus, the streetwall's two highest columns (the lantern towers) are limited to three stories. Professor Louis Naidorf, Dean of the Woodbury University School of Architecture and Design, testified that streetwalls are traditionally considered as architectural features: "Particularly in modern urban design, streetwalls are one of the basics of the architectural vocabulary, along with columns, windows, and doors."

The streetwall matches the building and gives the impression that the building continues to the end of the property line. The streetwall towers are designed to appear as part of the building; indeed, the court found based on considerable evidence that Hayes was a joint author with Leicester of the lantern and smoke towers. The bases of the towers are identical to those of the building pilasters for the first three floors, constructed with the same pink granite and green marble. The lanterns on the lantern towers match the lanterns attached to the building at its third floor level; they are made of the same material and are at the same height as those on the building. The streetwall towers are positioned to match the distance between any two pilasters of the building. Additionally, there is a streetwall consisting of three smoke towers on the opposite corner of the building on Eighth Street, placed the same distance apart as the pilasters. These towers are identical to the two streetwall smoke towers closest to the building on Figueroa. Leicester concedes that the Eighth Street towers are not part of the Zanja Madre. As Professor Naidorf observed, the lantern towers and smoke towers that form the Figueroa streetwall as well as the smoke towers on the Eighth Street side of the building serve "the architectural and urban design purpose of defining the street frontage and enhancing the pedestrian level of the complex." In addition, the Zanja Madre streetwall serves the functional purpose of channeling traffic into the courtyard, as metal gates, which open and close for control, latch onto the lantern towers.

Nevertheless, Leicester argues that the court erred when it concluded that because the towers were placed in alignment with the building to give a visual effect of a wall, used the same marble to give the impression that the building continued until the end of the property line, and had identically appearing base features and visually matching design features on the building, that the towers are therefore part of the building plan because those features at most contribute to the visual effect of the Zanja Madre. Leicester contends that visual effects cannot impart usefulness to the four towers, thereby making the Zanja Madre a "building." He points out that these visual effects are not "intrinsic" to the towers nor do they render the towers intrinsically inhabitable as a "building." For this reason, he submits, the court erred in relying on these features. We disagree that these points matter, however, given the district court's finding that the smoke and lantern towers are part of the architectural work and the building plan. In the relevant sense, "building" includes structures "that are used, but not inhabited by human beings," H.R. Rep. 101-735, at 20, and §101's protection of an "architectural work" extends to the "overall form as well as the arrangement and composition of spaces and elements in the design" of a building. The 801 Tower's streetwall seems plainly covered as an "arrangement and composition of spaces and elements" in the building's design. Leicester also submits that the district court erred by finding that the four columns functioned to direct and control traffic into a courtyard adjacent to the 801 Tower, but we don't see how as they clearly support the gates that control access both to the courtyard and to the building. While Leicester correctly points out that the aesthetic features of the smoke and lantern towers do not contribute to the access control function, we are not convinced that for this reason alone the district court incorrectly found that the towers should be considered as a unit and as part of the 801 Tower as a whole.

Leicester further maintains that the streetwall towers are a sculptural work which is "conceptually separate" from the building and thus independently entitled to copyright protection. Again, the district court found otherwise and we cannot say its finding lacks support. The streetwall towers were designed to extend the building visually, which they do along both Figueroa and Eighth. The Eighth Street smoke towers are equally integrated and serve the same purpose on Eighth as the Figueroa Street smoke towers do on Figueroa. This is powerful evidence that they (together with the additional two lantern towers on Figueroa) are part of the functional and architectural vocabulary of the building.

C

Because the streetwall towers are part of the architectural work, §120(a) applies. It allows the public the right to photograph public buildings including, in this case, the streetwall smoke and lantern towers unless, as Leicester contends, the 1990 amendments specifically provide for the continued separate protection of sculptural works attached to buildings. Leicester's position is that the Berne Convention did not require taking away copyright protection for PGS works, and Congress did not do so when it passed the AWPCA implementing the Convention. He relies in particular upon passages in the legislative history indicating that certain works of authorship which may separately qualify for protection as PGS works may be permanently embodied in architectural works, and that in such cases the author (if the same for both works) may elect whether to seek a remedy under §102(a)(5) or 102(a)(8). *See, e.g.*, H.R. Rep. 101-735, at 19 n. 41;[4] H.R. Rep. 101-735, at 19.

Whether or not Leicester may have some *other* claim for a *different* infringement of his copyright in the Zanja Madre towers as a sculptural work, we believe he has none for a pictorial representation of the 801 Tower and its streetwall embodying a protected architectural work. Otherwise, §120(a)'s exemption for pictorial representations of buildings would make no sense. When copyright owners in architectural works were given protection for the first time in 1990, the right was limited by §120(a) so that publicly visible buildings could freely be photographed. *See* H.R. Rep. 101-735, at 11-12, 21-22. This reflected a shift from the prior regime of relying on "ad hoc determinations" of fair use. *Id.* at 21-22. Having done this, it would be counterintuitive to suppose that Congress meant to restrict pictorial copying to some, but not all of, a unitary architectural work.

Accordingly, we agree with the district court that §120(a) applies.

[*Affirmed.*]

---

4. Footnote 41 of the Report states: "The subcommittee was aware that certain works of authorship which may separately qualify for protection as pictorial, graphic, or sculptural works, may be permanently embedded in architectural works. Stained glass windows are one such example. Election is inappropriate in any case where the copyright owner of a pictorial, graphic, or sculptural work embodied in an architectural work is different from the copyright owner of the architectural work."

TASHIMA, Circuit Judge, concurring:

I concur in the result and in most of the reasoning of the majority opinion. I disagree only with its conclusion that the district court found that the streetwall towers were *not* "conceptually separate" from the building. On this point, I agree with the dissent that the district court found only "that the four relevant towers are a portion of the architectural work which includes the building and those four towers." As the dissent further observes, the district court found it unnecessary to decide whether the streetwall towers were conceptually separable because it concluded as a matter of law that "the enactment of Section 120(a) had the effect of limiting the conceptual separability concept to situations not involving architectural works." The district court concluded its analysis of the Architectural Works Copyright Protection Act (AWCPA), Pub. L. No. 101-650, §§701-706, 1990 U.S.C.C.A.N. (104 Stat.) 5133, thusly:

> If this interpretation is correct, the former doctrine of "conceptual separability" as it applied to pictorial, graphic or sculptural work embedded as part of a building, has been modified by the 1990 amendments. The court adopts this interpretation of the Act.

*Id.* I agree with this conclusion as applied to the facts of this case.

. . .

In these factual circumstances, where a joint architectural/artistic work functions as part of a building, the district court concluded that §120(a)'s exemption applied to protect Warner Bros.' pictorial representation of the streetwall towers against a claim of copyright infringement. I agree with that conclusion in the narrow circumstances of this case.[2] To hold otherwise, as the dissent apparently would do, would completely eviscerate the purpose and protection of §120(a)'s exemption. I do not believe that that was Congress' intent in enacting the AWCPA.

There is ample support in the legislative history of the Act that the protection for architectural works in 17 U.S.C. §102(a)(8) is now the exclusive remedy for PGS works embodied in an architectural work—at least for those PGS works that are so functionally a part of a building that §120(a)'s exemption would be rendered meaningless for such buildings, if conceptual separability were applied to them. A contrary reading of the AWCPA would countermine Congress' intent in creating the "pictorial representation" exemption from copyright protection for architectural works. I thus read the AWCPA as rejecting application of the conceptual separability test where the architectural work and the artistic work are so closely and functionally intertwined as in this case.

Under the dissent's reading of the AWCPA, any copyrightable architectural work containing conceptually separable PGS elements (*e.g.*, stained glass windows) would receive full copyright protection under §102(a)(5), while those

---

2. I emphasize the narrow and unique circumstances of this case: Here, the disputed PGS work is the functional equivalent of a building wall, serving the architectural purpose of extending the building line itself, as architecturally-mandated by the CRA. This is a far cry from "the smallest painting on the front of a building," or "painting even a small work on a building," to which the dissent compares the streetwall. The case the dissent worries about is not before us, even assuming that the details of the "small painting" could be discerned in the type of pictorial representation of a building at issue here. I note also that the free-standing elements of the Zanja Madre are not at issue in this case.

containing "original design elements" which are not separable would be subject to the "pictorial representation" exemption. The difficulty with this interpretation is that it is completely unclear how a potential infringer—or an artist or architect, for that matter—would be able to distinguish between the two, especially considering that this circuit has never addressed the conceptual separability doctrine and there is no uniform standard elsewhere. To require one to wade through the morass of conceptual separability before he can exercise the right granted by §120(a) and be assured that his pictorial representation is non-infringing cannot be what Congress intended. [Judge Tashima cited legislative history in support of the conclusion that "functional PGS works embedded in a building are no longer eligible for conceptual separability treatment."]

The dissent relies heavily on the legislative history concerning the architect's right to elect to sue under §102(a)(5)—the "plans" provision—and §102(a)(8)—the "architectural work" provision—and concludes that, since an architect still may sue for the unauthorized use of his plans, a PGS copyright owner, by necessary implication, also must be able to sue under the old version of §102(a)(5). *See* H.R. Rep. No. 101-735, at 6950 ("An individual creating an architectural work by depicting that work in plans or drawing [*sic*] will have two separate copyrights, one in the architectural work (section 102(a)(8)), the other in the plans or drawings (section 102(a)(5)).").

It does not follow, however, that because Congress did not intend that the new statute would change the extent of protection for architectural plans and drawings, it also intended that the nature of the protection for PGS works attached to an existing building would remain static. It is altogether feasible to allow an architect to elect to sue for the unauthorized reproduction of his drawings as a separate artistic work entitled to its own copyright protection without running afoul of the pictorial representation exception mandated by Congress. Conversely, providing full §102(a)(5) protection to a PGS work embodied as a functional element in an architectural work would eviscerate the pictorial representation exception because one could not photograph, draw, paint, etc. (subject to the fair use doctrine) any building that had such a PGS work embodied in it. Congress specifically noted the "important public purpose" served by allowing pictorial representations of our nation's buildings. H.R. Rep. No. 101-735, at 6953 (noting that "numerous scholarly books on architecture are based on the ability to use photographs of architectural works"). Thus, we should not read the AWCPA in a way that would inhibit those important public uses.

Although the dissent condemns limiting copyright protection for PGS works embodied in an architectural work, its approach would limit the copyright protection afforded to architects. As the dissent reads the Act, architects who cannot prove that another reproduced his or her plans will no longer have protection against the reproduction of original design elements of their buildings if that building happens to contain a conceptually separable PGS whose copyright is owned by another. Moreover, the dissent's approach would necessitate—in every case in which ornamental elements appear in an architectural work—a determination of whether any part of the work constitutes a conceptually separable sculptural work entitled to PGS protection, which is precisely the result Congress sought to avoid. *See* H.R. Rep. No. 101-735, at 6951 ("[T]he *principal* reason for not treating architectural works as pictorial, graphic, or sculptural works is to avoid entangling architectural works in this disagreement.") (emphasis added).

. . . In the circumstances of this case, the more reasoned interpretation of the AWCPA is that §102(a)(8) now provides the sole source of copyright protection for functional PGS works embodied in an architectural work. This approach provides the same scope of protection to the architect and the artist, provides some certainty in the law, conserves judicial resources by eliminating the difficult-to-apply conceptual separability test, and more closely effectuates Congress' intent to reject the conceptual separability test as a device for determining the scope of protection for architectural works. Most importantly, it gives meaning and substance to the pictorial representation exemption Congress enacted in §120(a).

For these reasons, I agree with the majority's conclusion that Congress did not "mean[] to restrict pictorial copying to some, but not all of, a unitary architectural work," and, therefore, that §120(a) applies.

FISHER, Circuit Judge, dissenting:

I agree with the majority that the district court did not clearly err in finding as a factual matter—after a thorough and thoughtful inquiry—that the streetwall portion of the Zanja Madre is part of the larger architectural work of the 801 Building, but I do not believe that ends the inquiry. This is so because I do not believe this finding precludes a concurrent finding that the streetwall towers can also be considered conceptually separate from the building (as part of the rest of the Zanja Madre sculpture, for example). If the towers can be seen as conceptually separate from the 801 Building, then they are entitled to full copyright protection as a sculptural work under 17 U.S.C. §102(5), despite being part of an architectural work, unless we determine as a matter of law that the Architectural Works Copyright Protection Act (AWCPA), Pub. L. No. 101-650, §§701-706, 104 Stat. 5133 (codified at 17 U.S.C. §§101-102, 120), completely eliminated separate copyright protection for pictorial, graphic and sculptural works ("PGS works") that are a part of, but conceptually separate from, architectural works.

The majority avoids reaching this difficult question of statutory construction by concluding that the district court's factual finding that the streetwall is part of the architectural work also constitutes a finding that the streetwall is not conceptually separable from the building. The district court, however, did not make such a finding. . . . The district court properly recognized that, even if the towers are part of the architectural work, the section 120(a) exception permitting the photographing of architectural works would not apply if the towers are conceptually separable from the 801 Building and therefore subject to full copyright protection as a sculptural work. [But the district court concluded that the conceptual separability doctrine for PGS works incorporated into an architectural work did not survive the enactment of the AWCPA.]

This conclusion on a matter of statutory interpretation is a question of law that we review de novo. [cit.] As I discuss below, I believe the district court erred in concluding that the AWCPA eliminated separate copyright protection for

PGS works that are part of architectural works. Accordingly, I respectfully dissent.

## Discussion

Determining the AWCPA's effect on PGS works incorporated in buildings is not a simple endeavor. As I explore below, the statute and legislative history do not provide a definitive answer in either direction. I recognize that, given the lack of clear guidance from the statutory language and legislative history, reasonable people can arrive at opposite conclusions. Nonetheless, I would resolve any doubt or ambiguity in favor of protecting the rights of the PGS artist. Several considerations inform this position. First, although we generally try to give meaning to every provision of a statute, [cit], when the meaning of a statute is ambiguous, we should attempt to avoid damaging existing rights absent a clear statement of a congressional intent to do so. This is in keeping with the general notion that "an amendatory act is not to be construed to change the original act or section further than expressly declared or necessarily implied." [cit.]

Prior to the AWCPA, the prevailing legal view was that PGS works that were part of, but conceptually separable from, buildings were entitled to full copyright protection under the 1976 Copyright Act. *See* H.R. Rep. No. 94-1476, at 55 (1976) ("Purely non-functional or monumental structures would be subject to full copyright protection under the bill, and the same would be true of artistic sculpture or decorative ornamentation or embellishment added to a structure."); *accord* 1 Melville B. Nimmer & David Nimmer, *Nimmer on Copyright* §2.08[D][2][b], at 2-128 (1997). We should presume that Congress was aware of this legal context when it amended the Copyright Act through the AWCPA. [cit.] We should not construe the AWCPA as altering this established practice without a clear statement of legislative intent.

Second, as the AWCPA's legislative history emphasizes, the purpose of the Act was to add protection for architectural works. *See* H.R. Rep. No. 101-735, at 20 ("The sole purpose of legislating at this time is to place the United States unequivocally in compliance with its Berne Convention obligations."). The United States has consistently taken a minimalist approach to implementing the Berne Convention, "making only those changes in U.S. law absolutely required to meet our treaty obligations." 136 Cong. Rec. E259 (daily ed. Feb. 7, 1990) (statement of Rep. Kastenmeier). The Berne Convention required Congress to add copyright protection for buildings in constructed form. Nothing in the Berne Convention required Congress simultaneously to eliminate separate copyright protection for PGS works that are part of an architectural work, and those who would read the AWCPA as extinguishing those existing rights should have the burden of proving Congress' intent to so do. Significantly, there is nothing in the AWCPA warning artists that if they incorporate their PGS works into the publicly viewable portion of a building, they will no longer be able to prevent others from commercially exploiting their works.

Third, it would be odd to interpret the AWCPA as eliminating protection for certain works of PGS artists when, contemporaneously with the AWCPA,

Congress enhanced the rights of PGS artists through separate legislation. The bill that contained the AWCPA also included the Visual Artists Rights Act of 1990 ("VARA"). *See* Pub. L. No. 101-650, §§601-10, 104 Stat. 5089, 5128-33 (1990). VARA provided, for the first time in American copyright history, limited "moral rights" for authors of works of "visual art," a subset of PGS works. *See* 17 U.S.C. §106A. Moral rights "afford protection for the author's personal, non-economic interests in receiving attribution for her work, and in preserving the work in the form in which it was created, even after its sale or licensing." Jane C. Ginsburg, *Copyright in the 101st Congress: Commentary on the Visual Artists Rights Act and the Architectural Works Copyright Protection Act of 1990,* 14 COLUM.-VLA J.L. & ARTS 477, 478 (1991). Absent a clear statement of legislative intent, I would not interpret the AWCPA as destroying PGS artists' established intellectual property rights, when, at the same time, Congress was expressing through VARA a desire to enhance the rights of PGS artists.

I. The Architectural Works Copyright Protection Act

. . .

C. AWCPA's Effect on Separate Copyright Protection for PGS Works

Nothing in the text of the AWCPA expressly eliminates or retains separate PGS protection for conceptually separable PGS works attached to buildings. As previously noted, this absence of a clear statutory mandate favors preserving the existing, historical rights of PGS artists. The conclusion that Congress did not alter the availability of separate protection is buttressed by a reasonable interpretation of the legislative history. Although the legislative history is ambiguous, its discussion of the concept of "election of protection" and treatment of monumental works of architecture, in my view, support the conclusion that Congress did not intend to eliminate separate protection for PGS works attached to buildings. Moreover, I do not believe the elimination of the separability test to determine the copyrightability of architectural works and the limit of one architectural work per structure command a contrary result.

1. Election of Protection

[Judge Fisher cited legislative history stating that "[a]n individual creating an architectural work by depicting that work in plans or drawing [*sic*] will have two separate copyrights, one in the architectural work (section 102(a)(8)), the other in the plans or drawings (section 102(a)(5)). Either or both of these copyrights may be infringed and eligible separately for damages." That is, according to Judge Fisher, Congress intended to allow an architect to elect both forms of protection concurrently.]

This reading of the legislative history is consistent with the rationale underlying Congress' explicit decision to provide a blanket photograph exemption—section 120(a)—rather than relying on the fair use doctrine. *See* H.R. Rep. No. 101-735, at 22. As the House Report accompanying the AWCPA noted:

> Millions of people visit our cities every year and take back home photographs, posters, and other pictorial representations of prominent works of architecture

as a memory of their trip. Additionally, numerous scholarly books on architecture are based on the ability to use photographs of architectural works. These uses do not interfere with the normal exploitation of architectural works. Given the important public purpose served by these uses and the lack of harm to the copyright owner's market, the Committee chose to provide an exemption, rather than rely on the doctrine of fair use, which requires ad hoc determinations.

*Id.* Congress was aware of the commercial market for posters and postcards of famous or interesting buildings, and it did not want its extension of copyright protection to constructed architectural works to affect that market. But Congress did not address the commercial market for posters and postcards of specific, copyrighted PGS works that are embedded in, or in some other way a part of, a building. Entrepreneurs desiring to sell postcards that featured a building's attached artwork always needed to obtain a license from the PGS artist or risk a copyright infringement suit. In this way, the PGS artists were in a position to control the commercial exploitation of two-dimensional reproductions of their independent, creative contribution to a larger work. I interpret the absence of explicit congressional intent to eliminate that ability to be further evidence that the AWCPA was not intended to affect the separate copyrightability of PGS works incorporated into buildings.

2. Monumental Works of Architecture

[Judge Fisher then noted that] [w]hen Congress looked [at monumental, nonfunctional works of architecture], which under the 1976 Copyright Act had been afforded full copyright protection as sculptural works, *see* H.R. Rep. No. 94-1476, at 55, and intended to eliminate that protection and replace it with protection solely as architectural works, it made its intent clear in the legislative history. Logically then, if Congress similarly had intended the AWCPA to eliminate separate PGS copyright protection for PGS works imbedded in architectural works, it would have done so expressly as well.

. . .

Congress' treatment of monumental works makes sense because monuments, which are generally nonfunctional, frequently blur the line between sculpture and architecture. Significantly, the rationale for changing the treatment of monuments does not transfer well to conceptually separable PGS works attached to architectural works. Unlike monumental, nonfunctional works of architecture, which "are, nevertheless, architectural works," PGS works attached to an architectural work are not themselves works of architecture. Despite being attached to an architectural work, they are, nevertheless, PGS works and should be entitled to all of the exclusive rights Congress has extended to works of that classification.

3. Elimination of Separability Test for Determining Copyrightability of Architectural Works

According to the House Report:

> By creating a new category of protectable subject matter in new section 102(a)(8), and, therefore, by deliberately not encompassing architectural works as pictorial, graphic, or sculptural works in existing section 102(a)(5),

the copyrightability of architectural works shall not be evaluated under the separability test applicable to pictorial, graphic, or sculptural works embodied in useful articles. There is considerable scholarly and judicial disagreement over how to apply the separability test, and the principal reason for not treating architectural works as pictorial, graphic, or sculptural works is to avoid entangling architectural works in this disagreement.

H.R. Rep. No. 101-735, at 20 (footnotes omitted). While it is true that Congress did not want architects to have to survive the morass of separability in order to obtain copyright protection for their creations, there is nothing in the AWCPA that suggests Congress intended to prevent sculptors and other artists who created PGS works that were attached to buildings from attempting to satisfy the difficult separability test and thereby gain full PGS copyright protection for their works. I believe this distinction between the copyrightability of architectural works and the copyrightability of PGS features that are part of architectural works is critical. Because buildings themselves traditionally have been considered "useful articles," see 1 *Nimmer on Copyright* §2.08[D][2][a], at 2-121 to 2-122, it would be extremely difficult, if not impossible, for an architect to obtain a copyright in a functional building if he were forced to satisfy the conceptual separability test. See Michael F. Clayton & Ron N. Dreben, *Copyright Protection for Architectural Works: Congress Changes the Rules*, 4 J. PROPRIETARY RTS. 15 (Mar. 1992) ("Given the inherent difficulty of physically or conceptually separating a building's design from its 'utilitarian' aspect or function, copyright protection for structures in this country [was] virtually nonexistent [prior to the AWCPA]."). In contrast, there is nothing inherently more difficult about applying the conceptual separability test to PGS features that are part of buildings than to PGS features that are part of other useful articles, yet Congress has not eliminated the test in those other contexts. Absent clear instruction from Congress, I believe we should continue to apply the conceptual separability test to determine the 120(a)(5) copyrightability of PGS works that are in some way a part of an architectural work. This approach has been employed for years and gives meaning to the extant rights of artists and architects.

The concurrence reads the AWCPA as replacing the conceptual separability test for PGS works embedded in architecture with a clear, bright-line rule. Its interpretation of the Act, however, sheds little light on the complicated interaction between the copyright protection of PGS works and architectural works. The concurrence proposes two very different ways of treating PGS works attached to, or embedded in, architectural works. On the one hand, it suggests Congress intended to paint with a broad brush, using the AWCPA to wipe out entirely PGS rights for *all* works embedded in buildings. On the other hand, it suggests an entirely different, and far narrower, reading of the Act in which Congress intended only to draw a fine line separating PGS protection from architectural work protection. This, as I explain below, is not so different from the current conceptual separability scheme.

The first approach is unnecessarily broad and threatens to alter deeply the relationship between artist and architect, not to mention art and architecture. The concurrence believes the legislative history of the Act reveals that

Congress intended to make the new protection given to architectural works under section 120 "the exclusive remedy for PGS works embodied in an architectural work." Conc. at 1222. This reading of the Act suggests *any* PGS work that can be considered "part" of a building automatically loses its PGS identity and protection. Such a work is entitled to receive only the lesser degree of protection afforded to architectural works. The rule makes no consideration for size of the work or degree to which the work is incorporated into a building. If an artist created even the smallest painting on the front of a building, she would lose PGS copyright protection in that work. This provides a great disincentive for artists to collaborate with architects.

The second approach posited by the concurrence tries to avoid this problem by setting forth a narrower, functionality-based test. Under this view, the AWCPA applies only to PGS works that are "so functionally a part of a building" that application of the conceptual separability test would render the section 120(a) exception for reproduction of architectural works meaningless. But this approach hardly creates clarity. At best, it preserves the status quo by serving as a proxy for conceptual separability. After all, it, too, requires a trial court to make a factual determination as to the degree of functionality a PGS work retains once it is considered part of an architectural work. Here, the district court found only that the streetwall had "functional aspects" and that, therefore, it was part of the architectural work. It did not apply any sort of functionality test to discern whether the streetwall was "so functional" that granting it PGS protection would have rendered application of section 120(a) to the 801 building meaningless. In fact, we have no idea from the district court's findings whether Warner Bros. could have filmed the 801 building without capturing a part of Zanja Madre.

Moreover, a test based solely on functionality creates yet another element of confusion because, in the legislative history of the AWCPA, Congress utilizes the term "functionality" as part of its proposed test for determining the copyrightability of architectural works. *See* H.R. Rep. No. 101-735, at 20-21, and *supra* n. 6. According to the House Report, an architectural work is copyrightable only to the extent its design elements are not "functionally required." With this in mind, the application of a functionality test for PGS works embedded in architecture might produce an ironic result. Under the concurrence's view, if a PGS work is deemed a "functional" part of a building, it loses its PGS protection and gains architectural work protection. But the very fact it has been determined to be "functional" arguably may defeat the copyrightability of the building itself, since in order for the architectural work to be copyrightable its design elements may not be "functionally required."

I recognize there is, on the surface, a degree of uncertainty in leaving alone the current scheme of protection for PGS works. In extreme cases, it may allow an entire architectural work to gain PGS protection, a result seemingly in tension with the goal of the AWCPA. This would happen, for instance, where a PGS work so fully dominated an architectural work that reproduction of the architectural work would be impossible without infringing the artist's PGS copyright. This would seem to be a rare case, however, and the current regime is equipped to handle it. In such a circumstance, as has been the case until now, a trial court could find that the PGS work was so integrated into the architectural work that it was not conceptually separable and, therefore, effectively lost its PGS status. Upon this finding, the PGS work would be protectable only as part of the architectural work. This, of course, preserves ambiguities at the margins, but law cannot be applied to the arts with mathematical precision.

Other difficulties that might arise from my reading of the AWCPA, moreover, remain unresolved by the concurrence. The concurrence's view, for example, still forces a commercial exploiter to determine whether a PGS element of a building is separately copyrighted since the piece may not be "so functional" a part of the architectural work as to render applicability of section 120(a) meaningless. To a commercial exploiter, degree of functionality should be no easier to determine than conceptual separability.

Ultimately, the only way to maneuver cleanly around these admittedly difficult problems is to read (as the concurrence suggests) the AWCPA so broadly as to eliminate fully the rights of *any* PGS work that is even a modest part of an architectural work, with no attention given to size of the work, placement, impact on the building, degree of functionality or possible conceptual separability. I believe this goes too far. It would discourage an artist from painting even a small work on a building. A sculptor would rightfully be wary of placing a piece too close to a building, or on a pedestal made with the same themes or patterns as the architectural work. The AWCPA need not be read to compel such a drastic result.

. . .

D. Other Provisions in the Copyright Act

[Judge Fisher also pointed out that when Congress enacted the Visual Artists' Rights Act, discussed in more detail in section D of this chapter, Congress amended 17 U.S.C. §113, which governs the scope of exclusive rights in PGS works, to account for the removal of PGS works from buildings. For Judge Fisher, this was "strong evidence" the Congress intended that PGS works incorporated into buildings would continue to receive "full PGS copyright protection."]

Also, interpreting the AWCPA as eliminating separate PGS protection for works incorporated into buildings would subject what would otherwise be PGS works to U.S.C. §120(b), which permits "the owners of a building embodying an architectural work" to make changes or destroy the building "without the consent of the author or copyright owner of the architectural work." Without continued application of conceptual separability for PGS works incorporated into buildings, those works, as part of the "architectural work," could be altered or destroyed without the permission of their authors. This interpretation would have Congress acting simultaneously to enhance, through VARA, the rights of authors of works of visual art while reducing, through the AWCPA, the rights of authors whose works of visual art are part of a building. An interpretation that preserves PGS protection for works attached to buildings would avoid this inconsistency.[11]

---

11. *Cf.* Significantly, in his contract, Leicester retains the right to buy back the entire Zanja Madre sculpture, including the streetwall, should the 801 building ever be demolished. This suggests that both artist and architect, at least, considered the streetwall to be conceptually—and physically—separable.

Finally, the Copyright Act's continued reference to PGS works incorporated in buildings provides additional evidence that Congress did not intend the AWCPA to eliminate PGS protection for such works. The Copyright Act requires registration of all "United States work[s]" as a prerequisite for a copyright infringement action. *See* 17 U.S.C. §411. Included in the definition of a "United States work" is "a pictorial, graphic, or sculptural work incorporated in a building or structure" located in the United States. 17 U.S.C. §101. This explicit reference to PGS works incorporated in a building was added in 1988 by the Berne Convention Implementation Act. *See* Pub. L. No. 100-568, §4(a)(1)(C). If Congress viewed the AWCPA as eliminating separate PGS protection for post-1990 PGS works incorporated into buildings, then presumably Congress would have amended the definition of "United States work" to differentiate between pre- and post-AWCPA structures.

Conclusion

The language of the AWCPA did not explicitly eliminate separate PGS copyright protection for artistic works that are incorporated into buildings. A reasonable reading of the legislative history supports the view that such separate protection remains available. Consequently, a PGS work that is part of, but conceptually separate from, an architectural work can enjoy full PGS copyright protection. Because PGS copyrights are not subject to the AWCPA's photograph exemption codified in section 120(a), Warner Bros.' pictorial reproductions of Leicester's streetwall towers in the film *Batman Forever* would not be protected by that section if Leicester's streetwall towers are conceptually separable from the 801 Building. Therefore, I would reverse the decision of the district court and remand for that conceptual separability determination. If the streetwall towers are conceptually separable, Leicester would be able to proceed to a trial on the merits of his copyright infringement claim.

Today, we erect a legal wall on a weak foundation. Depriving artists of PGS protection if their works are part of an architectural work is a drastic change in the law. It threatens to deprive the public of innovative and challenging forms of artistic and architectural expression. This result seems inconsistent with the overarching goals of the AWCPA and the VARA, taken together. Because Congress did not speak clearly on this important copyright issue, and I am not persuaded it intended to so alter artists' PGS rights, I respectfully dissent.

## NOTES AND QUESTIONS

1. ***Boundary problems.*** Is a case such as *Leicester* the predictable result of defining rights in PGS works separately of rights in architectural works? Could Congress have avoided the boundary problem by expanding PGS protection to incorporate architectural works? Or is a separate category of architectural works still preferable? Are the boundary problems between PGS and architectural works any more puzzling than, say, the boundary problems between copyright and design patent? Copyright and trade dress?

2. ***The outcome in* Leicester.** How would you have decided the *Leicester* case? Do you find the extended analysis of the legislative history illuminating?

Or does the case illustrate the perils of plunging into legislative history to interpret statutes?

## E. WORKS OF VISUAL ART

### Martin v. City of Indianapolis
192 F.3d 608 (7th Cir. 1999)

Harlington Wood, Jr., Circuit Judge:

We are not art critics, do not pretend to be and do not need to be to decide this case. A large outdoor stainless steel sculpture by plaintiff Jan Martin, an artist, was demolished by the defendant as part of an urban renewal project. Plaintiff brought a one-count suit against the City of Indianapolis (the "City") under the Visual Artists Rights Act of 1990 ("VARA"), 17 U.S.C. §101 *et seq.* The parties filed cross-motions for summary judgment. The district court granted plaintiff's motion and awarded plaintiff statutory damages in the maximum amount allowed for a non-wilful statutory violation. *Martin v. City of Indianapolis*, 982 F. Supp. 625 (S.D. Ind. 1997), and *Martin v. City of Indianapolis*, 4 F. Supp. 2d 808 (S.D. Ind. 1998). Neither party is satisfied. It is necessary to see how this unique controversy came to be.

### I. Background

Plaintiff is an artist, but in this instance more with a welding torch than with a brush. He offered evidence to show, not all of it admitted, that his works have been displayed in museums, and other works created for private commissions, including a time capsule for the Indianapolis Museum of Art Centennial. He has also done sculptured jewelry for the Indiana Arts Commission. In 1979, at the Annual Hoosier Salem Art Show, plaintiff was awarded the prize for best of show in any medium. He holds various arts degrees from Purdue University, the Art Institute of Chicago and Bowling Green State University in Ohio. Plaintiff had been employed as production coordinator for Tarpenning-LaFollette Co. (the "Company"), a metal contracting firm in Indianapolis. It was in this position that he turned his artistic talents to metal sculpture fabrication.

In 1984, plaintiff received permission from the Indianapolis Metropolitan Development Commission to erect a twenty-by-forty-foot metal sculpture on land owned by John LaFollette, chairman of the Company. The Company also agreed to furnish the materials. The resulting Project Agreement between the City and the Company granted a zoning variance to permit the erection of plaintiff's proposed sculpture. An attachment to that agreement and the center of this controversy provided as follows:

> Should a determination be made by the Department of Metropolitan Development that the subject sculpture is no longer compatible with the existing land use or that the acquisition of the property is necessary, the owner of the land and the owner of the sculpture will receive written notice signed by the Director of the Department of Metropolitan Development giving the owners of the land and sculpture ninety (90) days to remove said sculpture. Subject to weather and ground conditions.

Plaintiff went to work on the project and in a little over two years it was completed. He named it "Symphony #1," but as it turns out in view of this controversy, a more suitable musical name might have been "1812 Overture." Because of the possibility that the sculpture might someday have to be removed, as provided for in the Project Agreement, Symphony #1 was engineered and built by plaintiff so that it could be disassembled for removal and later reassembled. The sculpture did not go unnoticed by the press, public or art community. Favorable comments admitted into evidence and objected to by the City are now an issue on appeal and their admissibility will be considered hereinafter.

The trouble began in April 1992 when the City notified LaFollette that there would be public hearings on the City's proposed acquisition of various properties as part of an urban renewal plan. One of the properties to be acquired was home to Symphony #1. Kim Martin, president of the Company and plaintiff's brother, responded to the City. He reminded the City that the Company had paid for Symphony #1, and had signed the agreement with the Metropolitan Development Corporation pertaining to the eventuality of removal. Martin stated that if the sculpture was to be removed, the Company would be willing to donate it to the City provided the City would bear the costs of removal to a new site, but that plaintiff would like some input as to where his sculpture might be placed. Plaintiff also personally appeared before the Metropolitan Development Commission and made the same proposal. This was followed by a letter from plaintiff to the Mayor reiterating the removal proposal. The Mayor responded that he was referring plaintiff's proposal to his staff to see what could be done.

The City thereafter purchased the land. At the closing, plaintiff again repeated his proposal and agreed to assist so Symphony #1 could be saved and, if necessary, moved without damage. The City's response was that plaintiff would be contacted in the event the sculpture was to be removed. Shortly thereafter, the City awarded a contract to demolish the sculpture, and demolition followed, all without prior notice to plaintiff or the Company. This lawsuit resulted in which summary judgment was allowed for plaintiff. However, his victory was not entirely satisfactory to him, nor was the City satisfied. The City appealed, and plaintiff cross-appealed.

## II. Analysis

Although recognized under the Berne Convention, the legal protection of an artist's so-called "moral rights" was controversial in this country. The United States did not join the Berne Convention until 1988 when it did so in a very limited way.[3] Then Congress followed up by enacting VARA in 1990, with this explanation found in the House Reports:

> An artist's professional and personal identity is embodied in each work created by that artist. Each work is a part of his or her reputation. Each work is a form of personal expression (oftentimes painstakingly and earnestly recorded). It is a rebuke to the dignity of the visual artist that our copyright law allows distortion, modification and even outright permanent destruction of such efforts.

---

3. *See* S. Rep. No. 100-352 (1988), *reprinted in* 1988 U.S.C.C.A.N. 3706.

H.R. Rep. No. 101-514, at 15 (1990), *reprinted in* 1990 U.S.C.C.A.N. 6915, 6925.

VARA seems to be a stepchild of our copyright laws, but does not require copyright registration. Some remedies under the Copyright Act, however, including attorney's fees, are recoverable. 17 U.S.C. §§504-05. VARA provides: "[T]he author of a work of visual art . . . shall have the right . . . to prevent any destruction of a work of *recognized stature,* and any intentional or grossly negligent destruction of that work is a violation of that right." 17 U.S.C. §106A(a)(3)(B) (emphasis added). The district court considered Symphony #1 to be of "recognized stature" under the evidence presented and thus concluded that the City had violated plaintiff's rights under VARA. That finding is contested by the City.

"Recognized stature" is a necessary finding under VARA in order to protect a work of visual art from destruction. In spite of its significance, that phrase is not defined in VARA, leaving its intended meaning and application open to argument and judicial resolution. The only case found undertaking to define and apply "recognized stature" is *Carter v. Helmsley-Spear, Inc.*, 861 F. Supp. 303 (S.D.N.Y. 1994), *aff'd. in part, vacated in part, rev'd in part,* 71 F.3d 77 (2nd Cir. 1995). Involved was an unusual work of art consisting of interrelated sculptural elements constructed from recycled materials, mostly metal, to decorate the lobby of a commercial building in a borough of New York City. *Carter II,* 71 F.3d at 80. Part of the work was "a giant hand fashioned from an old school bus, [and] a face made of automobile parts. . . ." *Id.* Although the Second Circuit reversed the district court and held that the work was not a work of visual art protected by VARA, *id.* at 88, the district court presented an informative discussion in determining whether a work of visual art may qualify as one of "recognized stature." *See Carter I,* 861 F. Supp. at 324-26. That determination is based greatly on the testimony of experts on both sides of the issue, as would ordinarily be expected. *See id.*

The stature test formulated by the New York district court required:

> (1) that the visual art in question has "stature," i.e. is viewed as meritorious, and (2) that this stature is "recognized" by art experts, other members of the artistic community, or by some cross-section of society. In making this showing, plaintiffs generally, but not inevitably, will need to call expert witnesses to testify before the trier of fact.

*Carter I,* 861 F. Supp. at 325.

Even though the district court in this present case found that test was satisfied by the plaintiff's evidence, plaintiff argues that the *Carter v. Helmsley-Spear* test may be more rigorous than Congress intended. That may be, but we see no need for the purposes of this case to endeavor to refine that rule. Plaintiff's evidence, however, is not as complete as in *Carter v. Helmsley-Spear,* possibly because Symphony #1 was destroyed by the City without the opportunity for experts to appraise the sculpture in place.

The City objects to the "stature" testimony that was offered by plaintiff as inadmissible hearsay. If not admitted, it would result in plaintiff's failure to sustain his burden of proof. It is true that plaintiff offered no evidence of experts or others by deposition, affidavit or interrogatories. Plaintiff's evidence of "stature" consisted of certain newspaper and magazine articles, and various letters, including a letter from an art gallery director and a letter to the editor of *The Indianapolis News,* all in support of the sculpture, as well as a program from the show at which a model of the sculpture won "Best of Show." After reviewing the City's objection, the district court excluded plaintiff's "programs and awards" evidence as lacking adequate foundation, *Martin I,* 982 F. Supp. at 631 n. 1, but nevertheless found Martin had met his "stature" burden of proof with his other evidence. *Id.* at 630-31.

Included in the admitted evidence, for example, was a letter dated October 25, 1982 from the Director of the Herron School of Art, Indiana University, Indianapolis. It was written to the Company and says in part, "The proposed sculpture is, in my opinion, an interesting and aesthetically stimulating configuration of forms and structures." *The Indianapolis Star,* in a four-column article by its visual arts editor, discussed public sculpture in Indianapolis. This article included a photograph of Symphony #1. The article lamented that the City had "been graced by only five pieces of note," but that two more had been added that particular year, one being plaintiff's sculpture. It noted, among other things, that Symphony #1 had been erected without the aid of "federal grants" and without the help of any committee of concerned citizens. Other public sculptures came in for some criticism in the article. However, in discussing Symphony #1, the author wrote: "Gleaming clean and abstract, yet domestic in scale and reference, irregularly but securely cabled together, the sculpture shows the site what it might be. It unites the area, providing a nexus, a marker, a designation, an identity and, presumably, a point of pride."

The district judge commented on the City's hearsay objection to plaintiff's admitted evidence as follows:

> The statements contained within the proffered newspaper and magazine articles and letters are offered by Martin to show that respected members of the art community and members of the public at large consider Martin's work to be socially valuable and to have artistic merit, and to show the newsworthiness of Symphony #1 and Martin's work. *These statements are offered by Martin to show that the declarants said them,* not that the statements are, in fact, true. . . . The statements contained within the exhibits show how art critics and the public viewed Martin's work, particularly Symphony #1, and show that the sculpture was a matter worth reporting to the public. Therefore, the statements contained within these challenged exhibits are not hearsay because they are not being offered for the truth of the matters asserted therein.

*Martin I,* 982 F. Supp. at 630 (emphasis added).

We agree with the assessment made by the district court. . . .

Next the City claims that the Project Agreement entered into pre-VARA by plaintiff and the City encompassed many of plaintiff's rights under VARA. Therefore, the City argues, that whereas plaintiff failed to remove his work within the time allowed in the contract, plaintiff waived any cause of action he might have had under VARA. That failure was the City's, not plaintiff's, as under the Agreement the City was obligated to give the owners of the land and the sculpture ninety days to remove the sculpture. The City, after discussing with the Company and plaintiff possible other uses for the tract and the removal proposal, failed to give the required notice and went ahead and demolished the sculpture. Nothing had happened between the parties prior to that which could constitute a waiver of any rights by the Company or plaintiff. Plaintiff had no notice of the City letting a contract for Symphony #1's demolition and no notice when that demolition would actually occur. After the preliminary and ongoing discussions plaintiff and the Company had with the City, when there was no immediate threat of imminent demolition, plaintiff had the right to continue to rely on the specific notice provided in the Agreement, unless it had been waived, which it was not.

Plaintiff and the Company had proposed a solution if the sculpture was to be moved. That proposal was still pending when the surprise destruction of Symphony #1 occurred. Prior to the demolition, nothing more had been heard from anyone, including the Mayor. Bureaucratic ineptitude may be the only explanation. Under 17 U.S.C. §106A(e)(1), an artist may waive VARA rights "in a written instrument signed by the author," specifying to what the waiver applies. There is no written waiver instrument in this case which falls within the VARA requirements. We regard this argument to be without merit.

In spite of the City's conduct resulting in the intentional destruction of the sculpture, we do not believe under all the circumstances, particularly given the fact that the issue of VARA rights had not been raised until this suit, that the City's conduct was "wilful," as used in VARA, 17 U.S.C. §504(c)(2), so as to entitle the plaintiff to enhanced damages. This appears to be a case of bureaucratic failure within the City government, not a wilful violation of plaintiff's VARA rights. As far as we can tell from the record, those VARA rights were unknown to the City. The parties proceeded under their pre-VARA agreement which the City breached. However, plaintiff retained his VARA rights. As unfortunate as the City's unannounced demolition of Symphony #1 was, it does not qualify plaintiff for damages under VARA.

MANION, Circuit Judge, concurring in part and dissenting in part:

Like my colleagues, I am not an art critic. So I begin with the well-worn adage that one man's junk is another man's treasure. No doubt Jan Martin treasured what the city's bulldozers treated as junk. At this point in the litigation this court is not in a position to attach either label (or perhaps one falling somewhere in between) to Symphony #1. For the Martin sculpture to receive protection under the Visual Arts Rights Act (VARA), it has to rise to the statutory level of "recognized stature." Because at this summary judgment stage, at least, it has clearly not merited the protection that goes with that description, I respectfully dissent.

Another well-worn adage advises that you should never look a gift horse in the mouth. Of course anyone who has ever accepted a gift horse that turns out to be lame or otherwise infirm quickly understands the error of that advice when the feed and veterinary bills arrive. When the City acquired several tracts of land for urban renewal, Martin's Symphony #1 remained in place on one of the tracts. Martin offered to donate the sculpture to the City if it would remove and relocate it to another site. The City examined this "gift" and determined it would have cost it $8,000 to relocate, so it declined the offer. But it did agree to notify Martin in advance of any renewal project so he could remove Symphony #1 if he so chose. Although it appears that Martin was fully aware that the sculpture's days were numbered, the City did not send him an official notice before the bulldozer moved in. If this were a simple breach of contract claim (albeit not a federal case), damages could well be in order. Instead, this is a federal claim under VARA, and different standards apply.

Of course, VARA was not designed to regulate urban renewal, but to protect great works of art from destruction and mutilation, among other things. 17 U.S.C. §106A(a). In order to restrict VARA's reach, the Act was limited to preventing destruction of works of art that had attained a "recognized stature." 17 U.S.C. §106A(a)(3)(B). The court correctly notes that a natural reading of this term indicates that it has two elements (which correspond to its two words): (1) merit or intrinsic worth; and (2) a public acknowledgment of that merit by society or the art community. As the district court in *Carter v. Helmsley-Spear, Inc.* stated: "the recognized stature requirement is best viewed as a gate-keeping mechanism — protection is afforded only to those works of art that art experts, the art community, or society in general views as possessing stature." 861 F. Supp. 303, 325 (S.D.N.Y. 1994), *rev'd in part and aff'd. in part,* 71 F.3d 77 (2d Cir. 1995). So I concur with the court on this point.

I dissent, however, because summary judgment is not appropriate here. A plaintiff cannot satisfy his burden of demonstrating recognized stature through old newspaper articles and unverified letters, some of which do not even address the artwork in question. Rather, as the district court stated in *Carter*, in "making this showing [of recognized stature] plaintiffs generally, but not inevitably, will need to call expert witnesses to testify before the trier of fact." 861 F. Supp. at 325. Instances where expert testimony on this point is not necessary will be rare, and this is not one of those exceptional cases where something of unquestioned recognition and stature was destroyed. Furthermore, where newspaper articles are admitted into evidence only to acknowledge recognition but not for the truth of the matter asserted (that the art in question was good or bad), a plaintiff needs more to overcome *a defendant's* motion for summary judgment on a VARA claim, much less prevail on his own summary judgment motion. While the very publication of newspaper articles on a work of art may have bearing on the "recognized" element, there has to be some evidence that the art had stature (i.e., that it met a certain high level of quality). The newspaper articles are hearsay and not admitted for the truth of the matter asserted in them. Construed in the light most favorable to the defendant, they cannot demonstrate by a preponderance of the evidence that the plaintiff's art was of a recognized stature, and that no reasonable jury could find otherwise. Experts need to weigh in here, and the trial court and perhaps this court need to come up with a clearer definition of when works of art achieve "recognized stature."

For now, however, those who are purchasers or donees of art had best beware. To avoid being the perpetual curator of a piece of visual art that has lost (or perhaps never had) its luster, the recipient must obtain at the outset a waiver of the artist's rights under VARA. *See* 17 U.S.C. §106A(e). Before awarding building permits for erection of sculptures, municipalities might be well advised to obtain a written waiver of the artist's rights too. If not, once destroyed, art of questionable value may acquire a minimum worth of $20,000.00 under VARA.

## MASSACHUSETTS MUSEUM OF CONTEMPORARY ART FOUNDATION INC. v. BÜCHEL
593 F.3d 38 (1st Cir. 2010)

LIPEZ, J.:

### I.

. . .

[Artist Christoph Büchel, who is known for his elaborate, large-scale art, conceived of an ambitious, football-field-sized art installation entitled "Training Ground for Democracy," which was to be exhibited at the Massachusetts Museum of Contemporary Art ("MASS MoCA," or "the Museum"). The exhibit was to evoke a "village" containing a number of elements through which a visitor could walk or climb, engaging in various behaviors associated with democracy (immigrating, voting, protesting, etc.). Büchel planned for the installation to include a variety of large components, including a movie theater, a house, a bar, a mobile home, various sea containers, a bomb carousel, and an aircraft fuselage. During the early stages of the project, Büchel was not in residence, but sent instructions to the Museum. It proved to be expensive and time-consuming for Museum personnel to gather and assemble the components, and disagreements soon arose between Büchel and the Museum. Although Museum personnel continued some work on the project, the relationship with Büchel eventually deteriorated to a point at which Büchel refused to complete the installation. The Museum placed tarpaulins over the unfinished components of the work. Due to the layout of the Museum and the size of the Büchel exhibit, patrons had to walk through the area where the unfinished components were stored in order to access other parts of the Museum.

The Museum initiated litigation, seeking a declaration that it was "entitled to present to the public the materials and partial constructions" it had collected for "Training Ground for Democracy." Büchel counterclaimed under VARA and the Copyright Act, seeking damages and an injunction that would prevent MASS MoCA from displaying the unfinished installation. The district court granted summary judgment for the Museum, and Büchel appealed.]

### II.

Passed in 1990, the Visual Artists Rights Act, 17 U.S.C. 106A, was an amendment to the Copyright Act that protects the "moral rights" of certain visual artists in the works they create, consistent with Article 6bis of the Berne Convention. [cit.] The "rubric of moral rights encompasses many varieties of rights," but the two most widely recognized are attribution and integrity. [cit.] We will discuss both of these in detail below, but note briefly now that the right of attribution protects the author's right to be identified as the author of his work and also protects against the use of his name in connection with works created by others. *Id.* The right of integrity "allows the author to prevent any deforming or mutilating changes to his work." *Id.* Although these moral rights "exist independent[ly] of the economic rights" granted to all authors under the

Copyright Act, 5 William F. Patry, Patry on Copyright 16:1 (2009), they are part of the same statutory framework.

. . .

### B. VARA

Beyond the Copyright Act's protections of certain economic rights, VARA provides additional and independent protections to authors of works of visual art. See [*Carter v. Helmsley-Spear, Inc.*, 71 F.3d 77, 81-83 (2d Cir. 1995)]. A work of visual art is defined to include "a painting, drawing, print, or sculpture,[7] existing in a single copy" or in a limited edition. 17 U.S.C. 101. The definition specifically excludes a number of works that are otherwise copyrightable, including motion pictures and other audiovisual works, books, posters, periodicals, works made for hire, and merchandising, advertising, promotional, or packaging materials. *Id.*

VARA's passage reflected Congress's belief that the art covered by the Act "meet[s] a special societal need, and [its] protection and preservation serve an important public interest." House Report at 5-6, as reprinted in 1990 U.S.C.C.A.N. at 6915-16. To encourage the creation of such art, VARA protects the "moral rights" of its creators. These are "rights of a spiritual, non-economic and personal nature" that exist "independently of an artist's copyright in his or her work" and "spring from a belief that an artist in the process of creation injects his spirit into the work and that the artist's personality, as well as the integrity of the work, should therefore be protected and preserved." *Carter*, 71 F.3d at 81. The recognition of moral rights fosters a " 'climate of artistic worth and honor that encourages the author in the arduous act of creation.' " *Id.* at 83 (quoting House Report at 6, as reprinted in 1990 U.S.C.C.A.N. at 6915). Although an artist may not transfer his VARA rights (as they are considered an extension of his personality), he may waive those rights by "expressly agree[ing] to such waiver in a written instrument." 17 U.S.C. 106A(e)(1).

---

7. The parties do not dispute that, if completed, "Training Ground for Democracy" would have been a sculpture and therefore a qualified "work of visual art" under VARA. . . .

VARA provides that, in addition to the exclusive rights provided by section 106 of the Copyright Act, but subject to certain limitations, the author of a work of visual art

(1) shall have the right—
 (A) to claim authorship of that work, and
 (B) to prevent the use of his or her name as the author of any work of visual art which he or she did not create;

(2) shall have the right to prevent the use of his or her name as the author of the work of visual art in the event of a distortion, mutilation, or other modification of the work which would be prejudicial to his or her honor or reputation; and

(3) subject to the limitations set forth in section 113(d), shall have the right—
 (A) to prevent any intentional distortion, mutilation, or other modification of that work which would be prejudicial to his or her honor or reputation, and any intentional distortion, mutilation, or modification of that work is a violation of that right, and
 (B) to prevent any destruction of a work of recognized stature, and any intentional or grossly negligent destruction of that work is a violation of that right.

17 U.S.C. 106A(a).

Also, "[a]ll remedies available under copyright law, other than criminal remedies, are available in an action for infringement of moral rights." *Carter*, 71 F.3d at 83 (citing 17 U.S.C. 506); see also 17 U.S.C. 501(a).

More specifically, by guaranteeing the moral rights of "attribution" and "integrity," VARA " 'protects both the reputations of certain visual artists and the works of art they create.' " *Carter*, 71 F.3d at 83 (quoting House Report at 6, as reprinted in 1990 U.S. C.C.A.N. at 6915). Before discussing the precise contours of these rights, we consider whether, as a threshold matter, the indisputably unfinished "Training Ground for Democracy" was a "work of visual art" within the meaning of VARA.

## C. Does VARA Apply to Unfinished Works of Art?

Büchel argues that the district court erred by failing to recognize that VARA applies with equal force to incomplete artistic endeavors that would otherwise be subject to VARA protection. He asserts that the Act's plain language compels such a conclusion, which he claims is confirmed by the legislative history and sparse case law interpreting the statute. . . .

The definition of a "work of visual art" for VARA purposes is stated "in terms both positive (what it is) and negative (what it is not)." *Carter*, 71 F.3d at 84. An unfinished sculptural installation such as "Training Ground for Democracy" is not one of the items specifically excluded from VARA protection,[9] and MASS MoCA wisely does not attempt to argue otherwise. Instead, we must determine whether the "positive" aspect of the definition of "work of visual art" includes an unfinished version of a "sculpture[] existing in a single copy." 17 U.S.C. 101.

The text of VARA itself does not state when an artistic project becomes a work of visual art subject to its protections. However, VARA is part of the Copyright Act, and that Act's definition section, which defines "work of visual art," specifies that its definitions, unless otherwise provided, control throughout Title 17. See 17 U.S.C. 101. That general definitional section of the Copyright Act states that a work is "created" when it "is fixed in a copy . . . for the first time." Further, "where a work is prepared over a period of time, *the portion of it that has been fixed at any particular time constitutes the work as of that time*." 17 U.S.C. 101 (emphasis added). A work is "fixed" when it has been formed, "by or under the authority of the author," in a way that is "sufficiently permanent or stable to permit it to be perceived, reproduced, or otherwise communicated for a period of more than transitory duration." *Id*.

---

9. As provided in 17 U.S.C. 106A(c)(3), VARA specifically excludes certain categories of artwork listed in section 101 of the Copyright Act:

> (A) (i) any poster, map, globe, chart, technical drawing, diagram, model, applied art, motion picture or other audiovisual work, book, magazine, newspaper, periodical, data base, electronic information service, electronic publication, or similar publication;
> (ii) any merchandising item or advertising, promotional, descriptive, covering, or packaging material or container;
> (iii) any portion or part of any item described in clause (i) or (ii);
>
> (B) any work made for hire

17 U.S.C. 101.

Not surprisingly, based on section 101's general definitions, courts have held that the Copyright Act's protections extend to unfinished works. [cit.]

Reading VARA in accordance with the definitions in section 101, it too must be read to protect unfinished, but "fixed," works of art that, if completed, would qualify for protection under the statute. . . .

Our conclusion that the statute's plain language extends its coverage to unfinished works makes it unnecessary to delve into VARA's legislative history. We nonetheless note that we have looked closely at that history, and it fully supports our reading of the plain language. Common sense points in the same direction. Moral rights protect the personality and creative energy that an artist contributes to his or her work. That convergence between artist and artwork does not await the final brush stroke or the placement of the last element in a complex installation. [cit.]

We thus hold that VARA protects the moral rights of artists who have "created" works of art within the meaning of the Copyright Act even if those works are not yet complete.

### III.

Given Büchel's right to protection under VARA for his artistic investment in a partially completed artwork, we must now assess the district court's ruling that Büchel failed to raise a genuine issue of material fact with respect to any of his claims. . . .

#### A. The Scope of VARA's Integrity and Attribution Rights

##### 1. The Right of Integrity

VARA's right of integrity, codified at 17 U.S.C. 106A(a)(3)(A), provides that an artist shall have the right "to prevent any intentional distortion, mutilation, or other modification of [his or her] work which would be prejudicial to his or her honor or reputation, and [that] any intentional distortion, mutilation, or modification of that work is a violation of that right." It thus allows artists to protect their works against intentional modifications that would be prejudicial to their honor or reputations. House Report at 6, as reprinted in 1990 U.S.C.C.A.N. at 6915.

There is arguably some uncertainty about the plaintiff's burden of proof in a case such as this because the second part of section (a)(3)(A) — stating that "any intentional distortion, mutilation, or modification of th[e] work is a violation" of the right of integrity — does not explicitly require a showing of prejudice when the alteration already has occurred and damages, rather than injunctive relief, would be the appropriate remedy. See 5 Patry, supra, 16:22 (noting the ambiguity). Because those VARA cases that make it to court are "generally . . . decided on threshold questions such as whether the artist's work is a work of visual art within the scope of the Act," [cit.] courts have had little occasion to give content to the rights that VARA guarantees. See Wu, supra, at 159 ("[C]ourts avoid construing the extent of VARA protection by finding that works do not meet the threshold requirements for 'visual art' protected by VARA."). Unsurprisingly, therefore, we have found no case law discussing a possible difference in the showing required for injunctive relief and damages for right-of-integrity claims.

Some courts, however, have assumed without analysis that the prejudice showing is necessary for both injunctive relief and damages. [cit.] At least one commentator likewise accepts, without discussion, that the damages remedy requires a showing of prejudice. See Melville B. Nimmer, 3-8D Nimmer on Copyright 8D.06[C][1] (noting that "an intentional and prejudicial mutilation is an integrity violation, remediable through not only an injunction, but damages as well"). Interestingly, Nimmer raises, and dismisses, a different imprecision in section (a)(3)(A):

> The statutory language "distortion, mutilation, or other modification of the work which would be prejudicial to his or her honor or reputation" is susceptible of a reading whereby the requisite prejudice applies only to "modification," not to the antecedents of "distortion" or "mutilation." Though not without ambiguity, the better view under the Berne Convention, from which this language is drawn, is that prejudice applies in all three instances.

*Id.*

We agree with Nimmer's view of the provision, including the application of the prejudice requirement to a claim for damages, and consider that construction soundly grounded in VARA's legislative history. Under the heading "Purpose of the Legislation," the House Report notes that the right of integrity "allows artists to protect their works against modifications and destructions that are prejudicial to their honor or reputations." House Report at 6, as reprinted in 1990 U.S.C.C.A.N. at 6915. The Report also notes that the rights provided by VARA are "analogous to those protected by Article 6bis of the Berne Convention," *id.*, which in turn describes the right of integrity as applicable to "certain modifications and other derogatory actions" that would be prejudicial to the artist's honor or reputation.[14] Given the stated purpose of the legislation and the similar depiction of the integrity right in the Berne Convention, we conclude that Congress intended the prejudice requirement to apply to the right of integrity whether the remedy sought is injunctive relief or damages.

Although VARA does not define the terms "prejudicial," "honor," [and] "reputation," the House Report recommended that the prejudice inquiry "focus on the artistic or professional honor or reputation of the individual as embodied in the work that is protected," and "examine the way in which a work has been modified and the professional reputation of the author of the work." House Report at 15, as reprinted in 1990 U.S.C.C.A.N. at 6925-26 (footnotes omitted). Relying on dictionary definitions of prejudice, honor and reputation, the district court in *Carter* concluded that it should "consider whether

---

14. Article 6bis of the Berne Convention, which is titled "Moral Rights," includes a heading that lists among those rights "to object to certain modifications and other derogatory actions." The provision itself states, in relevant part:

> (1) Independently of the author's economic rights, and even after the transfer of the said rights, the author shall have the right . . . to object to any distortion, mutilation or other modification of, or other derogatory action in relation to, the said work, which would be prejudicial to his honor or reputation.

Berne Convention for the Protection of Literary and Artistic Works art. 6bis, Sept. 9, 1986, S. Treaty Doc. No. 99-27, 1161 U.N.T.S. 30.

[the proposed] alteration would cause injury or damage to plaintiffs' good name, public esteem, or reputation in the artistic community." 861 F. Supp. at 323. We think this a useful approach, but emphasize that the focus is on the artist's reputation in relation to the altered work of art; the artist need not have public stature beyond the context of the creation at issue. See House Report at 15, as reprinted in 1990 U.S.C.C.A.N. at 6925 ("[A]n author need not prove a pre-existing standing in the artistic community.").

### 2. The Right of Attribution

VARA's right of attribution grants the author of a work of visual art the right, in part, (1) "to claim authorship of that work"; (2) "to prevent the use of his or her name as the author of any work of visual art which he or she did not create"; and (3) "to prevent the use of his or her name as the author of the work of visual art in the event of a distortion, mutilation, or other modification of the work which would be prejudicial to his or her honor or reputation." 17 U.S.C. 106A(a)(1), (2). The right "ensures that artists are correctly identified with the works of art they create, and that they are not identified with works created by others." House Report at 6, as reprinted in 1990 U.S.C.C.A.N. at 6915. In addition, if a work of visual art has been distorted or modified (and, unlike the integrity right, the original distortion or modification need not be intentional), associating the author's name with the distorted work against his wishes would violate his right of attribution.

The right of attribution under VARA thus gives an artist a claim for injunctive relief to, inter alia, assert or disclaim authorship of a work. Whether VARA entitles an artist to damages for violation of the right of attribution is a separate question. We find the answer in the difference between the statutory language on the right of integrity and the language on the right of attribution. Subsection (a)(3) of section 106A, which codifies the right of integrity, is further divided into two subsections: (A) confers the right to protect the work against intentional alterations that would be prejudicial to honor or reputation, and (B) confers the right to protect a work of "recognized stature" from destruction.[16] Although both subsections are framed as rights "to prevent" certain conduct, they both also contain an additional clause stating that the occurrence of that conduct is, at least in certain circumstances, "a violation of th[e] right" to prevent the conduct from happening. See 17 U.S.C. 106A(a)(3)(A) ("any intentional distortion, mutilation, or modification of that work is a violation of that right"); *id.* at 106(a)(3)(B) ("any intentional or grossly negligent destruction of that work is a violation of that right").

No such "violation" clause is included in the sections codifying the right of attribution. See Nimmer, supra, at 8D.06[B][1] ("The statute does not make any

---

16. Section 106A(a)(3) states that the author of a work of visual art shall have the right "(A) to prevent any intentional distortion, mutilation, or other modification of that work which would be prejudicial to his or her honor or reputation" and the right "(B) to prevent any destruction of a work of recognized stature."

provision to redress violation of any of the foregoing three attribution rights."). The legislative history sheds no light on this difference, but Nimmer speculates as follows:

> Perhaps the implication is that whereas an integrity violation could give rise to a monetary recovery, failure to attribute is remediable solely through injunction. If that conclusion were intended, Congress certainly could have expressed its intent less obliquely.

*Id.* We agree with Nimmer's surmise that VARA does not provide a damages remedy for an attribution violation. Where the statutory language is framed as a right "to prevent" conduct, it does not necessarily follow that a plaintiff is entitled to damages once the conduct occurs. The question is whether "doing" the act the artist has a right to prevent also triggers a damages remedy, and the statutory language indicates that Congress answered that question for the attribution right differently from the integrity right.

It is also noteworthy that Congress crafted a damages remedy for the destruction of a work of recognized stature that is narrower than the right to prevent destruction of such works. While an artist may "prevent *any* destruction of a work of recognized stature," only an "intentional or grossly negligent destruction of that work is a violation of that right." 17 U.S.C. 106A(a)(3)(B) (emphasis added). This narrowing further indicates that Congress did not intend a damages remedy to arise automatically from the right to prevent conduct. In failing to provide a damages remedy for any type of violation of the moral right of attribution, Congress may have concluded that artists could obtain adequate relief for the harms of false attribution by resorting to the Copyright Act and other traditional claims.

### B. Büchel's VARA Claims

With this legal framework in mind, we turn to the record before the district court. . . .

Büchel alleges that MASS MoCA violated his right to integrity in three distinct ways: first, by continuing to work on the installation without his authorization, particularly in early 2007, and by then exhibiting the distorted artwork to the public; second, by using tarpaulins to "partially cover[]" and thus modify and distort the installation, and allowing Museum visitors to see it in that condition; and third, merely by showing Büchel's work in its unfinished state, which he claims was a distortion. Büchel asserts that these actions caused prejudice to his honor or reputation. [As to the right of attribution claim, the court concluded that it was moot, because the statute only provided injunctive relief and the exhibit no longer existed.]

As we shall explain, we conclude that summary judgment was improperly granted to MASS MoCA because material disputes of fact exist concerning the first of Büchel's integrity claims, i.e., that MASS MoCA modified "Training Ground" over his objections, to his detriment. We further conclude that the record contains sufficient evidence to allow a jury to find that MASS MoCA's actions caused prejudice to Büchel's honor or reputation. The other integrity claims, however, are unavailing.

### 1. Continuing Work on "Training Ground"

Büchel asserts that, in the months following his departure from [the Museum site] in December 2006, the Museum encroached on his artistic vision by making modifications to the installation that in some instances were directly contrary to his instructions.

Although a jury might agree with the [trial] court's assessment, the evidence viewed in the light most favorable to Büchel would allow a finding that at least some of the Museum's actions violated VARA. The record permits the inference that, even during his time as an artist-in-residence at MASS MoCA, Museum staff members were disregarding his instructions and intentionally modifying "Training Ground" in a manner that he did not approve. . . .

Both in his deposition and in his affidavit, Büchel described ways in which he felt the Museum had knowingly disregarded his specific instructions. For example, MASS MoCA's decision to build a cinderblock wall through the Cape Cod-style house in the installation, despite Büchels expressed desire that the construction await his return, resulted in what Büchel considered a "big distortion of the meaning of that element." The record is replete with similar allegations concerning other components of the installation, including the cinema, the bomb carousel, the Saddam spiderhole, the police car and the mobile home. Indeed, even the Museum, in its August 31, 2007 memorandum of law in support of its motion for summary judgment, admitted that the installation "[m]aterials as they now stand *reflect significant aesthetic and design choices by MASS MoCA personnel,* including with respect to the layout of the [m]aterials, and with respect to the selection and procurement of pre-existing buildings and vehicles that have been modified and incorporated into the [m]aterials." (Emphasis added.)

MASS MoCA argues that the evidence, taken in its entirety, does not add up to a triable issue with respect to a violation of Büchel's right of integrity, but shows only that Museum personnel were attempting to carry out Büchel's vision based on his instructions. . . .

As we have noted, a jury may well accept the Museum's depiction of its intention and its actions. At this juncture, however, the record must be viewed in the light most favorable to Büchel. The evidence we have described would permit a jury to find that the Museum forged ahead with the installation in the first half of 2007 knowing that the continuing construction in Büchel's absence would frustrate—and likely contradict—Büchel's artistic vision. We thus conclude that a jury issue exists as to whether these actions effected an intentional distortion or other modification of "Training Ground" that subjected MASS MoCA to liability under VARA.

The record also contains evidence from which a jury could conclude that the Museum's alterations had a detrimental impact on Büchel's honor or reputation. An article in the Boston Globe reported that, in February, Museum officials had shown the unfinished project to a group of Museum directors and curators who were attending an arts conference in the area. See Geoff Edgers, Behind doors, a world unseen: Dispute cloaks massive installation at MASS MoCA, Boston Globe (March 28, 2007), available at www.boston.com/ae/theater_arts/articles/2007/03/28/behind_doors_a_world_unseen/ ("Behind doors, a world unseen"). Another journalist reported on observing the unfinished (and still untarped) work. See The Show Will Go On, supra.

Although the commentary generated by these visits is not all negative, there was sufficient evidence for a jury to find that the changes to "Training Ground" caused prejudice to Büchel. The New York Times noted that the exhibition would "certainly give people unfamiliar with his obsessive, history-driven aesthetic an inaccurate sense of his art, and this is indeed a form of damage." Is It Art Yet?, supra. A critic for the Boston Globe similarly observed that "many people are going to judge [Büchel] and his work on the basis of this experience." Ken Johnson, No admittance: MASS MoCA has mishandled disputed art installation, Boston Globe, July 1, 2007, at 1N. One viewer, writing in Commentary magazine, observed that "I am not sure that it suffers from being enveiled." Michael J. Lewis, The Cost of Transgression, http://www.commentarymagazine.com/blogs/index. php/lewis/499 (June 4, 2007). A review published in Berkshire Fine Arts subtitled "Crap Under Wrap" . . . concluded that it would be a "huge mistake" to uncover the installation, which offered "virtually nothing of substance or interest." Crap Under Wrap, supra.

The record thus shows that some viewers of the installation reacted unfavorably to the work in its allegedly modified and distorted form. A factfinder might conclude, of course, that it was Büchel's underlying concept (notwithstanding its unfinished state) rather than MASS MoCA's actions that elicited the negative reactions. However, a jury could also reasonably infer that the negative impressions resulted from the Museum's unauthorized modifications to "Training Ground," diminishing the quality of the work and thereby harming Büchel's professional honor or reputation as a visual artist.

In concluding that Büchel has adduced sufficient evidence to support a right-of-integrity claim, we reject the Museum's assertion that to find a violation of Büchel's right of integrity in these circumstances would make it impossible for parties to collaborate on large-scale artistic works. The Museum warns that, under Büchel's interpretation, "no one other than the artist himself . . . - may ever perform any work in fabricating visual art unless that specific task has been authorized by the artist." We disagree. Although the artist's vision must govern, that principle does not prevent collaboration at the implementation level so long as the artist's vision guides that implementation. Here, Büchel alleges a campaign of intentional distortion and modification to his work in which Museum personnel repeatedly ignored his express wishes. Our holding that the summary judgment record precludes an affirmance of the district court on this claim may serve as a cautionary tale to museums contemplating similar installations in the future—guiding them to document the terms of their relationship and obtain VARA waivers where necessary—but it does not prevent museums or other collaborators from working cooperatively with artists on such non-traditional artworks.

2. Showing "Training Ground" Covered with Tarpaulins

Büchel also claims that MASS MoCA improperly modified and distorted Training Ground when it partially covered it with the yellow tarpaulins and displayed it in that condition. He asserts that the record shows beyond dispute that visitors looked behind the tarps, that the tarp-adorned installation was "judged by others to be Büchel's work, and that his honor and reputation were harmed by it." In response, the Museum argues that the yellow tarpaulins were merely functional—a way of keeping people "out" of the installation—rather than an aesthetic modification of the artwork that gave MASS MoCA patrons a distorted view of it.

Although the tarpaulins did prevent visitors to the Museum from seeing the entire unfinished installation, the record shows that a number of people were able to form an impression of "Training Ground" despite the partial covering. For example, according to one observer,

> [the tarps] don't reach the floor, and they rise only about two feet above eye level, so they don't cover much. You can easily crouch down to slip your head underneath or peek through the slits between the vinyl sheets. Beyond the passageway formed by the tarps, the monumental elements of the installation rise all around you, plain as day—the cinderblock walls, the two-story house, the guard tower, the trailers, the carnival ride, all compacted together in a claustrophobic, politically surreal borough of hell, George Orwell by way of David Lynch.

Thomas Micchelli, Christoph Büchel Training Ground for Democracy, The Brooklyn Rail (September 2007), available at http://www.brooklynrail.org/2007/09/artseen/buchel. Another critic noted that the installation "under all the tarps is really kind of a conceptual peep show. It doesn't take much effort or imagination to see most of the work. . . . Mass MoCA is hiding an elephant behind a napkin," and called it a "wink, wink, wrap show." Crap Under Wrap, supra. Photographs in the record confirm that the covers did not obscure the general path and layout of the installation. Indeed, given the location of "Training Ground," visitors to "Made at MASS MoCA" could not avoid seeing the unfinished "Training Ground" bedecked in tarpaulins.

Nonetheless, although the installation unquestionably looked different with the tarpaulins partially covering it, we agree with the district court that the mere covering of the artwork by the Museum, its host, cannot reasonably be deemed an intentional act of distortion or modification of Büchel's creation. To conclude otherwise would be to say that, even if all had gone well, the Museum would have been subject to a right-of-integrity claim if it had partially covered the work before its formal opening to prevent visitors from seeing it prematurely.

. . . The right of integrity under VARA, however, protects the artist from distortions of his work, not from disparaging commentary about his behavior. In our view, a finding that the Museum's covering of the installation constituted an intentional act of distortion or modification of Büchel's artistic creation would stretch VARA beyond sensible boundaries.

### 3. Exhibiting "Training Ground" in Its Unfinished State

Büchel maintains that, even aside from the alleged modifications to Training Ground, merely exhibiting the work of art in its unfinished state, without the artist's consent, constitutes a distortion. We reject this claim. A separate moral right of disclosure (also known as the right of divulgation) protects an author's authority to "prevent third parties from disclosing [his or her] work to the public without the author's consent," and is not covered by VARA.

See Cyrill P. Rigamonti, Deconstructing Moral Rights, 47 Harv. Int'l L.J. 353, 373, 405 (2006) "([T]he VARA ignores the rights of disclosure and withdrawal and instead focuses on the rights of attribution and integrity. . . .").

Although Büchel proffered an expert who opined that showing an unfinished work without the artist's permission is inherently a distortion, we decline to interpret VARA to include such a claim where a separate moral right of disclosure is widely recognized in other jurisdictions and Congress explicitly limited the statute's coverage to the rights of attribution and integrity. See Amy M. Adler, Against Moral Rights, 97 Cal. L. Rev. 263, 268 (2009) (noting that most European countries "recognize a right of divulgation, giving the artist the right to decide when (and whether) the work is complete and can be shown"); Rigamonti, supra, at 356 ("The standard set of moral rights recognized in the literature consists of the author's right to claim authorship (right of attribution), the right to object to modifications of the work (right of integrity), the right to decide when and how the work in question will be published (right of disclosure), and the right to withdraw a work after publication (right of withdrawal)." (footnotes omitted)); 5 Patry on Copyright 16:23 (noting that VARA does not give the artist "a right to prohibit display of mutilated versions of his or her work, only the right to prohibit the mutilation itself"). Any right Büchel possesses to withhold display of his artwork must be found outside VARA.

[Affirmed in part, vacated in part, and remanded.]

## NOTES AND QUESTIONS

1. *Limited subject matter.* As the *Martin* case points out, the VARA provides limited "moral rights" to authors of qualifying works of visual art. However, many works that are ostensibly works in visual media do not qualify under the Section 101 definition of works of visual art. For example, motion pictures do not qualify, nor does "applied art" or any "promotional" item. *See Pollara v. Seymour*, 344 F.3d 265 (2d Cir. 2003) (mural did not qualify as a work of visual art because artist had created it to promote a charity event); *cf. Carter v. Helmsley-Spear, Inc.*, 71 F.3d 77 (2d Cir. 1995) (site-specific sculpture affixed to and incorporated into building lobby was not disqualified as "applied art"). Paintings or sculptures that exist in a single copy, or in signed and consecutively numbered editions of no more than 200 copies, do qualify. Review the Section 101 definition. What explains the boundaries that the definition sets?

2. *Nature of the moral rights: rights of integrity; rights of attribution.* The VARA provides two types of moral rights. The *integrity right* includes the right to prevent intentional distortion, mutilation, or modification of the work that would prejudice the artist's honor or reputation, and the right to prevent destruction of the work through an intentional or grossly negligent act. 17 U.S.C. §106A(a)(3). The right to prevent destruction applies only to works of "recognized stature," the primary issue in *Martin*. The *attribution right* includes the right to claim authorship of the work, the right to prevent the use of one's name as the author of someone else's work, and the right to

prevent the use of one's name as the author of a work that has been distorted, mutilated, or modified in a way that would prejudice one's honor or reputation. 17 U.S.C. §§106A(a)(1), (2).

3. *Contracting around moral rights.* Moral rights exist alongside, but separate from, copyright. Accordingly, an author who assigns a copyright interest in a work of visual art does not thereby part with moral rights in the work. Indeed, the moral rights are not transferable at all. They are waivable, but only by express waiver given in writing in accordance with the statutory prescription set out in 17 U.S.C. §106A(e). Does this solicitude for an artist's moral rights make sense? Is it overly paternalistic?

4. *Claims under copyright law?* Because moral rights under VARA exist separately from copyright interests, might an artist who fails under VARA nonetheless win under copyright claims? For example, in *Büchel*, independent of the fate of Büchel's VARA claims, should Büchel have a claim that the Museum violated his copyright in the installation by engaging in unauthorized public display in violation of 17 U.S.C. §106(5)? What about a claim that the installation in its unfinished state was an unauthorized derivative work in violation of 17 U.S.C. §106(2)? Or that the installation covered with tarpaulins was an unauthorized derivative work? What responses might you assert on behalf of the Museum? Among other possibilities, you may wish to consider the effect of 17 U.S.C. §109. The court discussed these issues in Part IV of its opinion (omitted from the excerpt). Of course, the artist must own the copyright in order to present such claims.

5. *Term of moral rights.* How long should moral rights in a work of visual art endure? For works created after the effective date of VARA (June 1, 1991), the Section 106A rights last for the life of the author. Sensible?

# PART V
## SUI GENERIS REGIMES

# CHAPTER 8
# SUI GENERIS DESIGN PROTECTION

Outside the United States, many countries have enacted regimes specifically aimed at the protection of designs, rather than (or in addition to) relying on copyright or trademark protection. Indeed, some such protection is mandated by the TRIPS Agreement, which we will discuss below. You should consider whether the protection offered under the design patent statute, *see supra* Chapters 5-6, fully implements U.S. obligations under TRIPS.

Efforts to introduce similar sui generis design legislation in the United States have been under way for the better part of a century (starting in 1914). For periods of time, bills were introduced in Congress almost on an annual basis, and many passed either the House or the Senate. The closest that such a bill came to enactment was in 1976, when Title II of the Copyright Revision Act would have introduced a sui generis regime offering protection to the design of useful articles. However, at the last minute, Title II was deleted. Although advocates of design protection continued to press for sui generis legislation, no broad-based regime has been adopted. Indeed, since 1992, Congress has paid little attention to a general design regime. Instead, Congress has enacted industry-specific protection to the design of boat hulls. And recent legislative debates have focused on extending similar industry-specific protection to fashion designs.

In the meantime, the European Union has adopted two instruments that have arguably established a model for a modern design regime. Certainly, that regime has been mimicked elsewhere. And there has been pressure in the United States to follow the example of the European Union. The European regime was based on two parallel pieces of legislation: a directive harmonizing the *registered* design laws of the member states of the European Union; and a Regulation creating EU-wide *registered* and *unregistered* design rights. In this chapter, we will discuss the EU regime (Section A). Then we will examine the industry-specific U.S. regime (Section B), which may supply the framework for a broad-based U.S. form of design protection.

## A. EUROPEAN DESIGN RIGHTS

Design protection in the European Union is governed in large part by two pieces of legislation. In 1998, a directive harmonized the *registered* design laws of the member states of the European Union. *See* Directive 98/71/EC of the European Parliament and of the Council of 13 October 1998 on The Legal Protection of Design, O.J. L 289 (Oct. 28, 1998). Three years later, a parallel regulation created unitary EU-wide design rights, consisting of a three-year *unregistered* design right that runs from the date on which a design is first made available to the public within the EU, and a *registered* right that could, with appropriate filings, endure for twenty-five years. *See* Council Regulation 6/2002/EC of 12 December 2001, O.J. L. 3 (Jan. 5, 2002). Protection of Unregistered Community Designs commenced as of March 6, 2002, and the Office for Harmonisation for the Internal Market (OHIM, which functions as the EU Trade Mark and Design Office) began accepting applications for Registered Community Designs in April 2003. The proposals that led to the two instruments are analyzed in detail in Graeme B. Dinwoodie, *Federalized Functionalism: The Future of Design Protection in Europe*, 24 Am. Intell. Prop. L. Ass'n Q.J. 611 (1996). For analysis of the adopted legislation, *see* David Musker, Community Design Law: Principles and Practice (2002). *See also* I-III Design Protection in Europe: Decisions of European and National Courts (Henning Hartwig ed., 2007-2009).

The EU legislation in combination addresses three different rights:

(1) The Registered Community Design Right;
(2) The Unregistered Community Design Right; and
(3) The national *registered* design rights that must exist under the laws of each member state once the member state implements the provisions of the Directive.

The basic principles underlying the Regulation and the Directive are the same and govern all three of these types of rights. The Regulation provides a producer with two separate, but related, EU-wide rights with which to protect its design: a Registered Community Design right, and an Unregistered Community Design right. The scope of the Directive, however, was less ambitious than that of the Regulation: although it sought to harmonize national *registered* design laws, it neither required member states to introduce unregistered design right protection at the national level, nor obliged the United Kingdom to make amendments to its existing unregistered design law. Accordingly, differences may still exist between forms of unregistered protection that exist at the national level (including not only unregistered design rights proper, but protection afforded by "slavish imitation" doctrines or copyright law). Although this chapter focuses on the regime installed by the European legislation, it also includes several comparative references to these other forms of protection. In particular, we have noted several aspects of the UK unregistered design right, which differs in several respects from the Unregistered Community Design but is clearly its forerunner.

***Responses to the Costs of Registration.*** To accommodate the concerns of industry regarding the costs and delay of design registration, the Regulation contains two departures from a full-blown registration system. First, the Unregistered Design Right has been included as an integral part of the EU-wide solution. Most member states had some form of registered design protection already—and those that did not (e.g., Greece) were required by the parallel Design Directive to establish such protection. But the introduction of the Unregistered Community Design right was an innovation, if one that is based largely on a similar right first introduced in the United Kingdom in 1988. The purpose of providing protection without registration was to accommodate industries that develop large numbers of designs, only a few of which are commercially exploited and whose products are short lived. For these industries, such as fashion and textiles, almost any registration process will remain an overly expensive, unduly time-consuming, and not particularly helpful proposition. The registration *process*, particularly if it involves a substantive examination, ordinarily extends beyond the commercial life of the design. For these industries, some form of automatic short-term protection against unauthorized reproduction is necessary (and largely sufficient). Second, the registration system is a "passive" registration (or deposit) system.[*] OHIM checks applications only for obviously inappropriate subject matter and formal deficiencies. *See* Official Commentary on Proposed Article 48, in Explanatory Memorandum Accompanying the Proposal for a European Parliament and Council Regulation on the Community Design, COM(93) 342 final-COD 463 (Brussels, 3 Dec. 1993). Indeed, over the course of the evolution of the proposals, the abolition of substantive examinations appears to have become a priority in the thinking of the European Commission. An application for Community Design Registration may be filed at the Community Design Office or at the central industrial property office of a member state. *See* Regulation, art. 37. Generally, the registration of the design leads to its publication. Provision is made, however, for the possibility of deferred publication in order to maintain the secrecy of the design. *See* Regulation, arts. 49, 50.

***Relationship between Registered and Unregistered EU-Wide Rights.*** Assertion of rights under the unregistered community design system does not prevent application for a Registered Community Design. The two forms of protection are granted on the same conditions and are subject to the same exclusions; as a general matter, any design that could be registered will be entitled to unregistered design protection. Indeed, one of the benefits of the structure put in place by the Regulation is the ability of the producer to test the design in the marketplace with the protection offered by the unregistered design right and, if the design proves successful, within one year (the applicable grace period) to seek registration of that design. *See* Regulation, art. 7(2)

---

[*]The use of passive registration mirrored the nature of the examination under design laws then in place in several countries of the European Union. For example, the registration proceedings in the Benelux countries did not involve substantive examination, nor did those in France, Italy, and Spain. The U.K. authorities did examine for substantive compliance with the requirements of their act. The concerns of industry regarding the costs and delay of design registration have largely been addressed in the regulation, where unregistered rights will be available and community-level registered rights will be granted after a relatively cursory examination. Accordingly, the directive did not compel member states (such as the United Kingdom) to dismantle any system of substantive examination used under their registered design laws.

(grace period of one year relevant to assessing novelty and individual character in the case of a Registered Community Design application).

The substantive provisions governing eligibility for protection under the Regulation—in either unregistered or registered form—are intended to mirror those made applicable to national registered designs by the Directive. The primary differences between the registered and unregistered rights relate to the date of commencement of protection, and the term and scope of protection obtained. The unregistered protection subsists upon the design being made available to the public within the European Union, whereas registered protection runs from the date of the filing of an application for registration. *See* Regulation, arts. 12-13. Like most registered design laws, registration will confer upon the holder the exclusive right to use the design and to prevent the unauthorized third party use of the design or designs that do not produce "on the informed user a different overall impression." Directive, arts. 9, 12. However, although the rights conferred by a design registration are in the nature of monopoly rights, the owner of the *unregistered* community design secures only the right to prevent the use in question if it results from copying the protected design. *See* Regulation, art. 19(2). That is to say, independent creation is a defense in an action for infringement of an unregistered, but not a registered, design. *See* Explanatory Memorandum Accompanying the Amended Proposal for a Council Regulation on Community Design, COM(2000)660 final/2 (Nov. 23, 2000) at 4. Unregistered protection lasts for three years; however, because the conditions for protection do not vary as between registered and unregistered designs, each design protected for three years can, by timely application, receive protection of a patent-like nature for up to twenty-five years. *See* Regulation, arts. 12-13.

***Definition of Design.*** For the purpose of both instruments, design is defined as "the appearance of the whole or a part of a product resulting from the features of, in particular, the lines, contours, colours, shape, texture and/or materials of the product itself and/or its ornamentation." Directive, art. 1(a); Regulation, art. 3(a); *see also* Regulation, art. 3(b) (defining "product" broadly and including "packaging" in that definition). The most important aspect of the definition of design, however, is what it does *not* include: it contains no reference to the aesthetic or the functional nature of the design. The United Kingdom had addressed this issue in 1988 in the enactment of its *unregistered* design legislation—which protected aesthetic and functional designs alike—but prior to the Directive U.K. law still did distinguish between aesthetic and functional designs by limiting *registered* protection to those designs that had "eye-appeal." The EU instruments went further than the U.K. reforms by requiring the *registered* design laws of member states to protect the external appearance of a product whether that appearance is pure decoration, has no aesthetic content, or is a combination of functional and aesthetic elements. There was no intention to restrict these new protections to designs that appeal to the eye. Instead of confining protection by restricting the universe of protectable subject matter, the Directive required the registered design laws of member states to circumscribe protection through application of prescribed thresholds and exclusions.

***Thresholds.*** The thresholds to community design protection follow a common structural model: a two-step test that assesses (1) whether the design is different from other designs, and (2) whether the development of the design beyond prior designs involves more than minimal creativity on the part of the designer. More specifically, to obtain protection, a design must be new, and have individual character. *See* Directive, art. 3(2); Regulation, art. 4(1). Novelty consists of no identical design or immaterially different design having previously been made available to the public as of the date of the filing of the application or, if priority is claimed, the date of priority (or the date that the design for which protection is claimed was made available to the public, in the case of an unregistered design). *See* Directive, art. 4; Regulation, art. 5; *cf.* Regulation, art. 11 (term of protection for unregistered right commences on date on which "design was first made available to the public in the Community"). Throughout the legislative process, the Commission intended that novelty for design purposes be a less difficult standard than the patent requirement of the same name. However, an absolute novelty standard (having regard to prior art anywhere) was ultimately enacted, *see* Directive, art. 6; Regulation, art. 7, subject to a so-called safeguard clause. That clause is discussed in the *Green Lane* case, excerpted below.

To avoid protecting designs that differ only in small details from a prior design, a supplementary threshold was instituted. A design will be protected only if it possesses "individual character." This is the concept that truly sets the outside parameters of prima facie protection. A design shall "be considered to have an individual character if the overall impression it produces on the informed user differs from the overall impression produced on such a user by any design which has [previously] been made available to the public." Directive, art. 5; Regulation, art. 6. Although the "individual character" standard is somewhat vague, the legislation explicitly mandates consideration of the degree of freedom that the designer enjoyed in developing the design. That is to say, in a crowded field a smaller advance from prior designs will more easily warrant the conclusion of individual character. *See* Directive, art. 5(2); Regulation, art. 6(2). Of course, the scope of protection that such designs receive will be correspondingly limited; if there is little room for exceptional creativity on the part of the first designer, he cannot be heard to complain if the same restrictions compel a later designer to create a design that bears a resemblance to his in some respect. *See* Directive, art. 9(2); Regulation, art. 10(2).

***Functionality.*** In a system that broadly envisages the protection of functional designs on conditions that intentionally do not approach those required of applicants for utility patents, the exclusions from protection assume paramount importance. Protecting the appearance of a functional design clearly raises the possibility of incidentally affecting the ability of others to practice that function. Thus, any features of a design that are "solely dictated by the technical function [of the product]" are excluded from protection by Article 7(1) of the Directive. *See also* Regulation, art. 8(1). Similar exclusions are found in many design laws throughout the world. The Commission argued that if the design is dictated by the function of the product, the creative choices exercised by the designer are necessarily minimized (or even nonexistent). Such an exclusion might also be justified, however, by recognition of the countervailing competitive concerns that are implicated by the protection of functional designs on standards less demanding than those imposed by patent law.

The EU proposals initially contained two additional exclusions from protection that bear confusingly similar popular labels (which were taken from the debates leading to the 1988 U.K. reforms): "must-fit" and "must-match." The must-fit exclusion deals with mechanical synchronicity, whereas the must-match provision deals with visual synchronicity. Article 7(2) of the Directive created an exclusion for mechanical interconnections, that is:

> [F]eatures of appearance of a product which must necessarily be reproduced in their exact form and dimensions in order to permit the product in which the design is incorporated or to which it is applied to be mechanically connected or placed in, around or against another product so that either product may perform its function.

*See also* Regulation, art. 8(2). The exclusion of interconnections reveals the continuing conviction of the Commission that interoperability and standardization will enhance the competitive environment. As the Commission's *Green Paper* explained:

> Consumers should, for example, be able to replace a vacuum cleaner hose of a given make by another hose which fits into the vacuum cleaner. In principle, the design of the vacuum cleaner hoses qualifies for design protection just as does the design of the vacuum cleaner itself. To ensure interoperability and competition in the spare parts aftermarket in respect of a wide range of household articles, motor vehicles, consumer electronics etc., it appears advisable to exclude from protection those features of a design which would have to be reproduced necessarily in their exact form and dimensions in order for the component part to fit into the complex product for which it is intended.

Green Paper on the Legal Protection of Industrial Design, Working Document of the Services of the Commission, ¶5.4.10.1 (1991).

The debate about must-match designs (initially defined as designs where "the product incorporating the design or to which the design is applied is a component part of a complex product upon whose appearance the protected design is dependent") played out in the context of a proposed "repair clause." In the different proposals prior to the adoption of the Directive, this clause addressed the scope of protection for the design of certain spare parts. The most commonly cited example of a must-match design, which also occasioned the greatest controversy, is the design of car body panels. Although there was broad agreement on the must-fit exclusion, the adoption of a must-match exclusion resulted in stalemate among EU member states. Article 14 of the enacted Directive provided that:

> Until such time as amendments to this Directive are adopted on a proposal from the Commission [as contemplated within four years by Article 18], member states shall maintain in force their existing legal provisions relating to the

use of the design of a component part used for the purpose of the repair of a complex product so as to restore its original appearance and shall introduce changes to those provisions only if the purpose is to liberalize the market for such parts [i.e., reduce protection].

*See also* Registered Designs Act 1949, as amended, §7A(5) (UK) (providing that the "design of a component part . . . of a complex product . . . is not infringed by the use [of that design to repair the complex product so as to restore its original appearance]"); *cf.* Copyright, Designs & Patents Act 1988, §213(3)(b)(ii) (excluding from the scope of U.K. unregistered design protection designs that "are dependent upon the appearance of another article of which the article is intended by the designer to form an integral part"). However, even before the directive was implemented, the Commission initiated a consultation exercise among interested parties (car parts manufacturers and insurance companies) in the hope of reaching a voluntary resolution of the dispute. The exercise has not yet produced an agreed amendment addressing spare parts. On December 12, 2007, the European Parliament approved a proposal that would ultimately deny protection to car spare parts by amending Article 14 of the Directive to include a harmonized repair clause. *See* Report on the Parliament on the Proposal for a Directive Amending Directive 98/71/EC on the Legal Protection for Designs, COM(2004)0582–C6-0119/2004-2204/0203 (COD), Nov. 22, 2007, proposed amended art. 14(1) ("protection as a design shall not exist for a design that is incorporated in or applied to a product which constitutes a component part of a complex product and is used within the meaning of Article 12(1) of this Directive for the sole purpose of the repair of that complex product so as to restore its original appearance"). However, those (fifteen) member states presently offering protection would be allowed to continue that protection for five years. *See id.*, proposed art. 1A. In contrast, Article 110 of the Regulation already includes a provision along these lines and excludes protection for "designs which constitute a component part of a complex product used . . . for the purpose of the repair of that complex product so as to restore its original appearance".

## Community Design Regulation

### Article 7: Disclosure

1. For the purpose of applying Articles 5 and 6, a design shall be deemed to have been made available to the public if it has been published following registration or otherwise, or exhibited, used in trade or otherwise disclosed, before the date referred to in Articles 5(1)(a) and 6(1)(a) or in Articles 5(1)(b) and 6(1)(b), as the case may be, except where these events could not reasonably have become known in the normal course of business to the circles specialised in the sector concerned, operating within the Community. The design shall not, however, be deemed to have been made available to the public for the sole reason that it has been disclosed to a third person under explicit or implicit conditions of confidentiality.

. . .

## GREEN LANE PRODUCTS LTD. v PMS INTERNATIONAL GROUP PLC
[2008] EWCA Civ 358

JACOB L.J.:

This appeal is from a judgment of Lewison J. . . . He determined a preliminary point of construction of Regulation 6/2002 on Community designs [2002] OJ L3/1 (the Regulation). The point was: "The correct meaning in law of 'the circles specialised in the sector concerned operating within the Community' as that phrase is used in Art. 7 of the Regulation."

The appeal arises out of assumed facts which, if they were not the subject of a real case, might be thought to have been devised for a student moot. They are these:

(1) Green Lane make and sell under the trade mark "Dryerballs" spiky plastic balls for use in tumble driers. There are blue ones with square nodes and pink ones with rounded nodes. They apparently have a beneficial effect, for instance, helping soften fabrics and reducing drying time by lifting and separating the laundry as it tumbles.

(2) Green Lane has registered the design of its Dryerballs as community registered designs (CRDs) under Nos. 000217187-0001-004 with an application date of 24th August 2004. Below I show 0001, consisting of the combination of one ball with square nodes and one ball with rounded nodes, there being no colour restriction. It is not necessary to illustrate the others.

(3) PMS marketed spiky plastic balls (made in China from a tool created for PMS) extensively in the EU from 2002. They were sold as massage balls, not as laundry balls. They look like this:

(4) In 2006 PMS decided to sell its balls (of exactly the same design as its massage balls) for other purposes too. One of these purposes is as a laundry ball, but other packages are marked "Massage, Hand Exerciser, Easy-Catch Toy, Dog Trainer."

Green Lane says PMS will infringe its CRDs if they continue to sell their product for anything other than use as a massage ball. PMS says the CRDs are invalid by reason of their prior sale of their massage balls. Green Lane says: (a) that such prior art is irrelevant as a matter of law and (b) even if it is relevant, their CRDs are nonetheless valid. We are concerned only with the first of these points. . . .

Green Lane says that the extent of its rights under its CRDs [is] defined by Art. 10 — any article, whatever its intended purpose, will infringe unless it does not produce on the informed user a different overall impression. The only reason why continued sales by PMS of balls for massage purposes do not infringe is that such sales are protected by Art. 22. Even then such sales are protected only to the extent provided by that Article.

PMS says the design registrations are not "new" within the meaning of Art. 5 or do not have "individual character" within the meaning of Art. 6. They say this is so because of their own prior sales in the European Union of what, for all practical purposes, is the very design complained of. In short they say the design is old.

Now absent Art. 7 one would say that PMS are right: that a design cannot be "new" or have "individual character" if it is the same or practically the same as an article previously used in trade. But, say Green Lane, a design may be new or have individual character even if it is [in] fact old: Art. 7 says that a prior design is not taken to be made available to the public, even if it in reality was, where:

> . . . [T]hese events [i.e., prior use in trade] could not reasonably have become known in the normal course of business to the circles specialised in the sector concerned, operating in the Community.

And, says Green Lane, the "sector concerned" means the sector for which the design was registered, not the sector of the alleged prior art.

Lewison J. rejected that submission. He ruled that:

1. 'The sector concerned' within the meaning of Article 7 of the Regulation is the sector that consists of or includes the sector of the alleged prior art.
2. 'The circles specialised in the sector concerned, operating within the Community' within the meaning of Article 7 of the Regulation are capable of consisting of all individuals who conduct trade in relation to products in the sector concerned, including those who design, make, advertise, market, distribute and sell such products in the course of trade in the Community.

I would uphold that ruling. . . .

### The Language of Article 7 Itself

I start first simply with the language of the first sentence of Art. 7 itself:

> For the purpose of applying Articles 5 and 6, a design shall be deemed to have been made available to the public if it has been published following

registration or otherwise, or exhibited, used in trade or otherwise disclosed, before . . . , except where these events could not reasonably have become known in the normal course of business to the circles specialised in the sector concerned, operating within the Community.

As Ward L.J. observed during the course of oral argument, if that is read alone, the only "circles" which could be referred to are those of the prior art—those in which the design has been "exhibited, used in trade or otherwise disclosed". One looks to see, therefore, whether the context or the purpose or the travaux indicate any other meaning. I think they most certainly do not—that they are all confirmatory of the meaning when the sentence is read on its own.

### The Context of the Language

[T]urning now to the requirements for protection, the basic rule is that a design must be "new" and have "individual character" (Art. 4(1)). Article 5 elaborates on what is meant by "new" and Art. 6 on what is meant by "individual character". In both cases the test involves consideration of an earlier design, that is, a design which "has been made available to the public."

This is a clear incorporation of a key concept and well-known language of patent law defining the prior art which may be used to attack validity of a patent. An invention is "new" if it is not part of the "state of the art". The ". . . state of the art shall be held to comprise everything made available to the public by means of a written or oral description, by use, or in any other way before [the relevant date]" (see Art. 54 of the European Patent Convention). I shall use the expression conventionally used for this test: "absolute novelty."

From time to time people have wondered whether the absolute novelty test in patent law is not a little harsh—it covers for instance a fanciful example I made up some time ago—a disclosure in a document written in Sanskrit and misplaced in the children's section of Alice Springs' public library is one which is "made available to the public."

[However, a] bright-line workable rule . . . has served the test of time. Expensive investigation of not only whether a piece of prior art was known but how well known it was is obviated. The small price of the occasional harsh decision is well worth it for the sake of a cohesive and predictable system.

This clear rule, which so far as I am aware, is virtually standard for patent systems throughout the world, not only for identifying prior art available to attack novelty but also that for basing an obviousness attack. . . .

Both sides accept that "made available to the public" in the conventional patent law sense is also the basic rule for identifying prior art which may be considered for the purpose of attacking the validity of designs. The question is what is the meaning of the exception?

Before moving on it should be noted that the same rule and the same exception applies both to UDRs and CDRs. And of course that the same design can be the subject of both kinds of right is an important part of the architecture [of the Regulation].

I go back to the architecture. The next thing to consider is the basic scope of protection. This is provided by Art. 10(1): "any design which does not produce on the informed user a different overall impression." The acts prevented (broadly commercial use) are set out in Art. 19(1). In the case of CDRs the right is a true monopoly, but in the case of UDRs the right is limited to cases of copying.

It is particularly important to realise that the scope of protection covers any use of the design for article [sic], whatever its intended purpose. The scope provision, unlike for instance the previous law of the United Kingdom (s. 7 of the Registered Designs Act 1949) does not limit infringement to "articles for which the design is registered" or anything like that. So if you register a design for a car you can stop use of the design for a brooch or a cake or a toy, or if you register a textile design you can stop its use on wallpaper, a shirt or a plate.

Having provided in effect that any commercial use will infringe, the Regulation goes on to provide exceptions. The Art. 20 exceptions are in part taken from similar exceptions to patent infringement set out in the (unimplemented) Community Patent Convention 1975. Article 21 provides for exhaustion of rights, corresponding to Art. 7 of Directive 89/104 to approximate the laws of the Member States relating to trade marks [1989] OJ L40/1 (the Trade Marks Directive) and Art. 28 of the Community Patent Convention. Article 22 provides for a right of prior use.

UDRs are short term. They last for three years "as from the date on which the design was first made available to the public in the Community" (Art. 11). Note that the same expression "made available to the public" is used as in the test for identifying the prior art. The term of CDRs is much longer, a maximum of 25 years.

The point of the short-term protection for UDRs is twofold. The first is explicitly referred to in recital (16)—for products having a short market life there is no need to register. The second is as a result of Art. 7(2). This provides a "grace" period of 12 months. It works this way. If the designer markets his design and within a year thereafter applies to register it, his earlier disclosure of the design does not count as prior art. This has the benefit that he can see how his design is initially received by the market—if well he can go on to register it, if not he need not bother.

The next part of the architecture is the conditions for invalidity. Article 25 sets out the possible grounds of invalidity and says these are the only such grounds. . . .

The last part of the architecture which is necessary to consider is some of Title IV, Application for a Registered Community Design. Article 36 sets out what the application "shall contain." Besides what are clearly important but clearly only administrative matters such as requirements for an application, identification of the applicant and a representation of the design, Art. 36(2) says: "The application shall further contain an indication of the products in which the design is intended to be incorporated or to which it is intended to be applied." A lot of the argument revolves around this provision.

Article 36 also specifies some optional matters to be included in the application. These include: "[3](d) the classification of the products in which the design is intended to be incorporated or to which it is intended to be applied according to class."

It is necessary to explain what is meant by "classification . . . according to class." There is an international agreement called the "Locarno Agreement Establishing an International Classification for Industrial Designs", originally signed in 1968. The idea is to have a single internationally agreed classification for industrial designs by classes, subclasses, a detailed list of goods in which designs are incorporated and an indication of the classes and subclasses into which they fall. There is a similar, older, system for trade marks (the Nice Agreement). Article 2(1) of Locarno says this:

> Subject to the requirements prescribed by this Agreement, the international classification shall be solely of an administrative character. Nevertheless, each country may attribute to it the legal scope which it considers appropriate. In particular, the international classification shall not bind the countries of the Special Union as regards the nature and scope of the protection afforded to the design in those countries.

Article 36 contains further administrative matters (about fees and so on) and concludes with the following: "6. The information contained in the elements mentioned in paragraph 2 and in paragraph 3(a) and (d) shall not affect the scope of protection of the design as such."

. . .

## The Recital (14) Argument*

[The] main argument [for the claimant] is that recital (14) compels one to the conclusion that the circles of the Art. 7 exception must be those for which the design was registered, or, in the case of a UDR, the circles into which the holder of the right sold his product . . .

What [counsel for claimant] submits is that the "individual character" test of Art. 6 is to be performed by the "informed user". Recital (14) requires this notional person to consider "the existing design corpus", "the nature of the product to which the design is applied", "the industrial sector to which it belongs." All these things, he submits, only make sense if the sector concerned is that for which the design is registered. As [counsel for claimants] put it: "the informed user cannot be expected to be informed across a whole myriad of different sectors."

I accept that there are real difficulties about recital (14). But I think [counsel for defendants] is right and clearly so, in submitting that they do not arise so far as Art. 7 is concerned. The exception simply rules out certain prior art from being considered at all, either for the purposes of novelty (in relation to which the informed user plays no part) or for the purposes of "individual character". Whatever the informed user should be considering and whatever his notional attributes is not material to the inquiry as to what prior art is to be excluded. The informed user only comes in once the prior art to be considered is identified.

I think this is confirmed by a series of considerations all going one way:

(i) Article 36 (the administrative provisions) both on its own and when considered in relation to the grounds of invalidity;

---

*Ed. Note: The text of EU legislation contains a series of recitals by way of preamble.

(ii) the travaux préparatoires in relation to Art. 7; and
(iii) the otherwise irrational results, results which are not obscure or unrealistic.

...

### The Travaux for Article 36(2)

I start with Art. 36(2). This provision is ... crucial for Green Lane's argument. An applicant has to indicate the products upon which he intends to apply his design. It is this indication which, it is submitted, tells you, or enables you to work out, what the "sector concerned" is. If there was no such indication the argument could not get off the ground—you simply would not be able to tell what the design is registered for—the designs in issue are of that sort. Even where you think you could work out what it is for, you could be wrong: suppose it looks a bit like a chair but the applicant intended it to be a toy or a brooch or a statue.

But I do not think Art. 36(2) is intended to affect legal rights at all, whether by way of the definition of scope of protection, or validity, which in a real sense is also part of scope of protection or otherwise. It comes in a title which has nothing to do with existence or extent of rights—"Application for Registered Community Designs". It comes under a section whose heading is likewise nothing to do with either of these matters—"Filing of applications and the conditions which govern them". Its own heading has nothing to do with them either—"Conditions with which applications must comply". All the other matters in Art. 36 are obviously administrative, so it is stretching the imagination to think that Art. 36(2) is intended to have an effect on substantive rights.

Next there is no sanction for a mistaken or misstated Art. 36(2) declaration. An applicant can say what he likes about what he intends to apply his design to, but whether he gets it wrong, even deliberately wrong, does not in the end matter. There is no ground of revocation available if he does (see Art. 25 "only in the following cases"). If rights or their validity depended on the declaration, one would surely expect a sanction for a misstated declaration. Besides a designer may in some cases have a particular kind of article in mind only later to realise that he can exploit his design for other kinds of article.

Now it is true that the Art. 36(2) statement is compulsory, but this should be seen in the context that there is also an optional Locarno class declaration (Art. 36(3)(d)). The scheme is that the applicant should identify the product and may also say what class it is in. If he chooses not to do the latter, then the Office can do the job for him. That is the way I understand the scheme to work. The only purpose behind all of this is so that the classification system can be used for searching purposes. Everyone has an interest in the classification system working: people need to know whether registrations are valid or not and for that purpose it is helpful to be able to search in a structured system—hence the use of the classification system.

Article 36(6) confirms this. It says that both the compulsory and voluntary information "shall not affect the scope of protection of the design as such".

I think it wholly unrealistic to read this as limited to "scope" without including "validity". An invalid registration has no scope.

. . .

Nor does the argument fit with the fact that the rule must be the same for UDRs. Necessarily these do not have a statement about intended use. The designer just puts his product on the market. [Counsel for Green Lane] says you work out what the sector is from that. But a man who puts a thing on the market will be happy to sell his product for any purpose. And he may, depending on the adaptability of the design, sell it for a variety of purposes. Why should he, having sold his article on the market for one purpose, find other possible uses foreclosed by some later UDR of someone else? Or suppose a man puts his article on the market for a particular use and, within the grace period, applies for a CDR specifying a different purpose? Is there to be different prior art for the two cases? The answer can rationally only be no.

More confirmation that Art. 36(2) is purely administrative comes from the fact that the Regulation must clearly be read in conjunction with the Directive. The idea is that you can get the same rights, governed by the same rules as to validity Community-wide as you can get nationwide via a national registration. The Directive came first. It contains no Art. 36 — indeed no applications provisions at all. It was left to Member States to decide whether the applicant should or should not specify the proposed use of his design. Doubtless many, if not all, Member States used the Locarno Convention and may have required the applicant to specify the nature of his intended use or at least the class of this intended use. But the fact that there was no obligation in [the] Directive for this is a major pointer to the conclusion that any such statement could not affect validity in any way.

The Travaux for Article 7

Originally it was Green Lane which suggested that the travaux for Art. 7 supported its case. It pointed to the early Green Paper and the passage [to the effect that "a design, to obtain protection, should not already be known to the specialists operating within the Community in the sector of marketable goods to which the design is intended to be applied"]. But much water passed under the bridge thereafter and one cannot say that the final document was intended to implement that idea. Far from it.

First, following consultation, the first proposal actually dropped the idea said by Green Lane to be the intention. Absolute novelty was chosen. The explanatory memorandum said this: "Novelty is to be assessed at the worldwide level. If it has been registered or otherwise has been made available to the public anywhere in the world, it is not new."

It is a fair inference that that is what the users wanted. So far as one can see there was never any further wide consultation which changed that general view. How then did the exception to absolute novelty come about? The travaux are clear about this. It came about by reason of a specific piece of lobbying by the textile industry. It was a concern about counterfeiting and nothing to do with an intention that prior art, obscure in the field of intended use, should be discounted.

The Economic and Social Committee (ESC) Opinion of 1994 said this when considering the novelty provision:

> 3.1.2 This provision, as worded, would be difficult to apply in many fields, and particularly in the textiles industry. Sellers of counterfeit products often obtain false certification stating that the disputed design had already been created in a third country.
> 3.1.3 In these circumstances, the aim should be dissemination to interested parties within the European Community before the date of reference.
> 3.1.4 In the light of the above considerations, Article 5(2) might be worded as follows:
>> A design shall be deemed to have been made available to the public if it has been published following registration, exhibited, used in trade or otherwise disclosed, unless this could not reasonably be known to specialist circles in the sector in question operating within the Community before the date of reference. . . .

This is clearly the forerunner of the exception in Art. 7. The ESC's suggestion was taken up, extended also to the individual character test and became the law. It is worthwhile quoting the Commission's explanation for the proposed exception contained in its [1996] Amended Proposal:

> The Article [6] has furthermore been amended in accordance with the wishes of the European Parliament and the Economic and Social Committee through the introduction of what is commonly known as the 'safeguard clause'. Its aim is to protect the design industry from claims that a design right is not valid because there was an earlier design in use somewhere in the world where the European industry could not possibly have been aware of it. The intention of this provision is to avoid the situation where design rights can be invalidated by infringers claiming that antecedents can be found in remote places or museums.

As [counsel for defendant] observes for the exception to work as intended, the sector concerned had to be that of the cited prior art. His example demonstrates this: "If the CRD was in respect of a design for, say, teapots and the alleged prior art was for Columbian textiles, it would be the textiles circles in Europe who would be in a position to know whether the 'certification' was genuine. Ex hypothesi the teapot circles would never know."

Moreover the exception was clearly conceived as narrow—it was aimed at obscure prior art only: it meant that forging this would not help an infringer.

Although there were further travaux before the ultimate Regulation, there was no significant relevant further change.

The only other thing to note is that at no time did anyone ever suggest there was any link between what became recital (14) and this proposal. Yet if the recital and this provision were linked as Mr Vaughan submits, there surely would have been. The same goes for the travaux leading to Art. 22. It cannot seriously be argued that because Art. 22 provides a limited defence of prior use, it follows that the Art. 7 exception is wide.

. . .

### The Absurd Consequence if Green Lane Were Right

Finally I turn to the absurd consequences if [counsel for claimants] were right. The judge identified some of these and I can do no better than borrow his description with gratitude:

[22] There are a number of potential consequences of Green Lane's interpretation which suggest that it is wrong. First, consider the form of the application. Suppose a designer produces a design of a product which can be used for a multitude of purposes or products, each of which is in a different product class. Call the classes A, B, C and D; and assume that circles specialised in one class do not know about designs in the other classes. The design is both old and well-known in circles specialising in class D. If Dr Lawrence [counsel for defendant] is right, then the registration will be invalid if the applicant for registration specifies all four classes (or class D alone); but it will be valid if he only specifies class A. Yet once registered, the registration gives him a monopoly extending across all four classes. So the canny applicant will specify the products to which the design is intended to be applied in the narrowest possible way, so as to avoid exposing his design to prior art, confident in the expectation that once the design has been registered he will obtain the wide protection given to him by the registration.

[23] Second, consider the consequences of registration. The use of the design in class D is old and well-known. But upon registration of a design specifying class A as the intended class of products, it becomes unlawful to use the design for products in class D without the consent of the holder of the registered design. It is common ground that the grant of intellectual property rights ought not to have the effect of making unlawful that which had previously been lawful. Dr Lawrence seeks to meet this by invoking Article 22. But Article 22 is very narrow. It protects a person who has himself begun use of a design before the filing date of the CRD or made serious and determined preparations to do so. So consider a person who operates within the field of Class D. He is well aware of the old design, but has not used or prepared to use it yet, although all his competitors have. Article 22 would not allow him to use it. But why should he not use an old and well-known design within his own field of operation?

[24] Take another example. A manufacturer of products within class D sells them through a distributor. Dr Lawrence would accept that the manufacturer can go on manufacturing and the distributor can go on distributing. But what if the manufacturer wants to change his distributor after the relevant date? The new distributor has not previously sold products to that design. Since the sale of products to the registered design is itself an infringement under Article 19 the new distributor cannot sell. He cannot bring himself within Article 22 because he has no prior use; and the manufacturer (who is probably within Article 22) is prohibited by Article 22.3 from granting the new distributor a licence to exploit the design. So if Dr. Lawrence is right, the pre-existing business arrangements are frozen.

[25] Third, consider the situation as the period of protection is coming to an end. The original registration specified class A as the class of products to which the design was intended to be applied. It is in fact capable of being applied to classes B, C and D as well (although it has not yet been applied to class C products). As the period of protection comes towards its end, the proprietor

of the registered design applies to register it specifying class C as the class of products to which it is intended to be applied. Prior art within class A, on Dr Lawrence's interpretation, does not count (assuming that the circles specialising in the respective classes do not know about each other's designs); so the registration is successful. The proprietor of the registered design thus extends his protection within class A by registering his design for class C. Yet this is contrary to Article 12 which limits the 'total term' of a registered design to twenty five years.

There are other examples one can think of too. . . .

These examples are realistic. [Counsel for claimant] did not really contend otherwise. And he could not find any fault with them. His answer was to suggest that the alternative construction also produced absurd results. First it would involve difficult questions of searching and secondly that the rightholder might find his registration lost by reason of prior art which he could not reasonably learn about because the validity of a design could be challenged on the basis of any prior art in any field unless it was obscure in its own field.

I do not accept either point as absurd. As to the practicalities of searching, it has always been the case that design searches are not easy—most prior designs are not registered and so not readily searchable as, for instance, patent literature is. Yet the system has worked well for a long time with absolute novelty in many countries, for instance under the prior UK system.

But of even more fundamental significance is this: the right gives a monopoly over any kind of goods according to the design. It makes complete sense that the prior art available for attacking novelty should also extend to all kinds of goods, subject only to the limited exception of prior art obscure even in the sector from which it comes.

. . .

Accordingly [I would dismiss the] appeal . . .

## COMMUNITY DESIGN REGULATION

### Article 10: Scope of Protection

1. The scope of the protection conferred by a Community design shall include any design which does not produce on the informed user a different overall impression.

2. In assessing the scope of protection, the degree of freedom of the designer in developing his design shall be taken into consideration.

### Article 19(1): Rights Conferred by a Community Design

A registered Community design shall confer on its holder the exclusive right to use it and to prevent any third party not having his consent from using it. The aforementioned use shall cover, in particular, the making, offering, putting on the market, importing, exporting or using of a product in which the design is incorporated or to which it is applied, or stocking such a product for those purposes.

## Procter & Gamble Co. v Reckitt Benckiser (UK) Ltd
[2007] EWCA Civ 936

Jacob L.J.:

This is an appeal from a judgment of Lewison J. He held Procter & Gamble's (P&G) registered Community design (RCD) No. 000097969-0001 valid and infringed. The indication of the products to which the design is intended to be applied is "sprayers". P&G use it in a number of countries (but not yet here) for an air freshener product called "Febreze". The Reckitt spray canister held to infringe is for their "Air Wick" room air conditioner.

### Evidence in Registered Design Cases

The most important things in a case about registered designs are: (1) the registered design; (2) the accused object; and (3) the prior art.

And the most important thing about each of these is what they look like. Of course parties and judges have to try to put into words why they say a design has "individual character" or what the "overall impression produced on an informed user" is. But "it takes longer to say than to see" as I observed in Philips Electronics NV v Remington Consumer Products Ltd (No.1) [1998] R.P.C. 283 at 318. And words themselves are often insufficiently precise on their own.

It follows that a place for evidence is very limited indeed. By and large it should be possible to decide a registered design case in a few hours. The evidence of the designer, e.g. as to whether he/she was trying to make, or thought he/she had made, a breakthrough, is irrelevant. The evidence of experts, particularly about consumer products, is unlikely to be of much assistance: anyone can point out similarities and differences, though an educated eye can sometimes help a bit. Sometimes there may be a piece of technical evidence which is relevant—e.g. that design freedom is limited by certain constraints. But even so, that is usually more or less self-evident and certainly unlikely to be controversial to the point of a need for cross-examination, still less substantial cross-examination.

In Thermos Ltd v Aladdin Sales & Marketing Ltd [2000] F.S.R. 402 at 404, I said:

> Most registered designs are for consumer articles, objects bought or to be appreciated by ordinary members of the public. I observed in Isaac Oren v. Red Box Toy Factory Ltd [1999] F.S.R. 785, at 791, that 'I do not think, generally speaking, that 'expert' evidence of this opinion sort, (*i.e.* as to what an ordinary consumer would see) in cases involving registered designs for consumer products is ever likely to be useful. . . . Much the most important matters in a registered design action are what the various designs look like. Everything else is secondary. It is, for instance, clear law that whether or not the defendant copied is irrelevant. . . . So it is irrelevant for the claimants' witness to throw down a challenge that he thought the defendant copied, as was done here, and it is equally irrelevant for the defendant to prove or to give disclosure about how his design was arrived at. Similarly, it is irrelevant for the claimant to prove, if it be the case, that he spent a fortune in arriving at his design. It

matters not whether he thought of it in the bath or by engaging the most prestigious design consultants in the world.' . . .

*Thermos* was decided in relation to the then UK domestic law of registered designs. This case is the first to reach this Court concerning a Community design registration (CDR) granted pursuant to Regulation 6/2002 (the Regulation). But everything I said then applies also to actions about CDRs too.

It follows that the design history of the P&G design, and whether Reckitt copied . . . was irrelevant. Of more relevance (though even this is secondary) is the fact that the P&G design (in the form of its physical embodiment) received some independent accolade. The judge records this at:

10. The Febreze product was well-received within the packaging community. At the end of 2004 it won the New Jersey Packaging Executives Package of the Year Award. In 2005 it won the Ameristar Award within the category of household products. The citation for the latter award said:

Febreze Air Effects is packaged in a uniquely shaped aerosol can that breaks category norms, stands out on the shelf, is easy to use and delivers a superb scent experience for consumers. Febreze redefines the difference a great product and a unique package can make in a customized container and actuator.

. . .

### The Registered Design (000097969-0001)

There are six representations shown.

The category of product is described as "sprayers". I have reproduced all six pictures. The judge left out the top and bottom views. Rightly everyone ignored these as having any real significance. I reproduce them only so that readers can see that for themselves.

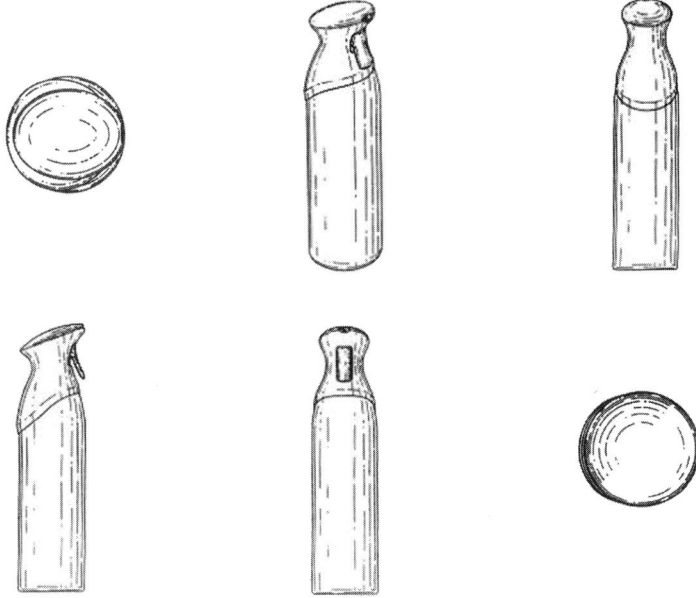

We also had physical embodiments of the design, both in plain white and in their actual Febreze get-up. It has long been the practice, where there is a physical embodiment of a registered design, for the court to look at that. Of course, one has to be very careful that the physical object is a true reproduction of the design. In the present case it was accepted that that was so, subject to some minor variation so trivial as to be hardly discoverable even on a close comparison between the registered design and the Febreze sprayer.

### The Accused Design

The judge reproduced pictures of this at [19]:

Unlike the registered design (which has a slightly tapered top to the can which blends with the top), this has a top which fits on a standard cylindrical canister. . . .

### The Informed User

By Art. 10(1), ". . . the scope of the protection conferred by a Community design shall include any design which does not produce on the informed user a different overall impression."

The Regulation does not tell us much about the notional "informed user". He/she is clearly not quite the same sort of person as the "person skilled in the art" of patent law. The equivalent to that person in the field of design would be some sort of average designer, not a user. Recital 14 assists a bit. It says:

> 14. The assessment as to whether a design has individual character should be based on whether the overall impression produced on an informed user viewing the design clearly differs from that produced on him by the existing design corpus, taking into consideration the nature of the product to which the design is applied or in which it is incorporated, and in particular the industrial sector to which it belongs and the degree of freedom of the designer in developing the design.

The recital is actually framed around the requirement for registrability—whether the design has "individual character"—rather than the test for infringement. Curiously the reference to the "existing design corpus, taking into consideration the nature of the product to which the design is applied" is not expressly carried over into the text of any of the actual Articles of the Regulation. But self-evidently it is relevant to their interpretation. What it tells us is that for the purposes of registrability the notional informed user is to be taken as aware of other similar designs which form part of the "design corpus". Further, the "overall impression" to the "informed user" is also a key ingredient of the infringement test. So for that test too the notional informed user must be taken to be aware of the "existing design corpus."

The recital uses another phrase not carried over into the Articles — "clearly differs". Only if the "overall impression" "clearly differs" from that of the "existing design corpus" will the design have an "individual character". Plainly that is relevant for registrability, even if Art. 6(1) does not expressly use "clearly differs". Does the phrase also apply to the infringement test? Does an accused design escape infringement only if its overall impression "clearly differs" from the registered design? All Art. 10(1) says is "different overall impression". Does that really mean "clearly different" — the word "clearly" requiring much blue water between the accused and registered design for non-infringement?

The judge thought it did. But I do not. Different policies are involved. It is one thing to restrict the grant of a monopoly right to designs which are shown "clearly" to differ from the existing design corpus. That makes sense — you need clear blue water between the registered design and the "prior art", otherwise there is a real risk that design monopolies will or may interfere with routine, ordinary, minor, everyday design modifications — what patent lawyers call "mere workshop modifications". But no such policy applies to the scope of protection. It is sufficient to avoid infringement if the accused product is of a design which produces a "different overall impression". There is no policy requirement that the difference be "clear". If a design differs, that is enough — an informed user can discriminate.

Actually the judge did not expressly, in his detailed consideration of infringement, import any requirement of "clearly differ". It probably, however, underlay some of his reasoning.

I move on to mention another point. The right conferred applies to any sort of product even though the registration contains an indication of the type of article for which it is intended, see Art. 36(2). Where the alleged infringement is a quite different sort of product from that indicated as being the intended type, there may be problems about identifying the attributes of the informed user — is he a user of the kind of article such as the alleged infringement or a user of the kind of intended article? Or both? But none of that applies here.

Here the "design corpus" of which the informed user is taken [to] be aware are other sprayers generally known — not just sprayers for air fresheners or even those of the kind purchased by ordinary consumers. There was no dispute about this.

The "informed user" test makes sense: a user who has experience of other similar articles will be reasonably discriminatory — able to appreciate enough detail to decide whether a design creates an overall impression which has individual character and whether an alleged infringement produces a different overall impression.

It follows that the informed user is not the same as the "average consumer" of trade mark law. The ECJ describes the attributes of this notional figure in Lloyd Schuhfabrik Meyer & Co GmbH v Klijsen Handel BV (C-342/97) [1999] E.C.R. I-3819:

> 26. . . . the perception of marks in the mind of the average consumer of the category of goods or services in question plays a decisive role in the global appreciation of the likelihood of confusion. The average consumer normally perceives a mark as a whole and does not proceed to analyse its various details. . . .
>
> 27. For the purposes of that global appreciation, the average consumer of the category of products concerned is deemed to be reasonably well-informed and reasonably observant and circumspect (see, to that effect, Case C-210/96 Gut Springenheide and Tusky [1998] ECR I-4657, paragraph 31). However, account should be taken of the fact that the average consumer only rarely has the chance to make a direct comparison between the different marks but must place his trust in the imperfect picture of them that he has kept in his mind. It should also be borne in mind that the average consumer's level of attention is likely to vary according to the category of goods or services in question.

The informed user of design law is more discriminating. Whilst I do not say that imperfect recollection has no part to play in judging what the overall impression of design is, it cannot be decisive. The judge placed more emphasis than I think is right on an "imperfect recollection" test or something like it. He accepted Mr Wyand's submission that, "the overall impression of a design is what sticks in the mind *after* [my emphasis] it has been carefully viewed". I would say that what matters is what strikes the mind of the informed user *when* it is carefully viewed.

I think the Higher Provisional Court in Vienna, in holding that P&G's design is not infringed by the Air Wick product (decision of December 6, 2006, overruling a lower court decision granting an interim injunction) was right when it said:

> The 'informed user' will, in the view of the Appeals Court, have more extensive knowledge than an 'average consumer in possession of average information, awareness and understanding', in particular he will be open to design issues and will be fairly familiar with them (Bulling/Langöhrig/Hellwig, Gemeinschaftsgeschmackmuster [Community designs], Rz 56).

Policy considerations point the same way. The main point of protection of a trade mark is to prevent consumer confusion or deception. The possibility of imperfect recollection plays a significant part in that. The point of protecting a design is to protect that design *as a design*. So what matters is the overall impression created by it: will the user buy it, consider it or appreciate it *for its individual design*? That involves the user looking at the article, not half-remembering it. The motivation is different from purchasing or otherwise relying on a trade mark as a guarantee of origin.

So the informed user is alert to design issues and is better informed than the average consumer in trade mark law. Things which may infringe a registered trade mark may not infringe a corresponding registered design. I cannot think of any instance where the reverse might be so.

Another thing is also clear. Where shapes are, to some extent, required to be the way they are by reason of function, the informed user is taken to know that. That is what Art. 6(2) (for validity) and Art. 10(2) (for scope of protection) require. Take an aspect of this case. Both products have a trigger and something of a "pistol grip". There is some constraint on design freedom for this—the product must be grippable so that the index finger can pull the trigger, the trigger must be shaped to fit the finger and have sufficient space behind it for it to be pulled. That is a given. The informed user must take those requirements into account when assessing overall impression.

Thus Art. 10(2) is a narrowing provision. Smaller differences will be enough to create a different overall impression where freedom of design is limited.

In this connection I have no doubt that the "freedom of the designer" referred to is not that of a particular party—it is the degree of choice a designer would have in creating his design, not particular constraints on a particular party. The judge so held. . . .

The judge considered the nature of the informed user at [paras. 30–41 of his opinion]. He considered a formulation by H.H. Judge Fysh in WoodHouse UK Plc v Architectural Lighting Systems (t/a Aquila Design) [2006] R.P.C. 1 and several decisions of the invalidity division of OHIM. I set the passages out for convenience here, though in the end I do not think they are saying anything different from the Austrian Court or what I have concluded above:

Judge Fysh in *Woodhouse*:

> First, this notional person must obviously be a user of articles of the sort which is the subject of the registered design—and I would think, a regular user at that. He could thus be a consumer or buyer or be otherwise familiar with the subject matter say, through use at work. The quality smacks of practical considerations. In my view the informed user is first, a person to whom the design is directed. Evidently he is not a manufacturer of the articles and both counsel roundly rejected the candidature of 'the man in the street'. 'Informed' to my mind adds a notion of familiarity with the relevant rather more than what one might expect of the average consumer; it imports the notion of 'what's about in the market' and 'what has been about in the recent past?' I do not think it requires an archival mind (or eye) or more than an average memory but it does, I think, demand some awareness of product trend and availability and some knowledge of basic technical considerations (if any). In connection with the latter, one must not forget that we are in the territory of designs and thus what matters most is the appearance of things; as Mr Davis reminded me, these are not petty patents. Therefore, focus on eye appeal seems more pertinent than familiarity with the underlying operational or manufacturing technology (if any).

Eredu v Arrmet (OHIM ref: ICD000000024; April 27, 2004 , a bar stool):

> The degree of freedom of a designer is limited by the fact that stools of the type to which the CD relates necessarily comprise a base, a central column and a seat in order that the stool fulfils its function.

The informed user is familiar with the basic features of stools. When assessing the overall impression of the design he/she takes into consideration the limitations to the freedom of the designer and weighs the various features consequently. He/she will pay more attention to similarities of non necessary features and dissimilarities of necessary ones.

In particular, the informed user is aware of the prior art known in the normal course of business to the circles specialised in the sector concerned. Therefore, he knows that that type of stool usually has a foot rest and a back.

. . .

### The "Different Overall Impression" Test

Once one has identified the notional "informed user" correctly and what he would know about the design corpus, one asks whether the accused product produces "a different overall impression" to such a person[.]

This test is inherently rather imprecise: an article may reasonably seem to one man to create "a different overall impression" and yet to another to do so. It is always so with the scope of rights in a visual work. You need to cover not only exact imitations, but also things which come "too close". Whatever words you choose, you are bound to leave a considerable margin for the judgment of the tribunal. Thus, in copyright the test for infringement is doing a forbidden act "in relation to the work as a whole or any substantial part of it" (s. 16(3) of the Copyright, Designs and Patents Act 1988) and for infringement of a UK registered design the test used to be doing a forbidden act in respect of, "an article, to which [the registered design] or a design not substantially different from it has been applied". The test of "substantiality" leaves just the same sort of margin as the "overall impression" test. Whether it is the same test or not I leave for others to consider. . . .

Having said that, however, there are some general observations that can be made:

i) For the reasons I have given above, the test is "different" not "clearly different."

ii) The notional informed user is "fairly familiar" with design issues, as discussed above.

iii) Next is not a proposition of law but a statement about the way people (and thus the notional informed user) perceive things. It is simply that if a new design is markedly different from anything that has gone before, it is likely to have a greater overall visual impact than if it is "surrounded by kindred prior art." (HHJ Fysh's pithy phrase in *Woodhouse* at [58]). It follows that the "overall impression" created by such a design will be more significant and the room for differences which do not create a substantially different overall impression is greater. So protection for a striking novel product will be correspondingly greater than for a product which is incrementally different from the prior art, though different enough to have its own individual character and thus be validly registered.

iv) On the other hand it does not follow, in a case of markedly new design (or indeed any design) that it is sufficient to ask "is the alleged infringement closer to the registered design or to the prior art", if the

former infringement, if the latter not. The test[] remains "is the overall impression different?"
- v) It is legitimate to compare the registered design and the alleged infringement with a reasonable degree of care. The court must "don the spectacles of the informed user" to adapt the hackneyed but convenient metaphor of patent law. The possibility of imperfect recollection has a limited part to play in this exercise.
- vi) The court must identify the "overall impression" of the registered design with care. True it is that it is difficult to put into language, and it is helpful to use pictures as part of the identification, but the exercise must be done.
- vii) In this exercise the level of generality to which the court must descend is important. Here, for instance, it would be too general to say that the overall impression of the registered design is "a canister fitted with a trigger spray device on the top." The appropriate level of generality is that which would be taken by the notional informed user.
- viii) The court should then do the same exercise for the alleged infringement.
- ix) Finally the court should ask whether the overall impression of each is different. This is almost the equivalent to asking whether they are the *same* — the difference is nuanced, probably, involving a question of onus and no more.

### Principles to Be Applied by the Court of Appeal

There was no dispute as to these. It must be shown that the judge has gone wrong in principle, see, e.g. Designers Guild Ltd v Russell Williams (Textiles) Ltd [2001] F.S.R. 11 where Lord Hoffmann said, speaking of the closely analogous question of substantiality in relation to copyright infringement: "[B]ecause the decision involves the application of a not altogether precise legal standard to a combination of features of varying importance, I think that this falls within the class of case in which an appellate court should not reverse a judge's decision unless he has erred in principle."

### The Outline of the Argument as to an Error of Principle

Mr Carr [counsel for defendant] contends that the judge did go wrong in principle: that he did so in the following way. He first correctly identified the overall impression of the P&G design. He also at some points identified the overall impression of the Air Wick product. But in the end he failed to compare the overall impression of the P&G design as he had found it to be, with the overall impression of the Air Wick product.

The judge having made that error, Mr Carr submits that we should form our own overall impression of the design and the accused sprayer and that we should conclude that the impressions are different.

Putting it another way, Mr Carr submits that on a proper analysis the judge actually found that the overall impression of each was different and he ought to have concluded that there was no infringement.

Before going on to consider this argument in detail, I should record that Mr Carr, under a little pressure from the Court, abandoned his point about decoration, rejected by the judge. He was right to do so. The registration is evidently for a shape. The proper comparison is with the shape of the alleged infringement. Graphics on that (or on the physical embodiment of the design) are irrelevant.

## The Detailed Argument

The judge first described the design thus:

> 8. The winning design was chosen because it had a very distinctive look. Important features which gave it that look were its narrowed neck; its angled and elliptical top; its integrated look, especially the way that the top blended in with the body of the container and its flowing lines. The ergonomic aspects of the design were also important. One of the reasons for the choice of the angled top was that it would signal to consumers the direction of flow of the spray exiting the nozzle. The top of the head of the spray was flared out more in later iterations. This had the advantages both of making the hand grip of the container easier and also provided a flange which helped in preventing the container from slipping through the user's grip. It was also said that the flanged top helped to support the weight of the product, thus avoiding fatiguing the wrist; but since the product is lightweight and not held for prolonged periods, this did not seem to me to be a particularly important feature. The curves of the can and the head merge around the neck giving the product an integrated feel. The narrowed neck, as well as being more aesthetically pleasing, also made the container sit more easily in the hand. However, the fact that the container was not a simple cylinder meant that it would have to be custom made. The container was in fact manufactured from aluminium, rather than the conventional tinplate.
>
> 9. Overall, the shape of the design had a smooth and dynamic feel, flowing lines, and an elegant sense of movement.

I have already set out how the judge records that it was received with acclaim.

Mr Carr submits that this description fairly embodies the essence of the design, its overall impression. If he had applied that as the overall impression he would have found the Air Wick product to give a different impression.

The first time the judge refers to the impression created by the Air Wick design was at [para 20 of his judgment]. He said: "There were few kind words said about the Air Wick design. Ms Nelson said that she would have rejected the design out of hand, because it did not have a 'light and airy' feel. Mr Treeby, Reckitt Benckiser's own expert said that it was 'a common canister with a plastic cap stuck on top'; and that it was 'not in the same league as regards quality'."

If that is right . . . , then surely it creates a "different overall impression."

Further, submits Mr Carr, when the judge came to consider the question of the overall impression he failed to apply his own earlier description. Instead he identified a list of features which were stated at too high a level of generality. The judge said:

> 65. In my judgment the dominant features of the registered design are:
>     (i) The angled, elliptical, sloping top culminating in the spray nozzle;
>     (ii) The slightly curved trigger protruding from the angled underside of the top, but remaining within the footprint of the base;

(iii) The recessed 'neck' opposite and around the trigger;
(iv) The sloping shroud intersecting with the body of the canister and, in particular forming a curve at the rear;
(v) The cylindrical main body.

This, Mr Carr submits, does not capture the overall impression the judge had found at [paras 8-9 of his judgment]. The Air Wick product does not have a "smooth and dynamic feel" or an "elegant sense of movement". Nor does it have "flowing lines". There is no curved canister. The error the judge made was to generalise too much. So for instance, item (iv) was described in [para. 8] in more detail — enough to convey the impression made: "The curves of the can and the head merge around the neck giving the product an integrated feel." Similarly at [para. 8] the judge referred to the "curves of the canister" but his item (v), said to be a "dominant feature" is just a cylindrical body — which would have seemed wholly unremarkable to an informed (indeed any) user.

So, submits, Mr Carr, it is not right to identify "dominant features" at such a level of generality that the overall impression is not captured.

The judge at [para. 67 of his judgment] identified differences between the registered design and the Air Wick Product but went on to say at [67]:

> However, in my judgment these are relatively insignificant details; and do not detract from the same overall visual impression created by each of the two designs. The similarities between the two are overwhelmingly greater than the differences. I accept that the registered design is of a far greater quality and more integrated than the Air Wick canister; but in my judgment that does not mean that it escapes infringement. If that were so then a poor quality imitation would escape infringement, despite creating the same visual impression.

In saying that "the registered design is of far greater quality and more integrated", Mr Carr submits that the judge was in fact finding that there was a different overall impression. And that he should have so held.

Mr Carr further submits that the judge was wrong about item (ii). It is not a dominant feature of the design that the trigger is within the footprint of the base — if you just look at the design pictures that is not a thing that sticks out at all. Moreover being within the footprint is a true technical consideration — if it sticks out there will be problems about packing the canister in a box. So it is an aspect which the informed user would discount when deciding what the overall impression is.

Mr Carr further submitted that there were real, significant differences between the Air Wick product and the registered design. Most importantly:

(i) The Air Wick product has something of a "hammer head". The top "lozenge" has depth. It is shaped something like a Foreign Legionnaire's kepi. You could not say the same about the top of the registered design. As the Austrian court put it: "The shape of head too is different: while the head of the Febreze sprayer — to draw a comparison from the animal kingdom — is reminiscent of a snake's head, the shape of the Airwick sprayer head is like a lizard's head."

(ii) The registered design has a much thinner, more elegant, "neck". That is indeed so, particularly in the front or back views.

(iii) The registered design top ellipse is significantly larger than that of the Air Wick product.
(iv) The triggers, given the design constraint that they have to be triggers, could hardly be more different.
(v) The "cape" of the registered design flows elegantly over the curved top of the canister. That of the Air Wick product just sits on the top and is cut off at much the same level as the front. There is no integration.

Moreover, he submitted, there were elements of functionality which the judge failed to consider:

i) I have already commented on the trigger/footprint point.
ii) Once you have decided on a trigger mechanism you will need some sort of flaring so that the trigger can be gripped without the product slipping from the hand. Both the design and Air Wick have flared necks which achieve this, although the Air Wick does not do it as well. One should, for functional reasons, concentrate on the detail rather than the existence of the flare. If one does that, the flares are different — that of the Air-Wick product being significantly less marked.
iii) The direction of the spray nozzle, angled up, is functional — if, as you naturally will, you hold the canister vertically you need the spray to go upwards. The general line needs to be angled up. So the fact of an upwards inclination should be discounted.

### P&G's Case

Mr Wyand [counsel for the claimant] emphasised the purpose of protection as set out in Recital 7:

> Enhanced protection for industrial design not only promotes the contribution of individual designers to the sum of community excellence in the field, but also encourages innovation and development of new products and investment in their production.

He submitted that this showed an intention that the scope of protection should be wide. He gets that from the word "enhanced". But I do not read it as referring to the scope of protection at all. It comes after a series of recitals about the patchwork nature of national design protection rules, the problems for free movement that creates and the need for an EU-wide system and before a recital about the need for a more accessible design-protection system. It is saying no more than that design protection is desirable for the reasons given. In fact, if design protection is too wide, even for a strikingly innovative design, you are likely to discourage innovation and investment. Different designs will be caught or under the threat of being caught. Merely drawing inspiration from prior designs will become dangerous.

Next, and this was Mr Wyand's main point, he drew attention to how different the P&G design was from anything that had gone before. And he was right about that. The attempt to invalidate the design by reference to the prior art to my mind only served to emphasise just how innovative the

P&G was. We decided to dismiss the appeal on validity without calling upon Mr Wyand. . . .

Mr Wyand went on to emphasise how little there was in reality of design restraint by reason of function. The very fact of the large difference between the registered design and anything in the prior art—the "existing design corpus" proved this. If all spray canisters had to have a generally similar appearance, it would not have been possible for the P&G design to be so different from anything that had gone before.

That too is right. A large departure from the prior design corpus is indeed an indication of design freedom. Where a departure is small that may be for two reasons: technical restraint or simply lack of imagination by prior designers. The present design is a case of the latter. Mr Carr's points about design restraint for technical reasons are rather a long way from showing that a trigger-operated sprayer must have anything like the general appearance of the P&G design. They are too general. Take, for instance, the point about the nozzle pointing upwards and being seen to do that. That in no way requires more than that the nozzle does in fact point up and that its housing should in some way indicate that. It need not be elliptical, or square, or any particular shape to do any of that. Similarly his point about the grip—any sort of grip will do. You could even have a shape like a real revolver.

Given all that freedom, Mr Wyand submitted that the scope of protection should be wide—that it should cover what gives a "slightly cheaper, or slightly coarser impression". It followed, he submitted, that the judge cannot be faulted in his conclusion about same overall impression. And that is all the more so given the principles governing an appeal about that type of decision.

## My Conclusion

I have come to the conclusion that the judge did err in principle, essentially for the reasons advanced by Mr Carr, excluding his submissions about functional design restraint. I think the judge erred in the following ways:

(i) in failing to apply the "overall impression" of the registered design he in effect had found at [8-9];
(ii) in failing to apply the overall impression of the accused product he had found (or summarised) at [20];
(iii) in failing, at the point where he was considering infringement, to state what the overall impression of the alleged infringement was;
(iv) in applying by implication a requirement that the accused product should give the informed user a clearly different impression;
(v) in applying a "stick in the mind" test rather than "what would impress now" test; and
(vi) in approaching the "dominant features" of the design at too general a level, a level such as not to convey in words the overall impression which would be given to an informed observer.

The judge was concerned about the possibility that "a poor quality imitation would escape infringement". I am not so concerned. We are here considering monopolies in designs, not trade marks. A "poor quality" imitation if it does not convey the same impression as the "original" will fail on its own design merits, or rather the lack of them. If it conveys the "same impression" then it can hardly be a "poor quality imitation" and will succeed for the same reason as the "original".

Accordingly, I am free to form my own view. I think the impression which would be given to the informed user by the Air Wick product is different from that of the registered design. I say that for the reasons advanced by Mr Carr which I need not repeat here. The Austrian Court put it well:

> In reality, even though the same features are found in both, there are clear differences between the two sprayers resulting from the different mode of their execution: the Febreze sprayer is smaller, has a slightly larger diameter and so looks more compact. The head of this sprayer is shallower but also broader, so that the Febreze sprayer fits the hand differently than the Airwick sprayer (with the Airwick sprayer, which has the considerably narrower head, there is a feeling that it could slip out of the user's hand). In contrast to the Airwick sprayer, the metal can of the Febreze sprayer tapers upwards, so that the waist begins lower down than in the Airwick sprayer. The 'train' goes down much further in the Febreze sprayer, so that the lower boundary of the plastic part echoes the angle of the head part far more markedly than in the Airwick sprayer. The shape of head too is different: while the head of the Febreze sprayer—to draw a comparison from the animal kingdom—is reminiscent of a snake's head, the shape of the Airwick sprayer head is like a lizard's head.

The similarities between the products are at too general a level for one fairly to say that they would produce on the informed user the same overall impression. On the contrary, that user would get a different overall impression.

Accordingly I would allow the appeal on infringement, but dismiss the appeal on validity.

### J Choo (Jersey) Ltd v Towerstone Ltd.
[2008] EWHC 346 (Ch)

Floyd J.:

This is an application for summary judgment in a case about handbags. The cause of action is infringement of registered and unregistered Community design right. The application is made by the first claimant, the proprietor of the relevant rights, against the first defendant only. . . .

The relevant Community registered design is No. 401484–0015. . . .

The main issues before me are whether a handbag sold by the first defendant from its Oxford Street shop infringes the rights so identified and, if so, whether the first claimant is entitled to damages or on account of profits. There are minor issues as to the appropriateness of injunction and certain other relief.

### Infringement

[T]here is . . . no dispute that the first defendant sold from its Oxford Street store a bag. . . . which I have examined in the form of a physical exhibit. I was also shown in the course of the hearing an example of a bag made in accordance with the rights relied on, the Ramona bag.

The extent to which it is legitimate to have regard to a physical representation of the design in dispute is explained by Jacob L.J. in Procter & Gamble Co v Reckitt Benckiser (UK) Ltd [2007] EWCA Civ 936. There was no dispute of substance here that the Ramona bag was a reproduction of the registered design. As explained in that case, the appropriate approach to determining infringement of a Community registered design is to identify the informed user and determine what he would know about the design corpus, then to identify the overall impression given by the design, to do the same for the alleged infringement, and to ask whether the impression given for the two are the same or different, rather than clearly different.

The informed user in the present case would be someone with a knowledge of handbag design; not the woman in the street, not a handbag designer. Such a person would know about the design constraints inherent in handbag design, what features were necessary and unnecessary, and so on. There is evidence to support the proposition that the most significant features of a handbag design are those on the front of the bag, the part which is visible in use because it is carried with that side pointing out. I accept this evidence and consider that it is a fact which I should bear in mind in making the assessment of overall impression whilst not forgetting that it is the overall impression which is relevant.

Ms Reid, for the claimant, pointed to the wide degree of freedom which a handbag designer has. . . . Mr Bartlett, on behalf of the defendant, accepted that this was so.

Miss Merritt's evidence is that the claimants invest substantially in producing new and unique designs. She says that the Ramona bag concentrates its distinctive features on the front of the bag, even though some continue around the back. The unchallenged evidence was that the Ramona bag, when it was launched, was seen as the "it" bag. There is also some evidence that the launch of the claimant's bag attracted attention and was given wide publicity, including being photographed as being carried by some celebrities.

The scope of protection afforded to a registered design may be affected by the existence of kindred prior art. [cit] In this case there is no formal attack on the validity of the registered design, any specific plea of prior designs, or indeed any evidence of any designs available in the prior art to which I should have regard. . . . In those circumstances, I have to approach the issue of infringement on the basis of the evidence before me, i.e. of a reasonably unique and distinctive design.

There was no real dispute as to the features of the claimant's registered design. I summarise them thus.

It is a large, bucket bag design made up of four panels: two side panels and a front and back. A prominent feature is the double layer of threaded eyelets running around the top. The eyelets are large and are threaded with a strip of fabric, forming a double belt around the top of the bag, which acts to gather the fabric to some extent. The double belt is adjustable by means of a single belt-type buckle. It has a horseshoe shape feature on the end of the strap. There is a gap in the threaded eyelets in the centre of the bag where a vertical or longitudinal strap comes across. At its end is one part of a two-part closure. There are two decorative rivets on the strap part of the clasp. Below the clasp is a piece of additional fabric in a bow shape, most clearly visible on the design document but also present in the registered design. Below the clasp and the additional piece of fabric the strap emerges again and appears to go around the whole bag. The strap narrows before it disappears underneath. It is not entirely clear from the design document or the registered design whether the strap is stitched to the bag at this point; in the bag as sold it is not. In the registered design we see the back of the bag where the longitudinal strap passes underneath the corresponding bow feature, this time with no clasp, and is additionally fixed by two rivets at the level of the eyelets. In the registered design there is an additional piece of fabric on the underneath of the bag, which acts as a belt loop for the strap. More strikingly, the handles, which are a double strap, are made integral with both rows of eyelets and are shaped in a lozenge shape around them with two additional studs or rivets above and below. The handles are of sufficient length to allow carrying over the shoulder or as a carry bag.

Standing back, it seems to me that the overall impression to be formed by an informed user at an appropriate level of generality is of a bucket bag with a double row of large eyelets threaded with a belt and interrupted by a clasp strap appearing to run along the bag longitudinally, and with handles which terminate in a lozenge shape integral with the eyelet design.

The defendants' bag is again a large bucket bag design made up of four panels: two side panels, a front and back. It has a double layer of threaded eyelets running around the top. The eyelets are threaded with two strips of fabric, forming a double belt around the top of the bag which acts to gather the fabric in to some extent. The double belt is adjustable by means of two belt-type buckles. The straps are terminated with rounded ends. There is a gap in the threaded eyelets in the centre of the bag where a vertical strap comes across. At its end is one part of a two-part closure. There are two decorative rivets on the strap part of the clasp. Below the clasp is a piece of additional fabric in a large bow shape. Below the clasp and the additional piece of fabric the strap emerges again and appears to go round the whole bag, although, on inspection of the bag, one finds that it does not. The strap narrows before it disappears underneath. It is stitched to the bag all the way to the bottom of the front panel. On the back of the bag one sees the rows of eyelets on the handle fixings, but the longitudinal strap presents only as far as the row of eyelets. There is no bow. The handles, which are a double strap, are made integral with both rows of eyelets and are shaped in a lozenge shape around them with two additional studs or rivets above and below. The handles are of sufficient length to allow carrying over the shoulder or as a carry bag.

The first defendant draws attention to the following differences between the two bags:

>   (1) the differences in texture between the Ramona bag and the first defendant's bag;

(2) the absence of a square panel of fabric behind the clasp;
(3) the fact that the longitudinal strap does not run all the way round the first defendant's bag, has no rivets at the rear, has no belt loop on the base and is sewn to the bag;
(4) some differences on the back of the clasp;
(5) differences in the number of eyelets—there are twice as many on the Ramona bag and the eyelets are somewhat larger;
(6) the absence of the horseshoe fitting at the end of the strap;
(7) the absence of the "Jimmy Choo" logo on the strip buckles; and
(8) a difference in the lozenge shapes at the end of the handles where they meet the eyelets.

The first, second, fourth and seventh differences are, in my view, irrelevant. They are not features of the designs. The differences in the longitudinal strap (difference (3)) are trivial when the bag is viewed from the front, as it must be for the unregistered design, and do not influence the impression given by the bag as a whole, given the evidence as to the dominance of the design on the front of the bag. The differences in the number of eyelets (difference (5)) also do not seem to me to affect the overall impression. It is not easy to determine the number of eyelets in the design. Neither does the absence of the horseshoe (difference (6)). The difference in the lozenge-shape strap ending (difference (8)) is barely noticeable.

I would characterise the impression given by the defendants' bag on an informed user, again at the appropriate level of generality, again as of a bucket bag with a double row of large eyelets threaded with a belt and interrupted by a clasp strap appearing to run around the bag longitudinally, and with handles which terminate in a lozenge shape and which are integral with the eyelet design.

Accordingly, whilst at the level of a highly detailed examination of features of the two designs there are some differences, the overall impression on an informed user is, in my judgment, exactly the same. It does not seem to me to be arguable that the differences relied on by the defendant could have the effect for which it contends.

Mr Bartlett relied on *Procter*, where Jacob L.J. (with whom Dyson L.J. and May L.J. agreed), said: "The Judge was concerned about the possibility that 'a poor quality imitation would escape infringement.' I am not so concerned. We are here considering monopolies in designs, not trade marks. A 'poor quality' imitation if it does not convey the same impression as the 'original' will fail on its own design merits, or rather the lack of them. If it conveys the 'same impression' then it can hardly be a 'poor quality imitation' and will succeed for the same reason as the 'original.'"

Mr Bartlett relies on what he says is the poorer quality of the defendants' bag. It is correct that a difference in quality may give rise to a different impression if it is a difference discernible by comparing the design and the alleged infringement. But here the differences in quality are really only discernible when comparing the two bags. Comparing the drawing and the representations of the design and the defendants' bag does not give rise to a different impression of quality, in my judgment.

It follows that, in my judgment, the defendants' bag is an infringement of the registered design. Infringement of unregistered design right requires copying to have taken place. Ms Reid submits that the evidence of similarity is sufficient to justify an inference of copying. That, she says, is sufficient to shift the burden onto the defendants. There being no alternative explanation put forward, I am entitled to find copying.

Mr Bartlett does not suggest that any evidence likely to be forthcoming at trial will alter the position. He accepts that the question reduces to whether the similarities are sufficient to justify a finding of copying.

Looking at the bags side by side, restricting my consideration to the features which appear in the design document, it seems to me that the inference of copying is overwhelming. The likelihood that these two designs could have been arrived at independently, given the large number of identical features in a design field as free as the present one, seems to me to be truly fanciful.

. . . .

## NOTES AND QUESTIONS

1. *Definition of "design."* The definition of design in the Design Directive and Regulation includes two- and three-dimensional design. Thus, both EU-wide rights and national registered design rights can protect either form of design. In contrast, the 1988 U.K. reforms, on which to some extent the EU legislation was patterned, did make some distinction between two- and three-dimensional designs with respect to unregistered design protection. *See* Copyright, Designs & Patents Act 1988, §213(2) (defining "design" for purposes of U.K. *unregistered* design protection as the "design of any aspect of the *shape or configuration* (whether internal or external) of the whole or part of an article") (emphasis added); *id.* at §213(3)(c) (excluding "surface decoration" from U.K. *unregistered* design right). Generally, three-dimensional designs are amenable to UK unregistered design right protection, and surface decoration can instead be protected by copyright law. *See Dyson Ltd. v. Qualtex (UK) Ltd.*, [2006] EWCA Civ. 166 at ¶76; *see also* Copyright, Designs & Patents Act 1988, §§4, 51-52 (UK) (copyright provisions). Although not explicit, in the United States, two-dimensional designs are more apt to receive copyright protection than three-dimensional designs. Are there reasons to treat two- and three-dimensional design differently?

2. *Claiming practice.* The definition of design in the European instruments encompasses the whole *or part* of a product; the part of the product whose design is sought to be protected need not have a commercial life of its own. This affords substantial latitude to the claimant to strategically define its design in numerous ways, including and excluding different parts of the product and combinations thereof. This is particularly useful in the context of unregistered design right, where the design is first identified in the context of litigation when the nature of the accused product is known. The U.K. courts have confirmed that (at least in the context of the U.K. unregistered right, which likewise protects the design of part of a product) it is acceptable for the plaintiff to define its design in this fashion. *See A Fulton Co. v. Totes Isotoner*, [2004] R.P.C. 16 (CA 2003) (UK); *cf. Dyson Ltd. v. Qualtex (UK) Ltd.*, [2006]

EWCA Civ. 166 at ¶22 (noting lack of similar flexibility in copyright law). We have seen in Chapter 2 that U.S. trademark courts are alert to the abuse that such "late claiming" can encourage (although design patent claimants in the United States have similar flexibility, as seen in Chapter 5). Should European courts incorporate such concerns into unregistered design right doctrine? *See Dyson Ltd. v. Qualtex (UK) Ltd.*, [2006] EWCA Civ. 166 at ¶122 ("it will be important that the claimant should identify with precision each and every 'design' he relies upon. Just claiming design rights in parts, for instance, will not do — each aspect said to constitute a 'design' should be spelt out. This will focus minds from the outset. Well-advised claimants will confine themselves to their best case 'designs.'").

3. *The thresholds for protection.* The Commission considered basing protection on a threshold of originality (the subjective notion of the design being original to the designer, and not copied, regardless of objective similarity to other designs). What arguments might have supported adoption of such a threshold? Why do you think that the Commission rejected that threshold? The Commission could also have adopted a modified copyright originality threshold, such as found in the Vessel Hull Design Protection Act, 17 U.S.C. §§1301(b), 1302(a)(2), the Semiconductor Chip Protection Act of 1984, 17 U.S.C. §§902(b) (1994) (protecting mask works that are original and that are not staple, commonplace, or familiar in the semiconductor industry), and in the U.K.'s unregistered design system. *See* Copyright, Designs & Patents Act 1988, §§213(1), 213(4) (providing unregistered design protection to designs that are "original" and not "commonplace in the design field in question at the time of its creation"); *Farmers Build v. Carrier Bulk Materials*, [1999] R.P.C. 461 (CA) (UK) (noting that original means "not copied" and that whether a design is "commonplace" requires an objective comparison of the design with earlier, well-known designs in the field). What are the advantages of each respective approach? What difficulties might arise from adopting a new threshold falling between the relatively well-understood thresholds of patent and copyright? In light of the diverse approaches to protectability in member states prior to the enactment of the directive, what institutional forces might help establish common understanding of these terms in practice? The courts might embrace certain conceptual approaches that would help. *See* Graeme B. Dinwoodie, *Federalized Functionalism: The Future of Design Protection in Europe*, 24 Am. Intell. Prop. L. Ass'n Q.J. 611, 662 (1996) (arguing that courts should link the showing of differences required to establish individual character with the showing of differences required to escape infringement).

4. *Prior art.* The prior art to be considered in the analysis of individual character and novelty is determined universally. As Lord Justice Jacob notes in *Green Lane*, the Commission in its Green Paper had suggested that "a test of universal objective novelty cannot be fulfilled and therefore should not be imposed." Why not? Why might a universal standard be inappropriate for designs? What dangers flow from the reversal of that policy? Are you persuaded by the reasons mentioned by Lord Justice Jacob in support of an absolute novelty standard? Does the safeguard clause in Article 6 of the directive and Article 7 of the Regulation undermine the benefits of absolute novelty? Is there anything left of the safeguard clause if the *Green Lane* decision is correct?

5. ***Absolute novelty and the commencement of Unregistered Community Design protection.*** Article 11(1) of the Regulation provides that Unregistered Community Design right runs from the date on which a design is "first made available to the public within the Community." That phrase is defined in Article 11(2) in terms that approximate the language of the safeguard clause in Article 7(1). What are the consequences of a designer first putting products bearing the design on the market *outside* the European Union? *See* Thane International Group's Application, [2006] ECDR 8 (LG Frankfurt, 2004) (Ger.) (holding that the claimant's design could not be protected by UCD right because it has been put on the market in the United States before being made available to the public in the EU, which had the effect of destroying the novelty of the design). If the German court is correct in *Thane* (which might be open to doubt; review articles 7(1) and 11(2)), how might a designer who has first put products on the market outside the EU secure protection within the EU?

6. ***Protection of functional designs.*** Why is it important that EU law makes no distinction between aesthetic and functional designs? What dangers does the inclusion of functional designs generate? Are the benefits received from their inclusion as protectable subject-matter worth the costs or risks? How might those costs or risks be controlled or minimized? One writer has suggested that the definition of "design" in the Directive — and, in particular, the use of the term "appearance" — defeats the Commission's stated objective of protecting modern functionalist industrial design. *See* Uma Suthersanen, *Breaking Down the Intellectual Property Barriers*, 2 INTELL. PROP. Q 267, 274-275 (1998); *cf.* 2 STEPHEN P. LADAS, PATENTS, TRADEMARKS AND RELATED RIGHTS 869 (1975) (suggesting broader conception of "appearance"). Review the definition of "design" in Article 1(a) in the Directive: What types of designs are excluded by the limitations built into the definition? Does it by its terms offer protection to functionalist design?

7. ***Designs solely dictated by function.*** The U.K. courts have narrowly interpreted the exclusion of designs solely dictated by function found in both European instruments. In particular, in *Landor & Hawa Int'l Ltd. v. Azure Designs*, [2006] EWCA 1285, the Court of Appeal held that the provision excludes protection only for design features that were the sole way to achieve a particular function. In two recent Board of Appeal decisions from OHIM, the Board has suggested that the exclusion does not require that there be no alternative means to achieve the function. Compare similar functionality exclusions in trademark law (Chapter 3) and design patent law (Chapter 5). Which approach makes most sense, and are they reconcilable?

8. ***Must-fit designs.*** Article 8(2) of the Regulation and Article 7(2) of the Directive exclude "features of appearance of a product which must necessarily be reproduced in their exact form and dimensions in order to permit the product in which the design is incorporated or to which it is applied to be mechanically connected or placed in, around or against another product so that either product may perform its function." There is also a so-called must-fit exclusion from U.K. unregistered design right (not subject to the European instruments). It denies protection to features that "enable the article to be connected to, or placed in, around or against, another article so that either article may perform

its function." *See* Copyright, Designs & Patents Act 1988, §213(3)(b)(i) (UK). Would you read these provisions to be of identical scope? *See Dyson Ltd. v. Qualtex (UK) Ltd.*, [2006] EWCA Civ. 166 (commenting that "it does not matter if there are two ways of achieving the necessary fit or connection between the subject article (the first one referred to in the sub-section) and the article to which it fits or with which it interfaces. If the design chosen by the design right owner is a way of achieving that fit or interface, then it does not attract design right no matter how many alternative ways of achieving the same 'fit' might be available. . . . [And t]he sub-section operates to exclude design right even if the relevant part of the design performs some function other than the function described in the sub-section — for example, it is decorative, or has an additional function not falling within the provision").

9. *Must-match exclusions.* Essential mechanical designs will, to a large extent, be caught by the must-fit exception or by the specific exclusion of so-called under the hood designs. *See* Directive, art. 3(3). Why should the protection of must-match designs — designs where "the product incorporating the design or to which the design is applied is a component part of a complex product upon whose appearance the protected design is dependent" — be restricted? Consider the prototypical case of car body panels. *See* Bernhard Posner, *The Proposed EC Industrial Design Directive and Regulation: An Update and Analysis*, 2 INT'L INTELL. PROP. L. & POL. at 46-10 (1998); *see also British Leyland Motor Corp. v. Armstrong Patents Co.*, [1986] 1 All E.R. 850, 864 (1986) (Lord Templeman) (noting that if copyright gives exclusive rights in spare parts for cars "the purchaser of a BL car sells his soul to the company store"). Are there any costs to allowing free copying of the design of spare parts? What does the term "complex product," with respect to which the must-match provision and its permission to copy in order to supply the repair market applies, mean? *See* Directive, art. 1(c). What products other than cars might be encompassed by this term? And what makes a design "dependent upon the appearance" of the complex product? In *Dyson Ltd. v. Qualtex (UK) Ltd.*, [2006] EWCA Civ. 166, the U.K. Court of Appeal analyzed in detail the must-match exclusion from U.K. unregistered design right in a case involving the design of parts of a vacuum cleaner. Section 213(3)(b)(ii) of the Copyright, Designs & Patents Act 1988 excludes protection for features of an article that "are dependent upon the appearance of another article of which the article is intended by the designer to form an integral part." The court held that whether the exclusion applies turns in large part on the question of "dependency," and that that question should be answered by considering whether the article upon which the design was alleged to be dependent would be "radically different in appearance" if the design for which protection was sought were different. *See id.* at ¶68. Moreover, if there was, as a practical matter, design freedom for the part, then there was likely no dependency. *Id.* at ¶63. In reaching this conclusion, the court rejected a broader reading of dependency, bearing in mind that the intention of the U.K. legislature (though expressed in tortuous language) had *not* been to deny protection for all spare parts. *See id.* at ¶64. Does the concept of dependency draw a useful line in terms of what designs can be protected? *Cf.* Registered Designs Act 1949, as amended, §7A(5) (UK).

10. ***Grace period.*** An important feature of the European regime is that the producer can market products bearing a design and make a decision whether to seek a Registered Community Design based on market response. Prior to filing for registered design protection, the producer can rely on Unregistered Community Design right. To make this work, the Regulation and Directive provide for a one-year grace period, which prevents the disclosure by the designer or his successor in title destroying novelty or individual character. *See* Regulation, art. 7(2). Nor will the acts of an infringer during that period be taken into consideration under either assessment. *See id.,* art. 7(3). U.S. design patent law contains a grace period incorporated from U.S. utility patent law. European utility patent law contains no such grace period. *See* European Patent Convention, arts. 54-55. Yet, European registered design law contains such a grace period. Why might European law treat utility patents differently from designs on this question, whereas U.S. law recognizes no such distinction?

11. ***Connection between thresholds and scope of protection.*** In *Procter & Gamble*, Lord Justice Jacob concluded that to demonstrate individual character a claimant must show that its design *clearly* differs from the prior art, whereas the defendant will escape liability by showing that its accused design produces a different overall impression (rather than a clearly different overall impression) from that of the claimant. Are you persuaded? *See* Henning Hartwig, *The Concept of Reciprocity in European Design Law*, 5 J. Intell. Prop. L. & Prac. 186, 187 (2010) (arguing to the contrary and noting legislative implementation of the directive that ignores the use of the term "clearly" in the relevant recital); Graeme B. Dinwoodie, *Federalized Functionalism: The Future of Design Protection in Europe*, 24 Am. Intell. Prop. L. Ass'n Q.J. 611, 655 n.123 (1996) (discussing relationship between thresholds and scope); *id.* at 662 (arguing for affirmative endorsement of link between degree of difference required to escape infringement and that required to demonstrate individual character).

12. ***Scope of protection: comparison to trademark.*** How does the scope of protection offered by a registered or unregistered community design compare with that afforded trademarks (under U.S. or EU law)? In *Procter & Gamble*, Lord Justice Jacob commented that "the informed user . . . is better informed than the average consumer in trade mark law. Things which may infringe a registered trade mark may not infringe a corresponding registered design. I cannot think of any instance where the reverse might be so." Do you agree? Would the same proposition hold true under U.S. law (with respect to trademark and design patent)? To what extent is the scope of trademark or design protection, respectively, a function of the awareness of the fictional person through whose eyes the comparison is made?

13. ***Scope of protection: comparison to design patent.*** Recall the *Egyptian Goddess/Gorham* standard from design patent law. To what extent does a finding of infringement under the Community regime depend on an inquiry into substantial similarity as viewed by an ordinary observer? Would the ordinary observer under *Egyptian Goddess* be deemed to be aware of the same prior art as the informed user under *Procter & Gamble*? *See* Lorna Brazell, Egyptian Goddess v. Swisa, Inc.*: Is Design Law in the US and EU Converging?*, 31 Eur. Intell. Prop. Rev. 576 (2009).

**14. *Scope of protection: across products.*** EU design protection extends to incorporation of the design in any products, and is not restricted to those on which the designer used or intended to use the products. How does this scope of protection compare with that offered by trademark, design patent, and copyright law in the United States?

**15. *Proving infringement.*** One of the few distinctions between the Registered Community Design and the Unregistered Community Design right is that the latter is dependent on proof of copying. In practice, how big a difference does this make, especially if courts assessing infringement of unregistered rights follow copyright jurisprudence and are willing to presume copying from access and probative similarity? Should courts indulge that presumption? Should it be modified when dealing with functional designs, and if so, in what ways? Why did the Commission wish to offer designers patent-like rights upon registration? Would producers' legitimate concerns have been addressed by a lesser scope of rights? What justifies the broader scope of protection for registered rights? Do those justifications extend to the type of registration envisaged by the Regulation? For example, why does copyright offer a lesser scope of protection than patent? Is the registered nature of patent rights the sole reason?

**16. *Infringement and technical constraints.*** Article 10(1) of the Regulation calls for infringement to be determined based on overall impression on an informed user. According to Lord Justice Jacob in *Procter & Gamble*, Article 10(2) requires the informed user to take into account the extent to which technical constraints limit the freedom of design. Is this a proper reading of Article 10? To what extent does Article 10(2) turn the informed user into someone akin to an expert? How far from an expert is the informed user described by Mr. Justice Floyd in *J. Choo*? In U.S. design patent law after *Egyptian Goddess*, does the "ordinary observer" also take into account the extent to which technical constraints limit the freedom of design?

**17. *Bright-line rules in infringement analysis.*** Lord Justice Jacob comments that the test for infringement is "inherently imprecise." Could the uncertainties be ameliorated by articulation of a series of bright-line rules? For example, should courts adopt the rule that a poor quality imitation of a protected design necessarily creates a different overall impression? Are *Procter & Gamble* and *J. Choo* reconcilable on the relevance of the quality of the defendant's product?

**18. *Unregistered rights.*** If the Commission wished to create an automatic, short-term protection against unauthorized copying, what options were available to it? Why do you think it chose to introduce the (relatively new) concept of an unregistered design right? What dangers flow from granting industrial property rights without registration? Do these justify insisting on registration before protection? What are the problems of using a novelty standard for unregistered rights? *See* Lionel Bently & Alan Coulthard, *From the Commonplace to the Interface: Five Cases on Unregistered Design Right*, 19 EUR. INTELL. PROP. REV. 401, 407 (1997) (discussing dangers of novelty standard).

**19. *Treatment of third-country designers.*** The U.K. government took the position that it could condition *its* unregistered design right on reciprocal protection without violating its obligations under either the Paris or Berne

Conventions. *See* CHRISTINE FELLNER, INDUSTRIAL DESIGN LAW 125-126 (1995) (explaining reasoning of the U.K. government); *see also* The Design Right (Reciprocal Protection) (No. 2) Order 1989, S.I. 1989, No. 1294 (not listing the United States or Japan as a country to whose nationals protection will be extended); Copyright, Designs & Patents Act 1988, §§217-220 (limiting availability of right by reference to nationality of designer or employer or commissioner or circumstances of first marketing). Although the TRIPS Agreement retained the exceptions to national treatment found in the Paris and Berne Conventions, *see* art. 3, commentators have suggested that the MFN obligations contained in Article 4 should void such conditions of material reciprocity. *See* J.H. Reichman, *Universal Minimum Standards of Intellectual Property Protection under the TRIPS Component of the WTO Agreement*, 29 INT'L LAW. 345, 349 n.27 (1995). The spirit of the TRIPS Agreement (and the Paris Convention) would suggest that design rights should be available on a national treatment basis, and that is accepted in the EU-wide regime. Would you support conditioning the Community rights on reciprocity?

20. **Link to the Hague Agreement.** As of January 3, 2008, a Registered Community Design can serve as the basis for an application under the Hague Agreement mentioned in Chapter 1. Likewise, applicants in other Hague countries can designate the European Union as a territory in which protection is sought via the Hague mechanism. *Cf.* Geneva Act of the Hague Agreement Concerning the International Registration of Industrial Designs, art. 27(1)(ii) (July 2, 1999).

## B. SUI GENERIS REGIMES UNDER U.S. LAW

In 1998, Congress enacted the Vessel Hull Design Protection Act (VHDPA) as Title V of the Digital Millennium Copyright Act. The VHDPA is now Chapter 13 of the Copyright title of the U.S. Code. According to the report of the relevant committee in the House of Representatives, the VHDPA sought to address the practice of "hull splashing."

> Boat manufacturers invest significant resources in the design and development of safe, structurally sound, and often high-performance boat hull designs. Including research and development costs, a boat manufacturer may invest as much as $500,000 to produce a design from which one line of vessels can be manufactured. When a boat hull is designed and the design engineering and tooling process is complete, the engineers then develop a boat "plug" from which they construct a boat "mold." The manufacturer constructs a particular line of boats from this mold.
> 
> In contrast, those intent on stealing the original boat design, such as Thunder Craft, can simply use a finished boat hull in place of the manufacturer's plug to develop a mold. This practice is referred to in the trade as "splashing a mold." The copied mold can then be used to create a line of vessels with a hull seemingly identical to that appropriated from the design manufacturer.
> 
> "Hull splashing" is a problem for consumers, as well as manufacturers and boat design firms. Consumers who purchase copied boats are defrauded in the sense that they are not benefitting from the many attributes of hull design,

other than shape, that are structurally relevant, including those related to quality and safety. It is also highly unlikely that consumer know that a boat has been copied from an existing design. Most importantly for the purposes of promoting intellectual property rights, if manufacturers are not permitted to recoup at least some of their research and development costs, they may no longer invest in new, innovative boat designs that boaters eagerly await.

H.R. Rep. No. 105-436 at 13 (1998).

Unlike the design patent system, the VHDPA is administered by the Copyright Office. Excerpts from the statute, as amended in 2008, follow.

## Vessel Hull Design Protection Act

### §1301. Designs protected

(a) Designs Protected. —

(1) In General. — The designer or other owner of an original design of a useful article which makes the article attractive or distinctive in appearance to the purchasing or using public may secure the protection provided by this chapter upon complying with and subject to this chapter.

(2) Vessel features. — The design of a vessel hull, deck, or combination of a hull and deck, including a plug or mold, is subject to protection under this chapter, notwithstanding section 1302.

. . .

(b) Definitions. — For the purpose of this chapter, the following terms have the following meanings:

(1) A design is "original" if it is the result of the designer's creative endeavor that provides a distinguishable variation over prior work pertaining to similar articles which is more than merely trivial and has not been copied from another source.

(2) A "useful article" is a vessel hull or deck, including a plug or mold, which in normal use has an intrinsic utilitarian function that is not merely to portray the appearance of the article or to convey information. An article which normally is part of a useful article shall be deemed to be a useful article.

(3) A "vessel" is a craft—

(A) that is designed and capable of independently steering a course on or through water through its own means of propulsion; and

(B) that is designed and capable of carrying and transporting one or more passengers.

(4) A "hull" is the exterior frame or body of a vessel, exclusive of the deck, superstructure, masts, sails, yards, rigging, hardware, fixtures, and other attachments.

(5) A "plug" means a device or model used to make a mold for the purpose of exact duplication, regardless of whether the device or model has an intrinsic utilitarian function that is not only to portray the appearance of the product or to convey information.

(6) A "mold" means a matrix or form in which a substance for material is used, regardless of whether the matrix or form has an

intrinsic utilitarian function that is not only to portray the appearance of the product or to convey information.

### §1302. Designs not subject to protection

Protection under this chapter shall not be available for a design that is—

(1) not original;

(2) staple or commonplace, such as a standard geometric figure, a familiar symbol, an emblem, or a motif, or another shape, pattern, or configuration which has become standard, common, prevalent, or ordinary;

(3) different from a design excluded by paragraph (2) only in insignificant details or in elements which are variants commonly used in the relevant trades;

(4) dictated solely by a utilitarian function of the article that embodies it; or

(5) embodied in a useful article that was made public by the designer or owner in the United States or a foreign country more than 2 years before the date of the application for registration under this chapter.

. . .

### §1304. Commencement of protection

The protection provided for a design under this chapter shall commence upon the earlier of the date of publication of the registration . . . or the date the design is first made public as defined by section 1310(b).

### §1305. Term of protection

(a) IN GENERAL. — Subject to subsection (b), the protection provided under this chapter for a design shall continue for a term of 10 years beginning on the date of the commencement of protection under section 1304.

(b) EXPIRATION. — All terms of protection provided in this section shall run to the end of the calendar year in which they would otherwise expire.

(c) TERMINATION OF RIGHTS. — Upon expiration or termination of protection in a particular design under this chapter, all rights under this chapter in the design shall terminate, regardless of the number of different articles in which the design may have been used during the term of its protection.

. . .

### §1308. Exclusive rights

The owner of a design protected under this chapter has the exclusive right to—

(1) make, have made, or import, for sale or for use in trade, any useful article embodying that design; and

(2) sell or distribute for sale or for use in trade any useful article embodying that design.

### §1309. Infringement

(a) ACTS OF INFRINGEMENT. — Except as provided in subsection (b), it shall be infringement of the exclusive rights in a design protected under this chapter for any person, without the consent of the owner of the design, within the United States and during the term of such protection, to—

(1) make, have made, or import, for sale or for use in trade, any infringing article as defined in subsection (e); or

(2) sell or distribute for sale or for use in trade any such infringing article.

(b) ACTS OF SELLERS AND DISTRIBUTORS. — A seller or distributor of an infringing article who did not make or import the article shall be deemed to have infringed on a design protected under this chapter only if that person—

(1) induced or acted in collusion with a manufacturer to make, or an importer to import such article, except that merely purchasing or giving an order to purchase such article in the ordinary course of business shall not of itself constitute such inducement or collusion; or

(2) refused or failed, upon the request of the owner of the design, to make a prompt and full disclosure of that person's source of such article, and that person orders or reorders such article after receiving notice by registered or certified mail of the protection subsisting in the design.

(c) ACTS WITHOUT KNOWLEDGE. — It shall not be infringement under this section to make, have made, import, sell, or distribute, any article embodying a design which was created without knowledge that a design was protected under this chapter and was copied from such protected design.

(d) ACTS IN ORDINARY COURSE OF BUSINESS. — A person who incorporates into that person's product of manufacture an infringing article acquired from others in the ordinary course of business, or who, without knowledge of the protected design embodied in an infringing article, makes or processes the infringing article for the account of another person in the ordinary course of business, shall not be deemed to have infringed the rights in that design under this chapter except under a condition contained in paragraph (1) or (2) of subsection (b). Accepting an order or reorder from the source of the infringing article shall be deemed ordering or reordering within the meaning of subsection (b)(2).

(e) INFRINGING ARTICLE DEFINED. — As used in this section, an "infringing article" is any article the design of which has been copied from a design protected under this chapter, without the consent of the owner of the protected design. An infringing article is not an illustration or picture of a protected design in an advertisement, book, periodical, newspaper, photograph, broadcast, motion picture, or similar medium. A design shall not be deemed to have been copied from a protected design if it is original and not substantially similar in appearance to a protected design.

(f) ESTABLISHING ORIGINALITY. — The party to any action or proceeding under this chapter who alleges rights under this chapter in a design shall have the burden of establishing the design's originality whenever the opposing party introduces an earlier work which is identical to such design, or so similar as to make prima facie showing that such design was copied from such work.

. . .

## §1310. Application for registration

(a) TIME LIMIT FOR APPLICATION FOR REGISTRATION. — Protection under this chapter shall be lost if application for registration of the design is not made within 2 years after the date on which the design is first made public.

(b) WHEN DESIGN IS MADE PUBLIC. — A design is made public when an existing useful article embodying the design is anywhere publicly exhibited, publicly distributed, or offered for sale or sold to the public by the owner of the design or with the owner's consent.

(c) APPLICATION BY OWNER OF DESIGN. — Application for registration may be made by the owner of the design.

. . .

(h) PICTORIAL REPRESENTATION OF DESIGN. — The application for registration shall be accompanied by two copies of a drawing or other pictorial representation of the useful article embodying the design, having one or more views, adequate to show the design, in a form and style suitable for reproduction, which shall be deemed a part of the application.

(i) DESIGN IN MORE THAN ONE USEFUL ARTICLE. — If the distinguishing elements of a design are in substantially the same form in different useful articles, the design shall be protected as to all such useful articles when protected as to one of them, but not more than one registration shall be required for the design.

. . .

### §1321. Remedy for infringement

(a) IN GENERAL. — The owner of a design is entitled, after issuance of a certificate of registration of the design under this chapter, to institute an action for any infringement of the design.

(b) REVIEW OF REFUSAL TO REGISTER. — (1) Subject to paragraph (2), the owner of a design may seek judicial review of a final refusal of the Administrator to register the design under this chapter by bringing a civil action, and may in the same action, if the court adjudges the design subject to protection under this chapter, enforce the rights in that design under this chapter.

(2) The owner of a design may seek judicial review under this section if—

(A) the owner has previously duly filed and prosecuted to final refusal an application in proper form for registration of the design;

(B) the owner causes a copy of the complaint in the action to be delivered to the Administrator within 10 days after the commencement of the action; and

(C) the defendant has committed acts in respect to the design which would constitute infringement with respect to a design protected under this chapter.

. . .

### §1329. Relation to design patent law

The issuance of a design patent under title 35, United States Code, for an original design for an article of manufacture shall terminate any protection of the original design under this chapter.

### §1330. Common law and other rights unaffected

Nothing in this chapter shall annul or limit—

(1) common law or other rights or remedies, if any, available to or held by any person with respect to a design which has not been registered under this chapter; or

(2) any right under the trademark laws or any right protected against unfair competition.

## NOTES AND QUESTIONS

1. *Design notice.* Under section 1306, whenever any design for which protection is sought is made public under section 1310(b), the owner of the design is required to mark the useful article with a prescribed design notice. Omission of the notice affects remedies available against any person who begins an undertaking leading to infringement without written notice of the design protection. *See* 17 U.S.C. §1307.

2. *Comparison with other regimes.* Examine the provisions of the VHDPA excerpted above. Identify the key features of the regime, bearing in mind those elements of other design protection regimes. In what ways does protection under the VHDPA differ from the protection offered under regimes previously discussed in this book (principally, trademark und unfair competition, design patent, and copyright law)? In what ways does it resemble (or differ from) the EU design regime discussed in section A of this Chapter?

3. *Further industry-specific extensions?* What about the design of boat hulls makes them the appropriate recipients of this form of special design protection? (Is such protection constitutional? *See Bonito Boats Inc. v. Thunder Craft Boats, Inc.*, 489, U.S. 1 (1989), *supra* Chapter 1.) To what extent do those conditions apply in other industries? Would you support the extension of the VHDPA to other industries where the same conditions pertain? Most recently, congressional attention has been focused on the possibility of protecting fashion designs with sui generis legislation. For example, H.R. 5055, 109th Cong. (2006) would have amended §1301(a) to provide that "a fashion design [be] subject to protection under this chapter" and amended §1302(b) to include "an article of apparel" in the definition of "useful articles" subject to protection. A "fashion design" would be the appearance as a whole of an article of apparel, including its ornamentation; "apparel" for purposes of Chapter 13 would mean "an article of men's, women's, or children's clothing, including undergarments, outerwear, gloves, footwear, and headgear; handbags, purses, and tote bags; belts; and eyeglass frames." Would you support the enactment of such an amendment? Would there need to be any further legislative changes given the different subject matter? *See* Design Piracy Prohibition Act, H.R. 2196, 111th Cong. (Apr. 30, 2009) (providing term of protection of three years, and providing registration grace period of six months rather than two years).

4. *The VHDPA as a model for broad-based design protection?* To what extent would the VHDPA serve as a model for broad-based (non-industry specific) design protection legislation? If it were to be extended generally, would any modifications be required?

5. *Title II of the Copyright Revision Act of 1976.* Title II of the bill that eventually became the Copyright Revision Act 1976 would have created a sui generis form of design protection. It was deleted by the House Judiciary Committee.

6. *Connections, and distinctions, between design protection and utility model protection.* Many countries offer "utility model" protection, a form of intellectual property protection that historically shared many characteristics

with design protection, but today may be more like utility patent protection. For example, in 1891, Germany introduced the *Gebrauchmuster* system, which limited the scope of eligible subject matter to movable articles having three dimensions—*Raumform-Efordernis*, frequently referred to as the spatial form requirement. A number of other countries enacted similar "utility model" legislation. In 1990, however, Germany eliminated the spatial form requirement, converting the *Gebrauchmuster* to a second-tier or "petty" patent regime— essentially a patent regime with a shorter term and less rigorous patentability requirements than those of the utility patent regime.

**7. *TRIPS compliance.*** Articles 25-26 of the TRIPS Agreement established international obligations with respect to the protection of designs. Consider the text below. Does the United States comply with these provisions?

## Article 25
### Requirements for Protection

1. Members shall provide for the protection of independently created industrial designs that are new or original. Members may provide that designs are not new or original if they do not significantly differ from known designs or combinations of known design features. Members may provide that such protection shall not extend to designs dictated essentially by technical or functional considerations.

2. Each Member shall ensure that requirements for securing protection for textile designs, in particular in regard to any cost, examination or publication, do not unreasonably impair the opportunity to seek and obtain such protection. Members shall be free to meet this obligation through industrial design law or through copyright law.

## Article 26
### Protection

1. The owner of a protected industrial design shall have the right to prevent third parties not having the owner's consent from making, selling or importing articles bearing or embodying a design which is a copy, or substantially a copy, of the protected design, when such acts are undertaken for commercial purposes.

2. Members may provide limited exceptions to the protection of industrial designs, provided that such exceptions do not unreasonably conflict with the normal exploitation of protected industrial designs and do not unreasonably prejudice the legitimate interests of the owner of the protected design, taking account of the legitimate interests of third parties.

3. The duration of protection available shall amount to at least 10 years.

## EPILOGUE

We have now discussed each of the different forms of intellectual property protection for designs. Is there one regime that you think most appropriate? If you had to devise a single regime, what features would it contain? Is it appropriate for design to be potentially protected under more than one regime? As you will have seen, as Professor Reichman suggested in the quote with which we started the book, design remains a puzzle—but one that offers insights into many contemporary intellectual property debates.

# TABLE OF CASES

*Main cases are in italics.*

A Fulton Co. v. Totes Isotoner, 560
A&H Sportswear, Inc. v. Victoria's Secret Stores, Inc., 270
Abercrombie & Fitch Co. v. Hunting World, Inc., 65
*Abercrombie & Fitch Stores, Inc. v. American Eagle Outfitters*, 160
Acad. of Motion Picture Arts & Sciences v. Creative House Promotions, Inc., 260
Adidas v. Marca Mode, 234
adidas-America, Inc. v. Payless Shoesource, Inc., 275, 293
Adobe Sys. Inc. v. Southern Software Inc., 464
Allen Eng. Corp. v. Bartell Indus., Inc., 199
Al-Site Corp. v. VSI Int'l, Inc., 360
*AmBrit, Inc. v. Kraft, Inc.*, 217, 219
AMF Inc. v. Sleekcraft Boats, 217
Amini Innovation Corp. v. Anthony California, Inc., 332, 409
Antioch Co. v. Western Trimming Corp., 156
Apple Computer, Inc. v. Microsoft Corp., 437
Applied Arts Corp. v. Grand Rapids Metalcraft Corp., 391
Arc'teryx Eqpt., Inc. v. Westcomb Outerwear, Inc., 409
Aro Mfg. Co. v. Convertible Top Replacement Co., 199

Ashley v. Weeks-Numan Co., 387
ASICS Corp. v. Target Corp., 173
Australian Gold, Inc. v. Hatfield, 217
*Au-Tomotive Gold, Inc. v. Volkswagen of America, Inc.*, 165
AutoZone, Inc. v. Tandy Corp., 216
Avia Group Int'l, Inc. v. L.A. Gear Cal., Inc., 333

Badger Meter, Inc. v. Grinnell Corp., 253
Baker v. Selden, 440
Baughman Tile Co. v. Plastic Tubing Inc., 172
Bd of Supervisors of La. State Univ. v. Smack Apparel Co., 170
*Benetton Group SpA v. G-Star International BV*, 181
Bernhardt, L.L.C. v. Collezione Europa USA, Inc., 463
Berry Sterling Corp. v. Pescor Plastics, Inc., 331, 332
Best Cellars, Inc. v. Wine Made Simple, Inc., 229
*Best Lock Corp. v. Ilco Unican Corp.*, 320
Black & Decker Inc. v. Pittway Corp., 362
Blisscraft of Hollywood v. United Plastics Co., 317
Boisson v. Banian, Ltd., 475
Bonazoli v. R.S.V.P. Int'l, Inc., 159, 169, 463

*Bonito Boats, Inc. v. Thunder Craft Boats, Inc.,* 28, 275, 297, 571
Boosey & Hawkes Music Publishers, Ltd. v. Walt Disney Co., 232
Boston Athletic Ass'n v. Sullivan, 214
Braun Inc. v. Dynamics Corp. of Am., 387, 430
*Bretford Mfg., Inc. v. Smith System Mfg. Corp.,* 204
Bristol-Myers Squibb Co. v. McNeil-P.P.C., Inc., 231
British Leyland Motor Corp. v. Armstrong Patents Co., 464
Brother Records, Inc. v. Jardine, 282
*Brunswick Corp. v. British Seagull Ltd.,* 129

Cairns v. Franklin Mint Co., 282
CareFirst of Maryland, Inc. v. First Care, P.C., 215
Carman Indus., Inc. v. Wahl, 311
Carter v. Helmsley-Spear, Inc., 523
Catalina Lighting, Inc. v. Lamps Plus, Inc., 390, 430
Century 21 Real Estate Corp. v. Lendingtree, Inc., 291
Champion Spark Plug Co. v. Sanders, 284
Chesebrough Mfg. Co. v. Old Gold Chem. Co., 230
City of Elizabeth v. American Nicholson Pavement Co., 353
In re Clay, 361
Compco Corp. v. Day-Brite Lighting, Inc., 27
Conopco, Inc. v. May Dept. Stores Co., 237
Contessa Food Prods., Inc. v. Conagra, Inc., 389, 408
Contico Int'l, Inc. v. Rubbermaid Commercial Prods., Inc., 317
Conwest Resources v. Playtime Novelties, 463
*Crescent Tool Co. v. Kilborn & Bishop Co.,* 46
*Crocs, Inc. v. International Trade Commission,* 410

Dastar Corp. v. Twentieth Century Fox Film Corp., 202
Dippin' Dots, Inc. v. Frosty Bites Distribution, LLC, 156, 158, 169, 170, 172, 217

*Door-Master Corp. v. Yorktowne, Inc.,* 335
Dorr-Oliver, Inc. v. Fluid-Quip, Inc., 262
Duraco Prods. v. Joy Plastic Enters., 76
Durdin v. Kuryakyn Holdings, Inc., 352
*Durling v. Spectrum Furniture Co., Inc.,* 355
Dyson Ltd. v. Qualtex (UK) Ltd., 560, 563
Dyson Ltd. v. Registrar of Trade Marks, 105

E. & J. Gallo Winery v. Gallo Cattle Co., 293
In re E. I. DuPont deNemours, 218
E. Kahn's Sons Co. v. Columbus Packing Co., 233
E.S.S. Entertainment 2000, Inc. v. Rockstar Video, Inc., 291
eBay Inc. v. MercExchange, L.L.C., 430
Eco Mfg. LLC v. Honeywell Int'l Inc., 142, 156, 159, 170, 202
Egbert v. Lippmann, 352
*Egyptian Goddess, Inc. v. Swisa, Inc.,* 341, 391, 392
Eliya v. Kohls Dept. Stores, 463
Elmer v. ICC Fabricating, Inc., 409
Eltra Corp. v. Ringer, 464
Enesco Corp. v. Price/Costco Inc., 283
*Enterprise Mfg. Co. v. Landers, Frary & Clark,* 45
*Eppendorf-Netheler-Hinz GmbH v. Ritter GmbH,* 147
EZ Dock, Inc., v. Schafer Sys. Inc., 353

Farmers Build v. Carrier Bulk Materials, 561
Feist Publ., Inc. v. Rural Telephone Service, 434
*Ferrari S.P.A. Esercizio Fabriche Automobili E Corse v. Roberts,* 255
*Flagg Mfg. Co. v. Holway,* 42
Fonovisa, Inc. v. Cherry Auction, Inc., 475
Ford Motor Co. v. Lloyd Design Corp., 171
Forschner Group, Inc., v. Arrow Trading Co., 293
Frisch's Rests. v. Elby's Big Boy Inc., 216

Frosty Treats, Inc. v. Sony Computer Entm't America Inc., 216
*Fuji Kogyo Co., Ltd. v. Pacific Bay Int'l, Inc.,* 149
Fun-damental Too, Ltd. v. Gemmy Indus., Inc., 77

Gateway Inc. v. Companion Prods., Inc., 157, 172
Gen. Motors Corp. v. Keystone Automotive Indus., Inc., 261
Gen. Motors Corp. v. Urban Gorilla, LLC, 262
General Motors Corp. v. Lanard Toys, Inc., 103, 156
*George G. Fox Co. v. Hathaway,* 43
*In re Gibson Guitar,* 156
Gibson Guitar Corp. v. Paul Reed Smith Guitars LP, 157, 262
Glasscraft Door I, L.P. v. Seybro Door & Weathership Co., Inc., 436
In re Glavas, 362
*Gorham Co. v. White,* 298, 305, 382
Graham v. John Deere Co., 359, 362
Gray v. Meijer, Inc., 237
Green Lane Products Ltd. v. PMS International Group Plc, 534
GTFM, Inc. v. Solid Clothing, Inc., 171

H.I. Ltd. P'ship v. Winghouse of Fla., Inc., 171
Haagen Dazs v. Frusen Gladje, Ltd., 171
Ex Parte Haig & Haig Ltd., 64
Hanover Star Milling Co. v. Metcalf, 41
Hansen Beverage Co. v. National Beverage Corp., 230
In re Haruna, 341
Helene Curtis Industries, Inc. v. Church & Dwight Co., 216
*Herbert Rosenthal Jewelry Corp. v. Kalpakian,* 437
*Herman Miller, Inc. v. A. Studio S.R.L.,* 277
Hermes Int. v. Lederer De Paris Fifth Ave., 262
Holmes Group v. Vornado Air Circulation Sys., 158, 197, 202
In re Honeywell, Inc., 159
*Hoop v. Hoop,* 301

In re Howard Leight Indus., 106
In re Hruby, 305
Hupp v. Siroflex of America, Inc., 331, 361, 387
Hybritech Inc. v. Monoclonal Antibodies, Inc., 363

I.P. Lund Trading ApS v. Kohler Co., 275
Incredible Techs. v. Virtual Techs. Inc., 159
Int'l Stamp Art, Inc. v. U. S. Postal Service, 282
*International Seaway Trading Corp. v. Walgreens Corp.,* 341
Interpace Corp. v. Lapp, Inc., 215
Inwood Labs., Inc. v. Ives Labs., Inc., 132, 332

*J Choo (Jersey) Ltd v. Towerstone Ltd.,* 556
J.M. Hollister, LLC v. American Eagle Outfitters, 66
In re Jabour, 362
Jada Toys, Inc. v. Mattel, Inc., 255
Jazz Photo Corp. v. Int'l Trade Comm'n, 424
JCW Investments, Inc. v. Novelty, Inc., 470
Joseph Schlitz Brewing Co. v. Houston Ice & Brewing Co., 228

Keds Corp. v. Renee Int'l Trading Corp., 214
Keene Corp. v. Paraflex Indus., Inc., 131
*Kellogg Co. v. National Biscuit Co.,* 108, 197
Kendall-Jackson Winery, Ltd. v. E. & J. Gallo Winery, 66, 132
Kewanee Oil Co. v. Bicron Corp., 36
KeyStone Retaining Wall Systems, Inc. v. Westrock, Inc., 390
King-Seeley Thermos Co. v. Aladdin Indus., Inc., 293
Knitwaves, Inc. v. Lollytogs Ltd., 76
*Kohler Co. v. Moen Inc.,* 48
*Koninklijke Philips Electronics NV v. Remington Consumer Products Ltd,* 174
KOS Pharm., Inc. v. Andrx Corp., 214

KP Permanent Make-Up, Inc. v. Lasting Impression I, Inc., 282
KSR Int'l Co. v. Teleflex Inc., 361

L.A. Gear, Inc. v. Thom McAn Shoe Co., 331, 360, 387
Landor & Hawa Int'l Ltd. v. Azure designs, 562
Landscape Forms, Inc. v. Columbia Cascade Co., 105
Lawman Armor Corp. v. Winner Int'l L.L.C., 391
Lee v. Dayton-Hudson Corp., 386, 409
*Lego Juris a/s v. Office for Harmonisation in the Internal Market,* 177
Lego Nederland BV v. Mega Brands Inc., 185
*Leicester v. Warner Brothers,* 491
Leviton Mfg. Co. v. Universal Sec. Instruments, Inc., 106, 158
Libman Co. v. Vining Indus., Inc., 229, 231
Litton Sys., Inc. v. Whirlpool Corp., 391
Logan Graphic Prods. v. Textus USA, Inc., 157, 173
Lois Sportswear, U.S.A., Inc. v. Levi Strauss & Co., 261
Louis Vuitton Malletier S.A. v. Haute Diggity Dog, LLC, 276, 292

Mag Jewelry Co., Inc. v. Cherokee, Inc., 474
Maharashi Hardy Blechman Ltd. v. Abercrombie & Fitch Co., 104, 169
Maker's Mark Distillery, Inc. v. Diageo North. Am., 106
Malaco Leaf AB v. Promotion in Motion, Inc., 106, 169
Malletier v. Burlington Coat Factory Warehouse Corp., 230, 253
In re Mann, 408
Markman v. Westview Instruments, 159, 408
*Martin v. City Of Indianapolis,* 507
Masquerade Novelty, Inc. v. Unique Indus., 463
*Massachusetts Museum of Contemporary Art Foundation Inc. v. Büchel,* 513

Mastercrafters Clock & Radio Co. v. Vacheron & Constatin-LeCoultre Watches, Inc., 260
*Mattel Inc. v. Walking Mountain Productions,* 284, 475
*Mazer v. Stein,* 310, 441
McKeon Prods. Inc. v. Flents Prods. Co., 237
McKernan v. Burek, 95
McLean v. Fleming, 82
McNeil Nutritionals, LLC v. Heartland Sweeteners, 235, 237
McNeil-P.P.C., Inc. v. Guardian Drug Co., 231, 237
Mega Blocks Inc. v. Lego Sys. A/S, 185
Merriam-Webster, Inc. v. Random House, Inc., 230
Midwest Indus., Inc. v. Karavan Trailers, Inc., 186, 202
Mishawaka Rubber & Woolen Mfg. Co. v. S.S. Kresge Co., 42
In re Mogen David Wine Corp., 309
Montwillo v. Tull, 436
*In re Morton-Norwich Products, Inc.,* 112
*Moseley v. V Secret Catalogue, Inc.,* 274
Munsingwear Inc. v. Jockey Int'l Inc., 262
My-T-Fine Corp. v. Samuels, 233

Nabisco, Inc. v. PF Brands, Inc., 275
In re Nalbandian, 359, 362
New Colt Holding Corp. v. RJG Holdings of Fla., Inc., 103, 104, 157, 170
New York Stock Exchange, Inc. v. New York, New York Hotel, LLC, 275
*Nike, Inc. v. Wal-Mart Stores, Inc.,* 425
Nora Beverages, Inc. v. Perrier Group of Am., Inc., 253
North American Medical Corp. v. Axiom Worldwide, Inc., 430

OddzOn Prods., Inc. v. Just Toys, Inc., 305, 387
Odegard, Inc. v. Safavieh Carpets, Inc., 475
Oreck Corp. v. U.S. Floor Sys., Inc., 215

Pagliero v. Wallace China Co., 124
Palm Bay Imports, Inc. v. Veuve Clicquot Ponsardin Maison Fondee En 1772, 218

Partido Revolucionario Dominicano (PRD) Seccional Metropolitana de Washington-DC, Maryland y Virginia v. Partido Revolucionario Dominicano, Seccional de Maryland y Virginia, 217
Payless Shoesource, Inc. v. Reebok Int'l Ltd., 387
Peaceable Planet, Inc. v. Ty, Inc., 208
Pebble Beach Co. v. Tour 18 I Ltd., 255
Peek & Cloppenburg v. Cassina, 475
*Peter Pan Fabrics, Inc. v. Martin Weiner Corp.*, 465
Pfaff v. Wells Electronics, Inc., 352
*PHG Technologies, Llc v. St. John Companies, Inc.*, 325
Philips Elec. BV v. Remington Consumer Prods., 106
Phillips v. AWH Corp., 340
*Pivot Point Int'l, Inc. v. Charlene Products, Inc.*, 446
Pizzeria Uno Corp. v. Temple, 215
Planet Hollywood (Region IV), Inc. v. Hollywood Casino Corp., 275
Playtex Products, Inc. v. Georgia-Pacific Corp, 214
Polaroid Corp. v. Polarad Elecs. Corp., 212, 214
Pollara v. Seymour, 523
Power Controls Corp. v. Hybrinetics, Inc., 330
Prestonettes, Inc. v. Coty, 42, 283
*Procter & Gamble Co. v. Reckitt Benckiser (UK) Ltd*, 544
Procter & Gamble v. McLane Company, 104, 234

*Qualitex Co. v. Jacobson Products Co., Inc.*, 78, 111, 132, 133

Rainforest Café, Inc. v. Amazon, Inc., 270
Re Marcio X, 475
Regal Jewelry Co. v. Kingsbridge Int'l Inc., 105
Rescuecom v. Google, 234
*Richardson v. Stanley Works, Inc.*, 417
Richmond Homes Mgmt., Inc. v. Raintree, Inc., 490
In re Right-On Co., Ltd., 96

Ringling Bros.-Barnum & Bailey Combined Shows, Inc. v. Utah Div. of Travel Dev., 271
Rogers v. Grimaldi, 291
Rosco, Inc. v. Mirror Lite Co., 330, 331
Rose Art Indus. v. Swanson, 105
Ross Cosmetics Dist. Ctr. Inc. v. United States, 276
Roth Greeting Cards v. United Card Co., 436
Roto-Rooter Corp. v. O'Neal, 215
Rowe v. Blodgett & Clapp Co., 318

Sally Beauty Co. v. Beautyco, Inc., 217
Samara Bros. v. Wal-Mart Stores, Inc., 159
Sanson Hosiery Mills v. S.H. Kress & Co., 387, 390
Sara Lee Corp. v. Kayser-Roth Corp., 215
Scott Fetzer Co. v. House of Vacuums Inc., 215
Seabrook Foods, Inc. v. Bar-Well Foods, Ltd., 67
In re Seagate Technology L.L.C., 430
*Sears, Roebuck & Co. v. Stiffel Co.*, 24, 391
Sebel Furniture Limited v. Acoustic & Felts Pty Limited, 235
Seiko Epson Corp. v. Nu-Kote Int'l, Inc., 331
Shakespeare Co. v. Silstar Corp. of America, Inc., 283
Shire US Inc. v. Barr Labs., Inc., 132
*In Re Slokevage*, 92
South Corp. v. United States, 315
Spinmaster Ltd. v. Overbreak, LLC, 463
Spotless Enters. v. A&E Prods. Group L.P., 390
SquirtCo v. Seven-Up Co., 216
Starbucks U.S. Brands LLC v. Ruben, 232
Straumann Co. v. Lifecore Biomedical Inc., 156
Stuart Hall Co. v. Ampad Corp., 76
Sullivan v. CBS Corp., 216
Sun Hill Indus., Inc. v. Easter Unlimited, Inc., 410
Sunbeam Prods., Inc. v. West Bend Co., 254

Talking Rain Beverage Co. v. South Beach Beverage Co., 157
Thane International Group's Application, 562
In re Thorington, 311
Tie Tech, Inc. v. Kinedyne Corp., 160
Titan Tire Corp. v. Case New Holland, Inc., 361
Tootsie Roll Indus., Inc. v. Sathers, Inc., 231
Top Tobacco, L.P. v. North Atlantic Operating Co., Inc., 255
*T-Peg, Inc. v. Vermont Timber Works, Inc.*, 483
*TrafFix Devices, Inc. v. Mktg. Displays, Inc.*, 135, 254
Truck Eqpt. Service Co. v. Fruehauf Corp., 63
*Two Pesos, Inc. v. Taco Cabana, Inc.*, 68
Ty Inc. v. Perryman, 274
*Ty, Inc. v. Gma Accessories, Inc.*, 466

Unette Corp. v. Unit Pack Co., Inc., 386, 387
Union Carbide Corp. v. Ever-Ready Inc., 232
United States v. Foote, 277
Universal Furniture v. Collezione Europe USA, 463

*Valu Engineering, Inc. v. Rexnord Corp.*, 143

*Versa Products Company, Inc. v. Bifold Company (Manufacturing) Ltd.*, 239
*Vornado Air Circulation Sys., Inc. v. Duracraft Corp.*, 186

*Wallace Int'l Silversmiths, Inc. v. Godinger Silver Art Co., Inc.*, 124
*Wal-Mart Stores, Inc. v. Samara Brothers, Inc.*, 85, 122
Web Printing Controls Co. v. Oxy-Dry Corp., 232
*In re Webb*, 312, 389
Whimsicality, Inc. v. Rubie's Costume Co., 463
Wilhelm Pudenz, GmbH v. Littlefuse, Inc., 202

*Yankee Candle Co., Inc. v. Bridgewater Candle Co., Llc*, 98
In re Yardley, 310, 445
Yokohama Rubber Co. v. Stamford Tyres International PTE Ltd., 363
Yurman Design, Inc. v. Golden Treasure Imports, Inc., 170
Yurman Design, Inc. v. PAJ, Inc., 104
*Yurman Studio, Inc. v. Castaneda*, 434

In re Zahn, 307
Zatarains, Inc. v. Oak Grove Smokehouse, Inc., 65

# *INDEX*

*Abercrombie* Spectrum
  generally, 65. *See* Distinctiveness
Anticipation
  all-elements rule, 337
  ordinary observer, 345
Apple, Inc.
  iPod, 4 *et seq.*
Article of manufacture
  design for, 301

Brother Billy
  builds leecher, 364
  designs computer icons, 312
  uses middle finger, 352

Claims
  construction in design patents, 403
  in design patents generally, 300
Community design protection
  scope of protection, 543
  validity of rights, 533
Copyrightability
  architectural works, 483
  idea/expression dichotomy, 437
  originality, 434
  pictorial, graphic and sculptural works, 440 *et seq.*
  typefaces, 464
Copyright scope
  ordinary observer, 465

public display right, 475
substantial similarity, 465 *et seq.*
works of visual art, 507 *et seq.*
Counterfeiting
  protection against, 276
  remedies, 276 *et seq.*
Cumulation/preemption problem
  *Bonito Boats* view of, 28
  *Dastar* view of (trademark/copyright), 202
  *Sears/Compco* view of, 24
  *Vornado* view of (trademark/utility patent), 186

Design
  definitions, 4
  overview of process, 5 *et seq.*
Dilution
  blurring, 274
  constitutional limits, 275
  tarnishment, 274
  trademark dilution revision act 2006, 271 *et seq.*
Dinwoodie and Janis
  as the Blues Brothers, 463
  depicted as Hercules, 440
  as Ernie and Bert, 463
  make pumpkin-shaped bags, 423
  in sausage races, 463
  sell chocolates in heart-shaped boxes, 123

as superheros, 463
as Ted Kennedy and Newt Gingrich, 463
Distinctiveness
   *Abercrombie* spectrum, 65
   packaging/design distinction, 77, 85 *et seq.*, 92 *et seq.*
   *Seabrook* analysis, 67
   secondary meaning, 96 *et seq.*

*Egyptian Goddess* Standard
   applied, 410 *et seq.*
   articulated, 402
Experimental use
   negation of public use bar to patentability, 352

Fair Use
   of copyrighted works, 475 *et seq.*
   of trade dress, 277
Functionality
   aesthetic features in trade dress, 123 *et seq.*, 160 *et seq.*
   *Berry Sterling* factors, 331
   design patents after *Egyptian Goddess*, 417
   design patents generally, 320 *et seq.*
   *Inwood/Qualitex* test, 132 *et seq.*
   in European Union design law, 531
   in European Union trademark law, 174
   *Morton-Norwich* factors, 119
   *Pagliero* standard, 124
   *Traffix* test, 139
   utilitarian features in trade dress, 143

*Gorham* Substantial Similarity Test
   enunciated, 384

Hague Agreement
   overview, 16

Initial Interest Confusion. *See* Likelihood of Confusion
*Inwood/Qualitex* Test. *See* Functionality

Likelihood of Confusion
   in cases on private label goods, 235
   factors tests, 212 *et seq.*
   initial interest, 262
   post-sale, 255
   in product design trade dress, 239
   in product packaging trade dress, 219

*Morton-Norwich* factors *See* Functionality
Matter of Concern Test
   in design patents, 314

Novelty
   in design patents, 335

Obviousness
   *Durling* analysis, 355
   ordinary designer, 356
Ornamentality
   in design patents, 312

Parody
   *Rogers v. Grimaldi* test, 286
   in trade dress dilution cases, 292
   in trade dress infringement cases, 284 *et seq.*
Pictorial, graphic and sculptural works
   separability analysis, 445 *et seq.*
Point of Novelty Test
   adopted, 391
   rejected, 392
Post-Sale Confusion. *See* Likelihood of Confusion
Priority
   in design patents, 364

Remedies
   design patent infringement, 425
   trade dress infringement, 292
Repair
   of design patented articles, 424
   in European Union design law, 532

*Seabrook* analysis
   generally, 67
Secondary meaning
   defined, 96. *See* Distinctiveness
Statutory Bar
   in design patents, 335
Sui Generis Design Protection
   in Europe, 528 *et seq.*
     U.S. Vessel Hull Design Protection Act, 566

Trade Dress Protection
   color as a mark, 78
   distinctiveness, 64 *et seq.*
   historical evolution in U.S., 42 *et seq.*
   Lanham Act section 45, 48 *et seq.*
Trips
   overview of articles concerning design, 16